ANCIENT GREECE

In this revised edition, Matthew Dillon and Lynda Garland have expanded the chronological range of *Ancient Greece* to include the Greek world of the fourth century. The sourcebook now ranges from the first lines of Greek literature to the death of Alexander the Great, covering all of the main historical periods and social phenomena of ancient Greece. The material is taken from a variety of sources: historians, inscriptions, graffiti, law codes, epitaphs, decrees, drama and poetry. It includes the major literary authors, but also covers a wide selection of writers, including many non-Athenian authors. Whilst focusing on the main cities of ancient Greece – Athens and Sparta – the sourcebook also draws on a wide range of material concerning the Greeks in Egypt, Italy, Sicily, Asia Minor and the Black Sea.

Ancient Greece not only covers the chronological, political history of ancient Greece, but also explores the full spectrum of Greek life through topics such as gender, social class, race and labour. This revised edition includes:

- Two completely new chapters - 'The Rise of Macedon' and 'Alexander "the Great", 336-323 BC'
- New material in the chapters on The City-State, Religion in the Greek World, Tyrants and Tyranny, the Peloponnesian War and Its Aftermath, Labour: Slaves, Serfs and Citizens, and Women, Sexuality and the Family

It is structured so that:

- Thematically arranged chapters are arranged to allow students to build up gradually knowledge of the ancient Greek world
- Introductory essays to each chapter give necessary background to understand topic areas
- Linking commentaries help students understand the source extracts and what they reveal about the ancient Greeks

Ancient Greece: Social and Historical Documents from Archaic Times to the Death of Alexander the Great. Third Edition, will continue to be a definitive collection of source material on the society and culture of the Greeks.

Matthew Dillon is an Associate Professor in Ancient History in the School of Humanities, University of New England, Australia. His main research interests are Ancient Greek History, and Religion.

Lynda Garland is Professor and Head of the School of Humanities, University of New England, Australia. Her main research interests are in the areas of Ancient History and Byzantine Studies.

ROUTLEDGE SOURCEBOOKS FOR THE ANCIENT WORLD

READINGS IN LATE ANTIQUITY: *SECOND EDITION, Michael Maas*

GREEK AND ROMAN EDUCATION, *Mark Joyal, J.C. Yardley and Iain McDougall*

THE REPUBLICAN ROMAN ARMY, *Michael M. Sage*

THE STORY OF ATHENS, *Phillip Harding*

ROMAN SOCIAL HISTORY, *Tim Parkin and Arthur Pomeroy*

DEATH IN ANCIENT ROME, *Valerie Hope*

ANCIENT ROME, *Matthew Dillon and Lynda Garland*

SEXUALITY IN GREEK AND ROMAN LITERATURE, *Marguerite Johnson and Terry Ryan*

ATHENIAN POLITICAL ORATORY, *David Phillips*

POMPEII, *Alison E. Cooley and M.G.L. Cooley*

GREEK SCIENCE OF THE HELLENISTIC ERA, *Georgia Irby-Massie and Paul Keyser*

WOMEN AND LAW IN THE ROMAN EMPIRE, *Judith Evans Grubbs*

WARFARE IN ANCIENT GREECE, *Michael M. Sage*

THE GOVERNMENT OF THE ROMAN EMPIRE, *Barbara Levick*

PAGANS AND CHRISTIANS IN LATE ANTIQUITY, *A.D. Lee*

ANCIENT GREEK LAWS, *Ilias Arnaoutoglou*

TRIALS FROM CLASSICAL ATHENS, *Christopher Carey*

GREEK AND ROMAN TECHNOLOGY, *John Humphrey, John Oleson and Andrew Sherwood*

ROMAN ITALY 388 BC – AD 200, *Kathryn Lomas*

THE ROMAN ARMY 31 BC – AD 337, *Brian Campbell*

THE ROMAN HOUSEHOLD, *Jane F. Gardner and Thomas Wiedemann*

ATHENIAN POLITICS, *G.R. Stanton*

GREEK AND ROMAN SLAVERY, *Thomas Wiedemann*

Forthcoming:

ANCIENT CITY OF ROME, *Christopher Smith, J.C.N. Coulston and Hazel Dodge*

WOMEN OF THE ANCIENT NEAR EAST, *Mark Chavalas*

GREEK RELIGION, *Emma Stafford and Karen Stears*

ANCIENT GREECE

Social and Historical Documents from Archaic Times to the Death of Alexander the Great

Third Edition

Matthew Dillon and Lynda Garland

LONDON AND NEW YORK

First edition published 1994
Second edition first published 2000
This third edition first published 2010 by Routledge
2 Park Square, Milton Park, Abingdon, OX14 4RN

Simultaneously published in the USA and Canada by Routledge
711 Third Avenue, New York, NY 10017, USA

Routledge is an imprint of the Taylor & Francis Group, an informa business

Typeset in Baskerville by Saxon Graphics Ltd, Derby

British Library Cataloguing in Publication Data
A catalogue record for this book is available from the British Library

Library of Congress Cataloging in Publication Data
A catalog record for this book has been requested

ISBN 10: 0-415-47329-2 (hbk)
ISBN 10: 0-415-47330-6 (pbk)
ISBN 10: 0-203-85455-1 (ebk)

ISBN 13: 978-0-415-47329-3 (hbk)
ISBN 13: 978-0-415-47330-9 (pbk)
ISBN 13: 978-0-203-85455-6 (ebk)

FOR ALL OUR STUDENTS , PAST, PRESENT AND FUTURE

CONTENTS

LIST OF TABLES AND MAPS

GENEALOGICAL TABLES

MAPS

GLOSSARY

acropolis:	citadel, the highest part of a city
agema:	the Macedonian guard
agoge:	the Spartan system of education
agora:	the market square, civic centre of a city-state
agoranomoi:	market magistrates at Athens
aisymnetes:	an elected tyrant
Amphictyonic Council:	representatives of the twelve states responsible for the upkeep and welfare of the sanctuary and games at Delphi
apoikia:	a colony or settlement (pl.: apoikiai)
architheoros:	the leader of a sacred embassy
archon:	a magistrate; the most important archonship in Athens was the eponymous archonship (the holder gave his name to the year)
Areiopagos:	a hill west of the acropolis; the council of the Areiopagos, which was composed of ex-archons, met here
atimia:	loss of citizen rights (adj.: atimos, pl.: atimoi)
boeotarch:	a chief magistrate of the Boeotian league
boule:	the council of a city; the bouleterion (council chamber) was its meeting place
chiliarch:	a Macedonian commander (of 1,000 men)
choregos:	a wealthy citizen who financed a dramatic chorus for a festival
cleruchy:	a colony where the settlers retained their original citizenship
Companions:	cavalry in the Macedonian army
decarchy:	a government of ten men
demagogue:	a popular leader or speaker (a fourth-century term)
deme:	a village; Kleisthenes divided Attica into 140 units called demes
demos:	the people of a city, the citizens; sometimes the assembly
dikasterion:	a jury-court (pl.: dikasteria)

dokimasia:	the scrutiny of a person's qualifications for office or citizenship
ekklesia:	the assembly of adult male citizens
Eleven, the:	the police commissioners at Athens
emporion:	a trading station (pl.: emporia)
ephor:	a Spartan magistrate; five were elected annually
epigonoi:	the successors of Alexander the Great
epimetelai:	supervisors
epoptes:	the highest grade of initiate at Eleusis (pl.: epoptai)
eunomia:	good order
eupatridai:	nobles, aristocrats
euthyna:	the examination of an official's conduct or accounts at the end of his term (pl.: euthynai)
genos:	a clan, group of families (pl.: gene)
gerousia:	a council of twenty-eight elders (gerontes) in Sparta plus the two kings
gnorimoi:	the notables, wealthy
harmost:	a governor imposed by Sparta
hegemon:	a leader or commander (as of the League of Corinth)
heliaia:	a court (generally of appeal) at Athens
hellenotamiai:	financial officials of the Delian League
helot:	a Spartan serf
hetaira:	a courtesan, higher-class prostitute
hetaireia:	a club, association of citizens (pl.: hetaireiai)
hieromnemones:	representatives on the Delphic Amphictyonic Council
hieropoioi:	sacred officials, temple overseers
hippeis:	cavalry; the second of Solon's four propertied classes in Athens
homoioi:	'equals'; a term used in Sparta for full citizens, the Spartiates
hoplite:	a heavily armed infantryman
hypaspistai:	Macedonian shield-bearers; a brigade of guards
isonomia:	equality of rights
King:	the (Great) King of Persia
kolakretai:	Athenian financial officials
komos:	a band of revellers; a celebratory procession
Lakedaimon:	Sparta; the Spartans were known as Lakedaimonians
Lakonia:	Sparta's immediate countryside; 'Lakonian' often means Spartan
liturgy:	public duty imposed on wealthy citizens, such as financing a dramatic chorus or paying for the maintenance of a trireme for a year
medise:	to support or collaborate with the Persians (Medes)

metic:	an immigrant, foreign resident
mystagogos:	someone who introduces others to the Eleusinian Mysteries
mystes:	an initiate, especially at the Eleusinian Mysteries (pl.: mystai)
neodameis:	new citizens (in Sparta); enfranchised helots
oikistes:	the founder of a colony (pl.: oikistai)
oikos:	a household (pl.: oikoi)
Olympiad:	the four-year period between one Olympic games and the next
penestai:	Thessalian serfs
pentakosiomedimnoi:	the 500 bushel-class, the first of Solon's four propertied classes
perioikoi:	neighbours; peoples subject to Sparta in the Peloponnese
pezetairoi:	foot-guards in the Macedonian army
phoros:	tribute contribution (e.g. to Athens from members of the Delian League)
phratry:	a brotherhood with social and religious associations
phyle:	a tribe; Kleisthenes organised the Athenians into ten tribes (phylai)
polemarch:	a war leader; one of the archons in Athens
polis:	a city-state (pl.: poleis)
politeia:	constitution; or (by extension) citizenship
poletai:	Athenian financial officials
prostates:	champion, leader of a political party; patron of metics
prytaneion:	town hall
prytany:	one-tenth of the Athenian administrative year, during which the representatives of one of the ten tribes (the fifty prytaneis) presided in the boule and assembly; the prytaneion was the town hall
Pythia:	the priestess at Delphi
Relatives:	an elite corps of Persians
rhapsode:	a bard, minstrel
sarissa:	the basic Macedonian weapon, a six-metre pike
satrap:	a Persian governor
skolion:	a drinking song (pl.: skolia)
Spartiate:	a full Spartan citizen
stasis:	civil dissension, factional disturbance; a party or faction
stele:	a slab; an inscription, such as a gravestone or decree (pl.: stelai)
strategos:	a general (pl.: strategoi); strategia is the command held by a stratego

synoikismos:	the union of several towns to form a single state (synoecism)
syssitia:	public messes at Sparta (also pheiditia)
tagos:	the chief magistrate of Thessaly
theoria:	a sacred embassy
theoroi:	sacred envoys
thetes:	the lowest of Solon's four propertied classes (sing.: thes)
the Thirty:	the oligarchs who ruled Athens in 404/3
tholos:	the round house; the headquarters of the prytaneis
trireme:	a warship with 170 rowers
trierarch:	the commander of a trireme
trittys:	a regional division of Attica (pl.: trittyes)
tyrant:	a ruler with no hereditary right to rule
tyrannos:	a tyrant (pl.: tyrannoi)
zeugitai:	the third of Solon's four propertied classes

SOME USEFUL DEFINITIONS

Athenian months

Hekatombaion (June/July)
Metageitnion (July/August)
Boedromion (August/September)
Pyanopsion (September/October)
Maimakterion (October/November)
Posideion (November/December)
Gamelion (December/January)
Anthesterion (January/February)
Elaphebolion (February/March)
Mounichion (March/April)
Thargelion (April/May)
Skirophorion (May/June)

The ten Athenian tribes in their official order

Erechtheis (I)
Aigeis (II)
Pandionis (III)
Leontis (IV)
Akamantis (V)
Oineis (VI)
Kekropis (VII)
Hippothontis (VIII)
Aiantis (IX)
Antiochis (X)

Attic coinage

6 obols (ob.) = 1 drachma (dr.)
100 dr. = 1 mina
2 minas = 1 stater
60 minas = 1 talent (T.)

Measurements of capacity

1 kotyle (jug) = 285cc
12 kotylai = 1 chous (3.4 litres)
12 choes = 1 metretes (41 litres)
192 kotylai = 1 medimnos (55 dry litres)

Measurements of distance

1 daktylos (finger) = approx. $^7/_{10}$ in.; 1.9 cm
24 daktyloi = 1 cubit (approx. 1 ft 5 in.; 45 cm)
1 orguia = 1 fathom (approx. 6 ft; 1.80 m)
100 orguiai = 1 stade (approx. 606 ft; 180 m)

Symbols used in documents

( )	explanatory addition to text
[ ]	letters or words in inscriptions restored by modern scholars
[[ ]]	enclosed letters or words deliberately erased
F	fragment

HOW TO USE AND CITE *ANCIENT GREECE*

Students frequently ask the authors about **the setting out of the documents** which are contained in *Ancient Greece*. This is best explained by taking the example given below. Here **3.90** is simply the document number of the extract in *Ancient Greece*: document number **90** in Chapter **3**. This has nothing to do with the ancient source itself. The document is taken from **Herodotos 8.144.2**, in which **Herodotos** is the name of the author and **8.144.2** refers to where the extract can be found in Herodotos' work: Book 8, chapter 144, paragraph 2. After comes a short title: **Religion as Part of the Greek Identity**. This is not a title drawn from Herodotos. Rather, it is a description given by Dillon and Garland to the document, to give the reader a quick idea of what the extract is about. Under the actual heading comes an indented comment by Dillon and Garland: once again this is not the ancient source itself but a brief introduction to the passage, intended to help elucidate its main features. In a larger font size, under this comment, comes the ancient source itself.

3.90 Herodotos 8.144.2: Religion as Part of the Greek Identity

When the Spartans heard that Mardonios had sent to the Athenians a proposal that they make terms with Persia, they sent envoys who were present when the Athenians gave their answer. This was the Athenians' reply.

8.144.2 There are many important reasons which prevent us from doing this, even if we so wished, the first and greatest being the burning and demolishing of the statues and temples of our gods, which we must avenge with all our power rather than making terms with the agent of their destruction. Furthermore there is the fact that we are all Greeks, sharing both the same blood and the same language, and we have the temples of our gods in common and our sacrifices and similar lifestyle, and it would not be right for the Athenians to betray all these.

Another question which is often asked is **how to give a traditional footnote or in text reference** to a document in *Ancient Greece*. Once again, taking the above example, we would suggest:

> Herodotos 8.114.2, in Dillon, M. and Garland, L. *Ancient Greece: Social and Historical Documents from Archaic Times to the Death of Alexander the Great*, London, 2002, doc. 3.90, p. 121–22.

An abbreviated form of this could be:

> Herodotos 8.114.2, in Dillon and Garland, *Ancient Greece*, doc. 3.90, p. 121–22.

PREFACE TO THE THIRD EDITION

This third edition of *Ancient Greece* has been expanded in its historical range down to the death of Alexander III 'the Great' of Macedon, and so has a new title: *Ancient Greece: Social and Historical Documents from Archaic Times to the Death of Alexander the Great.* Over the last ten years since the second edition of *Ancient Greece,* the authors have become convinced that it was necessary to give a fuller historical treatment of ancient Greece so that users of the book could learn what happened in Greece in the fourth century BC. This also means that the social history chapters could contain documents from this century, giving a fuller indication of what ancient Greek society was like.

In addition, we feel that there is a need for a textbook, appearing in conjunction with this third edition, which will give the full background to the texts translated in *Ancient Greece.* This textbook, *The Ancient Greeks: History and Culture from Archaic Times to the Death of Alexander,* has the same chapter titles as *Ancient Greece,* and will provide students with the necessary background knowledge and details for understanding each historical period and social aspect of ancient Greece. Accordingly, many of the extensive comments accompanying individual documents have been reduced in scope and size in *Ancient Greece* itself. What we aim to give in this edition is enough commentary on each document to make it comprehensible, with the overall background to be given in the textbook. Our teaching from *Ancient Greece* over the last fifteen years has also taught us that less is often more. We have tried to give the necessary background for each document but have not tried to 'overload' the students with information. As first-year undergraduates tend not to follow up the detailed references to modern authors given with the documents in the first and second editions, these have been taken out and replaced with a shorter more useable selection of reading for each chapter, to be found in the Bibliography.

We give a special thanks to all our students over the last fifteen years, not just at the University of New England, but those who have used this book in Australia, New Zealand, Britain, Ireland, Germany and the United States. We would like to thank Routledge most sincerely for the invitation to write a third edition and Brian E. Colles for allowing us to use his translation of the Bisitun Rock Inscription (doc.11.2).

Armidale, Australia
August, AD 2009

PREFACE TO THE SECOND EDITION

This second edition of *Ancient Greece: Social and Historical Documents from Archaic Times to the Death of Socrates* owes its existence to all those readers who found the first edition of use and who commented on its strengths and omissions. We have been prompted to write a second edition rather than reprinting the original *Ancient Greece* by these comments, which have led us to include many new documents, mainly on prostitution and homosexuality. The numbering of documents in the first twelve chapters of the new edition is the same as in the last; a new passage of Thucydides on the Greek colonisation of Sicily is included as 1.10.ii, and recently discovered material from Simonides' elegies on the Persian Wars as document 7.43.ii. A passage (8.4.ii) on Timokreon's views of his contemporary Themistokles is also included. It seemed better to include this new material as subsections with Roman numeration rather than to disturb the numeration of the original edition. Chapter thirteen contains many new documents; docs 1–64 are largely the same as in the first edition, but doc. 13.65 has now become 13.93, and documents 13.24, 13.52 and 13.56 have joined the sections on pederasty and prostitution as 13.70, 13.80 and 13.89, respectively. A new chapter has been added on the ancient sources themselves and their methodology to help students and readers in general become aware of the more important problems in using ancient authors as historical sources. The bibliographies and references accompanying the notes on individual documents throughout the book have been updated as much as possible. Finally, we would like to thank all those who have made encouraging comments on the first edition, and we hope that the second edition will prove to be equally useful.

Armidale, Australia
March 1999

PREFACE TO THE FIRST EDITION

This work was originally intended as a sourcebook for use with the first unit of Ancient History offered by the Open Learning Agency of Australia, Ancient Greece: Early History, which we wrote in 1993. But in the event it has developed into a sourcebook aimed at undergraduate students of Greek history at all levels, with some uses also as a research tool for the reader interested in further study. The period covered is that of the Greek world from the archaic period to the end of the fifth century and the documents have been carefully chosen to reflect contemporary views of the main issues of political and social history within that period. Any sourcebook is naturally open to criticisms regarding the selection of material: the authors have attempted impartiality in their choice of topics and documents but inevitably some imbalance of emphasis has probably occurred. Nevertheless the main areas of Greek social and political history have been covered in depth, with special focus on the manifestations in the archaic period of colonisation and tyranny throughout the Greek world and Athenian politics in the sixth century. The history of the classical period per se is represented by sections on the Persian Wars, the Delian League and Pentekontaetia and the Peloponnesian War, and Sparta's history and society in both archaic and classical times is covered by a separate section. These chapters, however, are also intended to be supplemented by the material in the so-called 'social' sections of this book. In these chapters on social history, we present a view of the realities of life in ancient Greece, with particular emphasis on the city-state and its relevance to Greek life and politics, labour, and the extent to which slaves, metics, serfs and citizens competed in the labour market, religion in all its manifestations, and women and sexual relationships in Greek society. The aim has been to give a wide range of material from contemporary sources, which will, if the authors' aim is achieved, be more than sufficient for study at an undergraduate level.

Since this book is intended to give a view of the Greek world as a whole, where possible documents have been chosen relating not simply to Athens and Sparta but to the lesser-known centres of Greek civilisation and culture, and the aim has been to keep the reader continually in mind of the geographical and chronological scope of Greek history and civilisation. A book covering so broad a subject must inevitably suffer from incompleteness in some areas, and we have had to limit not merely the topics covered, but the number of texts illustrating each section. We can only hope that our choice of material does not appear too arbitrary, and have tried to ensure that we have given references throughout to other useful passages which will direct the student to further documents of relevance in the area. We have also given suggestions for further reading on particular points of importance and envisage that the chapter bibliographies will enable students to pursue detailed research on particular topics.

In our translations we have followed the Greek as closely as possible, even to punctuation where this does not involve confusion, and poetry is as far as possible translated in lines following those of the original text. Present in our minds has been the thought that this would be a suitable text for use in a unit on 'Greek for historians', and to that end we have made comparisons of the translations with the original sources as easy as possible. For this reason we have carefully inserted all chapter and section numbers of the original sources in the text of our translations. For those students who do not as yet have Greek, we can perhaps hope that this study of some of the more important documents of Greek history will inspire them to attempt to acquire the language. Titles of ancient sources are given in English, but references to the texts used in our translations can be found in the index of ancient sources. There is probably no way to avoid the pitfalls inherent in the transliteration of Greek names and terms into English. Where possible a literal transliteration has been preferred, except where the names and terms might be thought to be better known to the reader in an anglicised form. This naturally has involved some arbitrary judgements and appearance of inconsistency, of which the authors are aware.

Our thanks are particularly due to two of our colleagues for their help and support: Professor Trevor Bryce, now Deputy Vice-Chancellor of Lincoln University in New Zealand, and Mrs Annette Ince, who has given us invaluable assistance with the formatting and presentation of this book. Our thanks are also due to Dixson Library, University of New England.

Armidale, NSW
June 1994

1

THE POLIS: THE GREEK CITY-STATE

The central focus of civilisation for the Greeks, after the oikos or family unit, was the polis (plural: poleis). Polis is usually translated as 'city-state' as a polis was generally an independent state, with its own laws, customs, political system, military force, currency and sometimes calendar. According to Aristotle those who did not live in a polis were 'tribeless, lawless, hearthless', and to the Greeks the fact that they lived in a city-state was proof that they were a civilised people (doc. 1.1). But the polis should also in Aristotle's opinion be limited in size and self-sufficient. He was the first to employ the metaphor of the 'ship of state'. Too few inhabitants and the polis could not be self-sufficient, too many and the ship would be too big, and the administration of the polis would be adversely affected (doc. 1.3).

Aristotle's well-known statement that 'man is a political animal' should in fact be translated as 'man is a creature who lives in a polis' (Arist. *Pol.* 1253a 2–3: doc. 1.1), while according to Thucydides (7.77.7) 'it is men who are the city, and not walls or ships with no men inside'. Much of the history of the Greeks is the history of the interaction between its cities. City-states were generally independent, and, though various cities at different times attempted to dominate the other cities in Greece, these attempts were generally short-lived. The cities, rather than uniting with each other, were prone to fight amongst themselves, and nearby neighbours were often the most implacable enemies, such as Sparta and Argos. While there was a concept of mutual identity when faced with an outside enemy, as when during the Persian Wars the Hellenic League was formed to combat Xerxes (docs 11.19, 11.24), most Greeks saw themselves not primarily as Greek, but as a member of their city-state. Aristotle viewed the Greeks as superior to other peoples; the Greeks attained the 'highest political development' and Greece 'could rule everyone else, if it could achieve political unity' (doc. 1.2). But such unity was achieved only under Philip and Alexander of Macedon.

Apart from links with a mother-city which had sent out a colony, individual communities preferred to be self-sufficient, though many states were members of leagues, larger organisations formed to protect smaller cities or contribute to the power of the largest city-state in the region, such as the Peloponnesian League and Boeotian federation (docs 1.57–58, cf. 6.62–63). Athens was to gain power over a number of cities through the Delian League. There could also be cultural and religious unions between different cities (docs 1.59–60). While the Greek states shared several cultural features, such as the same language, religious beliefs, and system of writing (doc. 3.90), there were still differences between states: there were dialectical variations, each state had its own tutelary deities with different cults, names and festivals, and there could be differences of alphabet (cf. doc. 2.10).

Athens was the largest mercantile and commercial centre but had a rival in Corinth whose position on the Isthmus made it a major shipping centre and trading depot, with goods being transferred across the Isthmus to avoid the longer sail around the Peloponnese (docs 1.61–62). From the available sources, it is possible to obtain a clear impression of some of the economic priorities of Greek city-states. Obviously by the fifth century the import of grain was of great importance to certain states like Teos (doc. 1.65), and there was legislation to stop corruption and consumer exploitation, as in the wine trade at Thasos, which not only regulated when wine could be sold, but specifically prevented adulteration and retail dealing, in terms which imply that these were a common occurrence (doc. 1.66). The most specific evidence for the economy of a city-state of course derives from Athens. Athens controlled trade (doc. 1.69), and levied customs duties (doc. 1.68), and had revenues drawn from a wide variety of taxes (doc. 1.28). All cities would have had their own system of taxation, both direct and indirect (doc. 1.47), and in the sixth as well as the fifth century BC most states would have had quite complex taxation and commercial systems in place.

Aristotle's discussions of the various types of government point to the diversity of political organisation in Greece: kingship, aristocracy and constitutional government (politeia), from which the 'deviations' were, respectively for him, tyranny, oligarchy and democracy (doc. 1.1). Naturally the constitutions of cities changed over time, and the *Athenaion Politeia* listed eleven changes in constitution (politeia) from Athens' earliest history down to the 320s BC (doc. 1.4). In a democracy, Aristotle notes that all the citizens 'must be equal'; each citizen is governed by the others but in turn governs them (through rotation of who holds the political offices). The majority of citizens should decide what is to be done (doc. 1.5). Theophrastos in discussing the laws of Eresos saw 'merit, adequate property and common sense' as defining the criteria for office (doc. 1.6), but Perikles summed up a different political ideology for democratic Athens: it was merit alone, not the property a citizen owned, which was the determining principle in political participation: no one was denied office because of being poor (doc. 1.17).

While the poorer citizens in a democracy did ensure that they enjoyed sacrifices and civic amenities (doc. 1.8, cf. 1.18), and Aristotle defined democracy as looking only to the 'interests of the poor' (doc. 1.1), citizenship carried specific obligations. Perikles in his Funeral Oration outlined the privileges citizens enjoyed: to stand for political office and to speak in the assembly, with the majority managing the affairs of the city and 'not just a few' (doc. 1.17). All citizens were to participate in Athenian affairs of state: Solon had passed a law against political apathy in 594/3 BC (doc. 8.21). More importantly, Perikles described the citizen who took no part in politics as 'totally useless' (doc. 1.17). A citizen had to be prepared to lay down his life for his city (cf. doc. 1.41); he had to look at Athens and become its lover (doc. 1.17).

Aristotle's concern that if the citizens are unknown to each other then the 'management of political positions' suffers (docs 1.1, 1.3) was overcome in Athens by the people having control over the officials, who were examined before they took office and had to give an account of their term of office when it was over (docs 1.19, 1.22). Widespread political participation by the citizens was ensured at Athens by paying the citizens for political duties, such as holding office, being a member of the boule, serving on a jury, and in the fourth century for attendance at the assembly (ekklesia). The vast majority of citizens had to work hard for a living and needed financial reimbursement for working time spent in political duties. In particular, payment for serving on juries was fundamental to Athenian practice because the law courts made so many decisions (doc. 9.23), particularly in the fourth century BC when laws proposed in the assembly could be declared illegal, with the juries deciding on the issue. Despite Aristophanes' comic caricatures of the jurors as cranky old men who loved deciding a lawsuit (docs 1.25–26, 1.28), the judicial system worked efficiently; arbitrary punishment, imprisonment, execution and confiscation of property were not hallmarks of the democracy but of the two periods of oligarchy in 411 and 404–403 BC.

Most of the evidence about the workings of city-states comes from Athens. This was an unusually large city, with several important urban areas, such as Eleusis, and various villages (demes) scattered throughout the territory of Attica (though Syracuse in Sicily was also larger and more important than many mainland Greek cities). Every citizen had the right to vote and also to speak in the assembly, which in fifth-century Athens was the decision-making body (doc. 1.18; cf. 7.26 for Mytilene). Nevertheless there were constitutional constraints on the assembly, and from Kleisthenes' time the agenda for the meeting was drawn up beforehand by the boule, the Council of Five Hundred, which served rather like a standing committee. Of the five hundred councillors, fifty were chosen from each of the ten tribes and one of the tribes was in office ('held the prytany', each prytany being one-tenth of the year) at any one time, the fifty councillors from that particular tribe being responsible for the day-to-day business that came up in the Council and procedure in the assembly, such as putting questions to the vote. But the procedure did not always run normally, as after the battle of Arginousai in 406 BC (doc. 1.20). In the seventh and sixth centuries the most important officials of Athens had been the archons: there were nine of these – the basileus (or king) archon, the eponymous archon, after whom the year was named, and the polemarch (war archon), plus six thesmothetai. In the time of Kleisthenes, the archons were joined by a tenth, the secretary of the thesmothetai, and now corresponded to the new ten tribes, with one archon was elected from each. In fact, in the fifth century the most important officials were the ten generals (strategoi), who were appointed annually, one from each tribe, but were eligible for re-election and thus became the real political leaders of Athens as well as the commanders of the armed forces.

Perikles' Funeral Oration is a valuable document for the Athenians' concept of the responsibilities of a citizen in a democracy as well as making clear the fact that Athens in particular prided itself on its independence and political system (doc. 1.17). Nevertheless, there was no 'model' for a city-state, despite Aristotle's theoretical propositions. It would be unwise to take Athens as representing the 'average' Greek polis: Sparta was in many respects the very antithesis of Athens, in political structure and constitution, society, economy and culture. All Greek city-states were different and possessed their own constitutions and social practices (cf. docs 1.45–54), but all were of course equally important to their inhabitants, whose lives revolved entirely around this integral component of Greek civilisation and culture.

THE GOVERNMENT OF THE CITY-STATE

1.1 Aristotle *Politics* 1252b28–1253a7, 1279a22–1279b10: Man Is a 'Political Animal'

The phrase 'man is a political animal' is a famous mistranslation of Aristotle's phrase: 'man is by nature a creature of the polis'. That is, man functions with and belongs to the city-state (the polis; pl.: poleis), which was the essential building block of Greek civilisation and one of its defining characteristics. Aristotle defines various types of government but what is crucial is that the individual citizen has a role in the polis; he here sees democracy, like that of fifth-century Athens, as a deviation from normal rule by the people. The amalgamation of villages into a single unit was synoikismos, synoecism (for which see docs 1.7, 1.55–56).

1252b28 The amalgamation of numerous villages creates a unified city-state, large enough to be self-sufficient or nearly so, starting from the need to survive, and continuing its existence for the sake of a comfortable lifestyle. So, the city is natural just like the earlier forms of society. It is the outcome of them, and the nature of a thing is its outcome, for what each thing is when its development has been completed we call this its nature, whether we are talking of a man, or a horse, or a household. Moreover the final cause and outcome of a thing is the best, and to be self-sufficient is the best outcome.

1253a2 From this it is clear that the state is a creation of nature and that man is by nature a creature of the polis. And anyone who by nature and not by chance is without a polis is either a bad man or far above humanity, and like the 'tribeless, lawless, hearthless' person whom Homer (*Iliad* 9.63) condemns, this man is by nature necessarily a lover of war, and may even be compared to an isolated piece in a board-game like draughts.

1279a22 Then, with regard to the different types of government, we have to find out how many there are, and what they are, and first of all what their true forms are — for when these are defined the deviations from them will at once become clear. The words constitution and government have the same meaning and the government, which is the supreme authority in poleis, must be in the hands of one, or of a few, or of the many, and the true forms of government therefore are those in which the one, or the few, or the many are ruling with a view to the common interest, while those which rule with a view to private interests, whether of the one, or of the few, or of the many, are deviations. For, the citizens, if they are truly so, ought to share in the benefits of government.

1279a32 Of the types of government which look to the common interest we normally call that in which one person rules kingship; that in which more than one but not many rule, aristocracy — either because the rulers are the best men, or because they promote the best interests of the state and citizens; and, when the many administer the state for the common interest, the government is called by its generic name – constitutional government … **1279b4** Of the above-mentioned types, the deviations from these are as follows: from kingship, tyranny; from aristocracy, oligarchy; from constitutional government, democracy. For tyranny is a kind of monarchy, which looks only to the interests of the ruler; oligarchy looks to the interests of the wealthy; and democracy to the interests of the poor: none of these looks to the common good of the people as a whole.

1.2 Aristotle *Politics* 1327b23–33: Greek Superiority over Other Countries

The Greeks are here seen as superior to other races by reason of the effect geography and climate have on their development, and their right to rule or enslave inferior peoples is implicitly accepted. Herodotos similarly praises the location of the cities of the Ionian Greeks on the coast of Asia Minor (doc. 1.59).

1327b23 Peoples in cold countries, especially those in Europe, are spirited but lack intelligence and skill; for this reason they remain mostly free, but do not attain political development and are unable to rule those near them. The peoples of Asia possess intelligence and skill, but they lack spirit, and for this reason they remain governed by others and enslaved. The Greek race, however, lying between these regions, shares the characteristics of both. It is spirited and intelligent, and for this reason remains at liberty and attains the highest political development, while it is able to rule everyone else, if it can achieve political unity.

1.3 Aristotle *Politics* 1326a40–b24: The Ideal City-State

The city-state, according to Aristotle, needs to be of a certain size and to be self-sufficient, while the citizens are to know each other so that the 'management of political offices' and judgements in law cases are sound. Despite his emphasis on the self-sufficiency of cities, most of them relied on imports, and Perikles boasts that Athens can afford imported goods from all over the world (docs 1.17, 1.69). Aristotle argues that in a large city foreigners and metics can more easily claim citizenship, but the Athenians overcame this problem by having the citizen rolls managed at the level of the small deme units (doc. 1.38). Stentor was the herald with a booming voice in Homer's *Iliad* (5.785–6).

1326a40 A boat that is the span of an outstretched hand in length will not be a boat at all, nor will one that is two stades in length. When a boat comes to a certain length it will be unseaworthy either because it is too small or because it is too big.

1326b2 It is the same with a polis: if it has too few inhabitants it will not be self-sufficient (a polis is necessarily self-sufficient), and if it has too many it will of course be self-sufficient, but as a country, not as a polis; for it will not easily acquire a government — for who would be a military commander of such an excessively large group of people, or who a herald, unless he had a voice like Stentor? So when the population first reaches the minimum size for self-sufficiency and prosperity in respect of its political community, it can continue growing larger in size than this and become a larger polis, but this, as we said, cannot go on indefinitely.

1326b11 It is easy to determine from how a polis works the limit of where this growth has to stop. The tasks of a polis belong to those who rule and those who are ruled, the tasks of the ruler being governing and giving judgement. But, for judging lawsuits and the allocation of offices according to merit, citizens have to know each other and what kind of people these others are, and where this is not the case the management of political positions and the judging of lawsuits obviously suffers. In both cases it is not proper to conduct these in a casual manner, as clearly has to happen where the population is too large. It also makes it easier for foreigners and metics to claim citizenship, as it is not difficult to escape detection because of the size of the population. So it is clear that a polis is of best size when it has a population large enough for a self-sufficient lifestyle but one that can be seen at a glance.

1.4 [Aristotle] *Athenaion Politeia* 41.2: The Eleven Constitutions of Athens

Writing in the 320s BC, the author of the *Athenaion Politeia* outlines eleven major constitutional changes at Athens, and sees the constitution as having become increasingly democratic throughout the fourth century. Voting for decrees in the ekklesia, and control of the law courts (dikasteria), are given as the two ways in which 'the many' govern the Athenian state.

41.2 The return from Phyle and the Piraeus (403 BC) was the eleventh change to the constitution. The first was the establishment of Ion and his companions when they came to settle at Athens, for it was then that the Athenians were divided for the first time into four tribes and the tribe-kings appointed. The second (the first after the original one which had a constitutional significance) took place in the time of Theseus, and deviated slightly from monarchy. After this came the one in the time of Drakon, in which laws were drawn up for the first time. The third was in the time of Solon following civil unrest, which saw the start of democratic rule. The fourth was the tyranny in Peisistratos' time. The fifth was that of

Kleisthenes after the overthrow of the tyrants, which was more democratic than that of Solon. The sixth followed the Persian Wars under the oversight of the Council of the Areiopagos. The seventh and subsequent change had been suggested by Aristeides, but was put into effect by Ephialtes when he dissolved the Areiopagos Council, during which owing to the demagogues and its naval empire the city committed its greatest mistakes. Eighth was the establishment of the Four Hundred, and after this came the ninth, when democracy was restored. Tenth was the tyranny of the Thirty and the Ten. The eleventh was the one that came into being after the return from Phyle and the Piraeus. From this time the constitution has continued down to that of the present day, and the power of the people has continuously increased throughout this period. For the people has made itself master of everything and administers everything through decrees and jury-courts in which the people has total control, for even the law cases tried by the Council have come across to the people. They appear to act correctly in so doing: for a few people are more easily corrupted by money and favours than the many.

1.5 Aristotle *Politics* 1317a40–b4: Aristotle on Democracy

Democracy, or the 'rule of the people', was the form of government at Athens from 508/7 to 322/1 BC. The Athenian government was a form of 'direct' democracy, in which all citizens were expected to participate, both by voting and speaking in the assembly and by standing for various offices and magistracies, or serving on Athens' council, the boule: Perikles praises this form of government in his Funeral Oration (doc. 1.17). Greek cities also possessed governments in the form of kingships (especially the dual kingship in Sparta), tyrannies (one-man rule), aristocracies ('the rule of the best') and oligarchies ('the rule of the few').

1317a40 A democratic polis presupposes liberty, and it is generally said that only in this type of state can liberty be enjoyed: **1317b1** people say that this is the aim of every democracy. One principle of liberty is that everyone is governed and governs in turn. This is because democratic justice means equality by numbers and not by merit, and this being so the majority must be the sovereign power, and whatever the majority decides must be the final decision and be just. Every one of the citizens, it is said, must be equal. In consequence, in democracies the poor have more power than the wealthy, as there are more of them and the decision of the majority is supreme. So this is one of the marks of liberty, which all democrats see as the distinguishing mark of their constitution: another is that everyone should live as he chooses. This, they affirm, is liberty in practice, since not living in accordance with your wishes constitutes the life of a slave. This is the second distinguishing mark of democracy, and in consequence of this there has evolved the desire not to be governed, by anyone if possible, and if not for government to be taken in turns, thus contributing to the concept of liberty founded on equality.

1317b17 As this is our foundation and starting point, the principle features of democracy are as follows: the election of all officials from the whole body; that everyone should govern each individual and that every individual should in turn govern everyone; that appointment to every position, or at least those that do not require experience and skill, should be made by lot; that no property qualification should be needed for officials or just a very low one; that the same person should not hold the same office twice, or not often, except in the case of military positions; that all positions, or as many as possible, should be limited in duration;

that everyone should be involved in the judicial system and selected out of everyone and judge all issues, or at least the majority of them and those of the greatest importance, such as the audit of accounts, the constitution, and private contracts, with the assembly the supreme authority over all of these, or at least the most important, with the magistrates having no responsibility over any of them or only a very few. Of all the magistracies, the Council is the most democratic when there is no way of paying everyone; but, if there is, the authority of the Council is lost as well, as the people when paid take over all the lawsuits themselves as I said in my discussion earlier. The next feature of democracy is that everyone gets paid, including assembly, courts, and magistrates, and, if this is not possible, then magistrates, courts, Council and the sovereign assemblies, or at the very least those magistrates who have to dine together. While oligarchy is defined by birth, wealth and education, the distinguishing factors of democracy seem to be the opposite of these, such as low birth, poverty and the lifestyle of a tradesman.

1.6 Theophrastos, *Laws for Eresos*: The Need for Experience in Public Life

Theophrastos (*c.* 370–288), a pupil of Aristotle's and his successor in the Academy, is here theorising about the best ways to appoint officials. Theophrastos' home was the city of Eresos on the island of Lesbos.

What is best is that someone should gain trust through his lifestyle and upbringing, not his property, and education and good customs in the state will bring this about. At any rate, the practice of basing office-holding on census classes seems in general too archaic because it would often debar the true leaders: neither Epameinondas, nor Pelopidas, nor Iphikrates and Chabrias from Athens would have become generals, nor those earlier and better men Aristeides and Themistokles. It appears, therefore, that there needs overall to be some consideration of which offices should be filled on the basis of wealth and merit or merit only or wealth only. For the treasury positions, as has been said, people look for wealth; for guarding the laws or some other such position one needs justice, and for the generalship, whether it is in charge of matters outside or within the city, sufficient fortune in addition to merit, as well as the third factor, mentioned before, experience. These are the three requirements for holding office: merit, adequate property, and common sense — assuming that goodwill is a common factor. The two first of these are needed for all, while common sense is appropriate for some, but essential for the most important offices. In some ways it is enough if one looks at both criteria honestly, for they are in general good at observing, and best at recognising, times of crisis; as a result people are chosen for their good fortune and ability, though some people do look at one or the other because they choose the best citizens, while most people who are poor at judging look to property. It is true, as said before, that some offices especially call for trustworthiness, some common sense and cleverness, and others attention to detail and aggression, even if this is distasteful. But it is not easy to assign a person to each by law, so that it has to be those who scrutinise the candidates who select the most suitable.

Since some offices, as has been said, require experience, it is a good idea always to introduce into these some of the younger men so they can be trained how to do things by those with the knowledge and so not cause any damage to the city's administration, as Hagnon once advised the Athenians to do in the case of their generals, using the example of hunting, where, he said, lovers of hunting always bring along puppies. And some of the well-administered smaller cities already do this, such as Karystos and Kythnos: they appoint three men who have already served as generals and two of the younger men. In this office in particular the most important crises are bound to arise, but nevertheless some mixture of this sort, combining the different age-groups, will result in good government and positive reinforcement from both ages, as in the gymnasiarchy: those who elect two men, one older, one younger, for this position do this in the right way, so that one provides the discipline for his share, while the other takes the lead in the fitness exercises when he strips off. Not that it is fair that both have exactly the same duties — but the overall responsibility belongs to them both, and what is needed for that is a high degree of attention to detail. Anyone, however, who intends to hold the higher magistracies should first hold other offices, as was said for the generalship. It would be ridiculous if a person who had not been a taxiarchos (leader of a tribal contingent) or phylarchos (leader of a tribe) went straight into being a general. As was said before, some offices can be tried out earlier, others should be left till later, for two reasons: in this system the man who expects office is made eager and ambitious to be tried out because of the status of the more important offices or, as used to happen in Epeiros, the delay (before they can be held). In some places the law states that candidates for higher offices have to be selected from the lower ones or from those supposed to lead to the higher ones, as in Phokis, where they select their generals from those who have been phylarchs and treasurers. Generally speaking no one should hold office without at least having been a member of the Council, as in Ambrakia.

ATHENS: 'THE VIOLET-CROWNED CITY'

'Rich, violet-crowned and famed in song,
Bulwark of Greece, glorious Athens.'

Pindar F64

Estimates of Attica's overall population in the fifth century are difficult to arrive at. It seems likely that that there were between 30,000 and 40,000 male citizens, with their wives and children, in addition to the resident foreigners, the metics. There were not large numbers of slaves, so an overall human population of 200,000–250,000 is probable.

1.7 Thucydides 1.10.2: A Comparison of Athens and Sparta

Sparta was made up of separate, geographically unconnected villages, and had not undergone a synoikismos into one community, unlike Athens (see doc. 1.56; and for Athens' great buildings, docs 1.9, 1.35).

1.10.2 If the Spartans' city were to become deserted, and only the temples and foundations of buildings were left, I think that the people of that time far in the future would find it difficult to believe that the Spartans' power had been as great as their fame implied (and yet they inhabit two-fifths of the Peloponnese, and are in command of all of it as well as of many allies outside it; nevertheless, it has not been synoikised into a city, nor does it possess costly temples and buildings, but consists of a number of villages in the early Greek manner, and would seem an inferior place), whereas if the same thing were to happen to Athens, from its visible remains one would assume that the city had been twice as powerful as it actually is.

1.8 [Xenophon] *Constitution of the Athenians* 2.9–10: The Amenities of Athens, c. 425 BC

The author is apparently annoyed that the people can enjoy benefits which the rich have to pay for themselves. At doc. 1.30 the author complains that it is the wealthy who pay for liturgies, and sees a popular motive behind it, so that the poorer citizens become wealthy and the rich poorer, which of course did not happen.

2.9 The people, realising that it is impossible for each of the poor to offer sacrifices, hold banquets, set up shrines and govern a great and beautiful city, have discovered a way of having sacrifices, shrines, festivals and sanctuaries. So the city sacrifices numerous victims at public expense, but it is the people who banquet and who are allocated the victims. **10** And while some of the wealthy have their own private gymnasia, baths and dressing-rooms, the people have built for their own use many wrestling-schools (palaistrai), dressing-rooms and bath-houses; and the ordinary people enjoy far more of these than the aristocrats and the wealthy.

1.9 Plutarch *Life of Perikles* 12.1–2: Perikles' Building Programme

Perikles' opponents in the assembly criticised his building programme as misuse of funds contributed by the allies. But it is unclear whether tribute funded the Parthenon, which itself probably only cost some 460–500 talents over several years and could have been paid for by internal revenues.

12.1 But what brought most pleasure and adornment to Athens, and the greatest amazement to the rest of mankind, and is the only evidence that the tales of Greece's power and ancient prosperity are not lies, was Perikles' construction of monuments. But this of all his measures was the one most maligned and slandered by his enemies in the assembly ... **2** 'Greece must be outraged,' they cried, 'and consider this an act of blatant tyranny, when she sees that with the contributions she has been compelled to make towards the war we are gilding and beautifying our city, like some vain woman decking herself in precious jewels and statues and temples worth thousands of talents.'

1.10 Thucydides 2.13.3–5: Athens' Resources at the Outbreak of War

Perikles is here pointing out the city's resources to the people of Athens at the outbreak of the Peloponnesian War. Compared to Sparta, Athens was financially well prepared for war, and in addition had a fleet of 300 triremes. The sacred monies could be used but were to be repaid, but Athens in the event did not repay them: cf. doc. 1.11 for the treasures in the Parthenon.

2.13.3 Perikles told the Athenians to take courage from the fact that the city had nearly six hundred talents a year coming in as tribute from the allies, quite apart from the rest of the revenue, and that they still had on the acropolis six thousand talents in coined silver (at its greatest the reserve had amounted to nine thousand seven hundred talents, from which they had paid for the propylaea of the acropolis and the other buildings and for Potidaea). **4** There was also uncoined gold and silver in the shape of private and public dedications and all the sacred accoutrements used in the processions and festivals, and Persian spoils and other things of the same kind, amounting to not less than five hundred talents. **5** And to this he added the many possessions of the other shrines, which they could make use of, and, if nothing else were available to them, the gold decorating the statue of the goddess herself. He pointed out that there was forty talents' weight of pure gold on the statue, all removable. But he said that if they used it to ensure their own safety, they had to replace no less an amount afterwards. **6** As to their finances then he told them to have confidence: as to hoplites there were thirteen thousand, not counting the sixteen thousand who manned the garrisons and city walls. **7** This was the number that was initially on garrison duty when the enemy were invading, comprised of the oldest and youngest citizens and those metics who were hoplites … **8** He pointed out that there were twelve hundred cavalry, including mounted archers, and three hundred seaworthy triremes.

1.11 *Inscriptiones Graecae* I^3 351: Inventory of the Treasures of the Parthenon, 422/1 BC

The treasures in the Parthenon were made up of dedications and war booty. Every four years an account had to be made of the treasures, to ensure that there had been no theft or embezzling: note the precise value given for specific objects. These treasures belonged to the goddess Athena, and while Perikles said the treasures could be borrowed the Athenians had to give back 'no less an amount' (doc. 1.10). Compare Croesus' dedications at Delphi: Hdt. 1.50 (cf. doc. 3.20), cf. 9.80. [*IG* I^2 280.]

1 Gods. The following was handed over by the four boards, who gave their account from the Great Panathenaia to the Great Panathenaia, to the treasurers, for whom Presbias son of Semios of Phegaia was secretary. The treasurers, for whom Presbias son of Semios of Phegaia was secretary, handed over to the treasurers for whom Nikeas son of Euthykles of Halimous was secretary, to Euphemos of Kollytos and his colleagues in the Parthenon: crown of gold, weight of this 60 drachmas; bowls (phialai) of gold, five, weight of these 782 drachmas; uncoined gold, weight of this 1 drachma, 4 obols; drinking-cup (karchesion) of gold, its base silver gilt, sacred to Herakles of Elaious, weight of this 138 drachmas; two nails, silver underneath, gilt, weight of these 184 drachmas; mask, silver underneath, gilt, weight of this 116 drachmas; phialai of silver, 138 drachmas; horn of silver; weight of these 2 talents, 3,307 drachmas.

By number as follows: short Persian swords set in gold, 6; standing crop set in gold, ears of corn, 12; breadbaskets wooden underneath, gilt, 2; censer, wooden underneath, gilt, 1; girl on a stele, gilt, 1; bed, wooden underneath, gilt, 1; gorgon mask, skull overlaid with gold; horse, griffin, front part of griffin, griffin, head of lion, necklace of flowers, serpent, these overlaid with gold; helmet, overlaid with gold; shields, overlaid with gold, wooden underneath, 15; beds, Chian work, 7; beds, Milesian work, 10; sabres, 9; swords, 5; breastplates, 16; shields with devices, 6; shields covered with bronze, 31; chairs, 6; foot-stools, 4; camp-stools (diphroi), 9; lyre, gilt, 1; lyres of ivory, 4; lyres 4; table inlaid with ivory; helmets of bronze, 3; feet of beds, overlaid with silver, 13; small leather shield; phialai of silver, 4; small cups, silver underneath, 2; horse of silver; weight of these 900 drachmas. Shields, overlaid with gold, wooden underneath, 2; short Persian sword, overlaid with gold, unweighed; phialai of silver, 8, weight of these 807 drachmas; drinking-cups (poteria) from Chalkis of silver, 4, weight of these 124 drachmas; flute-case from Methymne of ivory, gilt; shield from Lesbos, with device; helmet from Lesbos, of Illyrian bronze; phialai of silver, 2; drinking-cups (karchesia) of silver, 2; weight of these 580 drachmas. Lesbian cups (kotyloi) of silver, 3, weight of these 370 drachmas; crown of gold, weight of this, 18 drachmas, 3 obols; crown of gold, weight of this 29 drachmas; crown of gold of Athena Nike, weight of this 29 drachmas; crown of gold, weight of this 33 drachmas; crown of gold of Athena Nike, weight of this 33 drachmas; tetradrachm of gold, weight of this 7 drachmas, $2^1/_2$ obols; onyx on a gold ring, unweighed.

1.12 *Inscriptiones Graecae* I^3 458a: Pheidias' Statue of Athena, 440/39

This inscription provides for the purchase of materials for the cult-image of the Parthenon, which was begun in 447/6 and dedicated in 438 BC; cf. Thuc. 2.13.5; Plut. *Per.* 13.14. The total cost may have been between 700 and 1,000 talents. For the charges against Pheidias of impiety and embezzling gold and ivory intended for the statue, see Plut. *Per.* 31.2–5. [*IG* I^2 356.]

Kichesippos of the deme Myrrhinous was secretary for the commissioners of the statue. Receipt from the treasurers for whom Demostratos of Xypete was secretary: 100 talents. The treasurers were Ktesion, Strosias, Antiphates, Menandros, Thymochares, Smokordos, Pheideleides. Gold was bought, weight 6 talents, 1,618 drachmas, 1 obol; the cost of this was 87 talents, 4,652 drachmas, 5 obols. Ivory was bought: 2 talents, 743 drachmas.

1.13 *Inscriptiones Graecae* I^3 449: Building Accounts of the Parthenon, 434/3 BC

This is the best preserved of the Parthenon building accounts, of which the fifteen years 447/6 to 433/2 BC are recorded on the four sides of a marble stele on the acropolis. The accounts start with the balance from the previous year and the year's income of the board of annual commissioners, the main grant coming from Athena's treasurers (here less than normal at four talents as the project was nearing completion). [*IG* I^2 352.]

For the commissioners for whom Antikles was secretary in the (year of) the fourteenth Council in which Metagenes was first secretary, when Krates was the Athenians' archon. Receipts for this year are as follows:

1,470 dr.:	Balance from the last year
74:	Lampsakene gold staters
27 ⅙:	Cyzicene gold staters
25,000 dr.:	From the treasurers of the goddess's treasury for whom Krates of Lamptrai was secretary
1,372 dr.:	From gold sold off, weight 98 drachmas; payment for this
1,305 dr. 4 ob.:	From ivory sold off, weight 3 talents, 60 drachmas; payment for this

Expenditures:

… 200:	For purchases
—2 dr. 1 ob.:	

For wages:

1,926 dr. 2 ob.:	For the workers at Pentelikos and those who load the stone on the wagons

401		
	16,392 dr.:	Wages for the sculptors of the pediment-sculptures
	1,800 dr.:	For monthly wages
	..11 dr., 2 ob.:	
405	Balance for this Year	
	—	
	—	
	74:	Lampsakene gold staters
	27 ⅙:	Cyzicene gold staters

1.14 *Inscriptiones Graecae* I³ 49 : Care of Athens' Water Supply, c. 435 BC

This inscription concerns Perikles and his sons Paralos and Xanthippos (and other unspecified sons; cf. doc. 4.29) and the improvement of Athens' water supply, which was to receive first priority from the income from the tribute once Athena had received her one-sixtieth share (the 'first fruits'). Perikles and his sons had apparently offered to pay some of the costs themselves, but the people decided to use the money from the tribute instead. [*IG* I² 54.]

... Hipponikos proposed the motion: ... each ... are to receive pay of a drachma for each day, and they are to look after the spring and the conduit for the water ... Nikomachos proposed the amendment: that the rest be as resolved by the Council, ... so that they flow ... so that for minimum cost ... the prytaneis who by lot are the first to hold office, ... in the first of the regular assemblies immediately after the sacred matters. ... is good for the people of the Athenians ... not occur and it shall turn out for the Athenians ... proposed the amendment: that the rest be as Nikomachos proposed; and that Perikles and Paralos and Xanthippos and the (other) sons be commended; and expenditure (on this) shall be made from the money that is paid into the tribute of the Athenians, once the goddess has received from them her accustomed portion.

1.15 Demosthenes 43 *Against Makartatos* 71: Athens' Olive Trees

The defendant is accused of having cut down more than a thousand oil-producing olive trees in order to sell the wood while the inheritance of a minor's estate was still under adjudication. The prosecution claims that olive trees are so important to the state that the offence was not only against the owners of the estate but against Athens itself. Olive oil was used for food, lighting and bathing. It was also one of Athens' more important exports. The olive tree was sacred to Athena. Jars of oil from the sacred trees were presented as prizes at the Panathenaia in Athens and jars of olive oil were left on tombs: doc. 3.57.

71 If anyone digs up an olive tree at Athens, unless it is for a sanctuary of the Athenian state or a deme, or for his own use up to the maximum of two olive trees per year, or for the needs of a deceased person, he shall owe the treasury a hundred drachmas for each olive tree, with a tenth of this belonging to the goddess. In addition he shall owe the individual who prosecutes him a hundred drachmas for each olive tree. Cases concerning such matters are to be brought before the archons, according to their jurisdiction. The prosecutor shall deposit the court fees for his part. When a person is convicted, the archons before whom the case was brought shall make a written report to the collectors of the amount due to the treasury and to the treasurers of the goddess of the amount due to the goddess. If they do not make this report, they shall themselves be liable for the amount.

THE WORKINGS OF ATHENIAN DEMOCRACY

The two most important democratic institutions of Athens were the assembly (ekklesia) and the law courts (dikasteria); in the fifth century all citizens over eighteen years of age were members of the assembly, but in the fourth century citizens had to be at least twenty years of age. After Kleisthenes' reforms in 508 BC, the ekklesia made all of the political decisions, and, in the fourth century, indictments against proposed laws were aggressively pursued by political opponents in the dikasteria. The courts also possessed some political jurisdiction in the examination of the incoming and outgoing magistrates (dokimasiai and euthynai), who may have comprised some 700 (doc. 1.23). The Council, or boule, arranged the agenda for the assembly. In the fifth century the Council had 500 members, fifty from each tribe, each tribe presiding in turn: these presiding councillors were called the prytaneis and met in the prytaneion, the 'town hall'.

1.16 [Aristotle] *Athenaion Politeia* 43.1–6: Business Matters for the Council and Assembly

In the Athenian democracy it was axiomatic that any one citizen was as good as another and as capable of holding office – hence choosing by lot was an appropriate way of selecting officials. Exceptions, however, were made in the cases of financial officials, generals and those in charge of the water supply, showing not only that these were important functions, but that it was admitted that they needed skills not necessarily possessed by the 'average' citizen. The theoric fund was a festival account.

43.1 All the officials involved with routine administration are chosen by lot. The exceptions are: the treasurer of the military fund, those in charge of the theoric fund, and the superintendent of the water supply. All these are elected by show of hands, and those who are elected stay in office from one Panathenaia to the next. All military officials are also elected by show of hands. **2** The five hundred members of the Council are elected by lot, fifty from each tribe. Each of the tribes in turn presides, in an order decided by lot, with the first four holding office for thirty-six days each and each of the remaining six for thirty-five days, as the year is comprised of lunar months. **3** Members of the presiding tribe (the prytaneis) first dine in the prytaneion, receiving a payment from the city, and then convene meetings both of the Council and the people, with the Council meeting on every day except holidays, and the people four times in each prytany. The prytaneis give written notice of the business to be dealt with by the Council, and the agenda for each day, and the venue. **4** They also give written notice of assembly meetings: one sovereign meeting, at which there must be a vote on whether the magistrates appear to be performing their duties properly, and to deal with the food supply and defence of the country. On this same day those who wish to do so bring impeachments, and the inventories of confiscated property and claims to estates and heiresses are read out, so that no one is unaware of any vacant estate. **5** In the sixth prytany, in addition to the other matters mentioned, they take a vote on whether to hold an ostracism or not, and hear complaints about informers, both Athenians and metics, no more than three each, and whether anyone has failed to redeem a promise made to the people. **6** The second meeting is one for petitions at which anyone who wishes can place an olive-branch (on the altar) and address the people on any matter he chooses, whether private or public. The other two meetings deal with the remaining business and at these the laws lay down that three discussions of sacred matters must take place, three to do with heralds and embassies, and three to do with secular matters.

1.17 Thucydides 2.37.1–43.1: The Duties of a Citizen: Perikles' Funeral Oration

This speech was delivered by Perikles in 431/0 BC over the first Athenians who fell in the Peloponnesian War. Perikles is here stressing the ideals of democracy and praising the Athenian way of life. The essential nature of Athenian democracy is made clear: the majority of the citizens run the state, all are equal before the law and any citizen can stand for political office. There is a deliberate implicit comparison with Sparta: the Athenians 'love wisdom without cowardice'. The essential participatory nature of the democracy is made clear in the reference to the 'totally useless' citizen. Citizens are to 'love' their city: for the lover and beloved in Greek culture, see docs 4.72–89.

2.36.1 I shall speak firstly of our ancestors, for it is right as well as appropriate to give them the place of honour on such an occasion through the recollection of their deeds. For they handed down to us this country of ours, which the same people have inhabited continuously through successive generations up to this very day, free and independent through their valour. **2** And not only do they deserve praise, but our fathers deserve it even more, for, in addition to the inheritance that they were given, they acquired — and not without considerable trouble — the empire that we now possess and bequeathed it to those of us who are alive today. **3** And those of us now here, who are mostly still in the prime of life, have increased this empire even further in most respects and provided it with all the resources necessary to make it self-sufficient both in war and in peace. **4** I will not remind you of the military achievements by which our various possessions were acquired, whether it was ourselves or our fathers that valiantly repelled the approach of war, from barbarians and Greeks, as I do not want to speak at excessive length to those who already know the facts. But I do want to begin by describing the sort of training that has brought us to our present position, and the political institutions and way of life that have made our empire great, and then continue on to the praise of these men, as I consider that on the present occasion such statements are not unsuitable and that the whole crowd of both citizens and foreigners can listen to it with advantage.

2.37.1 We possess a constitution which does not imitate the laws of our neighbours: in fact we are an example to others rather than imitating anyone else. And the constitution's name is democracy, because the majority manage its affairs, not just a few; as regards the laws, everybody is equal when private disputes are being settled, and, as regards the criteria used to pick out anyone for office, what counts is not his belonging to a particular class, but his personal merit, while as regards poverty, as long as he can do something of value for the city, no one is prevented by obscurity from taking part in public life. **2** We conduct our political life with freedom, especially freedom from suspicion in respect of each other in our daily business, not being angry with our neighbour if he does as he pleases, and not even giving him the sort of looks which, although they do no harm, still hurt people's feelings. **3** But while we avoid giving offence in private life, in our public life it is primarily fear which prevents us from committing unlawful acts and makes us obey the magistrates and the laws, and in particular those laws made to protect those who are being unjustly treated and those which, though unwritten, bring acknowledged disgrace on people who break them. **2.38.1** Furthermore, we have provided numerous forms of relaxation and recreation for the mind: there are festivals and sacrifices throughout the year, and the elegance of our private dwellings and the pleasure we take in these day by day drives out any distress we might feel. **2** And because of the city's size, all kinds of things are imported from all over the earth, so that it seems just as natural to us to enjoy the goods of other men as those of our own production ... **2.40.1** We love good things without extravagance and we love wisdom without cowardice; we use wealth as an opportunity for action rather than as something to boast about, and there is nothing disgraceful for anyone in admitting poverty — what is disgraceful is not taking steps to escape it. **2** In the same people there is a concern at the same time for their own affairs and for those of the city, and even those primarily concerned with their own business are not deficient in their knowledge of the city's affairs; indeed, we are unique in considering the man who takes no part in the affairs of the city not as one who minds his own business, but as one who is totally useless ...

2.42.4 Not one of these men allowed either wealth, with the prospect of its continued enjoyment, to make him cowardly, or the hope which exists in poverty, that if you could only escape it you could become rich, to make him shrink from danger: they believed that vengeance on their enemies was more desirable than either, and also regarded such a risk as the most glorious of all, deciding to accept it and revenge themselves on the enemy, relinquishing their personal wishes and desires, and trusting to hope the uncertain chance of success, while in action, with regard to what faced them, they relied confidently on their own abilities. In that moment of combat, they thought it better to die in defending themselves than to yield and save their lives, and fled from dishonour, while standing firm in the face of physical danger, losing their lives in that brief moment ordained by fate, at the pinnacle not of fear but of glory.

2.43.1 And so these men conducted themselves as befits our city: and you who survive, though you pray the circumstances that will face you may be less hazardous, have to resolve that you will possess a spirit to resist the enemy no less brave than theirs. You have to judge the advantage of such a spirit not by words alone, though much could be said on this theme about all the benefits inherent in resisting the enemy — and you know all this without being told. No — you must actively keep before you the power of this city day by day, and become her lovers (erastai), and, when you are inspired by the vision of her greatness, remember that all this has been attained by men of courage who knew their duty and who, when it came to action, possessed a sense of honour. Even if they failed in an undertaking, they thought it right that their city should not be deprived of their valour, and offered it up to her as the most glorious contribution they could make. **2** They gave their lives for the common good, and in so doing won for themselves the praise which never grows old and the most distinguished of all tombs, not that in which they lie buried, but that in which their glory lies in eternal remembrance, on every occasion on which story or deed calls for its commemoration.

1.18 Aristophanes *Acharnians* 17–27: Assembly Procedure

Though the *Acharnians* was performed in 425 BC during the Archidamian phase of the Peloponnesian War when many country-dwellers were living together cramped up in the city, the vermilion-painted rope was still needed to pull people into the assembly. This perhaps shows the lack of attention of the people to public duty, or more probably simply the difficulty in getting citizens to the assembly so that it could start on time – the citizens were busy with gossiping and, as at all public functions, there was a problem getting everyone into the venue on time so it could commence. Dikaiopolis, a die-hard countryman, is speaking here.

Never, from the time when I began to wash
Have I been so tormented by soap under my eyebrows
As now, when a regular assembly is due to be held
At dawn, and the Pnyx here is deserted —
People are chatting in the agora and here and there
Avoiding the vermilion rope.
Even the prytaneis haven't come, but they'll arrive
Late, and then jostle as you'd expect
To try and get on the front bench,
All pouring in together; but that there'll be peace,
They don't care at all — O city, city!
I am always the first person to get to the assembly
And take my seat; then in my solitude
I groan, I yawn, I stretch myself, I fart,
Get bored, scribble, pluck my bead, do sums,
While I gaze out to the countryside, longing for peace,
Hating the city and longing for my own deme,
Which never told me to 'buy coal,'
'buy vinegar,' 'buy oil' — it didn't know the word!
It produced everything all by itself and that 'buy' word didn't exist.
So now I'm here absolutely ready
To shout, interrupt, and abuse the speakers,
If anyone speaks of anything other than peace!

1.19 Isocrates 7 *Areiopagitikos* 26–7: The Essence of Athenian Democracy

Isocrates (436–338 BC) praised Athenian democracy in this speech, which was probably delivered in 354; there is an implicit reference here to the rendering of the accounts of officials at the end of their term of office (the euthyna, or audit).

26 In short, our ancestors decided that the people, as the absolute power, should appoint the magistrates, punish those who failed in their duties, and act as judge in matters of dispute, while those who had the time and the means should devote themselves to public affairs like servants. **27** If they acted with justice they would be commended and be satisfied with this honour; if they governed badly they would receive no mercy but be subjected to the severest penalties. And yet, how could anyone discover a democracy with more stability or more justice than this one — which put the most competent men in charge of its government, but gave the people absolute power over them?

1.20 Xenophon *Hellenika* 1.7.9–15: The Trial of the Generals after Arginousai

In 406 BC the Athenians sent every available man (including slaves: doc. 5.23) to aid the Athenian fleet blockaded at Mytilene by the Spartans. They were victorious at Arginousai, but a storm prevented the Athenian generals from rescuing those cast into the sea. Six of the eight generals involved returned to Athens, and were brought before the assembly. Kallixenos secured passage in the Council of a resolution that the assembly should simply vote to acquit or condemn, by ballot, all six defendants together without further discussion. The Athenians soon regretted what they had done: Xen. *Hell.* 1.7.35. Socrates, who was a member of the Council at the time, was the only one to object (doc. 3.85). The Eleven were the jailers and executioners at Athens.

1.7.9 Then they held an assembly, to which the Council presented its proposal, Kallixenos bringing the motion as follows: since the Athenians have heard both those who brought charges against the generals and the generals' defence in the previous assembly, they are all to vote by tribes; and two urns will be provided for each tribe; and for each tribe a herald shall proclaim that whoever thinks the generals to be guilty of not picking up those who had won the naval battle shall place his vote in the first urn, and whoever thinks them to be not guilty, in the second. **10** And if it is decided that they are guilty, they shall be punished with death and handed over to the Eleven and their property confiscated, and a tithe to belong to the goddess ... **12** Euryptolemos and Peisianaktos and some others brought a charge against Kallixenos of having made an unconstitutional proposal. And some of the people commended this, but the majority shouted that it would be dreadful if the people were not allowed to do what they wanted. **13** In addition, when Lykiskos proposed the motion that these men should be judged by the same vote as the generals unless they withdrew their charge, the mob again created an uproar, and they were forced to withdraw their charges. **14** Some of the prytaneis declared that they would not put the question to the vote contrary to law, but Kallixenos again mounted the speakers' platform and made the same accusations against them. And the crowd shouted that all who refused should be taken to court. **15** The prytaneis, terrified, all agreed to put the question to the vote except for Socrates, son of Sophroniskos; he declared that he would not do anything against the law.

1.21 Antiphon 5 *On the Murder of Herodes* 69–71: A Hasty Judgement

This particular example, which occurred some time in the past and had become notorious, indicates that 'the exception proves the rule'; Athenian justice worked remarkably fairly over two centuries. The hellenotamiai ('Greek treasurers') administered the funds of the Delian League. The Eleven were Athenian officials in charge of the prison and the execution of criminals; they were appointed by lot.

69 The hellenotamiai of Athens were once wrongfully charged with embezzlement, as wrongfully as in the case against me today. All but one of them were executed, with anger overtaking rationality. The true facts later came to light. **70** The survivor, whose name is said to have been Sosias, had been condemned to death, but not yet executed. In the meantime it was revealed how the money had disappeared, and the fellow was rescued by the Athenian people although already in the hands of the Eleven, while the others who died were completely innocent. **71** The older ones amongst you remember this, I expect, while the younger ones like myself will have heard of it.

1.22 Aeschines 3 *Against Ktesiphon* 17–21: Athenian Auditors

As Aeschines notes in this speech dating to 330 BC, all Athenian officials of any kind, political, military or religious, had to undergo an audit (euthyna), an examination of their period in office, at the end of their term. The priestly families specifically mentioned, the Eumolpidai and Kerykes, were those involved in the Eleusinian Mysteries (docs 3.31–39). The trierarchs were those wealthy individuals made responsible for the costs of maintaining a warship – trireme – for one year (see docs 1.30–31).

17 In this our city, so ancient and powerful as it is, no one who has held any public office is exempt from audit. **18** I shall initially illustrate this with examples which you will find most unexpected. For example, the law requires priests and priestesses to be subject to audit, both collectively and each of them individually, and these are people who only receive perquisites and whose job is to offer prayers to the gods on your behalf — and they are subject not only individually, but whole clans together — the Eumolpidai, Kerykes and all the others.

19 The law again requires that the trierarchs are subject to audit, though they have not handled public funds, and do not withdraw large sums of your money and repay them with small ones, nor do they claim to be making donations when they are in fact paying back your money — in fact, they are acknowledged as having spent their family property in your service.

And not only the trierarchs, but the most powerful committees in the state come under judgement in the courts. **20** Firstly the law requires that the Council of the Areiopagos lodges its accounts with the auditors and submits to examination — yes, that grim supreme authority comes under your judgement ... Once again the legislator has made the Council of Five Hundred subject to audit. **21** And he so deeply distrusts persons subject to audit that he states at the commencement of the laws, 'An official', he says, 'who is subject to audit may not leave the country.' 'Herakles!', you might say, 'because I have held office, I am not allowed to leave the country?' No, in case you are making off with the city's money or public business. What's more, a person subject to audit may not consecrate his property, or make a dedication, or be adopted, or make a will disposing of his property, and many other prohibitions as well. In short the legislator keeps as security the goods of all those subject to audit until their accounts have been examined by the city.

1.23 [Aristotle] *Athenaion Politeia* 24.3: Public Salaries in Fifth-Century Athens

The *Athenaion Politeia* is here recording Aristeides' policy towards the populace, resulting in their 'taking control of the empire'. The 'prytaneion' refers to those, like victors at the pan-Hellenic festivals, who dined at public expense (doc. 1.78).

24.3 They also gave the populace a comfortable standard of living, as Aristeides had proposed. For it came about that more than 20,000 people were maintained from the tribute contributions, the taxes and the allies. For there were 6,000 jurors, 1,600 citizen archers, plus 1,200 cavalry, 500 members of the Council, 500 guards of the dockyards, plus 50 guards on the acropolis, about 700 officials at home, and about 700 abroad. In addition, when they afterwards went to war, there were 2,500 hoplites, 20 guard-ships, and other ships carrying the tributes with 2,000 men chosen by lot, as well as the prytaneion, and orphans, and jailers; for all of these received their maintenance from the state.

1.24 [Aristotle] *Athenaion Politeia* 41.2–3, 62.2: Payment for Citizen Duties in the Fourth Century

Due to the difficulties of achieving a quorum for meetings of the assembly, payment for attendance was introduced at the end of the fifth century (cf. doc. 1.18). The fact that the sum involved was soon raised implies that even payment did not entirely solve the problem. By the time of the writer of the *Athenaion Politeia* payment had been raised to a drachma or more. For Herakleides, see Plato *Ion* 541d.

41.3 At first they refused to grant payment for attending the assembly, but as people were not attending the assembly, and the prytaneis kept coming up with many ideas to get the populace to attend so that proposals could be ratified through their show of hands, Agyrrhios (403/2 BC) first introduced payment of an obol, after him Herakleides of Klazomenai, known as 'King', made it two obols, and then Agyrrhios again made it three…

62.2 Payment for public duties: first of all the people are paid a drachma for attending ordinary assemblies, and nine obols for a sovereign one; the jury-courts get three obols per day; the Council five obols. The prytaneis are given an extra obol for food. The nine archons each get four obols for food and have to keep a herald and flute-player; the archon for Salamis gets a drachma a day.

1.25 [Aristotle] *Athenaion Politeia* 50.1–51.4: Officials in the Athenian Democracy

Here are listed some of the officials in Athens responsible for the smooth running of the city, handling everything from the hiring of flute girls to the superintendence of the market regulations. The financial officials were established by Kleisthenes. The living conditions as described here show that the city had its less glamorous side (50.2).

50.1 Ten men are elected by lot as Repairers of Shrines, who receive thirty minas from the financial officials for the restoration of those temples that most require it, and ten as City-controllers. **2** Five of these hold office in the Piraeus and five in the city, and they supervise the female flute, harp and lyre players to ensure that they do not receive more than two drachmas, and, if more than one person wants to hire one, the officials cast lots and hire her to the winner. And they take care that none of the night-soil collectors deposits excrement within ten stades of the city wall and they prevent buildings being constructed in the streets so that balconies overhang the streets or overhead pipes overflow into the streets or windows open onto the streets. They also remove the bodies of those who die on the streets, and have public slaves for this purpose.

51.1 Ten Market-controllers are also elected by lot, five for the Piraeus and five for Athens itself. The laws assign these the responsibility of overseeing all merchandise, to ensure that only pure and unadulterated goods are sold. **2** Ten Measure-controllers are also elected by lot, five for the city and five for the Piraeus. They inspect all weights and measures to ensure that sellers use correct ones. **3** There used to be ten Grain-guardians as well, five for the Piraeus and five for the city, but now there are twenty for the city and fifteen for the Piraeus. Their duties are, first of all, to ensure that unground grain is for sale in the market at a reasonable price, and then that the millers sell barley-meal at a price related to that of barley and bakers their loaves at a price related to that of wheat, and that these weigh the amounts that the officials prescribe — for law prescribes that they determine the weight. **4** They also elect by lot ten harbour inspectors, whose job it is to supervise the markets at the harbour and ensure that the merchants bring the city two-thirds of the grain brought by sea that arrives at the grain-market.

1.26 Aristophanes *Wasps* 836–62, 894–97: A Satire on Jury-Court Procedure

The *Wasps*, performed in 422 BC, is in many respects a satire on the jury-courts and Aristophanes is in particular satirising Kleon's control of the jury-courts and his use of them against opponents (for Kleon as a dog, see doc. 13.18; his deme was Kydathenaion (cf. line 895): 'kyon' means dog). Labes is meant to represent the general Laches and this is a parody of Laches' trial before a court for embezzlement during his generalship in Sicily in 426/5 BC. Bdelykleon (Kleon-hater), whose father Philokleon (Kleon-lover) is a confirmed and obsessive juror, tries to keep him from the courts by setting up a mock trial at home. Philokleon is itching to inflict a harsh penalty by drawing a long furrow in his voting-tablet (cf. *Wasps* 106–08); if the defendant was found guilty the jurors then voted between the penalties proposed by the prosecutor and the defendant.

Bdelykleon: Whatever is the matter?
Sosias (a slave): Why, that dog Labes just
Rushed into the kitchen, snatched up
A fresh Sicilian cheese and ate the lot!
Bdelykleon: So this is the first case to be brought before
My father: you can be there as prosecutor.
Sosias: Not I indeed; actually the other dog has said
That he will prosecute, if someone brings the indictment.
Bdelykleon: Very well, bring them both here.
Sosias: I'll certainly do that.
Bdelykleon: What's that?
Philokleon: The pig-pen from the Hearth.
Bdelykleon: Do you want to commit sacrilege?
Philokleon: No, it's so that
846 I can begin right from the start and squash someone.
But come on, hurry up; I have my eye on condemning a defendant.
Bdelykleon: Hold on while I get the noticeboards and charge sheets.
Philokleon: Damn it, you're wasting time and driving me mad with these delays.
I'm longing to plough furrows in the space on my voting-tablet!
Bdelykleon: There you are.

Philokleon: Call the case.
Bdelykleon: Very well. Who's
The first?
Philokleon: Blast! I'm cross
That I forgot to bring out the urns.
Bdelykleon: Hey, where are you dashing off to?
Philokleon: To get the urns.
Bdelykleon: There's no need.
I brought these small jugs.
Philokleon: Splendid. Now we have everything
We need, except a water-clock.
Bdelykleon: Well, what's this? (He produces a chamber pot.) Not a water-clock?
Philokleon: You've provided everything, and all as smartly as an Athenian.
Bdelykleon: Let someone bring fire as quickly as possible
And myrtle-wreaths and incense from indoors,
So we can first pray to the gods.

The indictment:
Bdelykleon: Now hear the indictment. Prosecution by
The Dog of Kydathenaion against Labes of Aixone
That he wronged one Sicilian cheese by eating it
All by himself. Penalty a figwood dog-collar.

1.27 Aristophanes *Wasps* 605–12: The Delights of Jury Pay

Anyone over thirty years of age could serve as a juror, and the official number of jurors was 6,000 (600 from each tribe); see *Wasps* 662 (doc. 1.28), [Arist.] *Ath. Pol.* 24.3, 63.3. A full court for important public cases needed 501 jurors, private suits had 201 or 401. Perikles introduced jury pay of two obols a day, which was raised to three obols probably in 425 or 424. A family of four, living frugally, might have subsisted on less than two and a half obols a day for their food in the late fifth century, and jury pay would have been a useful source of support, especially for the elderly. Philokleon, the old and enthusiastic juror, is speaking here.

But the most enjoyable thing of all of these, which I had forgotten,
Is when I get home with my pay, and everyone joins
In welcoming me back for my money, and first of all my daughter
Gives me a wash and rubs my feet with oil and bends down to kiss me
And calls me daddy, and fishes out the three obols with her tongue,
While my wife brings me a barley cake to win me over
And sits down beside me and presses me: 'Eat this,
Try this.'

1.28 Aristophanes *Wasps* 655–64: Revenues at Athens

Here the character Bdelykleon lists Athens' revenues, to prove to his father that the jury-courts only receive a small proportion of the state's income; he is calculating on every juror serving 300 days a year, surely an overestimate.

Bdelykleon: Listen now, daddy darling, and relax your forehead a little.
First of all make a rough calculation, not with counters but on your fingers,
Of the tribute which comes to us from all the cities together,
Then apart from this the taxes, besides, and the many one-per-cents,
Court deposits, mines, market-taxes, harbour dues, rents for public land, confiscations;
From these we get a total of nearly 2,000 talents.
Now take away from this a year's pay for the jurors,
6,000 of them — 'for no more than these yet dwell in our land' —
And we get some 150 talents.

Philokleon: So the pay we've been getting is not even a tenth of the revenue!

1.29 Aristophanes *Knights* 162–67: The Basis of Power in Athens

Demosthenes the slave is here trying to persuade the sausage-seller to take over the government; performed in 424 BC, this is a bitter satire against Kleon, who was granted dining-rights in the prytaneion after his victory at Pylos (doc. 13.11). The sausage-seller is here promised Kleon's heritage — he can control the sources of Athens' prosperity and political power, override the Council, and cut the generals down to size in the courts at their euthynai (audits). The verb in line 167 has a very abusive tone even by the standards of Athenian comedy.

Demosthenes: Look over here,
Can you see the rows of all these people?

Sausage-seller: Yes I can.

Demosthenes: Of all of these you will be chief,
And of the agora and the harbours and the Pnyx;
You'll tread on the Council and humble the generals,
Throw people into prison, and suck penises in the prytaneion.

RICH AND POOR IN ATHENS

Solon took four existing property classes and made them the basis for political rights and privileges – the pentakosiomedimnoi (the wealthiest), the hippeis, zeugitai, and the poorest, the thetes. While there were clearly wealthy citizens, such as Nikias (doc. 5.16), and the hippeis and zeugitai were reasonably well off, the class of thetes consisted of the poorest citizens, who rowed in the navy and were the 'backbone' of the Athenian empire in the fifth century. Slave-owning was not as extensive as is often assumed by modern scholars and many Athenians worked hard for their living (see docs 5.53–64).

1.30 Lysias 21 *On a Charge of Taking Bribes* 1–5: Liturgies and the Wealthy

The defendant in this lawsuit, apparently on a charge of corruption, was eighteen in 411/0 BC and gives an account of his public services (liturgies) down to 404/3; he states that in eight years he spent over ten talents on liturgies. The richer individuals, those with estates worth more than three talents, financed certain state activities, and often reminded the jurors of this in lawsuits, as in this speech. The eisphora was a levy imposed on the wealthy from time to time to meet special military costs. There were about 100 liturgies for plays and other services in any one year, as well as the 300 trierarchies.

1 I was judged of age in the archonship of Theopompos, and was appointed choregos for tragedy, spending thirty minas, and, two months later at the Thargelia, 2,000 drachmas where I won with a male chorus, as well as 800 drachmas in the archonship of Glaukippos on pyrrhic dancers at the Great Panathenaia. **2** In the same archonship I also won with a male chorus at the Dionysia, spending 5,000 drachmas including the dedication of the tripod, and, in the archonship of Diokles, 300 on a cyclic chorus at the Lesser Panathenaia. In the meantime I was trierarch for seven years and spent six talents. **3** And though I have incurred such expenses and been daily in danger on your behalf on service abroad, nevertheless I made contributions, one of thirty minas and one of 4,000 drachmas, to special taxes (eisphorai). And when I returned in the archonship of Alexias, I immediately produced games at the festival of Prometheus, and won a victory, after spending 12 minas. **4** And afterwards I was made choregos for a children's chorus and spent more than 15 minas. In the archonship of Eukleides, I was choregos for comedy for Kephisodoros and won, spending, including the dedication of the costumes, 16 minas. I was also choregos at the Lesser Panathenaia with beardless pyrrhic dancers and spent 7 minas. **5** I have won a victory with a trireme in the competition at Sounion, spending 15 minas; and this is apart from sacred embassies and processions of maidens in honour of Athena Polias (arrhephoriai) and other such duties, in which my expenditure has been more than thirty minas. If I had wanted to perform my liturgies according to the actual regulations, I would have spent less than a quarter of what I have enumerated.

1.31 *Inscriptiones Graecae* II^2 1609 lines 83–111: A Trierarchy, 371/0 or 366/5 BC

The triremes in Athens' fleet all had feminine names, such as *Saviour* in the first entry. This inscription is one of many records of the shipyard superintendents at the Piraeus, Athens' harbour. A wealthy Athenian would act as a trierarch for each trireme, though sometimes two would share the duty, and the equipment which came with the ship when given to him was recorded. Many trierarchs provided all new equipment from their own resources as a mark of their pride in the state, and the trierarchs were expected to captain their ship for the year. Apart from the *Saviour*, the other ships appear to have been founding a cleruchy (an overseas settlement), and were presumably carrying colonists with Euktemon and Euthios as the oikistai (founders); *Good Renown* is apparently collecting tithes for Eleusis. Each trireme had 170 rowers: the 200 oar-timbers are to allow for wastage when the oars are made.

83 *Saviour*: trierarchs Apollodoros of Acharnai, Timokrates of Krioa. These have the complete set of wooden equipment that Archestratos of Alopeke contributed; of hanging equipment **85** they have a sail which Stephanos of Euonymon contributed, white sidescreens, two anchors that Pasion of Acharnai contributed, sidescreens of hide and other screens (a hypoblema and katablema) that Phil... of Acharnai returned, ropes that Pasion of Acharnai returned. During our term of office, this ship... light ropes, a sail, Na... contributed.

These triremes sailed out under Euktemon of Lousia and Euthios of Sounion, the leaders of the cleruchy:

Doric maid: trierarchs Apollodoros of Acharnai, Timokrates of Krioa. Of the wooden equipment this ship has two ladders, two poles, two supports.

Leadership: trierarchs Philinos of Lamptrai, Demomeles of Paiania. These took no equipment in our term of office.

Music: trierarchs Phanostratos of Kephisia, Dorotheos of Eleusis. These took no equipment in our term of office.

Victory: the work of Pistokrates, one of the new ships; trierarchs Deinias of Erchia, Leochares of Pallene. These have no equipment in our term of office.

Leadership: one of the new ships, the work of Lysikrates; trierarch Chabrias of Aixone. He has two hundred oar-timbers and in place of these oar-timbers he is to give back a full set of oars.

Good Renown: trierarch Kallippos of Aixone. He has hanging equipment and wooden, full sets. This ship was given to the collectors of tithes.

Backhante: one of the new ships, the work of Hierophon; trierarch Aristaichmos of Cholleidai. He has a complete set of hanging equipment and of the wooden two hundred oar-timbers. In place of these he is to give back a full set of oars. He also has a large mast.

Naukratis: one of the new ships, the work of Xenokles; trierarchs Timotheos of Anaphlystos, Theoxenos of Euonymon. These have of the hanging equipment a sail, a hypoblema, a katablema, light ropes, four anchor cables and of the wooden equipment two hundred oar-timbers. In place of these they are to give back a full set of oars.

Good Weather: one of the new ships, the work of Aristokles; trierarchs Charikleides of Myrrhinous, Kallistratos of Aphidna. These have the hanging equipment, a full set, and wooden, except for the spare mast. In place of the full set he (sic) took two hundred oar-timbers, on condition of giving back a full set.

Blameless: trierarchs Philippos of Kolonos, Polykles of Anagyrous. These have a full set of hanging equipment. Of the wooden they have a large mast, a large yardarm, ladders, two hundred oar-timbers. In place of the oar-timbers a full set of oars is to be given back. They have returned the hanging equipment except for the heavy ropes and the cables for the hull; of the wooden they have returned a full set of oars.

Rose-bed: trierarchs Kleotimides of Atene, Kephalion of Aphidna. These owe a full set of hanging equipment, and of the wooden a large yardarm, ladders. The rest Timotheos of Acharnai, Theodoros of Melite are to return.

1.32 *Inscriptiones Graecae* I^3 421h: Sale Prices of Alkibiades' Bedroom Furniture

After setting out on the Sicilian expedition, Alkibiades was recalled in 414 BC to stand trial for his alleged part in the mutilation of the hermai and profanation of the Mysteries; he escaped to Sparta and his property was sold. This is a sale-list of part of Alkibiades' bedroom furniture; twelve of the couches were made in Miletos; the garments were presumably nightclothes. For Alkibiades' wealth, see docs 3.27, 4.55. [*IG* I^2 330; Tod 1.80.]

--	A two-doored chest
--	A four-doored chest
90 dr.	11 Milesian-made couches
16 dr.	4 tables
17 dr.	A one-ended low couch
10 dr. 1 ob.	A plain coverlet
	A two-ended Milesian-made couch
	6 perfume containers
--	5 stools
1d 1 ob.	A seat-back
- 4 ob.	A wicker-basket
--	A reed-mat
--	A garment
--	A garment
--	A bedstead
--	Yellow wool
--	A bedstead
--	Two horsehair ropes
--	A wide box
--	3 boxes
--	A stuffed pillow
--	A stuffed pillow
--	4 bedspreads
--	4 bedspreads
--	4 bedspreads
--	4 bedspreads

1.33 Lysias 24 *On the Refusal of a Grant to an Invalid* 6: A Disabled Tradesman

This speech was probably written after the restoration of the democracy in 403 BC. Every year the Council examined the claims of disabled persons, and, if they could show cause, would allow them a pension of an obol a day. In this case a small tradesman who ran a shop has been accused of not being disabled.

6 My father left me nothing, and I ceased maintaining my mother on her death only two years ago, and I do not yet have any children to look after me. I possess a trade from which I can obtain only slight support, which I work at with difficulty, and I am as yet unable to procure someone to relieve me of this. I have no other income besides this pension and if you deprive me of it, I am in danger of ending up in the most dreadful position.

1.34 Theophrastos *Characters* 10: The 'Penny-Pincher'

Theophrastos, writing in Athens in the late fourth century, here describes some of the characteristics of a typical penny-pincher. A 'cent' here is a copper coin worth three-eighths of an obol.

10.5 When a slave breaks a pot or plate, the penny-pincher takes it out of his rations. **6** And if his wife drops a 'cent', he's the sort to move all the furniture, beds and chests and rummage through the floor-sweepings. ... **11** When he gives a dinner for his fellow demesmen he serves up meat cut into minuscule portions. **12** When he goes shopping, he comes home without having bought anything. **13** He forbids his wife to lend salt, or a lamp-wick, or cumin, or oregano, or barley, or garlands, or cakes for sacrifice, asserting that these small items add up to a lot during the course of a year.

1.35 Demosthenes 23 *Against Aristokrates* 206–209: Public versus Private Wealth

Demosthenes contrasts the public glories and honest politicians of the fifth century with the more lowly buildings and wealthier politicians of the fourth. The picture is probably exaggerated, but Athens' public buildings of the fifth century were not equalled by those in the fourth, and there were financial difficulties attendant upon military campaigning which had not been an issue when Athens had its financial reserves as recorded by Perikles (doc. 1.10). For Aristeides and his incorruptibility, see doc. 10.12.

206 In olden times the city was prosperous and magnificent in public, while in private no one stood higher than everybody else. **207** And the proof is this: if any of you know the sort of house that Themistokles or Miltiades or any of the other great men of that period possessed, he could see that it was no grander than anyone else's, but, as for the city's buildings and constructions, they were so large and of such quality that no chance of outdoing them was left to later generations — like the Propylaea, shipyards, porticoes, Piraeus, and all the rest which you see adorning the city. **208** But today everyone in public life has so much property that some of them have constructed houses that are more splendid than many public buildings, and some have acquired more land than all of you in this court possess between you. As for the public buildings you put up and whitewash, I am ashamed to say how small and shabby they are. Can you name anything you have acquired that you can leave to future generations, as they did the Chersonese, Amphipolis, and the glory of their noble achievements? It's *their* glory that citizens like these are throwing away as fast as they can, but they cannot hide it, men of Athens, and that is fair. **209** In those days when Aristeides had total control of organising the tributes, his own property did not grow by a single drachma, and when he died the city had to pay for his burial; if you needed anything you had more money in the treasury than any other Greek state, and as a result, for however long you decreed a campaign would last, you set out with pay for that whole period. But today those who manage public affairs start poor and end rich and have enough put by to maintain them in affluence for a long time, while you don't have enough in the treasury to pay for a single day on campaign, and if something has to be done, you do not have the money for it. In those days the people were the master of the politicians — now it is the servant.

CITIZENSHIP

The Greek word for citizenship was politeia, which also meant constitution and the body of citizen members: citizenship was the basis on which the constitution rested. There were clear political and legal distinctions between citizens on the one hand and metics and slaves on the other; one of the more severe punishments for a citizen was atimia, or loss of citizen rights. A citizen in Athens had the right to attend the assembly, and be a magistrate or juror when over thirty, to own property and attend all festivals, and had full access to the protection of the law.

1.36 [Aristotle] *Athenaion Politeia* 26.4: Perikles Changes the Law on Citizenship

More rigorous regulations regarding citizenship were brought in by Perikles in 451/0 BC, perhaps because of the growing size of the citizen body as indicated here, or so that Athenians could find citizen husbands for their daughters. There was possibly a large number of mixed marriages and dubious cases of citizenship at this point, and the law now became very clear on who could or could not become a citizen. There were strict penalties for breaking this law: doc. 4.56.

26.4 In the archonship of Antidotos (451/0 BC), because of the number of citizens, it was decided on a motion of Perikles that a person should not have citizen rights unless both of his parents had been citizens.

1.37 [Demosthenes] 59 *Against Neaira* 104: The Plataeans Become Athenian Citizens

The Plataeans allied themselves with Athens in 519 BC, and fought alongside them at Marathon. [Demosthenes] quotes a decree conferring citizenship on the Plataeans, after Plataea was destroyed by Sparta in 427 (Thuc. 3.68.3); rather than settle in Athens, most of them set up a new city at Skione. The conferral of citizenship was a great honour: see doc. 1.54.

Hippokrates proposed the motion: that the Plataeans are to be Athenians from today, with full rights like the rest of the Athenians, and share in all the things which the Athenians share, both sacred and profane, but they shall not be eligible for any priesthood or rite which belongs to a particular family or the nine archonships, but their descendants shall be. And the Plataeans shall be distributed among the demes and tribes. Once they have been so distributed, it will no longer be possible for any Plataean to become an Athenian, unless he is awarded the honor by the Athenian people.

1.38 [Aristotle] *Athenaion Politeia* 42.1–2: Registration as a Deme Member

Male youths were registered as deme members after their eighteenth birthday, when the deme members voted as to whether they were the correct age, and whether they were eligible for deme membership; if anyone was judged to be ineligible as not-free, he was allowed to appeal to the court. In the fourth century, the ephebes at the age of eighteen had two years of military service before being entered on the register of citizens (the pinax ekklesiastikos) of their deme. For the oath taken by the ephebes, see doc. 3.13.

42.1 The present arrangement of the constitution is as follows: those whose parents have both been citizens have the right to be citizens, and they are enrolled amongst the demesmen at the age of eighteen. When they are enrolled, the demesmen decide by vote under oath concerning them, first if they appear to be the legal age, and if they do not appear to be, they again return to the status of boys, and secondly if the candidate is free and has been born in accordance with the laws. When they decide that someone is not free, he appeals to the law-court, and the demesmen choose five men from amongst themselves as his accusers, and if it appears that he had no right to be enrolled, the city sells him (into slavery); but if he wins his case, the demesmen are compelled to enrol him. **2** After this the Council examines those who have been enrolled, and if anyone appears to be younger than eighteen years, it fines the demesmen who enrolled him. When the young men (ephebes) have been examined, their fathers assemble by tribes, take an oath, and elect three of their tribesmen over the age of forty, whom they consider to be the best and most suitable to supervise the young men, and from these the people elects by vote one from each tribe as guardian and from the other Athenians a superintendent for all of them.

1.39 Philochoros Atthis F35a: Phratry Membership

Phratries ('brotherhoods') were primarily concerned with the entitlement of potential members to membership and the ritual ceremonies which accompanied the acceptance of new members. The orgeones are members of the phratry, but their exact nature is unclear; homogalaktes means 'men of the same milk' (cf. Arist. *Pol.* 1252b16–18), gennetai 'members of clans (gene)'; possibly associations of orgeones, which were upper class in origin, offered sacrifices at their own expense on the altars of gods and heroes in Attica. This law possibly dates to 451/0 BC. For phratries in Attica in 621/0, see doc. 8.3. [*FGH* 328 F35a.]

Philochoros has also written concerning the orgeones: 'the phratry members are to be compelled to accept both the orgeones and the homogalaktes, whom we call gennetai.'

1.40 *Inscriptiones Graecae* II^2 1237: Of Zeus of the Phratry, 396/5 BC

The phratriarch was the president of the phratry, probably of the Dekeleians in this case, the Demotionidai being a privileged clan (genos) within that phratry. The Apatouria was an Ionian festival (Hdt. 1.147.2), lasting for three days during Pyanopsion, at which children were presented to the phratry members as new members. On the first day (Dorpia) the fellow phratry members feasted together; the second day was given over to sacrificing, especially in honour of Zeus Phratrios and Athena Phratria; and on the third day (Koureotis) young boys were admitted to the phratry, their change of status being celebrated by sacrifices (the meion and koureion), both of which probably took place on this day. The koureion sacrifice accompanied a dedication of a lock of the boy's hair to Artemis to celebrate his passage out of childhood, hence the name from 'kouros', boy. According to Andocides 1.127 the father had to swear on the altar that he was introducing a legitimate (gnesios) son to the phratry. Line 120 makes it clear that the mother's father's name and deme have to be recorded.

1 Of Zeus of the Phratry. The priest Theodoros son of Euphantides inscribed and set up the stele. The priest is to be given the following perquisites from sacrifices: **5** from every meion a thigh, a side-cut, an ear, and three obols of silver; from every koureion a thigh, a side-cut, an ear, a cake made from a choinix measure of flour, a half-kotyle of wine and a drachma of silver. **9** The following was resolved by the members of the phratry, when Phormio was archon of the Athenians and Pantakles of Oion was phratriarch. Hierokles proposed the motion: all those who have not been adjudicated on in accordance with the law of the Demotionidai **15** the members of the phratry shall immediately adjudicate on, swearing by Zeus of the Phratry and taking their ballot from the altar; whoever appears to have been admitted without being entitled to be a phratry member, the priest **20** and the phratriarch are to delete his name from the register of the Demotionidai and the copy, and the man who introduced the person who has been rejected shall be liable to pay a fine of 100 drachmas sacred to Zeus of the Phratry, and this money **25** the priest and the phratriarch are to exact or be liable to pay the fine themselves. In future the adjudication (on new members) is to take place in the year after the sacrifice of the koureion, on the koureotis day of the Apatouria. The (phratry members) are to take their ballot from the altar. **30** If anyone wishes to appeal to the Demotionidai regarding the grounds on which he has been rejected, he is allowed to do so; the house of the Dekeleians shall elect as judges five men over thirty years of age, **35** and the phratriarch and the priest shall take their oaths to undertake their duties most justly and not to allow anyone who is not entitled to phratry membership to belong to the phratry … **114** Menexenos proposed the amendment: that the rest be resolved by the phratry members regarding the introduction of the children in accordance with the previous decrees, but, so that the members of the phratry may know which men are going to introduce (new members), there is to be recorded with the phratriarch in the first year (of the child's life) or in that of the koureion his name and father's name and deme, and his **120** mother's father's name and deme, and the phratriarch is to make a record of the names submitted and set this up in a place which the Dekeleians frequent, and the priest is to record it on a whitewashed noticeboard and set it up in the sanctuary **125** of Leto. And this decree is to be recorded on the stele …

THE LESS THAN IDEAL CITIZEN

1.41 Theophrastos *Characters* 25 (*On Cowardice*): A Typical Coward

Military cowardice was punished both at Sparta (docs 6.10, 6.15) and at Athens (docs 1.42, 1.44): ancient Greek society required that all adult males be prepared to fight and die for their city when required (cf. Perikles' Funeral Oration: doc. 1.17).

1 Of course, cowardice is clearly when the soul becomes overwhelmed by fear. The coward is the sort of person, **2** who, when sailing, believes that the cliffs are pirate ships. When a wave strikes, he asks if anyone on board has not been initiated. With the helmsman, he looks up and asks him if they are halfway there yet, and how he thinks the sky is looking, and says to the man sitting next to him that he is frightened because of a dream he has had; and he takes off his tunic, hands it to his slave and begs to be put to shore.

3 When he is on military service and the infantry is sallying out, he tells everyone to stand near him first and have a look round, and says that their job is to discover which ones are the enemy. **4** When he hears an outcry and sees men falling, he says to those standing next to him that in his haste he forgot to get his sword, runs to the tent and sends the slave out to see where the enemy are, hides the sword under the pillow and then wastes a lot of time pretending he is looking for it. **5** While in his tent he sees one of his friends being brought in wounded, and runs up to him, tells him to bear up, picks him up and carries him. He looks after him, sponges him off, sits beside him shooing the flies away from the wound — anything rather than fight the enemy! When the trumpeter sounds the signal for battle, he sits in his tent saying, 'Go to the crows! He doesn't let a man have even a wink of sleep with all his signalling!' **6** Covered in blood from the other man's wound, he meets those returning from battle and recounts as if he'd been in danger, 'I saved one of our friends!' Then he brings in the members of his tribe to look at him lying there, while he tells each of them how he carried him into the tent with his own hands!

1.42 Aeschines 1 *Against Timarchos* 26–32: Inappropriate Conduct on the Speaker's Platform

Aeschines delivered this speech against Timarchos in 346 BC. Athenian law debarred from addressing the assembly those who mistreated their parents, were cowards or male prostitutes or who had squandered their inheritance. The private activities of a citizen were thought to reflect on their abilities to advise the state. For Timarchos as a male prostitute, see doc. 4.87.

26 Consider, men of Athens, the difference between Timarchos and Solon — along with those men of old I referred to a moment since. *They* considered it inappropriate to speak with their arm outside their cloak, whereas *he* not long ago — in fact just the other day — threw off his cloak in the assembly and, stripped to the skin, behaved like a wrestler in a pankration match — except that his heavy drinking and licentious lifestyle meant his torso was such a ghastly and shameful sight that respectable men, at least, covered their eyes in their shame for our city that our policy should be in the hands of advisers like this. **27** The legislator (Solon) had this type of conduct in mind when he clearly laid down rules as to those who could address the assembly and those who could not speak before the people. Solon does not exclude from the platform the man who has no ancestors who held office, or the man who earns his daily bread by pursuing a trade: in fact he welcomes these with enthusiasm and for this reason has the invitation put repeatedly, 'Who would like to speak?'

28 Who then does the legislator think should be barred from speaking? Those who have lived a scandalous life — he refuses to allow them to address the people. And where is the evidence for this? Where he says, 'The examination of public speakers: if anyone addresses the people who treats his father or mother with violence, or fails to maintain them, or refuses them a home, he is not allowed to make a speech.' And quite correctly in my view, by Zeus! Why? Because if a person behaves badly towards those whom he ought to respect like the gods themselves, how, he asks, will he treat those who are not of his family, or indeed the city as a whole?

Whom next does he bar from speaking? **29** 'The man who has failed to carry out all the military service required of him, or who has thrown away his shield.' And rightly so. Why? Well sir, if you do not take up arms on behalf of your country, or your cowardice prevents you from defending it, you have no right to act as one of its counsellors. Who is his third target? 'The man who has put himself in the position of a prostitute or hetaira,' he tells us. After all, the man who has sold his own body in violation of all rules of decency, he considered to be a person who would think little of betraying his city's interests.

30 Whom does he list in the fourth place? 'The man who has squandered his ancestral possessions or his inheritance.' He thought that the man who mismanaged his own household would behave in exactly the same way towards the interests of the city, and Solon could not envisage that the same man could be a scoundrel in private life but in public life a valuable citizen, and believed that public speakers should approach the platform prepared not only by what they have to say but by how they live their lives. **31** He considered that advice from a good and upright man would benefit his audience, even if awkwardly and simply delivered, while he thought that the words of a loose-living man, who has made his own body a laughing stock and inexcusably wasted his inheritance, would be of no benefit, however well delivered. **32** In consequence he debars them from the platform and forbids them to address the people.

1.43 Demosthenes 21 *Against Meidias* 47: *Hybris* in Athens

Individuals committing hybris – an act of violence by the stronger against the weak – could be indicted before the thesmothetai ('law givers' or junior magistrates) and a case brought to the heliaia, the Solonian court. Men, women and children, whether slave or free, were protected against hybris at Athens.

47 If a person commits hybris against anyone, whether child or woman or man, either free or slave, or commits any unlawful act against any of these, any Athenian citizen who wishes to do so may bring an indictment before the thesmothetai. And the thesmothetai shall bring him before the Heliaia within thirty days of the date of the indictment, unless some public business should prevent it, in which case they shall do so as soon as possible. Should the Heliaia condemn the offender, it shall immediately decide the penalty or fine he is thought to deserve. In cases where indictments are lodged in accordance with the law, if someone fails to prosecute, or following prosecution fails to obtain a fifth of the votes, he shall pay 1,000 drachmas to the treasury. If the penalty for the hybris is a fine and the offence was against a free man, the offender shall be imprisoned until he has paid it.

1.44 Demosthenes 24 *Against Timokrates* 105: Penalties for Serious Crimes

Solon's laws provided specific punishments for thieves, as well as for those who maltreated their parents and evaded military service.

105 If someone recovers the property which has been stolen, the penalty (for the thief) shall be twice its value; if it is not recovered, the penalty shall be ten times the value, in addition to the legal punishment. The thief shall be kept in the stocks for five days and nights, if the Heliaia imposes an additional penalty. The additional penalty may be proposed by anyone who chooses, when the question of punishment is under discussion. If anyone is arrested after being convicted of maltreating his parents or evading military service, or of entering any forbidden place after notice of outlawry, the Eleven shall imprison him and bring him before the Heliaia and anyone who chooses and is entitled to do so may prosecute him. If he is convicted, the Heliaia shall decide the penalty which he shall undergo, whether corporal or financial. And if the penalty is financial he shall be kept in prison until he has paid it.

CITY-STATES AND THEIR LAWS

1.45 Meiggs & Lewis 2: A Law from Dreros in Crete, *c*. 650 BC

This may be the earliest surviving Greek law on stone, and is the earliest which has survived complete. It forbids the repeated tenure of the office of kosmos, probably the chief magistracy, within ten years. The demioi (damioi) may be financial supervisors and the twenty perhaps the Council. The use of the word city may, or may not, imply the participation of the assembly.

May god be kind (?). The city has decided as follows: when a man has been kosmos, for ten years that same man shall not be kosmos; if he should become kosmos, whatever judgements he gives he shall himself owe double, and he shall lose rights to office as long as he lives, and whatever he does as kosmos shall be nothing. The swearers shall be the kosmos, and the damioi and the twenty of the city.

1.46 Meiggs & Lewis 8C: The Popular Council at Chios, 575–550 BC

The role of the people in Chios has already by this point become considerable, and the popular Council can apparently judge appeals; cf. doc. 8.19 for this inscription's possible relevance to the Council of Four Hundred of Solon at Athens. The Hebdomaia was a festival to Apollo celebrated on the seventh of every month.

Let him appeal to the Council of the people; on the third day after the Hebdomaia, the Council of the people with power to inflict penalties is to assemble, with fifty men chosen from each tribe; it shall transact the other business which concerns the people and in particular all the lawsuits which arise subject to appeal in the month …

1.47 *SIG*^{3} 4, lines 5–12: Immunity from Indirect Taxation at Cyzicus

This sixth-century BC inscription from the relatively small community of Cyzicus grants exemption (ateleia) from certain indirect taxes to the descendants of two citizens who died for their country. It was reinscribed in the first century BC, and was therefore presumably still current.

In the prytany of Maiandrios. The city has given the son of Medikes and the sons of Aisepos and their descendants exemption from taxes and maintenance in the prytaneion, with the exception of the nautos, the tax for the use of the public scales, the tax on the sale of horses, the tax of twenty-five per cent, and the tax on the sale of slaves; they shall be exempt from all the others; the people swore about these over the sacrificial victims. The city gave this stele to Manes son of Medikes.

1.48 Meiggs & Lewis 13 A & C: A Lokrian Community Settles New Territory

This law on a bronze plaque from western Lokris, dated to *c.* 525–500 BC, deals with the regulations concerning the settlement of new territory, including rules to protect the new settlers; it appears in particular to define pasturage-rights, but the term epinomia may instead refer to inheritance, as translated here; text C has also been inserted as an omitted line (see Meiggs & Lewis, p.23). The lots are only allowed to be sold in cases of real need, which implies the desire to keep the property (kleros) in the family, and the colony, not the mother-city, is to have the right of decision as to whether they need reinforcements under the necessity of war. The fact that they already have temples, elders and a citizen assembly suggests that these are not new settlers from another area, but members of an existing settlement who are assimilating a new stretch of agricultural land.

This law concerning the land shall be in force for the division of the plain of Hyla and Liskara, both the separate lots and the public ones. The right of inheritance (epinomia) shall belong to the parents and the son; if there is no son, to the daughter; if there is no daughter, to the brother; if there is no brother, by degree of relationship let a man inherit according to the law. If the heirs do not take the property, he shall have the right to bestow it on whoever he wishes. Whatever a man plants, he shall be immune from its seizure. Unless under compulsion of war a majority of the one hundred and one men chosen from the best citizens decides that at least two hundred fighting men are to be brought in as additional settlers; whoever proposes a division (of land) or puts it to the vote in the Council of elders or in the city or in the select Council or who causes civil dissension concerning the division of land, he and his family for all time shall be accursed and his property confiscated and his house be razed to the ground just as for the law on murder. This law shall be sacred to Pythian Apollo and the gods who dwell with him; on the man who transgresses it may there be destruction for himself and his family and his property, but may god be propitious to the man who observes it. The land shall belong half to the previous settlers, half to the additional settlers. Let them distribute the valley portions; exchange shall be valid, but the exchange shall take place before the magistrate.

1.49 Buck no. 58: A Treaty between Oiantheia and Chaleion

This treaty between two small states of western Lokris is recorded on a bronze tablet of the mid-fifth century BC. The first document guarantees reciprocal rights to the citizens of each when on the other's territory, specifically the prevention of seizure of persons or property in enforcement of existing claims on the other party; the second consists of regulations regarding the legal rights of foreigners. The proxenos ('guest-friend') presumably bears witness that the foreigner has been resident there for a month or more.

A No one is to carry off an Oiantheian foreigner from Chaleian territory, nor a Chaleian from Oiantheian territory, nor his property, even if anyone is making a seizure; but the person who has made the seizure may be seized with impunity. The property of foreigners may be seized at sea with impunity, except from the harbour of either city. If anyone makes a seizure unlawfully, (the penalty is) four drachmas; and if he holds what has been seized for more than ten days he shall be liable to pay half as much again as the value of what he seized. If a Chaleian resides in Oiantheia or an Oiantheian in Chaleion for more than a month he shall be subject to the legal procedure there. If the proxenos acts falsely as proxenos, he shall be fined double.

B If those who judge suits concerning foreigners are divided in opinion, the foreigner who brings the suit shall choose jurors from the best citizens, exclusive of his proxenos and private host, in suits involving a mina or more, fifteen men, in those involving less, nine men. If a citizen brings a suit against another citizen in accordance with the treaty, the magistrates shall choose the jurors from the best citizens after having sworn the five-fold oath. The jurors shall take the same oath and the majority is to prevail.

1.50 Buck no. 61: An Eleian Law, *c.* 500 BC

This law appears to free from liability the family and phratry of an accused person, and to prevent his maltreatment. The hellenodikai (sing.: hellenodikas) were 'hellenic judges', whose duties also included supervision of the Olympic festival.

1 The law (rhetra) of the Eleians. The phratry, family and property (of an accused man) shall be immune. If anyone makes a charge (against them), he shall be prosecuted as in (the case of) an Eleian. If he who has the highest office and the magistrates (basileis) do not exact the fines, each of those who fails to exact them shall pay a fine of ten minas sacred to Olympian Zeus. The hellanodikas shall enforce this, and the board of public workers (demiourgoi) shall enforce the other fines (which have not been exacted); if the hellanodikas does not enforce it, he shall pay double in his accounting. If anyone maltreats a man who is accused of a charge involving a fine, he shall be liable to the fine of ten minas, if he does so intentionally. And the secretary of the phratry shall incur the same (fine), if he wrongs anyone. The tablet sacred at Olympia.

1.51 Buck no. 64: A Sixth-Century Eleian Law

This is the conclusion of an inscription, the first tablet of which has been lost, from Elis. Compare the procedure in Sparta where the assembly was not allowed to propose changes to motions.

If he commits fornication (?) in the sacred precinct, he shall pay the penalty by sacrificing an ox and complete purification, and the official (?) (thearos) the same. If anyone gives judgement contrary to what is written, the judgement shall be invalid, and the rhetra of the people shall be final in judging; anything of what is written may be amended if it seems better with regard to the god, by withdrawing or adding with the approval of the whole Council of five hundred and the people in full assembly. Changes may be made three times (?), adding or withdrawing.

1.52 Meiggs & Lewis 17: An Alliance between Elis and Heraia, *c.* 500

Heraia is in western Arcadia; this was passed prior to Elis' synoikismos (synoecism) in 471/0 BC (see doc. 1.55). For a similar alliance, a Spartan treaty with Aetolia, see doc. 6.61.

The covenant (rhetra) of the Eleians and the Heraians. There shall be an alliance for one hundred years, starting with this year. If there shall be any need either of word or deed, they shall combine with each other both in other matters and in war. If they do not combine, a talent of silver is to be paid sacred to Olympian Zeus by the offenders. If anyone offends against these writings, whether private individual, official, or the state, he is to be liable to the penalty written here.

1.53 Meiggs & Lewis 42B: A Treaty Between Knossos and Tylissos, *c.* 450 BC

This is part of an inscription defining relations between Argos and the two Cretan states Knossos and Tylissos; Tylissos, possibly a dependency of Argos, is being protected against Knossos; the Argives do not have the power of veto when the two cities are in agreement, but are able to break a tied vote. This fragment, found at Argos, deals with the sharing of plunder and the export of goods.

2 … the land of the Acharnaians may be plundered by the Tylissians except for the parts belonging to the city of the Knossians. Whatever we both win together from the enemy, the Tylissians shall in a division have a third part of everything taken by land, and the half of everything that is taken by sea. The Knossians shall have the tithe of whatever we seize in common; the finest of the spoils shall be sent to Delphi by both jointly, and the rest shall be dedicated to Ares at Knossos by both jointly. Export shall be allowed from Knossos to Tylissos and from Tylissos to Knossos; but if a Tylissian exports beyond, let him pay as much as the Knossians, and goods from Tylissos may be exported wherever he desires. To Poseidon the Knossian priest shall sacrifice at Iutos. To Hera in the Heraion both shall sacrifice a cow jointly, and they shall sacrifice before the Hyakinthia …

1.54 *Inscriptiones Graecae* I^3 110: Commendation of a Proxenos at Athens, 408/7 BC

A proxenos was a foreigner who looked after the interests of another state in his home town, and the position was usually hereditary. In this case, Oiniades of Old Skiathos is officially made a proxenos of Athens for his services to Athenians on the island of Skiathos. This position was considered to be a great honour. This stele was discovered on the Athenian acropolis. [Meiggs & Lewis 90; *IG* I^2 118.]

Gods. Decree of the Council and people, the tribe Antiochis held the prytany, Eukleides was secretary, Hierokles presided, Euktemon was archon. Dieitrephes proposed the motion: since Oiniades of Old Skiathos is a loyal friend towards the city of the Athenians and eager to promote our interests in any way he can, and behaves well to Athenians who visit Skiathos, he is to be commended and inscribed as proxenos and benefactor of the Athenians, along with his descendants. The Council that is in power and the generals and the magistrate at Skiathos, whoever it might be, are to ensure that no wrong is done to him. The secretary of the Council is to have this decree inscribed on a marble stele and to have it set up on the acropolis. He is also to be invited to dinner at the prytaneion for tomorrow. Antichares proposed the amendment: all else to remain as proposed but the resolution be altered to read not Skiathos as written, but Oiniades of Old Skiathos.

LEAGUES, UNIONS AND FEDERATIONS

Synoikismos (synoecism) was the amalgamation of communities to form a single city-state. The advantages were that one single community could be walled and more easily defended, and a range of civic amenities, such as theatres, political meeting places and markets could be provided, as well as giving greater political, social and religious identity to the people who were united together in one place.

1.55 Diodorus *Library of History* 11.54.1: The Synoikismos of Elis 471/0 BC

In 471/70 BC the various villages and towns of Elis joined together – underwent synoikismos – into a single state. See docs 1.50–51 for laws passed by the Eleian cities prior to this.

When Praxiergos was archon in Athens and the Romans elected as consuls Aulus Verginius Trikostus and Gaius Servius Structus, in this year the Eleians who were living in a number of small cities were synoecised into a single city, which is called Elis.

1.56 Thucydides 2.15.1–2: The Synoikismos of Athens

Thucydides is here describing how, according to Athenian tradition, Theseus reorganised Attica, making Athens the single political centre. The Synoikia festival in honour of Athena celebrated

Athens' political union, and was held both as a state festival and also in individual demes, and even in the last years of the fifth century was celebrated by the four pre-Kleisthenic tribes (doc. 10.20).

2.15.1 In the time of Kekrops and the first kings down to Theseus, the people of Attica had always lived in cities, each of which had their own administrative building (prytaneion) and officials, and unless there were some danger they did not join in consultation with the king, but each of them would govern itself and make its own decisions; and some of these on occasion actually made war on Athens, like Eumolpos and the Eleusinians against Erechtheus. **2** But when Theseus became king, being an intelligent as well as a powerful man, he organised the country primarily by dissolving the Council chambers (bouleuteria) and governments of the other cities and bringing them together into the present city, making one council chamber and one seat of administration, and compelling everyone to belong to this one city, though they could look after their own affairs just as before. With everyone uniting in it, it was a great city that was handed down by Theseus to posterity; and he inaugurated the Synoikia (celebration of union), a festival in honour of the goddess, which the Athenians still keep at public expense even today.

1.57 Thucydides 5.38.1–3: The Boeotian Federation

Thebes took the lead of the Boeotian cities in about the seventh century BC; under Theban supremacy there was a federal army under the command of Boeotarchs (commanders of Boeotia); Thebes was only one of nine, later ten, league members, but there were eleven representational districts, for which doc. 1.58 provides details. The autonomy of the individual cities was limited by the compulsion to adopt a certain moderately oligarchic constitution; the government of the individual cities, and it seems of the league as well, was in the hands of a Council, divided into four sections, which took it in turns to transact business. This passage relates to 421/0 BC.

5.38.1 Meanwhile the Boeotarchs, Corinthians, Megarians and envoys from Thrace resolved to exchange oaths with each other that they would come to each other's help on any occasion when requested, and that they would not make war or peace without common consent, and that the Boeotians and Megarians (who were acting in concert) should conclude a treaty with the Argives. **2** But before the oaths were taken the Boeotarchs communicated these proposals to the four Councils of the Boeotians, which have the supreme authority, and advised them that oaths should be exchanged with all the cities who were willing to form a defensive alliance. **3** But the members of the Councils refused to agree to this proposal, fearing that they might be acting in opposition to the Spartans, by entering an agreement with the Corinthians who had revolted from them.

1.58 *Hellenica Oxyrhynchia* 16.1–4: The Boeotian Confederacy

Boeotia's alliance with Sparta led to its defeats at Tanagra and Oinophyta (docs 12.20, 6.60); later it was under Athenian control until the battle of Koroneia in 447. Boeotia now re-formed the Confederacy, which had come into being at the end of the sixth century, as described below.

16.1 In this summer the Boeotians and Phokians went to war. Some people in Thebes were mainly responsible for the bad feeling between them. Only a few years earlier the Boeotians had engaged in internal strife. **2** The situation at that time in Boeotia was as follows: at that period there were four Councils set up in each of the cities. Not all the citizens were allowed to participate in these, only those who possessed a certain degree of wealth. Each of these Councils in turn met and made decisions on policy matters, referring these decisions to the other three, and anything agreed by all of them was approved. **3** While they continued to administer internal affairs in this way, the Boeotian government was organised as follows: everyone there was divided into eleven areas, each of which provided a Boeotarch on this model: Thebes provided four, two for the city, and two for Plataea, Skolos, Erythrai, Skaphai and the other places previously associated with them but now under Theban control; Orchomenos and Hysiai provided two Boeotarchs; Thespiai along with Eutresis and Thisbai another two; Tanagra one; Haiartos, Lebadeia and Koroneia another one which each city provided in turn; similarly a Boeotarch was provided by Akraiphnion, Kopai and Chaironeia. **4** This was how the districts returned their magistrates. They provided sixty counsellors for each Boeotarch and covered their day-to-day expenses. With regard to the organisation of the army, each region had to provide about one thousand hoplites and one hundred cavalry — in simple terms, depending on the number of their magistrates, each region shared the common treasury, the taxes, provided jurors, and participated equally in public affairs, whether bad or good. This constitution applied to the whole of the Boeotian people and the Council and assemblies of the Boeotians met in the Kadmeia.

1.59 Herodotos 1.142.1–4, 1.148.1: The Panionion

Twelve of the Ionian cities and islands of Asia Minor formed a league (koinon) which met at the Panionion, from which other Ionians were excluded. At the Panionion, a temple dedicated to Poseidon on the north side of Cape Mykale, they celebrated a festival called the Panionia. Ethnic identity and solidarity found expression in religious unity.

1.142.1 These Ionians, who possess the Panionion, have founded their cities in places more favoured by weather and seasons than any other we know… **3** They do not all use the same speech but have four different dialects. Miletos is the most southerly of the cities, and after it Myous and Priene; these are settled in Caria and speak the same dialect. The following are in Lydia: Ephesos, Kolophon, Lebedos, Teos, Klazomenai and Phokaia. **4** These cities share a dialect completely different to those previously mentioned. There are also three remaining Ionian cities, of which two are on the islands of Samos and Chios, and one, Erythrai, is founded on the mainland. The Chians and Erythraians speak the same dialect, while the Samians have one peculiarly their own … **1.148.1** The Panionion is a sacred place on Mykale, facing north, jointly dedicated by the Ionians to Poseidon of Helikon; Mykale is a cape of the mainland running out towards Samos in a westerly direction, and here the Ionians from the cities used to gather and celebrate the festival, which they called the Panionia.

1.60 Herodotos 1.144.1–3: The Dorian Pentapolis

The Dorian pentapolis ('five cities') of Asia Minor and Rhodes shared a temple, the Triopion, where they celebrated the Games of Triopian Apollo.

1.144.1 The Dorians of what is now the country of the 'Five Cities', the same country which used to be called the 'Six Cities', refuse to let any of the neighbouring Dorians have admission to the Triopian temple, and even barred from using it those of their members who had broken the temple's regulations. **2** In olden times, at the festival of Triopian Apollo, they used to award bronze tripods to the victors and those who received them had to dedicate them there to the god and not take them home. **3** A man of Halikarnassos called Agasikles, when he was victorious, ignored this law and took the tripod home and nailed it to his wall. For this offence, the five cities — Lindos, Ialysos, Kamiros, Kos and Knidos — forbade the sixth city, Halikarnassos, from sharing the use of the temple.

TRADE AND COMMERCE

Colonisation led to an increase in trade and wealth (cf. doc. 7.3) and commercial treaties, symbola, were signed between city-states. Agriculture was the economic basis of Greek society, and most ancient Greeks would have been involved in growing foodstuffs. Athens imported a large amount of grain (docs 1.71–75) due to the heavily urbanised nature of its population.

1.61 Thucydides 1.13.2, 1.13.5: The Wealth and Power of Corinth

Corinth had long been a commercial emporion because of its position on the Isthmus, even when most communication was overland and before it had a navy; hence its wealth. When traffic by sea became more common, the Corinthians acquired a navy, put down piracy, and opened a market on both sides of the Isthmus (cf. doc. 7.8). The diolkos, the stone runway for moving ships and goods across the Isthmus, can still be seen (doc. 7.61); Homer described Corinth as 'wealthy' (*Iliad* 2.570).

1.13.2 The Corinthians are said to have been just about the first to involve themselves with naval matters along modern lines, and it was at Corinth, it is said, that the first triremes in Greece were constructed ... **1.13.5** As the Corinthians had founded their city on the Isthmus they had always possessed a trading-station (emporion), as the Greeks of ancient times travelled more by land than by sea, with those from within the Peloponnese and those outside of it having to pass through Corinthian territory to make contact with each other. And the Corinthians grew rich and thus powerful, as is shown by the early poets, who called the place 'wealthy'. And when the Greeks began to take more to the sea, the Corinthians acquired ships and put down piracy, and since they were able to provide a double emporion (for traders by land and sea) they made their city powerful with the money that flowed in.

1.62 Strabo *Geography* 8.6.20: 'Wealthy' Corinth

Malea is a dangerous promontory on the south coast of the Peloponnese, with a narrow strait separating it from the island of Kythera.

Corinth is called 'wealthy' because of its emporion, as it is situated on the Isthmus and controls two harbours, one of which leads to Asia and the other to Italy. The exchange of cargoes from both countries that are so far from each other is thus made easy. And just as in olden days the strait of Sicily was dangerous for sailors, as well as the high seas, the sea beyond Malea was especially so because of the contrary winds. From this comes the proverb: 'when you double Malea, forget your home!' So both merchants from Italy and those from Asia preferred to avoid the journey around Malea and instead unloaded their cargoes at

Corinth. In addition the taxes on items exported by land from the Peloponnese and imported to it belonged to those who held the keys. This has continued ever since, but the advantages to the Corinthians of later times further increased, as the Isthmian festival celebrated there drew huge crowds. And the Bakchiadai who became tyrants were wealthy and numerous and of distinguished family, and held power for nearly 200 years and enjoyed in security the profits from this trade.

1.63 Herodotos 3.57.1–2: Siphnos' Revenues Distributed

The islanders of Siphnos used to divide the proceeds of their mines amongst themselves every year. The context of this document is the joint expedition by Samian exiles and the Spartans against Polykrates (doc. 7.34); the Samians asked the Siphnians to lend them ten talents. When this request was refused they attacked the island and forced the Siphnians to pay them 100 talents (Hdt. 3.58.3–4). For the Thasians' revenue from their mines, see Hdt. 6.46.2–47.2.

3.57.1 The Samians who had made the expedition against Polykrates, since the Spartans were going to desert them, sailed off to Siphnos; **2** they were in need of money, and at that time Siphnos' affairs were at the height of their prosperity, and they were by far the richest of the islanders, in as much as their gold and silver mines on the island were so productive that with a tenth of their output they furnished a treasury at Delphi equal to the richest ones there; and every year they used to share out the yield of the mines amongst themselves.

1.64 Chadwick 35–36: The Berezan Lead Letter, *c.* 500 BC

This inscription on a lead tablet was found on the island of Berezan near Olbia, a Milesian colony on the Black Sea. It is a letter from Achillodoros, who was travelling on a business trip on behalf of Anaxagoras. His cargo has been confiscated by Matasys, who has attempted to reduce Achillodoros to slavery, presumably in order to settle an outstanding claim against Anaxagoras. Matasys claims that Anaxagoras has deprived him of what ought to be his, that Achillodoros is Anaxagoras' slave, and that he is therefore liable to seizure by Matasys as compensation. Achillodoros here writes to his son Protagoras to let him know what is happening and to tell him to inform Anaxagoras. He tells his son to get the rest of the family to safety in the city, where they can appeal to the magistrates against any attempt to enslave them; Euneuros may be another of Achillodoros' sons.

Protagoras, your father sends you this message: he is being wronged by Matasys, for Matasys is reducing him to slavery and has deprived him of his cargo vessel. Go to Anaxagoras and say to him: Matasys says that Achillodoros is the slave of Anaxagoras, and says, 'Anaxagoras has my property, male slaves, female slaves, and houses.' But Achillodoros complains loudly and says that there is nothing between him and Matasys, and says that he is free and that there is nothing between him and Matasys. But what there is between Matasys and Anaxagoras they themselves know between them. Tell this to Anaxagoras and Achillodoros' wife. Achillodoros sends you another message: take your mother and your brothers, who are among the Arbinatai, to the city, and Euneuros will come himself to him (?Achillodoros) and then go straight down. Reverse: The lead of Achillodoros; addressed to his son and to Anaxagoras.

1.65 Meiggs & Lewis 30: Public Imprecations at Teos, *c.* 470 BC

The following curses are to be pronounced three times each year by certain magistrates against those who endanger the community, including those who prevent the import of grain, showing its great importance to the community that imported it, and against pirates; the aisymnetes is apparently a magistrate. For Thucydides on piracy as a way of life in his own time amongst the Ozolian Lokrians, Aetolians, and Akarnanians, see Thuc. 1.5.1–6.2; cf. Hom. *Od.* 3.71–74.

A Whoever makes drugs that are poisonous against the Teians as a community or against an individual, that man shall die, both himself and his family. Whoever prevents grain being imported to the Teian land by any cunning or contrivance either by sea or by the mainland, or re-exports it after it has been imported, shall die, both himself and his family.

B … **8** Whoever in future is aisymnetes in Teos or in the territory of Teos … knowingly betrays the city and territory of Teos or the men on the island or on the sea hereafter or the Aroian fort; or who in future commits treason or robbery or receives brigands or commits piracy or receives pirates knowingly, who carry off (plunder) from the territory of Teos or from the sea; or who plots some evil against the Teian community knowingly either with Greeks or with barbarians shall die, both himself and his family.

1.66 Pleket *Epigraphica* I, no. 2: The Wine Trade on Thasos *c.* 425–400 BC

The wine trade was obviously of extreme importance to Thasos. The second part of the inscription forbids the import of foreign wine into the area of the mainland which the Thasians controlled, the Thasian peraia, and the Thasian landowners are presumably ensuring the sale of their own produce, free from foreign competition. In lines 12–13, the selling of wine retail (literally by the kotyle, or jug) is also forbidden, which aims at ensuring that wine sold came from amphorai specifically labelled as Thasian. Plynterion is a month on Thasos.

I Neither sweet wine nor wine from the crop on the vines shall be bought before the first of Plynterion; whoever transgresses and buys it, shall be bound to pay stater for stater, one half to the city and the other half to the prosecutor. The lawsuit shall be as for cases of violence. But if someone buys wine in wine-jars (pithoi) the purchase shall be valid, if (the seller) has stamped a seal on wine jars.

II … the penalties and deposits shall be the same. If no one puts down a deposit (does not prosecute), the commissioners of the mainland are to bring the case. Whenever they win, all the penalty is to belong to the city; but if the commissioners do not bring the case, though they have learned of the matter, they shall be liable to pay a double penalty; whoever wishes shall bring the case in the same way, and he shall have half the penalty, and the magistrates (demiourgoi) shall grant the case against the commissioners in the same way. No Thasian ship shall import foreign wine within Athos and Pacheia; if it does, (the owner) shall be liable to the same penalties as for adulterating the wine with water, and the helmsman shall be liable to the same penalty; and the lawsuits and the deposits shall be the same. Nor shall anyone sell wine by the kotyle either from amphorai or from a cask or from a false (non-regulation) wine-jar (pithos); and whoever sells it, the lawsuits and the deposits and the penalties shall be the same as for adulterating it with water.

1.67 Herodotos 3.6.1–2: The Mystery of the Missing Amphorai

3.6.1 From all of Greece, and from Phoenicia as well, earthenware jars full of wine are imported into Egypt throughout the year, yet one could say that not a wine jar is to be seen anywhere. **2** Obviously, one should ask, where are these disposed of? I will explain this. Each mayor (demarch) has to collect all the wine jars from his city and send them to Memphis, and the people of Memphis have to fill them with water and take them to the waterless regions of Syria.

1.68 Andocides 1 *On the Mysteries* 133–34: Customs Duties at the Piraeus

Like most other taxes, the 2 per cent customs duty levied by Athens was not collected by a government agency but farmed out to the highest bidder at the cost of thirty talents: at this percentage the volume of traffic was approximately 1,800 talents in 399 BC, and presumably was much greater under Athens' 'empire'.

133 Agyrrhios here, that honest man, two years ago was chief contractor for the tax of two per cent. He bid thirty talents for it and those people he meets under the poplar tree all had shares in it with him; you know the kind of people they are. I think they met there with two purposes, to be paid for not outbidding him and to get a share in a tax-collecting business sold at a low price. **134** When they'd made a profit of six talents and realized what they were onto and how valuable it was, they all combined, gave the other bidders a share and put in a bid for the tax again for thirty talents. Since no one else put in a rival bid, I came forward before the Council and kept raising their offer, until I got the contract for thirty-six talents. After getting rid of those men and providing you with guarantors, I collected the money and paid it over to the city, without making any loss by it, as my partners and I made some small profit; and I'd ensured that those men didn't share out between them six talents of your money.

1.69 [Xenophon] *Constitution of the Athenians* 2.11–12: Athenian Control of Trade

Athens had a long-standing need for timber, particularly during the days of its empire, for the construction of its fleet (Xen. *Hell.* 6.1.11).

2.11 They alone of Greeks and barbarians are able to possess wealth. For if a city is rich in timber for shipbuilding, where will it dispose of it unless it has the consent of the rulers of the sea? If a city is rich in iron, copper or flax, where will it dispose of these unless it has the consent of the rulers of the sea? But it is from these very things that my ships are made, timber from one place, from another copper, from another flax, from another wax. **12** In addition, they will not permit exports elsewhere to wherever any of our rivals are, on pain of not being allowed use of the sea. And I, though I do nothing, have all these things from the land because of the sea, while no other city has two of them; the same city does not have timber and flax, but where there is most flax the land is smooth and timberless; the same city does not even have copper and iron, nor do any two or three of the rest come from a single city, but one from this and one from that.

1.70 Bogaert *Epigraphica* 21: The 'Tester' of Silver Coinage, 375/4 BC

Public slaves at Athens included the Scythian archers (doc. 5.11), clerks for the jury-courts, and this dokimastes, or tester of coinage. Athens in the 370s BC had certain financial difficulties, hence the need to standardise the coinage and rate of exchange. The epimeletai were commissioners in charge of the docks; the thesmothetai are the six junior archons in charge of allocating the courts; the apodektai received the revenue and assigned it to various functions; the poletai, or sellers, sold or leased state property; and the syllogeis were members of the Council with policing functions. [*SEG* 26.72; Harding 45; R&O 25.]

Resolved by the nomothetai, in the archonship of Hippodamas; Nikophon proposed the motion: Athenian silver coinage is to be accepted when it is shown to be silver and carries the official die. The public tester, who sits among the (bankers') tables, is to test according to these regulations every day except whenever there is a payment of money, when he should test in the Council chamber. If anyone brings forward foreign currency which carries the same die as the Attic, if it is good he is to give it back to the one who brought it forward. But if it is bronze underneath or lead underneath or counterfeit, he is to cut it across and it is to be sacred to the Mother of the Gods and he is to deposit it with the Council. And if the tester does not sit (at his post) or does not test according to the law, he is to be struck with fifty blows of the whip by the Syllogeis of the people. If someone does not accept what silver currency the tester has approved, he is to have confiscated everything he has for sale on that day. Denunciations that coins are contraband are to be made in the grain-market before the commissioners for the grain-market (the Sitophylakes), in the agora and the rest of the city before the Syllogeis of the people, and in the trading-port (emporion) and Piraeus before the Epimeletai of the trading-port, except for those in the grain-market, as those in the grain-market are to be made before the commissioners for the grain-market. For all denunciations which are less than ten drachmas the magistrates have jurisdiction to give a verdict, but for those above ten drachmas they are to bring them into the law-court. The thesmothetai are to assist by granting them a court assigned by lot when they request one or be subject to a fine of ... drachmas. The informer is to receive one-half, if he gets a conviction. If the seller is a male or female slave, let him or her be beaten with fifty lashes of the whip by the magistrates to whom each denunciation has been allocated. If any of the magistrates does not act in accordance with the written regulations, anyone of the Athenians who chooses and who is allowed to do so may bring him before the Council. And if he is convicted, he is to cease being a magistrate and the Council is to fine him up to 500 drachmas.

In order that there may also be a tester in the Piraeus for the shipowners and merchants and all the others, the Council is to appoint one from among the public slaves ... or is to purchase one, and the Apodektai (receivers) are to apportion the price. The Epimeletai of the trading-port are to ensure that he sits at the stele of Poseidon and are to apply the law as has been stated in the case of the tester in the city. Inscribe this law on a stone stele and place one in the city among the tables and another in the Piraeus in front of the stele of Poseidon. The secretary of the Council is to report the price to the Poletai and let the Poletai bring it into the Council. The payment of the salary of the tester in the trading-port is to begin from when he is appointed in the archonship of Hippodamas, and the Apodektai are to assign him the same amount as for the tester in the city. In the future his salary is to come from the same source as for workers in the mint. If there is any decree inscribed anywhere contrary to this law the secretary of the Council is to pull it down.

THE GRAIN TRADE

1.71 Herodotos 7.147.2–3: Grain from the Black Sea

This passage is the earliest explicit reference to the grain trade (both wheat and barley: barley was the staple diet in Greek cities for the ordinary citizen: doc. 1.25). Half of Athens' supply came from the Black Sea region (doc. 1.74). Grain from the western Greeks was equally important: Gelon promised to ship sufficient grain to Greece for the duration of Xerxes' invasion (Hdt. 7.158.4).

7.147.2 When Xerxes was at Abydos he saw boats from the Black Sea sailing through the Hellespont with cargoes of grain, carrying it to Aegina and the Peloponnese. His counsellors, on learning that they were enemy ships, were prepared to capture them, and kept their eye on the King awaiting his order. **3** Xerxes asked them where the boats were sailing; they answered, 'They are carrying grain, sire, to your enemies.' His reply was, 'Are not we sailing there ourselves, equipped, among other things, with grain? So what harm are they doing in transporting our grain for us?'

1.72 Demosthenes 35 *Against Lakritos* 51: A Law on the Transport of Grain

According to this law it was illegal to contract a loan on a ship which did not bring grain to Athens on its return voyage or to lend money for transporting grain anywhere other than Athens. The grain supply was so important that it was a fixed item on the assembly's agenda each month ([Arist.] *Ath. Pol.* 43.4: doc. 1.16). The epimeletai here are superintendents of the grain supply.

51 It shall be illegal for any Athenian or metic living at Athens, or for anyone for whom they are responsible, to lend money on any ship which is not going to bring grain or any of the other items specifically mentioned back to Athens. And if anyone lends money contrary to this law, information and an account of the money shall be laid before the epimeletai in the same way as is provided with regard to the ship and the grain. And the merchant shall have no right to bring a case to recover the money which he has lent for a voyage to anywhere other than Athens, and no magistrate shall bring any such case to trial.

1.73 Demosthenes 35 *Against Lakritos* 10–13: Contract for a Maritime Loan

The terms of the loan are that the borrowers should sail to Mende or Skione in Chalkidike, and purchase 3,000 jars of wine which they would then transport to the Black Sea, where they would sell the wine and ship a return cargo (of grain) for sale in Athens. On their return they would then pay back the loan with interest (the rate of interest remains unchanged even if their return takes place in the following year, which in Athens commenced with the summer solstice).

10 Androkles of Sphettos and Nausikrates of Karystos have lent Artemo and Apollodoros, both of Phaselis, 3,000 drachmas in silver for a voyage from Athens to Mende or Skione and from there to the Bosporos, or if they wish as far as Borysthenes on the left-hand side of the Black Sea, and from there back to Athens, at a rate of 225 drachmas per 1,000, but if they set sail from the Black Sea to the Hieron after the rising of Arcturus (the dog-star) at the rate of 300 per 1,000. This is on the security of 3,000 jars of wine from Mende, which will be transported from Mende or Skione in the twenty-oared ship owned by Hyblesios. **11**

They give these as security, and do not owe any money on them to any other person, nor will they borrow anything further upon this security. And they will transport all the goods acquired by trade from the Black Sea back to Athens in the same ship. If the goods arrive at Athens safely, the borrowers will repay the lenders the money due in accordance with the contract within twenty days of their return to Athens, with no deductions except for any jettison made by all the passengers in agreement or for any money paid to enemies: otherwise they will pay in full. And they will give the lenders the security to hold unencumbered, until they have repaid the money due in accordance with the contract. **12** And if they do not repay it within the time agreed, it will be legal for the lenders to pledge or sell the security for its current value; and, if the money falls short of the sum which is due to the lenders under the contract, the lenders can proceed against Artemo and Apollodoros and against all their property, whether landed or maritime, wherever it might be, as if they had lost a lawsuit and were overdue with the payment, and either one or both of the lenders may do this. **13** And if they do not enter the Black Sea, but remain in the Hellespont for ten days after the rising of the dog-star, and unload their goods at a place where the Athenians do not have the right of seizure and from there complete their voyage to Athens, they shall pay the same interest as that written into the contract the year before. And if the ship in which the goods are conveyed is damaged beyond repair, but the security is saved, whatever survives is to belong jointly to the lenders. And with regard to these matters nothing is to have greater authority than the contract. Witnesses: Phormio of Piraeus, Kephisodoros of Boeotia, Heliodoros of Pitthos.

1.74 Demosthenes 20 *Against Leptines* 31–32: The Importance of Grain Imports

Delivered in 355 BC this speech shows the crucial nature of Black Sea grain for Athens as shown by the fact that Athens starved when Lysander blocked the arrival of grain from this area (doc. 13.35). Athens had granted exemptions for Leukon and his children from liturgies and war-taxes.

31 You're aware that more than any other people we depend on imported grain. The grain that comes to us from the Black Sea equals the amount that arrives from all other emporia. This is understandable: for not only does that region produce the greatest amount of grain, but Leukon, who controls the area, has granted exemption from taxes to those carrying grain to Athens, and has laid down that those sailing to you have priority in loading. For just as he has been granted exemption for himself and his children he grants it to all of you. **32** See what this amounts to. He takes a tax of one-thirtieth from those who export grain from his country. Now from that region there come to Athens some 400,000 bushels: anyone can check this by looking at the records of the grain-commissioners. So for each 300,000 bushels he gives us a present of 10,000 and from the other 100,000 roughly 3,000.

1.75 Tod 2.196: Cyrene supplies Greece with Grain, 330–326 BC

Cyrene in North Africa – one of Greece's most successful colonies (docs 2.28–30) — donated fifty-one shipments of grain to forty-one different Greek states (that is, some states received two separate shipments), and a further two to Olympias in Macedonia and Kleopatra (married to the ruler of Epiros), Alexander the Great's mother and sister respectively. The amounts are in medimnoi, measures of grain, with one medimnos equalling fifty-five dry litres, and were shipped during a grain crisis between *c.* 330–326 BC, which is known from other sources. Sparta is conspicuous by its absence from the list. Pindar described Cyrene as 'grain-bearing' (*Isthmian* 4.54). [*SEG* 9.2; Harding 196; R&O 96]

The priest was Sosias, son of Kalliades. To whom the city gave grain, when the grain shortage happened in Greece:

To the Athenians 100,000; to Olympias 60,000; to the Argives 50,000; to the Larisans 50,000; to the Corinthians 50,000; to Kleopatra 50,000; to the Rhodians 30,000; to the Sikyonians 30,000; to the Meliboians 20,000; to the Megarians 20,000; to the Tenians 20,000; to the Lesbians 15,000; to the Therans 15,000; to the Oitaians 15,000; to the Ambraciots 15,000; to the Leukadians 15,000; to the Karystians 15,000; to Olympias 12,600; to the Atragians of Thessaly 10,000; to the Kythnians 10,000; to the Opountians 10,000; to the Kydonians 10,000; to the Koans 10,000; to the Parians 10,000; to the Delphians 10,000; to the Knosians 10,000; to the Boeotians of Tanagra 10,000; to the Gortynians 10,000; to the Eleians 10,000; to the Palairaians of Akarnania 10,000; to the Megarians 10,000; to the Meliboians 8,500; to the Phleiasians 8,000; to the Hermionians 8,000; to the Oitaians 6,400; to the Troizenians 6,000; to the Plataians 6,000; to the Ioulietans on Keos 5,000; to the Aeginetans 5,000; to the Astypalaians 5,000; to the Kytherans 5,000; to the Hyrtakinians 5,000; to the Aeginetans 5,000; to the Karthaians on Keos 4,000; to the Kytherans 3,100; to the Keans 3,000; to the Illyrians (Elyrians of Crete?) 3,000; to the Koresians on Keos 3,000; to the Ambrakiots 1,500; to the Iketyrians 1,000; to the Knosians 900.

THE SUPERSTARS OF THE CITY-STATE

Cf. doc. 9.41 for perpetual dining rights in the prytaneion for all victors at the four pan-Hellenic festivals and for the descendents of the 'tyrannicides' Harmodios and Aristogeiton and other benefactors of the city of Athens, such as Kleon after his victory at Pylos (doc. 1.29).

1.76 Diodorus *Library of History* 13.82.5–8: Athletes Honoured in Sicily

Exainetos of Akragas in Sicily won the foot-race (stadion) at the Olympic Games in 412 BC. Sicily was noted for its luxury and extravagance: see docs 7.48, 7.52. Diodoros' description makes clear the enthusiastic reception accorded to the victors when they returned home and the importance of sports to Greek culture.

13.82.5 At that period there was an man-made lake outside the city, seven stades in circumference and twenty cubits deep; the inhabitants of Akragas channelled water into this and cleverly kept a vast number of fish of every kind for their public banquets. The fish attracted swans and an immense number of other kinds of bird, and so the lake was a great attraction to those who saw it. **6** The luxurious lifestyle of the locals is also shown by the extravagant cost of the monuments which they erected, some adorned with racehorses and others with the birds kept as pets by girls and boys, monuments which Timaeus says he had seen extant even in his own lifetime. **7** And in the Olympiad before the one under discussion, the ninety-second, when Exainetos of Akragas won the stadion, they escorted him into the city in a chariot and accompanying him (not to mention everything else) there were three hundred chariots each drawn by white horses, all of these belonging to citizens of Akragas. **8** In general, from their youth they enjoyed a luxurious lifestyle, wearing extremely delicate clothing and gold ornaments and even using strigils and oil-flasks made of silver and gold.

1.77 Athenaeus *Deipnosophistae* 412d–413a: A Healthy Appetite

The oxen-devouring athletes below were presumably those competing in physical events such as boxing, wrestling and the pankration. Milon proved his strength both by carrying around an ox on his shoulder as if it was a lamb and then by devouring it without assistance. The beasts would have been first offered in sacrifice to Zeus, and then eaten by the participants in the sacrifice; Pisa means Olympia.

412d Theagenes, the athlete from Thasos, finished off an entire bull on his own, as Poseidippos says in his epigrams:

> **412e** 'And for a bet I once ate a Maonian ox;
> My country of Thasos could not have provided a meal
> For Theagenes. Whatever I ate, I demanded more. And so
> I stand in bronze, holding out my hand.'

Milon of Kroton, as Theodoros of Hierapolis tells us in his work *On Athletic Contests*, used to eat twenty minas (weight) of meat and as many of bread and three jugs of wine. At Olympia he hoisted a four-year-old bull on his shoulders, **412f** and carried it right around the stadium, after which he cut it up and ate it all on his own in a single day. Tithormos of Aetolia competed with him in eating an ox for breakfast as a bet, as Alexander of Aetolia records. And Phylarchos says, in the third book of his *Histories*, that Milon devoured a bull while reclining in front of the altar of Zeus. In consequence the poet Dorieus wrote this in his honour:

> 'Such was Milon, when he lifted the weight from the ground,
> A four-year-old steer, at Zeus' festival,
> **413a** And on his shoulders the mighty beast, like a young lamb,
> He carried like a light-weight through all the spectators.
> That was amazing enough, but he accomplished a greater wonder than this
> Before the sacrificial altar at Pisa, stranger:
> The ox, not broken to the yoke, that he had carried round,
> He cut this up for meat and feasted on it all on his own.'

1.78 Xenophanes Poems F2: The Heroes of the City-State

Successful victors in the games could be awarded a state pension or a monetary reward by their city or dining rights in the prytaneion for the rest of their lives. For example, a victor from Athens at the Isthmian games was awarded 100 drachmas (cf. Plut. *Sol.* 23.3; Diog. Laert. *Sol.* 1.55: a victor at Olympia 500 drachmas). Socrates also asked for maintenance in the prytaneion for life (doc. 3.86 cf. 9.41, 1.29); the philosopher Xenophanes of Kolophon (*c.* 570–*c.* 475 BC) and Socrates seem to have had similar views of their own merits as opposed to those of athletes.

But if anyone were to win a victory through swiftness of foot
Or through competing in the pentathlon, in the precinct of Zeus
Beside the streams of Pisa at Olympia, or in wrestling
Or through possessing the painful art of boxing,
Or in that dreadful kind of contest which they call the pankration,
To the citizens he would be more glorious to behold
And would win a conspicuous seat of honour at the games
And would get maintenance out of public stores
From the city, as well as a gift for him to put by as treasure;
So too if he won with his horses, he would obtain all these things —
Though not deserving of them like I am. For better than the strength
Of men or of horses is my wisdom.
But opinion about this is random, nor is it right
To prefer strength to noble wisdom.
For even if there is a good boxer in the community
Or one good at the pentathlon or wrestling,
Or at swiftness of foot, which is most honoured
Of all the feats of strength in men's contests,
The city would not, for this reason, be better ordered.
Small delight would this be to a city,
If anyone were to compete and win beside the banks of Pisa!
These things do not enrich the store-chambers of a city.

2

COLONISATION

Greek history begins with the Mycenaean world, which comprised a chain of city-states across mainland Greece inhabited by the historical originals of Homer's warlords. Shortly after the capture of Troy — if that was indeed a historical event — Greece was to enter a Dark Age until the eighth century and the dawn of the history of archaic Greece. But, even in Mycenaean times, Greek states were not confined to the mainland. As early as the fifteenth century BC, there are records of Greeks in Western Anatolia (Asia Minor), and archaeology makes clear the fact that Greek expansion had already taken place, with evidence for settlements and trading centres along the Asia Minor coastline. From c. 1200 to c. 1000 BC a major wave of migration took place from mainland Greece to Asia Minor.

Greece always comprised far more than just the well-known cities of the Greek mainland. From the eighth to the sixth century BC, a period sometimes known as the 'Age of Colonisation', the Greeks of Asia Minor and the Greek mainland sent out large numbers of colonies, both east and west of their homeland. This, however, was not the only period during which colonies were settled, and Greek cities founded several important colonies in the fifth century and later (cf. docs 2.21, 2.24). In this way, Sicily and southern Italy, the Black Sea area, Africa, and even France and Spain provided sites for new Greek cities.

The reasons behind colonisation are frequently debated, but it appears that 'land-hunger', trading considerations, drought and political problems at home were the primary social and economic factors that impelled cities to send out settlements elsewhere. Certainly many of the colonies in the west were inspired by the availability of agricultural land, and the presence of fresh water and a good harbour was also important (doc. 2.11). While the specific choice of location for individual colonies, such as Pithekoussai (doc. 2.10), can still be the subject of much debate, good agricultural land in the vicinity would always have been an incentive, for colonists would have needed to be self-sufficient in food. Most colonies probably resulted from mixed motives; when the Phokaians established colonies in the far west, like the Teians in Thrace (doc. 2.13), they did so because they were fleeing from Persian domination. This provides a political explanation for their settlements, but it is also clear that the Phokaians both in Corsica and in Sicily made the most of opportunities for trading and for piracy.

The Spartans founded Taras in south-east Italy in the late eighth century to solve the pressing political problem of the partheniai, who were clearly Spartan in origin but without political rights (doc. 2.23), but Dorieus' attempt to colonise Africa and Italy was in essence a private venture, for he left Sparta because his half-brother Kleomenes was made king (doc. 2.22). Later colonies, such as Herakleia in Trachis, settled by Sparta in the fifth century, could have a partial political and strategic motive, for Herakleia was ideally suited as a base from which to attack Euboea (doc. 2.24). Nevertheless, it is important to realise how significant population size could be in Greek cities throughout this period: the people of Thera, when due to severe drought they drafted their colonists to settle Cyrene, cursed any of those who might attempt to return, and when they later did so attacked them and drove them away (docs 2.28–29).

The Greeks, naturally, took their way of life with them, and founded cities which were similar to the cities which they had left. Colonists apparently took with them fire from their mother-city (metropolis) and thus established continuity with their homeland (doc. 2.4). Relationships in general remained strong between mother-cities and colonies, and even a colony of a colony could claim aid from the original mother-city, as Epidamnos did from Corinth, while mother-cities expected that their colonies would maintain links with them. Each city had an oikistes, a 'founder' (pl.: oikistai), and sometimes more than one, whose role was to act as leader while the colony was being established. The tie of a colony with its mother-city was so important that when the colonies themselves sent out colonies, the oikistai for these were chosen from the original mother-city, as in the case of Epidamnos (doc. 2.8).

Colonies maintained their Greek way of life, and accounts were written of the establishment of colonies, presumably to preserve a record of their Greek origins (doc. 2.2). Different versions of a colony's founding could develop, however, as in the case of Cyrene (docs 2.25–26). Maintaining ties with the mother-city was also a way of remaining in touch with their ancestral origins. Colonies in the west tended to be concerned with their own pressing problems, especially with the Carthaginians and Etruscans (docs 7.44–46), but they participated in the pan-Hellenic festivals (doc. 2.30), and the Sicilians especially were several times victorious in the chariot races (docs 7.57–59).

When founding colonies, the Greeks often had to fight the native inhabitants for the land which they desired (docs 2.12, 2.26–27). But it is also clear that on other occasions the Greeks would compete against each other for sites, as the Athenians and Mytilenaeans did at Sigeion (doc. 2.18). There was often no feeling of mutual solidarity between Greek colonies even in areas where the locals were hostile, as in Sicily, and on the Black Sea coast Greeks dispossessed by later Greek settlers joined Scythian tribes, forming a Hellenic–Scythian culture (docs 2.33–34). Yet in many cases it is apparent that the local peoples became partially hellenised, and that there was interaction between local peoples and Greeks (docs 2.35–36). Thucydides is the most detailed source for the numerous – and prosperous – colonies of Sicily, and indicates that various Greek settlers were dispossessed by those that came later (doc. 2.12).

Socrates' opinion of the Greek world is a significant one for any understanding of Greek civilisation. He is recorded by Plato as thinking of the Greeks as living around the shores of the Mediterranean and Black Sea like 'ants or frogs around a pond' (doc. 2.37). The Greeks inhabited a world which was not restricted to the Greek mainland and coastline of Asia Minor but which reached from Spain to the far end of the Black Sea. Colonisation was an intrinsic part of Greek history from the eighth century, and one that had significant implications for the social, economic and military history of the Greek world.

2.1 Thucydides 1.3.1–3: The Greeks before 'Greekness'

Thucydides here discusses the fact that the term Hellenes, as used by the Greeks to refer to themselves, is relatively late and does not appear in the works of Homer. Terms such as the Argives and Achaeans continued in use to refer to Greeks of Argos and Achaea, both in the Peloponnese.

1.3.1 Before the Trojan War, Hellas (Greece), it seems, undertook no enterprise in common. **2** Indeed I think that as a whole it did not yet even have this name, but that before the time of Hellen, son of Deukalion, the name did not even exist, and that different tribes gave their names to different regions, with the Pelasgians having the most impact. But when Hellen and his sons became powerful in Phthiotis and were invited to come to the assistance of other cities, these one by one began to be called 'Hellenic' because of this association, though it was a long time before it replaced all other names. **3** Homer is the best proof of this. Although he lived a long time after the Trojan War, he does not anywhere use this name (Hellene) for all, or even for any of the Greeks except those with Achilles from Phthiotis, who were in fact the original Hellenes, but calls them Danaans and Argives and Achaeans. He did not use the term barbarians either, and I think that this is because the Hellenes were not yet separated off so as to share a common name.

2.2 Xenophanes of Kolophon FA1: Ancient Foundation Stories of Cities

Numerous accounts of the foundation of colonies and other cities were written by ancient authors, and this was a popular genre, with cities keen on having their foundation histories preserved. [Diog. Laert. 9.18, 20.]

9.18 He wrote both poems in epic verse and works in elegiacs and iambics against Hesiod and Homer, censuring the things they say about the gods … **20** He also composed a poem called *The Foundation of Kolophon*, and *The Settlement of the Colony of Elea in Italy*, comprising two thousand lines.

THE DELPHIC ORACLE

2.3 Lucian *Astrology* 23: Delphi and Colonisation

It was routine to undertake divination before major enterprises, and Delphi played an important role in Greek colonisation by providing divine approval for colonising ventures.

The men of former times were very much given to divination and considered it by no means incidental, but would not found cities, or surround themselves with walls, or kill anyone, or get married, before they had learned all the details from the diviners.

2.4 *Etymologicum Magnum* 694.28–31: Prytaneia: The Sacred Fire

There is no explicit evidence from the classical period about the transfer of sacred fire from the mother-city to a colony. The evidence is late, such as this entry from the *Etymologicum Magnum*. The prytaneion (plural: prytaneia) was the town hall.

Prytaneia: the sacred fire is kept there; and those who are at any time setting out to a colony, from there light a fire from the hearth, that is they 'kindle it'.

THE OIKISTES

The oikistes (pl.: oikistai) or founder was the leader of the colonists in their enterprise; there could be more than one oikistes for each colony. In the eighth to sixth centuries the oikistes will presumably have remained in the colony. They were often venerated after death in the colony they had established.

2.5 Homer *Odyssey* 6.1–12: The Duties of an Oikistes

This passage, despite its mythical setting, describes the main duties of the founder of a colony, the oikistes. Odysseus, after a shipwreck, has arrived at the island of Phaeacia and is going to encounter princess Nausikaa: doc. 4.7.

So the much-enduring godlike Odysseus lay there asleep,
Worn out by sleep and toil; but Athena
Went to the land and city of the Phaeacian people,
Who long ago used to dwell in spacious Hypereia,
Near the Cyclopes an overbearing people,
Who used to plunder them, and were stronger than they.
Godlike Nausithoos removed them from there and led
And settled them in Scheria, far from hard-working men,
And he drew a wall around the city, and built houses,
And made temples to the gods, and divided up the corn-lands.
But already overpowered by fate he had gone to Hades,
And Alkinoos now ruled, who had counsel from the gods.

2.6 Graham 1983, 21–22n.7: A Dedication to an Oikistes

This inscription from Gela in Sicily was scratched on an Athenian cup dating to the fifth century BC, indicating that the cup was dedicated to Antiphamos of Rhodes, who founded Gela in 688 BC. The cult of an oikistes could clearly survive in a colony well after his death.

'Mnasithales dedicated this to Antiphamos.'

2.7 Thucydides 5.11.1: Oikistai at Amphipolis: Hagnon and Brasidas

The Athenian colony (apoikia) at Amphipolis in Thrace, founded by Hagnon, dated to 437/6 BC, and the advantages of the site included its command of trade routes and an important crossing of the Strymon river; the district was also rich in timber, which Athens needed for its fleet, and in silver. When the Amphipolitans surrendered their city to the Spartan Brasidas, who died in the battle with the Athenians outside the city in 422 BC, the people of the city felt that Hagnon would no longer benefit them as their oikistes.

5.11.1 After this all the allies with their weapons publicly attended and buried Brasidas in the city in front of what is now the agora; henceforward the Amphipolitans, after enclosing his tomb, sacrificed to him as a hero and gave him the honour of games and yearly sacrifices, and attributed the colony to him as founder, pulling down the buildings of Hagnon and getting rid of anything which might still survive as a reminder of his settlement. They considered that Brasidas had been their saviour (at the same time, they were at that point fostering the alliance with the Spartans through fear of the Athenians), and also that, because they were at war with the Athenians, Hagnon could no longer be honoured with similar benefit or contentment.

MOTHER-CITIES AND THEIR COLONIES

2.8 Thucydides 1.24.1–26.2: Corinth and her Colony Corcyra

Corinth colonised Corcyra in the late eighth century and Corcyra had in turn colonised Epidamnos in 627 BC, but the oikistes for this had come, as was customary, from Corcyra's own mother-city, Corinth. The passage clearly exemplifies the normal relationship between mother-city and colonies, and even the colony of a colony could claim aid from the original mother-city. A mother-city could expect specific honours from its colonies.

1.24.1 Epidamnos is a city on the right as one sails into the Ionian gulf; Taulantian barbarians, an Illyrian race, dwell nearby. **2** The Corcyraeans colonised it, and its founder was Phalios, son of Eratokleides, a Corinthian from the family of the Herakleidai, who had been invited from the mother-city according to ancestral custom. Some Corinthians and others of the Dorian race joined in colonising it. **3** As time passed, the Epidamnians' power became great and populous; **4** but they were split by factional strife amongst themselves for many years, as it is said, because they had been ruined and deprived of most of their power through a war with the neighbouring barbarians. **5** Finally, before the (Peloponnesian) war, the people expelled those of influence and power, and so these attacked with the barbarians and plundered the inhabitants of the city by both land and sea. **6** Since the people in the city were hard-pressed, as they were Epidamnians they sent envoys to Corcyra, since it was their mother-city, begging that it would not suffer them to be destroyed, but would reconcile them with their exiles and put an end to the war with the barbarians. **7** They sat as suppliants in the Heraion and made this request. But the Corcyraeans did not accept their plea, sending them away unsuccessful. **1.25.1** When the Epidamnians realised that they were going to get no assistance from Corcyra, they were at a loss as to what they could do, and so they sent to Delphi and consulted the god as to whether they should hand over the city to the Corinthians as their founders and try to obtain some assistance from them. He replied that they should hand it over and make the Corinthians their leaders. **2** The Epidamnians went to Corinth and handed over the colony in accordance with the oracle, pointing out that their founder was from Corinth and making known the oracle's response, and begged that they would not suffer them to be destroyed, but come to their aid. **3** The Corinthians promised their assistance, feeling they had a right to do so, as they considered that the colony was no less theirs than the Corcyraeans', and motivated at the same time by the fact that they hated the Corcyraeans, inasmuch as they disregarded them though they were their colonists; **4** for they neither gave the Corinthians the customary honours in their common festivals, nor served Corinthians with the first portion of the sacrifices, as the other colonies did. Instead they despised the Corinthians because they themselves were both equal to the richest of the Greeks at that time in monetary power and more powerful in military resources, and boasted that they were far superior in their fleet … **1.26.1** So, having all these complaints against the Corcyraeans, the Corinthians were glad to send help to Epidamnos, bidding anyone who wished to go as a colonist, as well as guards of Ambraciots, Leukadians and their own citizens. **2** And they went by land to Apollonia, a Corinthian colony, for fear that they might be hindered by the Corcyraeans if they crossed by sea.

2.9 Thucydides 1.56.1–57.1: Athenian Interference with Potidaea

There were strong bonds between some mother-cities and their colonies, and the mother-city expected that the colonies would 'follow its lead'. Potidaea, founded by Corinth c. 625–585 BC, was still receiving annual magistrates from Corinth in 432. The context is, as for doc. 2.8, the outbreak of the Peloponnesian War.

1.56.1 Immediately after this the following differences also occurred between the Athenians and Peloponnesians which led to war. **2** For since the Corinthians were planning how to revenge themselves on the Athenians, the latter, suspecting their enmity, gave instructions to the Potidaeans, colonists of Corinth and their own tributary allies who live on the isthmus of Pallene, to demolish their wall on the side towards Pallene, give hostages, and expel the magistrates (epidemiourgoi) sent them by Corinth and not in future receive those sent every year. For the Athenians were afraid that the Potidaeans might revolt under the persuasion of Perdikkas and the Corinthians, and might draw into the revolt with them Athens' other allies in Thrace. **1.57.1** The Athenians took these precautions regarding Potidaea immediately after the sea-battle at Corcyra.

THE COLONISATION OF THE WEST: ITALY AND SICILY

The Greek colonies sent out to Sicily and southern Italy were spectacularly successful. The term *Magna Graecia*, 'Greater Greece' (Greek: Megale Hellas), is an ancient one; while it could be used of the entire Greek world, its particular application was to the Greek cities of Sicily and southern Italy. The Greek cities fought amongst themselves, and had to deal with the indigenous Sikels as well as the Carthaginian cities in the western part of the island. There was a further wave of Greek colonisation to Sicily in the fourth century BC organised by Corinth (doc. 7.55).

2.10 Meiggs & Lewis 1 : 'Nestor's Cup' from Pithekoussai

Pithekoussai was the earliest Greek colony in the west, jointly founded by the Euboean cities of Chalkis and Eretria probably *c.* 750–25 BC, on the island of Ischia (opposite the west coast of Italy). 'Nestor's Cup' (a 'kotyle', drinking cup, c. 720–710), has the longest eighth-century Greek inscription and one of the oldest examples of Greek writing. The inscription is particularly important as Pithekoussai's neighbour colony Cumae on the mainland opposite (founded *c.* 725–700) transmitted the Greek alphabet to the Etruscans, from whom the Romans adopted it, and from which in turn our own alphabet derives. The lines refer to Nestor's cup: see Homer *Iliad* 11.632–37. [Hansen 454.]

Nestor's cup was good to drink from,
But whoever drinks from this cup will immediately
Be seized with desire for beautifully-crowned Aphrodite.

2.11 Ephoros *Histern* F137: The Colonisation of Sicily

Although the motive for colonisation is sometimes debated, as in the case of Pithekoussai or Sinope (docs 2.10, 2.17), in the following case in Sicily land hunger was clearly the motivating force according to the fourth-century historian Ephoros, whose original works are now lost but whose material was later cited by Strabo. [*FGH* 70 F137; Strabo *Geography* 6.2.2.]

The cities along the side which forms the strait are first Messene, then Tauromenion, Catana and Syracuse; but those between Catana and Syracuse, that is Naxos and Megara, have been deserted. This is also the location of the outlets of the river Symaithos and all the others that flow down from Aetna into well-harboured mouths; here too is the promontory of Xiphonia. Ephoros says that these were the first Greek cities to be founded in Sicily, in the tenth generation after the Trojan War; for men before that were so afraid of the bands of Etruscan pirates and the savagery of the barbarians there that they would not even sail there for trade. But Theokles, an Athenian, who had been carried away by the winds to Sicily, observed the worthlessness of the people and the excellence of the land, and, as he was unable on his return to persuade the Athenians, he took with him when he sailed many Chalkidians from Euboea and some of the Ionians, and also Dorians, most of whom were Megarians; accordingly the Chalkidians founded Naxos, while the Dorians founded Megara, which was previously called Hybla. Though the cities are no longer in existence, the name of Hybla continues to last because of the excellence of the Hyblaian honey.

2.12 Thucydides 6.3.1–5.3: Thucydides on Sicilian Colonisation

Thucydides is the best ancient account for the colonisation of Sicily; the context is the lead-up to the Athenian expedition against Sicily launched in 415/4 BC. In his account, note especially the comments on oikistai, mixed populations, troubles between the Greek settlers, their attitude to the native Sikels, and the sending out of further colonies by the original colonies.

6.3.1 The first Greeks (in Sicily) sailed from Chalkis in Euboea with Thoukles their founder and founded Naxos, as well as building an altar of Apollo the Founder (Archegetes) which is now outside the city, at which, when religious envoys (theoroi) sail from Sicily, they first sacrifice. **2** In the following year Archias, one of the Herakleidai from Corinth, founded Syracuse, after first driving out the Sikels from 'the island', where now the inner city is, though no longer surrounded by sea; some time later the outer city was brought within the city wall and became populous. **3** Thoukles and the Chalkidians set out from Naxos in the fifth year after Syracuse had been founded, drove out the Sikels in a war, and founded Leontinoi, and then Catana; but the people of Catana themselves chose Euarchos as their founder. **6.4.1** At about the same time Lamis from Megara, who was bringing a group of colonists, also arrived in Sicily, and founded a place called Trotilos above the river Pantakyas, but later leaving there settled for a short time with the Chalkidians at Leontinoi, was expelled by them, founded Thapsos, and then died, while the others after having to leave Thapsos founded what is called Hyblaian Megara, Hyblon, a Sikel king, having given them the land and guided them there. **2** They dwelt there for 245 years, but were made to leave the city and its land by Gelon, tyrant of the Syracusans. Before they had to leave, 100 years after they had settled there, they sent out Pamillos and founded Selinous, Pamillos having come out from the mother-city Megara to found it with them.

3 Antiphemos from Rhodes and Entimos from Crete founded Gela, bringing out settlers in a joint venture in the forty-fifth year after the foundation of Syracuse. It was named after the Gela river, and the place where the city is now and which was first walled is called

Lindioi; they adopted Doric legal usages. **4** In about 108 years after their own foundation the people of Gela founded Akragas, naming the city after the Akragas river, and making Aristonous and Pystilos the founders, giving it the same usages as those of Gela. **5** Zankle was originally founded by pirates who arrived from Cumae, the Chalkidian city in Opicia, but later on a large crowd of people came from Chalkis and the rest of Euboea and divided the territory jointly amongst themselves; and its founders were Perieres and Krataimenes, the one from Cumae, the other from Chalkis. Its first name was Zankle (it had been called this by the Sikels, because the place is sickle-shaped in appearance; the Sikels called the sickle 'zanklon'), but later on they were driven out by Samians and other Ionians, **6** who put into Sicily as they were fleeing from the Medes, and shortly afterwards Anaxilas, the tyrant of Rhegium, drove out the Samians, colonised the city with a mixture of people, and renamed it Messene after his own original homeland.

6.5.1 And Himera was founded from Zankle by Euklides, Simos and Sakon, and the majority of those who came to the colony were Chalkidians, though exiles from Syracuse, called the Myletidai, whose party had had the worst of it, joined in with them; their dialect was a mixture of Chalkidian and Doric, and their usages primarily Chalkidian. **2** Akrai and Kasmenai were founded by the Syracusans, Akrai seventy years after Syracuse and Kasmenai nearly twenty years after Akrai. **3** And Camarina was first founded by Syracusans, some 135 years after the foundation of Syracuse; its founders were Daskon and Menekolos. After the Camarinans were made to leave by the Syracusans in a war because they had revolted, some time later Hippokrates, tyrant of Gela, took the land of the Camarinans as ransom for Syracusan prisoners of war, and himself became its founder and colonised Camarina. Its people were again made to leave by Gelon, and it was settled for the third time by the people of Gela.

2.13 Herodotos 1.163.1–169.1: The Peoples of Phokaia and Teos Flee the Persians

The Phokaians fled their city around c. 545 BC as the Persians invaded, but half of the population returned to their city. The remainder went to their colony Alalia, on Corsica, established *c.* 565, and settled themselves as pirates; the battle of Alalia against the coalition of the Carthaginians and Etruscans took place *c.* 537. The Teians also abandoned their city *c.* 545.

1.163.1 These Phokaians were the first of the Greeks to make long sea voyages, and they were the ones who discovered the Adriatic, Etruria, Iberia and Tartessos. **2** They sailed not in merchant ships but in pentekonters. (*Arganthonios, tyrant of Tartessos in Spain, failed to persuade them to settle in his country, but gave them money to build a wall around their city.*) **1.164.1** So the Phokaians' wall was constructed in this way, and Harpagos, who led the army against them and was besieging them, made the proposal that he would be satisfied if the Phokaians wished to pull down one battlement of the wall and to sacrifice one house. **2** The Phokaians, though aggrieved at slavery, said that they wished to consider for one day and then answer; and while they were deliberating they told him to lead his army away from the wall. Harpagos said that he knew well what they were planning to do, but that even so he would allow them to deliberate. **3** And while Harpagos was leading his army away from the wall, the Phokaians in the meantime hauled their pentekonters down to the sea, put their children and women and all their belongings aboard, as well as the statues from their temples and the other votive offerings, except what was of bronze or stone or paintings, and, after putting everything else aboard, embarked themselves and sailed towards Chios; and the Persians possessed Phokaia without its people.

1.165.1 As the Chians chose not to sell them the islands called the Oinousai when they offered to buy them, being afraid that they would become a trading centre, and their island might be excluded because of this, accordingly the Phokaians set out for Corsica (Kyrnos). For they had built themselves a city on Corsica on the advice of an oracle twenty years before these events, the name of which was Alalia. **2** At that point Arganthonios had already died. When they set out for Corsica, they first sailed back to Phokaia, killed the Persian guard who had taken the city over from Harpagos, and afterwards, so that this should be incumbent on them all, laid heavy curses on anyone of their number who should fail to accompany the fleet. **3** In addition to this, they dropped a lump of iron into the sea and swore they would never return to Phokaia until this reappeared. But while they were on their way to Corsica, half of the citizens were gripped by longing and regret for their city and their country's customs, and they made perjurers of themselves by sailing back to Phokaia. Those who kept their oath set out from the Oinousai and continued their voyage.

1.166.1 When they reached Corsica, they lived there for five years in common with those who had previously arrived there and erected temples. They continually plundered all their neighbours to such an extent that the Etruscans and Carthaginians came to an agreement and made an expedition against them each with sixty ships. **2** The Phokaians too manned their ships, which were sixty in number, and met them in what is called the Sardinian Sea. In the sea battle which followed their encounter, the Phokaians gained a sort of Kadmeian victory (where more was lost than gained). Forty of their ships had been destroyed, and the twenty surviving ones were useless; for their rams were bent back. **3** They sailed back to Alalia, took with them their children and wives and as much of their property as the ships were able to carry, and then left Corsica and sailed to Rhegium. **1.167.1** The Carthaginians and Etruscans drew lots for the men from the ships which were destroyed, and of the Etruscans the Agyllaioi obtained by far the largest share, and these they led out and stoned … **3** This group of Phokaians suffered this fate, while those who escaped to Rhegium used it as a base of operations from which they established a city in Oinotria, which is now called Elea …

1.168.1 The Teians' history closely resembles theirs; for when Harpagos captured their wall with his mound, they all embarked in their ships and sailed to Thrace and there they founded the city Abdera, which before them Timesios of Klazomenai founded but had no joy of, but was driven out by the Thracians and is now honoured as a hero by the Teians in Abdera. **1.169.1** These were the only Ionians who abandoned their native lands because they were unable to endure slavery; the other Ionians, except the Milesians, engaged Harpagos in battle, like those who left, and behaved valiantly, each fighting on behalf of his own home; but they were defeated and conquered and all remained in their countries and submitted to the orders given them.

2.14 Diodorus *Library of History* 5.9.1–5: Practical Socialism at Lipara

Lipara is an island off the west coast of Italy and the north coast of Sicily, founded by Knidos in 580 BC. This colony has been of great interest to Marxist historians (and their opponents). The Sikels and the

Sicani are the native inhabitants of Sicily as opposed to the colonists; the public messes, and the fact that they are from Knidos and Rhodes, suggest that the colonists are Dorians, like the Spartans.

5.9.1 After this the Sikels entrusted their leadership to their best men, while the Sicani were at variance concerning the sovereignty (dynasteia) and waged war against each other for a considerable time. But many years afterwards, when the islands were again becoming even more desolate, some men of Knidos and Rhodes, displeased at the harshness shown by the kings of Asia, decided to send out a colony. **2** Accordingly they chose Pentathlos of Knidos as their leader, who traced his family back to Hippotes, a descendant of Herakles, during the fiftieth Olympiad, in which Epitelidas the Spartan won the stadion, and Pentathlos and his companions sailed to the regions of Sicily around Lilybaion and came across the people of Egesta and Selinous fighting it out with each other. **3** They were persuaded to ally themselves with the Selinountians and lost many men in the battle, amongst whom was Pentathlos himself. Accordingly the survivors, since the Selinountians had lost the war, decided to return home again; after choosing as leaders Pentathlos' relatives Gorgos and Thestor and Epithersides, they sailed back across the Tyrrhenian Sea. **4** After sailing to Lipara and meeting with a kindly reception, they were persuaded to settle Lipara together with the inhabitants, approximately five hundred people who were left from Aiolos' colony. Later on, because they were being harassed by Etruscan pirates, they equipped a fleet and divided themselves into two groups, one of which cultivated the islands which they had made common property, and the other opposed the pirates; they also made their possessions common property and lived according to a system of public messes, continuing for some time to live communally. **5** Later on they shared out Lipara, where their city was also, between them, but farmed the other islands in common. Finally they divided all the islands amongst themselves for twenty years and drew lots for them whenever this period expired. After this they defeated the Etruscans in many sea-battles, and from the booty they often dedicated notable tithes at Delphi.

THE BLACK SEA AND PROPONTIS

Greek colonisation of the Black Sea area probably started in the eighth century BC to relieve the mother-cities of surplus population. Numerous successful colonies were established along its shores. By the fifth century the colonies there were purchasing grain from the native inhabitants to send back to Greece (Hdt. 4.17.2; see docs 1.71–75, 13.35).

2.15 Herodotos 4.144.1–2: Chalkedon: A City Founded by the 'Blind'

Byzantium was on the European side of the Hellespont, while Chalkedon was on the Asian side. Chalkedon was founded first, and the ancient view was one of surprise that the site of Chalkedon was founded before that of Byzantium, which was better placed for controlling trade in and out of the Black Sea. It would appear that the colonists at Chalkedon were primarily interested in land, but the hostility of the local peoples could also explain why Byzantium was not settled until seventeen years after Chalkedon. Both cities were founded by Megara in the early seventh century BC.

4.144.1 Megabazos made the following remark and left an undying remembrance of himself amongst the people on the Hellespont; **2** for when he was in Byzantium he learned that the Chalkedonians had settled there seventeen years earlier than the men of Byzantium, and when he learned this he said that the Chalkedonians must have been blind at the time; for with a finer one at hand they would never have chosen to settle on the worse site, if they had not been blind.

2.16 Anaximenes of Lampsakos F 26: Miletos' Impact as Coloniser

Miletos was one of the most powerful cities in Asia Minor, and founded many colonies between the eighth and sixth centuries BC, many as trading emporia, especially around the Black Sea. [*FGH* 72 F26; Strabo *Geography* 14.1.6.]

The city of Miletos is responsible for many achievements, but the greatest is the number of its colonies; for all the Black Sea has been colonised by the Milesians as well as the Propontis and many other places. At any rate, Anaximenes of Lampsakos says that the Milesians colonised the island Ikaros, and Leros, and near the Hellespont Limnai in the Chersonese, and Abydos, Arisba and Paisos in Asia; and Artake and Cyzicus on the island of Kyzikenai; and Skepsis in the Troad's interior.

2.17 Pseudo-Skymnos *Geographical Description* 986–97: Sinope Refounded

Sinope, on the south shore of the Black Sea, was founded in the mid-eighth century BC by the oikistes Habrondas (here called Abron) from Miletos, but he was killed by the Cimmerians from southern Russia, who overran the area from about 700–650 BC. The Greek settlement was re-established by Milesian exiles in 631 BC. Land, minerals and perhaps the fish of the Black Sea provided motives for colonisation. Pseudo-Skymnos was writing at some time between 138 and 75/4 BC, his aim being to describe the whole accessible world, especially the foundation of cities and colonies.

Then Sinope a city named for one of
The Amazons, who dwell nearby,
Which once noble Syrians inhabited,
And after these, they say, all those of the Greeks
Who crossed over in the time of the Amazons, Autolykos
And Phlogios, with Deileon, who were Thessalians,
And then Abron, a Milesian by race;
He is thought to have been killed by Cimmerians;
After the Cimmerians, Koos, and again Kretines,
Who were exiles from the Milesians;
These together settled it, when
The Cimmerian army overran Asia.

2.18 Herodotos 5.94.1–95.2: Mytilenaean and Athenian Conflict over Sigeion

Athens did not send out large numbers of colonists during the colonisation period, but her most important colony was at Sigeion, in the late seventh century, on the Asian shore of the Hellespont. Athens' presence here was contested by Mytilene; in a battle in 607/6 BC the Athenian general Phrynon was killed in single combat with Pittakos, tyrant of Mytilene, one of the seven 'Wise Men' of ancient Greece; for Pittakos, see docs 7.24–30.

5.94.1 This put an end to the matter, and as Hippias was departing Amyntas the Macedonian gave him Anthemous and the Thessalians gave him Iolkos. He took neither of these offers, and went back to Sigeion, which Peisistratos had taken in battle from the Mytilenaeans, and, after conquering it, had set up his own illegitimate son Hegesistratos as tyrant, whom he had by an Argive wife. Hegesistratos kept control of what he had received from Peisistratos, but not without a fight. **2** For from their bases of Achilleion and Sigeion the Mytilenaeans and Athenians kept issuing out to do battle over a long period of time, the Mytilenaeans demanding the site, and the Athenians not recognising their claim and pointing out that the Aeolians had no more right to a share of the Trojan country than they or any of the other Greeks who assisted Menelaos in avenging the abduction of Helen. **5.95.1** While they were waging war all sorts of things occurred in the battles, including an incident in which the poet Alcaeus, when the engagement took place and the Athenians were victorious, escaped by running away, and the Athenians kept his arms and hung them up in the Athenaion at Sigeion. **2** Alcaeus put this in a poem which he sent to Melanippos, a friend of his at Mytilene, recounting his accident. Periander (tyrant of Corinth), son of Kypselos, reconciled the Mytilenaeans and Athenians; they referred the matter to him as arbitrator; and he settled it thus, that each should keep what they possessed. Sigeion thus came under Athenian control.

2.19 Alcaeus 428: The Poet Alcaeus Runs Away

This incident took place when Pittakos of Mytilene was challenging Athenian control of Sigeion (doc. 2.18). Throwing away one's shield was a sign of cowardice: docs 1.42, 6.18.

Alcaeus is safe but the shield that protected him
The Athenians hung up in the temple of the grey-eyed goddess Athena.

2.20 Xenophon *Anabasis* 5.6.15–19: A Potential Athenian Colony in Asia Minor, 400 BC

Xenophon considered establishing a colony of the shore of the Black Sea with the Ten Thousand mercenaries who had tried to put Cyrus on the Persian throne; on Cyrus' death Xenophon took the lead and the force escaped northward, finally reaching the Black Sea. As they were all soldiers, the colony could easily have defended its position. Xenophon was making a sacrifice to examine the entrails, to see whether the gods would give support to his proposed colony.

5.6.15 At this point Xenophon saw the large number of Greek hoplites, and the crowd of peltasts, archers, slingers and cavalry, all highly efficient through long practice, there at the Black Sea where such a large force could not have been collected without great expense, and he thought that it would be a good idea to obtain territory and power for Greece by founding a city. **16** He considered that it would reach a great size as he calculated their numbers and those of the peoples dwelling around the Black Sea. He was making a sacrifice to gain guidance about this plan, before speaking of it to any of the soldiers, and had summoned Silanos the Ambraciote, who had been Cyrus' diviner. **17** Silanos was afraid that the plan would take effect and that the army would remain there, and so told the troops that Xenophon wanted the army to settle there and found a city to achieve fame and power for himself. **18** Silanos himself wanted to reach Greece as quickly as possible, for he had kept safe and sound the 3,000 darics he had received from Cyrus when he told the truth during a sacrifice about what was going to happen in the next ten days.

19 When the soldiers heard this report, some of the soldiers thought settling there a good idea, but the majority thought otherwise. And Timasion the Dardanian and Thorax the Boeotian said to some merchants who were there from Herakleia and Sinope that if they did not provide pay for the army so they could have provisions for the voyage, there would be danger that their great force would remain on the Black Sea.

2.21 *Inscriptiones Graecae* II^2 1629: An Athenian Colony in the Adriatic, 325/4 BC

Eleven fragments, some 1,162 lines, survive of this inscription concerning the establishment of an Athenian colony in the Adriatic area. The site of this colony is not identified. The first 164 lines of the inscription give the details of nine ships participating in the enterprise; Miltiades also had some quadriremes (line 167); he might have been considered an auspicious founder as he had the same name as the earlier Miltiades (doc. 9.27). Athens, according to the inscription, was attempting to secure its own grain supply and to establish an emporion. The apodektai are financial officials; for trierarchies, see docs 1.30–31. [Tod 2.200.]

Captured triakonter … the work of Eudikos. The trierarch was Demokles son of Krates of Melite, and his fellow trierarch was Euthykrates son of Charias of Kydathenaion; he has wooden equipment, a complete set; of hanging gear, girding ropes for a trireme in place of those that are not fit for service, they took two in accordance with the decree of the people proposed by Hagnonides from Pergase. This triakonter and the equipment were received by Miltiades of Lakiadai, the oikistes, in accordance with the decree of the people proposed by Kephisophon of Cholargos.

The decree: in accordance with which Miltiades took over the triremes and quadriremes and triakonters and equipment. Kephisophon son of Lysiphon of Cholargos proposed the motion: Good Fortune for the people of Athens; so that as soon as possible the resolution of the people may be accomplished concerning the Adriatic colony, let it be voted by the people that the shipyard supervisors should hand over to the trierarchs the ships and equipment in accordance with the resolution of the people, and the trierarchs who have been appointed shall bring the ships alongside the jetty in Mounichion before the tenth of the month and have them prepared for the voyage; the first to bring his ship alongside is to be crowned by the people with a golden crown worth 500 drachmas, the second with a crown worth 300 drachmas, and the third with a crown worth 200. And it is to be proclaimed by the herald of the Boule at the Thargelia about the crowns and the Apodektai shall allocate the money for the crowns so that the trierarchs' wish to honour the people shall be made clear. And in order that the pleas (of those contesting the liturgy) can be brought forward, the thesmothetai shall provide jurors for the lawcourts, to the number of two hundred and one, for the use of the general elected to be in charge of the symmories during Mounichion on the second and the fifth days of the month; the pay is to be given to the jurors by the treasurers of the goddess according to law. So that there shall be for the people for all time its own trading-station and grain supply, once its own anchorage has been prepared, there is to be a guard against the Etruscans, and Miltiades the oikistes and the colonists **225** may be able to use their own fleet, and those of the Greeks and barbarians who sail the sea may also be able to sail into **230** the anchorage of the Athenians in order to keep their ships and other goods in safety.

SPARTAN COLONISATION

2.22 Herodotos 5.42.2–45.1: Dorieus Fails to Colonise Africa and Sicily

Dorieus' colonisation venture, although it had the Spartan state's consent, was more a private than a public attempt. His failure in Africa underlines the uniqueness of Cyrene and its settlements as the only Greek centre on the African coast; the Phoenicians were too dominant along the Gulf of Syrtis to the west of Cyrene. Taras was Sparta's only official foundation in the 'colonisation period' (doc. 2.23). Sparta traditionally founded Thera, but this was in the mythical mists of time (see doc. 2.30). The Spartans conquered Messenia as a means of extending their territory.

5.42.2 When Anaxandridas died and the Spartans according to custom made Kleomenes, the eldest, king, Dorieus took this badly and not consenting to being ruled by Kleomenes asked the Spartiates for a body of men and took them off to found a colony, though he neither consulted the oracle at Delphi about which country he should go to for his settlement, nor followed any of the customary usages. Feeling very angry about the whole affair he went off with his ships to Libya; men from Thera guided him there. **3** Arriving there, he settled at Kinyps, a lovely spot belonging to the Libyans beside a river. In the third year he was driven out from there by the Makai, Libyans and Carthaginians and returned to the Peloponnese. **5.43.1** There Antichares, a man from Eleon, advised him in accordance with Laios' oracles to found Herakleia in Sicily, saying that all the country of Eryx (in western Sicily) belonged to the Herakleidai as Herakles himself had conquered it. After hearing this Dorieus went to Delphi to consult the oracle, to ask whether he would obtain the land for which he was setting out; the Pythia responded that he would obtain it. Dorieus took the expedition which he had led to Libya and travelled along the Italian coast. **5.44.1** At this time, according to the people of Sybaris, they and their king Telys were preparing to make war on Croton, and the Crotoniates in great fear begged Dorieus to help them, and obtained their request; Dorieus joined forces with them against Sybaris and helped them to capture it … **5.45.1** Each of them points out these proofs, the Sybarites a precinct and temple beside the dry river Krathis which they say Dorieus dedicated to Athena Krathias after helping to take the city, and the death of Dorieus himself they consider as the greatest proof, because he was killed for transgressing the instructions of the oracle; for if he had not gone beyond these instructions, and done what he had been sent to do, he would have taken the country of Eryx and held it, and neither he nor his army would have been destroyed.

2.23 Strabo *Geography* 6.3.2–3: The Spartan Partheniai Found Taras in Italy

Taras (Tarentum), in south-east Italy, was founded by Spartans who were not full citizens. The story of the partheniai may contain some semi-mythical elements, but it is clear that there were political differences of some sort between the Spartans and the partheniai, who were clearly of Spartan background but without full citizen rights; the traditional date of the foundation was 706 BC. From the fourth century Taras became the most prominent of the Greek cities in southern Italy. [Antiochos *FGH* 555 F13; Ephoros *FGH* 70 F216.]

6.3.2 When speaking about the foundation of Taras, Antiochos says that when the Messenian War took place those Spartans who did not take part in the campaign were adjudged slaves and named helots, and all children born during the campaign they called partheniai and decided that they should not have citizen rights; the partheniai did not tolerate this (for there were many of them) and plotted against the citizens … (*The plot is betrayed by Phalanthos.*) Telling the conspirators not to worry, the Spartans gave them into custody and sent Phalanthos to the god to ask about a colony. The response was:

> 'I have given you Satyrion, and the rich land of Taras
> To dwell in and become a bane to the Iapygians.'

So the partheniai went with Phalanthos, and both the barbarians and the Cretans who previously occupied the site welcomed them … **3** But Ephoros' account of its foundation is as follows: the Spartans were at war with the Messenians because they had killed their king Teleklos when he went to Messene to sacrifice, and they had sworn not to return home before they had either captured Messene or all been killed … (*In the tenth year, the Spartans sent home their youngest men to cohabit with the maidens; the children thus born were called partheniai, who on being denied citizen rights after the end of the war leagued with the helots, but were betrayed.*) The conspirators on learning that the deed had been disclosed held back, and the Spartans persuaded them through their fathers to leave and found a colony; and if they got possession of a satisfactory site they were to stay there, and, if not, they were to be assigned on their return the fifth part of Messenia. They were sent out, finding on their arrival the Achaeans waging war with the barbarians, and, after sharing their dangers, founded Taras.

2.24 Thucydides 3.92.1–93.2: Herakleia: A Fifth-Century Spartan Colony

Following the great age of colonisation there were colonisation enterprises in the fifth century, notably by Athens and even Sparta. Athens had not participated to a great extent in the colonisation movement, except for Sigeion and the Chersonese. In 426 BC the Spartans established Herakleia in Trachis (Herakleia Trachinia), consulting Delphi after making the decision; none of the three oikistai involved seem to have remained long in the colony.

3.92.1 It was at about this time that the Spartans established their colony Herakleia in Trachis for the following reason. **2** The Malians are comprised of three groups, the Paralians, Irieans and Trachinians; and of these the Trachinians had suffered badly in a war at the hands of their neighbours the Oitaians, and at first were going to ally themselves with the Athenians. Fearing, however, that they might not be reliable, they sent to Sparta, after choosing Teisamenos as their envoy. **3** The people of Doris, the Spartans' mother-city, joined in the embassy with the same request; for they too were suffering at the hands of the Oitaians. **4** When the Spartans heard this, they resolved to send out a colony, wishing to assist both the Trachinians and the Dorians. And at the same time the city appeared to them to be well situated for the war against the Athenians, for a fleet could be prepared there against Euboea, with the result that the crossing would be short, and would also be useful for the route to Thrace. So, all things considered, they were eager to found the place. **5** First of all, therefore, they consulted the god at Delphi, and at his bidding they sent out the colonists from both Sparta and their neighbours, and invited any of the other Greeks who wished to join them, except the Ionians and Achaeans and some other races.

Three Spartans led them as their oikistai, Leon, Alkidas and Damagon. **6** And they established and fortified the city from scratch, which is now called Herakleia and is approximately 400 stades from Thermopylai and twenty from the sea. They also started constructing dockyards and secured the side facing Thermopylai by building across the pass itself, so they might be well protected. **3.93.1** The Athenians, while this city was being settled, were at first afraid and thought that it was particularly aimed at Euboea, because it is only a short crossing to Kenaion in Euboea. However, things turned out quite contrary to their expectation; for no harm came of it. **2** The reason was that the Thessalians, who were dominant in those regions and whose land was being threatened by the settlement, were afraid that they would have very powerful neighbours and so kept causing destruction and continually waging war on the new settlers until they had worn down what had at first been a very large population — for everyone had gone with confidence, thinking that the city would be safe because it was being founded by Spartans. Not least, however, it was the magistrates sent out by the Spartans themselves whose arrival ruined matters and aided the decline in population, by frightening away the majority through their harsh and often unjust government, so that it was all the easier for their neighbours to prevail over them.

THE COLONISATION OF THASOS BY PAROS

The island of Thasos off the Thracian coast was rich in gold, which attracted the Phoenicians, as it did the Greeks of the island of Paros in the seventh century, probably about 680 BC, while valleys on the island were suitable for agriculture. This provided a double motive for its colonisation by the Greeks.

2.25 Stephen of Byzantium, *Lexikon* Thasos : The Foundation of Thasos

Archilochos' father had presumably consulted Delphi on the advisability of Paros founding a colony on Thasos and received the following foundation oracle.

That Thasos is very high is clear from the oracle that was given to Archilochos' father:

> 'Report to the Parians, Telesikles, that I bid you
> Found a far-seen city on a lofty island.'

2.26 Archilochos F5: Archilochos Throws Away His Shield

Archilochos was involved in fighting against the Saians, a group of Thracians on the mainland opposite Thasos. Archilochos' attitude here is contradicted by his supposed epitaph (Archilochos 1) in which he boasts of his achievements first as a warrior and only secondly as a poet: 'I am a servant of Lord Enyalios, And yet skilled in the lovely gift of the Muses'; for the war god Enyalios, see docs 9.40, 3.51. [Plutarch *Moralia* 239b.]

When Archilochos the poet went to Sparta, they immediately drove him out because they discovered that he had written in a poem that it was better to throw away your weapons than be killed:

> 'One of the Saians rejoices in my shield, which, beside a bush,

I unwillingly abandoned, though it was not at fault;
At least I saved myself. Why should I care about that shield?
Hang it! I'll get another one just as good.'

2.27 Archilochos FF20–21, 102: Archilochos' Opinion of Thasos

Archilochos found little to admire on Thasos; compare Archilochos 22, where he compares Thasos to Siris in southern Italy, to Thasos' disadvantage: 'for there is no spot as beautiful or desirable or lovely as the banks of the Siris.' In F20 the troubles of the Magnesians, attacked by the Cimmerians (cf. doc. 2.17), may have been bad but Archilochos thinks those of Thasos worse. Elsewhere (93a) he complains of the misfortunes which the quest for gold has caused.

20 'I lament the misfortunes of the people of Thasos, not those of the Magnesians.'

21 But we (see only one aspect of exile), like Archilochos, who disregards the fruitful lands and vineyards of Thasos and blames it for being rugged and mountainous, and who says:

'But it stands like an ass's backbone,
Crowned with wild forest.'

102 'The misery of all the Greeks has gathered on Thasos!'

THE GREEKS AT CYRENE

Thera (Santorini), a small volcanic island, sent out a small number of men to Libya in 637 BC who eventually founded Cyrene on the African coast in 631. Various other settlements sprang up on the nearby coast to create a series of Greek towns in the area known as Cyrenaica. Cyrene, Naukratis and the mercenary settlements in Egypt were the only Greek colonies in Africa. Later, as Cyrene expanded, there were conflicts with the Libyans.

2.28 Meiggs & Lewis 5: The Foundation Decree of Cyrene Is Reaffirmed

This inscription of the fourth century BC concerns the rights of a new group of colonists who have arrived from Thera and embodies what purports to be the original foundation decree for the colony. Scholars debate whether this decree is genuinely seventh century, or whether it is a forgery of the fourth century. The decree gave the colonists five years to establish the colony, and then they could return; in Herodotos, the colonists returning home prematurely had things thrown at them (4.156.3: doc. 2.29). [*SEG* 9.3.]

God. Good Fortune. Damis son of Bathykles proposed the motion: concerning the matters raised by the Therans (through their spokesman) Kleudamas son of Euthykles, so that the city may prosper and the people of Cyrene be fortunate, we grant the Therans citizenship according to ancestral custom, which our forefathers instituted, both those who founded Cyrene from Thera and those who stayed in Thera, just as Apollo gave to Battos and to the Therans who founded Cyrene good fortune if they abided by the oaths which our forefathers concluded with them when they sent out the colony in accordance with the injunction of Apollo the Founder (Archagetas).

With good fortune. It has been resolved by the people that the Therans should continue to have equal citizenship in Cyrene according to the same conditions; and that all Therans who dwell in Cyrene should take the same oath as the others once swore and shall be assigned to a tribe and phratry and nine hetaireiai. This decree shall be inscribed on a white stele of marble and the stele be placed in the ancestral temple of Pythian Apollo, and the sworn agreement shall also be inscribed on the stele, which the colonists made when they sailed to Libya with Battos from Thera to Cyrene. As to the expenditure which is necessary for the stone or inscription, let the superintendents of the accounts provide it from Apollo's revenues.

The sworn agreement of the settlers. It has been resolved by the assembly; since Apollo spontaneously told Battos and the Therans to colonise Cyrene, it has been decided by the Therans to send Battos to Libya as Founder (Archagetas) and as king, and for the Therans to sail as his companions; they are to sail on equal and similar terms according to family, and one son is to be enlisted ... the adults and of the other Therans the free-born ... are to sail. And if the colonists establish the settlement, any of their relatives who sail afterwards to Libya are to share in citizenship and magistracies and be allotted portions of the unowned land. But if they do not establish the settlement and the Therans are unable to assist it, and they are oppressed by hardship for five years, they shall depart from that land without fear to Thera to their own property and be citizens. Whoever refuses to go when the city sends him shall be liable to the death penalty and his property shall be confiscated. And the man who harbours or hides him, whether a father his son or a brother his brother is to suffer the same as he who refuses to sail. On these conditions oaths were sworn by those who were to remain there and those who were to sail to found the settlement and they cursed those who should transgress it and not abide by it, whether those settling in Libya or who stayed home. They made wax figures and burned them, calling down this curse, after everyone had gathered together, men and women, boys and girls: 'he who does not abide by these oaths but transgresses them shall melt away and dissolve just like the figures, both himself and his descendants and his property, but those who abide by these oaths, both those who sail to Libya and those who stay in Thera, shall have abundant good things, both themselves and their descendants.'

2.29 Herodotos 4.150.2–159.4: Herodotos' Account of the Foundation of Cyrene

The Therans founded the colony at Cyrene with two pentekonters of men. A pentekonter has fifty rowers, and other crew, so the number of colonists sent out was small, but enough to reduce the number of Therans to a level which the drought-stricken island could support. Cyrene flourished as the exporter of the plant silphion, the sap of which was highly regarded as a medicament throughout Greece, and as an exporter of wool.

4.150.2 Grinnos, son of Aisanias, who was a descendant of Theras and king of the island of Thera, arrived at Delphi with a hundred victims for sacrifice (a hecatomb) from his city; other citizens were with him including Battos, son of Polymnestos, one of the Euphemidai of the race of the Minyans. **3** And while Grinnos the king of the Therans was consulting the oracle about other matters, the Pythia gave the response that he should found a city in Libya. In reply he said, 'I, Lord, am already too old and inactive to set out; you should bid one of these younger men to do this.' As he spoke he pointed at Battos. **4** This is all that happened at that point, and they then went away and forgot about the oracle, neither knowing where on earth Libya was, nor daring to send out a colony to an uncertain destination. **4.151.1** For the next seven years there was no rain on Thera, during which all the trees on the island died of drought except one. And, when the Therans consulted the oracle, the Pythia proposed sending the colony to Libya. (**4.151.2–152.5:** *a purple-fisherman called Korobios from Crete guided them to the island of Platea, and the Therans returned home with this news.*) **4.153.1** When the Therans who had left Korobios on the island arrived at Thera, they reported that they had established a settlement on an island off the coast of Libya. The Therans decided to send a party with brother drawing lots with brother and including men from all the seven villages, with Battos as their leader and king. And thus they sent two pentekonters to Platea … **4.155.1** This is what the people of Thera and Cyrene say, but my opinion is different: **2** it is that he took the name of Battos when he reached Libya, choosing the name both as a consequence of the oracle's response at Delphi and because of the honour he had there; for to the Libyans 'battos' means 'king', and because of this I think that the Pythia when she was prophesying spoke to him in Libyan, knowing that he would be a king in Libya. **3** For when he reached manhood, he went to Delphi to ask about his speech; and when he made his inquiry the Pythia spoke to him thus:

> '*Battos*, you have come regarding your speech; but Lord Phoibos Apollo
> Sends you to found a city in Libya, feeder of sheep,'

as if she had said in Greek, '*King*, you have come regarding your speech.' **4** And he replied thus: 'Lord, I came to you to inquire about my speech, but you proclaim to me other things which are impossible, bidding me to found a colony in Libya — with what means, with what men?' But as she started to prophesy to him in the same way as before, Battos left in the middle of what she was saying and went to Thera. **4.156.1** But afterwards things continued to go badly for both him and the other Therans. Not knowing what was wrong the Therans sent to Delphi concerning their current troubles. **2** And the Pythia told them that if they joined with Battos in founding Cyrene in Libya they would fare better. After this the Therans sent off Battos with two pentekonters. When these had sailed to Libya, they could not decide what to do next, so they returned to Thera; **3** but the Therans threw things at them as they were putting ashore and did not allow them to land, but told them to sail back again. Thus compelled, they sailed back again and settled on an island lying off the coast of Libya, the name of which, as mentioned previously, was Platea. The island is said to be the same size as the city of Cyrene is now. **4.157.1** They lived there for two years, but nothing went well for them, so they left one of their number behind and all sailed to Delphi, and arriving at the oracle they inquired of it, saying that they had settled in Libya, and though they were living there they were no better off. **2** In reply the Pythia proclaimed this:

> 'If you know Libya, feeder of sheep, better than I,
> I who have been there, though you have not, I much admire your wisdom.'

When they heard this, Battos and his men sailed back again; for the god was not going to let them off from the colony before they had reached Libya. **3** When they arrived at the island and picked up the man they had left there, they settled a site in Libya itself opposite the island called Aziris, which is shut in on both sides by beautiful valleys with a river running past on one side. **4.158.1** They inhabited this spot for six years; but in the seventh year the Libyans offered to lead them to a better site and persuaded them to leave. **2** And the Libyans took them from there and removed them towards the west, and, so that the Greeks did not see the best of the sites as they passed through, they calculated the time of day so they passed by it during the night. The name of this site is Irasa. **3** And they took the Greeks to a spring said to be sacred to Apollo and said: 'Men of Greece, here is a fitting place for you to settle; for here the sky has holes in it.' **4.159.1** During the lifetime of Battos the founder, who ruled for forty years, and that of his son Arkesilas, who ruled for sixteen, the Cyrenaeans who lived there were the same number as had originally been sent to the colony; **2** but under the third king, called Battos the Fortunate, the Pythia in a proclamation encouraged all Greeks to sail to settle Libya with the Cyrenaeans; for the Cyrenaeans were inviting others to an apportionment of the land. **3** The words of the oracle were:

'Whoever comes to lovely Libya after
The land has been apportioned, I say will later regret it.'

4 A large crowd of people collected at Cyrene and the neighbouring Libyans, who were being deprived of a large amount of land, and their king, whose name was Adikran, because of their loss of land and insulting treatment from the Cyrenaeans, sent to Egypt and handed themselves over to the protection of Apries, the king of Egypt.

2.30 Pindar *Pythian Ode* 5: Pindar Honours Battos' Descendant Arkesilas IV

Pindar wrote three odes for victors who came from Cyrene in the sporting events at the Pythian festival celebrated at Delphi: one, *Pythian* 9, for Telesikrates, winner of the foot-race in full armour in 474 BC, and two, *Pythian* 4 and 5, for Arkesilas IV who won the four-horse chariot race in 462. Arkesilas' race was noted for the fact that forty of the chariots crashed. This ode below was sung at Cyrene on the return of the horses and charioteer, Arkesilas' brother-in-law Karrhotos (lines 23–53); lines 72–76 refer to the foundation of Thera, Cyrene's mother-city, by the Spartans: the Karneia, an important Spartan festival, was inherited by Thera and thence by Cyrene; prior to the arrival of the Therans, the local heroes of Cyrene were supposedly Trojans (lines 82–84). For tyrants and the pan-Hellenic games, see docs 7.57–59.

Yet after one thing and another, Battos' ancient prosperity still attends us,
A tower of the city and brightest light
To strangers. From him even loud-roaring
Lions fled in fear,
When he let loose on them his speech from overseas;
And Apollo Archagetas gave
The wild beasts to dread fear,
So his oracles for Cyrene's lord should not be unfulfilled …
And he (Apollo) celebrates in song my
Well-loved glory that comes from Sparta;
From there sprang
The Aigeidai who came to Thera,
My forefathers, not without the gods, but some destiny led them;
The feast abounding in sacrifices
We received from there,
Karneian Apollo, and

In your banquet we honour
The well-built city of Cyrene,
Which is held by bronze-armoured strangers,
Trojans, the sons of Antenor. For they came with Helen,
When they saw their fatherland in smoke
In war. With kindness that chariot-driving nation
Was welcomed with sacrifices by men who came with gifts,
Whom Aristoteles (Battos) led, in swift ships
Opening a deep path in the sea.
He built greater groves for the gods,
Made a straight-cut level path for Apollo's
Processions, which shield men from ill,
Sounding with the tramp of horses,
A paved road, where now apart at the far end of the agora
he lies in death.
He was blessed amongst men
While he lived, and afterwards a hero worshipped by the people.
And apart, before the palace, lie others who have found death,
Holy kings …

THE GREEKS IN EGYPT: TRADERS AND MERCENARIES

The Greeks had had trading connections with Egypt in the Mycenaean period, and these were renewed in archaic times. The Greeks sold wine to Egypt, and bought grain (Bacchylides *Fragment* 20b, 14–16: 'and wheat-bearing ships across the gleaming sea bring immense wealth from Egypt'), as well as importing Egyptian art, which had a profound influence on the development of Greek art. The mercenaries employed by the kings, and many of the traders at Naukratis, settled permanently in Egypt.

2.31 Herodotos 2.152.3–154.5, 178.1–181.2: Greek Settlers in Egypt

The Egyptian king Psammetichos I (664–610 BC), of Libyan origin, employed Carian and Ionian Greeks to establish him in power. These mercenaries settled down permanently in Egypt, being colonists of a specialised type, and Greek mercenaries may also have been employed by Necho II (610–594) in his Syrian campaign of 608 BC.

2.152.3 Psammetichos sent to the city Buto, where the Egyptians' most truthful oracle is, and received the response that revenge would come in the form of bronze men appearing from the sea. **4** Psammetichos was totally disinclined to believe that bronze men would come to his assistance; but not long afterwards necessity overtook men from Ionia and Caria who had sailed out in search of plunder and they were carried off course to Egypt; they disembarked and armed themselves in bronze and one of the Egyptians, who had not seen men armed in bronze before, arrived at the marshes and reported to Psammetichos that bronze men had come from the sea and were plundering the plain. **5** On learning that the oracle had been fulfilled, he made friends with the Ionians and Carians, promised them great rewards and persuaded them to be on his side; having persuaded them, with the help of his own Egyptian supporters and his mercenaries, he deposed the kings …

2.154.1 To the Ionians and Carians who assisted him Psammetichos gave sites to dwell in opposite each other, with the Nile in the middle, which were called the Camps. He gave them these sites as well as all the other things he had promised them. **2** Moreover he entrusted to them Egyptian boys to be taught the Greek language, and it is from these who were trained in the language that the current interpreters in Egypt are descended. **3** Both the Ionians and the Carians inhabited these sites for a long time; these sites are in the direction of the sea a little below the city of Boubastis on what is called the Pelousian mouth of the Nile. Some time afterwards King Amasis removed them from there and established them in Memphis as protection for himself against the Egyptians. **4** Once these had settled in Egypt we Greeks from our dealings with them have known with certainty all that has happened in Egypt from the time of King Psammetichos onwards; they were the first non-native speakers to be settled in Egypt. **5** In the places from which they were expelled the hauling-engines of their ships and the ruins of their houses still existed up till my time …

2.178.1 Amasis was well disposed towards the Greeks and, as well as the other favours he granted to some of them, he moreover gave to those who came to Egypt Naukratis as a city to settle in, while to those who sailed there but did not choose to live there he gave sites where they could set up altars and precincts to their gods. **2** The greatest of these precincts, which is also the best known and most frequented, is called the Hellenion, and these are the cities which jointly dedicated it: of the Ionians Chios, Teos, Phokaia and Klazomenai, and of the Dorians Rhodes, Knidos, Halikarnassos and Phaselis, and of the Aeolians only the Mytilenaeans. **3** The precinct belongs to these, and these cities provide the men in charge of the trading-station (emporion); as many other cities as lay claim to a share of it do so without justification. The Aeginetans independently dedicated a precinct to Zeus on their own, and the Samians another one to Hera and the Milesians one to Apollo. **2.179.1** In former times Naukratis was the only trading-station and there was no other in Egypt. And if anyone arrived at any of the other mouths of the Nile, he had to swear that he had not come there deliberately, and after denying this on oath sail ship and all to the Canopic mouth; or if it was impossible to sail against opposing winds he had to take his cargo round the Delta in flat-bottomed boats, until he reached Naukratis. This was the unique position held by Naukratis …

2.180.1 And when the Amphictyons farmed out the building of the temple, which is now at Delphi, for three hundred talents (for the one previously there had burned down accidentally), the Delphians had to provide a quarter. **2** And when the Delphians travelled round the cities collecting presents, in their travels they received not the least from Egypt. For Amasis gave them a thousand talents of alum, and the Greeks living in Egypt twenty minas. **2.181.1** Amasis concluded a treaty of friendship and alliance with the people of Cyrene. And he thought it right to take a wife from there, either because he desired to have a Greek wife or for other reasons to do with his friendship with the Cyrenaeans. **2** So he married, some say, the daughter of Battos son of Arkesilas, and others the daughter of Kritoboulos, a distinguished citizen, her name being Ladike.

2.32 Meiggs & Lewis 7: Greek Mercenaries as Sightseers in Nubia

Herodotos 2.161.1 mentions the expedition of Psammetichos II (594–589 BC) to Ethiopia in 591 BC (calling him Psammis). His Greek (and Carian) mercenaries carved inscriptions on the legs of the colossi of Ramesses II at Abu Simbel in Nubia, which indicate the mercenaries' origins. In line 5, Peleqos son of Eudamos, is literally, 'axe, son of nobody', that is, the implement with which the inscription was written: this must be one of the earliest examples of Greek humour in an inscription.

When King Psammetichos came to Elephantine,
This was written by those who, with Psammetichos son of Theokles,
Sailed and came above Kerkis, as far as the river permitted;
Potasimto commanded the non-native speakers, and Amasis the Egyptians;
Archon son of Amoibichos wrote us and Axe son of Nobody.
Helesibios the Teian.
Telephos the Ialysan wrote me.
Python son of Amoibichos.
... and Krithis wrote me.
Pabis the Kolophonian with Psammates.
Anaxanor ... the Ialysan when King Psammetichos ... marched his army the first time.

GREEKS AND INDIGENOUS POPULATIONS

There was often conflict between the Greeks and the local populations, who were usually displaced by the Greek colonists. There is also evidence, however, for cross-cultural influence and commercial interchanges between Greeks and the indigenous peoples. Clearly along the shores of the Black Sea in the Scythian area there was even intermarriage and so cultural interaction amongst Greeks and Scythians.

2.33 Herodotos 4.16.1–17.1: Graeco-Scythians in the Black Sea Region

Herodotos here writes of 'Greek Scythians', who lived west of the Borysthenes river on the Black Sea. Olbia, the best-known colony in the region, was of Milesian origin, and situated on the Borysthenes. The Kallippidai might have been dispossessed Greeks who had 'gone native' or an originally Scythian tribe which became partially hellenised.

4.16.1 Concerning this area which is now under discussion, no one knows accurately what is beyond it; for I have not been able to learn from anyone who says that he knows it at first hand ... **2** But as much as I was able precisely to learn by hearsay at a distance will all be recounted. **4.17.1** From the trading-centre at the mouth of the Borysthenes (for this is the midmost point of the whole Scythian coastline), from here the first inhabitants are the Kallippidai who are Scythian Greeks, and beyond them is another race called the Alizones. Both these and the Kallippidai have a way of life like that of the Scythians in other respects, but they also sow and eat grain, and onions, garlic, lentils and millet.

2.34 Herodotos 4.108.1–109.1: Greek Settlers 'Go Native' in Scythia

The Gelonoi were originally Greeks, but had been driven out of the emporia, presumably by other Greeks who came along later, and settled amongst the Boudinoi, a group of Scythians. The word *phtheir* (louse) can have a secondary meaning of 'pine nut', and Herodotos has possibly misunderstood his informant.

4.108.1 The Boudinoi, a populous and powerful nation, all have the very marked characteristics of grey eyes and red hair. In their territory there is a city built of wood, and the name of this city is Gelonos; each side of its wall has a length of thirty stades, being high and made of wood throughout, and their houses and temples are also made of wood. **2** There are temples of Greek gods there decorated in the Greek manner with statues, altars and shrines all of wood, and they celebrate a festival in honour of Dionysos with Bacchic rites every two years. For the Gelonoi were originally Greeks, who were expelled from the trading-stations and settled among the Boudinoi; and in language they speak half-Scythian and half-Greek. **4.109.1** The Boudinoi do not have the same language as the Gelonoi, nor is their way of life the same; for the Boudinoi are natives and nomads and have the unusual practice of eating lice, and the Gelonoi work the land and eat grain and keep gardens, and resemble them in neither appearance nor colouring.

2.35 Strabo *Geography* 5.4.7: Naples: A Mixed Greek and Campanian Population

The city of Naples or Neapolis (which is the Greek for 'New City') in southern Italy, founded before 650 BC, long retained its Greek character. The Emperor Augustus himself attended the contests there, while Nero performed there and addressed the crowd in Greek. Note the difficulties which the colony experienced with its indigenous neighbours, here solved by a compromise.

5.4.7 After Dikaiarchia there is Neapolis of the Cumaeans; later the Chalkidians settled a colony there with some of the Pithekoussaians and Athenians, with the result that it was called Neapolis for this reason. A monument of one of the sirens, Parthenope, is pointed out there, and an athletic contest is celebrated in accordance with an oracle. But later on, after some dissension, they accepted some of the Campanians as fellow settlers and were forced to treat their worst enemies as their closest friends, since their closest friends were now alienated. The names of their chief magistrates (demarchs) reveal this, the first being Greek, and the later ones Campanian mixed with Greek. Many traces of the Greek way of life are preserved there, gymnasia, and courts for wrestling (ephebeia), and phratries and Greek names, although the people are Romans. And at the present time a sacred contest is celebrated by them every four years both in music and athletics lasting for several days, which is equal to the most famous of those held in Greece.

2.36 Strabo *Geography* 3.4.8: Emporion in Spain

Emporion literally means 'trading-centre', and was situated on the Spanish coast and founded between 600 and 575 BC, south-west of its mother-city Massalia (modern Marseilles), itself a Phokaian colony, founded c. 600; the Massalians were well known for their treasury at Delphi (dated to 525). The city had good relations with the Celts of the interior and its oikistes Euxenos married a local princess.

3.4.8 Formerly the Emporitans used to live on a small offshore island, now called Old City, but now they live on the mainland. They have a double city, for it has been divided into two by a wall, since in earlier times it had as neighbours some Indiketans, who, although having their own government, wanted to have a wall shared with the Greeks encircling them for the sake of security; so the enclosed area was in two parts, divided by a wall in the middle.

But in time they united in the same constitution which combined barbarian and Greek usages, as has happened in many other cases.

2.37 Plato *Phaedo* 109a–b: Socrates' View of the Greek World

Phasis was the most easterly of the Greek colonies, situated at the extreme eastern end of the Black Sea; the Pillars of Herakles are the Straits of Gibraltar.

'And then,' said Socrates, 'I believe that the earth is extremely large, and that we who live between the pillars of Herakles and Phasis inhabit some small part of it around the sea, just like ants or frogs around a pond.'

3

RELIGION IN THE GREEK WORLD

'Let us begin our song with the Helikonian Muses' (doc. 3.1). The Muses dwelt on Mount Helikon and the great poets believed that their poetry was inspired by these divine beings. On the basis of this inspiration, Homer and Hesiod recorded numerous stories about the gods, and their works reflect many of the beliefs about the immortals held by the Greeks (cf. doc. 3.2). Hesiod described the origin of the gods, and especially the birth of Zeus, greatest of the gods the Greeks worshipped (doc. 3.2). He and his brothers and sisters were the Olympian gods, dwelling on Mount Olympus in northern Greece. They were corporeal beings, of flesh and blood, and anthropomorphic in nature, fashioned like human beings. They enjoyed eating and drinking and all the pleasures of life. Being human in form, they could be imagined and depicted, and the gold and ivory statue of Zeus at Olympia was one of the Seven Wonders of the Ancient World (doc. 3.3).

Not all agreed with this human-like conception of the gods: Xenophanes commented that if oxen, horses and lions had hands, then they would depict their gods as oxen, horses and lions (doc. 3.5). In addition to their human shape, the gods had human traits: theirs was not a life of untroubled ease and happiness, and they had many negative characteristics. In the *Iliad* the gods are jealous, capricious, cruel, selfish, devious, petty, vindictive and obstinate, behaving in fact exactly as human beings do and have always done. The traditional view of the gods in Homer was not without its sceptics and a number of the Presocratic philosophers as part of their questioning of conventional beliefs criticised the traditional mythology of the Olympian religion and its ceremonies and rites of worship (see docs 3.4–6; cf. 3.73–80). But these sceptics only serve to confirm the rule: most Greeks believed in the gods about which Homer and Hesiod wrote, and traditional Olympian religion remained the normal form of belief in the archaic and classical periods.

The gods were worshipped through sacrifice, which often took place at a festival, and prayer. Homer describes a sacrifice and all its component parts; in this case the goddess Athena came to receive the sacrifice (doc. 3.9). The gods would always receive their share of an animal killed for consumption: Athena received the thigh bones and fat (docs 3.10–11, 3.18). Festivals were held all year round, and to make sure the gods were not forgotten calendars of when the sacrifices were to be made were inscribed, recording when sacrifices were to occur and what the victim was to be, as well as the share the priests and others could expect for performing their religious duties (doc. 13.12).

Traditional Greek religion largely lacked written guidelines, and most Greek religious practices were handed down from generation to generation. Without a set of holy books, the Greeks sought to learn the will of the gods through the use of oracles, believing that they could consult the gods directly. There were several oracular centres throughout Greece, the most famous being at Delphi, where a priestess, the Pythia, sat on a tripod in the temple of Apollo, answering questions which were put to her by inquirers. She was the medium of Apollo, god of prophecy: when she spoke it was believed that the god was speaking through her. Consultants would customarily enquire about any number of problems: why there was a plague in their city, whether they should send a colony to Sicily, or why they were childless or their crops had failed (docs 2.3, 2.22, 2.29, 3.20–23). Another way to seek knowledge of the future was through sacrifice: the beast was killed and its guts examined. Smooth entrails, well-coloured gall bladders and symmetrical livers meant all was well (doc. 3.63). But incomplete entrails, or a fire that would not burn, portended evil (docs 3.17–18). The study of the flights of birds would also reveal the will of the gods (docs 3.14–15).

Pan-Hellenic festivals were very much a part of the Greek way of life and the right of worshippers to travel to and from these festivals was carefully protected (doc. 3.26). The major festivals attracted participants from all over the Greek world and even tyrants from Sicily and Greek kings from Cyrene regularly sent chariots to compete at the Olympic and Pythian games, while poets such as Pindar and Bacchylides celebrated their victories (docs 2.30, 7.57–59; cf. 3.27). There were also, of course, festivals held by individual cities for the benefit of their citizens, as well as festivals which were restricted to particular groups of Greeks. The Ionians had a cult centre on the island of Delos, and Thucydides, reflecting his particular interest in religion as it impinged on political events, has a long description of the festival there, and quotes extracts from the *Homeric Hymn to Apollo* which describe the festival on Delos in the archaic period, when the Ionians came together to give the god pleasure with boxing, dancing and singing (doc. 3.28; cf. 1.59).

In the *Odyssey* Homer paints a very gloomy picture of the afterlife (doc. 3.53; cf. 4.3). The souls of the deceased wander around in the underworld as spirits, leading a shadowy existence without pleasure. But this afterlife did not appeal to all of the Greeks, many of whom participated in ceremonies which gave them hopes for a better afterlife. These ceremonies are known as mystery celebrations, the most famous of which were the Eleusinian Mysteries, celebrated at Eleusis in Attica (docs 3.31–39), a personal approach to the problem of the afterlife in which an individual by participating in the rites of Demeter gained access to a happy life after death.

Another example of personal religion was the cult of the healing god Asklepios and it was to this god that the Greeks turned in cases of personal sickness. His main healing centre in Greece was at Epidauros, in the eastern Peloponnese, where the sick slept in a special building, the abaton, set aside for this purpose, and hoped that during the night the god Asklepios would appear to them in a dream and heal them. It was very much a case of faith healing: carrying out the proper rituals, praying, and then during the night hoping for a vision of the god which would bring about a cure (docs 3.42–44).

Between gods and mortals were the heroes: famous mythological figures were given cult honours at the place of their burial in the belief that they would come to the assistance of those who worshipped them (docs 3.45–46, 14.22). One of these heroes, Trophonios, also provided predictions of the future for those undertaking the required ceremonies at his cult centre (doc. 3.48).

While the role of women was often controlled, they did have specific religious duties, as in the worship of Dionysos (doc. 3.41). In particular they served important roles as priestesses, not just at Delphi, but at Athens as priestesses of Athena, the deity who was believed to protect the state and who had the most impressive temple and cult statue in the city (doc. 1.12), and a treasury of valuable items and money dedicated by individuals, as well as a share of the tribute that was collected by the state from the allies in the fifth century (docs 1.11, 12.28).

Some of the philosophers had different views, criticising the anthropomorphic conceptualisation of the gods and their behaviour (docs 3.4–5), but also seeing the gods as beyond human comprehension: it is 'Mind' that controls everything and has plotted the course of all that has happened, is happening and will happen (doc. 3.74). Socrates in 399 BC was prosecuted and executed for corrupting the youth of Athens, teaching them about new gods: in the popular imagination he was identified with the sophists, clever thinking and new gods (doc. 3.82).

Religion permeated the life of the city-state: the life of the citizen revolved around innumerable festivals, of the city, phratry (brotherhood) and deme (village) (cf. docs 1.38–40, 10.19–20). Public religion centred on the sacrifices offered at such festivals, involving public feasting which strengthened ties of kinship and solidarity within the polis. Each city had its own temples and shrines, as well as tutelary deities, and Athens was full of hermai, small representations of Hermes in stone outside individual houses (cf. doc. 13.22). Yet, despite the fact that the various Greek cities each had their own special deities and festivals, Herodotos defines two of the most important characteristics of the Greeks: their common language and shared religion (doc. 3.91). Religion was therefore a significant determinant of Greek identity and an important part of the common heritage which distinguished Greek from barbarian.

THE OLYMPIAN RELIGION AND ITS CRITICS

Greek religion was polytheistic, but the main gods were the 'Twelve Olympians': the gods who dwelt on Mount Olympus in northern Greece. These included the siblings Zeus, Hera, Demeter, and Poseidon; their brother Hades dwelt under the earth as king of the dead, while their sister Hestia, goddess of the hearth, was not usually included amongst the Twelve. In addition, there were Ares, Aphrodite, the twins Apollo and Artemis, Athena, Dionysos, Hephaistos and Hermes. There were also numerous lesser gods and local heroes ('demi-gods'), sometimes mortals who were divinised due to their greatness in this life. Prayer and, more importantly, animal sacrifice were intrinsic to the worship of these gods.

3.1 Hesiod *Theogony* 1–23: The Olympian Gods

In the *Theogony*, Hesiod gives the genealogies of the gods. The 'mighty son of Kronos' was Zeus, who overthrew his father Kronos and was the chief of the gods and more powerful than all of them combined.

Let us begin our song with the Helikonian Muses
Who dwell on Helikon, the great and holy mountain
And around the violet spring on their soft feet
Dance, circling the altar of the mighty son of Kronos.
When they have washed their tender bodies in Permessos
Or the Horse's fount or sacred Olmeios
On Helikon's peak they take their place in fair, lovely
Dances, moving on nimble feet.
From there they set out, veiled in thick mist,
Going by night to utter with lovely voice
Praise to aegis-bearing Zeus and queenly Hera
Of Argos, who walks on golden sandals,
And the daughter of aegis-bearing Zeus, grey-eyed Athena,
To Phoibos Apollo and Artemis who delights in arrows,
Poseidon, earth-holder and earth-shaker,
Revered Themis and quick-glancing Aphrodite,
Golden-crowned Hebe and fair Dione,
Leto, Iapetos and Kronos of cunning counsel,
Dawn, great Sun and bright Moon,

Earth and great Oceanos and black Night
And all the sacred race of the deathless immortals.
It was they who taught Hesiod beautiful song
As he shepherded his sheep under sacred Helikon.

3.2 Hesiod *Theogony* 466–73, 77–91: The Birth of Zeus

Ouranos (Sky or Heaven) was overthrown and castrated by his son Kronos (when his sperm hit the surf, Aphrodite sprang from the waves), who was to be the father of the Olympian gods; Kronos attempted to avoid the prophecy that he too would be overthrown by his offspring by swallowing his children, but his wife Rhea hid Zeus from him and he swallowed a stone instead.

Kronos kept no careless watch, but looked carefully
And swallowed down his children; and endless grief seized Rhea.
But when she was about to bear Zeus, father of gods and men,
Then she beseeched her dear parents,
Both Earth (Ge) and starry Heaven (Ouranos),
To devise with her some plan, so that she might unnoticed bear
Her dear child, and that Retribution might pay Kronos back for his own father
And the children great Kronos, crafty of counsel, had swallowed down.
...
477 They sent her to Lyktos, to the rich land of Crete
Where she was about to bear the last of her children
Great Zeus; mighty Earth received him from her
In broad Crete to nourish and to rear.
There she came bearing him swiftly through the black night,
First to Lyktos; and taking him in her hands she hid him
In a deep cave, in the secret places of divine earth,
On densely wooded mount Aigaion.
But in his place she wrapped a great stone in swaddling clothes and put it
In the hands of the great lord son of Heaven, king of earlier gods;
And he took it in his hands and placed it in his belly,
Wretch, not knowing in his heart that
In place of the stone his son, unconquered and unworried,
Was left behind, who by force and hands was soon to overcome
And drive him from his rank, himself to reign amongst the immortals.

3.3 Pausanias *Description of Greece* 5.11.1, 5.11.8–11: Pheidias' Statue of Zeus

The chryselephantine (gold and ivory) statue of the seated Zeus, over forty feet high, was housed in the temple at Olympia, built in the 460s BC; Pheidias made the statue about thirty years later and it was one of the Seven Wonders of the Ancient World: the others were the Pyramids of Egypt, the city wall and the Hanging Gardens of Babylon, the Mausoleum at Halikarnassos, the Colossus of Rhodes and the temple of Artemis at Ephesos.

5.11.1 The god sits on a throne and is made of gold and ivory; on his head is a garland in imitation of olive shoots. In his right hand he carries a Victory (Nike) also of ivory and gold, and she has a ribbon and on her head a garland; in the god's left hand is a sceptre adorned with every kind of metal, and the bird sitting on the sceptre is the eagle. The god's sandals are of gold, as is his cloak; on the cloak both figures of animals and flowers of the lily are embroidered. The throne has variegated decorations of gold and jewels, ebony and ivory, with figures painted and carved on it. ... **8** On the base supporting the throne and all the majesty of Zeus are figures in gold — the Sun mounted on his chariot, and Zeus and Hera, and Hephaistos with one of the Graces near him; then by her is Hermes, and close by Hermes Hestia; and after Hestia is Eros welcoming Aphrodite arising from the sea, with Aphrodite being crowned by Persuasion. There are also reliefs of Apollo with Artemis, Athena and Herakles, and at the end of the base Amphitrite and Poseidon, with the Moon driving what appears to be a horse ... **10** The whole floor in front of the statue is paved not with white but with black tiles, and the surround of Parian marble encircles the black stone to contain the oil that is poured in: olive oil is after all beneficial to the statue at Olympia and it is olive oil that stops the ivory from being damaged by the marshy nature of the Altis. On the Athenian acropolis the ivory of the 'Parthenon' as she is called is not improved by oil but by water — for the acropolis is so dry owing to its height that the image needs water or dampness. **11** When I enquired at Epidauros why they do not pour either water or olive oil on the statue of Asklepios they told me that both the god's statue and his throne were built over a cistern.

3.4 Xenophanes of Kolophon *Poem* 11: The Gods of Homer and Hesiod

Several philosophers criticised traditional anthropomorphic conceptions of the gods; their works only survive as fragments quoted by later writers. Xenophanes lived *c.* 570–*c.* 475 BC, and challenged traditional notions about the gods, particularly the attribution of human behavioural traits to them, but without questioning their existence.

Both Homer and Hesiod have attributed all things to the gods,
As many as are shameful and a reproach amongst mankind,
Thieving and adultery and deceiving each other.

3.5 Xenophanes of Kolophon *Poem* 15–16: 'In Their Own Image'

Xenophanes points out that humans portray the gods as anthropomorphic, but that there is no reason for supposing that they are. He perceives that different races attribute to the gods their own characteristics.

15 But if oxen and horses and lions had hands,
Or could draw with their hands and create works like men,
Horses would draw pictures of the gods like horses,
And oxen like oxen, and each would make their bodies
Just like the bodily form that they themselves had.

16 The Ethiopians say their gods are snub-nosed and black,
The Thracians that theirs have grey-blue eyes and red hair.

3.6 Herakleitos F5: Purification in Blood

Herakleitos of Ephesos, living *c.* 500 BC, criticised the nature of purification (presumably from homicide) by sacrifice involving the shedding of blood: the blood of the murder is washed away by the blood of the sacrifice, a reasoning he found illogical. He also criticised praying to statues, thus questioning whether a cult statue represented the god.

They purify themselves by defiling themselves with other blood, just as if one were to step into mud to wash off mud. A man would be thought mad if anyone were to observe him acting in this way. And they pray to their statues, as if one were to talk gossip to houses, not knowing at all of what nature gods or heroes are.

3.7 Sophocles *Antigone* 332–71: The Wonderful Achievements of Humankind

The Greeks were conscious of the uniqueness of humanity and what separated humans from beasts, and the attributes and qualities mortals shared with the gods.

There is much that exists that is wonderful, but
There is nothing so wonderful as man!
Over the grey sea
Blown by the winter wind
He moves, through the engulfing
Swells, and of the gods
The highest, Earth,
That never rests, he wears away,
With furrowing ploughs, year after year,
With his breed of horses turning up the soil.
The light-minded race
Of birds he captures,
And the various wild creatures
And the marine life of the ocean
In the woven meshes of his nets —
Man the intelligent. He masters
With his cunning devices the creatures
That roam the mountains;
The shaggy-necked
Horse he tames
With its neck under the yoke
And the tireless mountain bull.
And speech and wind-swift
Thought and the temperaments that rule cities
He has learned
And to escape being out in the open
In the inhospitable hills and
To avoid the stormy shafts of rain
With his inventive nature. He is without resource towards
Nothing for the future: from Hades alone

He will not find escape;
And from incurable diseases
He has contrived cures.
Skilful is the contrivance
Of his art beyond hope
And he proceeds
Sometimes to evil, at other times to good.
When he follow the laws of the earth,
The justice the gods have sworn,
He ranks high in the city: but outcast from his city
Is he whom evil attends because of his recklessness.

3.8 Pindar *Nemean* 6.1–7: Mortals and Gods Are Kin

This was written for Alkimidas of Aegina, winner in the boys' wrestling at Nemea; this was the twenty-fifth pan-Hellenic win for his family. The mother of both gods and men is Earth (Ge or Gaia). The sporting metaphor is very appropriate for an athlete.

One race of men, one of gods, but we both draw breath
From the same mother — yet a sundering power separates us
Totally, for the one race is nothing, while the bronze heaven remains a safe dwelling-place
For ever. But all the same we do somehow resemble
The Immortals, whether in greatness of mind or outward form,
Although we know neither by day nor by night
What course Destiny has marked for us to run

SACRIFICE AND PUBLIC WORSHIP

3.9 Homer *Odyssey* 3.430–63, 470–72: A Homeric Sacrifice

Telemachos is here visiting Nestor in search of news of his father Odysseus. This is the most extensive description of a Greek sacrifice (see also Homer *Iliad* 1.437–68). Important details include the adornment of the cow, the rituals leading up to the killing of the animal, particularly the washing of hands, the act of slaughter itself – simultaneous with the women crying out loud — the roasting of the entrails on the spits and then the feasting. Athena herself comes to enjoy the sacrifice. The barley is sprinkled on the victim's head so it nods, thus assenting to being sacrificed.

So Nestor spoke and they all went busily to work. The cow was brought
From the plain, and from the swift well-balanced ship came
The companions of great-hearted Telemachos. The smith too came
Holding in his hands the bronze tools, instruments of his craft,
Anvil, hammer and well-made fire-tongs,
With which he worked the gold. Athena came also
To receive the sacrifice. The old man, Nestor, driver of chariots,
Gave the gold and the smith spread it over the horns of the cow
After working it, so the goddess would rejoice when she saw the offering.

Stratios and godlike Echephron led the cow by the horns,
And Aretos, bringing water for the hands in a basin adorned with flowers
Came from inside the palace, while in the other hand he held barley grains
In a basket; Thrasymedes, steadfast in battle, stood by
Holding in his hand the axe to fell the cow.
Perseus held the bowl for the blood; then old Nestor, driver of horses,
Began the ceremony with the washing of hands and sprinkling of barley,
Making many prayers to Athena as he started the sacrifice by cutting off some hair from the head and throwing it on the fire.
When they had prayed and sprinkled the barley grains,
Nestor's son, the high-spirited Thrasymedes,
Stood near and struck the blow; the axe cut through the tendons
Of the neck, and released the cow's strength. The women cried aloud,
The daughters and daughters-in-law and revered wife
Of Nestor, Eurydike, eldest of the daughters of Klymenos,
While the men raised its head from the spacious earth
And held it; Peisistratos, leader of men, cut its throat.
When the black blood had flowed from her, and life had left her bones,
They immediately dismembered her, and cut out the thigh bones
All accordingly to procedure, and covered them with a double layer of fat,
And put the raw pieces on top of them.
The old man burned them on firewood, and poured on sparkling
Wine; and by him the young men held in their hands the five-pronged forks.
When the thigh bones were burned and they had tasted the entrails
They cut up the rest, put them on spits
And roasted them, holding the sharply pointed spits in their hands.
...
When they had roasted the outside pieces of meat and taken them off the spits
They sat down and dined, and noble men saw to their needs,
Pouring wine into goblets of gold.

3.10 Menander *Dyskolos* 393–406: A Reluctant Victim

The sacrificial butcher Sikon, a professional hired on this occasion, here enters with a very unhappy sheep for sacrifice, clearly an unwilling and intractable victim, which he will sacrifice to the god Pan. Sostratos' mother had a dream of the god Pan putting her son in chains and telling him to dig the neighbour's land; this sacrifice at Pan's shrine is to avert the ill-omened dream. The household brings with it pots and pans, baskets, water, sacrificial cakes, masses of rugs and a flute-girl (even so they forgot the cauldron). Here Sikon is speaking.

This sheep isn't your run-of-the-mill beauty.
Hell and damnation to it! If I lift it up
And carry it in the air, it fastens its teeth onto a branch
And devours the leaves off the fig-branches,
Tearing itself out of my arms.
While if you put it on the ground, it won't budge an inch.

Here's a contradiction for you! This thing's made mince-meat of me, the cook, who's had to haul it along the road.
But happily here's the shrine
Where we're to sacrifice. Hail Pan! Slave! Getas!
Why are you so far behind?
Getas: It's the four donkey-loads
Of stuff those wretched women have tied up
For me to carry!
Sikon: There's a mob of people coming,
It seems! What a terrible lot of rugs
You're carrying!

3.11 Menander *Samia* 399–404: The Gods' Share of Sacrifices

Nikeratos, who is poor and elderly, is here sacrificing a sheep and lists the parts assigned to the gods. Normally the participants would cook and share the remainder of the meat, but being poverty-stricken he cannot afford an animal with any spare flesh on it.

This sheep will provide all the standard offerings
For the gods and goddesses, when it's sacrificed.
For it has blood, an adequate gall bladder, great bones,
A large spleen – all that the Olympians need.
I'll cut up the fleece and send it to my friends
To taste – that's all that I'll have left!

3.12 *LSCG Suppl.* 10: The Athenian Calendar of Sacrifices, 403/2–400/399 BC

As part of the revision of Athenian laws which began in 410 BC, the Athenian religious calendar was examined and inscribed. This fragment of the calendar records biennial sacrifices in particular months (an earlier, damaged, tablet recorded annual sacrifices). The four pre-Kleisthenic tribes are mentioned (Argadies, Hopletes, Aigikoreis and Geleontes) and they clearly had religious duties. Various officials received parts of the sacrifices as payments for their duties, and victims are often specified as needing to be 'unblemished' or of 'high quality'. The cost of each victim to a particular deity is specified. Sacrifices were not cheap: one drachma a day was a good wage in the fifth century. Cf. Lysias 30, Andocides 3.81–5.

The following sacrifices are made in alternate years …

In Hekatombaion on the fifteenth from the (laws of) the tribe-kings for the tribe of the Geleontes, for the Leukotainians' trittys, a sheep unblemished (4 dr.) the priest's perquisite (4 dr. 2 ob.) for the tribe-kings for the back (1 dr.), to the herald for the shoulder, feet, head (4 ob.).

On the sixteenth from the (laws of) the tribe-kings for the tribe of the Geleontes, for Zeus Phratrios and Athena Phratria, two oxen unblemished (50 dr.) the priest's perquisite (16 dr.) for the tribe-kings the leg to the herald for the chest, feet, head (2 dr. 3 ob.). For the animals' rearer, of barley … bushels … To Themis a sheep (12 dr.); to Zeus of the forecourt a sheep (15 dr.); to Demeter a sheep (12 dr.); to Pherrephatta (Persephone) a ram

(17 dr.); to Eumolpos a sheep (15 dr.); to Melichos the hero a sheep (15 dr.); to Archegetes (Iackhos) a sheep (15 dr.); to Polyxen[os] a sheep (15 dr.); to Threptos (Triptolemos) a ram of high quality (17 dr.); to Dioklo[s] a sheep (15 dr.); to Keleos a sheep (15 dr.); the Eumolp[idai] make these sacrifices to the priestess [of Demeter] (100 dr.).

From the stelai: a young pig ... (3 dr.); to Hesti[a] a sheep (12 dr.); to Athen[a] a sheep (12 dr.); to the Gr[aces ...] (10 dr.); a sheep to Her[mes] presider over games (15 dr.); ... (10 dr.); to He[ra] a sheep (15 dr.); to Zeus a sheep (15 dr.) ...

3.13 Tod 20: The Oath of the Athenian Ephebes

The Athenian ephebes (Greek pl.: epheboi), eighteen-year-olds, who in the fourth century BC underwent military training for two years, swore an oath to various gods – several of them local to Athens – that they would stand firm in battle. The oath was inscribed in a dedication made by Dion son of Dion. Cf. Plut. *Alk.* 15.7-8.

Gods. The priest of Ares and Athena Areia, Dion son of Dion of Acharnai made the dedication. The ancestral oath of the ephebes, which must be sworn by the ephebes:

I shall not disgrace the sacred weapons, nor shall I abandon my comrade, wherever I shall be positioned (in the ranks); I will fight to defend things sacred and secular, and I shall not hand down a lesser fatherland, but one that is greater and stronger, both to the best of my power and with the assistance of all, and I shall willingly obey those governing prudently at any time and the laws which have been established, and any others which shall be established prudently at some future time. If anyone attempts to abolish them, I shall not permit this both to the best of my power and with the assistance of all, and I shall honour the ancestral shrines. Witnesses to this are the gods Aglauros, Hestia, Enyo, Enyalios, Ares and Athena Areia, Zeus, Thallo, Auxo, Hegemone, Herakles, the boundaries of my fatherland, wheat, barley, vines, olive trees, fig trees.

DIVINATION: OMENS AND ORACLES

Before major undertakings the Greeks would consult the gods regarding their wishes and intentions for the future (see doc. 2.3). This was divination, in Greek *manteia*, and took several forms: the gods could be consulted directly through prophetic mediums, most notably the Pythian priestess at Delphi. In addition, various other methods were employed: oionomanteia (the observation of the flight of birds), hieroskopia (examination of the internal organs of a sacrificed beast), and 'signs by the way' (doc. 3.16); a sneeze on the right was also favourable; and there was also the interpretation of dreams: oneiromanteia.

3.14 Hesiod *Works and Days* 826–28: Discerning the Omens

By observing the omens, and hence the will of the gods, mortals ensure they will not act against divine wishes.

He is fortunate and prosperous who, knowing all these things,
Does his work guiltless before the immortal gods,
Discerning the omens of birds and avoiding transgressions.

3.15 *LSAM* 30: Sixth-Century Divination at Ephesos

This is the only inscription which lists several possible bird movements and their interpretation. It seems to suggest an official site from which observations were taken (cf. doc. 3.18). Birds were so common a form of omen that the word for omen was often simply 'bird'. [*SIG*[3] 1167.]

... if (the bird) flying from right to left disappears (from view) (the omen is) favourable; if it raises its left wing, flies away and disappears (the omen is) unfavourable; if flying from left to right it disappears on a straight course (the omen is) unfavourable; but if after raising its right wing, it flies away and disappears (the omen is) favourable ...

3.16 Aeschylus *Prometheus Bound* 484–95: Prometheus Teaches Mortals Divination

Prometheus, amongst his other gifts to mortals, taught the art of divination, especially oionomanteia and hieroskopia. 'Signs by the way' were phenomena one encountered as one went about daily life, which could be interpreted as ominous: cf. doc. 3.72.

I marked out many ways of divination,
And was the first to discern among dreams those which must
Take place in reality, and doubtful utterances
I made known to them and signs by the way;
The flight of birds with crooked talons I distinguished
Exactly, those which by their nature are auspicious
And the ill-omened, and the mode of life
Each has, and what enmities
Towards each other and loves and companionships,
And the smoothness of entrails and what colour
The gall bladder should have to please
The gods, and the speckled symmetry of the liver's lobe.

3.17 Euripides *Electra* 826–29: Aegisthus' Doom Is Sealed

These signs portend the coming slaughter of Aegisthus by Orestes, to avenge his father Agamemnon, murdered by Clytemnestra and her lover Aegisthus (cf. docs 3.55, 4.68).

Taking in his hands the sacrificial parts
Aegisthus gazed at them. The liver-lobe was missing
From the entrails, and the portal veins and gall bladder nearby
Portended evil visitations to him examining them.

3.18 Sophocles *Antigone* 998–1011: Teiresias Learns the Gods' Wrath

Kreon, king of Thebes, has had Antigone entombed in a cave for burying her brother, who was technically an enemy, having attacked Thebes; she hangs herself and Kreon's son, her betrothed and heir to the throne, commits suicide. For her speech of justification to Kreon, see doc. 4.69; for her burial of her brother, see doc. 3.54.

You will know when you hear the signs of my craft!
For on my ancient seat of divination
I sat where every sort of bird gathers,
And heard the uninterpretable voice of birds, shrieking
Through some evil influence and unintelligibly;
And I realised that they were tearing at each other with murderous
Talons; for the flapping of wings was not without meaning.
Straightway I fearfully tried burnt offerings
With kindled altars; but from the sacrifices
Fire would not blaze forth, but onto the ash
The juices melted and dripped from the thighs,
Smouldering and spitting, and the gall bladders
Melted into air, and the dripping
Thighs lay bare of their covering fat.

3.19 Demosthenes 43 *Against Makartatos* 66: The Formula for Consulting an Oracle

As a result of a sign which appeared in the sky the Athenians consulted the Delphic oracle as to its significance. The response was a ritual prescription. This formula is said to date to the time of Solon (594/3 BC).

66 (The enquiry): the Oracle. Good fortune. The Athenian people are making enquiry about the sign which has appeared in the sky, what the Athenians ought to do or to which god they should sacrifice or pray so that the sign will turn out to their advantage.

(The response): concerning the sign in the sky, it is to the Athenians' advantage to sacrifice with good omens to Zeus 'Most High', Athena 'Most High', Herakles, Apollo 'the Deliverer', and send offerings to the Amphiones; they should sacrifice for good fortune to Apollo 'Guardian of the Streets', Leto and Artemis; they should fill the streets with the smell of sacrifice; they should provide bowls of wine and choruses; and they should wreath themselves with garlands in honour of all the Olympian gods and goddesses according to their ancestral practice, raising their right and left hands, and offer public thanksgiving according to their ancestral practice. And they should sacrifice and offer gifts to the hero-founder, after whom you are named, according to ancestral practice; and their relatives shall make offerings for the dead on the appointed day in accordance with the usual custom.

3.20 Herodotos 1.53.1–54.2: Croesus Consults Delphi

Croesus, concerned at the rising power of Persia, sent envoys to consult several Greek oracles; he was pleased with the responses of Amphiaraos in Boeotia and Apollo at Delphi; to the Delphians he granted two staters per man. The Delphians in return granted him promanteia, the right by which the Delphians granted to either individuals or communities the privilege of consulting the oracle first, before other enquirers. Consultations took place only once a month, and not during winter, and there were three Pythias who served in rotation. The response in this passage is a classic case of Delphic ambiguity: Croesos attacked the Persians and did destroy a mighty empire: his own; cf. the Pythia's similarly cryptic response to the Spartans as to whether they should attack Tegea (docs 3.46, 6.55).

1.53.1 Croesus instructed the men who were going to take these gifts to the shrines to ask the oracles if he should make war on Persia and if he should seek the help of another allied army. **2** When they arrived at their destinations, the Lydians dedicated the offerings, and consulted the oracles, asking, 'Croesus, King of Lydia and other countries, believing that these are the only oracles among mankind, has given you gifts worthy of your divination, and now inquires of you if he should make war against the Persians and if he should seek the help of another allied army'. **3** This is what they asked, and the response of both oracles was the same, prophesying to Croesus that, if he made war against the Persians, he would destroy a great empire; and they advised him to find out which of the Greeks were the most powerful and to ally himself with them. **1.54.1** When Croesus learned the oracles which had been delivered, he was delighted with the responses, and, as he confidently expected to destroy the kingdom of Cyrus, he sent yet another present to Delphi, after ascertaining the number of inhabitants, two gold staters for each man. **2** The Delphians in return gave Croesus and the Lydians in perpetuity the right of promanteia and exemption from dues and front seats at the festival, and allowed anyone who wished to become a citizen of Delphi.

3.21 Euripides *Ion* 299–306: A Husband and Wife at Delphi

In the play *Ion*, Kreousa, wife of Xouthos, has come with him to Delphi to enquire why they are childless. Unknown to her husband, she had previously borne a child to Apollo, Ion, himself now a priest, though she does not recognise him, nor does he know her. Ion's words seem to imply that Kreousa could personally consult the oracle (that is, a woman could do so). For Trophonios' oracle, see doc. 3.48.

Ion: Have you come with your husband or on your own as a consultant?
Kreousa: With my husband; he is delaying at the precinct of Trophonios.
Ion: As a visitor or for the sake of oracles?
Kreousa: He would like to learn one thing from him and from Apollo.
Ion: Have you come here concerning crops for the land or children?
Kreousa: We are childless, and have been long married.
Ion: Have you never borne a child, but are childless?
Kreousa: Apollo knows my childlessness.

3.22 Plutarch *Moralia* 51.438a–c: The Pythia Dies after a Disastrous Consultation

Apollo could be consulted via the Pythia once a month. Plutarch here describes a second-century CE consultation that went wrong. It is to be noted here that the Pythia's abnormal state is connected with the bad omen of the unwillingness of the sacrificial victim. Other accounts indicate that she was normally calm and sedate during consultations.

438a A delegation from abroad had arrived to consult the oracle and it is reported that the sacrificial victim remained unmoved and impassive in response to the initial libations. However, the priests kept persevering to an extreme in their eagerness to get a result, **438b** and only when the victim was deluged and nearly half-drowned did it give in. What then was the consequence for the Pythia? She went down into the oracular shrine unwillingly, they say, and with reluctance, and from her first responses it was immediately obvious from the roughness of her voice that she was not prophesying properly, but was labouring like an overladen ship and possessed by an incoherent and malevolent spirit. At length she became completely hysterical and with an unintelligible and fearful cry rushed to the exit and threw herself down, with the result that not only the delegation fled, but so did the prophetic interpreter Nikander and the other holy men present. Shortly afterwards, however, they went in and took up the Pythia, who was still conscious, **438c** and she only lived a few days longer.

3.23 *LSCG Suppl.* 39: The Cost of the Pelanos

Before consultation took place at Delphi an offering of the pelanos, a cake, had to be made outside and a full sacrifice was also necessary within the temple. In this inscription, which probably dates to the last two decades of the fifth century BC, the pelanos seems to have been commuted into a tax or a sum of money. The consultation fees, which seem to have varied from state to state, are here set down for the Phaselites.

1 These things (were resolved) by the Delphians: the Phaselites are to give seven drachmas two obols in Delphian currency for the pelanos for a public (consultation), a private individual four obols. **5** Timodikos and Histiaios were the theoroi (from Phaselis), Herulos the magistrate.

3.24 Thucydides 7.50.3–4: The Eclipse during the Sicilian Expedition

The Athenians, having suffered a disastrous defeat, were preparing to sail away when an eclipse of the moon took place and Nikias, their commander, insisted that they stay for the further twenty-seven days recommended by the seers; in this he followed the opinion of the majority of the troops: for the outcome, see docs 13.26–27. The eclipse occurred on 27 August 413 BC; see also Plut. *Nik.* 4.1–2; Pausanias also waited for favourable omens at Plataea, though under attack: Hdt. 9.61.3–62.1 (doc. 11.47).

7.50.3 When the Athenian generals saw that the Syracusans had been reinforced by another army and that their own position, far from improving, was daily becoming worse in every respect, and was becoming particularly difficult because of the sickness among the men, they regretted that they had not withdrawn earlier and as even Nikias was no longer so opposed to this, except that he did not approve of an open vote, they gave notice as secretly as possible for everyone to be prepared to sail out of the camp when the signal to do so was given. **4** And they were about to sail out, and everything was ready, when there was an eclipse of the moon, which happened to be full. Most of the Athenians took this so seriously that they bade the generals wait, and Nikias (who was rather too inclined to divination and such matters) said that he would not even discuss how the move should be made until, as the seers prescribed, they had waited thrice nine days. It was for this reason that the Athenians delayed and stayed on.

FESTIVALS

Festivals organised by the state brought the whole community together to worship the gods, through sacrifices, and dramatic and athletic contests. There were also the four pan-Hellenic festivals, attended by Greeks from all over the Greek world, from France to Asia

Minor to the Black Sea. By at least the eighth century BC an athletic contest was held at Olympia (the traditional date was 776 BC); by the early fifth century Delphi, Olympia, Corinth at the Isthmus and Nemea all had festivals (respectively, the Pythian, Olympian, Isthmian and Nemean), which formed an institutionalised festival circuit, known as the periodos, on the Greek mainland.

3.25 *LSCG Suppl.* 38: Provisions for an Andrian Choir Visiting Delphi

States would send official sacred embassies to represent them at sacred festivals, so ensuring that the gods were aware of their city's piety. The Aegean island of Andros sent a sacred embassy (theoria) to Delphi, and this fifth-century BC inscription makes detailed arrangements for the procedure to be followed. The architheoroi who were in charge of the theoria and the other officials had their food supplied for them. As there was a choir it is likely that the theoria was being dispatched to participate in the musical contests at the Pythian festival. The meaning of metaxenia is uncertain.

A ... **6** The following are not to pay for their grain or beans: the three architheoroi, the seer, the commander, the herald, the flautist, the helmsman, the boatswain, the steward. The following shall receive a skin: the herald, the flautist, the boatswain, each of the public priests. The (Delphians) are to provide food on the first day; barley-cake, meat, wine as much as they wish and the other things as suitable. For the (next) two days apart from grain let each put down both boy and man an Aeginetan obol for each day; and the architheoroi are to consecrate half (of these obols); the costs (of the cult) are: four obols for the pelanos, two for the metaxenia, six for the priest at each sacrifice. Let the private individual receive the third part of the skins which he sacrifices except for the ones sacrificed for consultation or purification, and all those on the embassy (theoria).

B The boule is to elect from those sailing to Delphi five men and take their oaths; they are to not pay for food on account of this office; and they are to have the power to fine the disorderly up to five drachmas for each day. Whomever they fine let them record (their names) in the Council.

3.26 Thucydides 5.18.1–3: Access to Pan-Hellenic Sanctuaries Guaranteed

The first clause, given below, of the Peace of Nikias in 421 BC during the Peloponnesian War allowed all Greeks to consult Pan-Hellenic oracles and attend festivals in safety even in wartime; cf. Thuc. 4.118.1.

5.18.1 The Athenians and Spartans and their allies made a treaty and swore to it, city by city, as follows: **2** 'Concerning the temples which are common to all, anyone who wishes may, in accordance with ancestral custom, offer sacrifices in them, travel to them, consult the oracle, and attend the festival, being guaranteed security by both land and sea. The sanctuary and the temple of Apollo at Delphi and the Delphians are to be independent and have their own taxes and courts, both the people and their territory, in accordance with ancestral custom. **3** This treaty is to be in force between the Athenians and their allies and the Spartans and their allies for fifty years, without deceit and without harm both by land and sea.'

3.27 Plutarch *Life of Alkibiades* 11.1–2, 12.1: Alkibiades at the Olympics

Alkibiades entered seven chariots in the same race at the Olympics; for a woman victor, see doc. 4.17. A win at the games was very prestigious for the city (cf. doc. 1.78; Thuc. 6.16.2).

11.1 The horses Alkibiades bred were renowned everywhere, as was the number of his chariots; for no one else, either a private individual or a king, had ever entered seven at the Olympics, and he was the only one to do so. **2** And to have won with them the first, second and fourth prizes, as Thucydides says, and the third according to Euripides, surpasses in brilliance and renown all ambition in this field … **12.1** This success was made all the more brilliant by the distinction shown him by the different cities. For the Ephesians erected for him a magnificently adorned tent, and the city of Chios provided fodder for his horses and a large number of victims for sacrifice, and the Lesbians gave him wine and other provisions which enabled him to give many people lavish entertainment.

3.28 Thucydides 3.104.1–4: The Delian Games

Delos was the sacred island of the Ionians, where Apollo and Artemis had been born, and was the original meeting place for Athens and its allies, whence the title 'Delian League' (doc. 12.4). The Ionians had previously held a festival at Delos and in 426 BC the Athenians revived it. For Peisistratos' purification, see doc. 9.17; Hdt. 1.64.2.

3.104.1 The same winter (426/5 BC) the Athenians purified Delos in accordance with some oracle. Peisistratos the tyrant had previously purified it, though not all of it, just as much of the island as could be seen from the temple; but at this time all of it was purified in the following way. **2** They removed all the graves of those who had died on Delos and proclaimed that for the future no one was to die or to give birth there, but had to be taken over to Rheneia … It was then after the purification that the Athenians first celebrated the Delian Games, which were held every fifth year. **3** There had also been in days of old a great gathering of the Ionians and neighbouring islanders on Delos; for they used to come to the festival with their wives and children, as the Ionians do now at the Ephesia, and they would hold a contest there in athletics and music and the cities would bring choruses. **4** Homer in particular shows that this was so in these verses, which come from his hymn to Apollo:

'But it was on Delos, Phoibos, that your heart especially took delight,
Where the long-robed Ionians gather together
With their children and wives on your sacred street;
There in boxing and dancing and singing
They think of you and rejoice, when they hold your contest.'

3.29 Aristophanes *Frogs* 1089–98: The Torch Race at the Panathenaia

One of the features of both the Greater and Lesser Panathenaia festivals in Athens was a torch race held on the first day. Aeschylus, in the underworld, has been complaining that due to Euripides' plays everyone in Athens is now out of training, both morally and physically, and that no one can even carry a torch any longer. Here the god Dionysos agrees with him.

No, by Zeus, they can't! As a result I was quite exhausted
With laughter at the Panathenaia, when
This slow chap was running head bent,
White, fat and quite left behind
Looking quite awful; and when the people at the Kerameikos
At the gates started beating his
Stomach and sides and flanks and buttocks
With the flat of the hand,
He farted,
Blowing on the torch, and ran off.

3.30 *Inscriptiones Graecae* V 1.222: The Karneia at Sparta

The Karneia was held in honour of Apollo, and was celebrated in Dorian cities, notably Sparta and Thera (doc. 2.30). Aiglatas commemorated his several victories in the athletic contests at this festival on a marble stele at Sparta, with a relief apparently representing a pair of ram's horns (the symbol of Apollo Karneios). The dolichos is the longer foot-race. [Friedländer 50.]

Aiglatas dedicated this offering to Karneian (Apollo)
After winning five times in the long race and he also ran
The dolichos three times, at the festival of Athena
... also the Smyrnaia

THE ELEUSINIAN MYSTERIES

Participants in the annual Eleusinian Mysteries held at Eleusis were bound to secrecy, on pain of death, not to reveal what took place in the nocturnal rites. But the ceremonies seem to have been based to some extent on the adventures of Demeter as related in the *Homeric Hymn to Demeter*, probably written down in the seventh century BC (doc. 3.31). Initiates, mainly Athenians, walked from Athens to Eleusis, and on the next evening there was a celebration at which the actual initiation took place, when the mystai gained access to a happy afterlife in the darkened hall called the telesterion.

3.31 *Homeric Hymn to Demeter* 198–211, 476–82: Demeter Grieves over Persephone

On arrival at Eleusis Demeter sat and neither laughed nor tasted food or drink, and it is probable, therefore, that the pilgrims to Eleusis fasted in imitation of the goddess. Her daughter Persephone had been abducted by Hades. According to Sophocles, the mysteries were locked 'by a golden key (of silence) on the tongue' (*Oed. Col.* 1051–52).

A long while Demeter sat upon the stool silent and mourning,
Nor did she greet anyone by word or sign,
But unsmiling, without tasting food or drink,
She sat pining with longing for her deep-girded daughter,
Until with jests true-hearted Iambe
Joked many times and turned the holy lady
To smile and laugh and have a joyous heart;

And afterwards also she delighted her with her moods.
Metaneira filled and gave her a cup of honey-sweet wine,
But she refused it; for she said it was not right
To drink red wine, but told them to mix
Meal and water with delicate pennyroyal and give it her to drink.
Iambe made the kykeon and gave it to the goddess as she bade;
And the lady Demeter received it for the sake of the rite.
. . .
To all Demeter revealed the conduct of her rites and mysteries —
To Triptolemos and Polyxeinos and Diokles as well —
Dread mysteries, which one may not in any way transgress or learn of
Or utter; for great reverence for the gods checks the voice.
Happy is he of mortal men who has seen these things;
But he who is not initiated in the rites, who has no part in them,
Has no share of such things, dead, down in mouldy darkness.

3.32 Aristophanes *Frogs* 312–36: The Revels of the Initiates

Here the god Dionysos and the slave Xanthias see in the underworld the happy life enjoyed by the initiates in the Eleusinian Mysteries. Dionysos (as Iakchos) was associated with the Eleusinian Mysteries: cf. docs 3.41, 3.69.

Dionysos: Didn't you hear it?
Xanthias: What?
Dionysos: A sound of flutes.
Xanthias: Yes I did, and a certain
314 Very mystical air of torches breathed on me.
Dionysos: Be quiet, let's crouch down and listen.
Chorus: Iakchos, O Iakchos!
Iakchos, O Iakchos!
Xanthias: That's it master — the initiates
Are sporting somewhere here, whom Herakles told us about.
320 At any rate they are chanting Iakchos, like Diagoras does.
Dionysos: I think so as well. It'll be best
To keep quiet, so we can know for sure.
Chorus: O Iakchos, highly honoured, who dwell here in your abode,
325 Iakchos, O Iakchos,
Come here to dance through this meadow
To your pious celebrants,
Shaking about your head
The full-fruited luxuriant
330/1 Myrtle garland, striking with bold
Foot the unbridled
333/4 Sportive rite,
Which has full share of the Graces, the pure and holy
Dance among your pious mystai.

3.33 Sophocles F837: The Eleusinian Afterlife

Thrice blessed are those mortals who after observing these rites
Journey to the halls of Hades. Only these
Have life there — for the others all that is there is wretchedness.

3.34 Andocides 1 *On the Mysteries* 11–12: The Assembly Cleared of Non-Initiates

On the eve of the sailing of the Sicilian Expedition in June 415 BC Alkibiades was accused of imitating and so mocking the secret Eleusinian Mysteries. He was recalled from Sicily to face charges: doc. 13.24.

11 'Athenians, you are sending out an expedition and so vast an armament, and are about to undergo danger; but I will prove that your general Alkibiades has been celebrating the Mysteries in his house with others, and if you grant immunity to the person whom I tell you, a servant, a non-initiate, belonging to one of the men here shall describe them to you; if it is not so, deal with me as you wish, if I am not speaking the truth.' **12** Alkibiades spoke at length in opposition denying the charge, and the prytaneis decided to remove all non-initiates from the meeting and to go themselves to fetch the slave whom Pythonikos had told them about.

3.35 Xenophon *Hellenika* 1.4.20–21: Alkibiades Returns to Athens in 407 BC

To celebrate the Greater Mysteries the Athenians traditionally made the journey from Athens to Eleusis by land, on the nineteenth of Boedromion, a distance of some twenty-two kilometres, but since the Spartan fortification at Dekeleia in 413 BC (doc. 13.25) they could not go by land and so went by sea instead. Alkibiades, however, in 407 BC led out the army by land, protecting the mystai during their procession to Eleusis.

1.4.20 When Alkibiades had spoken in his defence in the boule and assembly, saying that he had not committed sacrilege and had been wronged, after other such things had been said and no one spoke in opposition because the assembly would not have tolerated it, he was proclaimed commander-in-chief with supreme powers, on the ground that he would be able to restore the city's former power. First of all he led out all the soldiers and conducted by land the mysteries which the Athenians had been conducting by sea because of the war; **21** then he collected a force of fifteen hundred hoplites, and one hundred and fifty cavalry and one hundred ships.

3.36 *Inscriptiones Graecae* I^3 6B: Regulations for a Sacred Truce, *c.* 460 BC

There were sacred truces for the Eleusinian Mysteries, both Lesser and Greater, as well as for the major Pan-Hellenic events. The length of the truces for the mysteries was fifty-five days, covering the period before, during and after the celebration itself. The terms of the truce indicate that cities which did not observe the truce would not be allowed access to the mysteries. Sacred truces did not mean that warfare ceased throughout the Greek world, but ensured that those participating in the festivals involved were to be inviolable. The epoptai are those who have been admitted to the highest level of initiation. [*IG* I^2 9.]

... that **5** done inadvertently by a single, that done intentionally by a double penalty. There shall be a truce (spondai) for the initiates, **10** both the epoptai and for their followers and for the property of the foreigners **15** and for all the Athenians; the beginning of the period of the truce shall be **20** Metageitnion from the full moon through Boedromion and Pyanopsion **26** until the tenth of the month. The truce shall be in force in all those **30** cities which use the shrine and for the Athenians there in those **35** same cities. For the Lesser Mysteries the truce shall be from **40** Gamelion from the full moon through Anthesterion and Elaphebolion **46** until the tenth of the month.

3.37 *Inscriptiones Graecae* I[3] 6C: Regulations for the Mysteries, *c.* 460 BC

In order to be initiated, the initiates had to pay various fees to cult personnel. The Eumolpidai and the Kerykes were the Eleusinian families which had charge of the Mysteries; the hieropoioi were sacred officials. Groups of mystai had a mystagogos (a 'leader of initiates') to assist them with their initiation. [*IG* I[2] 9.]

5 ... obol ... the hieropoioi shall receive a half-obol each day from each initiate. The priestess of Demeter **10** shall receive at the Lesser Mysteries an obol from each initiate and at the Greater Mysteries an obol from each initiate; all the obols shall belong **15** to the two goddesses except 1,600 drachmas. From the 1,600 drachmas the priestess shall provide for expenses as **20** was done previously. The Eumolpidai and the Kerykes shall receive from each initiate five obols from men and three from women; it shall not be permitted to initiate an underage initiate **25** except for the one initiated from the hearth. The Kerykes shall initiate ... each of the initiates and the Eumolpidai the same; ... more they shall be fined 1,000 **30** drachmas. Those of the Kerykes and Eumolpidai who are adults shall perform the initiation; the sacred money ... the Athenians ..., as long as they wish, as for **35** the money of Athena on the acropolis; and the hieropoioi are to administer the money ... on the acropolis **39** ... **41** the orphaned children and the initiates each ... Those initiates at Eleusis ... in the hall within the sanctuary, **45** and those in the city ... in the Eleusinion. The priest of the altar and the cleanser of the two goddesses and the priest of ... shall each receive ... from **50** each initiate ...

3.38 *Inscriptiones Graecae* I[3] 78: The Offering of First Fruits at Eleusis, c. 422 BC

The administration involved in collecting 1/600 of all barley and 1/1,200 of all wheat grown in Attica and by Athens' allies, and possibly by other Greek cities as well, must have been complex. In 329/8 BC Eleusinian wheat was sold at prices fixed by the assembly, possibly below the market price. The hierophant was the most important of the Eleusinian officials, as he revealed the rites to the initiates. [*IG* I[2] 76.]

[Timo]tel[e]s of Acharnai was secretary. It was resolved by the boule and the people; (the tribe) Kekropis held the prytany, Timoteles was secretary, Kykneas presided: the commissioners (syngrapheis) drew up the following: that the Athenians are to offer to the two goddesses the first fruits of the grain in accordance with ancestral custom and the **5** oracle from Delphi, from every hundred medimnoi of barley not less than a sixth of a medimnos, from every hundred medimnoi of wheat not less than one twelfth of a medimnos; and if anyone produces more or less than this he is to offer first fruits in the same proportion. The demarchs are to collect (it) by deme and they are to hand it over to the hieropoioi from Eleusis at Eleusis. (The Athenians) are to construct at Eleusis three storage pits, in accordance with ancestral custom, wherever seems to be suitable to the hieropoioi and the architect from the money belonging to the two goddesses. They are to deposit there the grain which they receive from the demarchs. The allies are also to offer first fruits in the same way. The cities are to choose collectors for the grain, according to the way in which it seems to them best for the grain to be collected; when it has been collected, they are to send it to Athens; and those who bring it are to hand it over to the hieropoioi from Eleusis at Eleusis. If they do not receive it within five days after it has been reported, although those from the city from which the grain comes have offered it, the hieropoioi are to be liable to a fine of 1,000 drachmas each; and they are to receive it from the demarchs in the same way. The boule is to choose heralds and send them to the cities announcing what is now being decreed by the people, for the present as quickly as possible, and for the future whenever the boule decides. The hierophant and the torch-bearer (daidouchos) are to proclaim at the mysteries that the Greeks are to offer first fruits in accordance with ancestral custom and the oracle from Delphi. They are to record on a noticeboard the weight of the grain received from the demarchs according to each deme and that received from the cities according to each city and set it up in the Eleusinion at Eleusis and in the council chamber. The boule is also to make a proclamation to all the other Greek cities, in whatever way seems to be feasible, telling them how the Athenians and the allies are offering first fruits, and not ordering them but encouraging them to offer first fruits, if they wish, in accordance with ancestral custom and the oracle from Delphi. The hieropoioi are also to receive (grain) that anyone brings from these cities in the same way … And concerning the first fruits of olive oil Lampon shall draw up a draft and show it to the boule in the ninth prytany; and the boule shall be compelled to bring it before the people.

3.39 *Inscriptiones Graecae* I^3 79: The Crossing of the Stream near Eleusis

A decree of the Athenian people passed in 422/1 BC provided for the building of a bridge over the Rhetos stream: it was important for the priestesses, carrying the sacred objects, the hiera, to be able to cross in safety. 'The ruins of the ancient temple' refers to the destruction of the anaktoron by the Persians in 480 BC.

Prepis son of Eupheros was secretary. It was resolved by the boule and the people; (the tribe) Aigeis held the prytany, Prepis was secretary, Patrokles presided, Theaios proposed the motion: the Rhetos near the city is to be bridged using stones from Eleusis from the ruins of the ancient temple, which were left after use on the wall, so that the priestesses can carry the hiera most safely. They are to make the width five feet, so that wagons may not be driven across but those going to the rites can walk. They are to cover the streams of the Rhetos with stones in accordance with the specifications that Demomeles the architect draws up.

3.40 Herakleitos F14: The 'Unholy' Mysteries

The Christian writer Clement of Alexandria, here quoting the philosopher Herakleitos, was hostile to the Eleusinian initiates and other Greek religious groups. [Clement *Protreptikos* 22.]

Night-wanderers, magicians, Bacchants, Maenads, initiates: he threatens these with the things after death, he foretells for them the fire: for they are initiated in unholy manner in the mysteries customary amongst men.

3.41 Euripides *The Bacchai* 677–713, 723–747: The Maenads and Dionysos

Euripides in the *Bacchai* dealt with the myth of the introduction of maenadism to Greece in the city of Thebes. Dionysos (also known as Bromios and Iakchos) has himself come to the city and has made the Theban women frenzied — they have become maenads — so that they have fled to the hills to worship him. Pentheus, king of Thebes, rejects Dionysos' divinity, and a messenger reports to him the activities of the women, led by Pentheus' own mother and aunts. The messenger here relates that the rites were for women only, of all ages, and so not orgiastic, and describes their clothes and handling of tame snakes. The dismembering of wild animals described here was part of myth not actual ritual practice; for historical maenads in Phokis, see doc. 4.31.

Our grazing herds of cattle were just
Ascending to the hilltops, when the sun
Shed its beams to warm the earth.
I saw three bands (thiasoi) of female dancers,
One led by Autonoe, a second
By your mother Agaue, the third group by Ino.
All lay asleep, their bodies relaxed,
Some on their backs on fir branches,
Others with their heads on the ground and oak leaves,
Lying at random, decorously, not, as you maintain,
Drunk from the mixing bowl or the flute's playing,
Or in secret search of Aphrodite in the woods.
Your mother cried out, standing amidst
The bacchants, to rouse them from their sleep,
When she heard the lowing of the horned cattle.
They shook the deep sleep from their eyes,
And stood upright, wondrous to see in their decency,
Young women, and old, and girls still unmarried.
First they let down their hair to their shoulders,
While those whose fawn-skins had come unfastened
Retied them, the dappled skins being
Girdled with snakes that licked their cheeks.
Some in their arms held gazelles or wild wolf-cubs
Cradling them to give them the white milk
— Those young mothers with breasts full to bursting
Who had babies left behind. They crowned themselves
With garlands — ivy, oak and flowering bindweed.
One took and struck a thyrsos against a rock:
From there a dewy spring of water leapt forth.
Another stuck her fennel branch into the ground:
The god there brought forth a fountain of wine.
Those who desired to drink white milk

Dug in the earth with their fingertips
And milk streamed forth. From their ivy
Thyrsoi dripped streams of honey.
If you had been there to see it, the god whom you now disparage
You'd have approached with prayers.
723 At the appointed time,
They began to wave their thrysoi in Bacchic revelry,
Calling on Zeus' son Iakchos with a single voice
By the name Bromios. The whole mountain was equally possessed
And the wild beasts, and all was rapid motion.
Agaue's leaping brought her near to me
And I jumped up to seize her,
Leaving the thicket where I had hidden myself.
She cried out, 'My whirling hounds,
Men are hunting us! Follow me,
Follow with hands armed with thyrsoi!'
So we ran off, escaping
Being torn apart by the Bacchants, while they
Attacked grass-grazing cattle— but not with iron in hand!
You could have seen one with a fatted calf
Bellowing, tearing it apart with her hands;
Others tore heifers into pieces.
You'd have seen flanks and cloven hooves
Thrown here and there; hanging
From the fir trees were lumps of flesh dripping blood.
Bulls previously violent, with anger in their horns,
Were thrown to the ground
Dragged down by innumerable maidens' hands,
Their fleshy covering torn to pieces,
Quicker than you could blink your royal eyelids!

ASKLEPIOS THE HEALER

Sick individuals who consulted the healing deity Asklepios slept overnight in the abaton, an 'incubation' centre, and hoped that the god would appear to them in a dream and cure them, or prescribe a treatment. Consultation to Asklepios involved a preliminary sacrifice and the payment of a consultation fee. There were major Pan-Hellenic shrines to Asklepios (Asklepieia) at Epidauros, Kos in the Aegean and Pergamon in Asia Minor. Asklepios also had a shrine in the Piraeus and at the foot of the acropolis. Amphiaraos, a healing deity, had a sanctuary at Oropos, attracting the sick from both Boeotia and Attica.

3.42 *Inscriptiones Graecae* II^2 4960a: Asklepios is Introduced to Athens

Asklepios' popularity as a healing god spread throughout the fifth and fourth centuries BC. He was introduced to the Piraeus in the late 420s (Zea is a small harbour at the Piraeus) and from there to Athens, along with his sacred snake, in 420 BC. As well as his snake Asklepios also had sacred dogs, and the assistance of his daughter Hygieia (Health).

2 When the god came up from Zea at the time of the Great Mysteries he was taken to the Eleusinion **5** and having summoned his snake from his home he brought it hither in Telemachos' chariot. At the same time Hygieia arrived, **10** and in this way this whole sanctuary was established during the archonship of Astyphilos of Kydantidai (420 BC).

3.43 *Inscriptiones Graecae* IV^2 1, no. 121–22: Testimonia to Asklepios' Cult

The pilgrims who visited Epidauros left behind records of their cures as a thanksgiving; in the fourth century BC the priests at Epidauros gathered together the individual testimonia, the iamata and presumably also oral versions of cures, and had them inscribed on stone; some of these still survive. Some of the cures appear to be fantastic, but the cult at Epidauros functioned for nearly a millennium, and drew its clientele from all over the Greek world. No medical attention was available at the Asklepieia and the cult relied on autosuggestion and faith healing. A cure was an iama (pl.: iamata). [R&O 102.]

1 Kleo had been pregnant for five years. After she had been pregnant for five years she came as a suppliant to the god and slept in the abaton; as soon as she left it and was outside the sanctuary she bore a son, who as soon as he was born washed himself from the spring and walked about with his mother. In return for this she inscribed on her offering: 'The size of the tablet is not wonderful, but the god is, in that Kleo was pregnant with the burden for five years, until she slept in the temple and he made her healthy.' **4** Ambrosia of Athens blind in one eye. She came as a suppliant to the god. As she walked about in the sanctuary she laughed at some of the cures (iamata) as incredible and impossible, that the lame and blind should be made healthy just by seeing a dream. She slept and saw a vision: the god seemed to stand beside her and say that he would make her well, but that as payment he would require her to dedicate to the temple a silver pig as a memorial of her ignorance. When he had said this, he cut the diseased eyeball and poured in some drug. When day came, she left cured. **20** Lyson of Hermione a blind boy. While wide awake he had his eyes healed by one of the dogs of the temple and went away cured. **42** Nikasiboula of Messene slept (in the abaton) for the sake of offspring and saw a dream; it seemed to her that the god approached her with a snake creeping behind him, and that she had intercourse with it; and afterwards two sons were born to her within a year.

3.44 Aristophanes *Wealth* 659–671, 727–41: The God Wealth Is Healed by Asklepios

Aristophanes, in his play *Wealth*, gives a comic description of a night in an Asklepieion, where Ploutos, the god Wealth, is cured of blindness; here Karion, the slave of Chremylos, is reporting the success of Wealth's cure to Chremylos' wife. Ploutos first bathes in the sea (lines 656–58).

Karion: Then we went to the god's precinct.
And there on the altar our cakes and preparatory offerings
We dedicated, food for Hephaistos' flame,
And after putting Wealth to bed, in the proper way,
Each of us set our mattresses in order …
When he'd put out the lamps
And ordered us to go to sleep, the god's
Servant told us, if anyone heard a noise,

To be silent, so we all lay there in an orderly manner.
Karion: Then the god sat down beside Wealth;
First of all he examined his head,
Then taking a clean linen cloth
He wiped his eyelids; and Panacea
Covered his head with a purple cloth
And his whole face; the god then made a clucking noise
And two serpents rushed from the inner shrine —
They were absolutely enormous!
Wife: Dear gods!
Karion: They crept gently under the purple cloth
And appeared to lick his eyelids all round;
Before you could drink down ten cups of wine
Wealth was standing up, mistress, and could see!
I clapped my hands for joy
And woke up my master, and the god immediately
Disappeared, with the snakes, into the inner shrine.

HEROES

In the archaic and classical period, the discovery of Mycenaean and Dark Age tombs with warriors' bones and weapons led to the establishment of hero cults. The bones of Orestes and Theseus were 'discovered' and became the object of cults. Since power resided with the vestiges of the hero's mortality, the cult of a hero centred on those bones: the hero was a localised semi-divine figure. The heroes were chthonic deities, dwelling beneath the earth; other chthonic deities were Trophonios, who had an oracular centre at Lebadeia, and originally Asklepios.

3.45 Sophocles *Oedipus at Colonus* 1518–34: Oedipus Bequeaths His Bones to Athens

Heroes, with their bones in a particular locality, were thought of as tutelary (protective) deities. Oedipus here tells King Theseus that his grave will protect the Athenians and be a bulwark against the Thebans.

I will teach you, son of Aigeus, what
For this city will remain untouched by age.
I will myself straightway show you the place,
Without a guide's help, where I must die.
Never tell this to any man,
Either where it is hidden or whereabouts it lies;
And this will always serve for your defence
Better than many shields and the imported spear of neighbours.
But these mysteries, which may not be spoken of,
You will yourself learn, when you go there alone;
Since neither to any of your citizens might I reveal it
Nor to my own children, though I love them.

But you must always preserve it, and when to life's end
You come, only to your eldest son
Reveal it, while he should show it to his own successor.
And thus you will inhabit this city unmolested
By the men of Thebes.

3.46 Herodotos 1.67.2–68.6: The Bones of Orestes

An oracle helped the Spartans locate the bones of Orestes, son of Agamemnon. With his assistance, the Spartans were able to defeat the Tegeans. For the Spartan conflict with Tegea, and the Spartans' defeat in 560 BC, see doc. 6.55.

1.67.2 Because the Spartans were always being defeated in war by the men of Tegea, they sent consultants to Delphi to ask which god they should propitiate in order to be able to defeat the Tegeates in war. The Pythia gave them the response that they should bring home the bones of Orestes, son of Agamemnon. **3** Being unable to discover Orestes' tomb, they sent them again to consult the god and ask where the place was in which Orestes lay. The Pythia responded to the consultants in the following words:

> **4** 'On the level plain of Arkadia there is a place, Tegea,
> Where two winds blow continually through harsh necessity.
> Blow matches blow, and suffering lies upon suffering.
> There the life-giving earth holds the son of Agamemnon:
> Take him — and you will be master of Tegea.'

5 When the Spartans heard this they were no closer to finding what they were looking for, though they searched everywhere, until Lichas, one of the Spartiates known as 'Benefactors', finally found it … **1.68.1** Lichas discovered it at Tegea by a mixture of luck and cleverness. Sparta was on good terms with Tegea at the time, and when he went into a forge, he saw iron being worked and was amazed at seeing what was going on. **2** When the blacksmith saw that he was astonished, he stopped his work and said, 'Lakonian stranger, you are wondering at the forging of iron, but you would have marvelled far more if you had seen what I saw. **3** I wanted to construct a well in this courtyard, and as I dug I found a coffin seven cubits long. I couldn't believe that there had ever been men taller than those of today, so I opened it up and saw inside a corpse as long as the coffin. I then measured it and buried it back in the earth.' When the smith reported what he had seen, Lichas noted what he said and deduced from the oracular response that this must be Orestes, **4** arguing that the smith's two bellows he had seen must be the winds, the anvil and hammer the blow and counter-blow, and the worked iron the suffering lying upon suffering — he guessed this last because the discovery of iron has been detrimental to humankind. **5** After coming to this conclusion he returned to Sparta and told it all to the Spartans. They pretended to bring a charge against him and send him into exile, so he went to Tegea where he told the smith of his misfortune and tried to rent the courtyard from him. **6** The smith at first refused, but Lichas persuaded him in time, settled down there and opened the tomb and gathered the bones, which he then took to Sparta. Ever since this, the Spartans were far superior to the men of Tegea in all their engagements in war; indeed most of the Peloponnese was already under their control.

3.47 Pausanias *Description of Greece* 6.9.6–8: Kleomedes: The 'Last Hero'

Kleomedes was a mortal who died in 462 BC and was worshipped after death as a hero in order to placate his spirit.

6.9.6 At the Olympic festival before this (492 BC) they say that Kleomedes of Astypalaia while boxing with Ikkos of Epidauros killed him during the contest. When he was convicted of foul play by the umpires (hellanodikai) and deprived of his victory, he became mad through grief and returned to Astypalaia. There he attacked a school of some sixty children and overthrew the pillar which supported the roof. **7** The roof fell on the children, and he was stoned by the townsmen and took refuge in the sanctuary of Athena; he got into a chest standing in the sanctuary and pulled down the lid, and the Astypalaians laboured in vain in their efforts to open the chest. Finally they broke open the boards of the chest, but found no Kleomedes, either living or dead, so they sent men to Delphi to ask what had happened to Kleomedes. **8** They say that the Pythia gave them this response:

> 'Kleomedes of Astypalaia is the last of heroes:
> Honour him with sacrifices as he is no longer a mortal.'

So from this time the Astypalaians have paid honours to Kleomedes as a hero.

3.48 Pausanias *Description of Greece* 9.39.5–14: An Underground Hero-Shrine

Pausanias in the second century AD was himself a consultant of the oracle of the hero Trophonios at Lebadeia near Delphi. The ceremony would have been much the same in archaic and classical times. The method of consultation and the nature of the divination were very different from the oracular process at Delphi, and involved much more personal involvement – both physical and mental – than at Delphi; cf. doc. 3.21, where Kreousa's husband consults Trophonios before going to Delphi.

9.39.5 This is what happens at the oracle: when someone decides to descend to the oracle of Trophonios, he first stays for a certain number of days in a particular building, which is sacred to Good Spirit and Good Fortune. While he stays there, as well as observing other restrictions, he purifies himself by abstaining from hot baths, his bath being the river Herkyna. There is abundant meat from the sacrifices, for the people who descend sacrifice to Trophonios himself, and his children, as well as to Apollo, Kronos, Zeus named 'the King', to Hera the Charioteer and to Demeter whom they call Europa, saying that she was the nurse of Trophonios. **6** At each sacrifice a diviner is present who examines the entrails of the sacrificial victim and after the inspection prophesies to the person descending whether Trophonios is well disposed and will receive him propitiously. The entrails of the other sacrificial victims do not reveal the opinion of Trophonios so much, but on the night on which each person descends they sacrifice a ram over a pit, invoking the name of Agamedes. Even if the earlier sacrifices have appeared propitious no account is taken of them unless the entrails of this ram indicate the same; but if they concur then each person descends in high hopes, and makes his descent as follows. **7** Firstly he is taken at night to the river Herkyna, led by two boys of citizen parents who are about thirteen years of age, named Hermai, who anoint him with oil and wash him. It is these boys who wash the person descending and attend him in whatever ways are necessary. From there he is taken by the priests, not straight to the oracle but to springs of water, lying very close to each other. **8** Here he has to drink water which is called the water of Forgetfulness, so he may forget all the things he has been thinking of up to now, and then in turn drink another water, that of Memory, which makes him remember what he sees after his descent. He then views the statue which they say was made by Daidalos — it is not shown by the priests except to those going to consult Trophonios — and after seeing it, worshipping it, and praying, he proceeds to the oracle, wearing a linen tunic with ribbons around the waist and wearing locally made boots.

9 The oracle is beyond the grove, on the mountain. A circular surround of white marble encloses it, the circumference of the surround being the same as that of the smallest threshing-floor, while its height is rather less than two cubits. On the surround stand spikes, of bronze, as are the crossbars holding them together, through which has been made a double door. Inside this enclosure is a chasm in the earth, not natural but built skilfully and with very precise construction. **10** The shape of this structure is similar to that of a bread-oven; the breadth across the middle might be estimated as about four cubits, and the structure's depth, as far as one can guess, is no more than eight cubits. No way of descent to the bottom has been constructed, but when a person consults Trophonios they bring him a narrow, light ladder. When he has descended there is a gap between the floor and the structure; its breadth appears to be about two spans and its height one. **11** The person descending then lies down with his back on the floor holding barley-cakes kneaded with honey, and goes feet first into the gap, himself following and trying hard to get his knees through the opening. The rest of his body is immediately drawn in, just as the largest and swiftest river will catch a man in its eddy and draw him under. After this those who have entered the shrine learn the future, not always in the same way but sometimes by sight and at others by hearing. For those descending the return trip is through the same opening, their feet emerging first.

12 They say that no one who has made the descent has died, except for one of the bodyguards of Demetrios: they say, however, that he did not perform any of the customary rites in the sanctuary, and that he did not go down to consult the god, but in the hope of stealing gold and silver from the shrine. It is said that the man's corpse appeared in a different place and was not thrown out at the sacred mouth. Other accounts are given about this man, but I have related the most reliable. **13** After ascending from Trophonios, the priests then see to him, sitting him on the chair called Memory's, which stands not far from the shrine, and when he is seated ask him what he has seen and learned. After ascertaining this they then entrust him to his associates. These lift him and take him, overcome with terror and unconscious both of himself and his surroundings, to the house where he stayed earlier with Good Fortune and Good Spirit. Later, however, he will recover all his faculties no less than before and the ability to laugh will return to him. **14** I am not writing hearsay, but have myself consulted Trophonios and seen others do so. Those who descend into the shrine of Trophonios are required to write all that they have heard or seen on a tablet and make a dedication of it.

SANCTUARIES AND CULT REGULATIONS

Sanctuaries of the gods were often walled, to set them aside from the profane world of humans. There was usually a temple, with a cult statue of the god, and offerings made by grateful worshippers were housed here. There were often specific regulations for sanctuaries and they could not be used for sleeping unless they were dedicated to a healing god. The dress of worshippers was often subject to specific requirements, accommodation was confined to certain areas, sexual activity was restricted and the types of food which the worshippers could eat might also be prescribed; who was to have access to temples could also be restricted.

3.49 *LSCG Suppl.* 50: A Spring of the Nymphs at Delos

This inscription concerning the nymphs' sacred spring dates to the fifth century BC. The prohibition against dumping manure (presumably from sacrificial animals) was typical of Greek sanctuaries, and must have reflected a real problem.

Do not wash anything in the spring, or swim in the spring, or throw into the spring dung or anything else. Penalty: two sacred drachmas.

3.50 *Inscriptiones Graecae* I^3 977, 980, 982: Inscriptions from the Vari Cave near Athens

Archedamos of Thera was a nympholeptos, one 'seized by the nymphs'. In the fifth century he embellished a cave in Attica, near Vari, which can still be visited today. The interior has several wall reliefs as well as inscriptions, and Archedamos planted a garden for the nymphs, and built them a dancing floor. The entrails from sacrifices had to be washed out of the cave and the dung cleaned out. [*IG* I^2 784–85, 788–89; Hansen 321; *LSCG* 9.]

977A Archedamos of Thera planted (this) garden to the Nymphs.

977B Archedamos of Thera also built a dancing-floor for the dancing Nymphs.

980 Archedamos of Thera – raptured by Nymphs (the nympholeptos) – furnished the cave at the request of the Nymphs.

982 Wash the entrails outside and clean out the dung.

3.51 *LSCG Suppl.* 85: The Cult of Enyalios at Lindos on Rhodes

Enyalios was a war deity, probably to be equated with Ares; cf. doc. 9.40. Here all soldiers are to pay a tax to the cult and initially their general is made responsible for collecting the money to be paid from the soldiers. For the 'sixtieth' compare the one-sixtieth of the phoros (tribute) made over to Athena by the Athenians (doc. 12.28).

It was resolved by the boule and the people, Oi[...] presided, S[...] was secretary, Ag[ath]archos proposed the motion: those who make expeditions from Lindos either at public or at private expense should pay a sixtieth of their pay to E[nya]lios; the general is to exact the money and hand it over to the priest; and in future from the booty the individuals themselves are to hand it over to the priest; the priest is to give an account to the boule each year and is to hand (it) over to the incoming priest. The commissioners are to record both what the generals hold themselves and the rest, and those who make an expedition. A sacrifice to [Eny]alios is to be made by the prytaneis who are in office in the month of [Ar]ta[miti]on; they are to sacrifice to Enyalios a boar, a dog and a goat.

3.52 Xenophon *Anabasis* 5.3.7–13: Xenophon's Shrine near Sparta

The state built elaborate sanctuaries and costly temples to the gods. Private individuals also did so, but not on the same scale. Xenophon was at this point, after returning from Cyrus' ill-fated expedition and afterwards serving with the Spartans in Asia Minor, in exile from Athens and living as a 'colonist' of Sparta. He used his booty from the Asian campaign to buy and develop this idyllic estate.

5.3.7 While Xenophon was in exile and living at Skillous near Olympia, where the Spartans had placed him as a colonist, Megabyzos came to attend the festival at Olympia and gave Xenophon back the money he had left with him. On receiving it, Xenophon bought a piece of land for the goddess where the god (Apollo) instructed. **8** It happened that a river, Selinous, flowed through the estate, and at Ephesos a river Selinous also flows past the temple of Artemis. There are fish and mussels in both of them, and in the precinct at Skillous there are all kinds of wild beast that are hunted. **9** Here Xenophon erected an altar and temple with the sacred money, and from then on always took a tithe of the seasonal produce of the land and sacrificed this to the goddess, with all the citizens and neighbouring men and women camping and participating in the festival. The goddess provided the participants with barley, bread, wine and dried fruits, as well as a portion of the sacrificial victims from the sacred herd and of the animals killed in the hunt. **10** Xenophon's sons and the sons of the other citizens used to go hunting during the festival and any men who wished could join in with them: they caught their game partly from the sacred precinct itself and partly from Mount Pholoe — boars, gazelles and stags.

11 The place lies on the road which leads from Sparta to Olympia and is some twenty stades from the temple of Zeus at Olympia. In the sacred precinct there is meadowland and hills filled with trees, suitable for the raising of pigs, goats, cattle and horses, so that even the draught animals belonging to the people who attend the festival have a banquet of their own. **12** Surrounding the temple is a grove of cultivated trees which produce all kinds of seasonal fruits. The temple itself resembles that at Ephesos, though is small rather than large, and the image of the goddess is like that at Ephesos, though of cypress wood rather than gold. **13** A stele with the following inscription stands beside the temple: 'The place is sacred to Artemis. He who possesses it and enjoys its fruits must give a tithe each year in sacrifice, and from the rest must keep the temple in repair, and if anyone fails to do this it will be a matter for the goddess.'

DEATH AND FUNERARY PRACTICES

The dead were cremated or inhumed; cremation was the most popular form of burial at Athens in the last quarter of the fifth century BC. The ashes and bones from the funeral pyre were placed in an urn, which was then buried. The psyche, spirit or soul, was believed to exist after death, as a miserable shadow in Hades, or alternatively, if the person had been initiated into the Eleusinian Mysteries, a happy existence awaited it.

3.53 Homer *Odyssey* 11.473–505: Odysseus Visits the Underworld

The view of the afterlife represented in this passage was widely held, and it was to escape this that individuals were initiated into the Eleusinian Mysteries. If the mysteries had a Mycenaean origin, it is probable that the two versions of the afterlife had always existed side by side. The Homeric afterlife was more suited to the heroic lifestyle of the warrior chieftains of the *Iliad*: as Hades had nothing to offer, it was important to live gloriously and achieve immortality through heroic exploits. Odysseus has consulted the dead by a special ritual which does not appear to have classical counterparts, digging a pit, pouring libations of milk and honey, wine and water, sprinkling barley-meal and cutting the throats of the victims so their blood flowed into the pit (Homer *Odyssey* 11.23–36). The blood draws the dead, and when they drink it they remember their past life and can speak. The dead hero Achilles is speaking here.

'Son of Laertes, ordained by Zeus, Odysseus of many devices,
Dauntless one, what still greater deed can you devise in your heart?
How have you dared to come down to Hades, where the dead
Dwell without their wits, the shadows of outworn mortals?'
So he spoke, and I answered him in reply,
'Achilles, son of Peleus, bravest of the Achaeans,
I came in need of Teiresias, in case he might give me
Counsel how I might arrive at rocky Ithaka;
For I have not yet come near Achaea, nor set foot on
My island, but have always met with evils; but you, Achilles,
No man was ever more fortunate than you or ever will be.
For before, when you were alive, we honoured you like the gods,
We Argives, and now again you are a great ruler of the dead
Down here; you should not grieve at being dead, Achilles.'
This I spoke, and he immediately said in answer,
'Do not praise death to me, noble Odysseus.
I would rather be a serf (thes) labouring for someone else,
Even for a landless man, who had no livelihood,
Than be king over all the departed dead.'
And there I saw Minos, glorious son of Zeus,
Holding a golden sceptre, giving judgement to the dead,
Seated there; and those around put their cases to the king
Sitting and standing throughout Hades of the wide gates.
And after him I saw mighty Orion
Hunting wide beasts through a meadow of asphodel,
The same ones he had slain on the lonely mountains,
Holding in his hands an all-bronze club, always unbroken.
And I saw Tityos, the son of well-renowned Earth,
Lying on the ground; he lay over nine acres,
And two vultures, one on each side of him, plucked at his liver,
Digging their beaks inside; and he could not ward them off with his hands;

For he had done violence to Leto, glorious consort of Zeus,
As she was travelling to Delphi through Panopeus of the beautiful dancing grounds.

3.54 Sophocles *Antigone* 426–31: Antigone Buries Her Brother

After Oedipus, Antigone's father, died, bequeathing his body to Athens (doc. 3.45), her two brothers killed each other fighting for the kingship of Thebes. Kreon, Antigone's uncle, has decreed that Polyneikes, the invader and traitor, should remain unburied. Antigone, however, buries her brother's corpse and is caught by the guard; for her justification for breaking the laws in order to do this, see doc. 4.69. The guard who has captured Antigone in the act is speaking here.

Thus she, when she saw the body bare,
Cried out in lamentation, invoking
Dreadful curses on those who did the deed.
Straightway in her hands she carried thirsty dust,
And from a well-wrought brazen ewer
Honoured the corpse with threefold libations.

3.55 Aeschylus *Libation Bearers* 87–93: Prayers and Libations to the Dead

Electra is here at the tomb of her father Agamemnon, who had been murdered by his wife Clytemnestra on his return from Troy; see docs 3.17, 4.68.

How am I to pour these funeral libations?
How can I speak auspiciously? How am I to pray to my father?
Shall I say that I bring this to her dear husband,
From a loving wife? — from my mother!
Or shall I say this, as is mankind's custom,
Give back equal blessings on those who send these
Wreaths — a return worthy of their crimes!

3.56 *Inscriptiones Graecae* I^3 1179 II: The Dead at Potidaea, 432 BC

Potidaea was one of the conflicts immediately prior to the outbreak of the Peloponnesian War; the city revolted from Athens in 432 BC and was reduced two years later; this epitaph honours the Athenians who died in this campaign. [*IG* I^2 945 II; Clairmont 1.174–77; Hansen 10.]

Aether has received their souls and earth their bodies;
They died at the gates of Potidaea;
Some of their enemies have the grave as their portion, others fleeing
Put the wall as their truest hope of life.

3.57 *LSCG* 97A: Funerary Rites on Keos

This funerary law from Iulis on the island of Keos, dating to the second half of the fifth century, is sumptuary in nature (limiting ostentation at the funeral), and also has an the emphasis on the avoidance of pollution for the participants. [*SIG*^{3} 1218.]

These are the laws concerning the dead; bury the dead person as follows: in three white cloths, a spread, a garment, and a coverlet — there may be less — worth not more than 300 drachmas. Carry out the corpse on a wedge-footed bed and do not cover him completely with the cloths. Bring not more than three choes of wine to the tomb and not more than one chous of olive oil, and bring back the vessels. Carry the dead man, covered over, up to the tomb in silence. Perform the preliminary sacrifice according to ancestral custom. Bring the bed and its coverings from the tomb indoors. On the following day a freeman should first sprinkle the house with seawater, then wash it with water having scattered it with earth; when it has been sprinkled throughout, the house is purified and sacrifices should be made on the hearth. The women who go to the funeral are to leave the tomb before the men. Do not carry out the rites performed on the thirtieth day in honour of the deceased. Do not put a cup (kylix) under the bed, do not pour out the water, and do not bring the sweepings to the tomb. Whenever someone dies, when he is carried out, no women should go to the house other than those polluted (by the death). The mother and wife and sisters and daughters are polluted, and in addition to these not more than five women, children of the daughters and of the cousins, no one else. Those polluted after being washed from head to foot are to be purified with a pouring of water.

3.58 Plato *Republic* 614b–615c: Plato's 'Myth of Er'

Plato here outlines his doctrine of the immortality of the soul: after spending 1,000 years in the underworld the souls get to choose a new life on earth and are reincarnated, the good choosing to pursue righteousness and be 'dear to the gods' (621c). For Alkinoos, see Homer *Odyssey* 6.12; see also Plat. *Gorg.* 524a and *Phaed.* 107d, where souls are said to be judged after death.

614b 'I shall not tell you,' I said, 'the tale told to Alkinoos, but that of a valiant man, Er, the son of Armenios, a Pamphylian by race. Once upon a time he was slain in battle and when the bodies were taken up, already decayed, on the tenth day, he was found to be healthy, and, after he was taken home, during his funeral on the twelfth day he revived as he lay on the funeral pyre. After coming back to life he recounted what he said he had seen in the other world. He related that, after his soul had left his body, he journeyed with many others, **614c** and they arrived at a mysterious place where there were two chasms side by side in the earth and, above these, two others in the heaven, with judges sitting between these chasms. When they had given judgement, they told the just to journey to the right and upwards through the heaven, with signs attached to them in front indicating the judgement that had been made on them, while the unjust were to journey to the left and downwards, wearing tokens on their backs of all they had done. **614d** As he approached, they told him that he was to be the messenger to humankind, to tell them of that other world, and they instructed him to listen closely and observe everything in that place. And he said that here he saw through each chasm in heaven and earth souls departing after judgement had been passed on them, while through the other chasms there ascended from the one in the earth souls that were full of squalor and dust, and from the other there descended from heaven souls that were spotless. **614e** And as they kept arriving they seemed to have come from a long journey, so to speak, and happily went off to the meadow and encamped as if at a festival, where friends greeted each other. Those who ascended from the earth asked the others about the state of things up there, and those from heaven about what it had been like for those below. So they recounted their tales to each other, one group lamenting and weeping **615a** as they called to mind how many awful sufferings and sights they had met with during their journey under the earth — the journey lasted a thousand years — while those from heaven related their pleasures and visions of unimaginable beauty.

To give the whole story, Glaukon, would take a very long time; but the chief point, he said, was this: for all the wrongs which they had done to anyone, and for each individual they had wronged they had been punished ten times for each one, and this was measured in periods of a hundred years at a time, **615b** so that, taking this as the length of human life, the punishment had to be ten times the wrongdoing. So, for example, if people had caused many deaths, or betrayed cities or armies and had them enslaved, or had taken part in any other crime, they would receive in return tenfold sufferings for each, while those who had done good and been just and holy, **615c** were rewarded on the same principle.

WOMEN AND THEIR RELIGIOUS ROLE

Although excluded from the political life of the polis, women played a vital role in its religious life. Female deities usually had priestesses and numerous cults were under the jurisdiction of women; the most important priesthood in all of Greece was arguably that held by the Pythia. Priests and priestesses were responsible for the administration of sanctuaries and temples, purificatory rituals and the overseeing of sacrifices, and, generally, for the guardianship of the sanctuary's treasures; for these duties they were entitled to a share of the sacrifices.

3.59 Herodotos 6.134.1–135.3: Miltiades and Sacrilege on Paros

Following his triumph at Marathon, the Athenians granted Miltiades the Younger a fleet of seventy ships with which he attacked Paros, but unsuccessfully. In this episode he met with an accident, and returned home. Herodotos' account does not make clear exactly what Timo's advice to Miltiades was, but there are overtones of sacrilege in this incident. Demeter's title here is Demeter Thesmophoros: for the Thesmophoria, see doc. 3.64.

6.134.1 What I have so far narrated is what all the Greeks say happened, but from here on the account is that of the Parians themselves: as Miltiades was getting nowhere one of the prisoners, a Parian woman whose name was Timo, an under-priestess of the chthonic deities, approached him. When she saw Miltiades she counselled him, if he really wanted to take Paros, to do what she suggested. **2** After she had given him her advice, Miltiades went to the hill in front of the city and jumped over the fence around the sanctuary of Demeter Thesmophoros (the lawgiver) as he was unable to open the doors. After jumping over he went towards the shrine (megaron) to do something inside, whether to disturb in some way the things which ought not to be touched or something else; but when he got to the doors he was immediately overcome by terror and went back the way he had come, but in leaping down the wall he sprained his thigh. Some people say he struck his knee. **6.135.1** Miltiades was in a bad way as he sailed back to Athens, and he was returning without money for the Athenians and without having succeeded in taking Paros, having just besieged it for twenty-six days and ravaged the island. **2** When the Parians learned that Timo, the under-priestess of the goddesses, had instigated Miltiades' actions, they wanted to punish her for this, and sent messengers to Delphi as soon as they were free of the siege; they sent to inquire if they could put the priestess of the goddesses to death for giving information to the enemy which might have led to her country's capture and for revealing to Miltiades mysteries that ought not to be divulged to the male sex. **3** But the Pythia did not allow this, and said that Timo was not guilty of these offences, but it had been necessary for Miltiades to come to a bad end, and Timo had only put in an appearance to bring about his misfortunes.

3.60 Thucydides 2.2.1, 4.133.2–3: Chrysis, Priestess of Hera at Argos

Another priestess of importance was Chrysis, who served Hera for fifty-six and a half years at Argos. Thucydides uses her (together with the ephorate at Sparta and the archonship at Athens) to date the Theban entry into Plataea and the outbreak of war in 431 BC.

2.2.1 The thirty years' truce which was signed after the capture of Euboea remained in force for fourteen years; but in the fifteenth year (431 BC), which was the forty-eighth year of the priestess-ship of Chrysis at Argos, when Ainesias was ephor at Sparta and Pythodoros still had two months to go as archon at Athens, six months after the battle of Potidaea, at the beginning of spring, rather more than 300 Thebans (commanded by the boeotarchs Pythangelos, son of Phyleidas, and Diemporos, son of Onetorides) came armed at about the first watch of the night and entered Plataea in Boeotia, an ally of Athens … **4.133.2** Also in the same summer (423 BC) the temple of Hera at Argos burned down, after Chrysis the priestess had placed a lighted lamp near the garlands and then fallen asleep, which resulted in her not noticing that they had caught fire and were blazing. **3** Chrysis, afraid of the Argives, immediately fled by night to Phleious; and they appointed another priestess named Phaeinis according to the established procedure. Chrysis, at the time of her flight, had been in office for eight years of the war and half of the ninth.

3.61 Aristophanes *Lysistrata* 638–51: An Athenian Girl's Service to the State

Here a chorus of well-born Athenian women list their religious activities in which they have participated in the past, which include having been an arrhephoros (pl.: arrhephoroi), a bear at the Brauronia and a kanephoros at the Panathenaia (see docs 9.30–31). The arrhephoroi were young girls, seven to eleven years of age, who worked on the peplos (robe) for Athena which was carried in procession at the Panathenaia, and had other cult duties on the acropolis. They were also involved in the Arrhephoria: doc. 3.62. Certain Athenian girls served as arktoi, bears, at the sanctuary of Artemis at Brauron. A kanephoros carried a ritual basket in a festival procession. The Brauronia festival was celebrated every four years. A chorus of old women is speaking here.

For we, all you citizens, have been trying to give advice
Useful to the city;
Naturally, since it reared me splendidly in luxury.
As soon as I was seven years of age
I carried the symbols of Athena Polias;
Then when I was ten years old
I ground the corn for Artemis;
And then I was a bear at the Brauronia,
Wearing the saffron-coloured robe;

And as a beautiful girl I was a basket-carrier with a necklace of dried figs.
Do I not then owe it to the city to give it some good advice?
Even if I am a woman, do not begrudge me this,
If I introduce something better than the present state of affairs.
For I have a share in the contribution — I contribute men.

3.62 Pausanias *Description of Greece* 1.27.3: The Arrhephoria

Pausanias describes the ritual of the arrhephoria at Athens. The ritual was obviously in place in the fifth century as it is mentioned by Aristophanes (doc. 3.61; cf. 1.30).

1.27.3 I was very surprised at a ritual that took place there, which is not widely known, and so I shall describe it. Two girls live not far from the temple of Athena Polias, and the Athenians call them the arrhephoroi. They live for a time with the goddess, but when the festival comes round they carry out the following ritual at night. The priestess of Athena gives them objects to carry which they place on their heads, with neither the giver nor the bearers having any knowledge of what these are. Not far away, within the city, there is a precinct belonging to the goddess called Aphrodite in the Gardens, with a natural underground passage through it: by this the girls descend. They leave down there the objects they are carrying, and receive something else wrapped up which they bring back. The girls are then released from their duties and other girls are taken to the acropolis in their place.

3.63 Menander *Samia* 35–49: The Festival of Adonis

Moschion as a young man seduced a young girl, Plangon, during the celebration of the women's festival of the Adonia, which was held at his house. At Athens the Adonia took place in the spring in honour of Aphrodite's lover Adonis, who had been killed by a boar while a young man. As part of the rites, women sowed lettuce seeds in shallow flowerpots which they placed on their rooftops, the quickly withering plants being thought to symbolise Adonis' short life.

The girl's mother got on splendidly
With my father's Samian girlfriend, who
Spent much of her time with them, and
They with us. When I rushed in from the farm,
By chance I found them gathered in our house here
To celebrate the Adonia, with a number
Of other women too. The rites
Were a lot of fun, as you'd expect, and as I was there
(Unfortunately!) I watched what went on – I couldn't get to sleep
Because of the racket they were making.
They were carting their 'gardens' up to the roof,
Dancing, and having an all-night party.
I shrink from telling what happened next, perhaps ashamed
Without any need, but still ashamed —
The girl got pregnant!

3.64 Aristophanes *Thesmophoriazousai* 76–85, 623–33: A Male View of the Thesmophoria

The Thesmophoria was celebrated in honour of Demeter and Kore (Persephone) and was observed throughout Greece in autumn. In this passage Mnesilochos takes part in disguise to defend Euripides, whose 'slander' of women is a stock joke in Aristophanes (cf. *Frogs* 1050–51), as is their love of alcohol. Kleisthenes was notoriously effeminate, and is here shown on the side of the women.

Euripides: This very day it will be decided
Whether Euripides is to live or die!
Mnesilochos: How can it? The courts aren't going to be judging
Today, nor is the boule sitting.
80 After all, it's the second and middle day of the
Thesmophoria!
Euripides: It's this that I think is going to put an end to me.
The women have been plotting against me,
And today at the Thesmophoria they'll be holding
84 An assembly to plan my destruction!
Mnesilochos: What for?
Euripides: Because I write plays and say bad things about them.
Kleisthenes: Have you ever been up here before?
Mnesilochos: Of course!
624 Every year!
Kleisthenes: Who's your tent-mate?
Mnesilochos: Oh, what's-her-name.
Kleisthenes: That's no answer!
Woman (to Kleisthenes): Go away. I will question her properly
About last year's rites; you stand aside,
For, as a man, you may not hear. You there, tell me
629 Which of the rites was the first shown to us?
Mnesilochos: Well now, what did come first? We drank!
Woman: And what did we do after that?
Mnesilochos: We drank each other's health!
Woman: You heard that from someone! What came third?
Mnesilochos: Xenylla asked for a basin, as there wasn't a
chamberpot.

MYRRHINE, PRIESTESS OF ATHENA NIKE

Three inscriptions testify to the life and importance of Myrrhine, a priestess of Athena Nike; Myrrhine means myrtle-branch, or myrtle-wreath, an appropriate name for a priestess. The inscription appointing her as priestess was found on the acropolis; on the reverse side of the stele a further inscription dated to 424/3 (doc. 3.66) authorised payment of her salary. The priestess was appointed by lot from all Athenian women, so it was not an office confined to aristocratic families, unlike many of the traditional priestly offices; her epitaph, which proudly proclaims her status, shows that the incumbent served for life.

3.65 *Inscriptiones Graecae* I³ 35: The Appointment of the Priestess of Athena Nike

This inscription records the appointment of a priestess for Athena Nike and the provision for her of an annual salary of fifty drachmas (equal to 100 days' jury-pay for a citizen) and perquisites from the sacrifices. Kallikrates was one of the period's most famous architects. [Meiggs & Lewis 44; *IG* I² 24.]

(The tribe) Leontis held the prytany. It was resolved by the boule and the people: … presided, Glaukos proposed the motion: for Athena Nike a priestess, who is to be chosen by lot from all Athenian women, shall be appointed, and the sanctuary is to be furnished with doors in accordance with the specifications which Kallikrates draws up. The poletai are to let out the contract in the prytany of Leontis. The priestess is to be paid fifty drachmas and receive the legs and hides from public sacrifices. A temple shall be built, in accordance with the specifications Kallikrates draws up, and a stone altar. Hestiaios proposed the amendment: three men are to be chosen from the boule. These are to draw up the specifications with Kallikrates and indicate to the boule the way in which the contract will be let out …

3.66 *Inscriptiones Graecae* I³ 36: Payment of the Priestess of Athena Nike

1 It was resolved by the boule and the people: (the tribe) Aigeis held the prytany, Neokleides was secretary, Hagnodemos presided, Kallias proposed the motion: **5** to the priestess of Athena Nike the fifty drachmas which were written on the stele shall be paid by the kolakretai, **9** who are in office in the month of Thargelion, to the priestess of Athena Nike.

3.67 *SEG* 12.80: Epitaph for Myrrhine, Priestess of Athena Nike

This epitaph found on Mount Hymettos is dated to around 405 BC.

This far-seen tomb is that of the daughter of Kallimachos,
Who was the first to tend the temple of Nike;
Her name shared in her good fame, for by divine
Fortune she was called Myrrhine. Truly
She was the first who tended the statue of Athena Nike
Chosen by lot out of everyone, Myrrhine, by good fortune.

PERSONAL PIETY

3.68 Xenophanes of Kolophon *Poem* B1: Libations to the Gods at a Symposium

Xenophanes here describes his idea of the perfect, pious, dinner party.

For now the floor is clean and everyone's hands
And the wine-cups; one (boy) puts woven garlands on our heads,
Another offers fragrant unguent in a bowl (phiale);
The mixing-bowl stands full of cheer;

And another wine, which says it will never run dry,
Gentle and smelling of flowers, is ready in the wine-jars;
In the middle frankincense gives off its sacred odour,
And there is water, cold, sweet and pure;
Yellow loaves and a table of honour carrying cheese and rich honey are at hand;
And the altar in the middle is completely covered with flowers,
And singing and festivity fill the house.
First cheerful men should celebrate the god in hymns
With auspicious speech and pure words,
And they should make libation and pray for the power to do
What is righteous; and they should drink as much as will allow them
To arrive home without a servant, unless they are very old.
And one should praise the man who displays good qualities after drinking,
For having memory and energy in praising virtue,
Not conducting the battles of the Titans and Giants,
Nor the Centaurs, fictions of older days,
Nor of violent discords; there is nothing good in these:
What is good is always to have consideration towards the gods.

3.69 Friedländer 126: A Family from Sybaris Rescued off Lindos

A wooden group of cow and calf from the temple of Athena at Lindos on Rhodes, probably of the sixth century BC, was dedicated and inscribed by Amphinomos and his sons. When Diagoras of Melos (see doc. 3.32), an atheist who mocked the Eleusinian Mysteries, was on Samothrace and a friend pointed out the votive paintings, he retorted that those who perished at sea did not have the opportunity to dedicate pictures (Cicero *Nature of the Gods* 89).

Amphinomos and his sons from spacious Sybaris,
When their ship was saved, dedicated this tithe.

3.70 *Inscriptiones Graecae* 1^3 1014: Kalliteles' Descendants Replace His Dedication

A marble herm from Daphni in Attica; cf. doc. 7.12, Kallimachos' vowed offering was set up after his death. [Hansen 313; *IG* I^2 834.]

Previously Kalliteles made the dedication; this one
His descendants have set up, and to them make return.

3.71 Friedländer 143: Akeratos: A Leading Thasian

From Thasos, c. 500 BC, a base of local marble; cf. docs 2.25–27 for Paros' colonisation of Thasos.

Akeratos dedicated me to Herakles; he amongst the Thasians
And Parians was the only person who was archon of both.
He went on many missions for his city from nation to nation
Of men, because of his everlasting excellence.

3.72 Theophrastos *Characters* 16: The Superstitious Man

Theophrastos, writing in Athens in the late fourth century BC, here describes some of the characteristics of a superstitious man. Weasels were unlucky. The pareia, 'cheek' snake, was sacred to Asklepios. Just as Nikias was 'rather too inclined to divination' (doc. 3.24), some Athenians were too inclined to see the gods at work in even trivial matters.

16.1 The superstitious man is the type **2** who when he sees a crow washes his hands, has to sprinkle himself with water from a shrine, put a piece of laurel in his mouth and walk around like that all day. **3** If a weasel crosses his path he won't go any further until someone goes between them or he chucks three stones across the road. **4** And if he spots a snake in his house, he calls on Sabazios (if it is a reddish-brown cheek snake), but if it's a sacred snake he straightaway establishes a hero shrine on the spot. **5** When he goes past the oily stones at the crossroads he pours oil from his flask all over them, falls on his knees and prostrates himself before going on. **6** If a mouse gnaws a hole in a sack of barley, he goes to the diviner to ask what he has to do, and if the reply is to give it to the leather-worker to be sewn up he takes no notice but runs off and makes an expiatory sacrifice.

7 He tends to purify his house often, maintaining that Hekate has put a spell on it. **8** If owls hoot as he walks by, he panics and exclaims "Athena is mightier!" before going on. **9** He won't step on a grave, or visit a corpse or a woman in childbed, saying that it's better for him not to incur pollution.

10 On the fourth and seventh days of the month, he tells his household to boil wine and goes out to buy myrtle, frankincense and sacrificial cakes and comes back home to spend all day putting garlands on the hermaphrodites.

11 Whenever he has a dream, he goes to the dream interpreters, the prophets and the omen-diviners to ask which god or goddess he should pray to. Every month he goes with his wife to the Orphic initiators to be initiated, and, if she has not the time, takes his children and their nurse. **12** When people are meticulously sprinkling themselves at the sea, he makes sure he is seen there. **13** If he spots someone wreathed with garlic at the crossroads, he goes away to wash himself from his head down, summons priestesses, and orders a full-scale purification by squill or dog. **14** If he sees a madman or epileptic, he shudders and spits into his own chest.

SOCRATES AND THE 'NEW ATHEISM'

By the mid-fifth century Athens had become the acknowledged leader of Greece in intellectual matters and attracted a number of philosophers and sophists, who were a professional group who made a living as itinerant teachers, especially of rhetoric, the technique of winning over opinion in the assembly and courts. Since religion was both the cornerstone of morality and 'good order' and an integral part of the life and tradition of the city-state, the widespread questioning of traditional concepts of religion and conventional beliefs naturally provoked a dramatic reaction. The irony of Socrates' condemnation to death is that he was certainly not an atheist, though comic poets such as Aristophanes attribute such beliefs to him: in fact he was deeply religious and always listened to his personal daimonion (doc. 3.85). Nor was he a sophist: while his Socratic technique of questioning his interlocutors may well have upset people in Athens, he was utterly opposed to the sophists' priorities and teachings. Trials for impiety were a way of attacking those who did not entirely fit into Athenian society: such as Aspasia, Protagoras, Anaxagoras, Diagoras, the sculptor Pheidias and Phryne.

3.73 Empedokles of Akragas F117: Reincarnation

Empedokles wrote in the mid-fifth century BC, and his work *On Nature* provides a physical explanation of the universe (based on the belief that there were four eternally distinct substances, fire, air, water and earth). His belief in reincarnation, as given below, was often satirised; cf. doc. 3.58 for Plato's Myth of Er.

For already I have been born as a boy and a girl
And a bush and a bird and a dumb fish leaping out of the sea.

3.74 Empedokles of Akragas F134: 'Mind' as God

For Empedokles, 'God' was not anthropomorphic in character but an intellectual entity.

For he does not have the head of a man on the trunk of a body, nor do two branches shoot from his back, nor does he have feet, nor swift knees, nor any hairy genitalia, but he is Mind, sacred and beyond even a god's power to articulate, only Itself, rushing through the entire cosmos with Its swift thoughts.

3.75 Epicharmos F64: 'I Am Not a Corpse but a God'

Epicharmos of Syracuse (writing about 500-475 BC) wrote comedies in which he included philosophical comments. The following was supposedly his own epitaph.

I am a corpse. A corpse is excrement, and excrement is earth. If earth is a god, I am not a corpse but a god.

3.76 Anaxagoras F12: Anaxagoras of Klazomenai

Anaxagoras began his philosophical activity in Athens in 456/5 BC and remained there for twenty-seven years; Perikles and Euripides were among his pupils. His scientific speculations led to his being prosecuted for impiety and he died at Lampsakos.

12 For Mind is the finest of all things and the purest, and has all knowledge about everything and has the greatest power; and Mind controls everything, all things that have life, both the greater and the lesser. Mind also controlled the whole rotation, so that it began to rotate in the beginning. And at first it began to rotate from some small point, but now it rotates over a greater area, and it will rotate over a greater area still. And the things which are mixed together and separated off and divided are all known by Mind. And whatever was going to be and whatever that was then but is not now, and whatever is now and whatever will be, Mind arranged all of them, including this rotation in which now the stars rotate and the sun and the moon, and the air and the aether which are being separated off.

3.77 Diogenes Laertius *Lives of Eminent Philosophers* 9.51–2: Book-Burning in Athens

The Greeks believed in the gods and only a few, generally philosophers, were agnostics or atheists. Protagoras of Abdera, 490-420 BC, travelled throughout Greece and visited Athens on a number of occasions. According to Plato *Prot.* 317b, he had been the first to call himself a sophist and take fees for teaching. His most famous saying was that 'Man is the measure of all things'.

9.51 Protagoras was the first to assert that there are two sides to every question, which contradict each other; he used to develop arguments in this fashion and was the first to do so. He began one of his works with the following words: 'Man is the measure of all things, of things that are that they are, and of things that are not that they are not.' He used to say that the soul had no existence apart from the senses, as Plato states in the *Theatetos* (152a), and that everything is true. Another work he began with the words: 'Regarding the gods, I have no way of knowing whether they exist or whether they do not. There are many hindrances to knowledge — the obscurity of the topic and the brevity of human life.' **52** As a result of this book's introduction he was exiled by the Athenians, and they burned his books in the marketplace, after sending a herald to collect them from all the people who possessed a copy.

3.78 Antiphon F44: Nature versus Law

Antiphon, a fifth-century Athenian sophist, recommended a way of life capable of banishing misery and argued that nature (physis) should be followed rather than law (nomos); cf. Ar. *Clouds* 1075–78.

So justice is not transgressing the legal usages of the city in which one is a citizen. Accordingly, a man can best conduct himself in accordance with justice, if he upholds the great laws in the company of witnesses, and when alone without witnesses the dictates of nature; for the dictates of the laws are accidental, but those of nature compulsory; and the dictates of the laws are agreed by consent not by natural evolution, while those of nature have evolved naturally and have not been agreed upon. So if a man who transgresses legal usages does so unnoticed by those who have agreed on them he avoids both disgrace and punishment; otherwise he does not; but if someone violates against all possibility any of those laws implanted by nature, even if he does so unnoticed by all mankind, the evil is no less, and even if all see, it is no greater; for he is not harmed because of an opinion but because of truth.

3.79 Xenophon *Memorabilia* 1.6.1–3, 6.10: A Sophist's View of Socrates

Socrates was born in Athens in 469, the son of Sophroniskos, a stonemason or sculptor, and Phainarete, a midwife; Socrates believed that virtue was knowledge, and that no one does wrong willingly, for vice is only due to ignorance. Socrates was well known for wearing the same cloak summer and winter, and for going barefoot, for which he was satirised in the comic poets (see Ar. *Clouds* 103, 363; cf. *Birds* 1282).

1.6.1 Antiphon approached Socrates with the intention of taking his companions away from him, and in their presence spoke as follows: **2** 'Socrates, I always thought that philosophers ought to become happier people; but you seem to me to have derived the opposite from philosophy. At all events, you live in such a way that not even a slave under a master would be able to endure; your food and drink are of the poorest kind, and you not only wear a poor cloak, but wear the same one summer and winter, and always go barefoot and without a tunic. **3** Besides you won't take money, which gladdens its receivers and makes those who possess it live more freely and pleasantly. The teachers of other occupations try to make their students imitate themselves, but, if you are disposed to make your companions do that, you must think yourself a teacher of misery.' ... **10** 'You seem to think, Antiphon, that happiness comprises luxury and extravagance; but my view is that wanting nothing is divine, and to want as little as possible comes closest to the divine, and as that which is divine is supreme, that which approaches nearest to the divine is nearest to the supreme.'

3.80 Aristophanes *Clouds* 365–73: Socrates and the 'New Religion'

Aristophanes in his play *Clouds* made fun of Socrates and sophists. Socrates is here portrayed attempting to educate the ignorant old Strepsiades, who wants to learn the new rhetoric so he can win lawsuits and not pay back his debts. In this play Aristophanes is attributing to Socrates a number of beliefs and practices which actually belonged to sophists, such as Protagoras, and Presocratic philosophers, such as Anaxagoras and Diogenes of Apollonia. For Socrates' 'teaching' in the *Clouds*, see also doc. 3.82.

Socrates: The Clouds are the only goddesses, all the others are just nonsense.
Strepsiades: But Zeus! Come on now, doesn't the Olympian god exist?
Socrates: Who's Zeus? You're talking rubbish, there is no Zeus.
Strepsiades: What do you mean?
Who rains then? Tell me that first of all.
Socrates: Why, they do; and I can teach you this with clear proofs.
Come on, have you ever seen it raining without Clouds?
Yet he should be able to rain from a clear sky, when these are out of town.
Strepsiades: By Apollo! You've confirmed this by your argument;
Yet I really thought before that Zeus was pissing through a sieve!

3.81 Plato *Symposium* 219e–220d: Alkibiades' View of Socrates

Socrates took part in the Athenian campaign at Potidaea, which revolted from Athens in 432, and his endurance of hardship there became proverbial. Alkibiades is speaking at a symposium, for which see doc. 4.88. The quotation at 220c is from Homer *Odyssey* 2.242.

219e It was after this that we served together in the campaign against Potidaea and were mess-mates there. First of all he surpassed not only me but everyone else in his endurance of hardships; whenever we were cut off somewhere, as happens in campaigns, and had to go without food, **220a** the rest of us were nowhere near him in terms of endurance. And again when we had plenty of supplies no one enjoyed them more than he, and, though unwilling to drink, when forced to he outdid everyone, and most surprising of all — no human being has ever seen Socrates drunk. You will see the proof of this shortly if I'm not wrong. But it was in his endurance of winter — and the winters there are terrible — **220b** that he performed remarkable feats, including one occasion when there was a tremendous frost and everyone either stayed inside or, if any of us did go out, wrapped themselves up in a most remarkable way, and tied and swathed their feet in felt and sheepskin. But Socrates went out in those conditions with the short cloak he normally wore, and walked more easily over the ice barefoot than the rest of us did with shoes on. The soldiers viewed him with suspicion, for they thought he was looking down on them.

220c So much for that episode; and 'the next exploit that this high-enduring hero dared' one day while on service there is well worth hearing. A problem occurred to him at dawn and he stood still on the spot to think it through. When he couldn't find a solution he didn't give up but stood there considering it. By the time it was midday the men began to notice him and said to each other in amazement that Socrates had been standing there in deep thought since dawn. Finally in the evening some of the Ionians finished dinner and — **220d** it was summer this time — brought out their bedding and rested in the cool, while keeping an eye on him to see if he would stand there all night as well. He stayed standing there until dawn came and the sun rose, then prayed to the sun and walked off.

3.82 Aristophanes *Clouds* 218–48: The Socrates of the *Clouds*

Socrates was made fun of not only by Aristophanes in the *Clouds*, first performed in 423 BC, but by other comic poets as well. The portrayal of Socrates here is a conflation of the views of various contemporary thinkers. Clearly his behaviour was seen as unconventional, and therefore suspect.

Strepsiades: Tell me, who is this man hanging from the hook?
Student: It's him.
Strepsiades: Who's him?
Student: Socrates.
Strepsiades: Socrates! Could you give him a shout for me?
Student: You call him yourself! I haven't got the time.
Strepsiades: Socrates!
My dear little Socrates!
Socrates: Why do you call me, mortal creature?
Strepsiades: First, I entreat you, tell me what you're doing up there.
Socrates: I walk on air and contemplate the sun.
Strepsiades: If you want to be contemptuous of the gods, why do you do it
From a basket, and not from ground level?
Socrates: I would never discover the truth of astronomical phenomena
If I did not suspend my mind and combine
My fine thought with the air itself.
If I were on the ground and looked upward from below,
I would discover nothing; for the earth forcibly

Draws to itself the moisture from thought
In exactly the same way as happens with watercress.

Strepsiades: What?
Thought draws moisture into watercress?
Do come down to me, my dear Socrates,
And teach me what I've come for.

Socrates: What have you come for?

Strepsiades: I want to learn to be a good speaker.
Because interest rates and hard-hearted creditors
Are laying me waste, and my goods are being seized for debt.

Socrates: How did you manage to get into debt without noticing it?

Strepsiades: A horsey disease — terrible at devouring people! — has destroyed me.
But teach me the one of your two arguments,
Which never pays its debts. Whatever fee
You charge, I swear to you by the gods I'll pay it!

Socrates: What gods are you swearing by? The first thing to learn
Is that gods are not current coin with us.

3.83 Xenophon *Memorabilia* 1.2.39–46: Alkibiades Practises the Socratic Method on Perikles

Socrates' aim was to elicit definitions from his interlocutors, particularly of terms relating to ethical ideas such as justice, arete (virtue) and courage. Unfortunately many were angered by his conversational and dialectical abilities. Alkibiades was Perikles' nephew: Perikles' first wife (with whom he was unhappy) was perhaps Alkibiades' mother Deinomache, Perikles' cousin; Alkibiades grew up in Perikles' household.

1.2.39 While Kritias and Alkibiades were Socrates' associates they were out of sympathy with him for the whole of that time, and right from the very beginning what they were aiming at was leadership of the city. For even while they were Socrates' companions they tried to converse not with others, but mainly with leading politicians. **40** It is actually reported that Alkibiades, before he was twenty years of age, held the following conversation about the laws with Perikles, his guardian, and the city's champion. **41** 'Tell me, Perikles,' he asked, 'could you teach me what a law is?' 'Why, certainly,' replied Perikles. 'Then please teach me,' said Alkibiades. 'For whenever I hear men being commended for observing the laws, I think that no one can justly obtain this praise without knowing what a law is.' **42** 'Well, Alkibiades,' said Perikles, 'there is nothing very difficult about what you want, in your wish to understand what a law is; laws are all those things which the assembled people have approved and enacted, through which they declare what ought and ought not to be done.' 'Is this the case whether they think it right to do good or evil?' 'Good, of course, young man, but not evil.' **43** 'But if, as happens under an oligarchy, not the majority but a minority meet and enact what ought to be done, what's this?' 'All that, after deliberation, the sovereign power in the city ordains ought to be done, is called a law.' 'And if a tyrant controls the city and enacts what the citizens ought to do, is this also a law?' 'Yes, whatever a tyrant as ruler ordains is also called a law.' **44** 'But what is force, or the negation of law, Perikles? Isn't it when the stronger without persuasion forcibly compels the weaker to do whatever he chooses?' 'Yes, that is my view,' replied Perikles. 'Then whatever a tyrant enacts and compels the citizens to do without persuasion is the negation of law?' 'I believe so,' replied Perikles, 'and I withdraw my statement that whatever a tyrant enacts without persuasion is a law.' **45** 'And whatever the minority enacts, without persuading the majority but by using its power, should we call that force, or not?' 'Everything, I think,' replied Perikles, 'that a person compels someone else to do without persuasion, whether by enactment or not, is force rather than law.' 'So whatever the whole people enacts without persuasion, by using its power over the possessors of property, would be force rather than law?' **46** 'Alkibiades,' said Perikles, 'when we were your age we used to be very clever at these sorts of things too; for the sorts of things we studied and exercised our skill on then, are exactly the same as those that you seem to like practising now.' 'Perikles,' answered Alkibiades, 'I only wish I'd known you when you were really good at such debates!'

3.84 Plato *Apology* 20e–21a: Socrates and the Delphic Oracle

The Delphic oracle had confirmed that Socrates was wiser than anyone else, but as Socrates goes on to explain (*Apol.* 23a–b), the oracle's meaning was that Socrates' highly limited form of wisdom is the most that human beings can accomplish, and real wisdom is the prerogative of God. Socrates explains his habit of questioning others as his attempt to prove the oracle wrong.

20e Gentlemen, please do not interrupt me if I seem to be making an arrogant claim, for what I'm going to say is not my opinion; I'm going to bring forward an unimpeachable source. For as witness to my wisdom, such as it is, I am going to call the god at Delphi. Of course you know Chairephon. He was a friend of mine from boyhood **21a** and a friend to democracy and took part in your recent expulsion and restoration. You know what Chairephon was like, how impetuous he was over anything he had started. Well on one occasion he actually went to Delphi and dared to ask the oracle — as I said earlier gentlemen, please don't interrupt — whether there was anyone wiser than myself. And the Pythia replied that there was no one wiser. And as he is dead, his brother will give evidence about this.

3.85 Plato *Apology* 31c–32d: Socrates and his 'Daimonion'

Socrates was accused in 399 BC and brought to trial for refusing to recognise the gods of the state, and introducing new divinities, apparently his daimonion, his 'inner voice' that advised him; he was also said to be guilty of corrupting the youth. The *Apology* is the speech he made in his defence as presented by Plato. For his refusal to convict the generals, see doc. 1.20.

31c Perhaps it may seem to be strange that I should go around giving advice like this and taking an interest in private affairs, but not dare publicly to address your assembly and give counsel to the city. The reason for this is what you have heard me mention on many previous occasions, that I am subject to a divine and supernatural experience (daimonion), **31d** which Meletos made fun of in his indictment. It started in my childhood, a sort of voice, which when it comes always stops me from doing something that I was going to do, and never encourages me. This is what opposes my taking part in politics ... **32a** Gentlemen, I have never held any office in the city, except for being a member of the boule; **32b** and it happened that my tribe Antiochis was holding the prytany when you decided to judge en masse the ten generals who had not picked up the survivors in the sea battle, illegally, as you all realised later. On that occasion I was the only one of the prytaneis who opposed your acting against the laws, and voted in opposition; and while the orators were ready to inform against me and arrest me, with you ordering and clamouring for them to do so, **32c** I thought I ought to run the risk on the side of law and justice rather than support you in your unjust decision through fear of prison or death. This happened while the city was still a democracy; and when the oligarchy came to power (in 404 BC), the Thirty in their turn summoned me and four others to the tholos and ordered us to escort from Salamis Leon of Salamis for his execution, and they issued many similar orders to a number of other people, wishing to implicate as many people as possible in their crimes. On that occasion I, however, **32d** showed again not by words but by deeds that death was no concern at all to me, if that is not too strong an expression, but that I was entirely concerned not to do anything unjust or impious. That government, though it was so powerful, did not terrify me into doing anything unjust, but, when we left the tholos, the other four went to Salamis and arrested Leon, and I went off home. And I would probably have been executed for this, if the government hadn't shortly afterwards been overthrown.

3.86 Plato *Apology* 36b–e: Not a Potion, but a Pension

After the prosecution had proposed the death penalty, it was up to Socrates to propose a counter-penalty that the jury would accept. Socrates' eventual suggestion of a fine of a mina, guaranteed by his friends, who included Plato and Krito (38b), was reasonable. Socrates' statement that he deserved maintenance in the prytaneion was recognisably ironic and intended to remind the jurors of Xenophanes B2 (doc. 1.78).

36b So Meletos wants the death penalty. All right; what penalty shall I propose to you as an alternative, gentlemen? Clearly it must be deserved; so, what penalty do I deserve to suffer or what fine, in view of the fact that I have not led a quiet life, but have ignored what most people care for — making money, a comfortable family life, rank as a general or public speaker, other official positions, and political clubs and factions which are features of our city, considering myself **36c** to be too honest in reality to survive if I went in for such things, and so instead of going into something which was going to be of no benefit to either myself or you, I went to each of you in private to do you, as I think, the great possible service. I tried to persuade each of you not to care for his own interests before his own well-being, how he might become as virtuous and wise as possible, and not to care for the interests of the city before the city itself, and in all other concerns in the same way — **36d** so what do I deserve for behaving in this way? Some reward, gentlemen, if I have to propose what in truth I deserve; and also a reward which would be suitable for myself. Well, what suits a poor man who has benefited the city and who needs leisure for giving you exhortation? There is nothing more appropriate for such a person, gentlemen, than maintenance in the prytaneion, which is far more appropriate in fact for me than for any of you who has won at the Olympics with a horse or pair or team; such a person makes you seem to be successful, but I really do, and he does not need the maintenance, whereas I do. **36e** So if I have to propose a penalty in accordance with justice, I propose this, maintenance in the prytaneion.

3.87 Plato *Phaedo* 59d–60a: Socrates Dismisses Xanthippe

Socrates was condemned to death by drinking hemlock. While the sacred embassy sent to Delos was away, no executions could take place in Athens. Socrates has made his friends wait outside while he bids farewell to Xanthippe and his son.

59d We assembled earlier than usual on that occasion; for on the previous day, when we left the prison in the evening, **59e** we learned that the boat from Delos had arrived. So we encouraged each other to meet at the usual place as early as possible. When we arrived, and the porter who was accustomed to answer the door came out to us, he told us to wait and not to go in until he told us. 'The Eleven are releasing Socrates from his chains,' he said, 'and informing him that he is to die today.' After waiting a short while he came and told us to go on in. So we entered and found Socrates just released, **60a** and Xanthippe, you know her, holding his little boy and sitting beside him. When Xanthippe saw us, she wailed and made the sort of remark you'd expect from a woman: 'Socrates, this is the last time you and your friends will be able to talk together!' Socrates looked at Krito and said, 'Krito, let someone take her home.' And so some of Krito's servants led her away lamenting and beating her breast.

3.88 Plato *Phaedo* 117a–118: A 'Cock for Asklepios'

Socrates refused to allow his friends to arrange for his escape from prison (Plat. *Krito*, esp. 44b–46a), and he upbraided them for lamenting his impending death. The debt of the cock for Asklepios does seem to relate to the current situation, as if Socrates wants Asklepios thanked for release (through death) from the chilling effects of the hemlock.

117a Krito, after hearing this, made a sign to his servant who was standing nearby. The slave went out and after a considerable time came back with the man who was to administer the poison, carrying it already pounded up in a cup. When Socrates saw the man he asked, 'Well, my good fellow, you're the expert in these matters, what do I have to do?' 'Only drink it and walk around,' he replied, 'until your legs feel heavy, and then lie down; **117b** it will then act on its own.' As he said this he handed the cup to Socrates. Socrates took it quite cheerfully, Echekrates, without a tremor or change of colour or countenance, but looked up at the man with his usual bull-like gaze and said, 'What do you say about pouring a libation from this drink? Is it allowed or not?' 'We only make up, Socrates,' he replied, 'just as much as we think is a sufficient dose.' **117c** 'I see,' he said. 'But I suppose that I am allowed, and indeed ought, to pray to the gods that my migration from this world to the next might be prosperous. So this is my prayer and may it be granted.' As he said this he held his breath and drank it down calmly and with no sign of distaste. Most of us had up to this time been able to hold back our tears, but when we saw that he was drinking and then had actually drunk it, we were able to no longer, but my tears despite myself flooded forth, and I covered my face and mourned my loss — not for him, but for my own fate in losing such a friend. **117d** Even before me Krito had gone out because he wasn't able to restrain his tears. And Apollodoros, who even previously hadn't stopped crying, now roared aloud weeping and grieving so violently that he caused everyone present to break down except Socrates himself. 'Really, my friends,' he said, 'what an extraordinary way to behave! That was my main reason for sending the women away, so they wouldn't offend like this,

117e for I have heard that one ought to die in auspicious silence. Calm yourselves and be brave.' His words made us ashamed of ourselves and we restrained our tears. Socrates walked around and then said that his legs were feeling heavy and lay down on his back — that was what the man told him to do. This man, who was the one who had given him the poison, kept his hand on Socrates and after a little while examined his feet and legs, and then gave his foot a hard pinch and asked if he could feel anything, and Socrates said no. **118** He then did the same to the calves of both his legs, and moving upwards like this showed us that Socrates was becoming cold and numb. He then felt him again and said that when it reached his heart Socrates would be dead. The coldness was already nearly as far as his abdomen, when Socrates, who had covered his face, uncovered it and said (these were his last words), 'Krito, we ought to offer a cock to Asklepios; pay the debt, and don't forget it.' 'It shall be done,' said Krito. 'Is there anything else?' Socrates made no reply to the question, but after a little while he stirred and when the man uncovered him his eyes were fixed. When Krito saw this, he closed his mouth and eyes. This was the end, Echekrates, of our friend, who was, we might say, of all the people we knew of that time, not only the best, but in general the most discerning and upright.

3.89 Xenophon *Memorabilia* 4.8.11: Xenophon Remembers Socrates

Xenophon, like many aristocratic youths, was an associate of Socrates and wrote an account of his trial. Here, as elsewhere, he stresses Socrates' piety.

All those who knew what kind of man Socrates was pursue virtue and continue to this day to miss him above all others, as the greatest help in the search for virtue. For my own part I have described him as he was: so religious that he never did anything without seeking guidance from the gods, so honourable that he never did the smallest harm to any person, but gave the greatest assistance to all who had dealings with him, so self-disciplined that he never chose what was pleasant before what was right, so wise that he never erred in judging good and bad and had no need of advice from anyone else, relying on himself for his knowledge of them, and so competent at explaining and defining such parameters and at convicting others of their mistakes and turning them to virtue and noble conduct. This is how he appeared to me — exactly what a truly good and happy man should be. And if anyone disagrees with this, let him set the character of others beside his, and then judge.

THE GREEKS AND THEIR IDENTITY

3.90 Herodotos 3.38.1–4: Religious Differences across Cultures

Cambyses, the 'mad' Persian king who conquered Egypt and supposedly laughed at both religion and custom, came to the throne in 530 BC. The Greeks burned their dead, and the Persians, worshippers of Ahura Mazda (doc. 11.2), exposed theirs to be eaten by birds. Here Herodotos presents an open view on funerary practices and demonstrates the way the Greeks defined themselves in terms of their religious beliefs.

3.38.1 If someone were to propose to all humankind that they should select the best customs out of all those in existence, after consideration each would choose his own: for everyone thinks that his own customs are by far the best ... **2** I will put forward one of the many pieces of evidence that all people have this attitude towards their customs. **3** When Darius was ruling he sent for the Greeks at his court and asked them what money they would take to eat their fathers' corpses; they said they would not do so for any money. **4** Darius then sent for those Indians who are called Kallatiai, who eat their parents, and asked them in the presence of the Greeks who could understand what they said through an interpreter, what amount of money they would take to use fire to burn their fathers when they died; they cried out that he should not speak such inauspicious words. This shows the power of custom, and I think Pindar was correct when he said that custom was king of all.

3.91 Herodotos 8.144.2: Religion as Part of the Greek Identity

When the Spartans heard that Mardonios had sent to the Athenians a proposal that they make terms with Persia, they sent envoys who were present when the Athenians gave their answer. This was the Athenians' reply.

8.144.2 There are many important reasons which prevent us from doing this, even if we so wished, the first and greatest being the burning and demolishing of the statues and temples of our gods, which we must avenge with all our power rather than making terms with the agent of their destruction. Furthermore there is the fact that we are all Greeks, sharing both the same blood and the same language, and we have the temples of our gods in common and our sacrifices and similar lifestyle, and it would not be right for the Athenians to betray all these.

4

WOMEN, SEXUALITY AND THE FAMILY

Within the framework of tribes (phylai) and clans (gene) Greek society was essentially based on the family, on the oikos (or household), which was composed of a combination of free people and slaves. The family was under the power of the head of the household, and it was a tightly bound unit with complex hierarchical relationships. The term oikos covered not only the members of the nuclear family, but the whole physical and economic unit, including property, slaves and land, and there was strict limitation of succession by inheritance, to be broken only under specific circumstances. The oikos was also a religious unit, which placed particular emphasis on maintaining the tombs of the family's ancestors. Apart from their membership of the family, all or most Athenian males were enrolled in the phratry, or brotherhood, of their father. Indeed before the reforms of Kleisthenes in 508/7 BC citizenship depended on membership of a phratry. After this, while phratry membership was not legally necessary, failure to be able to prove it was considered suspicious and those whose claims to citizenship were disputed regularly demonstrated their membership of a phratry as well as of a deme (cf. docs 10.7, 1.38–40).

As the oikos was both family and property unit, questions of property, inheritance and marriage were inextricably linked, and to a great extent the legislation concerning heiresses and marriage was primarily concerned with the preservation of the family property and the survival of the oikos (docs 4.49–51). Generally a man would marry when the property was divided on the death or retirement of his father, and establish his own oikos, and thirty or thirty-five appears to have been a normal age for a man to marry (doc. 4.105, cf. 4.9); prior to this age a man might have indulged in a homosexual relationship with a young boy (cf. docs 4.72–89; cf. 9.21, 9.30–31). Athenian law provided that sons succeeded their fathers unless disinherited and all sons had a share in the inheritance, which could result in the creation of small estates (doc. 4.9; cf. 4.18 for Sparta). But often when there were no sons, estates were left in the possession of epikleroi (sing.: epikleros); these were heiresses, daughters who had no brother, natural or adopted, and in their case both the estate and the daughter together could and should be jointly claimed by the nearest male relative in an order of strict precedence (docs 4.49–51, 5.63); doc. 4.53 demonstrates how complex families could become as a result.

The legislation of Perikles in 451/0 decreed that in Athens a man's parents both had to be citizens for him to be a citizen likewise (doc. 1.36, cf. 4.56), resulting in a need for Athenians to be able to prove legitimacy. This meant that adultery on the part of a wife could threaten the legitimacy and standing of all of her children. It also meant that any attempt to pass off a metic or concubine as a citizen woman could have the direst consequences, and hence the penalties for those involved were extremely severe (doc. 4.56). Sexual misconduct on the part of citizen women had always of course been considered highly reprehensible (doc. 4.50, cf. 4.54), and adultery was an offence not just against the husband but against the oikos generally. Not merely the need for chastity but patterns of work made a basic spatial division between men and women the norm: it was expected that women should live inside the house and see to the care of the house, children and servants, as well as contributing to the household's economy through their weaving (docs 4.63–64). Nevertheless, many women of the lower socio-economic class did work (docs 4.59–62), and women on the whole were not confined at home except by their domestic duties. Poets of the archaic period, such as Hesiod and Theognis, give a realistic picture of the influence and status of a wife and her position in the family and are worth careful consideration. They are often used as evidence for a misogynistic viewpoint (such as doc. 4.8), but even the satirical work of Semonides (doc. 4.13) highlights the importance of a wife's contribution to the home's prosperity and comfort; they certainly do not imply that women in this period were generally kept in total seclusion. Similarly documents on Spartan women, while they often present an idealised picture of Spartan society, do not suggest that Spartan women were anything but respected within their families and they appear to have enjoyed freedom relatively unknown elsewhere in the Greek world (docs 4.14–24).

Many women in Greece would of course have been involved in providing sexual services for men: hetairai were the most prestigious here, of whom many would have had a luxurious lifestyle, like Theodote, whose livelihood came from 'any friend she might make who wished to be generous' (doc. 4.96). Most, however, would have been slaves in brothels giving their services for perhaps as little as an obol: there was clearly plenty of choice in Athens, and no stigma in making use of such opportunities, even for slaves if they had the ready cash (docs 4.99–104).

Greek citizen men, in fact, expected to have a range of sexual opportunities continually available to them; the only one which was labelled as 'criminal' was that of attempting to seduce another citizen woman: slaves, prostitutes, hetairai and liaisons with young boys (their eromenoi) were perfectly suitable alternatives, and in certain societies, like Sparta and Thebes, such homoerotic relationships were formalised as in the 'Sacred Band' at Thebes (doc. 14.17). These other opportunities were actually considered, at least by comic poets, to be 'virtuous' inasmuch as they prevented young men from trying to seduce married women (doc. 4.103). In certain parts of the Greek world homoerotic relationships were considered normative, as at the Macedonian court (docs 14.54, 15.21). The lovers in the Theban Sacred Band fought together, bonded by their relationship, and were annihilated at the Battle of Chaironeia (doc. 14.17), and the same ethos existed at Sparta. Indeed elsewhere in Greek cities, especially amongst the more leisured classes, such relationships seem to have been a normal part of the rites of passage of an adolescent boy (doc. 4.78).

Much of the discussion concerning attitudes towards women in classical Athens has centred around the works of the tragedians. If heroines such as Clytemnestra, Antigone and Medea (docs 4.68–71) are considered to have been directly modelled on the women of fifth-century Athens, then clearly such women can hardly have been secluded or down-trodden. But these awesome protagonists were originally pre-classical mythological figures, presented in the context of traditional tales. What is important in these cases is not only the choice of the plots in themselves, but the ways in which the tragedians presented the story and the conflicts in which they chose to portray women. Valuable evidence is also provided by the works of Aristophanes, who wrote in great detail about women and their activities for the amusement of his audiences. To take his humour literally would be to misinterpret his point of attack greatly: his jokes cannot be taken as entirely representing Athenian men's views of their wives, with their emphasis on women's propensity to drink and sexual misdemeanours (cf. docs 3.64, 4.65). Rather, it shows that the Athenians were prepared, in comic productions, not only to poke fun at their wives (or *other people's* wives), but also to present on stage characters such as Lysistrata, whose views on society and politics are meant to be taken seriously by both actors and audience alike (doc. 4.66). As with sources for all social history, each piece of evidence regarding women and the family must be considered in its social and historical context. Nevertheless, while women were politically and legally disadvantaged vis-à-vis their menfolk, it would be rash to assume that for this reason they were considered by their society to be inferior and negligible members of their families and households.

SAPPHO OF LESBOS

The poet Sappho was a contemporary of Alcaeus and the tyrant Pittakos; born on Lesbos *c.* 620, she is said, like Alcaeus and his brother, to have spent some time in exile. Some forty-one of her poems survive; her main theme is love, and her poetry in general is written for a circle of aristocratic girls and women, although some of her work is intended for a wider audience.

4.1 Sappho 31: The Intensity of Passion

The scene is a dinner party, the circumstances of which are unspecified. There are no grounds for the traditional view that this is a wedding scene and the man in this poem the bridegroom, and that Sappho is describing her feelings for her favourite pupil, who is leaving her for a husband.

1 That man seems to me to be equal to the gods, who sits opposite you and listens close to you to your sweet voice
5 And your lovely laughter, which flutters my heart in my breast. For when I look at you for a moment, then I no longer have the power to speak,
9 But my tongue has broken, at once a subtle fire has stolen under my skin, with my eyes I see nothing, my ears hum,
13 A cold sweat pours over me, a trembling seizes me all over, I am paler than grass, to myself I seem to be little short of death.
17 But all must be endured, since †even a poor man† …

4.2 Sappho 16: 'Whatever One Loves'

Helen of Troy is here seen as an autonomous subject, not a passive object traded between men or under the compulsion of the goddess Aphrodite.

1 Some say a host of cavalry, others of infantry, and others of ships to be the most beautiful thing on the black earth, but I say it is whatever one loves.
5 It is very easy to make this understood by everyone, for she that far surpassed mankind in beauty, Helen, her husband, who was best of all,
9 Deserted and went sailing off to Troy, with no thought at all of her child or dear parents, but (Love) led her astray …
13 … (?she) has reminded me now of Anaktoria, who is no longer near;
17 I would rather see her lovely walk and the bright radiance of her face than the Lydians' chariots and fully armed infantry.

4.3 Sappho 55: To an Uneducated Woman

Pieria, just north of Olympus, was the home of the nine Muses. As with the Homeric afterlife fame equalled immortality.

1 When you have died, there you will lie, and there will be
Recollection of you nor †longing† ever after; for you have no share in the roses
3 From Pieria. But unseen in the house of Hades also,
 you will go to and fro among the shadowy corpses,
Flown from our midst.

4.4 Sappho 132: On Her Daughter

For Gyges of Lydia (c. 680–645) and his wealth, see doc. 7.1; Hdt. 1.8–14.

I have a beautiful daughter, who resembles golden flowers,
My darling Kleis, for whom I would not exchange all of Lydia† or lovely …

4.5 Anacreon 358: The Girl from Lesbos

According to Athenaeus *Deip.* 599c the following lines were said to be addressed to Sappho by the poet Anacreon.

Once again, with his purple ball
Golden-haired Love (Eros) has struck me
And now with the girl in embroidered sandals
He invites me to play;
But she, for she comes from Lesbos, a lovely place
To dwell in, finds fault
With my hair, for it is white,
And is entranced with some other — girl.

4.6 Praxilla 747: 'Hymn to Adonis'

There were a number of women poets whose work has not survived. Praxilla of Sicyon wrote in the mid-fifth century and was famous for her drinking songs. However, her reputation as a poetess was not always of the best and the expression 'sillier than Praxilla's Adonis' was used of foolish people. Adonis in mythology was a mortal beloved by Aphrodite, who was killed boar hunting. Here he is listing what he most misses from the world above.

The most beautiful thing that I leave behind is the light of the sun,
The next the shining stars and the face of the moon
And also ripe cucumbers and apples and pears.

EARLY MORALISERS AND MISOGYNISTS

Despite the overall tone of the works of the poets of the archaic period (Hesiod was writing *c.* 700 BC, Semonides in the mid-seventh century, Theognis perhaps 640–600, Hipponax *c.* 540) it is important to note the specific causes of complaint with which some of these early writers charged women (both Semonides and Hipponax, like Archilochos, were renowned for their abusive talents). It is significant that wives are seen as having a very great impact on a man's comfort and livelihood, and the 'misogynistic' works do not treat women as a negligible factor in their lives; certainly there is little, if any, concept of women being kept in seclusion.

4.7 Homer *Odyssey* 6.149–59, 178–85: Odysseus and Princess Nausikaa

Odysseus has here been shipwrecked on the coast of Phaeacia, and the first person he sees is the young princess Nausikaa, who has left the palace to wash clothes.

'Lady, I entreat you — but are you some god or mortal?
If you are one of the gods, who dwell in the broad sky,
It is Artemis, the daughter of great Zeus,
To whom I liken you most in appearance, size and stature.
But if you are one of the mortals, who live on the earth,
Thrice blessed are your father and lady mother,
And thrice blessed your brothers; their hearts
Must glow with pleasure for your sake,
When they see such a relative joining the dance.
But he will be by far the most blessed of all,
Who prevails with his wedding gifts and leads you to his home.
. . .
Show me the town, and give me a rag to wrap round myself,
If only a wrapper you brought here for your clothes.
And in return may the gods grant you all that you desire in your heart:
A husband and a home and the accompanying unity of mind and feeling,
Which is so desirable; for there is nothing nobler or better than this,
When two people, who think alike, keep house
As man and wife; causing great pain to their enemies,
And joy to their well-wishers; as they themselves know best.'

4.8 Hesiod *Works and Days* 57–82: Pandora

Pandora (the 'all-endowed') was given by Zeus to mankind in revenge for Prometheus' theft of fire. She removed the lid from a storage jar, thus allowing all the evils to escape; only Hope remained. Here Zeus is speaking.

'I will give them instead of fire an evil, in which all
May delight in their heart and lovingly embrace it, evil though it is.'
Thus spoke the father of gods and men and laughed out loud;
And he told renowned Hephaistos as quickly as possible
To mix earth with water, and place in it human voice
And strength, and liken it in face to the immortal goddesses
With the lovely and beauteous form of a maiden; and bade Athena
Teach her handiwork, to weave the intricate web;
And golden Aphrodite to shed grace on her head
And painful desire and cares that gnaw the limbs;
While to place in her a shameless mind and wily nature
He charged Hermes the messenger and slayer of Argos.
So he spoke, and they obeyed the lord Zeus, son of Kronos.
Immediately the renowned Lame God (Hephaistos) fashioned from earth
The likeness of a modest maiden through the counsels of the son of Kronos;

The goddess grey-eyed Athena girt and clothed her;
The divine Graces and august Persuasion
Put necklaces of gold around her skin; and the
Lovely-haired Hours crowned her with spring flowers;
And Pallas Athena equipped her with all kind of adornment.
In her breast the messenger, the Argos-slayer,
Contrived lies and crafty words and a wily nature
At the will of loud-thundering Zeus; and the herald of the gods
Put speech in her, and named this woman
Pandora, because each of those who dwell on Olympus
Gave her a gift, a bane to men who eat bread.'

4.9 Hesiod *Works and Days* 370–78, 695–705: Maxims for Prosperity

Hesiod in the *Works and Days* clearly distinguishes between wives whom men choose for themselves and women who are simply out for what they can get.

See that the wage promised to a friend can be relied on;
Even with your brother smile and get a witness;
†For trust† and mistrust together have ruined men.
Do not let a woman who decorates her buttocks deceive you,
By wily coaxing, for she is after your granary;
Whoever trusts a woman, trusts thieves.
There should be an only son to preserve his father's house;
For thus wealth will increase in the home;
He who leaves another son should die old.
In the prime of life bring a wife to your home,
When you are not much short of thirty,
Nor yet much above: this is the right age for marriage;
Your wife should be four years past puberty, and be married in the fifth.
You should marry a maiden, so you can teach her diligent habits,
And marry especially one who lives near you
Looking well about you, so your marriage is not a source of malignant joy to your neighbours.
For a man acquires nothing better than a wife —
A good one, but there is nothing more miserable than a bad one,
A parasite, who even if her husband is strong
Singes him without a torch and brings him to a raw old age.

4.10 Theognis 457–60: Youth and Age Do Not Mix

A young wife is not suitable for an elderly husband;
For she is a boat that does not obey the rudder,
Nor do anchors hold her; and she breaks her mooring cables
Often at night to find another harbour.

4.11 Theognis 1225–26: A Happy Man

Theognis is here writing to his eromenos (beloved) Kyrnos, urging him too to marry; for Kyrnos, see doc. 4.74.

Nothing, Kyrnos, is sweeter than a good wife;
I am a witness to the truth of this, and you should become so for me.

4.12 Hipponax 68: A Woman's Two Best Days

Hipponax of Ephesos was a master of abusive writing, and many of his works would have been intended for performance at popular festivals.

There are two days on which a woman is most pleasing —
When someone marries her and when he carries out her dead body.

4.13 Semonides of Amorgos 7: The Many Faces of Woman

Semonides in this humorous poem portrays women in ten different guises modelled on animals: all are distinctly uncomplimentary, except for the 'bee'. The main emphasis of the poem seems to be primarily on creature comforts within the household: note the complaint that it is impossible to entertain a dinner guest properly once you are married (cf. doc. 4.30). This poem was presumably for the entertainment of a male audience, perhaps at a symposium.

God made the female mind separately
In the beginning. One he made from a bristly sow,
And everything in her house mixed with mud
Lies in disorder and rolls around the floor;
While she unclean in unwashed garments
Sits on the dunghills and grows fat.
Another he made from a bitch, a quick runner, daughter of her own mother,
Who wants to hear and know everything,
And peers and wanders everywhere
Barking, even if she sees no human being.
A man cannot stop her with threats,
Not even if in anger he knocks out her teeth
With a stone, nor if he speaks to her gently;
Even when she is sitting amongst guests,
She continuously keeps up her incurable yapping.
Another is the child of a dainty long-maned mare,
Who diverts menial tasks and toil to others.
She will neither touch a mill or pick up a sieve,
Nor throw the dung out of the house,
Nor sit at the oven avoiding the soot.
She makes her husband acquainted with necessity;
Every day she washes the dirt off herself
Twice, sometimes thrice, and anoints herself with perfumes,

And always has her thick hair
Well combed and garlanded with flowers.
Such a wife is a fine sight
For other men, but proves an evil to the one she belongs to,
Unless he is a tyrant or king
Who takes pride in such things.
Another is from a monkey; and she is pre-eminently
The worst evil that Zeus has given to men.
Her face is hideous; such a woman
Makes everyone laugh when she goes through the town;
She is short in the neck; she moves with difficulty;
She has no bottom, and is skin and bone. Wretched is the husband
Who embraces such an evil.
She knows all arts and wiles
Just like a monkey; nor does she mind being laughed at;
She will not do anyone a good turn, but looks
And considers all day
How she can do the worst possible harm.
Another is from a bee; the man who gets her is fortunate;
For on her alone no blame settles,
And his livelihood flourishes and increases because of her,
And she grows old with a husband whom she loves and who loves her,
Bearing him a fine and well-reputed family.
She is pre-eminent among all the women,
And a godlike grace plays around her.
Nor does she take pleasure in sitting amongst the women
Where they tell stories about love.
Such wives of those granted to men
By Zeus are the best and the wisest.
Where there is a woman, a man cannot even in his house
Heartily entertain a guest who has arrived.
And she that seems to be most prudent,
Turns out to be the most outrageous;
And while her husband is agape for her, the neighbours
Rejoice seeing that he too is deceived.
Each man takes care to praise his own wife,
And find fault with his neighbour's;
We do not realise that the fate of all of us is alike.
For this is the greatest evil that Zeus has made,
Binding us with an unbreakable fetter,
From the time when Hades received those
Who went fighting for a woman's sake …

SPARTAN WOMEN AND FAMILIES

Other documents of interest on Spartan women include docs 6.15–16, 6.18, 6.71–72, 6.74.

4.14 Alcman 1: A Spartan Girls' Choir

Alcman was a Spartan poet (though he was later said to have come from Sardis: cf. doc. 6.79). From internal evidence his works can be dated to the later seventh and perhaps early sixth century, as he mentions the Eurypontid king Leotychidas (*c.* 625–600 BC). He was especially noted for his hymns written for girls' choirs (partheneia). In this passage, the girls appear to be offering a robe to the dawn goddess. Most of the names mentioned are those of the girls in the choir, led by Hagesichora and Agido, the 'Pleiades': Hagesichora means choir-leader, the role that she fills as 'choragos', while Ainesimbrota may be the trainer of the girls, or the mother of the four girls mentioned in lines 74–77, or a sorceress. The Spartan ideal of a marriageable girl is clearly different from that of the Athenian: one could not imagine a young Athenian girl being eulogistically described as a 'strong, thunderous-hoofed prize winner of winged dreams'. For possible lesbianism in Sparta, see Plut. *Lyk.* 18.9.

39 I sing of the light of Agido: I see her like the sun, which Agido calls to shine on us as our witness; but our illustrious choir-leader (Hagesichora) does not allow me either to praise her (Agido) or to criticize her; for Agido appears to be preeminent as if one were to set a horse among grazing beasts, a strong, thunderous-hoofed prizewinner of winged dreams.

50 Do you not see? The racehorse (Agido) is Venetic; but the hair of my cousin Hagesichora blooms like unmixed gold; and her silver face — why do I tell you distinctly? This is Hagesichora; and the second in appearance after Agido runs like a Kolaxaian (Scythian) horse against an Iberian; for as we carry a robe to the Dawn Goddess (Orthia) the Pleiades rise through the ambrosial night like the star Sirius and fight us.

64 For so much excess of purple is not enough to defend us, nor cunningly wrought serpent of solid gold, nor Lydian headband, adornment of dark-eyed girls, nor the hair of Nanno, nor even godlike Areta, or Thylakis and Kleesithera, nor will you go to Ainesimbrota's house and say, 'If only Astaphis were mine, and Philylla were to look at me, and Damareta and lovely Ianthemis'; but Hagesichora oppresses me (with passion).

78 For is not Hagesichora of the beautiful ankles present here, and near Agido ... does she not praise our festival? Gods, receive their ... (prayer); for fulfilment belongs to the gods. Choir-leader, if I might speak, I myself am a young girl (parthenos), like an owl, I screech in vain from the roof; and I especially desire to please Aotis (?Dawn), for she was the healer of our pains; but because of Hagesichora the girls set foot on lovely concord.

92 ... and in a ship too one must listen to the helmsman; and she (Hagesichora) is not more melodious than the Sirens, for they are goddesses, but she sings

like ten over against eleven girls; she sounds like a swan on the streams of the Xanthos; and with her lovely blond hair ... (4 lines are missing).

4.15 Anacreon 399: To 'Dress Like a Dorian'

Accounts of the dress worn by Spartan women, or the lack of it, are substantiated by this fragment of Anacreon; the Dorians were the racial group of whom the Spartans were the best-known representatives. Spartan girls were noted for their scanty clothing, their 'nakedness' in religious processions and athletics (which probably meant clad in only an undergarment, or chiton, such as the revealingly split mini-chiton (chitoniskos) worn by the Spartan runner on the cover of this book).

For women to 'dress like a Dorian' means to show themselves naked, as when Anacreon says:

'Take off your chiton and dress like a Dorian.'

4.16 Xenophon *Constitution of the Spartans* 1.3–8: The Upbringing of Spartan Girls

Xenophon appears to be giving a reasonably accurate picture, despite perhaps a certain degree of gullibility, of the traditions which in his view had made Sparta great. He gives a useful contrast of the Spartan upbringing of girls with that found in the rest of Greece. However, his account of Spartan dual households (including elderly men inviting youngsters into their house to sire children), while generally accepted, is at variance with Herodotos' account of Anaxandridas' double marriage (doc. 6.72), and, despite his account of bachelors siring children out of wedlock, Spartiates were expected to marry or else suffer penalties (doc. 6.16).

1.3 First, to begin at the beginning, I will start with the begetting of children. Elsewhere those girls who are going to have children and are considered to have been well brought up are nourished with the plainest diet which is practicable and the smallest amount of luxury food possible; wine is certainly not allowed them at all, or only if well diluted. Just as the majority of craftsmen are sedentary, the other Greeks expect their girls to sit quietly and work wool. But how can one expect girls brought up like this to give birth to healthy babies? **4** Lykourgos considered slave-girls quite adequate to produce clothing, and thought that for free women the most important job was to bear children. In the first place, therefore, he prescribed physical training for the female sex no less than for the male; and next, just as for men, he arranged competitions of racing and strength for women also, thinking that if both parents were strong their children would be more robust ... **6** In addition he put a stop to each man marrying when he wished, and laid down that men should marry when in their physical prime, thinking that this too would contribute to the production of fine children. **7** He saw, however, that if an old man had a young wife, such men particularly guarded their wives, and wanted to prevent this; so he arranged that the elderly husband should bring in any man whose physical and moral attributes he admired to produce children. **8** And if anyone did not want to live with a wife, but desired remarkable children, he made it legal for him to have children by any fertile woman of noble birth he might see, providing he first persuaded her husband.

4.17 Pausanias *Description of Greece* 3.8.1: Kyniska, Olympic Victor in 396 BC

Kyniska, daughter of the Spartan king Archidamos, won the chariot race at the Olympic games in 396 and 392 BC, and is evidence of the fact that Spartan women controlled a large proportion of Sparta's wealth as early as 396 (cf. doc. 4.18). Paus. 3.15.1 states that there was a heroon (hero-shrine) to her at Sparta and a statue of her by Apelles at Olympia.

Archidamos also had a daughter whose name was Kyniska, who was extremely ambitious of winning at the Olympic Games and was the first woman to breed chariot horses and the first to win an Olympic victory. After Kyniska Olympic victories were gained by other women, particularly from Sparta, but no one was more distinguished for their victories than she was.

4.18 Aristotle *Politics* 1269b39–1270a8, 1270a23–1270a31: Aristotle on Spartan Women

In this passage Aristotle discusses the lack of control exercised over Spartan women and the problems caused in Sparta by the failure to limit the size of inheritances and dowries. Aristotle was writing his *Politics* between *c.* 335 and 323 BC, though the discussion about Spartiate numbers below relates to Sparta's defeat at Leuktra in 371.

1269b39 Now, this licence of the women, from the earliest times, was to be expected. **1270a1** For the men were absent from home for long periods of time on military expeditions, fighting the war against the Argives and again against the Arkadians and Messenians; when they were at leisure they gave themselves over to the legislator already prepared by military life (in which there are many elements of virtue), while they say that Lykourgos attempted to bring the women under his laws, but they resisted and he gave up his attempt ... **1270a23** And nearly two-fifths of the whole country is in the hands of women, both because there have been numerous heiresses, and because large dowries are customary. And yet it would have been better to have regulated them, and given none at all or small or even moderate ones. But at present it is possible for a man to give an heiress to whomever he chooses, and, if he dies intestate, the person whom he leaves as his heir may give her to whomever he wishes. Accordingly, though the land was able to support 1,500 cavalry and 30,000 hoplites, the number fell below 1,000.

4.19 Plutarch *Life of Lykourgos* 14.1–8: 'The Only Women Who Bear Men'

For the accuracy of Plutarch's account, note doc. 6.1, where Plutarch admits that he is unable to provide accurate details of Lykourgos' life and times, but nevertheless writes a biography. His *Life of Lykourgos* is, however, well worth reading.

14.1 Since Lykourgos regarded education as the most important and finest duty of the legislator, he began at the earliest stage by looking at matters relating to marriages and births ... **3** For he exercised the girls' bodies with races and wrestling and discus and javelin throwing, so that the embryos formed in them would have a strong start in strong bodies and develop better, and they would undergo their pregnancies with vigour and would cope well and easily with childbirth. **4** He got rid of daintiness and sheltered upbringing and effeminacy of all kinds, by accustoming the girls no less than the young men to walking naked in processions, and dancing and singing at certain festivals, when young men were present and watching … **7** The nudity of the girls had nothing disgraceful in it, for modesty was present and immorality absent, but rather it made them accustomed to simplicity and enthusiastic as to physical fitness, and gave the female sex a taste of noble spirit, in as much as they too had a share in valour and ambition. **8** And so they came to speak and think in the way Leonidas' wife Gorgo is said to have done. For when some woman, who must have been a foreigner, said to her, 'You Lakonian women are the only ones who can rule men,' she replied, 'That is because we are the only ones who give birth to men.'

4.20 Plutarch *Life of Lykourgos* 25.8–9: The Mother of Brasidas

For Brasidas, who died in 422 BC, see docs 2.7, 13.20. Spartans were noted for their taciturnity and brevity of speech and Spartan women for their concept of honour and their willingness to see their sons die for Sparta.

25.8 Brasidas' mother, Argileonis, when some of the Amphipolitans came to Sparta and visited her, asked them if Brasidas had died nobly and in a manner worthy of Sparta. **9** When they extolled her son and said that Sparta had no one else like him, she said, 'Don't say that, strangers — Brasidas may have been noble and brave, but Sparta has many better men than he.'

4.21 Aristophanes *Lysistrata* 77–82: Lampito: A Typical Spartan Woman?

Lysistrata has called together the women of Athens to reveal her plans for making peace with Sparta, and with her friend Myrrhine is awaiting the arrival of women from other Greek cities.

Myrrhine: Here's Lampito approaching now.
Lysistrata: Dearest Lakonian! Welcome, Lampito!
How beautiful you appear, darling.
What lovely colour you have, what physical vigour!
Why, you could throttle a bull!
Lampito: I think I could, by the two goddesses.
For I keep in training and practise my buttock-jumps.

4.22 Pollux *Onomastikon* 4.102: Spartan Buttock-Jumps

'Bibasis' was a kind of Spartan dance, in which prizes were awarded not only to children but also to girls; one had to leap and touch the buttocks with one's feet, and the jumps were counted, hence the (anonymous) inscription in honour of one of these girls,

'Who once did a thousand at bibasis, the most ever done'.

4.23 Plutarch *Life of Lykourgos* 16.1–2: The Trials of a Spartan Baby

This passage seems at variance with the necessary qualifications for Spartiate status — completion of the agoge and ability to pay the mess contribution. Nevertheless it may well reflect Spartan attitudes in terms of eugenics, and Greek views generally, towards deformity in newborn children. Plutarch also relates that in Sparta babies were washed in wine to test whether they were epileptic, swaddling-clothes were not used, and children were not allowed to be fussy about their food or afraid of the dark; Spartan wet nurses were very much in demand elsewhere in Greece.

16.1 The father of a newborn baby did not have the power to decide whether to rear it, but carried it to a certain place called a meeting-place (lesche), where the eldest of his fellow tribesmen sat. They examined the infant, and if it was sturdy and robust, they told him to rear it, and allocated it one of the 9,000 lots of land. **2** But, if it was weak and deformed, they sent it off to the so-called Place of Exposure (Apothetai), a place like a pit by Mount Taygetos, considering it better for both the child itself and the city that what was not properly formed with a view to health and strength right from the very beginning should not live.

4.24 Plutarch *Life of Alkibiades* 23.7–9: Alkibiades and Queen Timaia

After his condemnation in absentia for profaning the Eleusinian Mysteries in 415, Alkibiades went to Sparta, where, according to Plutarch, he had an affair with Timaia, wife of the Eurypontid king Agis, while Agis was on campaign. There was presumably some truth in this account as Agis disowned Timaia's son Leotychidas, who was thought to be Alkibiades' child (though recognising him on his deathbed), and was succeeded by his brother Agesilaos (Plut. *Lys.* 22). This passage demonstrates the freedom of action which both Plutarch and Aristotle saw as possible for Spartan women, though the succession dispute in fact owed much to the intervention of Lysander.

23.7 While King Agis was away on campaign, Alkibiades seduced Timaia, Agis' wife, and as a result she became pregnant and did not attempt to deny it, giving birth to a male child who was called Leotychidas in public, while the name which was privately whispered by the mother to her friends and attendants was Alkibiades, so completely did love control the woman. **8** Alkibiades himself boasted that he had not done this as an insult, nor under the influence of desire, but so that his descendants might rule over the Spartans. Many people reported what had happened to Agis. **9** But it was the time factor which convinced him, because, frightened by an earthquake which took place, he had run from his wife's chamber, and had then not had intercourse with her for ten months, at the end of which period Leotychidas was born, whom he therefore refused to accept as his child. And because of this Leotychidas was later deprived of the kingship.

THE 'HISTORICAL' WOMAN

It is unwise to take literally any perceptions of society even when depicted by a contemporary author. The well-known passage in the Funeral Oration delivered by Perikles, and its brief comment on the duties of women who have lost their husbands, has to be taken in the context both of the funeral speech as a whole and of the aims and message of Perikles (as perceived by Thucydides) in delivering it at this point (doc. 4.27).

4.25 Herodotos 8.87.1–88.3 : Artemisia Strikes Again

Artemisia was tyrant of Herodotos' own city, Halikarnassos, and thus a Greek and ruler of Greeks, the power having passed into her hands on the death of her husband. She sailed with Xerxes' fleet, even though she had a grown-up son, furnishing five ships of war. She was the only one of his commanders who advised Xerxes not to fight at sea (Hdt. 7.99.1–3; 8.68.1–69.2) and the Greeks set a special reward of 10,000 drachmas for her capture (8.93.1–2).

8.87.1 The following actions of Artemisia increased her reputation with the King even more. **2** When the King's side had reached a stage of total disorder, Artemisia's vessel was at that point being pursued by an Athenian ship; as she was unable to escape it (for in front of her there were other friendly ships, and hers happened to be the nearest to the enemy), she decided to act as follows, and this turned out to be much to her advantage; while she was pursued by the Athenian ship, she drove straight at one of her own side's vessels, one from Kalynda, which was carrying the Kalyndian king Damasithymos. **3** Whether she had had some quarrel with him while they were still in the Hellespont I cannot say, nor if she did this deliberately, or whether the Kalyndian ship just happened to be in the way by chance. **4** Anyway she rammed and sank it, and was lucky enough to gain a twofold advantage by so doing; for when the trierarch of the Athenian ship saw her ramming one of the barbarians' ships, he thought that Artemisia's ship was a Greek one or was deserting from the barbarians and fighting for the Greeks, and so turned to attack others. **8.88.1** This then was one benefit, that she escaped and was not killed, and the other was that she happened, in injuring her own side, to gain an even better reputation with Xerxes. **2** For it is said that the King was watching and saw her ramming the ship, and one of the bystanders remarked, 'Sire, do you see how well Artemisia is fighting and that she has struck an enemy ship?' He asked if it really was the work of Artemisia, and they said that they knew her ship's figurehead very well; they thought that the ship which had been sunk belonged to the enemy. **3** She was also lucky, as was said, that no one from the Kalyndian ship was saved to accuse her. Xerxes' remark on what was told him is said to have been, 'My men have become women, my women men.'

4.26 Herodotos 5.87.1–88.3: Athenian Widows Make Their Point

According to Herodotos, who is describing the supposed origins of the enmity between Athens and Aegina, when the Athenians attacked Aegina to recover the statues of Damia and Auxesia originally made of Attic olive wood, which the Aeginetans had taken from Epidauros, all the Athenians except one were killed. The sole survivor also came to a bad end; as a result the women's dress was changed from a pinned peplos to an unpinned chiton. Clearly in times of crisis women were freely able to take to the streets. For aggression by Athenian women, see Hdt. 9.4–5, where Lykidas suggests that Mardonios' proposals be put before the assembly; the Athenians stoned him to death and the Athenian women got together, ran to his house, and did the same to his wife and children.

5.87.1 This is what is said by the Argives and Aeginetans, and the Athenians agree that only one of their men was saved and reached Attica; **2** but according to the Argives this one man survived after they had destroyed the Athenian army, and according to the Athenians it was an act of god, and even this one man did not survive but was killed in the following way. He arrived at Athens and reported the disaster. When the wives of the other men who had gone on the expedition to Aegina learned this they were angry that he alone out of all of them should have been saved, so they surrounded the fellow and jabbed the brooches from their dresses into him, each of them asking him where her husband was. **3** In this way he was killed, and this deed by their women seemed to the Athenians to be even worse than the disaster. The only way in which they could punish the women was to change their style of dress to the Ionian; for before this Athenian women wore Dorian dress, very similar to that at Corinth, but they now changed it to a linen tunic so the women would not use brooches ... **5.88.2** The Argives and Aeginetans then passed this law that in both their countries brooch-pins should be made half as long again as they had been and that in the sanctuary of these deities (Damia and Auxesia) women should particularly dedicate brooches ... **3** And the Argive and Aeginetan women because of the conflict with Athens, from that time up to the present, have worn even longer pins than in the past.

4.27 Thucydides 2.45.2: Women in Perikles' 'Funeral Oration'

For a consideration of this much-quoted passage it is essential to look at the funeral speech as a whole (2.34.1–46.2; cf. doc. 1.17) and to see Perikles' advice in the context of consoling those who have lost their sons (or brothers or fathers), who have died with honour. In context, it could be argued that Perikles is advising women here, as the widows of men who have died nobly, to restrain their grief as much as possible, rather than generally proclaiming that women should always be neither seen nor heard.

2.45.2 'I should perhaps say something about the virtue appropriate to women, to those of you who will now be widows, and I shall simply give one brief piece of advice. Your renown will be great if you do not behave in an inferior way to that natural to your sex, and your glory will be to be least mentioned amongst men concerning either your virtue or your faults.'

4.28 Thucydides 3.74.1: Women Fight in the Corcyraean Civil War

When the Corcyraeans were split by civil war in 427 BC, women joined in the fighting; cf. Thuc. 2.4.2, where women and slaves at Plataea threw stones and tiles from the roofs at the invading Thebans.

3.74.1 The women also joined in the fighting with daring, throwing down roof-tiles from their houses and enduring the uproar in a manner unnatural to their sex.

4.29 Plutarch *Life of Perikles* 24.2–9: Everyday with a Kiss

Plutarch's picture of the metic Aspasia is somewhat romanticised and apparently dependent on the satirical attacks of comic poets. Perikles had been unhappily married to a near relative (perhaps Alkiabiades' mother), whom presumably he had married as an epikleros, and whom he divorced *c.* 445 BC. Aspasia bore Perikles a son, Perikles junior, who had no citizen rights, because of Perikles' law of 451/0, but was made a citizen at Perikles' request after the death of his legitimate sons in the plague.

24.2 It seems that Perikles took these measures against the Samians to please Aspasia, so this would be a suitable place to discuss this woman and the art or power she possessed by which she won over all the leading citizens and even provided the philosophers with a subject for long and important discussions. **3** It is agreed that by birth she was a Milesian, the daughter of Axiochos; and they say that she was trying to rival Thargelia, an Ionian woman of times of old, in setting her sights on the most influential men ... **5** They say that

Perikles was attracted to Aspasia because of her wisdom and political awareness; and Socrates used to visit her sometimes with his acquaintances, while his close friends used to bring their wives to listen to her, even though she practised a calling that was neither decent nor respectable, since she brought up young girls as hetairai ... **7** Perikles' affection for Aspasia seems to have been quite romantic. **8** For his wife was a relation of his, who had been married first to Hipponikos, to whom she bore Kallias the wealthy, while to Perikles she bore Xanthippos and Paralos. When they found that they could no longer live together, Perikles handed her over to another man with her consent, and he took Aspasia as his companion and loved her to an unusual degree. **9** And they say that every day, when he left home and when he returned from the agora, he used to greet her with a kiss.

4.30 Xenophon *Symposium* 2.8–10: An Untrainable Wife: Socrates and Xanthippe

Xanthippe, whose name, with its 'hippos' (horse) termination, may suggest that she was from the aristocracy, is said once to have scolded Socrates and overturned the dinner table when he brought home an uninvited guest, Euthydemos, from the palaistra. Euthydemos was about to leave in anger, when Socrates said, 'At your place, the day before yesterday, didn't a hen fly in and do precisely this? — yet we weren't annoyed at it' (Plut. *Mor.* 461d; cf. Xen. *Mem.* 2.2.1–14, Socrates' advice to his eldest son Lamprokles, when irritated with his mother). For Xanthippe's dismissal from the room prior to Socrates' death, see doc. 3.87.

2.8 Then another girl began to accompany the dancing-girl on the flute and a boy stood beside her and handed her the hoops until he had given her twelve. She took them and as she was dancing kept throwing them whirling in the air, observing the proper height to throw them so as to catch them rhythmically. **9** And Socrates said, 'What this girl is doing is only one proof among many others that woman's nature happens to be no worse than man's, although lacking in judgement and bodily strength. So if any of you has a wife, let him confidently teach her what he would like to have her know.' **10** At which Antisthenes said, 'So how is it, Socrates, that you think like that and do not train Xanthippe, but live with a wife who is the most difficult to live with of all women in existence, and, I think, of all women past and future as well?' 'Because,' he replied, 'I see that those who wish to become horsemen do not acquire the most docile horses but high-spirited ones. For they think that if they can manage these, they will easily handle all the others. And I want to deal with and associate with mankind and I have got her, knowing well that, if I can stand her, I can easily live with all the rest of mankind.'

4.31 Plutarch *Fine Deeds of Women* 239e–f: The Women of Phokis

This incident took place during the Third Sacred War in the mid-fourth century (doc. 14.32). For women as maenads, including Olympias, mother of Alexander, see docs 3.41, 15.1.

239e When the tyrants at Phokis had taken control of Delphi, and the Thebans were fighting what has been called the Sacred War against them, the female devotees of Dionysos, who are called Thyades, unexpectedly arrived in their state of possession by the god and their ramblings by night at Amphissa. As they were exhausted and had not yet returned to a state of rationality, they threw themselves down in the marketplace, here and there, and lay there asleep. **239f** The wives of the men of Amphissa were afraid that, because their city had an alliance in place with the Phokians and large numbers of the tyrant's soldiers were stationed there, the Thyades might meet with ill treatment, and so they all ran out into the marketplace and stood round them in silence. They did not approach them while they were asleep, but, when they awoke, each took care of one of them and made sure they had food. Finally, after getting their husbands' consent they accompanied them to the borders, escorting them there in safety.

INSCRIPTIONAL EVIDENCE

Grave monuments provide useful evidence about the ways in which mothers, sisters, wives and daughters were seen by their families.

4.32 Simonides 36: Xanthippe, Periander's Great-Great-Grand-Daughter

For Periander and the Kypselid tyrants of Corinth, see docs 7.8–18; for Archedike, daughter of Hippias, see doc. 9.34. In this epitaph it is the stele which is speaking to the passer-by. (This is not the same Xanthippe as in doc. 4.30.)

> I shall mention her; for it is not right that here the glorious wife of Archenautes
> Should lie in death unnamed,
> Xanthippe, great-great-grandchild of Periander, who once in high-towered
> Corinth, where he was sovereign, commanded the people.

4.33 Friedländer 32: Thessalia

A marble stele possibly of the sixth century BC from Thessaly. In the first two lines Thessalia speaks for herself; Acheron is a river in the underworld.

> I died when an infant and did not yet reach the flower of my youth,
> But came first to tearful Acheron.
> Her father Kleodamos, son of Hyperanor, and her mother Korona
> Set me here as a monument to their daughter Thes(s)alia.

4.34 Friedländer 60: Learete of Thasos

Dated to the early fifth century BC.

> Truly beautiful is the monument which her father erected over dead
> Learete; for we shall no longer see her alive.

4.35 *Inscriptiones Graecae* I[3] 1261: Phrasikleia

An epitaph on a statue base for an otherwise unknown girl, from Attica, probably *c.* 540. [*IG* I[2] 1014.]

> The tomb of Phrasikleia; I shall be called maiden forever,
> Because I won this name from the gods instead of marriage.
> Aristion of Paros made me.

4.36 *Inscriptiones Graecae* IV 801: Amphidama of Troizen

This inscription is on an octagonal pillar, possibly of the seventh century.

For Damotimos this tomb was wrought by his dear mother
Amphidama; for no children were born in his house.
And the tripod, which he won in the footrace at Thebes ...
... Unharmed, and she set it up over her son.

4.37 Friedländer 140: Timarete for Her Dear Dead Son

A stele from Eretria, probably sixth century or slightly later.

Hail, passers-by; I lie here in death.
Come hither and read what man is buried here:
A foreigner from Aegina, his name Mnesitheos.
My dear mother Timarete set up this monument for me,
An imperishable stele on the top of the mound,
Which will say these words to passers-by for ever,
'Timarete set this up for her dear dead son.'

4.38 *Inscriptiones Graecae* IX 2.255: A Mother for a Valiant Son

A broad marble slab from near Pharsalos, probably of the early fifth century.

Echenais, his mother, set up this momument for Diokles
Mourning greatly that he, a valiant man, died untimely.
Alas, Diokles, your brother is without laughter;
Let everyone lamenting a valiant man go his way.

4.39 *Inscriptiones Graecae* I^3 1226: A Mother's Command

A block of poros from the Wall of Themistokles at Athens, dating probably to the mid-sixth century.

Splendid ... son of ... rylides, whose tomb here
His sons constructed at their mother's command.

4.40 Friedländer 74: Potalis for Her Husband

A stone, with outlines of figures, of perhaps the late sixth or early fifth century from Tanagra in Boeotia. If the restoration of Potalis in line 1 is correct, Mantitheos' wife Potalis was afterwards buried with him.

[Potalis] placed this stele over her dear dead husband
Mantitheos, who was skilled in hospitality and horsemanship.
Potalis.

4.41 *Inscriptiones Graecae* I^3 1210: Gnatho's Sister

A marble disc with spiral inscription; Attic, perhaps *c.* 530. [*IG* I^2 975]

This is the tomb of Gnatho. His sister buried him after nursing him in mental illness.

4.42 Archilochos 326: A Parian Girl Marries

This epigram is probably from Paros, where there was a temple of Hera and was copied in antiquity from an actual dedication. The unveiling of the bride was one of the formal elements of the wedding ceremony, and the veil could be consecrated to Hera, goddess of marriage. [*Anth. Pal.* 6.133]

Alkibia dedicated the sacred veil for her locks
To Hera, when she attained lawful wedlock.

4.43 [Anacreon] *Epigrammata* 7: A Royal Offering

The label on a garment dedicated in an unknown temple in Thessaly by Praxidike and Dyseris, wife of Echekratidas ruler of Larissa, at the beginning of the fifth century. [*Anth. Pal.* 6.136.]

Praxidike made and Dyseris designed
This garment; the skill of both is united.

4.44 Friedländer 166: A Western Greek Dedicates a Mirror to Athena

An early fifth-century dedication of a female bronze statuette on an Ionic capital, part of a mirror stand, from Poseidonia (Paestum) in Italy.

From Phillo, daughter of Charmylidas, a tithe to Athena.

4.45 Friedländer 46: From Nikandra, Prominent amongst Women

This inscription was carved on the right thigh of an archaic female statue at Delos dedicated to Artemis and is dated to *c.* 650–625 BC.

Nikandra dedicated me to the Far-Darter who delights in the arrow,
The daughter of Deinodikes of Naxos, prominent amongst other women,
The sister of Deinomenes, and now wife of Phraxos.

4.46 Friedländer 144: A Prayer by Man and Wife

Possibly early fifth century, or before, from Paros.

Demokydes and Telestodike having made a vow in common
Erected this offering to virgin Artemis

On her sacred ground, the daughter of aegis-bearing Zeus;
To their family and livelihood give increase in safety.

4.47 Friedländer 177: Inscriptions on Possessions

A seventh-century lekythos from Cumae in Italy.

I am Tataia's flask: whoever steals me will become blind!

Possibly a lover's gift from one young man to another. [*CIG* 545]

The cup of Kesiphon; if anyone breaks it
He shall pay a drachma, because it is a gift from Xenyllos.

Hansen 446. A black drinking cup (kantharos) from Thespiai, dated to the second half of the fifth century. [*IG* VII 3467]

Mogeas gives this cup as a gift to his wife Eucharis
Daughter of Eutretiphantos, so she may drink her fill.

An Attic black-figure cup, found at Taras (Tarentum), with the inscription scratched on the foot.

I am Melosa's prize; she beat the girls in carding.

4.48 Theophrastos *Characters* 21 (On Petty Ambition): Commemoration of a Lapdog

Pet birds and lapdogs from Malta were frequently depicted on Attic tombs, especially those of children.

6 He's likely to keep a jackdaw as a pet and buy it a little ladder and make it a bronze shield for the jackdaw to hold as it hops up the ladder… **9** When his Maltese lapdog dies he constructs a monument and little pillar, with the inscription 'Offshoot (Klados) of Malta'.

THE LEGAL STATUS OF WOMEN

Generally in Greece women inherited in preference to more distant male relatives, but they were excluded by men of the same degree of relationship as themselves; the position of daughters (but not sisters) in the Gortyn Law Code is exceptional.

4.49 Willetts *The Law Code of Gortyn*: The Gortyn Law Code

This law code from Crete, a Dorian society like Sparta, dates to *c.* 450 BC, and seems to be the result of a revision of earlier laws by the legislative body of Gortyn; its provisions differ somewhat from Athenian practice. Daughters had a specific portion of the inheritance rather than a dowry, and in some cases heiresses could have a say in whom they married. The apetairoi were not full citizens, but had a relatively free economic status. They may have included those unable to pay their mess contribution, or have been the sons of a citizen and a serf or slave. One stater is worth two drachmas.

Rape, seduction, adultery

(col. II.2) If a person commits rape on a free man or free woman, he shall pay one hundred staters, and if on someone belonging to the house of an apetairos ten; and if a slave on a free man or woman, he shall pay double; and if a free man on a male or female serf, five drachmas; and if a male serf on a male or female serf, five staters. If a person seduces by force a female slave belonging to the house, he shall pay two staters; but if she has already been seduced, one obol if in daytime, two obols if at night; and the slave's oath shall have precedence. If a person attempts to have intercourse with a free woman who is under a relative's guardianship, he shall pay ten staters if a witness testifies. If someone be taken in adultery with a free woman in her father's house or brother's or husband's, he shall pay one hundred staters; but if in someone else's house fifty; and if with the wife of an apetairos ten; but if a slave with a free woman he shall pay double; and if a slave with a slave five. The captor should proclaim in the presence of three witnesses to the relatives of the person caught that he must be ransomed within five days; and to the owner of the slave in the presence of two witnesses; but if he is not ransomed, the captors may deal with him as they wish; but if anyone declares that he has been taken by deceit, the captor is to swear in a case involving fifty staters or more with four others, each calling down curses on themselves, and in the case of an apetairos with two others, and in the case of a serf the master and one other, that he captured him in adultery and not by deceit.

Divorce

If a husband and wife should be divorced, she is to keep whatever property she came to her husband with and half of the produce, if there is any, from her own property, and half of whatever she has woven within the house, and if her husband is the cause of the divorce she is to have five staters; but if the husband should proclaim that he is not the cause, the judge shall decide on oath. **(col. III)** If the wife carries away anything else belonging to the husband, she shall pay five staters and whatever she may carry away; and let her restore whatever she may have stolen.

Widowhood

17 If a man dies leaving children, if the wife so wishes she may marry, keeping her own property and whatever her husband may have given her according to what is prescribed, in the presence of three adult free witnesses; but if she takes away anything belonging to the children, that is grounds for a trial. And if he leaves her childless, she is to have her own property and half of whatever she has woven within the house and is to obtain her portion of the produce in the house along with the lawful heirs as well as whatever her husband may have given her as is prescribed; but if she takes away anything else, that is grounds for a trial. And if the wife dies childless, he is to return her property to the rightful heirs and half whatever she has woven in the house and half of the produce, if it is from her own property.

Provisions for children

44 If a woman who is divorced should bear a child, it is to be brought to the husband in his house in the presence of three witnesses. And if he does not accept it, the child shall be in the mother's power either to rear or to expose; and **50** the oaths of the relatives and witnesses shall have precedence … **(col. IV.8)** If a woman who is divorced should expose her child before presenting it as is prescribed, she shall pay fifty staters for a free child, twenty-five for a slave. And if the man has no house to which she can bring it or she does not see him, there is to be no penalty if she exposes the child … **31** And if a person should die, the city houses and whatever there is inside the houses in which a serf does not reside, and the small and large cattle which do not belong to a serf, shall belong to the sons, but all the rest of the property is to be divided fairly, and the sons, **40** however many there are, shall each receive two parts, while the daughters, however many there are, shall each receive one part. If the mother dies, her property shall also be divided, in the same way as is prescribed for the father's. But if there is no property other than the house, the daughters shall receive their share as prescribed. And if the father, while alive, wishes to give to a married daughter, **50** let him give according to what is prescribed but not more. Any daughter to whom he gave or promised before is to have these things, but shall receive nothing else from her father's property … **(col. VI.31)** And if a mother dies leaving children, the father is to have control over the mother's estate, but he may not sell or mortgage unless the children consent and are of age … **44** And if he marries another woman, the children are to have control of their mother's property.

Heiresses

(col. VII.15) The heiress is to be married to the brother of her father, the oldest of those living. And if there are more heiresses and brothers of the father, **20** they are to be married to the next eldest. And if there should be no brothers of the father, but sons of the brothers, she is to be married to the one who is the son of the eldest. And if there are more heiresses and sons of brothers, they are to be married to the next after the son of the eldest. The groom-elect is to have one heiress and not more. **30** While the groom-elect or heiress is too young to marry, the heiress is to have the house, if there is one, and the groom-elect is to receive half the revenue from everything. But if the groom-elect does not wish to marry the heiress, though they are both old enough to marry, on the grounds that he is still a minor, all the property and produce shall be at the heiress's disposal until he marries her. **40** But if the groom-elect as an adult does not wish to marry the heiress who is old enough and willing to marry him, the relatives of the heiress are to take the matter to court and the judge is to order the marriage to take place within two months. And if he does not marry her as prescribed, the heiress is to have all the property and marry the next in succession, if there is one. **50** But if there is no groom-elect, she shall be married to whomever she wishes of those who ask from the tribe. And if the heiress, though old enough, does not wish to be married to the groom-elect, or the groom-elect is too young and the heiress is unwilling to wait, **(col. VIII)** the heiress is to have the house, if there is one in the city, and whatever is in the house, and she is to receive half of the rest and be married to whomsoever she wishes of those who ask from the tribe; but she is to give a share of the property to that man (whom she rejected). And if there are no kinsmen of the heiress as defined, **10** she is to have all the property and be married to whomever she wishes from the tribe. And if no one from the tribe should wish to marry her, the relatives of the heiress are to proclaim throughout the tribe, 'Does no one wish to marry her?' And if someone marries her it should be within thirty days from the time of the proclamation, but if not she can be married to another, whomever she can. And if a woman becomes an heiress after her father or brother has given her in marriage, if she does not wish to remain married to the one to whom they gave her, even if he is willing, as long as she has borne children she may be married to another of the tribe, dividing the property as prescribed. But if there are no children, she is to be married to the groom-elect, if there is one, and take all the property, and if there is not, as prescribed. If a husband dies leaving children to an heiress, she may marry whomever in the tribe she can, if she so wishes, but there is no compulsion. But if the deceased has left no children behind, she is to be married to the groom-elect as prescribed … An heiress is someone who has no father or brother by the same father. And while she is not old enough to marry, her father's brothers are to be responsible for the administration of the property, while she receives a half share of the produce. But if there should be no groom-elect while she is not old enough to marry, the heiress is to have control of the property and the produce and as long as she is not old enough to marry is to be brought up with her mother; and if she should have no mother, she is to be brought up with her mother's brothers … **(col. XII.9)** And where the heiress, there being no groom-elect or judges in the affairs of orphans, is brought up with her mother, her relatives on both sides who have been nominated are to administer the property and the revenue to the best of their ability until she is married. And she is to be married when she is twelve or older.

4.50 Plutarch *Life of Solon* 20.2–23.2: Legislation on Marriage and Inheritance

Solon introduced a law permitting a man who had no sons to adopt a son by will and make him his heir, rather than leaving his property to other members of his family; however, a daughter could not be deprived of her rights as epikleros. Under Solon's legislation an illegitimate son was not obliged to support his father, and according to Plutarch sons who had not been taught a trade were similarly freed from this obligation (see doc. 8.27). Some of Plutarch's statements here should be taken with caution: heiresses in Athens married into their own not into their husband's family, and it is also unlikely that dowries would have been completely abolished. 21.6 is aimed at the employment of hired mourners, as opposed to family members; cf. doc. 3.57. Note that an adulterer caught in the act could be killed, but a rapist, it seems, could not (cf. doc. 4.54) and the implication that prior to Solon's legislation unmarried girls could be sold as slaves.

20.2 Another law which seems out of place and ridiculous is that which allows an heiress, in the case of her lawful husband being unable to have intercourse with her, to be married by one of his next of kin. But some say that this was a sensible move against those who were impotent, but married heiresses for the sake of their property and used the law to do violence to nature. … **3** It was also a good idea that an heiress should not be allowed to choose anyone for a husband but whomever she wished of the relatives of her husband, so that her offspring might be of his household and family (genos) … **6** In all other marriages he abolished dowries, ordering the bride to bring with her three changes of clothing and household possessions of small value, and nothing else, for he did not want marriage to be a matter of profit or purchase, but the dwelling together of man and wife for the purposes of child-bearing and love and affection … **21.3** Solon also was well thought of for his law concerning wills. For before his time they were not allowed, and the property and house of the deceased had to remain in the family; but he, by allowing anyone who had no children, to leave his property to whomever he wished, honoured friendship more than kinship and goodwill more than compulsion, and made property the possession of those who owned it. **4** On the other hand he did not allow bequests to be totally uncomplicated and without restraint, but only those not made under the influence of illness or drugs or imprisonment or compulsion or through a wife's persuasion ... **5** He also made a law concerning women's appearances outside their house, as well as their mourning and their festivals, to prevent disorder and licence: when they went out he laid down that they were not to have more than three garments, nor carry more than an obol's worth of food or drink, or a basket more than a cubit in size, nor to travel at night except in a wagon with a lamp in front. **6** He also forbade laceration by mourners at funerals and using set dirges and lamenting anyone at the funeral ceremonies of other people ... **22.4** Even harsher was his regulation that sons born from a hetaira were not compelled to maintain their father, as Herakleides of Pontos narrates. For he who neglects the honourable state of marriage is clearly having a relationship with a woman not for the sake of children, but for pleasure, and forfeits his reward, and has lost the right of free speech towards his sons, since he has made their very birth a reproach to them. **23.1** In general, Solon's laws concerning women seem extremely incongruous. For he allowed anyone who caught an adulterer to kill him; but if anyone seized and raped a free woman, he laid down a penalty of one hundred drachmas, and, if he seduced her, twenty drachmas except for those women who openly sell themselves, meaning the hetairai; for they go openly to those who pay them. **2** He did not allow anyone to sell his daughters or sisters, unless he discovered that a virgin had consorted with a man.

4.51 Demosthenes 43 *Against Makartatos* 51, 54, 75: Athenian Laws on Heiresses

Athenian inheritance laws protected the rights of heiresses and ensured the survival of the family line; here dowries are stipulated for an heiress whose next of kin chooses not to marry her. If there was no heiress, male relatives had precedence in inheriting over females, and nearer relatives over more distant family members. Cf. Isaeus 7.20 for the same law.

51 If a man dies without having made a will, if he leaves female children, the property shall go with them, but, if not, the following shall be entitled to the estate: if there are brothers by the same father, and if there are legitimate sons of brothers, they shall take the share of the father. But if there are no brothers or sons of brothers then sisters from the same father and their children shall inherit in the same way. Males and sons of males shall have precedence, both if they are of the same ancestors and if they are of remoter kinship. If there are no relatives on the father's side within the degree of children of cousins, those on the mother's side shall inherit in similar fashion. But if there are no relatives on either side within this degree of relationship, the nearest of kin on the father's side shall inherit. No illegitimate child, whether male or female, shall have rights of inheritance in either sacred or secular matters from the year Eukleides was archon (403/2 BC)...

54 With regard to all heiresses in the class of thetes, if their next of kin does not wish to marry her he is to give her in marriage with a dowry of 500 drachmas if he belongs to the class of pentakosiomedimnoi, or 300, if he is one of the hippeis, or 150, if he is one of the zeugitai, in addition to her own property. If there are several kinsmen in the same degree of relationship, they shall all contribute proportionately to the heiress's dowry. And if there is more than one heiress, it shall not be necessary for a single kinsman to give more than one in marriage, but in each case the nearest kinsman shall give her in marriage or marry her himself. If the nearest kinsman does not marry her or give her in marriage, the archon shall compel him to either marry her or give her in marriage. If the archon does not compel him to do so, he shall be fined a thousand drachmas, which are to be sacred to Hera. Anyone who wishes shall lay information with the archon against anyone who does not comply with this law...

75 The archon shall be responsible for the orphans and heiresses and families which are in danger of becoming extinct, and for the women who remain in the households of their deceased husbands claiming that they are pregnant. He shall be responsible for these and not permit anyone to maltreat them. If anyone does maltreat them or behave unlawfully towards them in any way, he shall have the authority to impose a fine on this person up to the maximum allowed by law. And if this person seems to him to deserve a more severe penalty, he shall summon him to the court of the heliaia, giving him five days' notice and writing in the indictment the penalty which he considers to be appropriate. And if the person is convicted the Heliaia shall lay down for the convicted person the penalty, whether corporal or financial.

4.52 Antiphon 1 *Prosecution of the Stepmother* 14–17, 19–20: A Second Clytemnestra

Antiphon wrote this speech for the deceased's son, who is prosecuting his stepmother for murdering her husband by poison. The wife is supposed to have secured the services of a concubine (pallake) belonging to Philoneos, a friend of her husband, persuading her to serve the poison to both men in the belief that it was a love potion. The case at this point, *c.* 420 BC, is being revived after several years; the concubine was arrested at the time and executed for the crime; concubines could either be slaves, or, if kept 'with a view to free children', might be free women of non-citizen birth like Aspasia.

14 There was an upper room in our house, which Philoneos used to occupy when he visited Athens. He was a gentleman and a friend of our father's. Philoneos had a concubine, whom he intended to place in a brothel. My brother's mother made this woman her friend. **15** On hearing of the wrong she was going to be done by Philoneos, she sent for her, and when she came told her that she too was being wronged by our father. If she chose to follow her instructions, she said, she would be able to restore Philoneos' love for her and my father's love for herself, saying that she would find a way to do it, while the concubine's role was to carry this out. **16** So she asked her if she were willing to serve as her assistant, and the concubine, as I imagine, readily promised. Later on Philoneos happened to be involved in a sacrifice to Zeus Ktesios in the Piraeus, while my father was about to sail to Naxos. It seemed an excellent idea to Philoneos that in the same trip he should accompany my father, his friend, to the Piraeus and at the same time perform his sacrifice and give him a feast. **17** Philoneos' concubine accompanied him to assist at the sacrifice. And when they were at the Piraeus he of course performed the sacrifice. When the victims had been sacrificed, then the female began to deliberate how to give the drug, whether before dinner or after dinner. As she considered, it seemed to her to be best to give it after dinner, thus carrying out the instructions of this Clytemnestra ... **19** Philoneos' concubine, while she poured out the wine for the libation to accompany their prayers, which were not to be fulfilled, jurors, poured in the poison. Thinking that she was doing something clever she gave more to Philoneos, probably so that if she gave him more, she would be more beloved by Philoneos; for she did not yet know that she had been deceived by my stepmother, until she was already involved in the mischief; and she poured in a smaller portion for my father. **20** So they poured their libation, grasped their own destroyer, and drank down their last drink. Philoneos expired on the spot, while our father was seized with an illness from which he died on the twentieth day. For this, the woman who was carrying out orders when she did the deed has got the punishment she deserved, even though she was not at all responsible — she was broken on the wheel and handed over to the public executioner — and as for the woman who was responsible and planned it all, she too will get her punishment, if you and the gods are willing.

4.53 Lysias 32 *Against Diogeiton* 11–15: A Widow Fights for Her Sons' Rights

This speech, probably delivered in 400 BC, concerns the widow of a rich merchant named Diodotos, who had been killed in battle in 409. Diogeiton, who was the guardian of the estate, the widow's father, and also her husband's brother, is accused of having mishandled the property during her sons' minority, and, represented by her son-in-law in court, she charges him with having cheated her sons. Presumably the prosecution is being brought now because her eldest son has come of age. The grain mentioned in (15) was presumably interest on the investment of the 2,000 drachmas made in the Chersonese.

11 It would take too long to tell how much grief there was in my house at that time. Finally their mother begged and beseeched me to bring together her father and friends, saying that, even though she had not formerly been accustomed to speak amongst men, the size of their misfortunes compelled her to reveal to us everything concerning their troubles ... **12** And when we assembled, the woman asked Diogeiton how he could have the heart to think it right to treat the children in such a way: 'You are their father's brother, and my father, and their uncle and grandfather. **13** Even if you're not ashamed before any man, you ought,' she said, 'to fear the gods; for you received from him, when he went off to war, five talents as a deposit. And I am willing to swear to this on the lives of my children, both these here and my younger ones in any place you may name.' ... **14** In addition she convicted him of having recovered seven talents and 4,000 drachmas from bottomry loans and produced the records of these; for in the removal, when he was moving from Kollytos to the house of Phaidros, her sons came upon the register which had been mislaid and brought it to her. **15** And she proved that he had recovered 100 minas which had been lent at interest on a mortgage on land, and another 2,000 drachmas and some very valuable furniture, and that grain had come to them every year from the Chersonese.

4.54 Lysias 1 *On the Murder of Eratosthenes* 6–10: Death of an Adulterer

Euphiletos killed Eratosthenes, alleging that he had caught him in the act of adultery with his wife, in accordance with Solon's law (see doc. 4.50), but was then prosecuted by Eratosthenes' relatives for premeditated murder and entrapment. Euphiletos' domestic arrangements (the women's quarters being upstairs, but with the wife moving downstairs to be with the baby) and his relationship with his wife are supposed to sound normal and reasonable to an Athenian jury. It is significant that it was at Euphiletos' mother's funeral that his wife was seen by Eratosthenes, implying that funerals were one of the occasions on which a woman could be seen by men outside her family.

6 When I, Athenians, decided to marry and brought a wife into my household, for some time my attitude was that I did not wish to annoy her, but neither was she to be able to do exactly what she liked, and I watched her as much as possible, and kept an eye on her as was reasonable. But once my child had been born, I had confidence in her and handed over to her all my possessions, believing that this was the greatest sign of marital intimacy. **7** Well, in the beginning, Athenians, she was the best of wives; she was a clever, economical housewife, and precise in her management of everything; but when my mother died, her death was the cause of all my misfortunes. **8** For, when my wife was attending the funeral, she was seen by this man, who in time seduced her; for he kept a lookout for the maid-servant going to market and paid addresses to my wife which were her ruin. **9** Firstly, jurors (for I have to tell you this), my house has two storeys, the upper equal in space to the lower, divided into the women's quarters and the men's quarters. When our child was born, his mother nursed him; but so that when she had to bath him she did not run the risk of going down the stairs, I used to live upstairs, and the women down below. **10** And so by this point it had become quite customary for my wife often to go downstairs to sleep with the baby, so she could give him the breast and stop him crying. Things went on in this way for some time, and I suspected nothing, but was foolish enough to think that my wife was the most chaste woman in the whole city.

4.55 [Andocides] 4 *Against Alkibiades* 13–15: Hipparete Fails to Divorce Alkibiades

Despite the fact that in Athens women were unable to undertake legal actions in their own right, from this passage it appears that formal provision was made for a wife to initiate a divorce, which in this case was frustrated by the husband because of the large twenty-talent dowry, which would have had to have been returned to the wife's family (or interest be paid on it at the rate of 18 per cent per annum). According to Plut. *Alk*. 8.4–5, Hipparete left Alkibiades to live with her brother Kallias, and it was only on her petitioning for divorce that Alkibiades interfered. Kallias was here powerless to assist his sister, but, as the chief priest, oversaw the Eleusinian Mysteries, which Alkibiades was accused of profaning in 415.

13 I am amazed, too, at those who believe that Alkibiades is a lover of democracy, the type of constitution which more than any other aims at attaining equality — but they are not observing him from the point of view of his private life, though they can see his self-aggrandizement and arrogance, for he married the sister of Kallias for the agreed dowry of ten talents, but when Hipponikos was killed as a general at Delion he demanded the same amount again, on the grounds that Hipponikos had agreed to add that amount when Alkibiades should have a child by his daughter. **14** After obtaining such a dowry, greater than any other Greek's, he behaved so outrageously, introducing hetairai, both slave and free, into his own house, that he compelled his wife, who was an extremely decent woman, to leave him, and go before the archon according to law. He then gave particular proof of his power; for he summoned his friends, and snatching his wife carried her off from the agora by force, showing everyone his contempt for the archons, the laws and the rest of the citizens. **15** Moreover this was not enough for him, but he also plotted the murder of Kallias, to gain possession of Hipponikos' estate, as Kallias accused him before all of you in the assembly; and Kallias gave his wealth to the people, should he die childless, through fear that his property might cost him his life.

4.56 [Demosthenes] 59 (*Against Neaira*) 16, 52: Cohabiting with Foreigners

Only Athenians were permitted to intermarry (or those to whom this right was specifically granted, such as Perikles and Aspasia (doc. 4.29), and the Plataeans for their help against the Persians; Thuc. 2.71–8, 3.20–4, 3.52–68). At 104 (doc. 1.37) the orator implies that the Plataeans' descendants would be eligible for the archonships if their mothers were Athenian women. These laws were formulated in order to protect the rights of citizens from being widely disseminated.

16 If a foreigner cohabits as husband with an Athenian woman in any way or manner whatsoever, he shall be indicted before the thesmothetai by any Athenian who chooses and is entitled to do so. If he is convicted, he shall be sold, both himself and his property, and one-third of it shall belong to the person who ensured his conviction. The same shall apply to a foreign woman who cohabits with an Athenian man, and the Athenian who lives with the foreign woman so convicted shall be fined a thousand drachmas.

52 Anyone who gives a foreign woman in marriage to an Athenian man, claiming that she is related to him, shall lose his citizen rights and his property shall be confiscated and one-third of it shall belong to the person who ensured his conviction. Anyone entitled to do so may bring an indictment before the thesmothetai, just as in cases of those who usurp the rights of a citizen.

4.57 [Demosthenes] 59 (*Against Neaira*) 87: Penalties for Adulteresses

In Athens a man who caught an adulterer with his wife and killed him could plead justifiable homicide; adulterous wives had to be divorced and could not take part in religious rites.

87 When a person has caught the adulterer, it shall not be permitted for the person who has caught him to continue living with his wife; if he does continue to live with her, he shall be deprived of his rights as a citizen. Nor shall it be permitted for the wife who has been caught in adultery to attend the public sacrifices; if she does attend them, she may be made to suffer any penalty whatsoever, short of death, with complete impunity.

4.58 Pouilloux (1954) 371, no. 141: Dowries for Daughters of Thasian Heroes

This late fifth- or early fourth-century inscription BC from Thasos concerns the children of those who have died in war. There were similar provisions for the children of state heroes at Athens: Thuc. 2.46.

7 The polemarchs and the secretary of the boule are to inscribe their names and fathers' names on the list of Heroes, and summon **10** their fathers and sons whenever the city sacrifices to the Heroes … **16** All of them who leave behind children, when they come of age, the polemarchs are to give them each, if they are boys, greaves, a breastplate, dagger, helmet, shield and spear worth not less than three minas, at the games at the Herakleia, and proclaim their names; and if they are daughters, for a dowry ... when they become fourteen years old ...

THE WORKING WOMAN: AT HOME AND ABROAD

While little is known about working women in fifth-century Athens, it is clear that most working women were concerned primarily with 'women's work', such as spinning and weaving. But there is evidence that women were also employed in the market, as sellers of bread or garlands, and could be found as innkeepers.

4.59 Homer *Odyssey* 2.337–47: The Archaic Storeroom

Telemachos, Odysseus' son, needs supplies of wine and barley for his journey from Ithaka to Pylos and Sparta, where he intends to ask for news of his father.

Telemachos went down to his father's high-roofed treasure chamber,
A spacious room, where gold and bronze lay in piles
And clothes in chests and stores of fragrant olive oil;
Huge jars (pithoi) of wine, old and sweet,
Stood there, within them the unmixed divine drink,
Arranged in rows beside the wall for when Odysseus
Should return home after his many painful labours.
The closely fitted double doors were shut;
And there both night and day a woman housekeeper
Stayed there, keeping a close guard over everything, a woman of much wisdom,
Eurikleia, daughter of Ops, son of Pisenor.

4.60 Aristophanes *Thesmophoriazousai* 443–58: A Myrtle-Wreath Seller

The women of Athens are assembled to celebrate the festival of the Thesmophoria (cf. doc. 3.64). Aristophanes fantasises that they are planning revenge on the poet Euripides for supposedly revealing on stage their secrets and behaviour at the festival. Here a second woman, a seller of myrtle-wreaths worn at sacrifices and drinking parties, makes a speech against Euripides at the women's 'assembly'. For another citizen woman seller of ribbons in the market, see doc. 5.63; a woman bread-seller, Myrtia, also appears in *Wasps* 1388–98. Women clearly could work in the market, though it was nothing to be proud of: Euripides is frequently attacked by Aristophanes on the grounds that his mother sold vegetables (*Ach*. 478, *Knights* 19, *Thesm*. 387, *Frogs* 840).

I've only come forward to say a few words.
This lady's charges have covered just about everything;
I just want to tell you what I've been through myself.
My husband died in Cyprus,
Leaving me with five little children, and it's with difficulty
That I've fed them by making garlands in the myrtle-wreath market.
At least, before, I managed a pretty miserable existence,

And now he, by putting on his tragedies,
Has persuaded people that there aren't any gods;
As a result we don't sell even half what we used to.
I tell you all, on my advice,
Punish this man for many reasons;
For he treats us quite savagely, ladies,
Probably because he was brought up among those wild vegetables.
Well, I must be off to the agora — I've got twenty wreaths
To plait which gentlemen have specially ordered.

4.61 Aristophanes *Frogs* 549–78: Lady Innkeepers in the Underworld

The god Dionysos, in his journey to the underworld with his slave Xanthias, has attempted to disguise himself as Herakles. While there he unfortunately meets two ladies whose bill Herakles had omitted to discharge on an earlier visit. These women are metics, as the prostates, mentioned in line 569, was the patron which every metic needed in court.

Lady Innkeeper: Plathane, Plathane, come here, here's the villain
Who came into our inn one day
And ate up sixteen of our loaves.
Plathane: By Zeus,
That's the man.
Xanthias: Evil's coming to somebody!
Lady Innkeeper: As well as twenty pieces of boiled meat
At half an obol each.
Xanthias: Someone's going to be for it!
Lady Innkeeper: And all that garlic.
Dionysos: Woman, you're talking nonsense,
You don't know what you're saying.
Lady Innkeeper: So you didn't expect me
To know you, wearing those buskins?
Well, then? I haven't even mentioned all that dried fish.
Plathane: Too true!, nor all that fresh cheese, you rogue,
Which you gulped down baskets and all.
Lady Innkeeper: And when I asked him for the money,
He gave me this sour look and bellowed.
Xanthias: His conduct exactly! He's always like that.
Lady Innkeeper: And he drew his sword, as if he'd gone mad.
Plathane: Yes, you poor woman.
Lady Innkeeper: And the two of us were so scared
That we had to run straight upstairs;
And he rushed off taking the sleeping-mats with him.
Xanthias: That's just like him as well!
Plathane: We ought to do something!
Lady Innkeeper: You go and call Kleon, my patron.
Plathane: And you get Hyperbolos for me, if you meet him,

So we can crush this chap.
Lady Innkeeper: You horrible throat,
How I'd enjoy knocking out with a stone
Those molars you used to devour my merchandise.
Plathane: And I'd like to throw you into a pit.
Lady Innkeeper: I'd like to get a sickle and cut out that windpipe
Which swallowed down that tripe.
Plathane: I'm off to get Kleon, he'll summons him today
And wind all this out of him.

4.62 Aristophanes *Lysistrata* 13–19, 456–58: The Many Duties of Women

At the beginning of the play Kalonike explains to Lysistrata that the women of Athens are slow in answering her summons because of their domestic duties. Later, when their stronghold on the acropolis is attacked, Lysistrata calls for the help of her supporters — by definition Athenian citizen women — many of whom appear to have been in the retail professions.

Lysistrata: They've been told to meet here
To discuss a matter of great importance,
But they're asleep and haven't come.
Kalonike: But, my dear,
They will. It's difficult for women to get out of the house.
For one will be running around for her husband,
Another waking up a slave, or with the baby
Putting it to bed, or washing it, or feeding it.
Lysistrata: My women allies, come quick from inside,
You seed-pulse-and-vegetable-market-sellers,
You garlic-innkeeping-bread-sellers!

4.63 Xenophon *Oeconomicus* 7.4–23, 7.35–37, 10.10–13: A New Bride

In this description of a marital relationship, Ischomachos is here trying to treat his young wife, married at fourteen, if somewhat patronisingly, as an equal. Cf. also 9.2–8, for Ischomachos' advice to his wife when she starts wearing white lead and rouge for her complexion, and heels to make her taller; for make-up and beauty aids, see Ar. *Lysistrata* 42–48. Xenophon seems to imply that gluttony is a common vice among Greek women (7.6). For other advice by Ischomachos to his wife as reported to Socrates, see doc. 5.13. Socrates is speaking here.

7.4 'But Ischomachos,' I said, 'that's what I would really like to hear from you, whether you trained your wife yourself to be what she ought to be, or whether she knew how to manage her duties when you took her from her father and mother?' **5** 'How could she have had any knowledge when I married her, Socrates?' he replied. 'She wasn't yet fifteen when she came to me, and up to then she had lived in a sheltered environment, so that she might see as little as possible, hear as little as possible, and say as little as possible. **6** It's surely not to be wondered at if when she came she only knew how to take wool and produce a cloak and had seen how the spinning work was given out to the maidservants? Concerning how much she ate, Socrates, she had been very well trained, and this seems to me to be the most important training both for a man and a woman.'... **10** 'Well, Socrates, as soon as she was amenable and we were sufficiently familiar with each other that we could carry on a conversation, I asked her the following question: "Tell me, my wife, have you thought why I took you for my wife and your parents married you to me? **11** You must clearly see that we would have had no problem in finding someone else to sleep with. I on my own behalf and your parents on yours decided who would the best partner of home and children that we could find: and so I chose you and your parents chose me, it seems, as the best to be found. **12** Should God grant us children we will then consider together how best we shall educate them. For this blessing is one we will share — the acquisition of the very best of allies and comforters to us when we are old; and this household is now ours to share. **13** For I am giving you a share in all my possessions while you have put in everything you brought with you. And we should not calculate which of us has given the greater amount, but should be aware that whoever makes the better partner provides the greatest contribution."

14 'My wife's answer to this, Socrates, was, "How can I possibly help you? What power do I have? Rather, everything depends on you. My mother told me that my duty is to show discretion."

15 'Yes indeed, my wife; my father said the same to me. But discretion in a husband and wife means so to act that their possessions are in the best state possible and that as much as possible be added to them by fair and honourable means.'

16 ' "And what do you see me as doing to improve our household?" asked my wife ...

22 'Since both the indoor and outdoor tasks need hard work and diligence, god, it appears to me, adapted woman's nature from the first towards indoor duties and responsibilities, and man's to those outdoors.

23 'For he made the man's body and mind more able to endure cold and heat and journeys and expeditions, and accordingly gave him the outdoor tasks. And because he made her body less capable of enduring these, it seems to me that god assigned the indoor tasks to the woman.'

35 'It will be your duty', I said, 'to stay indoors and to send outside those of the servants whose work is outside, **36** and to superintend those whose work is inside, and to receive what is brought in, and to distribute what of this has to be expended, and to take thought for and watch over what has to be stored, so that the sum laid by for the year is not expended in a month. And whenever wool is brought in to you, you must see that there are cloaks made for those who need them. And you must take care that the dry provisions are properly edible. **37** However, one of the duties that will fall to you,' I said, 'may perhaps seem thankless, as you will have to see that any of the servants who is sick is cared for.' "Not at all," said my wife, "it will be most pleasing, if those who have been well looked after will be grateful and even more well-intentioned than before." ... **10.10** And I advised her, Socrates, not to be always sitting down like a slave, but with the help of the gods to try to stand before the loom like a mistress to teach what she might know better than another, and if she knows less, to learn, and to keep an eye on the baking-woman, and to stand by the housekeeper when she is measuring out, and to go round and see if everything is in its right place. I thought that this would give her a walk as well as occupation. **11** And I said that it was good exercise to mix and knead and to shake and fold cloaks and bedding. I said that with this exercise she would eat better and be healthier, and have a better natural colour ... **13** On the other hand those (wives) who spend all their time sitting about in a haughty manner expose themselves to comparison with decorated and fraudulent women.'

4.64 Xenophon *Memorabilia* 2.7.6–12: Socrates' Advice Starts a Home Industry

Aristarchos, a once-wealthy Athenian, has lost his farm, and his town properties have been abandoned by his tenants because of the disorders of 404/3 BC; a number of female relatives have come to live with him, and he is unable to feed all his household. Socrates ascertains that Aristarchos' womenfolk are able to cook and make clothing and proceeds to give good advice about putting them to work to produce marketable goods.

2.7.6 'Don't you know that from one of these occupations, making barley-groats, Nausikydes maintains not only himself and his household, but lots of pigs and cattle as well, and has enough left over to undertake liturgies for the city? That Kyrebos from baking keeps his whole household and lives in luxury, as does Demeas of Kollytos from making capes, and Menon by making cloaks, while most of the Megarians make a living out of tunic-making?' 'That's true,' replied Aristarchos, 'but they possess barbarian slaves they have bought and compel them to make whatever is convenient, whereas mine are free and relatives.' **7** 'Well, because they are free and relatives of yours, do you think they should do nothing else but eat and sleep? ... **10** If they were going to do something disgraceful, death would be better than that; but, it appears, what they understand is thought the finest and most suitable occupation for women. And everyone does what he understands with the greatest ease and speed and pleasure and the finest result. So do not shrink from suggesting this to them, as it will be profitable both to you and them and be something that, very probably, they will willingly undertake.' **11** 'Indeed,' said Aristarchos, 'your advice seems so good, Socrates, that I think I can now bear to borrow capital to make a start on this, whereas before I couldn't allow myself to borrow, knowing that when I had spent it I would not be able to pay the loan back.' **12** As a result the capital was provided, wool was bought, and the women worked through their midday meal and dined when they'd finished working. They were cheerful instead of gloomy, and looked pleasantly at each other instead of with jealousy, and loved him as a guardian, while he was fond of them because they were productive. Finally he came to Socrates and cheerfully told him all this, as well as the fact that they now criticized him, because he was the only one in the household who ate without working.

WOMEN IN GREEK DRAMA

Conflicts which involve women frequently feature in Greek tragedy. It would be rash to assume that the tragedians directly portrayed women of their own time on stage, but it could be argued that, while the Athenians would not normally expect their womenfolk to act so forcefully or articulately, they could envisage their doing so, *if* they were placed in situations of similar dramatic conflict. While the evidence of tragedy regarding the seclusion of women is ambivalent, clearly women in comedy could go out of the house, and their husbands knew they did, even if they were not supposed to.

4.65 Aristophanes *Clouds* 39–55, 60–74: An Ill-Matched Couple

Strepsiades is a diehard countryman, married (perhaps somewhat improbably) to an aristocratic wife from the Alkmeonid family and afflicted with a spendthrift son, who is encouraged in his expensive habits by his mother. This son is asleep near him dreaming of chariot-racing; '(h)ippos' means horse, whereas 'pheidon' means parsimonious; Koisyra is a female name in the Alkmeonid family, and the name Megakles has obviously become a byword for aristocratic breeding; Pheidippides may be a portrait of Alkibiades. Strepsiades is here speaking to his sleeping son.

You just carry on asleep. But remember that these debts
Will one day fall on your own head.
Oh dear!
I wish that match-maker would die a miserable death,
Who persuaded me to marry your mother;
My lifestyle in the country was delightful —
Unwashed, no bugs, lying around at my ease,
With my fill of bees and sheep and pressed olives.
Then I married Megakles son of Megakles'
Niece — her a city girl, while I was from the country,
Ladylike and used to luxurious living just like a Koisyra.
When I married her I went to bed with her
Smelling of unfermented wine, dried figs, wool and profit,
While she smelt of perfume and saffron and sexy kisses,
Expense and gluttony and Aphrodite Genetyllis.
I don't say that she was lazy, she wove all right.
But I used to show her this cloak and
Take occasion to say, 'Wife, you're weaving us out of house and home.'
Later on, when this son here was born to the two of us,
To me and my good wife,
From then on we quarrelled about what to call him;
She wanted to add something horsey to his name —
Xanthippos or Charippos or Kallippides,
While I wanted to name him Pheidonides after his grandfather.
So we kept arguing about it; and then in time
We compromised and called him Pheidippides.
She used to take the boy and caress him, saying,
'When you're grown up and drive your chariot to the city,
Just like Megakles, wearing your lovely robe.' And I'd say,
'When you drive the goats from Phelleus,
Just like your father, wearing your leather jerkin.'
But he never listened to anything I said,
He just infected all my affairs with this equine disease.

4.66 Aristophanes *Lysistrata* 507–20, 565–97: The Women's Solution

The *Lysistrata*, like the *Thesmophoriazousai*, both of which were produced in 411 BC, is full of jokes against women's predilection for drink and sex. Yet in her argument with the magistrate, as elsewhere when she speaks of the war, Lysistrata is meant to be taken seriously: even though her final lines reflect the way women in particular have suffered from the war, obviously her remarks also struck home to a primarily male audience.

Lysistrata: In the last war we bore with you men
Because of our modesty, whatever you did.
Nor did you allow us to complain. Yet we didn't approve.
But we kept a close eye on you, and often when we were indoors
We'd hear that you'd made a bad decision on some important matter;
Then we'd be upset inside, but would ask you with a smile,
'What have you decided to inscribe on the stele about the peace treaty
In the assembly today?' 'What's that to you?' my husband would say.
'Won't you shut up?' And I did.
Woman: I wouldn't have kept quiet!
Magistrate: And you'd have howled if you hadn't!
Lysistrata: Accordingly I kept quiet at home.
And then we'd hear of some even more worthless decree you'd passed;
So we'd ask, 'How is it, husband, that you manage things so foolishly?'
And he'd glare at me and say that, if I didn't weave my web,
I'd really have a headache to complain about: 'For war should be men's concern!'
Magistrate: So how would you be able to end so many muddled affairs
In the different countries and resolve them?
Lysistrata: Quite easily.
Magistrate: How? Show us.
Lysistrata: Just as we take our thread, like this, when it is tangled,
And draw it out with our spindles, this way and that,
That's how we'll put a stop to this war, if we're allowed to,
After sending our embassies, this way and that.
Magistrate: Do you think that with wool, threads and spindles you can end
Such a dreadful problem, you foolish women?
Lysistrata: Yes, and if you had any sense,
You'd manage the whole city on the principle of our wool.
Magistrate: How? Let me see.
Lysistrata: You ought first, just as in a bathtub
You wash away the dirt of a fleece, to beat out from the city
All the knaves and pick out the burrs,
And all those who form associations and stick close together
To get the magistracies you should pull them out and pluck their heads;
Then you should card all public goodwill into a basket, mixing up
All the metics, and any other foreigner who's your friend,
And anyone who's indebted to the state, and stir these all in together;
All the cities that are colonies of this country
You must certainly see that these are lying like flocks of wool
All separate; you should take the wool from all of these,
Bring it here and gather it into one, and then make
A huge ball, and then out of it weave a cloak for the people.

Magistrate: Isn't it dreadful that these women should 'beat out' and 'make balls'
Who've had no share in the war at all!
Lysistrata: What! you accursed fool,
We bear more than twice as much of it as you do: first we've borne sons
And sent them off as hoplites.
Magistrate: Silence! don't remind us of our miseries.
Lysistrata: And then when we ought to be having fun and enjoying our youth,
We've got to sleep alone because of the expeditions; and even if you leave us aside,
I grieve for the young girls who grow old in their bedchambers.
Magistrate: Don't men grow old as well?
Lysistrata: By heaven, that's not the same at all!
For when a man returns home, even if he's grey, he soon marries a young girl;
But a woman's time is short, and if she doesn't take advantage of it,
No one wants to marry her, and she sits at home looking for omens.

4.67 Aristophanes *Birds* 785–96: Could Athenian Women Attend the Theatre?

The *Birds* was produced at the Dionysia festival in 414 BC. In this passage the chorus addresses the audience on the advantages of possessing wings. On the whole it seems most likely that some women could and did attend the theatre, but these may primarily have been hetairai, while 'respectable' women, like the wife of the member of the boule below, would almost certainly have stayed at home.

There's nothing better or nicer than to grow wings.
For as soon as any of you spectators acquired wings,
When he was hungry and tired of the tragic choruses,
He could fly off home and have lunch,
And once he was full up he could fly back again to watch us.
And if some Patrokleides amongst you wanted to shit,
He wouldn't have to soil his cloak, but just fly away,
Fart, get his breath again and fly back.
And if one of you who happened to be having an affair
Spotted the lady's husband in the councillors' seats,
He could fly away from you, wings flapping,
Have his screw and then fly back here again.

4.68 Aeschylus *Agamemnon* 1377–98: Clytemnestra Murders Agamemnon

After ten years of war against Troy, Agamemnon has returned home triumphant. Before sailing to Troy he had sacrificed his daughter Iphigeneia to obtain favourable winds: Clytemnestra's fury and frustration over this have long festered, and she has planned her revenge, taking as her lover Aegisthus, Agamemnon's cousin. Clytemnestra is here describing how she has killed Agamemnon to the elders of Argos, the chorus in the play.

For me this contest, long pondered from time past,
Came from an ancient quarrel, but in time it came;

There where I struck I stand with the deed accomplished.
Thus I acted, nor do I deny it,
So he could neither flee nor ward off fate;
An inextricable casting-net, just as for fish,
I threw round him, an evil wealth of garment;
And then I struck him twice, and after uttering two cries
His limbs went limp, and as he lay
I gave him a third stroke, to Zeus below the earth,
Saviour of the dead, in thanks for prayers accomplished.
So falling he gasped out his life
And, spouting forth a swift gush of blood,
He struck me with a dark shower of bloody dew,
And I rejoiced no less than, at the heaven-sent moisture,
The sown field exalts in the bursting of the bud.
So things stand, elders of Argos:
You may rejoice, if you choose, but I am exultant;
And if it were fitting over a dead man to pour libation,
It would be just, and more than just;
For in the house this man filled a mixing-bowl of evil
Curses, which he has returned and drained himself.

4.69 Sophocles *Antigone* 441–70: Antigone Defies King Kreon

The *Antigone* probably dates to 442 BC. Antigone's two brothers have killed each other fighting for the kingship of Thebes. Kreon, Antigone's uncle, now king of Thebes, has decreed that Polyneikes, the invader and traitor, should remain unburied. Antigone has buried his corpse and been caught by the guard (see doc. 3.54). In this passage she confronts Kreon; despite the fact that she is betrothed to Kreon's son Haimon, Kreon has her entombed in a cave. Teiresias the diviner eventually persuades Kreon to release her, but when found she has hanged herself, whereupon Haimon commits suicide.

Kreon: You, who bend your head towards the ground,
Speak — do you deny that you did this deed?
Antigone: I admit that I did it and I deny it not.
Kreon (to the guard): You, take yourself off, where you wish,
Free of this heavy charge.
(to Antigone) You there, tell me, not at length but concisely,
Did you know it had been proclaimed that this should not be done?
Antigone: I knew it: why was I not likely to know? It was made clear.
Kreon: And did you indeed dare to break these laws?
Antigone: Yes, for it was not Zeus who laid down these commands,
Nor did Justice, who dwells with the gods below,
Ordain these laws amongst mankind;
But I did not consider that your proclamations possessed
Such power that you a mortal could override
The unwritten and immutable observances of the gods;

They did not come into being today or yesterday, but live
Always and for ever, and no one knows from where they came.
I was not likely, I who feared no man's anger,
To be punished by the gods for breaking these.
I knew that I was going to die; how not?
Even if you had not proclaimed it; and if I die
Before my time, then I count this as gain.
For whoever, like myself, lives in great
Misery, why should he not count death as profit?
And so for me in meeting this my destiny
There is nothing painful. But if I had endured
That my mother's son should remain a corpse unburied,
I would have grieved at that; but I am not unhappy now.
And if I now seem to you to have acted foolishly,
It might be said that I incur the charge of folly from a fool.

4.70 Euripides *Medea* 465–95: Medea Speaks Her Mind to Jason

The *Medea* was performed in 431 BC. Despite the fact that Medea has left her home for Jason she has been deserted by him, and he has arranged to marry the daughter of the king of Corinth. Medea betrayed her family for Jason, helping him to steal the Golden Fleece, and killing her younger brother to hinder pursuit; she persuaded the daughters of Pelias, Jason's enemy, to kill their father, by pretending that by chopping him up and boiling him they would renew his youth; at the play's denouement she sends the princess Glauke (her rival) a robe dipped in poison which kills both Glauke and her father. Medea has the status of a metic, not a citizen: she has no rights and no family to defend her, and is here attacking Jason for his infidelity.

You utter scoundrel! For that's the greatest insult
I can put into words regarding your cowardice;
Have you come to me, have you really come, you, who've become
The gods' worst enemy, and mine, and that of all the human race?
This is not courage, nor is it daring
To look friends whom you have wronged in the face,
But the greatest of all diseases amongst men —
Shamelessness! But you did well to come;
For my heart will be relieved by speaking
Ill of you and you will be grieved at hearing it.
I'll begin right at the beginning:
I saved you, as all the Greeks know
Who embarked on that same ship, the Argo, with you,
When you were sent to master the fire-breathing bulls
With yokes and sow the deadly field;
And the dragon, which encircled the golden fleece
With twisted coils and sleeplessly guarded it,
I slew, and raised for you the light of deliverance.
And I betrayed my father and my home

Coming to Iolkos under Mount Pelion
With you, showing more eagerness than wisdom;
And I killed Pelias, by a most distressing death,
At the hands of his own children, and wiped out the entire house.
And though you were treated like this by me, basest of men,
You betrayed me, and found yourself a new marriage-bed,
Even though we had children — for if I were still childless,
Your lusting after this marriage would be pardonable.
But respect for oaths is forgotten! nor do I know
If you think the gods of old no longer reign
Or that new customs apply nowadays to mankind,
Since you know well you have not kept the oath you swore to me!

4.71 Euripides *Alcestis* 150–84, 189–98: Alcestis Dies for Her Husband

The *Alcestis* is Euripides' earliest surviving work, produced in 438 BC. Its theme is the self-sacrificing love of a wife for an unworthy husband, for when Admetos was doomed to die, Alcestis volunteered to die for him, when even his elderly parents refused to take his place; at the end of the play she is rescued from the underworld by Herakles. While she is a worthy wife, the real tragedy of the play is that to the spectators at least he is obviously not a husband worth dying for. A maidservant here reports Alcestis' actions as she prepares for death.

Chorus: Let her know this, that in dying she will at least be renowned
As the best of wives by far beneath the sun.
Servant: How could she not be the best? Who could contradict it?
What would the woman have to be who could surpass her?
How could any wife more clearly show
That she honours her husband than by being willing to die for him?
The whole city knows that!
You will be amazed when you hear what she did in the house.
For when she learned that her appointed day
Had come, she washed her white skin with water
From the stream, and taking from the cedar chests
Clothes and adornments she dressed herself fittingly.
Standing before the altar of Hestia she prayed:
'Mistress, since I am going beneath the earth,
In this the last time that I will worship you, I beg you
Take care of my orphaned children; wed my son
To a loving wife, and my daughter to a noble husband;
Let not my children die before their time,
As I who bore them perish, but be fortunate
And live out a long and happy life in their native land.'
All the altars, throughout Admetos' palace,
She visited and garlanded and prayed,
Stripping foliage from myrtle branches,
Without tears or lamentation, nor did the approaching evil

Change the lovely colour of her complexion.
And then in her bedroom, throwing herself on the bed,
There she indeed wept and spoke these words:
'O bed, where I lost my maidenhead
To this husband, for whom I die,
Farewell; I do not hate you; you alone have destroyed me;
For it is in dread of betraying you and my husband
That I die. Some other woman will possess you,
Not more faithful than I, though perhaps more fortunate.'
She fell on the bed and kissed it, and all the bedding
Grew wet with the tears flooding from her eyes.
Her children, clinging to their mother's dress,
Wept; and she, taking them in her arms,
Embraced them first one and then the other, like one about to die.
All the servants were crying throughout the house
Pitying their mistress; and she stretched
Her right hand to each, nor was there any so base
That she did not speak to him and he again to her.
Such are the miseries in the house of Admetos.
If he had died, he would have perished, but by escaping death
He has acquired a grief that he will never forget.

HOMOSEXUALITY AND PEDERASTY

There is no clear reference to male homoeroticism in Homer or Hesiod. Pederasty appears to have become widely accepted during the seventh century, especially in aristocratic circles: to the Greeks themselves Laios, father of Oedipus, was the first homosexual, and Euripides produced a tragedy on this theme, the *Chrysippos*, in 411–409 BC. The gods themselves were depicted as given to pederasty, with Zeus abducting the young Ganymede and Poseidon Pelops. Homosexuality in Greece normally meant the love of an adult male, the erastes (pl.: erastai), who was perhaps in his twenties, for an adolescent, the eromenos or beloved (pl.: eromenoi), who was the passive recipient of his affection. By convention at Athens, intercourse was supposed to take place between the thighs of the eromenos (this 'intercrural' copulation is frequently depicted on Attic vases, especially in the second half of the sixth century), and anal penetration was seen as an outrage, especially when submitted to by an adult citizen, even though it must have occurred in pederastic relationships.

4.72 Aeschylus *Myrmidons* F135: Achilles and Patroklos

Homer nowhere describes an erotic relationship between Achilles and Patroklos and it is not necessary to assume that their relationship in the *Iliad* was homosexual. Later Greeks, however, such as Aeschines (1.142), explicitly saw it as such and Aeschylus wrote a trilogy on the Achilles story, in which he depicted Patroklos as Achilles' beloved. Clearly, in the reference to 'thighs' Aeschylus here, as in *Fragment* 136, where Achilles recalls his 'reverent converse with your thighs', is referring to intercrural sex, in which the pederastic lover rubbed his erect penis between the youth's thighs while both were standing.

And you felt no compunction for my holy reverence of your thighs,
Ungrateful for our many kisses.

4.73 Solon F25: Solon on Pederasty

Solon was numbered among the Seven Sages of antiquity and seen as one of Athens' most important statesmen and lawgivers. Pederasty was part of the social structure of the polis, and, according to Pausanias in Plato *Symp*. 182c, tyrants tried to suppress pederasty because it gave rise to noble ideals that threatened their power (as in the case of Harmodios and Aristogeiton). The earliest scenes of homosexual courtship on Attic black-figure vases are contemporary with this fragment, and homosexual eros had become socially accepted by the end of the seventh century. For Solon's supposed legislation on male prostitution and institution of public brothels, see docs 4.85, 4.99, cf. 5.34.

When he falls in love with a boy in the lovely flower of youth,
Desiring his thighs and sweet mouth.

4.74 Theognis 1319–68: Theognis, Pederast and Pedagogue

A large proportion of the corpus of Theognis' poetry is addressed to the youth Kyrnos, advising him on how to become a good aristocrat (cf. docs 4.11, 16.13), and Theognis' poetry extols boy-love. Theognis clearly expects his verses immortalising Kyrnos to be sung at symposia, even far in the future. Ganymede, and his abduction by Zeus, was a favourite subject in homoerotic vase painting; cf. Homer *Iliad*. 5.265–67.

Since, boy, the goddess Kypris (Aphrodite) has given you beauty which incites desire,
And all the young men take an interest in your appearance,
Listen to these words and nurture favour for me in your heart,
As you know how hard a thing love is for a man to bear.
While your cheeks are smooth, boy, I will never cease to fawn over you,
Not even if I am foredoomed to die.
It's honour still for you to give, and no disgrace to me who desire you
To ask. So I entreat you by our parents,
Respect me, fair boy, and grant me favour, or else if you should ever happen
To crave a gift of the violet-crowned Cypriot-born (goddess),
And approach another (with your request), may god grant
That you meet in return the same response as you give me.
Happy the lover who can exercise at home,
Sleeping all day long beside a beautiful youth!
To love a youth has been a pleasant thing, since even Zeus,
The son of Kronos, king of the immortals, once loved Ganymede,
And snatching him up brought him to Olympus, and made him
A god, while he had the lovely bloom of youth.
So do not wonder, Simonides, if I too
Have been shown to be overpowered with love for a beautiful youth.
1367 A youth shows gratitude, but a woman companion is never faithful —
She always loves the man who is present.

4.75 *Inscriptiones Graecae* I³ 1399: An Oath for Love of a Boy

A slab of marble from the Attic countryside, with crude archaic lettering, *c.* 500 BC, recording the heroic love of Gnathios for a younger boy, for whom he swore an oath that he would go to war; the boy presumably erected this as a memorial to Gnathios. [*IG* I² 920.]

Here a man swore a solemn oath for love of a boy
To mingle in strife and tearful war.
I am sacred to Gnathios, who lost his life in war …

4.76 *Inscriptiones Graecae* I³ 1401: Lysitheos Loves Mikion

This inscription from the acropolis at Athens may have been written by the beloved about his older lover, which would make it unusual. [*IG* I² 924.]

Lysitheos says he loves Mikion more than anyone in the city since he is brave.

4.77 *Inscriptiones Graecae* XII.3 543, 537, 538, 536: Obscene Inscriptions from Thera

A number of archaic graffiti from boulders on the island of Thera, perhaps dated to the early or mid-seventh century, celebrate homosexual relationships and sexual conquest, often linked with excellence in the dance. Thera had connections with both Sparta (Thera was colonised by Lakonians c. 850 BC) and Crete, and the Therans celebrated the rites of Apollo Karneios near the site of the inscriptions. These graffiti read like malicious boasts and slanders: (iv) appears to have been written by a youth called Empedokles, with an unfinished interpolation by Empylos on the second line, while the term 'faggot!' or 'pathic!' (pornos) referring to him has been added by Empedokles or another companion. There are fifty-eight non-scurrilous pederastic rock inscriptions from Thasos, perhaps from the fourth century, in which the same names frequently recur.

i Barbax dances well and he gave me pleasure(?) (*IG* XII.3 543).

ii By Apollo Delphinios, right here Krimon fucked So-and-so, the son of Bathykles, brother of So-and-so (*IG* XII.3 537).

iii Here Krimon fucked Amotion (*IG* XII.3 538).

iv Pheidippides fucked. Timagoras and Empheres and I fucked.
Empylos did? this too.
Faggot!
Empedokles inscribed this, and he danced by Apollo (*IG* XII.3 536)!

4.78 Ephoros *History* F149: Abduction on Crete

The fourth-century BC historian Ephoros recorded traditions of pederastic abduction on Crete, where ritualised homosexual rape of an eromenos (beloved) by a worthy erastes was considered an honour; only if the youth's friends considered the erastes socially unworthy was the youth taken away from him; cf. Plat. *Laws* 636a–b, where Plato implies that Sparta and Crete were unusual in their institutionalism of homosexuality. As in Sparta, male citizens in Crete were segregated into messes and barracks, which encouraged homosexual behaviour. [*FGH* 70 F149; Strabo *Geog.* 10.4.21.]

They have an unusual custom with regard to love affairs; for they win their eromenoi not by persuasion, but by abduction. The erastes tells the youth's friends three or more days beforehand that he is going to effect the abduction, but for them to hide the youth or not to allow him to travel the appointed road is extremely disgraceful, a confession, as it were, that the youth is unworthy to gain such an erastes ... The erastai consider as a worthy object of love he who is distinguished not by his beauty, but by his courage and propriety. And after giving the youth presents the erastes takes him away to any place in the country he wishes; and those who were present at the abduction follow, and after feasting and hunting together for two months (for it is not permitted to keep the youth for a longer period) they return to the city. The youth is released after receiving gifts of a military costume, an ox, and a drinking-cup (these are the gifts laid down by law) and other numerous and costly presents, to which the friends contribute because of the number of the expenses. The youth sacrifices the ox to Zeus and feasts those who returned with him; then he reveals the details of his intercourse with his erastes, whether he had welcomed it or not, the law allowing this in order that, if any violence was used on him during the abduction, he then has the chance to take his revenge and get rid of his erastes. For those youths who are fair in appearance and of distinguished ancestry not to obtain lovers is disgraceful, and considered a result of their character. But the parastathentes (for that is what they call those who have been abducted) receive honours: in both the dances and races they have the most prestigious positions, and they are allowed to dress differently from the others, in the clothes which have been given them by their lovers.

4.79 Xenophon *Constitution of the Spartans* 2.12–14: Spartan Pederasty

While Xenophon is here trying to portray Spartan pederasty as purely spiritual, he has to admit that this was not generally believed; cf. Plut. *Lyk.* 17–18, where women too indulge in same-sex love affairs, and where an erastes is fined for his beloved's crying-out in a fight. According to Xen. *Symp.* 8.34–35, in Elis and Thebes erastes and eromenos stood next to each other in line of battle, and the Sacred Band of Thebes, formed *c.* 378, was composed of pairs of homosexual lovers: see doc. 14.17.

2.12 I think I ought to say something too about men's love for youths, since this is also related to their education. Well, some of the other Greeks, like the Boeotians for instance, live together, man and boy, as if they were married, or, like the Eleians, win the youth by means of favours; on the other hand there are some who entirely prevent potential erastai from conversing with youths. **13** Lykourgos' views were in contrast to all of these, for, if a respectable man admired a youth's character and tried to make him a friend in all innocence and associate with him, he commended this and considered it the finest form of education; but if someone appeared to desire a boy's body, he thought this to be quite disgraceful and laid it down that at Sparta erastai should refrain from molesting boys no less than parents refrain from sleeping with their children and brothers with their sisters. **14** I am not surprised, however, that some people do not believe this; for in many cities the laws do not oppose passionate attachments to boys.

4.80 Aristotle F98: A Popular Song from Chalkis

The following song is said by Plutarch to have been quoted by Aristotle, perhaps Aristotle of Chalkis, *FGH* 423, a historiographer of the fourth century, rather than the philosopher. It refers to the Lelantine War between Eretria and Chalkis in the eighth century, in which Kleomachos of Pharsalia was killed fighting for Chalkis; a funerary column for Kleomachos stood in the agora of Chalkis, probably erected in the sixth century. Plutarch records a version of the tale in which Kleomachos' eromenos watched the battle, and states that until this point the Chalkidians had frowned on pederasty, but they now honoured it more than others. The song possibly dates back to archaic times. [Page *PMG* 873; Plut. *Mor.* 761a–b.]

O youths, all you who possess grace and noble fathers,
Do not grudge brave men converse with your bloom;
For, together with courage, Eros the limb-relaxer
Flourishes in the cities of Chalkis.

4.81 Anacreon 357, 359, 360, 407: Anacreon's Lovers

In the sixth century BC Anacreon created a tradition of poetry about the pleasures of sex and wine, and according to Athenaeus (*Diep.* 540e) while on Samos rivalled the tyrant Polykrates in his liaisons with boys: doc. 7.37. Note the attraction of modesty in youths, when approached by erastai.

357 O Lord, with whom Love the subduer
And the blue-eyed nymphs
And rosy Aphrodite
Play, as you roam
The high mountain peaks;
I beseech you, with good will
Come to me, hear my prayer
And find it acceptable;
Be Kleoboulos' good
Counsellor, Dionysos,
And make him accept my love.
359 Kleoboulos is the one I love,
Kleoboulos I am mad about,
Kleoboulos I ogle.
360 O youth with the girlish glance,
I seek you, but you do not listen,
Not knowing that you are the charioteer of my soul!
407 But pledge me as a toast,
Dear boy, your slender thighs.

4.82 Anacreon 396: Symposia and Drinking Songs

At symposia, youths were often present and were expected to help entertain the company with poetry and skolia, drinking songs, which could deal with pederastic love; the poems of Theognis, for example, were performed at symposia. For the procedures involved in symposia and in singing skolia, see Ar. *Wasps* 1208–48; a collection of twenty-five is preserved by Athen. *Diep.* 694c–695f.

Bring water, bring wine, boy, bring us flowery
Garlands; bring them, so I can box with Eros.

4.83 Aristophanes *Clouds* 973–80: Aristophanes and the 'Good Old Ways'

In the *Clouds* Aristophanes presents a contest between Right and Wrong, in which Right criticises the tendency of modern youth to march around acting as their own pimps, and mourns the passing of the good old days when boys were modest and disciplined, in the process showing himself as an aggressive old-fashioned pederast.

When they were sitting at their tutor's, the boys had to put one thigh forward
So as not to show anything cruel to those outside;
Then, when a boy got up again, he had to brush the sand together and take care
Not to leave an impression of his youth for his lovers.
And no boys in those days would anoint themselves with oil below the navel
To make moisture and down bloom upon their genitals as on apples.
Nor would they make their voice effeminate to attract their lovers,
Or walk about prostituting themselves with their eyes.

4.84 Aristophanes *Birds* 137–42: The Ideal Polis

The *Birds* was produced at the Dionysia in 414 BC, but it ignores the Peloponnesian War, instead presenting a fantasy picture of an ideal city built by the birds in the clouds. In this play, Peisthetairos' ideal of the perfect state is one where the worst that could happen would be a neighbour's anger when Peisthetairos failed to proposition his neighbour's young son.

I would like a city where the father of a beautiful youth meets me
As if he's suffered an injury, with the complaint,
'That's a nice way, Stilbonides, to treat my son!
You met him coming home from the gymnasium after his bath,
And you didn't kiss him, or address him, or embrace him —
You didn't even tickle his balls, and you an old friend of the family.'

4.85 Aeschines 1 *Against Timarchos* 9–11, 13–14, 19–20: 'Solon' on Male Prostitution

While it may be doubted that Solon laid down the laws cited by Aeschines below, it is clear that they were considered to be of long standing and so must date to at least the fifth century BC; they certainly predate 424 BC because Aristophanes *Knights* 877 refers to a law against male prostitution. Athenians who had prostituted themselves were deprived of certain citizen rights, and death or a fine was the punishment for prostituting a citizen youth or even a male slave (Aesch. 1.16). Aeschines is not attacking the practice of pederasty, which was acceptable legally (though slaves were forbidden to be lovers of free youths under penalty of fifty blows of the public lash); the point at issue here is that of male prostitution for citizens involving anal intercourse.

9 Look first at what the legislator says about teachers, to whom we of necessity have to entrust our children. Their livelihood depends on their integrity, with anything less meaning poverty — yet he still appears to distrust them, for he specifically lays down, first, at what time of day the freeborn boy is to go to school, then how many boys are to go with him, and when he is to go home. **10** He forbids the teachers to open schools or trainers the wrestling schools before sunrise, and tells them to close them before sunset, being highly suspicious of seclusion and darkness. He lays down who should go to school and at what age, provides for an official who shall superintend them, and for the superintendence of slave-attendants and festivals of the Muses in the schools and of Hermes in the palaistrai, and finally regulates the associations between the boys and their cyclic dances. **11** He also lays down that the choregos, a man who is going to expend his own money on your entertainment, should be more than forty years of age, so that he may have reached the most sensible period of one's life before he comes into association with your children…

13 Now after this, gentlemen of the jury, Solon legislates regarding great crimes, which actually occur, I believe, in our city. For the fact that unacceptable things were being done was the reason why our ancestors made these laws. At any rate the law states that if anyone is hired out as a prostitute by his father or brother or uncle or guardian, or anyone at all of his legal guardians, prosecution is to lie not against the youth himself, but against the man who put him up for hire and the man who hired him, against the first because he put him up for hire, and against the second, he says, because he hired him. And the penalties for both have been made the same, and a youth, when he comes of age, is not obliged to support his father or provide a home for him, if the father has hired him out as a prostitute; but he has to bury him when he has died and perform the other customary rites. **14** Consider how appropriate this is, gentlemen of the jury. While the father is alive he is deprived of the benefit of parenthood, just as he had taken away his son's right of political speech, but when he is dead, and unconscious of the service he is receiving, and law and religion are honoured instead, the lawgiver instructs the son to bury him and perform the other customary rites. And what other law has been laid down to protect your children? That against procurers, for the heaviest penalties have been imposed if anyone prostitutes a freeborn child or woman … **19** If any Athenian, says the lawgiver, should have acted as a prostitute, he is not to be permitted to become one of the nine archons, because, I suppose, the office involves wearing a wreath, nor to act as a priest, since he would not be pure of body, nor, he states, can he be one of the state's public advocates, nor can he hold any office whatever either at home or abroad, whether filled by lot or elected; **20** nor can he act as a herald or an ambassador, nor can he prosecute those who have been ambassadors, nor can he be a hired informer, nor can he even speak his opinion in either the boule or the assembly, not even if he were the best speaker in Athens. And if anyone acts contrary to this, the lawgiver has provided for prosecution on the charge of prostitution and has laid down the heaviest penalties.

4.86 Ion of Chios *Foundation of Chios* F6: Susceptible Sophocles

The fifth-century author Ion of Chios relates that he met 'boy-loving' Sophocles on Lesbos, where he had sailed as a general in 440 BC and where he was entertained by a Chian friend, Hermesilaos, whose wine-pourer was a handsome youth who took Sophocles' fancy. Perikles appears to have disapproved of Sophocles' behaviour: according to Plutarch (*Per.* 8.8), when Sophocles praised a handsome boy during this expedition Perikles told him that a general had to keep his eyes clean, as well as his hands. [*FGH* 392 F6; Athen. *Deip.* 604c–d.]

As the youth was trying to remove a piece of straw from the cup with his little finger, Sophocles asked him if he could see it clearly. When he said he could, Sophocles said, 'Then blow it away, so your finger doesn't get wet.' As he brought his face to the cup, Sophocles drew the cup nearer to his own mouth, so their heads would be closer to each other. When he was very near the youth, he took hold of him with his arm and kissed him. Everyone applauded with laughter and shouted because he had led the youth on so well, and Sophocles remarked, 'Gentlemen, I am practising my generalship, since Perikles told me that I knew how to write poetry, but not how to be a general. Don't you think my stratagem was very successful?'

4.87 Xenophon *Symposium* 1.8–9, 8.21–23: The 'Chaste' Lover

In the *Symposium*, written *c.* 380 BC, Xenophon purports to describe a dinner party held in 421 by the wealthy aristocrat Kallias, brother-in-law of Alkibiades, in honour of his eromenos Autolykos, who had just won the pankration at the Panathenaic games. Lykon, Autolykos' father, is also present and Kallias is considered to have behaved properly by inviting him as well. Socrates' discourse on homosexual affection (8.21) stresses the importance of the spiritual aspect of such relationships, as opposed to the purely physical, and in *Xen. Mem.* 1.3.11 he again takes an idealised view of pederastic relationships, even forbidding kissing; similarly, he considers that a youth who offers himself for money is a prostitute, while a youth who becomes the friend of a virtuous and good man is 'chaste': *Mem.* 1.6.13; cf. doc. 4.104.

1.8 Anyone who noticed what took place would have straightway considered that beauty is by its nature something kingly, especially when its possessor combines it with modesty and discretion, as in the present case of Autolykos. **9** For in the first place, just as a light which appears in the night draws the eyes of everyone, so now the beauty of Autolykos drew the gaze of everyone to himself … **8.21** 'For a youth does not, as a woman does, share with the man in the pleasure of the intercourse, but looks on sober at the other's intoxication by Aphrodite, and consequently it is not to be wondered at if he should become contemptuous of his erastes … **23** for he who teaches proper speech and conduct would be honoured like Cheiron and Phoenix by Achilles, but he whose desire is for the body would correctly be treated as a beggar. For he is always following his eromenos around, begging and beseeching either a kiss or some other caress.'

4.88 Plato *Symposium* 219b–d: Alkibiades Attempts to Seduce Socrates

Plato's *Symposium*, written after 385 BC, is set in 416, the year of the tragedian Agathon's first victory and the year before the disastrous Sicilian expedition. It describes a dinner party to celebrate Agathon's triumph, at which Agathon, Aristophanes and Socrates were present. The dialogue is about love, primarily pederastic relationships, and Alkibiades, who has arrived late and in a state of intoxication, describes Socrates' ability to withstand hardships and temptation by showing how he had attempted unsuccessfully to seduce Socrates, by wrestling with him in the gymnasium, by conversation and by sleeping with him after dinner in Alkibiades' own house.

219b Without allowing him to say anything else, I got up and covered him with my own garment (himation) — for it was winter — and then laid myself down under his worn cloak and threw my arms round this really superhuman and wonderful man, **219c** and lay there the whole night. Here again, Socrates, you have to say that I am not lying. But despite my doing this he was so superior to my attractions and despised them and put them to scorn and insulted me in the very point I prided myself on, gentlemen of the jury — for you are the judges in this case of Socrates' arrogance. For you should be aware, by all the gods and goddesses, that when I got up after sleeping with Socrates nothing more had happened **219d** than if I had been sleeping with my father or elder brother.

4.89 Lysias 3 *Against Simon* 4–6: Homosexual Rivalry

This speech, delivered for the defence before the Areiopagos at some time after 394, concerns the amorous rivalry of Simon and the defendant for the possession of a young Plataean, Theodotos, who was clearly not a citizen, as he could give evidence under torture (33). Theodotos was in a semi-permanent relationship with one of the men: Simon claimed that he had made a contract with Theodotos and given him the large sum of 300 drachmas (22).

4 If I am guilty, I expect no pardon; and if I can show that I am not guilty of the things Simon swore against me, and I appear to you foolishly attached to the youth for a man of my age, I beg you not to think anything the worse of me, knowing that to feel desire is innate in all mankind, and that he may be the best and most prudent person, who can bear his misfortunes most decently … **5** We felt desire, councillors, for Theodotos a lad from Plataea, and while I thought it right to make him my friend by being kind to him, this man by insulting and ill-using him thought to compel him to do what he wished. It would take a long time to tell you all that the youth has suffered from him; but I think that you ought to hear all the offences he has committed against me. **6** For when he learned that the youth was at my house, he came to my house at night drunk, and broke down the doors and entered the women's quarters, inside of which were my sister and nieces, who have lived so decently that they are even ashamed to be seen by their male relatives.

PROSTITUTION

The open sale of sexual services was a fact of life in Greek cities: in fourth-century BC Athens there was a prostitute tax paid to the state by both male and female prostitutes (Aesch. 1.119–20, 1.123–24). The ranks of those who provided sexual services were wide, though it can be difficult to draw distinctions between the various classes of women. At the bottom of the scale were the prostitutes (pornai), generally foreign-born slaves, who staffed the brothels and were controlled by a pimp, or pornoboskos, who was responsible for the payment of tax on their income. They could also walk the streets in search of clients. At the top of the scale were the hetairai ('companions'), like Theodote (doc. 4.96); the most famous hetaira was said to have been Aspasia, who became Perikles' partner *c.* 445.

4.90 Anacreon 446; Archilochos 209: Because the Lady Is a Whore

The seventh-century BC poet Archilochos of Paros was renowned in antiquity for his wit and for his scurrilous and erotic recitations, many of which were presumably fictional rather than autobiographical. These fragments from Archilochos and Anacreon are testimony to negative attitudes towards prostitutes, pornai, in seventh- and sixth-century poetry. [Suda 3.429.]

'Defiled', used of a prostitute by Archilochos. Anacreon has 'giving herself to everyone' and 'public highway' and 'sex-mad'.

4.91 Herodotos 2.134.1–135.5: The Courtesans of Egypt

Herodotos here praises the hetairai of Naukratis. He is here anachronistically identifying Rhodopis, who lived in Naukratis in Amasis' reign (*c.* 570–525 BC), with Doriche, a contemporary of Sappho. This is the first attested use of the word hetaira as courtesan.

2.134.1 There are some of the Greeks who say indeed that the pyramid of Mykerinos belongs to the hetaira Rhodopis, but in saying this they are not correct. **2** They do not even seem to me to know who Rhodopis was (for if they did, they would not have attributed to her the erection of a pyramid, in which countless thousands of talents, so to speak, must have been consumed), as well as the fact that she flourished in the time of King Amasis, not that of Mykerinos. **3** Rhodopis lived very many years later than the kings who left the pyramids, and by birth was a Thracian, the slave of Iadmon son of Hephaistopolis, a Samian, and fellow-slave of Aesop the story-writer ... **2.135.1** She was brought to Egypt by Xanthos the Samian, having come to practise her profession, and was freed from slavery at great cost by a man from Mytilene, Charaxos son of Skamandronymos and brother of Sappho the poet. **2** In this way Rhodopis was freed and remained in Egypt, and, being fascinating, acquired a fortune (for her at least), but not enough to build such a pyramid. **3** The tenth of her money can still be seen even today by whoever wishes, but a great fortune should not be attributed to her. For Rhodopis desired to leave behind in Greece a memorial of herself, and made a temple-offering that no one else had thought of, and dedicated this at Delphi in remembrance of herself. **4** So with a tenth of her money she bought as many iron spits as a tenth would allow (the spits being large enough for a whole ox), and sent them to Delphi; and they are still even now heaped together behind the altar dedicated by the Chians, opposite the temple itself. **5** And somehow the courtesans in Naukratis tend to be fascinating; for in the first place the woman of whom this story is told became so renowned that even all the Greeks learned the name of Rhodopis, and, after her, the one called Archedike became celebrated in song throughout Greece, though less talked about than the other.

4.92 Strabo *Description of Greece* 8.6.20: Corinthian Prostitutes as a Tourist Attraction

Corinth was known for its hierodouloi, sacred prostitutes at the temple of Aphrodite Ourania, and Corinthian prostitutes as a whole were proverbially expensive: see doc. 4.104. This proverb, which implies that not everyone could afford a trip to Corinth, also occurs in a fragment of Aristophanes (Kassel & Austin 3.2, F928), Strabo *Geog.* 12.3.36 and elsewhere. Athenian prostitutes were, in comparison, relatively cheap: see doc. 4.99. For Corinth's wealth as an economic and trading centre, to which the presence of the temple courtesans and other prostitutes contributed, see docs 1.61–62.

The temple of Aphrodite was so rich that it owned more than a thousand temple slaves (hierodouloi), hetairai whom both men and women had dedicated to the goddess. And therefore it was on account of these women as well that the city was crowded with people and grew rich; for instance, the ship-captains freely squandered their money, and hence the proverb, 'Not for every man is the voyage to Corinth.' Moreover, it is recorded that a certain hetaira replied to a woman who reproached her for not loving women's work or touching wool: 'But even so I have already taken down three erections in this short time!'

4.93 Pindar F122: Xenophon of Corinth Dedicates Temple Slaves

In 464 BC Xenophon of Corinth promised to dedicate 100 sacred prostitutes, hierodouloi, to Aphrodite if she helped him to victory in the Olympic games. He won both the foot-race and pentathlon, and commissioned Pindar to write a victory ode (*Ol.* 13) as well as this skolion to celebrate his dedication. The skolion was sung at the sacrificial feast, at which the prostitutes were also present. For an epigram by Simonides, which may refer to a dedication by temple prostitutes at Corinth during the Persian Wars, see doc. 11.43. [Athen. *Deip.* 573f–574b.]

Young girls, who welcome many strangers, handmaidens
Of Persuasion in wealthy Corinth,
You who burn the golden tears of fresh frankincense,
Often flying to the heavenly mother of desires,
Aphrodite, in your thoughts.
To you without the chance of refusal she has granted,
O children, that in lovely beds
You shall have the fruit of your soft bloom plucked.
And with necessity everything is beautiful.
. . .
But I wonder what they will say of me, the Isthmus'
Lords, when they find such a beginning of the honey-minded skolion,
As a husband of common women.
We have taught the nature of gold with a pure touchstone.
. . .
Mistress of Cyprus, here to your grove
Xenophon has brought a hundred-bodied herd of grazing girls,
Rejoicing in his fulfilled vows.

4.94 Alexis of Samos *Samian Annals* F1: A Profitable Profession

Perikles' successful eight-month siege of Samos took place in 440 BC, after Samos stopped contributing ships to the Delian League. For the siege of Samos, see Thuc. 1.115.2–117.3; doc. 12.24.

These prostitutes seem to be independent sex-workers, unlike the porne in Lysias 4, who, according to the defendant, is jointly owned by himself and the prosecutor, who have come to blows over who owns her, and the pallake (concubine) in doc. 4.52 who is going to be put into a brothel by her owner. The date of Alexis is unknown. [*FGH* 539 F1: Athen. *Deip.* 572f.]

Alexis of Samos in the second book of his *Samian Annals* says, 'The Aphrodite on Samos, whom some call "In the reeds", and others "In the swamp", was dedicated by prostitutes who had accompanied Perikles when he besieged Samos, as they had made a good profit from their charms.'

4.95 Aristophanes *Acharnians* 524–29: Aspasia's Girls

Aspasia, Perikles' partner from *c.* 445 BC, was later reputed to have trained young girls as prostitutes and entertainers (doc. 4.29) and the comic poets Kratinos and Eupolis attack her as a pallake and porne. The first mention of Aspasia as a brothel-keeper appears in this passage, where Aristophanes gives a fantastic story to account for Perikles' ban, perhaps in 432, on Megarian access to the Athenian agora and harbours in the empire. Kottabos was a game played by throwing the dregs from cups of wine at a target.

Going to Megara some young men,
Drunk from too many games of kottabos, stole a prostitute named Simaitha;
Then the Megarians, garlicked-up like fighting-cocks by this painful occurrence,
Stole in return two prostitutes of Aspasia's;
And that was the beginning of the war which broke out
All over Greece over three cock-suckers.

4.96 Xenophon *Memorabilia* 3.11.4: Theodote, a Wealthy Hetaira

Xenophon relates the visit of Socrates to a hetaira, Theodote, who was noted for her beauty, and who allowed artists to paint her portrait ('showing them as much as decency allowed'). In a classic definition of the hetaira, she is described as 'the sort of woman who would associate with any man who persuaded her' (3.11.1: Socrates questions her about the art of seduction and gives her advice as to how to retain her 'friends').

Socrates then noticed that Theodote was expensively dressed, that her mother, who was present, had fine clothes and attendants, that there were many good-looking maidservants who were carefully dressed, and that her house was also lavishly furnished. 'Tell me, Theodote,' he said, 'do you have a farm?'

'No, I don't,' she said.

'Or a house, perhaps, that gives you an income?'

'No, not a house.'

'Perhaps you own craftsmen?'

'Not craftsmen.'

'From where, then, do you get your livelihood?'

'My livelihood is from any friend I might make who wishes to be generous.'

4.97 Athenaeus *Deipnosophistae* 590d–591d: Phryne Shows All

The courtesan Phryne was nearly executed in the late fourth century for exotic religious practices; she was acquitted because she was seen by the jurors, because of her beauty, to be a priestess of Aphrodite. Clearly an hetaira could amass considerable wealth and influence.

590d Phryne came from Thespiai. When she was prosecuted by Euthias for a capital offence she was acquitted, and Euthias was so enraged by this, Hermippos tells us, that he never brought another case to court. **590e** When Hyperides was defending Phryne and was making no headway with his speech, when the jurors were clearly going to convict her, he had her brought out into the open, ripped open her undergarments and exposed her breasts, breaking into such piteous lamentations at the sight of her in his speech that he caused the jurors to experience superstitious fears of this expounder and attendant of Aphrodite and so they gave way to their compassion and refrained from putting her to death. After she had been acquitted, a decree was passed that no one speaking on anyone's behalf was to break into lamentation and that no man or woman being prosecuted was to have their body bared during the trial. **590f** As a matter of fact Phryne was more beautiful in the parts not usually seen. Because of this it was not easy to see her naked, for she always wore a close-fitting tunic and did not make use of the public baths. At the festivals of the Eleusinia and Poseidonia, in the sight of the entire Greek world, she only removed her cloak and let down her long hair before stepping into the sea: it was from her as his model that Apelles painted his 'Aphrodite Rising from the Sea'. **591a** Praxiteles the sculptor was in love with her and used her as his model for his Knidian Aphrodite, and on the base of his statue of Eros below the stage of the theatre, had inscribed:

'Praxiteles has portrayed to perfection the Eros which he suffered,
Drawing the model from his own heart,
Giving Me to Phryne as the price of Me. I cast love-spells
No longer shooting my arrows, but from My being gazed upon.'

591b He gave her a choice of his statues, whether she wanted to take his Eros or his Satyr which stood in the Street of the Tripods. She chose the Eros and dedicated it in Thespiai. Of Phryne herself her neighbours had a golden statue made which was set up at Delphi on a pillar of Pentelic marble; Praxiteles was the sculptor. When the cynic philosopher Krates saw it he said that it was a dedication to the Greeks' lack of self-control. The statue was set up between that of Archidamos king of Sparta **591c** and that of Philip son of Amyntas, with the inscription 'Phryne, daughter of Epikles, of Thespiai'; this is what Alketas states in the second volume of his work *On the Dedications at Delphi*. Apollodoros in his work *On Hetairai* records that there were two Phrynes, one of whom was called 'Tears and Laughter', the other 'Nile-perch'. Herodikos in the sixth book of his *Persons Who Appear in Comic Plays* says that the one was called Sestos by the rhetoricians because she 'sifted' and stripped bare all those who consorted with her, while the other was the Thespian. **591d** Phryne was extremely wealthy and used to promise that she would build a wall around Thebes if the Thebans would inscribe on it that 'Though Alexander demolished it, Phryne the hetaira had it rebuilt', as Kallistratos records in his work *On Hetairai*.

4.98 [Demosthenes] 59 *Against Neaira* 18–19, 28–32: Neaira's Career

Apollodoros and Theomnestos brought an indictment against Stephanos and Neaira, alleging that Neaira was an alien (and an ex-slave and prostitute), and hence should not be the wife of an Athenian citizen (cf. doc. 4.56); Neaira's daughter had also been married to two Athenian husbands as if she were herself a citizen woman. If this allegation was upheld Neaira would be sold as a slave and Stephanos fined 1,000 drachmas. Nikarete is the pimp or brothel-owner who originally owned Neaira, according to the prosecution. The speech dates to the mid-fourth century BC. According to this document Neaira's full purchase price was thirty minas, or 3,000 drachmas.

18 Nikarete, the freedwoman of Charisios the Eleian and the wife of his cook Hippias, acquired these seven girls when they were young children. She was clever at spotting potential good looks in young girls and knew from experience how to bring them up and educate them, as she practised this as her profession and made her living from them. **19** She called them her daughters so that, by pretending they were free women, she could extract the highest fees from the men who wished to sleep with them. When she had harvested the youthful prime of them all, she sold the persons of all seven of them together — Anteia and Stratola and Aristokleia and Metaneira and Philia and Isthmias and Neaira here…

28 Deposition: Hipparchos of Athmonon declares that Xenokleides and himself hired Neaira, the present defendant, in Corinth as a hetaira who prostituted herself for money, and that Neaira used to drink at Corinth in the company of himself and Xenokleides the poet.

29 Neaira then had two lovers, Timanoridas the Corinthian and Eukrates from Leukas. Since Nikarete was expensive in what she charged, demanding that they cover all the daily expenses of the household, they paid out thirty minas as the price of Neaira's person and purchased Neaira from Nikarete to be their slave in accordance with the law of the city.

30 They kept her and made use of her for as long as they wanted, and when they were going to get married they told her that they did not want to see their own hetaira working in Corinth or in the hands of a brothel-keeper, but they were happy to take less money than they had paid for her and see her reaping some benefit for herself. So they offered to remit 1,000 drachmas from the price of her freedom, 500 each, and told her, when she had found the money, to pay them the twenty minas. When she heard this suggestion from Eukrates and Timanoridas, she invited to Corinth men who had previously been her lovers, including Phrynion of Paianiea, the son of Demon and brother of Demochares, who was leading an outrageous and extravagant lifestyle, as the older ones among you will recall. **31** When Phrynion arrived, she told him about the offer that Eukrates and Timanoridas had made to her and gave him the tributes she had collected from her other lovers as a contribution towards the cost of her freedom, along with whatever she had saved up for herself, and asked him to make up the rest of the sum of twenty minas and pay it to Eukrates and Timanoridas so she could be free. **32** He was happy to listen to this proposal of hers, took the money which had been paid to her by her other lovers and after adding the balance himself paid Eukrates and Timanoridas the twenty minas as the price of her freedom and on condition that she should not practise her trade in Corinth.

4.99 Philemon F3: Prostitution as a Democratic Ideal in Athens

The institution of a system of public brothels in Athens was later ascribed to Solon, and the fourth-century comic poet Philemon, in his play *Brothers* (*Adelphoi*), praises the innovation by which even the poorest citizens could enjoy the services of a prostitute. The price of an obol here seems very low, and may be slang for 'dirt cheap'. [Athen. *Deip.* 569d.]

But you invented a law for all mankind;
For they say that you were the first, Solon, to envisage
This democratic and salutary thing, by Zeus!
(And it's appropriate for me to comment on this, Solon).
Seeing the city full of young men
And that these had their necessary natural urges
And were going wrong in the direction of what did not belong to them,
You set up women you had bought in various places
To be common to all and ready for action.
They stand there naked, so you're not deceived: look at everything.
Suppose you're not doing well, you're feeling
Erotic. The door's open.
One obol; jump in. There's no prudery,
No nonsense, she doesn't snatch herself away,
But you can immediately have whichever one you want how you want.
Then you leave; tell her to get lost, she's nothing to you.

4.100 Alexis *Fair Measure* F1: Beware of Prostitutes

Alexis, a poet of Middle and New comedy (*c.* 375–275), was born at Thourioi but lived mostly at Athens and wrote some 245 plays. [Athen. *Deip.* 568a–c.]

568a Alexis in his play entitled *Fair Measure* outlines the efforts engaged in by hetairai and the embellishments they make use of in these words:

Firstly they're concerned with making a profit and plundering their neighbours;
Everything else is unimportant — they're sewing up everyone else in plots.
And when they're rich they take in new hetairai, who are not experienced in the profession,
And quickly refashion them so they have totally different manners and looks from before.
568b Suppose one's rather short — a cork sole is stitched into her shoes.
One is tall — she wears a thin slipper
And puts her head to one side when she's out walking.
This reduces her height. One has no hips:
She works on a structure that ensures her bottom
is applauded by all who see her. One has a thick waist:
They give her tits made of the props comic actors use,
when they pad themselves out and
568c drag forward the covering of their stomachs by implements like punting poles.

One woman has eyebrows that are too red: they paint them with soot. Another is
Too dark: they paint them with white-lead.
One is too pale: she rubs on rouge.
A part of one's body is beautiful — this is shown naked.
This one has lovely teeth, so of course she has to laugh
So everyone there can see what a pretty mouth she has.

4.101 Aristophanes *Wasps* 500–2: A Democratically Minded Prostitute

In the *Wasps*, the slave Xanthias visits a prostitute, which implies that their services could be exceptionally cheap (unless this is itself a joke).

Xanthias: Like that prostitute I visited yesterday at midday,
When I told her to get on top, she got mad at me
And asked if I wanted to set up a tyranny like Hippias.

4.102 Athenaeus *Deipnosophistae* 695e: A Drinking Song

Athenaeus preserves an anonymous skolion, drinking song, together with twenty-four others, which may date back to the archaic period.

The prostitute and the bathman always have the same custom:
They wash the good and the bad in the same tub.

4.103 Xenarchos F4: A Plethora of Choice

As in doc. 4.99, consorting with prostitutes is seen as perfectly acceptable, and the fourth-century comic poet Xenarchos in his play *Pentathlos* recommends young men to visit them rather than pursue adulterous affairs with citizen women. [Athen. *Deip*. 569a.]

Terrible things, terrible, and not to be tolerated
Are being done by young men in the city.
For there are very good-looking young girls
In the brothels, who can be seen
Basking in the sun, their breasts uncovered,
Naked and lined up in rows ready for battle;
Of these you can choose whatever pleases you,
Thin, fat, round, tall, shrivelled,
Young, old, middle-aged, fully ripe.
You don't have to set up a ladder and enter in secret,
Nor crawl down in through the hole in the roof,
Nor be carried in craftily in a heap of straw.
They themselves use force and pull you in
Calling any old men
'Daddy', and the younger ones 'little brother'.
And each of these can be visited fearlessly, cheaply,
During the day, in the evening, in any way you like.

4.104 Aristophanes *Wealth* 149–59: The Price of Sexual Gratification

Chremylos and his slave Karion are here discussing the uses of money. Anal intercourse was used by prostitutes and hetairai as a form of contraception, and seems to have been normal in Corinth: anal intercourse with hetairai is frequently depicted on Athenian vases.

Chremylos: And they say that the Corinthian hetairai,
When any poor man tries their chances with them,
Just ignore him, but if a rich man arrives
They turn their anus to him right away!
Karion: They say the youths do the same too
Not for their erastai but for the money.
Chremylos: Only the male prostitutes, not the well-born boys;
They don't ask for money.
Karion: What do they ask for, then?
Chremylos: One asks for a good horse, another for hunting hounds.
Karion: They're probably ashamed to ask for money
So they disguise their wickedness with another name.

EPILOGUE

4.105 Solon 27: The Ten Ages of Man

The youthful boy loses the first row of teeth
He grew while a baby in seven years;
When god has completed the next seven years for him
He shows the signs that his youthful prime is on its way;
In the third seven, while his limbs are still growing
His chin grows downy with the bloom of changing skin.
In the fourth seven every man is at his best
In strength, when men give proof of valour.
In the fifth it is time for a man to think of marriage,
And seek a family of children to come after him.
In the sixth a man's mind is now disciplined in everything,
And he no longer wishes to do reckless deeds.
In the seventh he is now at his best in mind and tongue,
And in the eighth, that is fourteen years in total.
In the ninth he is still able, but less powerful than before
In both his speech and wisdom in matters of great prowess.
And if anyone comes to complete the tenth in full measure,
He will not meet the fate of death unseasonably.

5

LABOUR: SLAVES, SERFS AND CITIZENS

Slavery and servile labour played a very important part in the economy and society of Greek city-states throughout Greek history, and slaves are in fact documented as early as the Mycenaean age in the Linear B tablets. Without slaves, metics and serfs, Greek society would have been very different, and they were an essential component of Greek life throughout the archaic and classical periods. It is difficult to estimate the actual numbers of slaves in any city at any given time, but Thucydides states that when the Spartans fortified Dekeleia in Attica in 413 BC more than 20,000 Attic slaves from the countryside deserted, a large number of them skilled manual workers (doc. 5.25). This figure in itself might be an estimate, but it seems that there was a reasonably large slave population in Athens and Attica; however, there is no indication that it greatly outnumbered the free population of the city.

To the Greeks there was a very important distinction between slave and free and there was little or no moral dilemma for the Greeks about owning slaves. For Aristotle, slavery was natural (doc. 5.1). The oikos, the household, was the constituent part of the polis and was made up of free people and slaves. The slave belonged totally to the master. But Aristotle does point out that some writers argue that 'the rule of the master is against nature'. So while there was no move to abolish slavery, clearly at least a few writers (who probably owned slaves) did consider that the master–slave relationship was wrong (doc. 5.1). Slaves belonged so fully to the master that they were expected to be loyal, and to share in the joys and sorrows of their masters (doc. 5.66): to share their owners' emotions, rather than having their own independent feelings.

Slaves might be free people who had been captured in war, and it was quite acceptable to enslave fellow Greeks, though not those of one's own city (docs 5.4–7). Some slaves had been born and bred in the house or on the estate (cf. docs 5.10, 5.13) and so were an integral part of the family. Ischomachos notes that slaves who had children within the house were generally loyal (doc. 5.13). In addition, some slaves might have been unwanted newborn children who had been exposed by their parents, but there would in these cases be the difficulties of bringing up such slaves (who might die in infancy or early childhood) and there might be several years before they could do profitable work. A further means of enslavement was through piracy and kidnapping (docs 5.2, 5.8–9). Moreover, while Solon had put an end to agricultural debt-slavery in Athens in 594/3 BC, it obviously still existed elsewhere in the Greek world, as can be seen in the Gortyn Law Code (doc. 5.27). Kidnapping and the slave trade were profitable occupations: Herodotos describes how the Chian Panionios made his living by castrating and selling good-looking boys (doc. 5.2, cf. 7.14). Yet while death was the penalty for abducting people as slaves (see doc. 5.8), the slave trade and slave traders were simply a fact of life (docs 5.3, 5.8–9).

A slave could be an expensive commodity: Nikias, the wealthy estate owner and general, is said to have paid a talent for an overseer for his silver mine (doc. 5.15, cf. 5.19, 4.98), the equivalent of

12,000 days' pay for a juror (doc. 1.27). For those with large numbers of slaves, renting them out to those who could not afford them was obviously a profitable way to make money. Nikias was paid an obol per slave per day for the 1,000 men he rented out to Sosias, who worked the mines with them (doc. 5.16). If any of these slaves died while hired out, Sosias had to replace these slaves, so it was not in his interest to work them to death. In addition, that Sosias had to rent the slaves and did not buy them for himself shows that they were not a cheap or disposable 'commodity'. A list of slave prices from an auction actually survives from Athens and the amounts paid for these slaves are relatively high; ordinary Athenians could hardly have afforded any of the slaves being auctioned (doc. 5.18).

Slaves carried out a variety of occupations (docs 5.10–14, 5.26, 5.33). With the exception of working in the mines, most tasks which slaves carried out were also performed by free men. A common situation would be for a free man and his slave to work side by side at the same task. The fluting of columns on the Athenian acropolis was carried out by slaves and free men (doc. 5.42): there was no stigma attached to working with and alongside slaves. Slaves tended to complement free labour and certainly did not replace it. In times of war slaves were sometimes, but not usually, a useful source of military manpower. Those slaves who fought in wartime might be given their freedom, and sometimes even citizenship. The first slaves are recorded as fighting for Athens at the time of the first Persian invasion in 490 BC, and those slaves who served as rowers at Arginousai in 406 were given their freedom (docs 5.21–24).

The legal position of slaves did of course vary between different states. The Gortyn Law Code (doc. 5.27) provides information about the status of slaves and serfs in Crete, as well as clearly showing the status of children born to slaves or serfs (col. VI). Slaves in general were subject to the whims or wishes of their master, whose rights were almost absolute, though it appears that masters were not allowed to kill their slaves. Socrates lists the punishments of idle or recalcitrant slaves with no hint of disapproval (doc. 5.30), and in Athens slaves could only give evidence in a judicial case under torture (doc. 5.29). But Ischomachos, in discussing the choice of a new slave housekeeper, speaks of rewarding her if she pleased his wife and himself (doc. 5.13). The author of the *Economics* advises that slaves should be rewarded for good behaviour and that they will work better knowing that they will be so (doc. 5.32).

Athens and a number of other Greek cities also included a class of metics (immigrants, or resident foreigners). By the fifth century metics at Athens had become a large and important group; while not citizens (or slaves), they had specific and very well-protected rights, and in return contributed a great deal to the state's revenues as well as serving in the fleet and as hoplites (docs 5.36–43). Lysias, the orator, and his brother Polemarchos, were metics who owned a shield factory (doc. 5.41). Another well-known metic was Aspasia, who was said to run her own business training young girls as hetairai (docs 4.29, 4.95). Under certain specific conditions, metics could be granted citizenship: those metics who helped restore the democracy in 403 appear to have been made citizens and their occupations are listed in the decree which honoured them (doc. 5.43).

Crete was not the only Greek state to possess a class of serfs. The best known of such states was Sparta, which depended on its helots for agricultural production, but there was also a similar class, the penestai, in Thessaly (docs 5.51–52). The Spartans were also surrounded by the perioikoi, literally 'neighbours', who were politically subject to Sparta but had their own cities and some internal independence. Tyrtaeus, the Spartan poet of the Second Messenian War, provides details of the regime imposed on the helots by the Spartans after their final conquest of Messenia (see docs 5.44). There were, therefore, various types of slavery and forced labour in the Greek world. That slaves were an essential part of Greek life can be seen by the important part slaves play in Greek drama, and most dramatic productions include one or more slave characters who are integral to the plot (docs 5.65–70). These plays present slaves to an Athenian audience in a variety of environments and situations and show how deep rooted an institution slavery was in Greek society.

Naturally, of course, free Greeks themselves also worked in various ways. In certain classes of society agriculture, rather than trade, was considered the business of a 'gentleman' (docs 5.58–60), and even in the heyday of fifth-century BC Athens traders in the sense of retail manufacturers could be looked down on, and were to a large degree metics who had been encouraged to settle in Athens. Nevertheless, Solon and Hesiod mention a number of occupations in the archaic period (docs 11.53–56), and while a 'citizen economy' like that of Athens was made up of a myriad of small farming households, obviously a large proportion of Athenian citizens were also traders, artisans and workmen. The existence of slaves did not give citizens ample free time in which to run the state or engage in philosophical pursuits. The vast majority of free Greeks worked hard to support themselves and their families.

5.1 Aristotle *Politics* 1253b1–1254a24: Slaves by Nature and Slaves by Circumstance

Aristotle views the polis as a combination of households (oikoi), with these households containing free and slave members. The slave is defined completely as a possession, and as such by nature.

1253b1 Since it is clear that the polis is composed of constituent parts, we must speak first of the management of the household (oikos): for the city is made up of households. The parts of household management correspond to the persons who make it up, a complete household being made up of freemen and slaves. We should first begin by examining everything in its fewest elements, and the first and fewest parts of a household are master and slave, husband and wife, and father and children, and we have to consider what each of these relationships is and should be. These are: the master–slave relationship, the husband–wife one (for there is no name for the conjunction of woman and man), and thirdly the procreative relation (which also does not have its own proper name). These are the three we have spoken of. And there is a fourth part of the household, the so-called art of moneymaking, which to some is the same as household management and which others consider to be a very important part, and this we will have to consider.

1253b14 Let us first speak of master and slave, in order to see this in terms of real-life practicalities, and also to see if we can find a better theory of their relationships than exists at present. Some believe that the rule of a master is a science, and that household management and the rule of slaves are the same as political and monarchical rule, as we said at the beginning. Others state that the rule of a master is against nature — that the difference between slave and free is a question of law not of nature — and therefore is not just as it is imposed by force…

1254a11 The master is only the master of the slave, and does not belong to him; but the slave is not only the slave of the master but belongs to him totally. So it is clear from this what the nature and capacity of a slave is: a human being who by nature belongs not to himself but to another man is by nature a slave; and a human being who is also a possession may be said to belong to another man, a possession being an instrument of action, distinct from the possessor.

1254a17 But let us consider whether anyone is intended to be a slave by nature, for whom it is better and just for him to be someone's slave or not, or is all slavery contrary to nature? It is not difficult to solve this question both by reasoning and by fact. For that some should rule and others be ruled is not only essential, but beneficial, and at the point of birth people are divided into those to be ruled and those who rule.

ENSLAVEMENT AND THE SLAVE TRADE

The main sources of supply for slaves were warfare and piracy, as well as the sale by traders of non-Greeks. The slave population was continually augmented, from both Greek and non-Greek sources.

5.2 Herodotos 8.105.1–106.4: A Slave Trader Meets His Just Deserts

Herodotos' account of Hermotimos' revenge for his castration highlights the way Greeks felt about the castration of slaves, but does not mean that they saw anything improper or cruel in slavery as an institution or in slave-trading as a profession. The eunuchs were for the 'eastern market'.

8.105.1 Hermotimos had been captured by enemies and sold, and Panionios, a man from Chios, bought him, who made his living by the most vile profession; for he used to acquire boys who possessed a degree of beauty, castrate them and take them and sell them at Sardis and Ephesos for a lot of money. **2** For amongst the barbarians eunuchs are more highly regarded for their complete trustworthiness than the uncastrated. Amongst the many whom Panionios had castrated in the course of his profession was Hermotimos. But Hermotimos had not been entirely unfortunate, because he was sent from Sardis to the King with other gifts and as time passed was more highly valued by Xerxes than all his other eunuchs. **8.106.1** Now when the King was at Sardis, launching his Persian expedition against Athens, Hermotimos went down on some business to a part of Mysia, which the Chians own, called Atarneus, and there he found Panionios. **2** Recognizing him, he spoke to him for a long time in a friendly manner, first narrating to him all the benefits which he had had from what Panionios had done, and then promising to do the same for him in return if he brought his family (to Sardis) and settled there; Panionios gladly accepted the offer and brought his children and wife. **3** And when Hermotimos had him with his whole family in his power, he spoke as follows: 'You have made your living by the vilest profession practised by all mankind. What evil had I or any of my family ever done to you or yours that you should make me a nothing instead of a man? You thought that your actions then would escape the notice of the gods; but they are just and have brought you, whose actions were so vile, into my hands, so that you cannot complain of the vengeance I am going to take.' **4** After reproaching him like this, he had Panionios' sons brought before him, and Panionios was compelled to castrate all four of them, which he did; and when he had done that, his sons were compelled to castrate him. In this way Hermotimos got his revenge on Panionios.

5.3 Herodotos 5.6.1: The Thracians Sell Their Own Children

In his lively account of the people of Thrace Herodotos gives the following information about their trade in their own children. Apparently they exported them, though their most well-known sources of income were war and plunder.

5.6.1 The rest of the Thracians have this custom: they sell their children for export. They do not keep watch over their young girls, but allow them to mix with any men they like. But they guard their wives strictly; and they buy their wives from their parents for large sums.

5.4 Thucydides 5.116.2–4: Athens Captures Melos

The Dorian island of Melos was initially non-aligned with either Athens or Sparta and when faced with hostility from Athens went over to Sparta; the Athenians blockaded the island and took it in 416/5 BC, enslaving the women and children.

5.116.2 At about the same time the Melians captured another part of the Athenians' blockading wall, where there were not many guards. **3** As this had happened, another force came out later from Athens, with Philokrates, son of Demeas, in command, and as they were heavily besieged, and some treachery took place, the Melians surrendered of their own accord unconditionally to the Athenians. **4** And the Athenians killed all the Melian men they took in the prime of life, and enslaved the children and women; and they settled the spot, later on sending out five hundred colonists.

5.5 Thucydides 6.62.3–4: Athens Takes Sicilian Slaves

The Athenians, in Sicily in 415 BC, sailing to Egesta and Selinous, captured Hykkara, a Sicanian city in northern Sicily, and reduced its population to slavery. Note that though it was only a small town the Athenians still received 120 talents for their captives.

6.62.3 On their way they captured Hykkara, a Sicanian town at war with Egesta, on the coast. And they enslaved the inhabitants and handed the city over to the Egestaians (for their cavalry had come to help them). They then went back with the army through the country of the Sikels until they reached Catana, while the ships sailed round the coast carrying the slaves. **4** Nikias had sailed straight round from Hykkara to Egesta and after transacting other business there and receiving thirty talents he rejoined the expedition; and they sold the slaves and received one hundred and twenty talents for them.

5.6 Xenophon *Hellenika* 1.6.13–15: An Athenian Garrison Enslaved in 406 BC

Kallikratidas, the Spartan commander besieging the Greek city of Methymna, sold its Athenian garrison into slavery; while his allies told him to enslave the Methymnaians as well, he chose not to do so.

1.6.13 When the Methymnaians did not choose to surrender, for there was an Athenian garrison there and those in charge of affairs were supporters of Athens, Kallikratidas attacked the city and took it by storm. **14** The soldiers seized all its property as plunder, but Kallikratidas gathered all the captives in the agora, and when his allies told him to sell them, the Methymnaians as well, he said that while he was leader none of the Greeks should be enslaved if he could help it. **15** On the next day he let them go free, but sold the members of the Athenian garrison and all the captives who were slaves.

5.7 Xenophon *Hellenika* 2.2.3–4: The Athenians Fear Enslavement

When in 405 BC news came of the Athenian naval disaster at Aigospotamoi and it became clear they had at last lost the war with the Spartans, the Athenians feared that they would now, in turn, be enslaved.

2.2.3 The ship Paralos arrived at Athens at night and the disaster was reported, and lamentation passed from the Piraeus along the Long Walls to the city, one man telling the news to another. As a consequence, no one slept during that night, because they were grieving not only for those who were lost, but far more than that for themselves, as they thought that they would now suffer the same as they had done to the Melians, who were colonists of the Spartans, after subduing them by siege, and to the Histiaians and Skionaians and Toronaians and Aeginetans and many others of the Greeks. **4** On the next day they held an assembly, at which they resolved to block up all the harbours except one, repair the walls, station guards and make the city ready for a siege in all other respects as well.

5.8 Lysias 13 *Against Agoratos* 67: Death for Slave Abduction

Agoratos, by birth a slave and an informer for the Thirty, is being tried *c.* 399 BC under the restored democracy for the murder of one of the Thirty's victims. Here Lysias, in attacking his character and family, is describing one of Agoratos' brothers as a kidnapper of slaves.

Now there were four brothers, jurors. One of them, the eldest, was caught in Sicily making secret signals to the enemy and was crucified on a plank by Lamachos. The next abducted a slave from here to Corinth, and was caught again abducting a young female slave from there, and was thrown into prison and put to death.

5.9 Aristophanes *Wealth* 509–26: Thessalian Kidnappers as Social Necessities

In this, the last play of Aristophanes, produced in 388 BC, Chremylos plans to have Ploutos, the blind god of wealth, cured by the god Asklepios so that in future, being able to see, he will share his gifts out equally to everyone. Poverty, however, tries to argue him out of this plan on the grounds that no slave-traders will bother to traffic in slaves when everyone is equally wealthy.

Poverty: If what you desire happened, it certainly wouldn't benefit you.
For if Ploutos could see again to divide himself up evenly,
No person would study a craft or skill any more;
And with both of these vanished who would want
To be a smith or build ships or sew or make wheels,
Or make shoes or bricks or do the laundry or tan hides,
Or break up the earth with his plough and harvest the fruits of Demeter,
If you could live in idleness and neglect all these things?
Chremylos: You're talking nonsense. All the things you've just mentioned
Will be done by our servants.
Poverty: So where will you get servants from?
Chremylos: We'll buy them with money of course.
Poverty: But who's going to sell them,

When he's got money?
Chremylos: Someone who wants to make a profit,
A merchant from Thessaly from amongst all those kidnappers.
Poverty: But there won't even be a single kidnapper
According to your plan. What wealthy man would want
To risk his life doing something like that?
So you'll have to do the ploughing yourself and dig and all the rest
And you'll have a much more painful life than now.

SLAVES: THEIR OCCUPATIONS AND TRAINING

Slave-owning, given the prices of slaves and the fact that most tasks were performed by free individuals, sometimes with slave assistance, was not as extensive in Athens and elsewhere as is often stated. There is certainly no evidence for a huge number of slaves, and an estimate of 30,000–40,000 slaves in Athens seems reasonable. Slaves fulfilled a wide range of duties; mining, and at Athens the Scythian policing force, were the only exclusively slave occupations.

5.10 Sophocles *Oedipus Tyrannus* 1121–41: Slaves as Shepherds

This episode leads to the revelation that Oedipus has killed his own father, Laios, and married his own mother, Iocasta: Oedipus is questioning Laios' former shepherd (a trusted servant, born in the household), and asking whether he knows the Corinthian shepherd to whom the former shepherd had originally given Oedipus, rather than exposing him on the slopes as instructed.

Oedipus: You there, old man, look at me now and answer
What I ask you. Did you once belong to Laios?
Servant: Yes, not a purchased slave, but reared in his house.
Oedipus: What task or occupation was your care?
Servant: For most of my life I tended the flocks.
Oedipus: And which regions did you most frequent?
Servant: Sometimes Kithairon, and sometimes the neighbouring country.
Oedipus: Then you must have known this man, at least from report?
Servant: Doing what? What man do you refer to?
Oedipus: This one here; have you encountered him before?
Servant: Not enough for me to speak straightway from memory.
Corinthian: And no wonder, master. But I will definitely
Remind him, though he knows me not. For I know well that
He remembers when in the region of Kithairon —
He had two flocks, and I had one —
I associated with this man for three whole years
From spring till Arcturus rose for six months at a time;
When winter came to the sheepfold
I would drive mine back, and he his to Laios' farmstead.
Did this happen as I say or did it not?
Servant: You speak the truth, although of long ago.

5.11 Scholiast to Aristophanes *Acharnians* 54: Public Slaves, The Scythian Archers

The archers, who kept order in Athens in the assembly and boule, were owned by the state.

The archers were public slaves, a thousand in number, who originally lived in tents in the middle of the agora, but later moved to the Areiopagos. They were called Scythians or Peisinians.

5.12 Hesiod *Works and Days* 405–6: A Slave Woman Is More Useful than a Wife

Hesiod is giving advice to the small farmer, to buy a slave first before marrying. The woman's chief task would have been that of preparing food, especially grinding wheat and barley and helping with the oxen. Compare lines 502–3, 765–67 and 602–3, where he recommends acquiring a servant-girl with no children (for a servant nursing a child is a nuisance).

First of all you should acquire a house and a woman and an ox for the plough,
A female slave, not a wife, who can follow the oxen as well.

5.13 Xenophon *Oeconomicus* 9.5, 9.11–12: Successful Household Management

Ischomachos here relates to Socrates how he showed his new wife her home (cf. doc. 4.63). Particularly important for the smooth running of the household was the choice of housekeeper.

9.5 I showed her the women's quarters as well, divided from the men's quarters by a bolted door, so that nothing could be taken out from within which ought not to be and so that the servants did not produce children without our approval. For good servants who have produced children are for the most part more loyal, but the bad ones who have found a mate become more ingenious at doing mischief … **9.11** When we appointed our housekeeper, we considered which woman seemed to us to be the most temperate with regard to her stomach, wine, sleep and consorting with men, and additionally the one who appeared to us to have the best memory and the forethought not to annoy us by her carelessness, and to think how she might earn a reward by gratifying us. **12** We taught her to be well disposed towards us by sharing our joys with her when we were pleased, and if something made us miserable by calling on her sympathies. And we trained her to be eager that our household should prosper by making her acquainted with it and sharing our success with her.

5.14 [Demosthenes] 47 *Against Evergos and Mnesiboulos* 55–6: A Devoted Servant

The speaker thinks that his kindness to the old slave of the family will create sympathy amongst the jurors. The fate of the old slave – with no one to care for her – shows that manumission could leave a slave without a livelihood or protector. For an old, faithful nurse in tragedy, see doc. 5.65.

55 Worse than this, jurors, my wife happened to be having lunch with the children in the courtyard with an elderly woman who had been my wet nurse, a kindly devoted soul, who had been set free by my father. She lived with her husband when she had been freed, but after he died, when she was old and there was no one to look after her, she came back to me. **56** I couldn't bear to see either my nurse or the slave who attended me as a boy to be in want.

SLAVE PRICES AND EARNINGS

The price of a slave could vary markedly, depending on her or his skills and age, but it is clear that there were no cheap slaves. Factories staffed by slaves were very profitable (docs 5.19, 5.41); it was also common to leave a slave to work on his own at his trade and be responsible for his keep, while he paid a regular sum to his master; the term for this was 'living apart'. Slaves could also be hired out to another employer (docs 5.16, 5.42).

5.15 Xenophon *Memorabilia* 2.5.2: Nikias Pays a Talent for a Slave

Nikias paid a large amount for a mine overseer, and skilled slaves could obviously fetch high prices. The hetaira Neaira, in the fourth century, was allegedly worth thirty minas or half a talent (doc. 4.98).

2.5.2 'Antisthenes,' said Socrates, 'do friends have certain values, like servants? For one slave may be worth perhaps two minas, another less than half a mina, another five minas, and another even ten; Nikias, son of Nikeratos, is said to have paid a talent for an overseer for his silver-mine.'

5.16 Xenophon *Revenues* 4.14–15: Mineworkers Hired out by Nikias

Xenophon refers here to three groups of mining slaves, totalling 1,900 slaves. There will have been more slaves in the mines than this, perhaps a workforce of 5,000 or so. Sosias had to replace any of the slaves that died; this, and the fact that he had to hire the slaves in the first place (he could not afford to buy them himself), shows that it was in his interest to ensure that slaves were not worked to death. Conditions in the mines would have been harsh but not life-threatening.

4.14 Those of us who have been interested in the matter have long ago doubtless heard that Nikias, son of Nikeratos, once acquired one thousand men in the silver mines and that he hired them out to Sosias the Thracian, on condition that Sosias paid him a clear obol a man a day, and always kept the numbers constant. **15** And Hipponikos too had six hundred slaves let out on the same terms, who brought him a clear mina a day, while Philemonides had three hundred who brought him half a mina.

5.17 Herodotos 6.79.1: The Spartans Ransom Their Prisoners

The going rate for ransoming hoplites captured in war was two minas (cf. Hdt. 5.77.3; Thuc. 5.49.1).

6.79.1 Kleomenes then acted as follows: from some deserters whom he had acquired he learned the names of the Argives who had taken refuge in the sanctuary; he sent a herald in to invite them out by name, saying that he had received their ransoms; two minas is the sum set by the Peloponnesians as the ransom for each prisoner. About fifty of the Argives whom Kleomenes had called forth came out one by one and were killed.

5.18 *Inscriptiones Graecae* I^3 421, col. I: The Auction of Confiscated Slaves

The property of the men accused of having mutilated the hermai in 415, the hermokopidai ('hermai-cutters'), was confiscated and auctioned, as in the case of the sixteen domestic slaves belonging to Kephisodoros, a metic. The majority of the slaves were barbarians, and the average price per slave is 157 drachmas (or nearly half a year's wages for the average citizen), though this may have been below full market value. The first column represents the sales tax paid by the buyer, the second the price, and the third the sex and ethnic origin of the slave. [Meiggs & Lewis 79A.]

Property of Kephisodoros, a metic living in the Piraeus

2 dr.	165 dr.	A Thracian woman
1 dr. 3 obols	135 dr.	A Thracian woman
2 dr.	170 dr.	A Thracian
2 dr. 3 obols	240 dr.	A Syrian
1 dr. 3 obols	105 dr.	A Carian
2 dr.	161 dr.	An Illyrian
2 dr. 3 obols	220 dr.	A Thracian woman
1 dr. 3 obols	115 dr.	A Thracian
1 dr. 3 obols	144 dr.	A Scythian
1 dr. 3 obols	121 dr.	An Illyrian
2 dr.	153 dr.	A man from Colchis
2 dr.	174 dr.	A Carian child
1 dr.	72 dr.	A little Carian child
3 dr. 1 obol	301 dr.	A Syrian
2 dr.	151 dr.	A Melittenian (man or woman)
1 dr.	85 dr. 1 ob.	A Lydian woman

5.19 Demosthenes 27 *Against Aphorbos* 1.9–11: Slave Factories

Demosthenes' father left a large estate with two productive factories, a widow, a son of seven years and a daughter of five. The slaves were skilled and valuable, bringing in a good income and part of an extensive portfolio of earnings and investments. Demosthenes was engaged in a legal battle between 363 and 361 BC to recover his inheritance from his guardians. See also doc. 4.64, where Socrates lists a number of successful slave-run businesses.

9 My father, jurors, left two workshops, both of decent size, one with thirty-two or three sword-makers, mostly valued at five or six minas, and none less than three, from whom he received a clear income of thirty minas a year. The other consisted of twenty bed-manufacturers, pledged as security for a forty-mina debt, which gave him a clear twelve minas in income. In cash he left as much as a talent, loaned out on the interest of a drachma (per mina) a month, the interest on which came to more than seven minas a year. **10** This was the capital he left which brought in interest, as the defendants will themselves admit: the principal comprised four talents and 5,000 drachmas, and the interest on this to fifty minas a year. In addition, he left ivory and iron, for use in the workshops, and wood for beds worth about eighty minas, and oak-gall and copper bought for seventy minas. There was also a house bought for 3,000 drachmas, and furniture and drinking-cups, and jewellery and clothes, my mother's apparel, worth in all 10,000 drachmas, and eighty minas of cash in the house. **11** All this was what he left at home: there were also seventy minas in maritime loans, loaned out to Xouthos, 2,400 drachmas in Pasion's bank, 600 in Pylades', 1,600 in the possession of Demomeles, son of Demon, and roughly a talent lent out to different people in sums of two or three hundred drachmas. The total of these last amounts comes to more than eight talents and fifty minas, and you will find on investigation that taken all together the amount comes to about fourteen talents (actually 13 talents and 46 minas).

5.20 Plato *Laws* 914e, 916a–c : Utopian Legislation Regarding the Purchase of Slaves

The *Laws* were written in the 350s and early 340s BC, and were an idealisation of existing custom. Plato's 'laws' regarding slaves are, if anything, more severe than existing legislation in Athens. Cf. doc. 5.27 (column VII of the Gortyn Law Code) for the purchaser's culpability for slave misbehaviour.

914e Anyone who wishes, providing he is not mad, can seize his own slave and treat him as he wishes, within the limits of what is lawful; and he can seize a runaway on behalf of one of his relations or friends to keep him safe. And if anyone claims as free someone who is being seized as a slave, the taker should release him but the one who claims him as free should give three substantial guarantors, and on these terms he can be released, but on no others ... **916a** If anyone sells a slave suffering from consumption or gall-stones or strangury or the so-called 'sacred disease' (epilepsy) or some other illness either of body or mind, not obvious to the majority, which is long-standing and difficult to cure, and if the purchaser is a doctor or trainer, he has no right to return him on these grounds, **916b** not even if he were told the truth before the sale was made. But if a professional should sell such a slave to a private citizen, the buyer can take him back within six months, except in the case of the 'sacred disease', in which case he can have a year within which to return him. It should be arbitrated by a bench of doctors, nominated and chosen jointly by the two sides; and the losing party should pay a fine twice that of the selling price. If a private citizen sells to a private citizen, **916c** there should be a right of return and a hearing as said previously, but the loser should pay just the simple price. If someone knowingly sells a murderer to someone who is also aware of this, there shall be no right of return for such a purchase, but if the buyer did not know then he shall have the right of return when he becomes aware of this.

SLAVES IN WAR

It was customary to have slaves with the army, to carry the baggage and perform menial tasks, like preparing the food; cf. Thuc. 4.101.2 (Delion), 7.13.2, 7.75.5 (Sicily). At Potidaea in 428, there were 3,000 slaves, one for each Athenian hoplite in the garrison, for each of whom their master received one drachma a day for maintenance (Thuc. 3.17.4). Defence of the city, including rowing, was a citizen's duty, particularly for the thetes (Thuc. 1.14.3). In desperate circumstances when slaves fought either in the army or with the fleet they could be freed.

5.21 Pausanias *Description of Greece* 1.29.7: Slaves Fight Against Aegina, c. 491 BC

Pausanias is here describing the monuments outside Athens.

1.29.7 And there is the grave of the Athenians, who fought against the Aeginetans before the Persians invaded. Even for a democracy it was certainly a just decree, when the Athenians granted their slaves the right to be publicly buried and have their names recorded on a stele; it proclaims that in the war they behaved bravely in respect of their masters.

5.22 Pausanias *Description of Greece* 1.32.3: Slaves at Marathon

When the Persians landed at Marathon in 490 BC, the situation was desperate and slaves fought alongside their Athenian masters.

1.32.3 There is a village, Marathon, equidistant from the city of the Athenians and Karystos in Euboea; it was here that the barbarians landed in Attica and were defeated in the battle and lost some of their ships as they were putting off. There is a grave for the Athenians on the plain and on it are stelai with the names of the dead, each according to their tribes, and another grave for the Plataeans of Boeotia and for the slaves — for that was the first occasion on which slaves fought as well.

5.23 Xenophon *Hellenika* 1.6.24: Slaves at Arginousai

The situation at Arginousai in 406 BC was desperate, and the slaves – and even hippeis – rowed the ships. Each trireme had 170 oarsmen (and a total of 200 crew in total). The Athenians won the battle. The hippeis were the cavalry: see doc. 8.16.

1.6.24 When the Athenians heard of what had happened and about the blockade, they voted to go to the rescue with a hundred and ten ships, embarking all those who were of age, both slaves and free men; and they manned the hundred and ten ships in thirty days and set sail. Many of the hippeis even went aboard.

5.24 Aristophanes *Frogs* 687–99: Slaves Gain Citizen Rights

Aristophanes is here arguing that those who supported the oligarchical revolution of 411 BC should be restored to citizenship, since citizenship had been given to slaves: the chorus is speaking here. Hellanikos *FGH* 323a F 25: 'Hellanikos says that those who fought with them (at Arginousai) were freed and immediately became Plataeans and masters instead of slaves and were enrolled like the Plataeans as fellow citizens with them' (cf. doc. 1.37).

So first we propose
That you put all the citizens on a level and remove their fears,
And if anyone has erred after being deceived by Phrynichos' tricks,
Those who went wrong then, I say, should be allowed
To put up a case and be rid of their former mistakes.
Next, I say that no one in the city should be without civil rights:

For it's a disgrace that those who fought in one sea battle
Should immediately become Plataeans and masters instead of slaves.
Not that I mean to say that that was a bad decision —
In fact I commend it, as the only sensible thing you've done.
But additionally, it is only fair that those who with you —
And their fathers too — have often fought at sea, and our kinsmen too,
Should be forgiven this one fault when they ask you.

5.25 Thucydides 7.27.5: Slaves Desert in the Peloponnesian War

Dekeleia had been fortified by the Spartans in 413 BC and used as a permanent hostile post against Attica (doc. 13.25), which caused Athens great hardship from devastation to the countryside and loss of manpower, including the desertion of a large number of slaves. Thucydides obviously believed that this was a great blow to Athens; the numbers of skilled workmen (cheirotechnai) who deserted perhaps give some clue as to the total number of slaves in Attica, though this may be no more than an estimate by Thucydides.

7.27.5 For the Athenians were deprived of the whole of their country, and more than 20,000 slaves deserted, of whom the majority were skilled manual workers, and they lost all their flocks and draught animals.

5.26 Thucydides 3.73: Slaves as Agricultural Workers on Corcyra

During the civil war on Corcyra in 427 BC both sides sent out to the country districts to attempt to win the support of the slaves by offering them freedom. The great majority joined the democratic side.

3.73 On the next day there was some fighting at long range and both sides sent round to the country, inviting the slaves to join them and promising them freedom; the majority of the slaves joined the side of the people, while eight hundred mercenaries from the mainland came to the help of the others.

THE LEGAL POSITION OF SLAVES

Slaves did have legal rights, as indicated by the Law Code of Gortyn and the laws of Athens. The slave could not bring lawsuits for being mistreated — and could be beaten by their masters — but they could not be killed with impunity. The situation with helots, who were not slaves but serfs, was very different.

5.27 Willetts *The Law Code of Gortyn*: Serfs and Slaves at Gortyn

Crete possessed a tradition of patriarchal slavery, long after commercial slavery had become the dominant form of servitude in other parts of Greece, as can be seen in the Gortyn Law Code, inscribed in the mid-fifth century: the serfs had rights, such as that of tenure of the house in which they lived, and were seen as part of the estate. They possessed money, could marry and divorce, and their wives had their own property. A serf could even marry a free woman. But chattel-slaves and the slave market are also mentioned below; and clearly in Crete slavery for debt was still possible. In Crete, a stater was worth two drachmas.

Suits concerning ownership of actual or alleged slaves

(col. I) Gods. Whoever is going to contend whether someone is a free man or a slave is not to seize him before trial. But if he seizes him, (the judge) is to condemn him to pay ten staters for a free man and five for a slave, whoever he belongs to, and he is to give judgement that he should release him within three days. But if he does not release him, he is to pay a stater for a free man and a drachma for a slave for each day until he does release him; and the judge on oath is to decide as to the time. But if he denies that he seized him, the judge is to decide on oath, unless a witness testifies. And if one side contends that he is a free man and the other that he is a slave, those who testify that he is a free man are to win. And if they contend about a slave, each saying that he is his, if a witness testify, the judge is to judge according to the witness, but is to decide on oath if they testify for both sides or for neither. After the one who has him is defeated, he is to release the free man within five days and give back the slave in hand. But if he does not release nor give back, (the judge) is to judge that the (winning side) should receive in the case of a free man fifty staters and a stater per day until he releases him, and in the case of a slave ten staters and a drachma per day until he gives him back in hand.

56 But one who seizes a man condemned (for debt) or a man who has **(col. II)** mortgaged himself is to be immune from punishment.

Property rights of serfs

(col. III.40) If a female serf be separated from a serf while he is alive or if he should die, she is to have her own property; but if she takes away anything else, that is grounds for a trial … **52** And if a female serf should bear a child while separated, it is to be taken to the master of the man who married her, in the presence of two witnesses **(col. IV)**. And if he does not accept it, the child shall belong to the master of the female serf; but if she marries the same man again within a year, the child is to belong to the master of the male serf; and the oaths of the one who brought it and the witnesses shall have precedence … **18** If a female serf who is unmarried conceives and bears a child, the child shall belong to the master of her father; but if her father is not alive, it shall belong to the masters of her brothers.

Ransomed prisoners

(col. VI.46) If anyone of necessity gets a man, who is away from home, set free from another city at his request, he shall belong to the one who ransomed him until he pays what is owed. But if they do not agree about the amount, the judge is to decide on oath with reference to the pleas.

Mixed marriages

(col. VI.56) If a slave goes **(col. VII)** to a free woman and marries her, their children shall be free. But if the free woman goes to the slave their children shall be slaves. And if there are free and slave children of the same mother, if the mother dies and there is property, the free children are to have it; but if she had no free children, the heirs are to have it.

Purchase of slaves in the slave-market

(col. VII.10) If someone buys a slave from the marketplace and does not terminate the agreement within sixty days, the one who has acquired the slave will be liable if he (the slave) has done any wrong before or after (the purchase).

5.28 Antiphon 5 *On the Murder of Herodes* 29–32: Slaves Give Evidence under Torture

This speech was probably delivered c. 415 BC. In Athens slaves could only give evidence in a law court under torture. A party to a lawsuit could refuse the challenge to have one of his slaves tortured; otherwise, the methods of torture employed were drawn up in an arrangement between the parties involved, which made provision for compensation to be paid to the slave's master if the slave were permanently disabled as a result.

29 When they found the blood, they said that it was there that Herodes had been killed; but when this was not possible, as it turned out to belong to the animals for sacrifice, they desisted from that line of argument and seized and tortured the men. **30** The first whom they tortured there straightaway said nothing foolish about me; the other whom they tortured a number of days later, and who had been in their company during the preceding period, was the one who was persuaded by them to tell lies about me. I will produce witnesses to this. (Witnesses) **31** You have heard evidence as to how much later the man was tortured; now pay attention to the torture itself, what it was like. For the slave, to whom they had doubtless promised his freedom and who had to look to these men for putting an end to his sufferings, hoped to gain his freedom and wanted to be delivered immediately from the torture. I think you know already that with regard to those who do the greatest part of the torturing **32** it is in their favour that the tortured say whatever is going to gratify them; for in them lies their possible advantage, especially if those about whom they are lying do not happen to be present. But if I had ordered him to be stretched on the rack for not telling the truth, that in itself would doubtless have deterred him from telling lies about me.

5.29 Antiphon 5 *On the Murder of Herodes* 46–48, 69: Murder and Corporate Guilt

This speech makes clear that it was illegal for individuals to kill a slave. Even if a slave killed someone, it was the responsibility of the authorities, not the master, to punish them. From this passage it appears that if the owner was murdered, and the culprit not known, all the household slaves were executed.

46 None of you should forget this, that they killed the informer, and took care that he should not come before you, and that when I was present I should not be able to take the man and torture him. **47** And yet this would have been in their favour. Instead they bought the man, the informer, and privately and on their own initiative killed him, with no decree on the part of the city, and though he was not guilty of having murdered the man himself.

They should have kept him chained up, or given him to my friends on security, or handed him over to your magistrates so there could have been a vote on what was to happen to him. But instead you condemned him and killed him yourselves; not even the city is allowed to do that, to punish someone with death without the consent of the Athenian people. You thought that the jurors were fit to be judges of his statements, but of his deeds you became the judges yourselves. **48** And yet not even those slaves who have killed their masters, even if they are caught red-handed, can be killed by their master's relatives, but are handed over to the authorities in accordance with your ancestral laws. But if it is possible for a slave to give evidence against a free man in a case of murder, and for a master, if he chooses, to prosecute someone on behalf of his slave, and if the jury's vote is as equally applicable to the murderer of a slave as to the murderer of a free man, then it would have been right for this slave to have had a trial and not to have been killed by you without one...

69 Not long ago, a slave boy, not yet twelve years of age, attempted to murder his owner. And if he had not taken fright when the victim cried out, leaving the knife in the wound and fleeing, instead of staying where he was, all the slaves in the household would have been killed, as no one would have thought the boy responsible for such a bold action. But he was captured and later admitted his guilt.

5.30 Xenophon *Memorabilia* 2.1.15–17: Appropriate Punishments

As part of an exhortation on the virtues of self-control, Socrates is here explaining to Aristippos, a rather intemperate and independent companion of his, that his beliefs and taste for high living would not prevent his being enslaved by wrongdoers and asking how he would treat recalcitrant slaves.

2.1.15 'Who would want to have in his household a man who didn't want to work and who enjoyed a luxurious lifestyle? **16** Let us consider how masters treat such servants. Do they not control their lecherousness by starving them? Prevent them stealing by locking up anywhere they might steal from? Stop them running away by putting them in fetters? Drive out their laziness with beatings? What do you do when you find one of your servants is like this?' **17** 'I punish them with every kind of misery until I can compel them to behave like a slave should.'

5.31 Xenophon *Oeconomicus* 12.18–19: Slave Management

Ischomachos is discussing with Socrates the qualities and training needed for an overseer, a 'promotion' to which a good slave could sometimes look forward (cf. doc. 5.32). Ischomachos is relating his experiences; cf. doc 4.63. Note, however, that a bailiff could also be a hired citizen, and this was not necessarily a slave's occupation (doc. 5.60).

12.18 It is difficult to do something well when the teacher sets a bad example, and when a master sets an example of being careless it is difficult for a servant to become careful. **19** To put it briefly, I don't think I have come across good servants belonging to a bad master; but I have seen bad ones belonging to a good master, but not unpunished. If you want to make people fit to be managers you have to oversee their work and examine it and be willing to reward those responsible for whatever is done well and not shrink from giving the punishment deserved to someone who has been careless.

5.32 [Aristotle] *Economics* 1344 a35–b21: Rewards for Good Behaviour

1344a35 There are three areas of importance in dealing with slaves: work, punishment and food. Not being punished and not being made to work, but having food makes slaves insolent. Yet being made to work and being punished but not having food is an act of violence and makes the slave unable to work. So the solution is to give him work and sufficient food. It is not possible to manage slaves without payment, and the payment for slaves is food. As with other people as well, who, when they get nothing better for behaving better, and when there are no rewards for good behaviour or punishments for bad behaviour, behave in a worse manner, so this is also the case with slaves.

1344b7 So it is necessary to maintain surveillance and distribute and withhold everything according to what they deserve, food as well as clothing, and leisure, and punishment, and to imitate in both word and deed the power of physicians in writing prescriptions, observing as well that food, unlike medicine, must be taken regularly.

1344b12 The nationalities that are best for work are those that are neither excessively cowardly nor excessively brave, for both can behave badly — those that are excessively cowardly do not stick to their work, and the high-spirited are difficult to manage.

1344b15 It is also necessary to lay down some potential outcome for everything, as it is both fair and beneficial to offer freedom as a reward. The slaves will be willing to work when a reward and the time frame for it are set. It is also necessary to let them have children, as hostages. Also, do not acquire many slaves of the same nationality, as they do in the cities. In addition, celebrate sacrifices and holidays for the slaves' sake rather than for the free men, as free men have more of such occasions, and it is for their sakes that these occasions were established.

5.33 Xenophon *Oeconomicus* 5.14–16: Management of Farm Workers

Socrates here advises Kritoboulos that farming is an excellent pursuit in that the experience in training workers to co-operate is valuable practice for army commanders. For Socrates' view of agriculture as the only fit occupation for a 'gentleman', see doc. 5.58.

5.14 Farming also helps to train men to co-operate with each other as a team. When you make an expedition against the enemy you use men, and working the land needs men as well. **15** So if you are going to be a good farmer you have to make your workers both eager and willing to obey; and anyone who leads men against an enemy has to work towards achieving the same results, by rewarding those who do what brave men should and punishing the undisciplined. **16** And the farmer needs to encourage his workers often, no less that the general his soldiers; slaves need something good to hope for no less than free men, in fact rather more, so they want to stay with him.

5.34 Aeschines 1 *Against Timarchos* 138–39: Solon Legislates against Slave Activities

Citizen pursuits were closed to slaves by Solon; slaves could not be lovers of young men, ensuring that Athenian males only had sexual relations with other free males; cf. Plut. *Sol.* 1.6.

138 Our fathers, when they were legislating on our everyday pursuits and what nature compels us to do, forbade slaves to do the things they thought ought to be done by free men. 'A slave,' says the law, 'is not to take exercise or anoint himself in the wrestling schools (palaistrai)' … **139** Again the same lawgiver said, 'A slave shall not be the lover of a free boy nor follow him around or else receive fifty lashes from the public scourge.'

5.35 [Xenophon] *Constitution of the Athenians* 1.10–12: Slaves, Metics and Citizens

This was written c. 425 BC by an author of very oligarchic views who attributed his political treatise to Xenophon. A legal indictment for hybris (the 'graphe hybreos') could be made if a citizen struck a citizen, and it was a crime to treat a citizen as if he were a slave.

1.10 Slaves and metics are allowed the greatest licence at Athens, and you are not allowed to strike any of them there, nor will a slave stand aside for you. Why this is the local custom, I will tell you: if it were the law that a slave or metic or freedman could be struck by a free man, you would often hit an Athenian thinking that he were a slave; for the people there are no better dressed than slaves and metics, nor is their appearance any better. **11** If anyone should be amazed by the fact that at Athens they allow the slaves to live in luxury and let some of them have a splendid lifestyle, it would appear that this too is done deliberately. For when a country is a naval power, it is necessary for financial considerations to be slaves to your slaves, in order to take their earnings and let them go free. Where there are wealthy slaves there is no longer any reason for my slave to fear you. In Sparta my slave would fear you; but if your slave fears me he is likely to hand over his money to avoid danger to himself. **12** For this reason we have put slaves on terms of equality with free men and metics with citizens, because the city needs metics on account of its numerous trades and its fleet. For this reason we quite reasonably have given metics equal rights.

METICS

Metics were foreigners who were permanent residents of a city other than their own. At Athens, they could be granted citizenship only in return for extraordinary services to the state. They paid taxes, performed liturgies, served in the army but lacked the full political and legal rights of citizens and could not own their own land or houses. Athenian writers realised the contributions metics made to the state.

5.36 Aristophanes of Byzantium F38: The Definition of a Metic

Aristophanes of Byzantium (*c.* 257–180 BC) provides a specific definition of a metic. [F38 Nauck.]

A metic is anyone who comes from a foreign city and lives in the city, paying tax towards certain fixed needs of the city; for a number of days he is called a parepidemos (visitor) and is free from tax, but if he outstays the time laid down he becomes a metic and liable to taxation.

5.37 Xenophon *Revenues* 2.1: Xenophon on Metics

Xenophon, in the *Revenues*, written *c.* 355 BC, is suggesting ways in which the status of metics and the part they played in the state might be improved, with a view to aiding the economy.

2.1 For all these things, as I said, I think the state itself is responsible. And in addition to the indigenous benefits we might first pay attention to the metics; for this seems to me to be one of the finest sources of revenue since they maintain themselves, and though conferring many benefits on cities, they receive no payment but actually pay the metic tax.

5.38 Thucydides 2.31.1–2: Metics Serve in the Armed Forces

Perikles at the outbreak of war in 431 BC summarised Athens' manpower resources as 13,000 hoplites plus another 16,000 in garrison posts and on the battlements; this latter force was drawn from the eldest and youngest of the citizens and the metics who were qualified as hoplites (doc. 1.10). Metics clearly constituted an important source of hoplites for the city and were completely loyal to the city.

2.31.1 In the autumn of this year, the Athenians with their whole force, both themselves and the metics, invaded the Megarid, with Perikles son of Xanthippos in command. When the Athenians that had sailed round the Peloponnese in the hundred ships (for they happened to be already at Aegina on their way home) heard that the whole force had left the city and was at Megara, they sailed over to them and joined forces. **2** This was the greatest Athenian army that had ever been assembled, the city still being in her prime and not yet suffering from the plague; there were not less than 10,000 citizen hoplites (not including the 3,000 who were at Potidaea), and not less than 3,000 metic hoplites joined in the expedition, and this did not include the rest of the light-armed troops who were considerable in number.

5.39 Aeschylus *Suppliant Women* 600–14: The Danaids as 'Metics' in Athens

Danaos had fifty daughters, the Danaids, and his brother Aigyptos fifty sons, who tried to force the Danaids to marry them; the Danaids, the chorus here, fled to Argos with their father, and Aeschylus, in this play written *c.* 460 BC, imagines their being granted metic status in Argos.

Danaos: Children, take heart; the decrees of this country's
People have resolved everything well.
Chorus: Greetings, old man, who bring me welcome news.
Tell us in what way it was finally decided,
How the people's sovereign hand prevailed.
Danaos: It was resolved by the Argives, with no wavering,
So as to make my old heart young again;
The whole people, with right hands raised,
Made the air quiver as they brought these words to pass:
We are to be metics of this land, free and
Protected, with complete inviolability,
And no one, inhabitant or stranger, can
Remove us; and if violence be used,
Any of the landowners who does not help us
Will lose his rights, exiled by popular decree.

5.40 Thucydides 7.63.3–4: Crisis in Sicily

On the eve of the final defeat in Sicily in 413 BC, Nikias addressed the troops. In this passage he turns to 'those who have been considered Athenians' – the metics – who are serving as sailors in the fleet.

7.63.3 And as for the sailors I advise you — indeed I entreat you — not to be overly depressed by our disasters, since the armaments we have on our decks now are better and our ships more numerous. Keep in mind, those of you who up till now have been considered Athenians, without actually being so, how well worth preserving is the pleasant feeling that because of your knowledge of our language and imitation of our ways you have been admired throughout all of Greece, and shared in the benefits of our empire no less than ourselves, and even more with respect to the fear paid you by our subjects and your freedom from injury. **4** So that you, the only people with whom we freely share our empire, do not betray it now, despise the Corinthians whom you have often defeated, and the Sicilians, none of whom thought of resisting us when our fleet was in its prime, and beat them off, and show that even in sickness and disaster your skill is better than anyone else's strength, which is a matter of luck.

5.41 Lysias 12 *Against Eratosthenes* 4–11, 19–20: The Thirty and the Metics

Lysias was himself a metic, and owner of a shield factory with his brother Polemarchos. For the financial benefits which metics brought to Athens, see Xen. *Revenues* 2.1; for the Thirty, see doc. 13.40.

4 My father Kephalos was persuaded by Perikles to come to this country and lived here for thirty years, and neither he nor any of us ever appeared as prosecutor or defendant in any lawsuit. In fact we lived under the democracy so as to avoid giving any offence to other people or being wronged at their hands. **5** But when the Thirty, those scoundrels and informers, established their regime, stating that the city had to be purged of unjust men while all the other citizens had to incline themselves to virtue and justice, they were bold-faced enough not to put these professions into practice themselves, as I shall try to remind you by speaking first of my affairs and then of yours.

6 Theognis and Peison stated in front of the Thirty that there were some metics who were hostile to their regime, and that they thus had the perfect pretext for appearing to punish them, while in fact making money; in any case, the state was impoverished and the government needed cash. **7** They had no trouble in persuading their audience, for they thought nothing of putting people to death, and a great deal of making money. They therefore decided to arrest ten metics, of whom two would be poor, so they could explain to the others that this action had not been taken in order to make money but for the benefit of the state, just as if they were doing some other justifiable action. **8** So they divided up the households and began their visits: they found me entertaining guests whom they drove off before handing me over to Peison; the others went into the workshop and made a list of the slaves. I asked Peison if he would take money to save me. He agreed, provided it was a lot. **9** So I said that I was prepared to give him a talent of silver and he agreed to do this. I knew that he thought nothing of gods or men, but decided under the circumstances that it was still essential to have his oath on this. **10** When he had sworn that he would take the talent and save me, calling down utter destruction on himself and his children if he broke his oath, I went into my room and opened the chest. Peison noticed this and came in, and when he saw what was inside he called two of his servants, and told them to take what was in the chest. **11** He had now not what was sworn, jurors, but three talents of silver and four hundred cyzicenes, a hundred darics and four silver cups … (**16–17**: *Polemarchos, Lysias' brother, is arrested and made to drink hemlock.*) **19** They had 700 shields of ours, they had all that silver and gold, copper, jewellery, furniture and women's cloaks, more than they had ever thought to acquire, and 120 slaves, of whom they took the best, and gave the rest to the state, and showed the degree of insatiability and disgusting greed they had reached in this revelation of their characters: for the golden earrings of Polemarchos' wife, which she happened to be wearing, Melobios took from her ears as soon as he came into the house. **20** And we did not find any mercy at their hands even in regard to the smallest part of our property. But they injured us because of our money as much as others might have done through anger at great crimes, and we did not deserve this from the city, but had defrayed the cost of all our choruses (as choregoi), and contributed to many special taxes (eisphorai), and shown ourselves to be well-conducted, and performed all the duties laid on us, and had not made a single enemy, as well as ransoming many Athenians from the enemy.

5.42 *Inscriptiones Graecae* I^3 476: A Mixed Workforce

Citizens, metics and slaves are listed in this inscription as having been paid for taking part in the fluting of a column of the Erechtheum on the Athenian acropolis in 408/7 BC. Citizens are given their deme of origin, metics are described as living in a deme, and slaves as belonging to a particular person. Of the workmen, the status of 86 can be identified: 24 are citizens, 42 metics and 20 slaves. The rate of pay was a drachma per day for skilled labour, and citizens and metics have their slaves working alongside them. [*IG* I^2 374.]

199 The next (column): Simias living in Alopeke 13 dr.; Kerdon 12 dr. 5 ob.; Sindron belonging to Simias 12 dr. 5 ob.; Sokles belonging to Axiopeithes 12 dr. 5 ob.; Sannion belonging to Simias 12 dr. 5 ob.; Epieikes belonging to Simias 12 dr. 5 ob.; Sosandros belonging to Simias 12 dr. 5 ob. The next: Onesimos belonging to Nikostratos 16 dr. 4 ob.; Eudoxos living in Alopeke 16 dr. 4 ob.; Kleon 16 dr. 4 ob.; Simon living in Agryle 16 dr. 4 ob.; Antidotos belonging to Glaukos 16 dr. 4 ob.; Eudikos 16 dr. 4 ob. The next: Theugenes of Piraeus 15 dr.; Kephisogenes of Piraeus 15 dr.; Teukros living in Kydathenaion 15 dr.; Kephisodoros living in Skambonidai 15 dr.; Nikostratos 15 dr.; Theugiton of Piraeus 15 dr.

5.43 *IG* II^2 10: Metics Become Citizens, 401/0 BC

Thrasyboulos, a democrat who defeated the Thirty in 403 BC by entering the Piraeus and seizing Mounichia, was joined by metics, to whom he seems to have promised citizenship. [Osborne 1981–82, D6.]

A

Lysiades was secretary, Xenainetos was archon. It was resolved by the boule and the people: (the tribe) Hippothontis held the prytany, Lysiades was secretary, Demophilos presided,

Thrasyboulos proposed the motion: so that the foreigners who took part in the return from Phyle or who assisted those who returned in the return to the Piraeus should be awarded suitable honours, **5** it is to be decreed by the Athenians that they and their descendants are to have citizenship, and they are to be allocated immediately to the tribes in ten parts. The magistrates are to apply the same laws to them as to the other Athenians. And all those who came afterwards, and joined in the battle at Mounichia, and preserved the Piraeus, and all those who stood by the demos in the Piraeus when the reconciliation took place, and did what was ordered, who are domiciled in Athens, are to have isoteleia in accordance with the pledge given just as for the Athenians. And they …

B

Chairedemos, a farm(er)
Leptines, a (coo)k (mageiros)
Demetrios, a carp(enter)
Euphorion, a mulet(eer)
Kephisodoros, a buil(der)
Hegesias, a garden(er)
Epameinon, a donkey (driver)
… opos, an olive(…)
Glaukias, a farm(er)
… n, a nut(…)
Dionysios, a farm(er)

Bendiphanes, a dig …
Emporion, a farm(er)
Paidikos, a bake(r)
Sosias, a full(er)
Psammis, a farm(er)
Ergesis
… m … o
Eukolion, a hired labour(er)
Kallias, a statue (maker)
Of (the tribe) Aigeis
Athenogiton …

HELOTS, PERIOIKOI AND SERFS

Unlike the slaves providing dependent labour in Greek states, helots were not foreigners, but a subject people, the Messenians, working their own lands in a state of servitude to the Spartans. They had property rights of a kind, after paying half their produce to the Spartans, and were a self-perpetuating class of serfs with their own families and possessions, greatly outnumbering the Spartiates. While slaves in Athens were manumitted on serving in the armed forces, Sparta depended on helots in her army, with 35,000 fighting at Plataea (see Hdt. 9.28.2, 29.1, cf. doc. 11.47). The perioikoi lived in the cities around, practising agriculture but also providing Spartans with their industrial needs. They also served as hoplites, as at Plataea (see Hdt. 9.11.3, 28.2).

5.44 Tyrtaeus *Poems* 6, 7: Messenian Tribute and Servitude

For the amount each allotment (kleros) was supposed to produce, see Plut. *Lyk.* 8.7, 24.2. For mourning for Spartan kings, see Hdt. 6.58. [Paus. 4.14.4–5.]

4.14.4 The Messenians themselves were treated by the Spartans in the following way: first they made them take an oath that they would never rebel against them or attempt any form of revolution. Secondly, while the Spartans imposed no fixed tribute on them, they used to bring half of all their agricultural produce to Sparta. It was also laid down that at the funerals of kings and other magistrates both men and women should come from Messenia in black clothes; and a penalty was imposed on transgressors. **5** As to the punishments with which they maltreated the Messenians, this is written in the poems of Tyrtaeus (F6):

Just like donkeys oppressed with great burdens,
Bringing to their masters of grievous necessity
Half of all the produce their land bears.

That they were compelled to join in their mourning (for their masters) he has shown in these lines (F7):

Lamenting their masters, both their wives and themselves,
Whenever the baneful fate of death should overtake one.

5.45 Plutarch *Sayings of the Spartans* (*Moralia* 223a): Helots as Farmers

The main role of the helots, farming, is made clear here; for Kleomenes, see docs 6.72–78.

223a Kleomenes son of Anaxandridas said that Homer was the poet of the Spartans, and Hesiod of the helots; for the first had given instructions as to how to fight, and the second as to how to farm.

5.46 Plutarch *Life of Lykourgos* 28.8–9, 11–12: The Spartans' Callous Treatment of Helots

Cf. docs 6.46–47 for Spartan attitudes to alcohol; the quotation at 28.11 is from Kritias F37 (Diels II). For the helot revolt, see docs 12.9, 12.11.

28.8 In other ways too the Spartiates treated the helots harshly and brutally; for example they would compel them to drink a large quantity of unmixed wine and then would bring them into the messes to show the young men what drunkenness was like, **9** and used to order them to sing songs and perform dances which were ignoble and ridiculous, but to refrain from those appropriate for free men ... **11** This distinction can be clearly seen in the saying that at Sparta a free man is really free and a slave really a slave. **12** I believe that such harsh treatment on the part of the Spartiates came later, particularly after the great earthquake, when the helots are said to have risen up with the Messenians, done terrible damage to the country, and posed a serious threat to the city.

5.47 Myron of Priene F2: Helot Bondage

For Myron of Priene, see Paus. 4.6.1–5, who considers him an unreliable source; for Spartan clothing see doc. 6.17. [*FGH* 106 F2; Athen. *Deip.* 657c–d.]

That the Spartans used the helots insolently is also related by Myron of Priene in the second book of his *History of Messenia*, where he writes as follows: 'They assign the helots every insulting task which leads to every disgrace. For they decreed that each man should be compelled to wear a dog's-skin cap and wrap himself in leather and receive a certain number of strokes every year without having committed any crime, so that they would never unlearn that they were slaves. Additionally, if any of them surpassed in vigour their servile appearance, they inflicted the death penalty on them and a fine on those owners who did not reprove those who were becoming fat.'

5.48 Thucydides 4.80.2–5: Drastic Measures for Dealing with Helots

The Spartan general Brasidas in 424 BC proposed taking a small force against Athens' possessions in Thrace, one of his reasons being to keep the helots occupied.

4.80.2 At the same time they were glad of an excuse to send out some of the helots, as they were afraid, in the present state of affairs with Pylos in enemy hands, that they might start some sort of revolution. **3** Also on one occasion, because they were afraid of the difficulties they could cause and their numbers (for the Spartans' measures respecting the helots have concentrated almost entirely on security), they proclaimed that the helots should pick out all those who claimed to have done best service to Sparta in their wars, implying that they would be freed, but they were actually conducting a test, as they considered that those with spirit who came forward first to claim their freedom would also be those most likely to turn against Sparta. **4** So they picked out about 2,000, who crowned themselves with garlands and made the round of the sanctuaries as if they were now free, but not long afterwards they caused them to disappear and no one knows in what way any of them died. **5** And so on this occasion the Spartans were glad to send out 700 hoplites with Brasidas, while the rest of the army he took with him from the Peloponnese he had hired as mercenaries.

5.49 Thucydides 5.34.1: Helot Fighters Freed in 421 BC

The Spartans voted in 421 that the helots who had fought with Brasidas be freed and allowed to live where they wished, and settled them shortly afterwards at Lepreon with the neodamodeis, who were presumably liberated helots, on the border between Lakonia and Elis. For the neodamodeis, see Thuc. 5.67.1, 7.19.3, 7.58.3, 8.5.1.

5.34.1 That same summer the soldiers who had gone to Thrace with Brasidas returned, who had been brought home by Klearidas under the peace treaty, and the Spartans decreed that the helots who had fought with Brasidas should be free and live where they wished, and not long afterwards they settled them with the neodameis at Lepreon, which lies between Lakonia and Elis, the Spartans already being on terms of hostility with Elis.

5.50 Plutarch *Lykourgos* 28.1–5, 28.7: The Krypteia: The Spartan 'Secret Service'

Service in the krypteia was part of the training of Spartan youths. The killing of helots out at night could suggest that there was a curfew imposed on them. [Aristotle F538.]

28.1 In all this there is no trace of the injustice or arrogance, of which some accuse Lykourgos' laws, considering that while they are well equipped to produce valour, they fail to produce justice. **2** Their so-called 'krypteia', if this really was one of Lykourgos' institutions, as Aristotle says, may have given Plato as well this idea of Lykourgos and his constitution. The krypteia was like this: **3** the supervisors of the young men from time to time would send out into the countryside in different directions those who appeared to be the most intelligent, equipped only with daggers and basic provisions. **4** During the day they would disperse into obscure places to hide and rest, but at night they would make their way to the roads and kill any helot they caught. **5** Often too they would go through the fields and do away with the sturdiest and most powerful helots … **28.7** And Aristotle also says specifically that the ephors, when first they took up office, would declare war on the helots, so that killing them would not involve ritual pollution.

5.51 Theopompos F122: Thessalian Serfs

Local peoples who were conquered had been enserfed by the Spartans and by the Thessalians, whereas the Chians were the first to purchase slaves from outside as dependent labour, according to Theopompos. [*FGH* 115 F122; Athen. *Deip.* 265b–c.]

After the Thessalians and Spartans, the Chians were the first of the Greeks to use slaves, but they did not acquire them in the same way as these. For, as we shall see, the Spartans and Thessalians constituted their slave population out of the Greeks who had previously lived in the territories which they now hold, the Spartans taking over the Achaean territory, the Thessalians that of the Perrhaiboi and the Magnesians, and they call the people they enslaved helots and penestai respectively. But the Chians acquired barbarians as slaves and paid money for them.

5.52 Phylarchos F8: Serfs in Asia Minor

[*FGH* 81 F 8; Athen. *Deip.* 271b–c.]

Phylarchos in the sixth book of his *Histories* says that the Byzantines made themselves masters of the Bithynians, just like the Spartans of the helots.

CITIZEN LABOUR

There were of course, in Athens and probably in most Greek cities except Sparta, large numbers of free men engaged in labour, either manufacture, or retail trade, or working their own land. The ideal lifestyle for the Athenian citizen was to own a farm and support a family on the produce from that land, while having sufficient freedom from work to engage in social and political life. Slaves did not provide free citizens with time they could devote to leisure and politics: even citizens who owned slaves still generally worked.

5.53 Hesiod *Works and Days* 20–26: Maxims for Prosperity

While Hesiod assumes that the farmer will have slave labour, he also sees it as necessary for the farmer to work hard – and the potters and craftsmen as well. For Hesiod, hard work is necessary for the accumulation of wealth and he attaches no stigma to it.

Moreover Strife rouses even the helpless to work;
For a man craves work when he looks at the next man
Who is rich, who hastens to plough and plant

And set his house in good order; and neighbour is jealous of neighbour
As the latter hastens after riches; this strife is good for mankind.
And potter is angry with potter, and craftsman with craftsman,
Beggar envies beggar and minstrel envies minstrel.

5.54 Theognis 173–78: Avoid Poverty at All Costs

The seventh-century poet Theognis of Megara was clearly concerned about changing social conditions, that 'good men' were being ousted by the 'base' in Megara, and about the prevalence of social disruption (see docs 7.19–20). Part of his complaint concerns changing standards of wealth, and it is clear that those who were previously outsiders have now become the rulers. Here he warns the reader against poverty, implying that the poor man, however well born, has no political power.

Poverty overpowers a good man more than anything else,
Even more than grizzled old age or ague, Kyrnos;
To escape it he should throw himself into the yawning
Sea or down from precipitous rocks.
For a man overpowered by poverty can say or do
Nothing, and his tongue is tied.

5.55 Hesiod *Works and Days* 225–37: Justice Brings Prosperity

Hesiod links the observance of justice with prosperity and agricultural and human fertility.

Those who to strangers and locals give judgements
That are upright and do not deviate from what is just,
Their city prospers, and the people in it flourish;
Peace, who rears children, is throughout the land, nor does
Far-seeing Zeus ordain for them cruel war;
Famine does not accompany men who give right judgement
Nor destruction, but with festivity they reap the fruit of the work which is their care.
For them the earth bears much subsistence, and on the mountains the oak
Bears acorns at its peak and in its midst bees;
Their woolly sheep are weighed down with fleeces;
Their wives bear children as their parents did;
They prosper continually with what is good, nor do they go
On ships, for the fruitful land bears them fruit.

5.56 Solon *Poem* 13: The Professions

Solon, the Athenian reformer of 594 BC, here lists the ways that men can justly acquire wealth. Being a trader, farmer, hired labourer, or craftsman are all approved of: it is doctors who are criticised.

All exert themselves in different ways: one wanders the fishy sea
Desiring in his ships to bring home gain,
Tossed by dreadful winds,
Quite unsparing of his life;

Another ploughs the land abounding in trees every year
And works for hire, his care the curved ploughs;
One who has learned the works of Athena and Hephaistos skilled in many crafts
Brings in his livelihood with his hands,
Another through being taught the gifts of the Olympian Muses,
And who knows full measure of lovely wisdom;
Another person Lord Apollo the Far-shooter has made a diviner;
He knows the evil that comes to a man from afar,
For on him the gods attend; but what is destined
No bird (omen) or sacrifices will in any way ward off.
Others have the work of Paian (the gods' healer), who knows many drugs,
Doctors: but they have no efficacy;
For often from a small ache comes great pain,
And no one can relieve it by giving soothing drugs;
Although he can touch a man disordered by dreadful diseases
And with his hands suddenly make him well.
Fate brings both evil and good to mortal men,
And the gifts of the immortal gods cannot be avoided.
There is danger in all forms of work, nor does one know
Where a matter once begun will end.

5.57 Xenophon *Constitution of the Spartans* 7.1–2: The Spartan Way of Life

Ancient Greeks worked at a variety of occupations, aiming to earn money as Solon makes clear (doc. 5.56). Only at Sparta was attention to be given solely to military and political matters and the citizens were not supposed to concern themselves with wealth (but this last ideal was lost in the late fifth and fourth centuries).

7.1 In other states, I suppose, everyone makes as much money as they can; for one person farms, another owns ships, another is a merchant, and others support themselves by different crafts. **2** But at Sparta Lykourgos forbade free men to touch anything to do with making money, and instructed them only to think about those activities which provide cities with freedom.

5.58 Xenophon *Oeconomicus* 4.2–3, 6.8–9: Socrates on Artisans and Agriculture

Despite the views of Socrates here, a large number of Athenians supported themselves by labour of various sorts, and contempt for 'banausic' occupations (involving craftmanship) was limited in Athens to the aristocratic class: everyone else had to work. Note Perikles' statement in the Funeral Oration that poverty is no disgrace: what is disgraceful is not taking steps to escape it (Thuc. 2.40.1; doc. 1.17).

4.2 'Well said, Kritoboulos,' replied Socrates. 'For the trades of artisans as they are called are decried and are understandably held in contempt in our cities, for they disfigure the bodies of those who work at them and supervise them, compelling them to remain seated and stay within doors, and sometimes to spend all day at the fire. When bodies become enervated, the souls become much more sickly. **4.3** And moreover these artisans' trades as they are called leave no free time for attending to one's friends and the city, with the result that such men appear to be inadequate both in their relationships with friends and as defenders of their countries. And in some cities, and especially those which have a warlike reputation it is not permissible for any of the citizens to work at the trades of artisans.' ... **6.8** So we decided that for a gentleman the best occupation and science is agriculture, from which men obtain what they need. **6.9** For this work seems to be both the easiest to learn and the most pleasant to work at, to make the body most beautiful and robust, and to leave the mind the greatest amount of spare time for looking after the interests of one's friends and city.

5.59 Herodotos 2.166.2–167.2: Contempt for Trade among Barbarians and Greeks

Egyptian warriors (the Kalasirians) were not allowed to practise any trade, and Herodotos suggests that the Greeks — especially the Spartans — may have copied them. Here he lists societies which view trade as unsuitable for a citizen.

2.166.2 The Kalasirians are not allowed to practise any craft (techne), but they have a purely military training, passed from father to son. **2.167.1** Whether the Greeks learned this from the Egyptians, I cannot accurately determine, seeing that the Thracians and Scythians and Persians and Lydians and nearly all the barbarians consider those who learn a craft and their descendants as inferior to other citizens, while they consider those who are exempted from manual work to be noble, and especially those who concentrate on war. **2** All the Greeks have certainly learned this, the Spartans in particular, while the Corinthians are the ones who look down on craftsmen least of all.

5.60 Xenophon *Memorabilia* 2.8.1–6: Eutheros Falls on Hard Times

Eutheros was a man of property who has fallen on hard times (cf. doc. 4.64). Socrates suggests that he should hire himself out as an estate manager; clearly Athenians of this class were reluctant to take on paid employment, but obviously it was a possibility, and bailiffs were not always slaves.

2.8.1 On seeing another old friend after a long time, Socrates said, 'Where have you come from, Eutheros?' 'From abroad when the (Peloponnesian) War ended, Socrates,' he replied, 'And now I'm living here. Since we lost our foreign property, and my father left me nothing in Attica, I'm now compelled to stay here and engage in physical labour to obtain my provisions. I think that that's better than begging from anyone, especially as I have nothing against which I can borrow.' **2** 'And how long,' said Socrates, 'do you think your body will be strong enough to earn your provisions by working for hire?' 'By Zeus,' he said, 'not long.' 'And when you get older it is clear that you will need to spend money, but no one will be willing to give you a wage for physical labour.' **3** 'That's very true.' 'Then wouldn't it be better for you to take up at once the sort of work that would also be viable for you when you're older, and approach someone who has more property who needs someone to assist him, and supervise his tasks and help bring in the crops and look after his estate, helping yourself by helping him?' **4** 'I would find it hard to endure slavery, Socrates.' 'But those who are in charge in the cities and look after public affairs are not thought more servile on that account, but are thought even more free.' **5** 'Yet, Socrates, I could never undertake to become accountable to anyone.' 'But, Eutheros, it is not at all easy to find a job where one does not have some censure … **6** So you should try to avoid fault-finders and look for those who are considerate and undertake those things you are able to perform, and keep away from any that you can't, and whatever you do give it your best and most zealous attention. In this way, I think, you are least likely to find censure, and you are most likely to find help in your difficulties, and live most easily and in greatest security and with a good competence for your old age.'

5.61 Plutarch *Perikles* 12.5–6: Perikles and Citizen Labour

Perikles' building programme would have provided employment for a number of skilled workers, at least some of them citizens, but these projects cannot have employed a large workforce because they were not large enough in scope. Plutarch's 'undisciplined artisan mob' did not exist; moreover, the projects employed metics and slaves, so their main purpose was clearly not as citizen employment projects.

12.5 The military campaigns provided incomes from public funds for those who had their youth and strength, but Perikles wished that the undisciplined artisan mob should also have a share in the payments. He did not want it to receive pay for being lazy and idle, so he brought before the people great construction projects and undertakings which would require the involvement of many crafts for works that would take a long time to complete, so that those who stayed at home, no less than those who were with the fleet or on garrison duty or on expeditions, should have a reason for benefiting from and sharing in the public funds. **6** The raw materials to be used were stone, bronze, ivory, gold, ebony and cypress-wood, while the trades which fashioned this material were to be those of carpenters, modellers, coppersmiths, stonemasons, gilders, workers in ivory, painters, embroiderers and engravers, as well as the carriers and suppliers of these materials — merchants, sailors and pilots by sea, and by land cartwrights, keepers of draught animals, muleteers, rope-makers, weavers, leatherworkers, road-makers and miners.

5.62 Xenophon *Education of Cyrus* 8.2.5–6: Specialisation in the City-State

Xenophon, along with other Greek mercenaries, attempted to put Cyrus on the Persian throne in 401 BC. After Cyrus' death, Xenophon served with the Spartans and wrote many works in praise of Sparta. In his *Cyropaedia*, or *Education of Cyrus*, he gives Persia Spartan characteristics. The workmen here, while apparently free, could also have been slaves or metics.

8.2.5 Just as all other crafts achieve exceptional quality in large cities, so the food in the King's palace is of this high standard. In small cities the same person makes beds, doors, ploughs, tables — and he often does building jobs as well. Even so he is happy if he can find sufficient work to support him. And of course it is impossible for a man who pursues many trades to be good at them all. In large cities, however, there is a great demand for every form of trade, and one craft, or often even just a part of one, is enough to provide work: one person, for instance, makes shoes for men, and another for women; in some places a person may even make a living by just stitching shoes, another by cutting them out, one by simply sewing the uppers together, while yet another engages in none of these activities but instead assembles the various parts. So anyone who spends time at a very specialised task is bound to achieve excellence at it.

6 The same thing is also true in relation to the preparation of food. Where one person makes up the dining couches, lays the table, bakes, and prepares all sorts of different dishes, naturally everything has to take its chance; but where one man is totally occupied in boiling meat, another in roasting it, one in poaching fish and another in baking it, one man in making bread — and he does not even make all kinds, but has enough to do if he is known to be an expert at one special type — naturally everything prepared like this is going to be of exceptional quality.

5.63 Demosthenes 57 *Against Euboulides* 30–31, 33–35, 40–42: The Poorer Citizens

Many citizen women had to work for a living: see docs 4.59–64. Euxitheos is here appealing a decision of his deme Halimos that he is not a citizen but a resident alien; Euboulides is prefect of the deme. The case probably dates to 345, the year after Demosthenes' purge of the citizen lists. Metics had to be registered and pay metic-tax to work in the market.

30 Men of Athens, in criticising us for working in the market Euboulides has not only acted against your decree, but also against the laws, which state that anyone, who uses the fact that they work in the market against any male or female citizen, shall be liable to the penalties for slander. **31** We admit that we sell ribbons and do not live in the manner we would like. And if you think this is proof, Euboulides, that we are not Athenians, I will prove to you the very opposite — that metics are not allowed to do business in the market…

33 In my view, that we work in the market is the strongest proof that the accusations he is bringing against us are false. **34** He states that my mother sells ribbons and that she is known to everybody. Well then, there ought to be a lot of people who know her and who can give evidence who she is, and not just from hearsay. If she was a metic they should have examined the records of market-taxes, and shown whether she paid the metic-tax, and which country she was from; if she was a slave then the person who bought her, or if not, the person who sold her should have come to give evidence against her, or if not them, then someone else to prove that she had been a slave or had been set free. However, Euboulides has proved none of these points, but in my view has simply thrown abuse at her in every possible way. This is the way an informer works: he makes all sorts of accusations, and proves nothing.

35 He has also charged my mother with having been a wet nurse. We don't deny that this happened at the time when the city was in crisis and everyone was badly off; but I will clearly explain to you how and why this happened. And do not take this to our discredit, men of Athens, for you will find many Athenian citizen women today acting as wet nurses, whom I can mention by name if you want me to. If we were wealthy, of course we would not be selling ribbons or be in any sort of difficulties. But what does this have to do with my family's background? Nothing at all, in my view.

40 My mother, jurors, had a daughter by her first husband, Protomachos, to whom she was given in marriage by her brother Timokrates, who shared with her the same father and mother, and then had myself by my father. I have to give you an account of how she married my father; and the background to all the charges regarding Kleinias and my mother having been a wet nurse I shall also clearly explain to you. **41** Protomachos was a poor man, but inherited an heiress and her estate and therefore wanted to marry my mother to someone else. So he persuaded my father Thoukritos, a friend of his, to take her and my father received my mother in marriage from the hands of her brother Timokrates of Melite, in the presence of both his own uncles and other witnesses: those who are still alive will give evidence before you. **42** Some time later, when she now had two children, and my father was away on campaign with Thrasyboulos, she was in difficulties and so became wet nurse to Kleinias son of Kleidikos. This was not, by Zeus, very lucky for me in terms of the threat to me which has resulted (from it was from her position as wet nurse that all this slander about us has arisen), but in terms of the poverty she was experiencing, what she did was perhaps both necessary and appropriate.

5.64 *Inscriptiones Graecae* I^3 766: A Craftsman Dedicates a Tithe to Athena

This inscription praises craftsmanship; it is on fragments of a base of Parian marble from a dedication to Athena on the acropolis at Athens, *c.* 500–450 BC. The craftsman appears to have dedicated his own work (perhaps a statue) as a tithe from the proceeds of his profits. [*IG* I^2 678; Friedländer 134; Hansen 230.]

It is good for the skilled to exercise their skill according to their craft;
For he who has a craft has a better life.
This is a tithe to Athena.

THE DRAMATIC SLAVE

5.65 Aeschylus *Libation Bearers* 747–65: The Old Nurse of Orestes

Orestes returns to Mycenae planning to murder his mother Clytemnestra and her lover Aegisthus. To make his task easier, he arrives in disguise, and reports that he (Orestes) is dead. Slave wet nurses (tithai) and nannies (trophoi) had an important role in caring for the children of wealthy parents.

Nurse: Well I've never yet endured such a blow!
I've borne my other troubles with endurance,
But dear Orestes, my soul's care,
Whom I took from his mother and brought up –
The times he cried and got me out of bed!
The many tedious things I went through
For nothing; a baby knows no better and you've got
To nurse it like an animal; why not? It's how it thinks;
For a babe still in swaddling clothes can't say
If it's hungry or thirsty or wants to pee.
Children's insides are young and act instinctively.
I used to foretell these, but often
I'd be wrong, and I'd be washing the baby clothes,
For laundress and nurse were both the same person.
And I had these two duties
When I took Orestes from his father;
And now I'm wretched to hear that he's dead!

Well, I'll go to that man who's this house's
Ruin; he'll be pleased to hear of this.

5.66 Euripides *Helen* 722–33: Helen's Loyal Servant

Aristophanes has many lazy and unreliable slaves in his comedies; tragedy prefers its slaves to be loyal and upstanding in their relationship with their masters.

Now I remember again your wedding
And recall the lamps which I carried as I ran
Beside the four horses yoked together; and you in your chariot
As a bride with Menelaos left your happy home.
It's a base slave that does not revere his masters' affairs
And rejoice with them and share in their troubles.
I would be, a servant though I am,
Numbered amongst the noble
Slaves — not free in name,
But at least in mind; for this is better than for one man
To suffer two ills — to have a base mind
And to hear himself called slave by those around him.

5.67 Homer *Iliad* 6.447–463: Hector Foresees Andromache's Fate

Here Hector foresees Troy's capture by the Greeks and Andromache's future fate as a slave. Andromache will be enslaved, and have to weave and fetch water for a mistress.

'For I know this well in my heart and mind:
There will be a day when sacred Ilium will be destroyed
And Priam and the people of Priam of the good ashen spear.
But I do not feel so much grief for the Trojans,
Nor for Hekabe herself or lord Priam,
Or my brothers, who many and brave as they are
Will fall in the dust at the hands of the enemy,
As much as for you, when one of the bronze-clad Achaeans
Leads you off in tears, robbing you of the day of freedom.
And when you are in Argos weaving the web for some other woman,
And carrying water at Messene or Hypereia
Not of your own will but forced by strong necessity,
Someone will see you as you weep and say,
"That is the wife of Hector, who was the best fighter
Of the horse-taming Trojans, when they were besieging Ilium."
So they will say; and that will cause you yet another pang
From the need of such a man to ward off the day of slavery.'

5.68 Euripides *Trojan Women* 235–52, 272–78: The Fate of Women in Wartime

Hekabe (Hecuba), wife of Priam and queen of Troy, after the capture of Troy hears her own fate and that of her daughters and daughters-in-law from Talthybios, the Greek herald.

Talthybios: Hekabe, you know me from my frequent journeys to Troy,
Coming here as herald from the Greek host,
Known to you, lady, formerly,
I, Talthybios, come to announce news.
Hekabe: Dear women, this was our former fear.
Talthybios: You have now been allocated, if this was what you feared.
Hekabe: Alas! For what
City of Thessaly or Phthia
Or the land of Kadmos are we destined?
Talthybios: You have each been assigned to a different man, not all together.
Hekabe: Who is assigned to whom? Which Trojan woman does good luck await?
Talthybios: I know; but you must learn one at a time, not all together.
Hekabe: My child then,
Tell me, wretched Cassandra, who has obtained her?
Talthybios: King Agamemnon chose her specially.
Hekabe: For his Spartan wife
To be a slave? O misery!
Talthybios: Not so, but for his bed as a concubine.

Hekabe: What of the wife of bronze-hearted Hector,
Poor Andromache, what is her fate?
Talthybios: The son of Achilles too chose her especially.
Hekabe: And whose servant am I, who leans on her stick
With her aged hand as if on a third foot ?
Talthybios: Odysseus, king of Ithaca, has obtained you as his slave.
Hekabe: Oh woe!

5.69 Krates *The Wild Animals* F16: Life without Slaves

This is from a fifth-century BC comedy, of which fragments remain; here automation is promised as an alternative to slaves. [Athen. *Deip.* 267e–f.]

A: Then won't anyone own a male or female slave?
Will each man, even old people, have to look after themselves?
B: Not at all; I am going to give everything the ability to move around.
A: So what will that achieve?
B: Each piece of equipment
Will come when called for. 'Set yourself beside me, table.'
'That one — get yourself ready.' 'Get kneading, bread basket.'
'Pour, ladle.' 'Where's the cup? Go and wash yourself out.'
'Barley cake, rise.' 'The pot ought to disgorge the beets.'
'Fish, get moving.' 'But I'm not cooked yet on the other side.'

'Then why don't you turn over and give yourself some oil and a sprinkle of salt?'

5.70 Aristophanes *Frogs* 1–20: Slaves as a Stock Joke in Comedy

Obviously to bring on a slave or slaves with stock jokes to commence a comedy had become a stereotyped convention, and harsh treatment of slaves in plays appears to have been considered amusing.

Xanthias: Shall I tell one of the usual jokes, Master,
Those at which the audience always laugh?
Dionysos: Yes, whatever you like — all except 'what a load I've got!':
Watch that one; I feel sick enough already.
Xanthias: What about some other joke?
Dionysos: Anything but 'what a bad way I'm in!'
Xanthias: Then what? Shall I say something really funny?
Dionysos: Yes
With confidence; but just don't say —
Xanthias: What?
Dionysos: Shift your load and say you want to 'ease yourself'.
Xanthias: Not even that I'm carrying such a tremendous load that
If someone doesn't remove it I'm going to fart?
Dionysos: Definitely not, please — keep it for when I'm about to vomit.
Xanthias: So why did I have to carry all this baggage,
If I can't make any of the jokes that
Phrynichos and Lykis and Ameipsias always do,
Each time they have baggage carried on in a comedy?
Dionysos: Well, you can't; when I'm a spectator
And see one of these stage-tricks,
I come away more than a year older.
Xanthias: This thrice-wretched neck of mine —
It's 'in a bad way' and can't say anything funny.

6

SPARTA

Sparta lies in the south-east Peloponnese, on the Eurotas river, with the Taygetos mountain range to the west separating it from Messenia. There were four villages making up Sparta, or Lakedaimon: Pitana, Mesoa, Limnai and Kynosoura; Amyklai, to the south, was incorporated at an early stage into Spartan territory (cf. doc. 1.7). The immediate territory was known as Lakonia. Athens and Sparta were the two most powerful and important cities of ancient Greece. Their social and political organisation, however, differed markedly in several key areas. Sparta's political system consisted of two kings reigning simultaneously, a council of elders known as the gerousia, which consisted of twenty-eight members and the two kings, a board of five ephors and the Spartiates, full Spartan citizens, the assembly of which was known as the ekklesia. There were two branches of the royal family, the Agiad and the Eurypontid, with a king from each line; the Agiad was the senior. The Spartiates, Spartan citizens, were known as homoioi, 'equals', but within Lakonia were two other main groups, the perioikoi and the helots, who greatly outnumbered the Spartiates.

Central to Spartan history was the figure of Lykourgos, but whether he was a mythical or perhaps a historical figure is uncertain (doc. 6.1). He was the lawgiver who supposedly established both the 'Great Rhetra' and the military system which was the basis of Spartan power. Lykourgos was said to have modelled the Spartan constitution on that of Crete (docs 6.2–3); similarities between the two, however, would have been due to the fact that both societies were Dorian. While the Spartans saw him as a historical figure, it is more than possible that he was in fact a legendary creation. For while Tyrtaeus refers to the Spartan constitution which Delphi recognised, indicating that the reforms of Lykourgos were in existence when Tyrtaeus was writing during the Second Messenian War, he fails to mention Lykourgos himself (docs 6.6, 6.8–11). Nevertheless, it is convenient to speak of the reforms of Lykourgos, and it is now usual to date the so-called Lykourgan reforms to shortly after the Second Messenian War.

As early as the late eighth century BC Sparta had begun a series of wars to extend its territory; the First Messenian War is usually dated to 740–720 BC, and was won under King Theopompos (doc. 6.8). The Messenians later revolted in what is termed the Second Messenian War, which took place about the middle of the seventh century, and in which Tyrtaeus was a general (doc. 6.52, cf. 6.12). Many scholars date the development of Sparta's military system to the aftermath of this conflict. The system adopted by the Spartans meant that they were always in a state of military preparedness, which makes sense only if there were some immediate and pressing threat. In taking Messenia they had also acquired a subject population which required constant vigilance. The helots, in fact, become the 'millstone' around the Spartans' neck, especially when the Spartans were away on campaign, and the helots' tendency to revolt was a factor which had to be considered in all Spartan foreign policy. In addition to adopting a military way of life to keep the helots under control, the Spartans also buttressed their control over the Messenians by a system of alliances (docs 6.56, 6.61), in which their allies had to come to their assistance if the helots revolted; in this way many Peloponnesian states came within Sparta's sphere of influence by the end of the sixth century. In the Peloponnesian War Sparta was able to rely on many of the Peloponnesian states as allies in its war against Athens (docs. 6.62–63). So, beginning with wars in the eighth century, Sparta had by the end of the sixth century established leadership over most of the Peloponnese.

Plutarch (relying on Aristotle) considers the 'Great Rhetra' as the work of Lykourgos, which subsequently had a 'rider' attached to it by the kings Polydoros and Theopompos. It is possible, however, that the 'rider' was in fact an original part of the Great Rhetra. Plutarch, who records the Great Rhetra, provides some explanatory notes about it and the difficulties of interpretation suggest that this probably does reflect an authentic decree (doc. 6.5). The Spartan ekklesia, like the Athenian ekklesia, had the final say about the proposals brought before it, but according to the Great Rhetra only the 'elders and kings' could bring these proposals: the gerousia, in preparing the agenda, had a 'probouleutic' role. But the so-called rider to the Great Rhetra (doc. 6.6) provided that the assembly should not in any way alter the proposals but could only discuss those before it and vote on them; altered proposals were invalid. This meant that what the assembly was able to vote on was restricted. The rider, like the rhetra itself, indicates that the 'people' had 'sovereign authority' in the state, as they voted and made decisions: this is compatible with a hoplite system, in which the hoplites fought and had political power, and consequently the rhetra must date to a period when the military was organised along hoplite lines. The Spartan system had the training of the hoplite soldier as its focus, and the adoption of hoplite tactics and armour took place in the Greek world from c. 750 to 650 BC (cf. doc. 6.10). This is another argument for the reforms of the Spartan state taking place in the mid-seventh century, and not several centuries earlier, when hoplite warfare did not yet exist.

The Spartan political system had several elements: monarchy (the kings), democracy (the ekklesia) and oligarchy (the gerousia), as Aristotle saw it (doc. 6.25). Plato saw having two kings as a way of 'contracting' the power of the monarchy, and the gerousia and the ephors as a check on the power of the kings (doc. 6.21, cf. 6.32). Plutarch thought that the way in which the different elements in the constitution worked together was the key to Sparta's political stability (doc. 6.20). The kings had specific duties and privileges (doc. 6.26), with their main role being that of war leaders (doc. 6.29). Kings however could be reprimanded and fined, especially for failing to bring about expected military results (doc. 6.33). Despite the praise of some ancient authors, Aristotle had specific criticisms about the kings, gerousia, ephors and the messes (docs 6.37–44).

The Spartans were suspicious of democracies, feeling safer when their allies were ruled by oligarchies, and often opposed tyranny (docs 6.57–58, 7.7), though Kleomenes did attempt to impose Isagoras as 'tyrant' of Athens in 505 BC. This attempt was prevented by the Corinthians who left the expedition, followed by the other Spartan king, Demaratos (doc. 10.5). The Spartans also came to regret deposing the tyrant Hippias at Athens and Kleomenes attempted to restore him to power, but again the Corinthians successfully opposed this move (doc. 6.59). While oligarchies most closely resembled their own 'balanced' constitution, the Spartans feared Athens far more as a democracy than as a tyranny ruled by a pro-Spartan tyrant Isagoras.

The Spartans evolved a military system which set them apart from the rest of the Greeks, not so much because of its general aim but because of its single-minded pursuit of military principles and practices. Those who were found at birth to be physically inferior were exposed (doc. 4.23). From early childhood they trained in the arts of war; this system was the agoge, an intensive training method designed to toughen up the boys so that they would endure hardship and deprivation; flogging ensured discipline (doc. 6.49). Boys were whipped in the cult of Artemis to stain her altar with blood (doc. 6.51), and a similar well-known example of Spartan toughness is that of the boy who held a fox cub under his tunic and endured it lacerating his stomach and so died rather than admit that he had it (doc. 6.50). They learned marching songs and Tyrtaeus' poems by heart (doc. 6.12), inculcating a sense of military pride and self-sacrifice. Cowardice was punished (doc. 6.15), and those who did not die in battle when they had the chance to do so also faced social ostracism, but could redeem themselves (docs 11.30, cf. 11.27). Mothers played a key role in expecting bravery from their sons (doc. 6.18). According to Xenophon, the Spartans were the 'only craftsmen in warfare' (doc. 6.30). Aristotle accused the training of producing 'wild beasts' (doc. 6.81). But the Spartans were not without culture, celebrating festivals with dances and choirs (doc. 6.19, cf. 6.13, 4.14).

Spartan society was sober in comparison with that of Athens. Lykourgos stopped compulsory binge drinking (doc. 6.47). The older Spartans in particular had a sparse diet, enjoying the famous Lakonian broth, which others could not stomach (docs 6.45–46). The messes, in each of which small groups of Spartans ate together, were instituted to ensure that there would be conformity and uniformity of lifestyle amongst them (doc. 6.48). The agoge was intended to create professional soldiers and this system worked well for some two centuries. Victory in the Peloponnesian War brought money to Sparta (docs 6.68–71), contrasting with the incorruptibility of King Kleomenes in the sixth century (doc. 6.73). By the end of the fifth century there were signs that the Spartan system was breaking down and this was particularly reflected in the influx of wealth into Sparta and the decreasing number of Spartiates (doc. 6.37). Sparta invaded Boeotia but was defeated by the Thebans at the battle of Leuktra in 371 BC, and in 370 the Thebans liberated the Messenian helots and refounded the Messenian state, building a new capital for it called Megalopolis (docs 14.18–24). But true to their ideals the Spartans would not be led by another (that is, Alexander) into war against the Persians in 334 BC; and they revolted against him, unsuccessfully, in 330 BC, with King Agis III dying in battle (doc. 15.19).

LYKOURGOS 'THE LAWGIVER'

Plutarch *Life of Lykourgos* 1 records the opinions of ancient writers about Lykourgos: that he was contemporary with the establishment of the Olympic festival in 776 BC or earlier, that there were in fact two reformers called Lykourgos at different times, or that he was contemporary with the first kings. Herodotos (doc. 6.2) has him as the regent for Leobotas, which gives an approximately ninth-century date. The military system ascribed to Lykourgos, however, makes best historical sense in the aftermath of the Second Messenian War, dating to about the mid-seventh century, after which the Spartans had a subject population of helots to keep under control.

6.1 Plutarch *Life of Lykourgos* 1.1: Lykourgos, Man or Myth?

1.1 In general nothing can be said concerning Lykourgos the lawgiver that is not disputed, since there are different versions of his birth, travels abroad, death and above all his work on the laws and constitution, and least of all is there agreement about the times in which the man lived.

6.2 Herodotos 1.65.2–66.1: Lykourgos Reforms the Spartan Constitution

According to Xenophon *Constitution of the Spartans* 8.5, Lykourgos took his laws to Delphi, where they were approved by Apollo. While Herodotos attributes the ephorate to Lykourgos, the Great Rhetra does not mention it, and in fact this office was a later addition.

1.65.2 The change towards good government (eunomia) happened like this: Lykourgos, an esteemed Spartiate, went to Delphi to consult the oracle, and as he entered the shrine the Pythia immediately spoke as follows:

3 'You have come, Lykourgos, to my rich temple,
You who are dear to Zeus and all who have homes on Olympus.
I am in doubt whether to proclaim you a god or mortal;
But I hope that you are a god, Lykourgos.'

4 Some say that the Pythia in addition to this also revealed to him the Spartiates' constitution as it exists at the present time, but the Spartans themselves say that Lykourgos who was regent for Leobotas, his nephew, king of Sparta, brought the institutions from Crete. **5** For as soon as he became regent, he changed all the laws and made sure that these should not be transgressed. After this Lykourgos established military organisation, the divisions (enomotiai), companies of thirty (triakades) and messes (syssitia), as well as the ephors and elders. **1.66.1** By these changes they became a well-ordered state, and they dedicated a temple to Lykourgos when he died and revere him greatly. Living in a fertile country and with a numerous population of men, they immediately expanded and flourished.

6.3 Aristotle *Politics* 1271b24–26: Lykourgos and Crete

For the Spartan tradition that Lykourgos brought the Spartan constitution from Crete, see doc. 6.2 (Hdt. 1.65.4). For a much more detailed account, see Plut. *Lyk*. 4. According to Plut. *Lyk*. 3.6 and Arist. *Pol*. 1271b25–26, Lykourgos' ward was Charillos (also ninth century on traditional genealogies); for the modelling of the Spartan constitution on that of Crete, cf. Plut. *Lyk*. 4.1–3.

1271b24 They say that Lykourgos, when he gave up the guardianship of Charillos and went abroad, then spent most of his time in Crete and its neighbourhood because of their close relationship (between Crete and Sparta).

6.4 Xenophon *Constitution of the Spartans* 8.5: Lykourgos Consults Delphi

Xenophon states that Lykourgos took his laws to Delphi, where they were approved by Apollo, and this gave them religious backing. Cf. doc. 6.2; Plut. *Lyk*. 5.

8.5 Of the many other good plans instituted by Lykourgos so the citizens would be willing to obey the laws, this seems to me amongst the best, that before delivering his laws to the populace, he first went with the most important Spartans to Delphi and asked the god (Apollo) if it would be preferable and better for Sparta to obey the laws he had made. When Apollo replied that it would be better in every way, then Lykourgos put them into force, laying down that not to obey the laws given by Apollo was not only illegal but also impious.

6.5 Plutarch *Life of Lykourgos* 6.1–4, 6.6–9: The Great Rhetra

There were originally three tribes (phylai), at Sparta (as was normal for Dorian states such as Crete): Hylleis, Pamphyloi and Dymanes. The obai, villages, have been identified by some scholars as the four villages of the 'polis' Sparta itself, plus nearby Amyklai. 'From season to season to apellaze' (6.2) means to celebrate the festival of Apollo, the Apellai, and according to Plutarch to summon the assembly. Plutarch continues by quoting Tyrtaeus (doc. 6.6).

6.1 Lykourgos was so eager for this form of government (the elders) that he brought an oracle from Delphi about it, which they call a 'rhetra'. **2** It runs as follows: 'After dedicating a temple to Zeus Skyllanios and Athena Skyllania, forming tribes (phylai) and creating obai, and setting up a gerousia of thirty including the archagetai (founder-leaders), then from season to season apellaze between Babyka and Knakion so as to introduce and rescind (measures); to the people should belong the agora and the power.' **3** In this, 'forming phylai' and 'creating obai' refer to the division and allocation of the populace into groups, of which the former he named phylai, the latter obai. The kings are meant by archagetai, and to 'apellaze' is to hold an assembly, because he referred the origin and cause of his constitution to Pythian Apollo. **4** They now call Babyka … and Knakion Oinous; and Aristotle says that Knakion is a river and Babyka a bridge … **6** When the populace was assembled, Lykourgos allowed no one except the elders and the kings to put forward a proposal, but the people had the supreme authority to decide upon one which these laid before them. **7** Later on, however, when the people distorted and did violence to the motions by taking bits away and adding to them, the kings Polydoros and Theopompos added this to the rhetra: **8** 'If the people should choose a crooked ordinance ('rhetra'), the older-born and leaders are to set it aside,' that is they should not ratify it, but withdraw it entirely and dismiss the assembly, since they were altering and remodelling the proposal contrary to what was best. **9** And they persuaded the city that the god had commanded this addition, as Tyrtaeus perhaps recalls in these lines.

6.6 Tyrtaeus *Poem* 4: Apollo Proclaims the 'Rhetra'

Lykourgos himself is not mentioned by Tyrtaeus (but he does describe the Spartan political system: kings, gerousia and assembly). It seems likely that the 'Great Rhetra' was enacted in the mid-seventh century and that some time between Tyrtaeus and Herodotos, the Spartans credited these reforms to a figure they called Lykourgos. Diodorus 7.12.6 gives two extra lines (following line 2 of this document: 'For thus the Lord of the Silver Bow, Far-shooting Apollo, / The Golden-Haired spoke from his rich shrine').

They listened to Apollo and brought home from Delphi
The oracles of the god and his words of sure fulfilment:
The god-honoured kings shall begin the counsel,
For in their care is the lovely city of Sparta,
And the firstborn old men; then the common men
Answering them with straightforward ordinances
Shall both speak what is good and do all things right,
Nor give this city any crooked counsel;
And victory and might shall attend the people.
For concerning this Apollo proclaimed thus to the city.

THE SPARTAN ETHOS

Tyrtaeus described the Spartans as the 'descendants of invincible Herakles' (doc. 6.10). They focused on military training and abhorred cowardice. Sparta's need to control a large subject population led it to be cautious before declaring and going to war. They were also extremely scrupulous with regard to any omens that the gods might send which might be interpreted to mean that the gods wanted them to stop a particular campaign. The Corinthians in a speech made at Sparta just prior to the Peloponnesian War unfavourably contrasted the Spartan mentality with that of the Athenians, in order to provoke war: see doc. 13.3.

6.7 Ephoros *History* F117: Sparta Acquires a Subject Population

The Dorian conquest of the Peloponnese was traditionally dated to *c.* 1100 BC. The twins Eurysthenes and Prokles, descendants of Herakles, were supposed to be the fathers of Agis and Eurypon respectively, the 'founders' of the two royal families, the Agiads (the senior branch) and the Eurypontids (the lesser). The Spartans then expanded their territory by conquering Messenia, including the supposed city of 'Helos', and so gained a subject population — the helots. [*FGH* 70 F117; Strabo *Geog.* 8.5.4.]

8.5.4 Ephoros tells us that the Herakleidai, Eurysthenes and Prokles, took possession of Lakonia, divided it into six parts, and established cities in the countryside… Although all of the neighbouring people (the perioikoi) were subject to the Spartiates, they still had legal equality and shared citizenship and the right to public office. Agis, however, the son of Eurysthenes, deprived them of these equal rights and ordered them to pay tribute to Sparta. Everyone obeyed, except for the Heleians who lived at Helos and were called helots, who rose in rebellion. They were forcibly subjugated in war and condemned to slavery, on the specific condition that no owner was allowed to set them free or sell them beyond the borders. This was called the 'War against the Helots'. And it could be said that Agis and his associates were the instigators of the helot system that lasted right down to the period of Roman supremacy, in which the Spartans kept these men in a sort of public slavery, assigning them places to live and specific duties.

6.8 Tyrtaeus *Poem* 5: Victory over Messenia

In the second half of the eighth century BC Sparta began a series of wars to extend its territory. The last Messenian victory in the Olympic games took place in 736 BC; this, and the first Spartan victory in 716 at the Olympic games, as well as the approximate dates of Theopompos' reign in the eighth century, gives a rough date for the First Messenian War, perhaps *c.* 740–720. Following this, Messenia was divided up amongst the Spartans and ceased to be an independent state.

To our king, Theopompos, friend of the gods,
Because of whom we took spacious Messene,
Messene good to plough, good to plant;
They fought for it for fully nineteen years
Unceasingly and always stout of heart
The spearmen fathers of our fathers;
And in the twentieth, leaving their rich fields,
The Messenians fled from the great mountains of Ithome.

6.9 Tyrtaeus *Poem* 10: An Exhortation to Fight for Your Country

The Second Messenian War broke out in the mid-seventh century, presumably when the Messenians revolted, perhaps as a result of the Argive victory over the Spartans at Hysiai (see doc. 6.54). Tyrtaeus, a contemporary of this conflict, exhorts the Spartans to victory, making clear the consequences of defeat: shameful penury and exile.

To die after falling in the vanguard is a good thing
For a brave man doing battle on behalf of his native land.
But to leave his city and rich fields
To go begging is of all things the most painful,
Wandering with a dear mother and aged father
And with small children and a wedded wife.
Hateful shall he be amongst those, to whom he comes
Giving way to poverty and hateful penury,
And he shames his family, and belies his noble form,
And every dishonour and misery follow.
Thus there is no concern for a wanderer
Nor respect nor posterity hereafter.
Let us fight with courage for our country, and for our children
Let us die and never spare our lives.
Young men, remain beside each other and fight,
And do not begin shameful flight or fear,
But make your spirit great and brave in your heart,
And do not be faint-hearted when you fight with men;
Your elders, whose knees are no longer nimble,
Do not flee and leave them, those who are old.
For this is shameful, that fallen in the vanguard
An older man should lie before the youngsters,
His head already white and his beard grizzled,
Breathing out his brave spirit in the dust,
Holding his bloody genitals in his own hands —
Things shameful for the eyes and a sight to inspire wrath,
His flesh naked; but all things are seemly for a young man,
While he has the splendid flower of lovely youth,
Wondrous for men to behold, and desirable to women
While he is alive, and handsome when he has fallen in the vanguard.
But let each man plant himself stoutly and stay with both feet
Firmly stood upon the ground, biting his lip with his teeth.

6.10 Tyrtaeus *Poem* 11: The Spartan Phalanx

Tyrtaeus stresses that cowardice brings disgrace, and that bravery is shown in hand-to-hand combat in the front line. Note the use of hoplite tactics and armour.

You are descendants of invincible Herakles,
So have courage; Zeus has not yet turned his neck aside;

Do not fear a mass of men, do not be afraid,
But let each man hold his shield straight towards the vanguard,
Reckoning life as hateful, and the black
Fates of death dear as the rays of the sun.
For you know that the deeds of much-lamented Ares are destructive,
And have learned well the temperament of painful war;
You have been with those fleeing and those pursuing,
Young men, and of both you have had your fill and more.
Those who dare to remain beside each other
And go into hand-to-hand combat and the vanguard,
Fewer of these die, and they save the people afterwards;
But all valour is lost for those who flee from fear;
No one would ever finish recounting each misery,
All those that befall a man, if he should become disgraced.
For painful it is to pierce through from behind the back
Of a man running away in destructive war;
And the corpse lying in the dust is dishonoured
With his back struck from behind by a spear-point.
But let each man plant himself stoutly and stay with both feet
Firmly stood upon the ground, biting his lip with his teeth,
His thighs and calves below and breast and shoulders
Covered with the belly of his broad shield;
In his right hand let him shake his mighty spear,
And let him wave the dreadful crest above his head;
In the doing of mighty deeds let him learn to do battle,
And not stand beyond the missiles holding his shield,
But let each man go close hand-to-hand and with his long spear
Or his sword let him wound and take his foe.
Let him set foot beside foot, rest shield against shield,
Crest on crest, and helmet on helmet
And let him fight his man with breast approached to breast,
Holding either his sword hilt or his long spear.

6.11 Tyrtaeus *Poem* 12: The Rewards of Courage

This is prowess, this the best prize amongst men
And the fairest for a young man to win.
This is a common good for the city and all the people,
When a man remains standing firm in the vanguard
Unceasingly, and forgets shameful flight entirely,
Making his soul and heart steadfast,
Standing by his neighbour with words of encouragement;
Such a man is good in war.
He quickly turns the phalanxes of the hostile
Enemy; and eagerly checks the wave of battle,
And he who falls in the vanguard and loses his dear life
Has brought honour to his city and his people and his father,

Many times through his breast and bossed shield
And breastplate pierced through from the front.
Young and old together lament him,
And all the city mourns with deep regret;
His tomb and children are notable amongst men
And his children's children and all his family after;
His great glory and his name will never perish,
But even though underground he becomes immortal,
For it was while he nobly stood and fought
For country and children that raging Ares took him.
But if he escape the fate of death that brings long woe,
And victorious wins the glorious boast of his spear,
All honour him, young and old alike,
And he after much contentment goes to Hades;
As he ages he has distinction amongst the citizens, nor does any
Wish to harm either his reputation or his right.
All alike in the seats of council, both the young, his age group,
And his elders, give way to him.
Now let every man strive to reach the peak of this prowess
And in his heart let him never relax from war.

6.12 Philochoros *Atthis* F216: The Songs of Tyrtaeus Instruct Spartan Warriors

As well as being a poet Tyrtaeus was also the general responsible for the defeat of the Messenians in the Second Messenian War. The polemarch was the war leader. [*FGH* 328 F216; Athen. *Deip.* 630–31.]

The warlike nature of the (pyrrhic) dance shows it to be a Spartan invention. The Spartans are warlike, and their sons learn by heart the marching songs (embateria), which are also called martial songs (enoplia). In addition, the Lakonians themselves in their wars sing the songs of Tyrtaeus from memory and move in time to them. Philochoros says that when the Spartans defeated the Messenians through Tyrtaeus' generalship they made it a custom in their expeditions, whenever they were dining and singing paeans, that one at a time they should sing the songs of Tyrtaeus; and the polemarch was to judge and give a prize of meat to the victor.

6.13 Plutarch *Life of Lykourgos* 21.1–2: Spartan Music

The Spartans did train in poetry and music, even though later writers, such as Aelian (doc. 6.79), follow a tradition that they were totally 'inartistic'. Their taste was for songs relating to military virtues and practices, such as the poetry of Tyrtaeus. Philostratos *Gymnastika* 19 describes a Spartan dance in which the participants threw and avoided spears.

21.1 Their training in lyric poetry and music was no less serious than the good style and purity of their speech, and further their songs had a stimulus to rouse the spirit and inspire enthusiastic and effective action; their style was simple and unpretentious and their themes serious and character-building. **2** They were for the most part praises of those fortunate men who had died for Sparta, and censure of cowards, as living a wretched and miserable life, and promises or boasts of their bravery, as befitted their ages. As an example, it might not be a bad idea to quote one. They used to have three choirs at their festivals, corresponding to the three age groups; the choir of old men would begin, singing:

> 'We once were valiant young men.'

The choir of those in their prime would respond with,

> 'We are so now: if you wish observe and see.'

And the third choir, that of the boys, would sing,

> 'One day we will be far mightier men than both.'

6.14 Plutarch *Spartan Traditional Practices* 17 (*Moralia* 238c): Spartan Conservatism

If anyone transgressed any of the rules of ancient music, the Spartans did not permit it; even Terpander, who was one of the older musicians and the best cithara-player of his time and who praised heroic deeds, was nevertheless fined by the ephors who took his cithara and nailed it up to the wall because he fitted a single extra string to vary the sound; for they approved of only the more simple melodies.

6.15 Xenophon *Constitution of the Spartans* 9.1–6: The Penalties for Cowardice

In Sparta, where there was so much emphasis on preparing for warfare, the coward was the object of social ostracism; see doc. 2.26 (Archilochos). The Spartans who had surrendered at Sphakteria lost their citizenship (doc. 13.11), though this was later reversed. Cowards could not hold office (Thuc. 5.34.2). Xenophon implies that membership of a mess would cease; they had to wear a cloak with coloured patches and have their beard partially shaven, and were forbidden to marry (Plut. *Ages*. 30.2–4).

9.1 This achievement of Lykourgos also is worthy of admiration, for he brought it about that in Sparta a fine death was to be preferred to a disgraceful life; and anyone who considered the matter would find that fewer of the Spartans die than of those who choose to retreat from danger. **2** To speak truth, staying alive for the most part goes with bravery rather than with cowardice; for bravery is easier and pleasanter and more inventive and effective. It is clear that glory in particular goes with bravery; for everyone wants to ally themselves with the brave. **3** However, I should not omit an account of the way in which he brought this about. Lykourgos clearly arranged that the brave should have prosperity, and cowards misery. **4** For in other cities whenever anyone shows himself to be a coward, he is only called a coward, and the coward goes to the agora in the same way as the brave man, and sits beside him, and exercises at the gymnasium with him, if he wants to; but in Sparta everyone would be ashamed to have a coward associated with him as a mess-mate, or as an opponent in a wrestling bout. **5** Often such a person is left out unassigned when sides are picked for opposing teams in a ball game, and in choruses he is banished to the disgraceful positions, and even in the streets he has to make way, and on the benches give his place even to younger men. He has to maintain the girls of his family at home and give them the reason for their unmarried condition, while he has to suffer a hearth without a wife and pay a fine for that as well; he cannot cheerfully stroll around, or behave like a man of blameless lifestyle or he has to submit to being whipped by his betters. **6** When such dishonour is imposed upon cowards I do not wonder at their preferring death to such an ignominious and shameful life.

6.16 Plutarch *Life of Lykourgos* 15.1–3: Penalties for Bachelors

15.1 There were also incentives towards marriage in these customs — I mean the processions of girls wearing little clothing and their athletic contests in the sight of the young men, who were impelled not by the necessities of geometry, but by the necessities of the heart, as Plato says. Furthermore, Lykourgos also imposed dishonour on those who did not marry. **2** They were excluded from observing the young people at their exercises; in winter, the magistrates ordered them to march round the agora wearing only their tunics, and as they marched they sang a song specifically written for them, the gist of which was that they were being justly treated for disobeying the laws; **3** and they were also deprived of the honour and attentions young men paid to their elders — for when the following remark was made to Derkyllidas, even though he was a well-respected general, no one found fault with it; as he approached, one of the young men refused to give up his seat, with the words, 'You have fathered no one who will give up his seat to me.'

6.17 Xenophon *Constitution of the Spartans* 11.3, 13.8–9: Spartan Battle Dress

The Spartan hoplite traditionally wore a red cloak and carried a polished bronze shield; Agesilaos' army appeared all bronze and crimson (Xen. *Ages*. 2.7). For Spartan attention to their hair, see doc. 11.29 (Thermopylai). According to Arist. *Rhet*. 1367a28–32 long hair among the Spartans was the sign of a free man, since long hair hinders the performance of most manual tasks.

11.3 Regarding their equipment for battle, Lykourgos devised that they should have a crimson cloak and a bronze shield, thinking that the former has least in common with women's dress, and is most warlike; the latter can be very quickly polished and tarnishes very slowly. He also allowed those who had reached adulthood to wear their hair long, considering that they would thus appear taller, more noble, and more terrifying … **13.8** And the following practices instituted by Lykourgos with regard to the actual fighting are also, I consider, very advantageous. When the enemy are close enough to see, a she-goat is sacrificed, and it is laid down that all flautists present are to play their flutes and no Spartan is to be without a garland; an order is also given to polish weapons. **9** Young men are also allowed to enter battle with their hair groomed and looking both cheerful and noble.

6.18 Plutarch *Sayings of Spartan Women* 16, 20: 'With Your Shield or On It'

Saying 16 is one of the most quoted — and misquoted — sayings from Greek history and overlooks the fact that most Spartans who were killed in battle were buried where they fell (Plut. *Ages*. 40.4). Both of the following *Sayings* stress the role expected of Spartan mothers and serve as good examples of Spartan unwillingness to waste words (cf. docs 4.19–20); for similar reactions to death in battle, see doc. 14.20. [*Mor*. 241f–242a].

16 Another woman, handing her son his shield and encouraging him, said, 'Son, either with this or on this.' … **20** Another woman, hearing that her son had died in battle, on the spot where he had been positioned, said, 'Bury him and let his brother fill his place.'

6.19 Aristophanes *Lysistrata* 1296–1320: 'Good Old' Spartan Traditions

This is the conclusion to Aristophanes' play *Lysistrata*, which was performed to Athenians at war with Sparta, at the Lenaia festival in 411 BC; it won the first prize. While a comedy, with many parenthetical jokes against women and Spartans, Lysistrata's message was still meant to be taken seriously, and the chorus, after the Spartan envoys have been entertained in the prytaneion ('city hall'), sings of the Sparta which was Athens' ally in the 'good old days', and of Sparta's glorious traditions and festivals; cf. doc. 11.57. For girls' choirs in Sparta, see doc. 4.14; this passage specifically features Spartan deities: Athena of the Brazen House, Apollo of Amyklai and the Tyndaridai, who accompanied Spartan kings into battle.

Now leaving lovely Taygetos
Come, Lakonian Muse, come to glorify
The god of Amyklai (Apollo)
Whom we revere
And the Lady of the Brazen House (Athena),
And the brave Tyndaridai (Castor and Pollux),
Who sport beside the Eurotas.
Come, come quickly,
Come, jump lightly,
So we can celebrate Sparta,
Who loves the choruses of the gods
And the sound of feet,
Where the maidens, like fillies,
Beside the Eurotas
Dance, with their feet often
Bounding,
And their tresses waving
Like those of the Bakchai when they brandish the thyrsos and play.
The daughter of Leda (Helen) is at their head,
A pure and comely leader.
But come, bind your hair with a fillet,
And dance hand and foot
Like a stag; at the same time
Make a noise to help the dance along,
And celebrate again in song the almighty, all-conquering goddess of the Brazen House.

THE SPARTAN CONSTITUTION

The Spartan constitution comprised two kings, the gerousia (or council of elders), the ephorate (five annual magistrates) and an assembly of Spartiates, ruling over the perioikoi and helots. In addition to these, there was a system of upbringing, the agoge, and the mess system, participation in both of which was a prerequisite for citizenship. These features were found in other, particularly Dorian, Greek states, but at Sparta they were combined to effect a unique system: a state ruled by an elite of Spartiates whose prime concern was military preparedness.

6.20 Plutarch *Life of Lykourgos* 5.10–11: The Stability of Sparta's Constitution

It is interesting to note that both Plato (doc. 6.21) and Plutarch here make the gerousia Lykourgos' main achievement, rather than the Great Rhetra. Plutarch interprets the gerousia as the middle or balancing element of the constitution. The gerousia consisted of the two kings and twenty-eight elders elected for life.

5.10 Of the numerous reforms of Lykourgos, the first and most important was the institution of the elders, which Plato says, because it was mixed with the 'fevered' rule of the kings and had an equal vote with them in important matters, provided stability and common sense. **11** For the state was unstable, at one moment inclining towards the kings and tyranny, and at the next to the populace and democracy, and by placing the office of the elders in the middle as a kind of ballast, and making it balanced, he ensured the safest organisation and constitution, with the twenty-eight elders taking the side of the kings when it was a question of resisting democracy, and alternatively strengthening the people to avoid the development of a tyranny.

6.21 Plato *Laws* 691d–692a: The Reasons for Sparta's Success

Plato views the dual nature of the kingship as a check on absolute monarchy; the 'double race' are the Agiad and Eurypontid royal houses. The third 'saviour' mentioned here is Theopompos (*c.* 720–*c.* 670 BC), supposedly responsible for the institution of the ephorate (doc. 6.23); cf. Plut. *Lyk.* 7.1–3.

691d It seems as if there was some god who took care of you, who foresaw what was going to happen and engendered a double race of kings for you out of your one, thus contracting its powers to reasonable limits. **691e** And again, after this, a person (Lykourgos) whose human nature was mingled with some divine power, noticed that your government was still fevered, and so blended the prudent power of age with your natural audacious vigour, **692a** by giving the twenty-eight elders equal voting power in important matters to that of the power of the kings. Your third saviour saw that your government was still wanton and restive, so he imposed on it the power of the ephors as a kind of bridle, which was almost a power held by lot; and because of this measure your kingship, inasmuch as it had become a mixture of elements and a moderating power, has survived and itself been the reason for the preservation of the rest of the constitution.

6.22 Plutarch *Life of Lykourgos* 26.1–5: The Election of the Gerousia

The powers of the gerousia were wide and it judged cases involving capital punishment, loss of citizen rights or exile: cf. Xen. *Const. Spart.* 10.2. Voting by shouting was a democratic element, in which the majority view was easily 'heard'. The Spartan assembly also decided by acclamation, as in 432 BC when it voted for war under the influence of the ephor Sthenelaidas, against King Archidamos' advice (Thuc. 1.87.1–2).

26.1 Lykourgos, as has already been said, himself appointed the elders at first from those who had been involved in his plan; later on he arranged that, when an elder died, the man whose merits were judged to be best of all of those over the age of sixty should be appointed in his place. **2** And of all contests amongst mankind this seemed to be the most important and the one most worth fighting for; in it a man was judged not as the swiftest of the swift, nor as the strongest of the strong, but as the best and most prudent of the good and wise, and would have as a lifelong prize for his merits, so to speak, total authority in the state, with supreme powers over death and loss of citizen rights and the most important issues generally. **3** The selection took place in this way: when the assembly had gathered, chosen men were shut up in a building nearby, where they could neither see out nor be seen, but could only hear the shouts of those in the assembly. **4** For, as in other matters, they judged the competitors by shouting, not all together but each man being brought forward as decided by lot and walking through the assembly in silence. **5** The men who were shut up had tablets, and so in each case they noted the volume of the shouting, not knowing whom it was for, except that he was the first or the second or the third or whatever of those brought forward. And whoever received the greatest shouting and the loudest they proclaimed to be elected.

6.23 Plutarch *Life of Lykourgos* 7.1–3: The Institution of the Ephors

There were five ephors, elected annually by the Spartan assembly: there was no restriction on who could stand. King Theopompos, victor in the First Messenian War, supposedly instituted the office of the ephors; Herodotos attributes them to Lykourgos (doc. 6.2).

7.1 Although Lykourgos combined the elements in his constitution in this way, later Spartans, seeing the oligarchic element as undiluted and dominant, or 'inflated and restive', as Plato says, 'imposed on it the power of the ephors as a kind of bridle', the first ephors, Elatos and his colleagues, being appointed round about a hundred and thirty years after Lykourgos in the time of King Theopompos. **2** They say that when Theopompos was being criticised by his wife because the royal power he would hand on to his sons would be less than when he had received it, he answered, 'No, it will be greater, because it will last longer.' **3** And in fact, by escaping excess, and the jealousy that accompanies it, royalty at Sparta avoided its dangers, and as a result the Spartan kings did not suffer the same fate as the ones inflicted by the Messenians and Argives on their kings, who refused to yield or relax any of their power in favour of the people.

6.24 Xenophon *Constitution of the Spartans* 8.2–4: The Powers of the Ephors

The five ephors were elected annually, and there was no restriction on who could stand.

8.2 Even the most important people in Sparta are very deferential to the magistrates and take pride in being humble and in running and not walking to answer them whenever they are summoned, thinking that if they lead the way in strict obedience others also will follow; and this is what has happened. **3** It is also likely that these same men helped to establish the power of the ephorate too, since they realised that obedience is the greatest good, whether in a city, an army or a household; for the greater the power held by the magistrates, the more they considered that this would also impress the citizens with the need for obedience.

4 So the ephors have the power to fine whomever they wish, and have the authority to exact immediate payment, as well as the authority to put an end to magistrates' terms of office and even to imprison and put them on trial for their lives.

6.25 Aristotle *Politics* 1294b19–34: Sparta, Democracy or Oligarchy?

Aristotle here points out the democratic and oligarchic features of the Spartan constitution. His judgment in this passage is less unfavourable than his specific criticisms of Sparta's constitution and social system (docs 6.37–44, 6.81; cf. *Politics* 1271a18–26). He views Spartan kingship as having lasted so long because of its restricted powers: *Politics* 1313a18–33 (doc. 6.32).

1294b19 Many people try to describe it as a democracy because its system has many democratic elements, for example, to begin with, the education of children (for the sons of the rich are brought up in the same way as those of the poor, and are educated in a manner which is also possible for the sons of the poor), and the same is the case in the next age group, and when they become men (for thus there is no distinctive mark of being rich or poor) the arrangements for eating in the common messes (syssitia) are the same for everybody, and the rich wear such clothing as any of the poor could afford. Additionally, of the two most important offices the people choose the members of one and share in the other (for they elect the elders and share in the ephorate). Those who call it an oligarchy do so because of its many oligarchic features, for example that everyone is elected and no one chosen by lot, and that a few people have supreme authority to give sentences of death or exile, and many other similar points.

SPARTAN KINGSHIP

Herodotos gives the most detailed account of the dual kingship (Hdt. 6.52–55). The kings' power was not absolute, but was checked by both the gerousia and the ephorate. The heirs to the two thrones appear to have been exempt from the agoge required of other Spartiates: Plut. *Ages.* 1.4.

6.26 Herodotos 6.56–60.1: The Prerogatives of Spartan Kings

Herodotos in this passage lists the privileges of the kings in war and peace. Not only did the king get parts of sacrificial beasts (6.57.1), but 'enough good land belonging to the cities of the perioikoi to ensure moderate means without excessive wealth' (Xen. *Const. Spart.* 15.3). The Pythioi were officials who consulted the Delphic oracle on public affairs when the Spartans decided, probably in their assembly, to do so (6.57.2). Kleomenes had brought back from Athens the collection of oracles that the Peisistratidai had kept on the acropolis (6.57.4). Spartans who died in battle were buried where they fell, but the bodies of kings were brought back to Sparta for burial. The ceremony involving a bier presumably only took place when the body of the king could not be recovered (6.58.3-59); Leonidas was buried at Thermopylai, but his bones were later transferred to Sparta.

6.56 The Spartiates have given their kings these prerogatives: two priesthoods, of Zeus Lakedaimon and Zeus Ouranios, and the power to declare war against any country they might choose; none of the Spartiates is allowed to hinder this, and if one should, then he is put under a curse. When they take the field, the kings are the first to go and the last to return; on campaign they are guarded by a hundred picked men; and on their expeditions they can use as many animals as they wish, and they keep for themselves the skins and chines of all that are sacrificed. **6.57.1** This is in war, and in peacetime their other prerogatives are as follows: whenever a sacrifice takes place at public expense, the kings are the first to sit down to dinner and are the first served, each being given twice as much of everything as the other guests; theirs is the right of making the first libation and they get the skins of the sacrificed animals. **2** On the first and seventh days of every month each of them is given by the state a perfect victim for sacrifice at the temple of Apollo and a bushel of barley and a Lakonian quart of wine, and at all public games they have the privilege of specially reserved seats. It is their duty to appoint whomever of the citizens they wish as proxenoi and each of them chooses two Pythioi; the Pythioi are officials sent to Delphi, and they eat with the kings at public expense. **3** If the kings do not attend dinner they are each sent at their houses two choinikes of barley and a kotyle of wine, and when they are present they are given double rations of everything; they are awarded this same honour when they are invited to dinner at the houses of private citizens. **4** They guard the oracular responses, and the Pythioi also have knowledge of these. The kings have the sole right to make decisions on specific matters: concerning an heiress whom she should marry, if her father has not betrothed her, and concerning public roads. **5** And if anyone wants to adopt a child, he must do it in the kings' presence. And they sit beside the elders in council, of whom there are twenty-eight; and if the (two) kings are not present, those of the elders who are most closely related to them have the prerogatives of the kings and cast two votes and a third for themselves … **6.58.3** If one of the kings dies in war, they prepare a likeness of him and carry it to burial on a finely strewn bier. And when they bury a king, no public business takes place for ten days and no election is held, but they spend all these days in mourning. **6.59** They also have another custom corresponding to Persian usage; when the king has died and another king is installed, the new incumbent cancels the debts of any of the Spartiates who owes money to the king or treasury. Amongst the Persians also when a king comes to the throne he remits outstanding tribute owed by all his cities. **6.60.1** The Spartans also have the following custom which corresponds to Egyptian usage: their heralds and flautists and slaughterers (mageiroi) carry on their fathers' professions, and the son of a flautist becomes a flautist and the son of a slaughterer a slaughterer and the son of a herald a herald.

6.27 Herodotos 7.3.1–3: The Rules of Spartan Succession

Darius had succession problems with his two sons Artabazanes and Xerxes, Artabazanes having been born before Darius' succession to the kingship. Later Demaratos went to Greece with Xerxes in 480-479 BC, in return for which Xerxes gave Demaratos cities in the Troad to rule (Xen. *Hell.* 3.1.6); his descendants still reigned there in the fourth century (Xen. *Hell.* 3.1.6, *Anab.* 7.8.17).

7.3.1 Darius had not yet revealed his decision, when, at this very time, Demaratos son of Ariston happened to arrive in Susa, after being deprived of the kingship in Sparta and having left Sparta for voluntary exile. **2** Report has it that, when he learned of the difference between Darius' sons, he went and counselled Xerxes to say, in addition to what he was already saying, that he was born when Darius was already king and ruler of Persia, while Artabazanes was born while Darius was still a commoner; **3** so it was neither reasonable nor just that anyone else should hold the sovereignty before him, since in Sparta also, said

Demaratos as part of his advice, it was customary that if the firstborn sons were born before their father came to the throne, and there was a later son born afterwards while his father was ruler, then the succession to the kingship would belong to the later-born son.

6.28 Thucydides 1.20.3: Contemporary Misconceptions about Spartan Kingship

Thucydides asserts that the kings have only one vote in the gerousia (see doc. 6.2). Thucydides, in stating that there was no 'Pitanate lochos', is clearly disagreeing with Hdt. 9.53.2. As he is making a definite statement correcting widespread misconceptions, it is probably best to accept his view.

1.20.3 The rest of the Greeks have misconceptions about many other things as well, not just those forgotten through time, but those which are still in existence today, for example that the Spartan kings do not have one vote each but two, and that the Spartans have a band of men called 'Pitanate', which has never existed.

6.29 Aristotle *Politics* 1285a3–14: 'Death is Mine to Command!'

Aristotle's statement that the kingship was a 'perpetual generalship' indicates the military nature of Spartan kingship, and also reflects Spartan history: kings who were good generals and dealt successfully with the military problems facing Sparta had great influence within the state, whereas kings who were militarily unsuccessful tended to be overshadowed. The provision whereby the king could execute cowards in wartime will have been important for maintaining military discipline.

1285a3 Kingship in the Spartan constitution seems especially to be a kingship according to law, and is not supreme over everything, though when a king leaves the country he is leader of all to do with war; religious matters are also handed over to the kings. So this kingship is like a perpetual generalship held by personal authority, for he does not have the power to kill, except for cowardice, as in ancient times on military expeditions, under martial law. Homer makes this clear: for Agamemnon (*Iliad* 2.391–93) endured being reproached in assemblies, but when they were on an expedition he had the authority to kill; at least he says, 'Anyone I meet away from the fighting … he will have no hope of escaping the dogs or the birds; for death is mine to command.'

6.30 Xenophon *Constitution of the Spartans* 13.1–5: 'Craftsmen in Warfare'

The omens were taken before crossing Sparta's frontiers when leading the army to war; these were known as the diabateria. Unfavourable omens could prevent a Spartan army from marching out.

13.1 I will also give an account of the power and honour which Lykourgos gave a king on campaign. First of all, the city maintains the king and his staff while on service; the polemarchs share the same mess with him, so that they can always be at his side and take common counsel, if there should be need. Three of the homoioi (Spartiates) also share the king's mess and take care of all the provisions for the others, so that they can give all their time to military matters. **2** But I will go back to how the king sets out with an army. First, while at home, he sacrifices to Zeus the Leader (Agetor) and the gods connected with him; and, if the omens are favourable, the fire-bearer takes fire from the altar and leads the way to the frontiers of the country; there the king again sacrifices to Zeus and Athena. **3** Only when the sacrifices to both gods show favourable omens does he cross the country's frontiers; and the fire from these sacrifices leads the way without ever being put out, and all kinds of beasts for sacrifice follow. Whenever he offers a sacrifice, he always begins this work before daylight, wishing to be the first to win the god's goodwill. **4** The sacrifice is attended by polemarchs, captains, commanders of fifty men, commanders of foreign troops, commanders of the baggage train, and any of the generals from the allied cities who chooses to be present; **5** two of the ephors are also present, who do not interfere with anything, unless the king calls on them; they watch what each man does and see that everyone behaves properly. When the sacrifices are finished, the king summons everyone and gives the orders as to what has to be done. So, seeing these things, you would think that all others are novices in soldiering and the Spartans in reality the only craftsmen in warfare.

6.31 Herodotos 5.75.2: A New Law for Kings on Campaign

Kleomenes and Demaratos went as far as Eleusis in their invasion of Attica in 506 BC, when the Corinthians decided to withdraw, followed by Demaratos (doc. 10.5); in official actions before this point it was normal for both kings to be with the army (doc. 6.75). For the images of the Tyndaridai accompanying the army, see doc. 11.48.

5.75.2 Because of this difference of opinion a law was made in Sparta that both kings should not accompany an army on campaign, for until now both used to go with the army; now one of them was exempted from military service and had to remain behind as well as one of the two Tyndaridai (Castor and Pollux); for before this both of these too were invoked as allies to accompany the army.

6.32 Aristotle *Politics* 1313a18–33: Why Kingship Has Survived in Sparta

For Theopompos as the supposed instigator of the ephorate, see also docs 6.21, 6.23. Molossia was one of the states in Epiros in northern Greece.

1313a18 Kingships and tyrannies are clearly maintained, to put it simply, by opposing methods, kingship by becoming increasingly moderate. For the less the kings' areas of supreme authority, the longer all their power necessarily survives; they become less despotic and increasingly like their subjects in their behaviour, who then are less jealous of them. Because of this the Molossian kingship has lasted so long, and that of Sparta, both because power there from the beginning has been divided into two parts, and because Theopompos moderated it in other respects and in addition established the office of the ephors; the removal of power in time augmented the kingship, so in a way he made it more and not less important.

6.33 Thucydides 5.63.1–4: King Agis II Is Reprimanded

This incident dates to 418 BC. The advisory board appointed to oversee Agis (*c.* 427–400 BC) curtailed his rights to begin wars, and the incident underlines the accountability of the kings, while the threatened fine of 100,000 drachmas points to the fact that the kings could acquire wealth.

5.63.1 When the Spartans returned from Argos after making the four months' truce, they blamed Agis very heavily for not having conquered Argos for them, for such a good opportunity, they thought, had never occurred before, as it was not easy to assemble so many allies of such quality. **2** But when it was also reported that Orchomenos had been captured, they became even more incensed and immediately decided in their rage, contrary to their usual procedure, that they ought to raze his house to the ground and fine him 100,000 drachmas. **3** However, he begged them to do neither of these things, saying that when he next went to war he would atone for his faults by some noble deed, or they could then do as they wished. **4** So they held off carrying out the fine and demolishing his house, and for the time being made a law, which had not previously existed; this was that they should choose ten Spartiates as his associates and advisers, without whom he should have no authority to lead an army out of the state.

6.34 Xenophon *Constitution of the Spartans* 15.6–9: The Oath of the Kings and Ephors

15.6 Everyone rises up from their seats for the king except the ephors from their chairs of office. **7** And every month they exchange oaths with each other, the ephors on behalf of the city, and the king on his own behalf. The king's oath is that he will rule according to the established laws of the city, and the city's that while he holds to his oath they will keep the kingship undisturbed. **8** So these are the honours given to the king at home while he is alive, and they do not in any way greatly exceed those of private persons; for Lykourgos did not wish to inspire tyrannical pride in the kings nor to implant envy of power in the citizens. **9** But in the honours given to the king when he is dead the laws of Lykourgos wish to show that they have especially honoured Spartan kings not as men but as heroes.

6.35 Thucydides 1.130.1–133.4 (Simonides 17): Pausanias' Colourful Career

Pausanias provides the first evidence of a phenomenon noted by Xenophon (*Const. Spart.* 14.1–4; doc. 16.5): Spartans abroad went 'bad', as there were opportunities for personal enrichment and a more relaxed lifestyle (1.130.1). The skytale at 1.131.1 was a length of wood for sending cipher messages; see Plut. *Lys.* 19.7–12; doc. 14.5. For the tripod and serpent column at Delphi, see doc. 11.49. Pausanias was tricked into betraying his treachery, but before the ephors could arrest him he took refuge in the temple of Athena of the Brazen House on the Spartan acropolis, where they walled him up, removing him only when on the point of death, *c.* 470 BC (1.132.5–134.4) [Simonides 17.].

1.130.1 Pausanias had even before this been held in high esteem by the Greeks because of his generalship at the battle of Plataea, but when he received this letter (from Artabazos) he then became far more conceited and was no longer able to live in the conventional way, but used to go out of Byzantium dressed in Persian attire and a bodyguard of Persians and Egyptians would escort him as he travelled through Thrace; his banquets were held along Persian lines and he was unable to hide what he intended, but clearly showed in unimportant matters what he planned to do later on in affairs of more importance. **2** He made himself inaccessible and everyone alike found him so difficult to deal with that no one was able to approach him; it was not least for this reason that the allies turned to the Athenians. (**1.1131.1–132.1**: *Pausanias was recalled again and imprisoned by the ephors but released through lack of evidence.*) **1.132.2** He had given rise by his transgression of the laws and imitation of the barbarians to many suspicions that he did not wish to conform to conventional standards, and they began an investigation into all his actions to see if he had deviated at all from established rules of behaviour, as in the case of the tripod at Delphi, which the Greeks had dedicated as the first fruits of their Persian victory, on which he had thought fit on his own initiative to have this couplet inscribed:

> 'Since as leader of the Greeks he destroyed the Persian army,
> Pausanias dedicated this memorial to Phoibos (Apollo).'

3 The Spartans had immediately had this couplet obliterated from the tripod and they inscribed on it by name all the cities that had united in defeating the barbarian and erected the offering; even at the time this had seemed to be a crime of Pausanias', and after his recent conduct it appeared to be very much in line with his current intention. **4** They also learned that he was intriguing in some way with the helots, and this was so: for he was promising them liberation and citizenship, if they would join him in revolt and help him to achieve all his aims.

5 But as they did not rely on their helot informants they did not think it right to inflict any injury upon him, in accordance with the usage that was their custom towards their own people, that they should never be quick to make any fatal decision where a Spartiate was concerned, without incontrovertible proof. (*However, when the messenger Argilios, who was Pausanias' former lover, was given Pausanias' letter to carry to Artabazos, he broke the seal; finding as expected a postscript that he should be put to death on arrival, he turned informer.*)

1.133.1 When he showed this to the ephors, they were more convinced by the letter, but still wanted proof with their own ears by hearing Pausanias himself saying something incriminating, so by arrangement the man went to Tainaros as a suppliant and built himself a hut divided in two by a partition, in which he hid some of the ephors, and when Pausanias came to him and asked why he was there as a suppliant, they heard everything clearly. The man complained to Pausanias of the things Pausanias had written about him and revealed all the other details one by one, saying that he had never once risked Pausanias' interests in his contacts with the King, but that he was to be rewarded just like the many other messengers by being killed; Pausanias admitted all this and persuaded him not to be angry at what had happened, but pledged his good faith by raising him from his position as suppliant and asked him to get going as quickly as possible and not to hinder the negotiations. **1.134.1** After accurately hearing all this the ephors went away, intending, now that they knew all the facts, to arrest Pausanias in the city. It is said that he was on the point of being arrested in the street, but, when he saw the face of one of the ephors who was approaching, realised why he was coming, while another out of goodwill gave him a secret sign revealing their intent, and that he ran to the temple of Athena of the Brazen House (Chalkioikos) and escaped them; the precinct was nearby. He entered a small room which belonged to the temple, so he should not suffer hardship by being out in the open air, and stayed there quietly. **2** For the moment the ephors were too late in their pursuit, but they then took off the roof of the room, and having observed that he was inside, walled up the doors and barricaded him inside, and stationed themselves to wait until he was forced to give himself up from starvation. **3** And when they perceived that he was on the point of dying, they brought him out of the temple, just as he was in the room, still breathing, and once brought out he immediately died. **4** They were going to throw him into the Kaiadas, where they throw criminals; then they decided to bury him somewhere nearby. The god at Delphi afterwards told the Spartans to transfer him to where he had died (and he now lies there in front of the precinct, as is shown inscribed on the stelai there) and, as the deed had brought a curse on them, to give back two bodies instead of one to the Goddess of the Brazen House. So they made two bronze statues and dedicated them in place of Pausanias.

6.36 Nymphis F9: Pausanias 'Ruler of Spacious Greece'

The serpent column was not the only dedication of the time on which Pausanias arrogantly recorded his exploits. [Simonides 39: Page 254–55; *FGH* 432 F9: Athen. *Deip.* 536a–b.]

Nymphis of Herakleia, in the sixth book of his work on his native land, says, 'Pausanias, who conquered Mardonios at Plataea, departed from Spartan customs and gave himself to arrogance. When he was staying at Byzantium, he dared to inscribe, as if he himself had dedicated it, the bronze bowl devoted to the gods whose shrines stand at the mouth (of the entrance to the Black Sea), and which happens to still exist today, with this epigram, forgetting himself through his luxurious lifestyle and arrogance:

> This memorial of his prowess is dedicated to Lord Poseidon
> By Pausanias, ruler of spacious Greece,
> At the Black Sea, by birth a Spartan, son
> Of Kleombrotos, of the ancient family of Herakles.'

ARISTOTLE'S CRITICISMS OF THE CONSTITUTION

Although the Spartan constitution was widely admired by writers such as Xenophon and Plutarch, Aristotle in the *Politics* identified numerous defects in the Spartan system, judging it by its failure to maintain Spartan supremacy in the fourth century.

6.37 Aristotle *Politics* 1270a29–b6: Spartiate Numbers Decline

Prior to this passage Aristotle discusses the inequality of property ownership in Sparta (doc. 4.18). This shortage of men, oliganthropia, is reflected in the known figures of Spartiates. Lykourgos was said to have redistributed the land amongst 9,000 Spartiates (see doc. 6.66); Hdt. 7.234.2 has 8,000 Spartiates in 480 BC; and 5,000 of these fought in 479: Hdt. 9.10.1, 11.3, 28.2, 29.1, cf. 12.2. Xenophon has 700 Spartiates at Leuktra in 371, of whom 400 fell (Xen. *Hell.* 6.4.15, 17); there were 700 Spartiates in 243 (Plut. *Agis* 5.6).

1270a29 So although the land was able to support fifteen hundred cavalry, and thirty thousand hoplites, the number fell below one thousand. And events have themselves shown that the system was faulty: for the city could not withstand a single blow (Leuktra), but was destroyed because of the shortage of men. They say that in the time of the earlier kings they gave others a share in the citizenship, and so there was then no such shortage of men, although they were at war for so much of the time. They also say that there were once some ten thousand Spartiates; but whether these statements are true or not, it is better for the city to keep its numbers up through the equalisation of property. However, the law concerning the procreation of children is contrary to this amendment. **1270b1** For the lawgiver, wishing there to be as many Spartiates as possible, offers inducements to the citizens to have as many children as they can; for they have a law that anyone who has three sons is exempt from military service, and anyone with four is exempt from tax. Yet it is clear that if many are born, and the land is correspondingly divided, inevitably many become poor.

6.38 Aristotle *Politics* 1271a18–26: The Flaws in Spartan Kingship

Obviously here the problem which Aristotle sees is that kingship is inherited: he must be thinking in terms of an elective kingship. As with the gerousia, he considers that the offices should be held by those 'worthy of the office' (doc. 6.40). In referring to the use of enemies of the kings as envoys, he presumably means ephors. A good example of discord between kings is that between Kleomenes and Demaratos, but, in that case, Kleomenes negated the intended effect of the opposition by deposing his fellow king (docs 6.31, 6.75).

1271a18 Regarding kingship, we can consider elsewhere whether it is better for states to have kings or not; but it would be better not to have kings in the present fashion, but for each of the kings to be chosen with regard to his personal life. It is clear that even the lawgiver himself does not think that it is possible to make them really good men; at any rate he has no confidence in their being good men enough; that is why the Spartans used to send their enemies with them as fellow envoys, and think that the well-being of the state lay in discord between the kings.

6.39 Aristotle *Politics* 1270b6–35: The Ephorate

Aristotle's claims that the ephors were liable to corruption because they were often poor men seems to be overstated as they were frequently of the wealthy class. For the election of ephors, see also Arist. *Pol.* 1272a27–33.

1270b6 Moreover, the arrangements concerning the ephorate are also at fault. For this office has supreme authority in the most important matters, but its members come from the whole people, so that frequently men who are extremely poor get onto this board, and their poverty used to make them open to bribery. This has often been demonstrated in the past, and recently in the affair of the Andrians, in which certain ephors had been so corrupted by money that as far as was within their power they destroyed the entire city. And because the office is extremely powerful and equal to that of a tyrant, even the kings are compelled to curry favour with them, which has further harmed the constitution; for an aristocracy has turned into a democracy. **1270b28** The ephors also have supreme jurisdiction in cases of importance, although being there by chance, and accordingly it would be better for them to decide them not on their own judgement but according to the written rules, that is the laws. The ephors' lifestyle, too, is not in accordance with the aims of the state; for it is excessively relaxed, while for the rest it is far too excessive in its austerity, with the result that they are unable to endure it but secretly evade the law and enjoy bodily pleasures.

6.40 Aristotle *Politics* 1270b35–1271a18: The Gerousia

Aristotle has numerous criticisms of the gerousia, while Xenophon and Plutarch saw it as having a balancing effect on the constitution. The lawgiver referred to is presumably Lykourgos: cf. Xen. *Const. Spart.* 10.1; Plut. *Lyk.* 5.10–11.

1270b35 Their arrangements concerning the powers of the elders are also not faultless. One might suppose that as long as they are respectable men and sufficiently trained in manly virtue they would benefit the state, but it should be doubted whether they should possess for life supreme jurisdiction in cases of importance (for the mind, like the body, is subject to old age); **1271a1** and when they have been trained in such a manner that the lawgiver himself has no confidence in their being good men, it is dangerous. For those who have had a share in this office have manifestly been guilty of taking bribes and have been corrupt enough to give away a lot of public property. Accordingly it would be better if they were accountable; but now they are not … **1271a9** As for the election of the elders, the way it is decided is childish, and it is wrong that someone who is going to be thought fit for office should himself canvass it; for whether he wants it or not the man worthy of office is the man to hold it. Here the lawgiver is clearly doing what he does elsewhere in the constitution; for he makes the citizens ambitious and uses this in the election of the elders; for no one would canvass office unless he were ambitious. And yet nearly all deliberate crimes are caused by men's ambition and greed.

6.41 Aristotle *Politics* 1271a37–41: Naval Commanders

It is probable that Aristotle here is thinking of Lysander in particular, who as commander of the Spartan fleet engineered the destruction of the Athenian empire and acquired great power and was accorded semi-divine honours by the Samians (docs 13.35–39).

Some others have also criticised the law about naval commanders (nauarchoi), and their criticisms are justified. It is indeed a cause of dissension; for in addition to the kings, who are perpetual generals, the naval command has been established nearly like another kingship.

6.42 Aristotle *Politics* 1271a26–37, 1271b10–17: Spartan Financial Problems

Lykourgos instituted the practice whereby each of the homoioi – Spartan citizens – had to make an equal contribution to the mess. The inability of poorer Spartiates to make these contributions resulted in a declining number of citizens, particularly from the late fifth century onwards. Aristotle points out that the Spartan word for 'messes' was phiditia, not syssitia (andreia and syskenia were also found). See Arist. *Pol.* 1272a12–16, cf. 1330a 6–8; Xen. *Const. Spart.* 7.3; Plut. *Lyk.* 12.1–11.

1271a26 Nor have the regulations concerning the common meals (syssitia), which are called 'phiditia', been well framed by the person who first established them. For the gatherings should have taken place at public expense, as in Crete; but amongst the Spartans each man has to contribute, even though some of them are extremely poor and unable to afford this expense, with the consequence being the opposite of the lawgiver's intention. For he wanted to make the system of common meals democratic, but under the current regulations it is not democratic at all. For it is not easy for the very poor to share in them, but this is their ancestral definition of citizenship, that anyone who is unable to pay their contribution cannot be a citizen … **1271b10** The Spartiates' public finances are also badly managed. There is never anything in the state's treasury even though they are compelled to carry on great wars, and they are bad at paying taxes; because most of the land belongs to the Spartiates they do not look very closely at each other's contributions. The outcome has been quite the opposite of the beneficial state of affairs intended by the lawgiver; for he has made his city moneyless and its individuals greedy.

6.43 Aristotle *Politics* 1271a41–1271b6: Spartans Unable to Cope with Leisure

Aristotle here refers to Plato *Laws* 1.630; cf. 666e, 688a, 705d.

1271a41 The aims of the lawgiver could also be criticised in this way, as Plato does in the *Laws*: **1271b1** The whole system of their laws is geared towards only a part of virtue, that regarding war; this of course is useful in conquest. Accordingly they were stable while at war, but started to decline once they had become supreme, because they did not know how to be at leisure and had never experienced any other training superior to that of warfare.

6.44 Aristotle *Politics* 1333b5–26: Reasons for the Failure of the Spartan Constitution

Aristotle bases his assessment of the Spartan constitution on its failure to maintain Spartan power. From the historical perspective, however, the Spartans had maintained direct control of Messenia for several centuries, losing it only in 370 BC, when the Messenians revolted and the Thebans under Epameinondas created the city of Messene, and called on Messenians abroad to return to their homeland. The real failure of the Spartan system came with its inability in the subsequent decades after the Theban victory at Leuktra to deal with Sparta's new position, despite the efforts of Spartan reformers.

It is clear that those of the Greeks who today have the reputation for having the best forms of government and those of the lawgivers who instituted these constitutions did not organise their constitutional system with the best end in mind, or their laws and education with regard to all the virtues, but turned aside in a vulgar way to those that seemed useful and more profitable. In a similar fashion, some later writers have expressed the same view: for they praise the Spartans' constitution and admire the lawgiver's purpose, in that all his legislation was directed towards conquest and war. But this can be easily refuted by reasoning and in present times has been already refuted by facts. Just as most men desire the mastery of many others, because this brings about a great abundance of good fortune, so Thibron too clearly admires the Laconians' lawgiver (Lykourgos), as do each of the others who have written about this constitution, as they rule many others because they have been trained to meet dangers; and yet it is clear that, since the Spartans' rule no longer exists today, they are not fortunate, nor was their lawgiver a good one. It is indeed ridiculous, if while they kept his laws, and no one stopped them using these laws, they lost the power of living well.

COMMUNITY LIFE IN SPARTA

6.45 Xenophon *Constitution of the Spartans* 5.2–4: The Public Mess System

As Xenophon notes, the Spartans did not have drinking bouts (cf. docs 6.47, 5.46; Plat. *Laws* 637a). Their main food was barley-bread (*cf.* doc. 11.53).

5.2 Lykourgos then noticed that the Spartans just like the rest of the Greeks were living at home, and, realising that this was responsible for their taking most things too easily, brought the common messes (syskania) out into the open, considering that this would reduce disobedience of orders to a minimum. **3** He assigned them a ration of corn, so that they would be neither gorged nor hungry. But they get many additional foods supplied from hunting expeditions; and there are times when the rich also contribute wheaten bread instead; so the table is never bare until they separate and go to their quarters, but neither is it extravagantly supplied. **4** He also put an end to the compulsory drinking of wine, which undoes both body and mind, and allowed each man to drink when he was thirsty, thinking that this would be the least harmful and most pleasurable way of drinking.

6.46 Plutarch *Life of Lykourgos* 12.1–14: The Spartan Messes

The normal Greek diet consisted primarily of barley bread and porridge, supplemented by various vegetables and fruits, cheese and oil. This was enlivened with what were called 'relishes', such as olives, pickles and dried fish. A medimnos measured 74 litres, a chous 4.62 litres and a mina 618 grams. The most famous Spartan food was the 'black broth' eaten in the messes.

12.1 The Cretans call the public messes 'andreia', but the Spartans use the word 'phiditia'... **3** They used to meet in companies of fifteen, or slightly more or less, and each of the mess-mates would contribute every month a medimnos of barley meal, eight choes of wine, five minas of cheese, two and a half minas of figs, and also a small amount of money for relishes. **4** In addition, whenever anyone made a sacrifice of first fruits or had been hunting he would send a portion to the mess. For if someone was out late because he had been sacrificing or hunting he was permitted to eat at home, while the others had to be present. **5** For a long time they rigidly preserved the custom of eating in messes. King Agis once returned home from a campaign in which he had defeated the Athenians and wanted to dine with his wife. He sent for his portion, but the polemarchs would not send it, and on the next day, when he was too angry to conduct the usual sacrifice, they fined him.

6 Boys also used to come to the messes, as if they were attending schools of good behaviour. They would listen to political discussions and see examples of how free men of education behaved. There they became used to playing and joking without rudeness and to be laughed at without resenting it. **7** For this was thought to be a particularly Spartan characteristic, to put up with being the subject of jokes, but if anyone was unable to stand it he simply asked and the joker stopped. **8** As each person came in the eldest pointed to the door and said, 'Through that door no word spoken here passes.' **9** They say that anyone who wanted to join a mess was examined as follows: each of the mess-mates took in his hand a piece of soft bread and when a servant came along carrying a bowl on his head they silently threw it in like a vote—just as it was if the thrower approved, but squeezed tightly in the hand if he disapproved. **10** And even if just one of these was found they did not admit the candidate because they wanted all of them to enjoy each other's society... **12** Of their dishes the black broth is most highly esteemed by them and so the elderly men do not ask for even a bit of meat but leave it for the youngsters, while they dine on the broth that is poured out for them. **13** The story goes that one of the kings of Pontus bought a Spartan cook for the sake of this broth; when he tasted it he disliked it, at which the cook said, 'O King, those who appreciate this broth must first have bathed in the Eurotas.' **14** After drinking in moderation they go away without a torch. They are not permitted to walk with a light, on this or any other occasion, so they get used to walking with confidence and without fear in the dark of night. This is how they organise their messes.

6.47 Kritias F6: Drinking Customs at Sparta

Kritias of Athens (c. 460–403 BC), who wrote a *Constitution of Sparta* now lost, praised Spartan moderation in drinking, each man using his own cup and drinking at his own pace; Kritias also praised Spartan shoes, cloaks and goblets (which had an incurving rim to catch impurities, as the soldier often had to drink impure water): F34; Plut. *Lyk*. 9.7–8. [Athen. *Deip*. 432d.]

This also is a custom and practice at Sparta,
To drink from the same cup of wine,
Not to hand it round when you propose a toast,
Nor pass it to your right hand around the company.
...
But the Spartan youths drink just enough
To bring each mind to merry thought
And tongues to cheerfulness and moderate laughter.
Such drinking is beneficial to body,
Mind and property; and it suits well the works of Aphrodite
As well as sleep, the retreat from toil,
And Health most pleasurable of the gods to men
And Piety's neighbour Prudence.
For drinking healths in wine-cups beyond measure
Straightway delights yet causes pain for all time;
But the Spartan habit is evenly disposed,
To eat and drink proportionately to prudence
And capacity to work; there is no day appointed
For intoxicating the body with unmeasured drinking.

6.48 Xenophon *Constitution of the Spartans* 6.1–3: Communal Ownership

Communal responsibility for the discipline of boys at Sparta was intended to provide for strictness and conformity and was an important provision in a society in which fathers were absent from the home; see also Xen. *Const. Spart*. 2.10. For Spartan hunting dogs, see Xen. *Ages*. 9.6.

6.1 In other cities each man has the charge of his own children, servants and property; but Lykourgos wished to ensure that, without doing any harm, the citizens might get some benefit from each other, and so gave each man authority over other people's children just like his own ... **2** If a boy is beaten by another's father and reports this to his own father, it is disgraceful if he does not give his son a further beating; to such a degree they trust each other not to give their children any disgraceful order. **3** He also permitted them to use other people's servants as well, should there be need. And he made hounds common property; so those who need some ask to take them on the hunt, and if their owner is not at leisure himself he is pleased to send them along. Similarly they also make use of each other's horses.

6.49 Xenophon *Constitution of the Spartans* 2.1–8: The Agoge

According to Plutarch, the weak and deformed were exposed at birth (doc. 4.23). At seven years, boys were assigned to groups, each known as a boua, 'herd of cattle'. Spartan boys could be joined in the agoge by others who were not Spartans or full Spartans, referred to as mothakes or mothones: Xen. *Hell*. 5.3.9. Some of these may have been sons of foreigners, sent to train in the Spartan system (such as Xenophon's own sons: Plut. *Ages*. 20.2). Cf. Plut. *Lyk*. 16–19.

2.1 Other Greeks who claim to be educating their sons in the best possible way, as soon as the boys understand what is said to them straightway set over them servants as their escorts (paidagogoi), and send them to masters to learn letters and music and the exercises of the wrestling-school. In addition they soften their sons' feet with sandals, and coddle their bodies with changes of clothes; and they allow them as much food as their stomachs can take. **2** But Lykourgos, instead of each man privately appointing slaves as paidagogoi, gave the responsibility of the boys' charge to one of those from whom the most important offices are appointed, who is called the supervisor of education (paidonomos). He gave him the authority to muster the boys and oversee them, correcting them severely if any of them were lazy. He also gave him some of the older youths as scourge-bearers, so that they could punish them, when need be, and the result is that great self-respect and obedience are present in Sparta hand in hand. **3** And instead of softening their feet with sandals he ordered them to strengthen them by going barefoot, thinking that if they practised this they would go much more easily uphill, and descend more safely downhill, and that someone barefoot, if he were practised, would jump and spring and run more quickly than one in sandals. **4** And instead of being coddled with clothing, he thought that they should become accustomed to one cloak a year, considering that in this way they would be better prepared to face cold and heat.

5 He ordered the prefect (eiren) to provide just so much food that they would neither be weighed down from repletion nor lack experience of going hungry, thinking that those trained in this way would be better able, if they should have to, to toil without food, and last a longer time on the same food, if it were commanded, and need less cooked food, and be more tolerant of every kind of food and stay more healthy. He also considered that a regimen which made their bodies slim would do more to increase their height than one which dilated them with food. **6** On the other hand, so that they were not too distressed by hunger, though he did not allow them to take what they desired without trouble, he permitted them to relieve their hunger by occasionally stealing. **7** It was not because he was at a loss what to give them that he permitted them to contrive to provide their own food — no one, I think, could fail to see that. It is clear that anyone who is going to steal must both stay awake at night, and be deceitful and wait in ambush during the day, and have spies prepared if he is going to steal something. So all this shows that he trained the boys like this because he wanted them to be more devious at procuring supplies and more warlike. **8** Someone might say, 'Why, then, if he thought stealing a good thing, did he impose many strokes on one who was caught?' 'Because', I reply, 'whatever men teach, they punish whoever does not do it well. So, the Spartans punish those who are caught for stealing badly.'

6.50 Plutarch *Life of Lykourgos* 18.1: The Incredible Incident of the Boy and the Fox

In this incident, a example of Spartan toughness and endurance, the virtue of stealing without being detected is emphasised. The reasons for stealing a fox are not exactly clear. For a longer version of this story, see Plut. *Mor.* 234a (*Sayings of the Spartans* 35); cf. Plut. *Lyk.* 17.5–6.

18.1 The boys take great care over their stealing, as is shown in the story of one who had stolen a fox cub and had it hidden under his cloak, for he endured having his stomach lacerated by the beast's claws and teeth, and died rather than be detected.

6.51 Pausanias *Description of Greece* 3.16.7, 3.16.9–11: The Rites of Artemis Orthia

Plutarch states that he had personally seen boys dying under this treatment (*Lyk.* 17.1; cf. Xen. *Const. Spart.* 2.9, where the connection of Artemis Orthia with the stealing of cheeses from her altar under whip blows appears to be a later addition).

3.16.7 The place called Limnaion ('Marshy') is sacred to Artemis Orthia. The wooden statue there is said to be the one that Orestes and Iphigeneia stole from the land of Tauris, and the Spartans state that it was brought to their land because Orestes ruled there as well ... **9** There is further evidence in my view that the Orthia in Sparta is the statue which had belonged to the barbarians: first of all, Astrabakos and Alopekos, sons of Irbos, son of Amphisthenes, son of Amphikles, son of Agis, immediately went mad on finding the statue; next, the Spartiate Limnatians, the Kynosourians, and the people of Mesoa and Pitane began quarrelling while sacrificing to Artemis, which escalated to bloodshed, with a number of people dying at the altar and disease accounting for the rest. **10** They were then given an oracle that they should stain the altar with human blood. In the past they used to sacrifice the person upon whom the lot fell, but Lykourgos changed this to the practice of scourging the boys, and it is in this way that the altar has its fill of human blood. The priestess stands beside them holding the statue: at other times it is light, because of its size, **11** but, if the men who wield the scourges strike with restraint because of a boy's beauty or rank, the priestess immediately finds that the statue becomes heavy and hard to lift, and blames the scourgers, saying it is their fault that she is being weighed down. So the image retains the pleasure in human blood which it had in the sacrifices in the Tauric land.

SPARTAN FOREIGN AFFAIRS

After failing to conquer Tegea in the first half of the sixth century BC, Sparta created a system of alliances, forming the Peloponnesian League, the 'Lakedaimonians and their Allies'. According to Hdt. 1.68.6 Sparta had subdued most of the Peloponnese by *c.* 550; the allies were autonomous, and could speak and vote in the league assembly, but only the Spartans could convene an assembly, and the allies were bound by a majority vote.

6.52 Strabo *Geography* 8.4.10: Conquest of the Messenians

The Dorian conquest of the Peloponnese was traditionally dated to *c.* 1100 BC. Eurysthenes and Prokles were supposed to be the fathers of Agis and Eurypon, the 'founders' of the two royal families: cf. doc. 6.7. Tyrtaeus here clearly identifies himself as a Spartan, though, according to later tradition, like many other poets he was 'imported' to Sparta. According to Strabo 8.4.10, this is part of an elegy entitled *Eunomia* (Good Government: F2); cf. Arist. *Pol.* 1306b37–1307a2.

8.4.10 The Spartans often went to war as a result of the Messenians' revolts. Tyrtaeus says in his poems that the first conquest of Messenia took place in the time of his fathers' fathers, and the second at the time when the Messenians chose the Argives, Heleians, Pisatans and Arkadians as allies and rose in revolt, with the Arkadians supplying Aristokrates, king of Orchomenos, as general, and the Pisatans Pantaleon the son of Omphalion. Tyrtaeus tells us that he was the Spartans' general in this war and says that he came from there in his elegiac poem called *Eunomia*:

'For the son of Kronos himself, spouse of Hera of the beautiful crown,
Zeus, has given this city to the Herakleidai,
With whom we left windy Erineos
And came to the broad island of Pelops'.

6.53 Meiggs & Lewis 22: A Spartan Dedication

This elegiac couplet was inscribed on the base of a statue discovered at Olympia. Pausanias dates it to the Second Messenian War (*c.* 650–630) and the archaic nature of the dedication fits such a date. The statue of Zeus would have been dedicated in thanks for victory against the Messenians. [Paus. 5.24.3; Hansen 367; Buck no. 68; *LSAG* 196, no. 49.]

Accept Lord, Son of Kronos, Olympian Zeus, a fine statue
From the Spartans with propitious spirit.

6.54 Pausanias *Description of Greece* 2.24.7: The Battle of Hysiai, 669/8 BC

In the early seventh century Argos was more powerful than Sparta and won a battle at Hysiai in 669/8 BC. Kenchreas was a son of Poseidon and the nymph Peirene. He also gave his name to Corinth's Aegean harbour.

2.24.7 When returning to the road that leads (from Argos) to Tegea, there stands Kenchreai on the right-hand side of what is called the Wheel. They do not say why this place was given that name, unless it was so-called because of Kenchreas, son of Peirene. Here lie the common graves of the Argives who defeated the Spartans in battle at Hysiai. The conflict took place, I found out, when Peisistratos was archon at Athens, in the fourth year of the twenty-second Olympiad, when Eurybotos, an Athenian, won in the stadion (foot-race). As you descend to a lower level you find the ruins of Hysiai, which was once a city in the Argolid, and it is here they say that the Spartans met with their misfortune.

6.55 Herodotos 1.66.1–67.1: Tegea Defeats Sparta, *c.* 560 BC

This follows the success of Lykourgos' reforms. The Spartans were probably hoping to enslave the Arkadians as they had done the helots. According to legend, the finding of Orestes' bones (doc. 3.46) gave them eventual success. These early defeats, along with concern about the helots, helped shape the Spartan constitution. For a similarly enigmatic response from Delphi, see doc. 3.20.

1.66.1 Because they had fertile land and a good population, they soon began to flourish and prosper, and they were no longer satisfied with remaining quietly at home, but, being certain that they were superior to the Arkadians, consulted the Delphic oracle with regard to conquering the whole of Arkadia. **2** The Pythia replied as follows:

> 'Do you ask me for Arkadia? You ask a great deal, and I shall not give it.
> In Arkadia there are many men, acorn-eaters,
> And they will keep you out. But I do not begrudge you everything:
> I will give you Tegea to dance in with stamping feet
> And its fine plain to measure out with the line.'

3 When the Spartans heard this reply reported back, they ignored the rest of Arkadia and marched against the men of Tegea, carrying fetters, trusting in the deceitful oracle, and expecting to enslave the Tegeans. **4** It was they, however, who were defeated in the engagement and those who were taken captive had to work the Tegeans' plain and 'measure it out with the line', wearing the fetters themselves. The fetters with which they were bound were still safe at Tegea in my time, hanging up in the temple of Athena Alea. **1.67.1** So in the former war the Spartans were continuously defeated in their struggle with Tegea, but in the time of Croesus and the kingship of Anaxandrides and Ariston at Sparta, the Spartans gained the upper hand in the war.

6.56 Plutarch *Greek Questions* 5: A Treaty between Sparta and Tegea, *c.* 560 BC

Orestes' bones were found in Tegea in accordance with the prophecy from Delphi; henceforth the Spartans were victorious, and compelled Tegea to make a treaty in *c.* 560 BC. The Alpheios is the river at the sanctuary at Olympia. Chrestoi ('good'): the Tegeates are not to make the Messenians citizens, the Messenians are not to be 'good men'. [*Mor.* 292b; Aristotle F592.]

Question: Who are the 'good' (chrestoi) among the Arkadians and the Spartans?

When the Spartans had been reconciled to the Tegeates they made a treaty and set up a stele common to them both on the Alpheios, on which among other things was written, '(The Tegeates) are to expel the Messenians from the country, and it is not permitted to make them "good".' Aristotle in explaining this says that they should not be killed because of the help given to the Tegeates who supported Sparta.

6.57 Thucydides 1.18.1: Sparta's Attitude towards Tyrannies

Thucydides here points to Sparta's general anti-tyrant policy, and notes that tyranny had ceased in mainland Greece prior to the battle of Marathon (490 BC). For fourth-century Sicilian tyrants, see docs 7.40–56. In the sixth century the Spartans pursued a policy of putting down tyranny. In the case of Athens, they needed some persuasion to do so, and later, according to Herodotos, proposed to restore Hippias (doc 6.59). The phrase 'only a few years afterwards' in fact covers a period of twenty years from 511/10 to 490.

1.18.1 Eventually the tyrants of Athens and the rest of Greece as well (at least most of them and the last to be ruling), where in general tyrannies had been established long before that in Athens, were overthrown by the Spartans, with the exception of those in Sicily. For Sparta, following the settlement there of the Dorians who currently inhabit it, suffered from political discord for the longest period of all the places we know, despite the fact that from the earliest times good laws had been established and it was always free from tyrants. For nearly four hundred years or a little more, down to the end of the Peloponnesian war, the Spartans have enjoyed the same constitution; and this is why they became powerful and determined the affairs of other cities as well. It was not many years after the overthrow of the tyrants in Greece that the battle was fought at Marathon between the Athenians and the Persians.

6.58 Plutarch *On the Malignity of Herodotos* 21: Sparta Liberates Greece from Tyrannies

In response to Herodotos' story (3.47.1) that the Spartans wanted to depose Polykrates because the Samians had seized a mixing-bowl which the Spartans were sending to Persia, Plutarch lists the tyrannies which the Spartans had been instrumental in putting down. 'On the Malignity of Herodotos' points out a number of incredible and contradictory stories in Herodotos, but Plutarch sometimes misinterprets him. [*Mor.* 859b–e.]

859b In his third book, when Herodotos recounts the Spartan expedition against the tyrant Polykrates, he says that the Samians themselves think and say **859c** that the Spartans went to war for the sake of repaying them for their help against Messene, restoring those citizens who were in exile and making war against the tyrant; but he says that the Spartans deny this to be the reason and say that they were neither helping nor liberating the Samians, but went to war to punish them, since they had misappropriated a mixing-bowl (krater) the Spartans had sent to Croesus and also a breastplate that was being brought to them from Amasis. And yet we know that no city in those times so loved honour or hated tyranny as that of the Spartans. **859d** For the sake of what breastplate or mixing-bowl did they expel the Kypselids from Corinth and Ambracia? Lygdamis from Naxos? The sons of Peisistratos from Athens? Aeschines from Sicyon? Symmachos from Thasos? Aulis from Phokis? Aristogenes from Miletos? And put an end to the dynasty in Thessaly after King Leotychidas deposed Aristomedes and Agelaos? These events have been more accurately narrated by others; but according to Herodotos the Spartans went to an extreme of both cowardice and fatuity, if they denied the best and most righteous reason for their expedition **859e** and admitted that they attacked wretched and unfortunate people because of malice and pettiness.

6.59 Herodotos 5.90.1–92a.1, 5.93.2: The Spartans' Attempt to Restore Hippias

In 507 BC the Spartans had summoned their allies and invaded Attica to set up Isagoras as tyrant, going as far as Eleusis; when informed of the expedition's purpose, the Corinthians pulled out (doc. 10.5). The allies had joined the Spartan expedition when called upon without knowing the mission's purpose, and so must have been under treaty obligations to come when summoned by Sparta. Later, learning that their expulsion of Hippias had been prompted by bribery of the Pythia, the Spartans planned to restore him, *c.* 505–501 BC. They summoned their allies to Sparta and their plans were attacked by the Corinthian representative Sokles.

5.90.1 The Spartans had learned of what the Alkmeonidai had contrived regarding the Pythia and what she had done against both themselves and the Peisistratidai, and they considered it a double disaster in that they had expelled from their country men who had guest-ties with themselves and that though they had done so the Athenians felt no gratitude towards them. **2** Moreover, they were further impelled by oracles which said that they would suffer much hostility from the Athenians, these being previously unknown until they discovered them when Kleomenes brought them to Sparta. Kleomenes had acquired the oracles from the Athenian acropolis, and the Peisistratidai had formerly possessed them but left them in the temple when they were expelled; Kleomenes took them from there, where they had been left. **5.91.1** Then when the Spartans gained possession of the oracles and saw that the Athenians were increasing in power and were not at all prepared to obey them, they realised that if the people of Attica were free it would be well matched with their own, but if it were under the power of a tyranny it would be weak and obedient. So after learning all this, the Spartans summoned Hippias son of Peisistratos from Sigeion on the Hellespont (where the Peisistratidai had taken refuge). **2** When Hippias had arrived in response to the invitation, the Spartiates summoned envoys from their other allies as well and addressed them … (**5.91.2–92.1**: *the Spartans acknowledge that they made a mistake in giving power to the Athenian people and plan to restore Hippias.*) **5.92.1** The majority of the allies did not approve of this speech, but while the rest kept quiet, Sokles the Corinthian spoke as follows: **5.92a.1** 'The sky will soon be beneath the earth and the earth in mid-air over the sky, and men live in the sea and fish live like men used to, now that you, Spartans, are preparing to put down democracies and install tyrannies in cities, than which there is nothing more unjust or more bloodthirsty among mankind' … **5.93.2** The rest of the allies had meanwhile kept quiet, but when they heard Sokles speaking freely, everyone of them spoke up and supported Sokles' view, and called on the Spartans not to bring calamity to any Greek city. This concluded the matter.

6.60 Meiggs & Lewis 36: A Dedication for the Victory at Tanagra in 458/7 BC

This inscription from Olympia is very heavily restored. The Argives and Athenians fought against the Spartans at Tanagra, the Ionians as allies of the Athenians; cf. Thuc. 1.107.5 (doc. 12.20). [Hansen 351; Paus. 5.10.4.]

The temple has a golden shield, which in Tanagra
The Spartans and their alliance dedicated
As a gift taken from the Argives and Athenians and Ionians,
The tithe for victory in the war.

6.61 Meiggs & Lewis 67 (bis): A Fifth-Century Spartan Treaty with Aetolia

This is 'the first inscribed classical Spartan treaty' and was set up on the Spartan acropolis (Meiggs & Lewis p. 312). It is probable that the treaty was directly with the Erxadieis, who were a group of Aetolians (on the northern side of the Corinthian Gulf). The obligations of the Erxadieis outweigh those of the Spartans; while the Erxadieis must take part in Spartan offensives, the Spartans are under no obligations to reciprocate. The obligation to have the same friends and enemies was a standard clause in Spartan alliances.

Treaty with the Aetolians. On the following terms there is to be friendship and peace towards the Aetolians for ever and alliance. … nmonos was seer … They shall follow wherever the Spartans lead both by land and by sea, having the same friend and the same enemy as the Spartans. They will not put an end (to the war) without the Spartans, and shall send fighters against the same (opponent) as the Spartans. They shall not receive exiles who have participated in crimes. If anyone leads an expedition against the land of the Erxadieis for the purpose of making war, the Spartans shall assist them with all the strength in their power; and if anyone leads an expedition against the land of the Spartans for the purpose of making war, the Erxadieis shall assist them with all the strength in their power.

6.62 Thucydides 2.9.2–3: Sparta's Allies in 431 BC

Sparta was able to draw on numerous allies, some of them outside the Peloponnese.

2.9.2 These were the Spartans' allies: all the Peloponnesians inside the Isthmus except the Argives and Achaeans (these were on good terms with both sides; of the Achaeans the Pellenians were the only ones who joined in the war on the Spartan side at the beginning, though all of them did later), while outside the Peloponnese there were the Megarians, Boeotians, Lokrians, Phokians, Ambraciots, Leukadians, and Anaktorians. **3** Of these, the Corinthians, Megarians, Sicyonians, Pellenians, Eleians, Ambraciots and Leukadians supplied ships; the Boeotians, Phokians and Lokrians supplied cavalry; and the other cities provided infantry.

6.63 Thucydides 5.57.1–2: Spartan Allies in 419/18 BC

This passage describes the Spartan alliance in 419/18 BC and Thucydides here gives figures for the contingents sent by allies, indicating the numbers the Spartans could rely on for their campaigns. Note the changes in alliances from the list at doc. 6.62. Agis was king of Sparta *c.* 427–400 BC.

5.57.1 In the middle of the following summer, as the Epidaurians, their allies, were in difficulties and of the other states in the Peloponnese some were in revolt and others not on good terms with them, the Spartans thought that if they did not take some prior action the situation would get still worse. They and the helots therefore marched with their whole army against Argos; Agis, son of Archidamos, a Spartan king, was in command. **2** With them marched the Tegeates and all the other Arkadian allies of the Spartans. The allies from the rest of the Peloponnese and outside of it assembled at Phleious, five thousand hoplites from Boeotia and the same number of light-armed troops and five hundred cavalry and the same number of infantry, and two thousand hoplites from Corinth, and the rest had their several contingents, though the Phleiasians came with their whole force because the army was in their country.

6.64 Plutarch *Life of Lykourgos* 30.1–3: Sparta as 'Herakles'

For the Spartan attitude to money, in both tradition and reality, see docs 6.65–71. For the traditional role of Sparta as deposer of tyrants, see docs 6.57–58.

30.1 It was in the reign of Agis that coined money first poured into Sparta, and with this money arrived greed and a desire for wealth through the agency of Lysander, who, though himself incorruptible, filled his country with a love of wealth and luxury, by bringing back gold and silver from the (Peloponnesian) war and thus undermining the laws of Lykourgos. **2** While these formerly prevailed, Sparta had not so much the constitution of a city but the lifestyle of a trained and wise man, and in fact, just as the poets tell stories of Herakles with his lion-skin and club roaming the world, punishing lawless and bestial tyrants, so this city with just a dispatch-staff (skytale) and cloak ruled a willing and obedient Greece. She used to put down unjust oligarchies and tyrannies in the city-states, and arbitrate wars and put an end to civil strife, often without moving a single shield, but just by sending one envoy, whose orders everyone immediately obeyed, like bees swarming together and taking up their positions when their leader appears. **3** So outstanding was this city's good order (eunomia) and justice!

THE SPARTAN ECONOMY AND VIEW OF MONEY

6.65 Tyrtaeus *Poem* 1: Tyrtaeus on Spartan Unrest

Aristotle here refers to a fragment of Tyrtaeus which supposedly concerns Spartan discord and economic distress at the time of the Messenian Wars. The Lykourgan reforms and the conquest of Messenia brought political and economic stability to Sparta. [Arist. *Pol.* 1306b36–1307a2.]

Discords also arise when some are too poor and others are well off. And this particularly happens in wartime; for this occurred in Sparta at about the time of the Messenian War; and this is clear from Tyrtaeus' poem called *Eunomia*; for some were in such distress because of the war that they demanded a redistribution of land.

6.66 Plutarch *Life of Lykourgos* 8.1–8: Lykourgos' 'Redistribution of Land'

There are several reasons for rejecting the notion that Lykourgos distributed the land into 9,000 lots. It is not found in early writers (such as Herodotos, Xenophon or Aristotle) and may well have been invented in the third century BC when such redistribution was proposed to help solve Sparta's decline as a military power (see esp. Plut. *Agis* 7). There was certainly inequality in the distribution of land in the fourth century; cf. docs 6.37, 6.42; 4.18. Liquid produce means wine and oil (as opposed to grain) at 8.7: *cf.* doc. 6.46.

8.1 A second and very revolutionary reform of Lykourgos was his redistribution of the land. **2** For there was dreadful inequality and many people who were penniless and without property were pouring into the city, and wealth was completely concentrated in the hands of a few. **3** So to drive out arrogance, envy, wrongdoing and luxury and those even older and greater political diseases, wealth and poverty, he persuaded them to pool the whole country and divide it up afresh, and to live with each other all as equals with the same amount of property for their subsistence, giving the first place by merit, **4** since there would be no difference or inequality between people, except what censure for base deeds and praise for good ones would determine. **5** Following his words by action, he allotted the rest of Lakonia to the perioikoi in 30,000 lots, and that tributary to the city of Sparta into 9,000; this was the number of lots for Spartiates. **6** But some say that Lykourgos allotted 6,000, and Polydoros added 3,000 afterwards; and some that Polydoros allotted half the 9,000 and Lykourgos the other half. **7** Each man's lot was enough to produce a return of seventy medimnoi of barley for a man, and twelve for his wife, and proportionate amounts of liquid produce. **8** He thought this would suffice for them, and that they needed sufficient food for vigour and health, and nothing more.

6.67 Plutarch *Life of Lykourgos* 9.1–5: Spartan Currency

There was no independent Spartan silver coinage before the late fourth century, but individual Spartans could possess silver and gold. Kings could be fined by the ephors, and Spartans were susceptible to bribery, so there were obviously inequalities of wealth. Plutarch, however, gives here the traditional view of the Spartan economy.

9.1 He attempted to divide up their movable property as well, to remove completely any inequality and diversity, but when he saw how badly they accepted its outright removal, he took another way and devised constitutional measures against their greed. **2** He first made all gold and silver coinage invalid and ordered that they should only use iron currency; and he gave a slight value even to a great weight and bulk of this, so that a sum worth ten minas needed a large storeroom in a house and a yoke of oxen to carry it. **3** When this coinage came into force many kinds of crimes in Sparta went into exile. For who would thieve, or accept as a bribe, or steal, or plunder that which could neither be hidden nor be thought of as an enviable possession — and not even cut to bits for any monetary advantage? For, it is said, vinegar was used to cool the red-hot iron, making it lose its strength and worthless for any other purpose, once it was brittle and hard to work. **4** He next banished as foreign useless and superfluous crafts. And even with no one banishing them, the majority of them would probably have been driven out by this common currency, since there was no way of selling their products. **5** For the iron money could not be exported elsewhere in Greece, nor had it any value there, but was laughed at; as a result it was impossible to buy any foreign or trumpery goods, no cargo of wares sailed into their harbours, and Lakonia was visited by no rhetoric teacher, vagabond diviner, keeper of hetairai, or any craftsman of gold or silver ornaments, because there was no coinage.

6.68 Poseidonios F48c: Sparta Becomes Wealthy in 404 BC

Despite Gylippos' great services to the state in Sicily (see Thuc. 7 passim), he was nevertheless disgraced; later the accumulation of money became routine (cf. doc. 6.76), and there was an influx of gold and silver into Sparta after the establishment of Spartan control in 404 BC over what had previously been the Athenian empire: Xen. *Const. Spart.* 14.1–4. [*FGH* 87 F48c; Athen. *Deip.* 233f–234a.]

The Spartans, though they were prevented by their customs, as the same Poseidonios relates, from introducing into Sparta and acquiring gold and silver, nonetheless acquired it, and deposited it with the Arkadians, their neighbours; later on they had them as enemies instead of friends, so that because of this enmity their breach of faith could not be called to account (by their government). In fact they relate that any gold and silver in Sparta before this had been dedicated to Apollo at Delphi, and when Lysander brought it into the city as public property he became the cause of many evils. For report says that Gylippos, who had liberated the Syracusans, starved himself to death after being convicted by the ephors of having stolen from Lysander's money. It is not easy for a mortal to be contemptuous of what has been dedicated to a god and given to him, I suppose, as his adornment and possession.

6.69 Bogaert *Epigraphica* 3.29 A & B: A Spartiate Deposits Money at Tegea, *c.* 450 BC

This bronze plaque, originally from the temple of Athena Alea at Tegea, Arkadia, contains two contracts, one cancelled by deliberate erasure, presumably when replaced by the second. It is likely, as the dialect is not true Arkadian, that Xouthias was one of the Spartiates evading Spartan currency regulations by depositing money at Tegea. [*LSAG* 212–13 (27), pl. 41; Buck 267, no.70.]

A

For Xouthias, son of Philachaios, 200 minas are deposited; if he comes himself, let him take it; but if he dies, it shall belong to his children, when they are five years after the age of puberty. If none of his offspring survive, it shall belong to those who are judged his heirs. The Tegeates are to decide according to the law.

B

For Xouthias, son of Philachaios, are deposited 400 minas of silver. If he is alive, let him take it himself; but if he is not alive, let his legitimate sons take it, when they are five years after the age of puberty; and if they are not alive, let his legitimate daughters take it; and if they are not alive, let his illegitimate sons take it; and if his illegitimate sons are not alive, let his nearest relations take it; and if they dispute about it, the Tegeates are to decide according to the law.

6.70 Xenophon *Constitution of the Spartans* 14.1–4: Decline in Moral Standards

The expulsion of foreigners was called xenelasia (Thuc. 1.144.2, 2.39.1; Ar. *Birds* 1013-16). Xenophon contrasts the Spartans' former insularity with their eagerness to enrich themselves by serving outside Sparta. Traditionally, Spartans were to be kept to their traditional way of life by excluding foreign influences.

14.1 If anyone were to ask me, if still today the laws of Lykourgos appear to continue unchanged, this, by Zeus, I would not be able to assert with confidence. **2** For I know that previously the Spartans chose to stay at home with a moderate livelihood and associate with each other rather than be corrupted by governing other cities and flattery. **3** And I know that formerly they were afraid to be seen to be possessing gold; and now there are some who even pride themselves on acquiring it. **4** I also know that because of this foreigners were formerly expelled and living abroad was not permitted, so that the citizens might not be filled with self-indulgence through contact with foreigners; now I know that those who are thought to be the first among them are eager never to stop being governors abroad (harmosts).

6.71 Plutarch *Life of Agis* 4.1–5.7: Social Decay in Fourth-Century Sparta

Plutarch here summarises the decline of Sparta in the fourth century BC. See Arist. *Pol.* 1270a for Spartan land willed away from the family line. This is the third-century BC Spartan king, Agis IV, who reigned 262–241 BC.

4.1 Agis was not only far superior in his native disposition and high spirit to (his fellow-king) Leonidas, but to almost all the kings who had ruled after the great Agesilaos (*c.* 445–359). Even before he turned twenty, despite the fact that he had been brought up among the wealth and luxury of women, such as his mother Agesistrata and his grandmother Archidamia, the wealthiest of all the Spartans, **2** he at once opposed indulgence in pleasure, refused to wear all the adornment that suited the grace of his figure, and avoided and recoiled from every extravagance, taking pride in his short Spartan cloak, following Spartan traditions in terms of meals, baths and lifestyle, and declaring that he did not want the kingship unless he could make use of it to restore the laws and ancestral agoge.

5.1 The beginning of the decline and decay in the Spartan state came soon after their destruction of the Athenian hegemony, when Sparta was flooded with gold and silver. **2** But while the number of households instituted by Lykourgos were still preserved in transmission, and fathers left their estates to their sons, the continuation of this constitution and its equality between citizens to some extent protected the city from its other mistakes. **3** Then a certain powerful man, named Epitadeus, became ephor. He was self-willed and had a violent temper and as a result of a quarrel with his son introduced a law (rhetra) which permitted a man to give his oikos and kleros to whomever he wished, either while he was alive or by bequest after his death. **4** In doing so he indulged his own revenge in introducing this law, while the others, who welcomed it because of their greed, ratified it, thus destroying the best of institutions. **5** Men in authority started acquiring estates unscrupulously, ejecting the true possessors from their inheritances, and very soon the wealth of the state flowed into the hands of a few and the city was impoverished. This brought with it a lack of time for noble pursuits, and servility, along with envy and hatred of those who had property. **6** So no more than seven hundred of the Spartiates were left, and of those perhaps one hundred possessed land and estate. **7** The rest of the mass of people, without resources or rights, remained in the city fighting off wars apathetically and unenthusiastically, but always looking for some opportunity for change and revolution.

KLEOMENES: THE 'MAD' SPARTAN KING

Kleomenes was a crucial figure in Greek history of the late sixth and early fifth century. His first known act was in 519 BC when he advised the Plataeans to ally themselves with Athens (Hdt. 6.108; Thuc. 3.55.1–3, 68.5), and his reign is usually dated therefore to *c.* 521/20–491/90. Herodotos' account of the king clearly followed two divergent traditions, one of which was reasonably positive, but his negative remarks indicate that he had a hostile Spartan source, possibly either the relatives of Kleomenes' half brothers or of Demaratos.

6.72 Herodotos 5.39.1–42.2: The Unusual Circumstances of Kleomenes' Birth

Kleomenes had three younger half-brothers: Dorieus (cf. doc. 2.22), Leonidas and Kleombrotos (Table IV). The ephors apparently had an interest in ensuring that the kings produced offspring; in one incident, the ephors fined Archidamos for marrying a short wife, as kinglets (basileidia), not kings (basileis), would be born of such a union (Plut. *Ages*. 2.6).

5.39.1 Anaxandridas, son of Leon, was no longer king of Sparta; he had died, and Kleomenes, son of Anaxandridas, held the kingship, not because of his merit but by right of birth. For Anaxandridas had been married to his sister's daughter, of whom he was very fond, but had no children. **2** This being so, the ephors summoned him and said, 'Even if you do not look after your own interests, we cannot permit the family of Eurysthenes to become extinct. You now have a wife, but as she is not bearing children, get rid of her and marry another one; and by doing this you will please the Spartiates.' He in reply said that he would do neither of these things, and that they were giving him very improper advice in suggesting that he should send away his present wife, who had done him no wrong, and marry another one; nor would he obey them. **5.40.1** In response to this the ephors and the elders consulted and made the following proposal to Anaxandridas: 'Since, then, we see that you are attached to the wife you have, do the things we suggest and do not object, otherwise the Spartiates might think up something for you less acceptable. **2** We do not ask you to divorce the wife you have, and you can continue to give her all the privileges she now has, but take another wife as well as her to give you children.' Anaxandridas agreed to their suggestion and after this had two wives and lived in two different households, which was in no way typical of Sparta. (**5.41.1–3**: *Not long afterwards the second wife gave birth to Kleomenes; Anaxandridas' first wife then became pregnant, giving birth to Dorieus, followed later by Leonidas and Kleombrotos.*) **5.42.1** Kleomenes, it is said, was not of sound mind and on the verge of madness, whereas Dorieus was pre-eminent amongst all his age group and very confident that he would hold the kingship because of his merit. **2** So, feeling like this, when Anaxandridas died and the Spartans according to custom made the eldest Kleomenes king, Dorieus took this badly and, as he would not consent to being ruled by Kleomenes, he asked the Spartiates for a body of men and took them off to found a colony.

6.73 Herodotos 3.148.1–2: Kleomenes Proves Incorruptible

Polykrates delegated the tyranny of Samos to Maiandrios, but Maiandrios was expelled *c.* 515 BC by the Persians (Hdt. 3.142–147) and Polykrates' brother Syloson put into power (docs 7.31–32, 7.36). Maiandrios is here trying to regain power.

3.148.1 Maiandrios escaped from Samos and sailed to Sparta; he arrived there, bringing the things he had taken with him at his departure from Samos, and used to act as follows: he would set out gold and silver drinking cups and, while his servants were polishing them, would get into conversation with Kleomenes, son of Anaxandridas, who was currently king of Sparta, and bring him home; and whenever Kleomenes saw the cups he would be deeply amazed and impressed, and Maiandrios would tell him to take away with him as many of them as he wanted. **2** Though Maiandrios said this on two or three occasions, Kleomenes was the most upright of men and did not think it proper to accept what was offered, but realising that if Maiandrios were to offer them to some of the other citizens he would get assistance in his plan of vengeance, he went to the ephors and said that it would be better for Sparta if the Samian visitor were to leave the Peloponnese, before he managed to persuade either him or another Spartiate to become corrupt. They took heed of this and Maiandrios was banished by public proclamation.

6.74 Herodotos 5.49.1–51.3: Three Months from the Coast!

Between Maiandrios' and Aristagoras' visits, Kleomenes was active in Athenian affairs, deposing Hippias in 511/10 BC, and attempting to support Isagoras in 508/7 BC, with a further abortive invasion in 507. In 499 Aristagoras visited both Sparta and Athens seeking aid from mainland Greece for the cities of Asia Minor (cf. docs 11.3–6).

5.49.1 Aristagoras, tyrant of Miletos, arrived at Sparta when Kleomenes was ruling, and, according to the Spartans, went to talk to him taking with him a bronze map, on which the extent of the whole world was engraved including all the sea and every river. (**5.49.2–8**: *Aristagoras asks Kleomenes to rescue the Ionians from slavery and tells him how easy Persia will be to conquer and how wealthy it is.*) **5.49.9** Aristagoras said this, and Kleomenes answered him with these words: 'Milesian, I will put off answering you for two days.' **5.50.1** This is as far as they went at that point; when the day appointed for the decision came and they met as arranged, Kleomenes asked Aristagoras how many days' journey it was from the Ionian coast to the Great King. **2** Aristagoras, who had in other respects been clever and misled him well, in this made a mistake: if he wanted the Spartiates to invade Asia he ought not to have told him the truth, but he said that the journey took three months. **3** Kleomenes cut short the rest of his speech which Aristagoras had started to make about the journey, and said: 'Milesian, you must depart from Sparta before sunset; your proposal is totally unacceptable to the Spartans, for you want to take them a three months' journey from the sea.' **5.51.1** After saying this Kleomenes went home, and Aristagoras took a olive-branch and went to Kleomenes' house, and on entering begged Kleomenes, like a suppliant, to send away the child and listen to him; for Kleomenes' daughter, whose name was Gorgo, was standing beside him; she happened to be his only child and eight or nine years of age. Kleomenes told him to say what he wished and not hold back because of the child. **2** Thereupon Aristagoras began by promising him ten talents, if he would do what he requested. When Kleomenes refused with an upward motion of his head, Aristagoras went on offering more and more money, until he had promised him fifty talents at which the little child spoke out, 'Father, the stranger will corrupt you, if you don't go away.' **3** Kleomenes was pleased with his daughter's advice and went into another room and Aristagoras left Sparta for good, not getting another chance to speak about the journey to the Great King.

6.75 Herodotos 6.49.2–50.3, 6.61.1–66.3: Antagonism between Kleomenes and Demaratos

When the Persian designs on mainland Greece became obvious Kleomenes played an active part in dealing with the medising of Aegina. Kleomenes and Demaratos had previously fallen out during the abortive 506 BC campaign to Attica (doc. 6.31).

6.49.2 The Athenians at once reacted violently against the Aeginetans for doing this, believing that they had given (signs of submission) out of hostility to themselves, and that they would join the Persian expedition against them. So they gladly made use of the excuse and sent to Sparta accusing the Aeginetans of having acted like this as traitors to Greece. **6.50.1** In response to this accusation Kleomenes, son of Anaxandridas, king of the Spartiates, crossed to Aegina, intending to arrest the Aeginetans who were most responsible. **2** When he tried to arrest them, some of the Aeginetans opposed him, and amongst them particularly Krios (Ram), son of Polykritos, who said that he would not succeed in arresting a single Aeginetan; for he was doing this without the knowledge of the Spartiate people, persuaded with bribes by the Athenians; for otherwise the other king would have assisted him. **3** He said this at the command of Demaratos. As Kleomenes was driven from Aegina, he asked Krios his name; he told him what it was. And Kleomenes replied: 'You'd better cover your horns in bronze, Mr. Ram, as you're going to meet big trouble!' ... **6.61.1** At this point, Demaratos was discrediting Kleomenes, who was in Aegina and working towards the common good of Greece; Demaratos was not doing this out of concern for the Aeginetans but through envy and malice. When Kleomenes returned from Aegina, he started considering how he might put an end to Demaratos' kingship, and used the following affair as his means of attack: when Ariston was king of Sparta, even though he had married twice, he had no children ... (**6.61.2–62.2**: *Ariston falls in love with a friend's wife and tricks him into giving her up.*) **6.63.1** In this way Ariston married his third wife, after divorcing his second. In a fairly short time, not having fulfilled her ten months, his wife gave birth to Demaratos. **2** One of his servants reported to him that his son had been born, when he was sitting on his chair of office with the ephors. He knew the date at which he had married his wife and, counting up the months on his fingers, said with an oath: 'He can't be mine!' The ephors heard this, but did not at that point make anything of it; as the boy grew up, Ariston regretted what he had said; for he thought that Demaratos really was his son ... **6.64** As time went on Ariston died, and Demaratos held the kingship. As it seems, it was fated that these events were to be publicly known and deprive Demaratos of the kingship, through his quarrel with Kleomenes, first when Demaratos led the army back from Eleusis and then when Kleomenes went over to deal with the Aeginetans who had medised. **6.65.1** So, eager to pay him back, Kleomenes came to an agreement with Leotychidas, son of Menares and grandson of Agis, who was of the same house as Demaratos, on condition that, if he made him king instead of Demaratos, he would assist him against the Aeginetans. **2** Leotychidas was a particular enemy of Demaratos because of the following affair: Leotychidas had been betrothed to Perkalos, daughter of Chilon son of Demarmenos, but Demaratos schemed to deprive Leotychidas of his marriage, and got in first by carrying Perkalos off and marrying her. **3** For this reason Leotychidas hated Demaratos, and so now, at Kleomenes' desire, Leotychidas accused Demaratos on oath, saying that he ought not to be king of the Spartiates, as he was not Ariston's son ... **6.66.2** When this was referred to the Pythia by Kleomenes' design, Kleomenes then won over Kobon, son of Aristophantos, an extremely influential person at Delphi, and Kobon bribed Periallos the prophetess to say what Kleomenes wanted. **3** So the Pythia, when the messengers put the question to her, responded that Demaratos was not Ariston's son. But later this became publicly known and Kobon was exiled from Delphi, and Periallos deprived of her office.

6.76 Herodotos 6.70.3–71.1, 6.72.1–2: Leotychidas and His Son Go to the Dogs

Demaratos fled to Persia, where he was welcomed by Darius. Leotychidas was soon exiled on a charge of treason, being succeeded as the Eurypontid king by Archidamos (469–427 BC), who played an important part in the Peloponnesian War, the first phase of which was called after him.

6.70.3 Such was the fate of Demaratos who in this way reached Asia, he who had been quite outstanding among the Spartans in both actions and statesmanship, and had given them the honour of an Olympic victory in the four-horse chariot race, the only one of all the Spartan kings to have done this. **6.71.1** When Demaratos was deposed, Leotychidas, son of Menares, succeeded to the kingship; he had a son Zeuxidemos, whom some of the Spartiates called Puppy ('Kyniskos'). Zeuxidemos did not become king of Sparta; he died before Leotychidas, leaving a son Archidamos ... **6.72.1** Nor did Leotychidas grow old in Sparta, but Demaratos was avenged in the following way: when he was general of a Spartan army against Thessaly, and was just about to bring everything under his control, Leotychidas accepted a very large bribe. **2** He was caught red-handed in his camp, sitting on a glove full of coins, and was brought before a court and exiled from Sparta, and his house was razed to the ground; he took refuge in Tegea and died there.

6.77 Herodotos 6.73.1–84.3: Kleomenes and the Unkindest Cut of All

Kleomenes by deposing Demaratos laid himself open to a charge of corruption. The campaign against Argos probably took place in 494 BC, or a little earlier. The Argive army was defeated at Sepeia, and the survivors fled into a wood: Kleomenes lured some out, and then burned the wood; the Argives lost 6,000 men and used this to excuse themselves from participation in the war against the Persians. After Darius' invasion of Scythia in *c.* 513 BC, a Scythian embassy visited Kleomenes, proposing a joint attack on Persia.

6.73.1 After his attack on Demaratos had succeeded, Kleomenes immediately took Leotychidas with him and went to deal with the Aeginetans, as he bore them a grudge because of their insulting treatment of him. **2** The Aeginetans, now both kings had come to deal with them, thought it best not to oppose them any longer, and the kings selected ten of the most distinguished Aeginetans in both wealth and birth, amongst whom were Krios son of Polykritos and Kasambos son of Aristokrates, who were the most powerful men there, and they took them to Attica and put them in the charge of the Athenians, who were the Aeginetans' worst enemies.

6.74.1 After this, Kleomenes' schemes against Demaratos were detected and he became afraid of the Spartiates and retired secretly to Thessaly. From there he went to Arkadia where he began stirring up trouble, uniting the Arkadians against Sparta and making them take oaths that they would follow him wherever he might lead them ... **6.75.1** When the Spartans learned what Kleomenes was doing, they were afraid of him and brought him back home to the same power as before. He was slightly crazy even before this, but as soon as he returned he was overcome by madness: in fact when he met any of the Spartiates he used to thrust his sceptre into their faces. **2** Because of this lunatic behaviour his relatives put him in the stocks; as he was imprisoned there, when he saw that his jailer was on his own he asked him for a knife; at first the jailer did not wish to give it to him, but Kleomenes threatened what he would do once he was released, and fearing his threats the jailer (who was one of the helots) gave him a knife. **3** As soon as Kleomenes had the weapon he began mutilating himself from the shins; for he sliced his flesh into strips, proceeding from his shins to his thighs, and from his thighs to his hips and flanks, until he reached his stomach and while he was mincing this up he died. Such a fate, according to many of the Greeks, was owed to his bribing the Pythia to say what she did about Demaratos, but the Athenians say it was because he invaded Eleusis and destroyed the precinct of the goddesses, and the Argives for calling the Argive fugitives from the battle out of the shrine of Argos and massacring them, as well as holding the grove itself in such disrespect that he burned it down ...

6.84.1 The Argives say that it was because of this that Kleomenes went mad and died miserably, but the Spartiates themselves say that Kleomenes was not sent mad by any divine agency, but, because of his association with the Scythians, he had become a drinker of neat wine and this sent him mad. **2** For the Scythian nomads, when Darius invaded their country, were eager to be revenged on him and sent to Sparta to make an alliance ... **3** They say that when the Scythians came with this purpose in mind, Kleomenes associated with them too closely and from more contact with them than was proper learned from them to drink his wine neat; and the Spartiates think he went mad because of this ... but in my view it was retribution on Kleomenes for what he did to Demaratos.

6.78 Aristophanes *Lysistrata* 256–85: The Chorus Prepare to Besiege Lysistrata

This passage, where the chorus of the *Lysistrata* prepares to besiege the heroine and her women colleagues on the acropolis, refers to Kleomenes' attempt to install Isagoras and his supporters as an oligarchy a century before (see doc. 10.3). The length of time supposedly involved — a siege of six years — is an obvious exaggeration. The chorus here is one of elderly Athenian citizens; the tetrapolis was a group of four cities in the Marathon region of Attica (line 285).

Truly, many unexpected things
Happen during a long lifetime, alas!,
Since who would ever have expected,
Strymodoros, to hear that
Women, whom we have maintained
At home as a manifest evil,
Would take possession of the sacred image
And seize my acropolis,
And with bolts and bars
Make fast the propylaia?
...
By Demeter, they shall not laugh at us while I'm alive;
Since not even Kleomenes, who was the first to seize it,
Departed scot-free, but
Though breathing Spartan fury
Delivered up his arms to me and left,
With his tiny threadbare cloak,
Hungry, filthy, unplucked,
And unwashed for six years.
Thus I savagely besieged that man,
Sleeping seventeen shields deep at the gates.
And these enemies to Euripides and to all the gods
Shall I not, as I am here, restrain them from such impudence?
No longer then may my trophy still be in Tetrapolis!

LATER VIEWS OF THE SPARTANS

6.79 Aelian *Varia Historia* 12.50: The Spartans Import 'Professionals'

The traditional view that after the Lykourgan reforms Sparta became a cultural and material desert is not completely accurate. The Spartans still had their festivals and contests and they competed at the Olympic games. Aelian's judgement, like that of many modern historians, is too harsh as Tyrtaeus, at least, was a Spartan; for Alcman, see doc. 4.14.

The Spartans were ignorant of music; for their concern was with athletics and weapons. If they ever needed the help of the Muses in sickness or madness or any other public crisis, they used to send for foreigners such as doctors or purifiers in accordance with a response from the Delphic oracle. For instance they sent for Terpander, Thaletas, Tyrtaeus, Nymphaios of Kydonia and Alcman (for he was a Lydian).

6.80 Plutarch *Life of Lykourgos* 19.6–20.8: Spartan Taciturnity

19.6 Lykourgos himself seems to have been given to brevity of speech and pointed utterances, if his recorded sayings can be taken as an indication. **7** For example what he said about government to someone who wanted to make the city a democracy: 'Make your own household a democracy first.' ... **20.5** Demaratos, when a miserable fellow was troubling him with untimely questions and kept on asking him, 'Who is the best of the Spartiates?' answered, 'The one most unlike you'. ... **20.7** Theopompos, when a certain stranger was displaying his goodwill, and kept saying that amongst his own citizens he was called a friend of Sparta, said, 'It would be better, stranger, for you to be called a friend of your fellow citizens.' **20.8** And Pleistoanax son of Pausanias, when an Athenian orator called the Spartans uneducated, replied, 'Your point is quite correct; for we are the only Greeks who have learned nothing bad from you Athenians.'

6.81 Aristotle *Politics* 1338b9–19: Spartan Training Produces Wild Beasts

Aristotle's view of Sparta is of course conditioned by the time at which he is writing and contrasts with the more favourable views of Xenophon and Plutarch. For Aristotle's other adverse comments on Spartan training, see *Politics* 1271a41–b6, 1333b11–21, 1334a40–b3, 1338b24–38.

In our times those states which have the best reputations for taking care of their children aim at creating the condition of an athlete, ruining both their appearance and their bodily growth, while the Spartans, who have not fallen into this error, make them like wild beasts by their physical exertion, on the grounds that this is particularly beneficial to courage. And yet, as I have often said, this care should not be directed towards one virtue only, nor to this one in particular; and even if it should be directed towards this virtue they do not achieve even this. For neither amongst other animals nor foreign races do we see courage accompanying the most savage, but rather the gentler and lion-like dispositions.

7

TYRANTS AND TYRANNY

Tyranny in ancient Greece was not confined to a particular period, and tyrants are found ruling Greek cities from the seventh until the second century BC, the time of the Roman conquest of Greece. However, the seventh and sixth centuries were a period when numerous tyrannies arose, particularly in the Peloponnese, and this is accordingly sometimes referred to as the 'Age of Tyrants'. This ended on the Greek mainland with the expulsion of the tyranny of the Peisistratidai from Athens in 511/10 BC. Tyranny had a longer history in Sicily, and the tyrannies there, in the absence of Spartan interference, lasted until 466, the death of Hieron's brother. A new age of tyranny developed in Sicily with the accession of Dionysios I of Syracuse (405–367), and this period is often referred to as the time of the later tyrants. In Asia Minor, tyranny survived the Persian conquest, with the Persians using tyrants to rule Greek cities for them. The first appearance of the word 'tyrannis', tyranny, is in the poetry of Archilochos (doc. 7.1), who uses it to describe the reign of Gyges, the usurper of the Lydian throne, and tyrants in Greece resemble Gyges inasmuch as they usurped power. Many of them were ostentatious figures, and, just as Gyges was wealthy, it is possible that this was one of the connotations of the word for the Greeks. The first time the word 'tyrannos', tyrant, is applied to a specific Greek ruler in the surviving sources is in the work of another poet, Alcaeus, and is used of Pittakos of Mytilene (doc. 7.29). The main character of tyranny was the usurpation of power, because the tyrants overthrew the existing political system and replaced it with one-man rule.

Tyrannies arose in the Greek cities for a variety of reasons. They rarely lasted beyond two or three generations (doc. 7.70), often but not always because of Spartan interference in the sixth century. The Spartans not only had a policy of putting down tyrannies on the Greek mainland, but in fact sent an expedition to Samos in an unsuccessful attempt to overthrow the island tyranny of Polykrates of Samos, and succeeded in deposing Lygdamis of Naxos (docs 7.7, 7.34, 6.57–58). According to Thucydides, tyrannies arose at a time when the nature of Greek society was changing with the creation of new wealth (doc. 7.3). While the growth of tyrannies was part of the breakdown of the traditional aristocratic government, most of the tyrants came from an aristocratic background. The support of the people was often important for the tyrants (doc. 7.40), but they themselves were not from the lower socio-economic class of society, though they were sometimes accused of having been of low birth (doc. 7.29). Solon's attempts to defuse Athens' socio-political crisis centred around relieving the poor from economic oppression. His reforms were significant, but not enough to relieve the poor of all of their grievances, and they found a leader in the aristocrat Peisistratos, who became tyrant, while Theagenes of Megara also seems to have come to power by attacking the wealthy (doc. 7.19; cf. 7.10, 9.2, 9.11). At Athens, possibly as elsewhere, tyranny arose out of dissension within the state, not just between rich and poor, but also between rival aristocratic leaders.

There are numerous reasons for the development of tyrannies in the seventh and sixth centuries, and various theories have been put forward to account for the rise of tyranny. Ambition was clearly a factor, doubtless connected with the acquisition of new wealth, for many tyrants, such as Polykrates, enriched themselves and enjoyed a luxurious lifestyle (docs 7.37–39, cf. 7.6). Kylon attempted to seize Athens, probably in the 630s, apparently simply because he wanted to be tyrant: there is no evidence of aristocratic rivalry or championing of the poor (docs 7.21–23). Kypselos of Corinth and Orthagoras of Sicyon had shown that one-man rule was in fact a possibility. Yet if ambition was one factor, the political climate in which it was possible to entertain the idea of seizing power must have been favourable. Military power, or its equivalent, was clearly important in the usurpation of power by tyrants. Both Orthagoras and Kypselos were polemarchs in their cities (docs 7.5, 7.10); Gelon was commander of the cavalry (doc. 7.43); Theagenes of Megara (doc. 7.19) and Peisistratos at Athens in his first attempt at tyranny (docs 9.3–4), used the services of a bodyguard to obtain power; Theron used slaves (doc. 7.41); and Kylon had a force of men from his father-in-law Theagenes in his attempted coup at Athens (doc. 7.21). Dionysios I had a bodyguard, and is specifically compared to Peisistratos (doc. 7.49). Kylon's failed coup hints at the conditions necessary for the establishment of a tyranny, for the Athenian people united against Kylon's bid for power. Similarly, Peisistratos' first tyranny was aborted when two rival groups, those of Lykourgos and Megakles, joined forces. Presumably, when Kypselos and Orthagoras took over at Corinth and Sicyon, they could do so because there was no group strong enough to oppose them.

Tyranny largely ended in the Greek mainland by the end of the sixth century BC but Sicily experienced it beyond that date. Hieron was tyrant of Syracuse in 478–467 BC, and sent several chariot teams to compete in the Pan-Hellenic festivals (docs 7.57–59). A period of democracy intervened, but under pressure from Carthaginian attacks on Greek cities, Dionysios I became tyrant of Syracuse in 405 BC, using military force as his power base and having specific strategies with which he maintained control (docs 7.49–50). He made an alliance with Athens in 367 BC and was honoured by that city (doc. 7.51). His son, Dionysios II, was less successful and Timoleon of Corinth deposed him (docs 7.54–56). Sicily more than any other part of Greece was dominated by tyranny throughout its archaic and classical history.

Despite the fact that by the fifth century and perhaps earlier the word tyrant had acquired a pejorative meaning, many of the tyrants were clearly no worse rulers than the aristocrats who had held power before them, and some were obviously better. The worst ones, like Phalaris of Akragas (doc. 7.58), no doubt helped to give tyranny a bad name. But even in democratic Athens, Peisistratos' tyranny could be looked upon as the Age of Kronos, the mythical utopian age (doc. 9.16), and both Pittakos of Mytilene and Periander of Corinth were numbered among the Seven Sages. Tyranny under the social conditions prevailing in the seventh and sixth centuries was not necessarily seen as a political evil at the time, and it was only later that tyranny came to have unacceptable connotations for Greek society as a whole.

7.1 Archilochos 19: The First Use of the Word *Tyrannis* (Tyranny)

The poet Archilochos was the first Greek to use the word tyranny. In the following passage concerning Gyges of Lydia, who reigned *c.* 680–640 BC, the word tyranny presumably refers to absolute rule: cf. Arist. *Rhet.* 1418b27–31; Hdt. 1.12.2. Gyges was himself a usurper (Hdt. 1.8.1–12.2), and the word in subsequent history is used in the sense of an individual who seized power for himself. Tyrannos, tyrant, is a loan word from Lydia. When the term tyranny became derogatory is debated. As Gyges was wealthy, it is also possible that this was one of the connotations of the word for the Greeks (cf. doc. 12.26 for Kimon).

To me the possessions of Gyges rich in gold are of no concern;
Envy has not seized me, and I do not look with jealousy
On the works of the gods, nor do I passionately desire great tyranny;
Such things are far from my eyes.

7.2 Aristotle *Politics* 1310b14–31: The Origins of Tyranny

At *Politics* 1305a7–27 Aristotle notes that the champions of the people, like Peisistratos and Theagenes, aimed at tyranny with the people's support (doc. 8.38). Solon was clearly aware that had he wished he could have become tyrant in Athens (doc. 8.11). But some tyrants were clearly aristocrats who then had to take action against their fellow aristocrats in order to maintain power. Panaitios was ruler of Leontinoi in the early sixth century, Kypselos had been polemarch, and Dionysios strategos autokrator, general with absolute powers, in 406/5 BC: Diod. 13.94.5: doc. 7.49.

1310b14 Nearly all tyrants started out as popular leaders (demagogoi), it is fair to say, who were trusted because they spoke against the distinguished. Some tyrannies were established in this way, when cities had increased in size, while some, before these, were kingships which deviated from ancestral practices and grasped at more despotic powers; some again were from elected officials who then aimed at authoritarian rule (for in old times the populace used to set up long-term offices and embassies to religious sites), and others from oligarchies choosing one person as supreme over the highest positions. In all these ways achieving the object was easy, and only needed to be desired, because of the power existing either in the kingship or in the magistracy. For example Pheidon of Argos was one of several tyrants who set up tyrannies from an existing kingship; a number of Ionian tyrants and Phalaris did so from magistracies; and Panaitios in Leontinoi, Kypselos in Corinth, Peisistratos in Athens, and Dionysios in Syracuse, as well as others in the same way, got their start from being popular leaders.

7.3 Thucydides 1.13.1, 17.1: Tyranny and the Achievements of Tyrants

In this passage, Thucydides relates the development of trade and a growing economy to the emergence of tyranny. He notes that tyrannies were widespread, and in the seventh and sixth centuries they do in fact seem to have been one of the most common forms of government. Thucydides seems to equate successful tyranny with the military achievements of the states over which the tyrants ruled, seeing combinations of cities as dynamic, and will no doubt have been influenced in this by the achievements of the Athenians as the head of the Delian League.

1.13.1 As Greece became more powerful and the acquisition of money still more important than before, tyrannies were established for the most part in the cities, and as the revenues were increasing (previously there were hereditary kingships based on established prerogatives), Greece began to build its navies and turned even more to the sea … **1.17.1** In the Greek cities governed by tyrants, the tyrants' only concern was for themselves, that is for their physical safety and increasing the power of their family. As a result they governed their cities as far as possible with a view to security. So no deed worthy of note was done by them, except in relation to their own immediate neighbours, which allowed the Sicilian tyrants to rise to great power. Thus the situation everywhere in Greece was such that nothing remarkable was being achieved by joint action and even the individual cities were lacking in enterprise.

7.4 Ephoros *History* F115: Pheidon of Argos

Pheidon of Argos, ruling in the first half of the seventh century BC, is mentioned by Herodotos as introducing a system of weights and measures for the Peloponnesians, and as assuming control of the Olympic games; he also calls him a tyrannos (Hdt. 6.127.3). Aristotle states that Pheidon's tyranny developed from an existing kingship; this would explain why the term tyrant is used for Pheidon, who was a hereditary ruler (doc. 7.2). [*FGH* 70 F115; Strabo *Geog.* 8.3.33.]

Pheidon the Argive, who was tenth in descent from Temenos, and who surpassed all the men of his time in power, through which he both recovered the whole inheritance of Temenos which had been broken up into many parts, and invented the measures which are called 'Pheidonian' as well as weights and stamped coinage from both other metals and silver, in addition to this attacked the cities that had been captured by Herakles and claimed for himself the right to hold the contests which Herakles had established, the Olympic Games being one of these; and he attacked and forcibly celebrated the games himself, as the Eleians did not have weapons with which to prevent him, because of the peace, and all the rest were under his sovereignty; however, the Eleians did not publicly record this celebration, but because of this obtained weapons and began to defend themselves; and the Spartans also joined in with them, either because they had been jealous of their prosperity on account of the peace, or because they thought they would have their help in deposing Pheidon, who had deprived them of the hegemony over the Peloponnesians which they had previously possessed; and the Eleians did help to depose Pheidon; and the Spartans helped the Eleians establish power in Pisatis and Triphylia.

TYRANNY AT SICYON: THE ORTHAGORIDS, 656/5?–556/5? BC

Diodorus records that the Sicyonians at Delphi received an oracle that they would be 'governed by the scourge' for 100 years: this was Orthagoras and his descendants who ruled Sikyon as tyrants (8.24). Aristotle (doc. 7.70) also states that the tyranny lasted 100 years and was the longest Greek tyranny. That the tyranny lasted this long seems possible, but the figure is not necessarily precise. Most of the information comes from Herodotos on Kleisthenes, while *FGH* 105 F2 preserves an account of how Orthagoras rose to power *c.* 676 BC on the basis of his military reputation and position as polemarch. Military power, however, or armed force, was clearly important in the usurpation of power by tyrants.

7.5 Herodotos 5.67.1–68.2: Kleisthenes' Anti-Argive Policy

The main thrust of many of Kleisthenes' policies, *c.* 600–560 BC, was anti-Argive and the only trace of internal tensions here are the insulting names given to the Dorian tribes of Sicyon. The other main event of Kleisthenes' career was his participation in the 'First Sacred War', *c.* 595–591 BC. Adrastos was a mythological figure, one of the heroes of the ancient epic the *Thebaid*, now lost, and of Aeschylus' *Seven against Thebes*; Melanippos was one of the Theban champions who opposed and defeated the Seven, and Kleisthenes planned to introduce Melanippos by building him a shrine. The implication of the term 'stone-thrower' is clearly derogatory, a light-armed soldier as opposed to a hoplite.

5.67.1 Kleisthenes, after making war against the Argives, stopped the rhapsodes from competing at Sicyon in their recitations of the Homeric epics because the Argives and Argos are highly commended throughout them; and there was, and still is, in the agora at Sicyon a shrine of Adrastos son of Talaos, whom as he was an Argive Kleisthenes desired to expel from the country. **2** So he went to Delphi and asked the oracle if he should expel Adrastos; but the Pythia's response was that Adrastos was King of the Sicyonians while he was merely a stone-thrower. Since the god did not allow this he returned home and considered a scheme which would bring about Adrastos' departure. When he thought he had found one he sent to Boeotian Thebes, saying that he wanted to introduce Melanippos son of Astakos (to Sicyon); and the Thebans gave permission. **3** Kleisthenes therefore introduced Melanippos and assigned him a precinct in the town hall (prytaneion) itself and settled him there in the greatest possible security. Kleisthenes introduced Melanippos (for this should be explained) as being Adrastos' greatest enemy, as he had killed Adrastos' brother Mekisteus and his son-in-law Tydeus. **4** When he had assigned him the precinct, he took away the sacrifices and festivals of Adrastos and gave them to Melanippos ... **5.68.1** He also changed the names of the Dorian tribes, so the Sicyonians and Argives should not be called the same. As a result he had a very good laugh at the Sicyonians; for he gave them names derived from the words pig and donkey and piglet, just changing the endings, except for his own tribe; this he named from his own sovereignty. These were called Rulers of the People (Archelaoi), and the others Pig-men (Hyatai), Donkey-men (Oneatai), and Piglet-men (Choireatai). **2** The Sicyonians used these names of the tribes while Kleisthenes was in power and for another sixty years after his death.

7.6 Herodotos 6.126.1–131.1: The Marriage of Kleisthenes' Daughter Agariste

The suitors for Agariste came from throughout the Greek world (though none from Ionia), indicating Kleisthenes' importance. Megakles of Athens, leader of the coastal party and opponent of Peisistratos, was the successful suitor; their son Kleisthenes was probably archon in Athens in 525/4 BC (see doc. 9.24); their great-great-grandson was Perikles (see Table I).

6.126.1 Later, in the next generation, Kleisthenes tyrant of Sicyon raised the family (of the Alkmeonidai) so it became far more renowned in Greece than it had been before. Kleisthenes, son of Aristonymos, grandson of Myron, and great-grandson of Andreas, had a daughter whose name was Agariste. He wanted to find the best of all the Greeks and give her to him in marriage. **2** So during the Olympian games, when he had won the four-horse chariot race there, Kleisthenes had it proclaimed that any Greek who thought himself worthy of being Kleisthenes' son-in-law should come on the sixtieth day or before to Sicyon, as Kleisthenes would celebrate the marriage within the year following that sixtieth day. **3** Then all the Greeks who were proud of themselves or their descent came along as suitors; Kleisthenes had had a racetrack and wrestling-ring made for them for this purpose. **6.127.1** From Italy came Smindurides son of Hippokrates from Sybaris, who of all men had reached the peak of luxurious living (for Sybaris was especially prosperous at this time), and Damasos, son of Amyris who was known as 'the wise', from Siris. **2** These came from Italy, and from the Ionian Gulf came Amphimnestos son of Epistrophos of Epidamnos; he came from the Ionian Gulf. From Aetolia came Males, brother of that Titormos who surpassed all Greeks in strength and had fled from human company to the limits of Aetolia.

3 From the Peloponnese came Leokedes, son of Pheidon, tyrant of the Argives, Pheidon who invented weights and measures for the Peloponnesians and committed the greatest outrage of all Greeks, for he expelled the Eleian judges and ran the games at Olympia himself, and there was also Amiantos, son of Lykourgos, an Arkadian from Trapezous, and Laphanes, from the city of Paios in Azania, son of Euphorion who is said in Arcadia to have received the Dioskouroi (Castor and Pollux) in his house and after this welcomed all men as his guests, and the Eleian Onomastos son of Agaios. **4** These came from the Peloponnese and from Athens arrived Megakles son of that Alkmeon who visited Croesus, and also Hippokleides son of Teisander, who excelled all other Athenians in wealth and good looks. From Eretria, which at that time was prosperous, came Lysanias; he was the only one from Euboea. From Thessaly came Diaktorides, one of the Skopadai from Krannon, and from Molossia Alkon. **6.128.1** These were the suitors. When they had all arrived on the appointed day Kleisthenes first inquired about the descent and family of each of them, and then kept them for a year and made trial of their bravery, temper, education and manners, conversing with them individually and all together; he took all the younger ones to the gymnasia, but the most important thing was his trial of their behaviour in company and, for as long as they were his guests, he kept up his investigations and simultaneously entertained them magnificently. **2** Of the suitors he was especially pleased with those who came from Athens, and of these in particular Hippokleides, son of Teisander, preferring him for his bravery and because he was connected by descent with the Kypselids in Corinth.

6.129.1 On the day appointed for the celebration of the marriage and Kleisthenes' decision as to whom he chose of them all, Kleisthenes sacrificed 100 oxen and sumptuously entertained the suitors and all the Sicyonians. **2** When dinner was over, the suitors held a competition in music and speaking in company. As the drinking progressed Hippokleides, who was winning easily, ordered the flautist to play him a tune, and when the flautist obeyed he danced. Doubtless he was pleased with his dancing, but Kleisthenes who was watching the whole affair looked on with suspicion. **3** After Hippokleides paused for a while he ordered a table to be brought, and when the table arrived first danced Spartan dance figures on it and then Attic, and thirdly supported his head on the table and gestured in the air with his legs. **4** During the first and second dances Kleisthenes abhorred the thought of Hippokleides becoming his son-in-law because of his dancing and his lack of self-respect, but restrained himself, not wishing to lose his temper with him; but when he saw him waving his legs in the air he was no longer able to restrain himself and said, 'Son of Teisander, you have danced away your marriage.' To which Hippokleides replied, 'It doesn't worry Hippokleides': **6.130.1** hence the common saying. Kleisthenes called for silence and spoke to the company as follows: 'Suitors of my daughter, I commend you all and, were it possible, I would gratify you all, not choosing one of you as exceptional or rejecting the rest; but as I only have one daughter I cannot deal with you all as you would wish, so to those of you who are rejected for this marriage I give a present of a talent of silver for wanting to marry into my family and to compensate for your absence from home, while I betroth my child Agariste to Megakles, son of Alkmeon, according to Athenian customs.' When Megakles said that he accepted the betrothal the marriage was formalized by Kleisthenes. **6.131.1** This was what happened in the trial of the suitors and in this way the Alkmeonidai became celebrated throughout Greece.

7.7 *Rylands Papyrus* 18: The Overthrow of the Orthagorid Tyranny

The Rylands Papyrus 18 claims that Aeschines of Sicyon was deposed in the ephorate of the Spartan Chilon, which Diog. Laert. 1.68 dates to the 55th Olympiad, i.e. 556/5–553/2. It is further testimony to the Spartan opposition to tyranny (docs. 6.57–8). [*FGH* 105 F1.]

Chilon the Spartan as ephor and Anaxandridas as general put down the tyrannies amongst the Greeks; Aeschines in Sicyon, in Athens Hippias (son of) Peisistrat[os].

TYRANNY AT CORINTH: THE KYPSELIDS *c.* 658–c. 585 BC

Tyranny emerged at Corinth *c.* 658 BC when Kypselos as polemarch (military leader) seized power from the powerful Bakchaidai family. He was succeeded by his son Periander in 627 BC, and he in turn briefly by his nephew Psammetichus from 588 to 585 BC. Periander became known in history as the archetypal oppressive tyrant. These tyrants pursued a vigorous foreign policy and Periander at least was a patron of the arts.

7.8 Strabo *Geography* 8.6.20: The Bakchiadai

The family of the Bakchiadai dominated Corinth for nearly 200 years, according to Strabo, although it is incorrect for him to call them tyrants; Hdt. 5.92b.1 describes them as an oligarchy (doc. 7.9).

The Bakchiadai, who became tyrants (of Corinth), were wealthy and numerous and of distinguished family, and held power for nearly two hundred years and enjoyed in security the profits from this trade; and when Kypselos overthrew them he became tyrant and his house lasted for three generations. Evidence for the wealth of this house is Kypselos' dedication at Olympia, an immense statue of hammered gold.

7.9 Herodotos 5.92b.1–92f.1: The Oracles Regarding Kypselos' Birth

The first of the dynasty of tyrants at Corinth, Kypselos, came to power in the 650s BC. There is no reason to accept the oracles surrounding Kypselos' birth as genuine and they are presumably *post eventum* fabrications, as they portray the Bakchiadai in a hostile light. Note the character of Kypselos' reign according to Hdt. 5.92e.2–f.1.

5.92b.1 The Corinthian political system was as follows: it was an oligarchy, and the family called the Bakchiadai ruled the city, who married only amongst themselves. Amphion, one of them, had a daughter who was lame; her name was Labda. None of the Bakchiadai wanted to marry her, so Eetion son of Echekrates, a man from the village of Petra but in descent one of the Lapithai and Kaineidai, married her. **2** He had no children by this wife or any other woman, so he set out to Delphi to enquire about a heir. As he entered, the Pythia immediately addressed him in these words:

> 'Eetion, no one honours you, who are worthy of high honour.
> Labda is pregnant, and she will bear a boulder; it will fall upon
> Men who rule on their own (monarchoi) and will bring justice to Corinth.'

5.92b.3 These prophecies made to Eetion were betrayed to the Bakchiadai, to whom an earlier oracle about Corinth had been meaningless, but which bore on the same thing as that of Eetion, and which said this:

> 'An eagle ('aetios') in the rocks is pregnant, and will bear a lion,
> A powerful eater of raw flesh; he will loose the knees of many.
> Now ponder these things well, people of Corinth, you who live
> Around beautiful Peirene and Corinth on the steep rock.'

5.92c.1 This earlier oracle had baffled the Bakchiadai, but then, when they heard the one given to Eetion, they immediately realized that it was in accordance with that one. Now they realized what was meant, they kept quiet, intending to kill the child to be born to Eetion. As soon as Labda had given birth, they sent ten of their number to the village in which Eetion lived to kill the child … (**5.92c.2–e.1:** *The assassins were unable to kill the baby as when they picked it up it smiled at them. They later returned, but Labda had overheard their plan and hidden the baby in a chest.*) **5.92e.1** Eetion's son grew up and as he had escaped this danger by means of the chest (kypsele) they gave him the name Kypselos. After Kypselos had reached manhood, he consulted the oracle at Delphi where he received an ambiguous answer, relying on which he made a successful attempt to seize power in Corinth. **5.92e.2** The prophecy was as follows:

> 'Fortunate is this man who goes down into my house,
> Kypselos son of Eetion, king of famous Corinth,
> He and his sons, but not his sons' sons.'

This was the prophecy, and Kypselos became tyrant and behaved like this: he exiled many Corinthians and deprived many of their property, and a lot more by far of their lives. **5.92f.1** After ruling for thirty years he finished his life in prosperity, and his son Periander succeeded him in the tyranny.

7.10 Nicholas of Damascus F57: Kypselos Seizes Power

In this account Kypselos has been sent from Corinth to Olympia for safety as a child. Nicholas' reference to Kypselos as a king is his way of expressing the term tyrant. For Kypselos' treasury at Delphi, see docs 7.11–12. [*FGH* 90 F57.4–6.]

4 In the course of time Kypselos wanted to return to Corinth and consulted the oracle at Delphi. He received a favourable response and without delay went to Corinth and was soon especially admired by the citizens, as he was brave and sensible and seemed to have the popular interest at heart when compared to the other Bakchiadai, who were arrogant and violent. **5** He became polemarch and was even more greatly loved, being the best by far of those who had ever held office there. For he did everything rightly, including the following: the Corinthians had a law that those who had been convicted in court should be taken before the polemarch and be imprisoned because of the damages assessed, of which he also took a share. But Kypselos neither imprisoned nor put any citizen in chains, but accepted the guarantors of some and let them go, and became the guarantor of others himself, and to them all gave up his own share; because of this he was particularly liked by the populace. **6** Seeing that the Corinthians were hostilely disposed towards the Bakchiadai, and that they did not have a champion, whom they might employ to overthrow the Bakchiadai, he offered himself and conciliated the populace, telling them of the oracle which said that it was fated that the Bakchiadai would be overthrown by him, for which reason in the past they had hastened to do away with him and now were plotting against him; but they would not be able to avert their doom. The people gladly believed his words, being inimical to the Bakchiadai and well disposed to him and considering that the deed would surely be accomplished because of his bravery. Finally having formed a party (hetairikon) he killed the ruler Hippokleides who was lawless and oppressive. And the people quickly set him up as king in his stead.

7.11 Herodotos 1.14.1–2: Kypselos' Treasury at Delphi

This was the treasury which the Corinthians re-christened after the overthrow of the tyranny. Kypselos' treasury will have advertised the power and prosperity of the tyrant and his city.

1.14.1 Gyges when he became tyrant sent numerous dedicatory offerings to Delphi, and most of the silver offerings there came from him, and besides the silver he dedicated boundless gold, of which especially worthy of mention are the six golden mixing-bowls there. **2** These stand in the Corinthian treasury and have a weight of thirty talents; but in truth the treasury does not belong to the people of Corinth but to Kypselos, son of Eetion.

7.12 Plutarch *The Oracles at Delphi* 13: Kypselos' Treasury Rededicated

By Pisa, Plutarch means Olympia, and the sense of the passage is that when the Eleians objected to the Corinthian request the Corinthians retaliated by refusing to allow Eleians to participate at the Isthmian festival. [*Mor.* 400d–e.]

400d After this Sarapion asked the guides why they did not call the house that of Kypselos who had dedicated it but of the Corinthians. **400e** When they were silent, as it appeared to me because they had no reason to give, I laughed and said … 'We heard them saying earlier that when the tyranny was overthrown the Corinthians wanted to inscribe their city on both the golden statue at Pisa (near Olympia) and the treasure-house here (Delphi). Accordingly the people of Delphi granted it and agreed and because the Eleians were jealous and did not, the Corinthians voted that they should not take part in the Isthmian Games.'

7.13 Herodotos 5.92f.1–92g.1: Periander and Thrasyboulos

Kypselos' son Periander had a much more colourful career than his father: for the anecdote of his murdered wife's ghost and his necrophilia with her corpse, see Hdt. 5.92g.2–4. But the tradition is not universally condemnatory: he had a favourable taxation policy (doc. 7.16) and according to Diogenes Laertius 1.98 was one of the Seven Sages of Greece; Pittakos, tyrant of Mytilene was one of the others, along with Solon of Athens, the philosopher Thales of Miletos, Chilon from Sparta, Kleoboulos from Lindos on Rhodes and Bias of Priene.

5.92f.1 Periander was initially milder than his father, but he then had contact through messengers with Thrasyboulos, tyrant of Miletos, after which he became much more bloodthirsty than Kypselos. **2** For he had sent a herald to Thrasyboulos to learn what was the safest way to ensure control of affairs and best govern the city. Thrasyboulos took the man who had come from Periander outside the city and entered a field of arable land. As he passed through the crop questioning and cross-examining the herald about why he had come from Corinth, he kept cutting off any of the ears of corn he saw which stood above the others, and threw them away, until in this way he had destroyed the best and most abundant of the crop. **3** After he had gone through the field in this way and uttered no word of advice he sent the herald away. When the herald returned to Corinth Periander was eager to learn his advice. But the herald said that Thrasyboulos had given no advice and that he was surprised at being sent to such a man, who was mad and who ruined his own property, describing what he had seen Thrasyboulos do. **5.92g.1** Periander understood what was meant and, realizing that Thrasyboulos had advised him to murder the pre-eminent citizens, from then on displayed his evil side to the citizens. Whatever Kypselos had omitted in the way of murder or banishment Periander accomplished for him.

7.14 Herodotos 3.48.2–53.7: Periander and the Three Hundred Boys

In this incident Periander attempted revenge on the Corcyraeans for their murder of his son; it also shows his concern with controlling Corinth's most important colony, Corcyra. Periander had killed his wife Melissa, daughter of Prokles, tyrant of Epidauros, and thus became estranged from his younger son, Lykophron, who was sent to Corcyra. Periander towards the end of his life wanted Lykophron to succeed him. But when the Corcyraeans learned of this, they murdered Lykophron to prevent Periander coming to Corcyra (Hdt. 3.49.2–53.7). Periander attacked Epidauros, and captured it and Prokles as punishment for what his father-in-law had said to his sons (Hdt. 3.50–52). The 300 boys were perhaps to be sold as slaves; but they might well have been a gift.

3.48.2 Periander, son of Kypselos, had sent three hundred boys, the sons of the leading men in Corcyra, to Alyattes at Sardis to have them made eunuchs; the Corinthians conveying the boys put in at Samos, and when the Samians learned the reason why they were being taken to Sardis, they first told the boys to take sanctuary in the temple of Artemis, **3** and then did not allow the Corinthians to drag the suppliants from the temple. When the Corinthians shut them up without food, the Samians instituted a festival, which they still keep even today in the same way; after nightfall, for the whole period that the boys were in sanctuary, they organised dances of maidens and youths, and, when organising the dances, they made it a custom to carry sweetmeats of sesame and honey, so that the Corcyraean boys could snatch these and obtain food. **4** This continued until the boys' Corinthian guards left and went home; and the Samians then took the boys back to Corcyra.

3.49.2 Periander selected the sons of the leading Corcyraeans and sent off them to Sardis to have them made eunuchs to get his revenge; for the Corcyraeans were the first to begin in this matter by committing a reckless crime. **3.50.1** For when Periander killed his own wife Melissa, yet another disaster was to follow the first. By Melissa he had two sons, one seventeen and one eighteen years old. **2** Their mother's father Prokles, who was tyrant of Epidauros, summoned them and treated them with kindness, as befitted his daughter's sons. When he escorted them at their departure he said, **3** 'Do you know, boys, who killed your mother?' The elder of them took no account of this speech, but the younger, whose name was Lykophron, was so distressed on hearing it that on arrival at Corinth he would not even speak to his father as he was his mother's murderer, nor would he respond when talked to nor answer his questions. Finally Periander was so angry that he drove him from the house…

3.52.6 When Periander realised that his son's trouble was unmanageable and unalterable he sent him away out of his sight by ship to Corcyra, **7** which was also under his control. After sending him off, Periander made war against his father-in-law Prokles, on the grounds that he was responsible for the current situation, and captured Epidauros and Prokles himself, taking him captive. **3.53.1** As time passed and Periander had grown old and realised that he was no longer able to oversee and manage affairs, he sent to Corcyra and invited Lykophron to return and be tyrant; for he saw no ability in his elder son, who seemed to him to be slow-witted. **2** Lykophron did not even consider the bearer of the message worth an answer. Periander badly wanted the young man and next sent the boy's sister to him, his own daughter, thinking that he would most likely listen to her. **3** When she arrived, she said to him, 'Boy, do you want the tyranny to fall into the hands of other people and your father's house to be plundered rather than that you should come back to Corinth and have them as your own? … **4** Tyranny is a difficult thing; many are desirous of it, and he is already an old man and past his prime; do not give your own possessions to other people.' **5** She used the arguments she had been taught by their father to convince him, but he in reply said that he would never come to Corinth while he knew his father to be alive. **6** When she reported this, Periander for the third time sent a herald saying that he was willing to go to Corcyra himself and ordering him to come to Corinth and on arrival succeed him in the tyranny. **7** When the boy agreed to these conditions, Periander made ready to go to Corcyra and his son to Corinth. But when the Corcyraeans learned all the details they killed the young man so Periander would not come to their country. It was for this that Periander was taking revenge on the Corcyraeans.

7.15 Nicholas of Damascus F58.1: Further Evidence for Periander's Methods

Other sources relate that Periander did not allow those who wished to do so to live in the city (Ephoros *FGH* 70 F179; Arist. F516; cf. doc. 9.16). According to Diogenes Laertius 1.98, Periander was the first tyrant to have a bodyguard; both Diogenes and Nicholas saw this as changing the nature of his rule (though, once again, Nicholas incorrectly describes the tyrants as kings). [FGH 90 F58.].

Periander, son of Kypselos, King of Corinth, took over the kingship from his father by right of inheritance and through his savagery and violence turned it into a tyranny and had a bodyguard of three hundred men. He prevented the citizens from acquiring slaves or having leisure time, always inventing jobs for them. And if anyone should be sat down in the agora, he used to fine him, fearing that he might be plotting something against him.

7.16 Aristotle F611.20: Periander's Attacks on Corruption and Luxury

Despite his attacks on luxury, Periander was a patron of the arts, and Arion, the best cithara-player of that time, lived at his court before departing for Sicily and Italy (Hdt. 1.23–24.1); for the episode of Arion and the dolphin, see Hdt. 1.23.1–24.8.

Periander first established his government by having a bodyguard of spear-bearers and not allowing people to live in the city, completely putting a stop to the acquisition of slaves and a luxurious way of life. He was moderate in other respects, in exacting no other tax and in being satisfied with those from the agora and harbours. He was also neither unjust nor arrogant, but a hater of corruption, and threw in the sea all the brothel madams. Finally he set up a council, which did not permit the expenditure to exceed the revenues.

7.17 Theognis 891–94: Kypselid Military Activities in Euboea

Theognis writes of Corinthian military activity in Euboea in the time of the Kypselids, but this is otherwise unattested. Kyrinthos was a city in Euboea, and Lelantos is a reference to the Lelantine Plain.

891 Alas for weakness! Kyrinthos has been destroyed,
The good vineyard of Lelantos is cut down;
The noble are in exile, the base manage the city.
If only Zeus would destroy the race of the Kypselids!

7.18 Nicholas of Damascus F60.1: The Overthrow of Tyranny at Corinth

The Kypselid tyranny lasted into a third generation; Psammetichos (or Kypselos II) reigned from 588 to 585 BC. For the throwing out of the bones of enemies, cf. doc. 7.22. For Periander's family in later times, see doc. 4.32, the epitaph of his great-great-grand-daughter. [*FGH* 90 F60.1.]

Periander left Kypselos, the son of his brother Gorgos, as successor to the kingship. When he arrived from Corcyra, he ruled Corinth as tyrant until some of the Corinthians rose up and killed him, after he had held the tyranny for a short time, and liberated the city. The people razed the houses of the tyrants to the ground and made their belongings public property, and exposed Kypselos unburied and dug up the tombs of his ancestors and threw out the bones.

THEAGENES AND TYRANNY IN MEGARA, c. 640 BC

According to Aristotle (*Pol.* 1305a24–27: doc. 7.65), Theagenes seized power after attacking the flocks (presumably of sheep) of the wealthy. Plut. *Mor.* 295c–d states that Theagenes was later overthrown; perhaps this occurred in the wake of Kylon's attempt at tyranny in Athens (see doc. 7.22).

7.19 Theognis 39–42, 43–52: Theognis on Tyranny and Social Discord

The poet Theognis of Megara flourished *c.* 640–600 BC. Clearly in Megara the traditional social hierarchy was undergoing change, as at Athens, where the rich and poor were in conflict; certainly Theagenes was said to have achieved power through use of an armed bodyguard (Arist. *Rhet.* 1357b31–33). The term 'monarchos' (mounarchos in Ionic) means monarch or sole ruler, and can be used of both kings and tyrants; this is the first time that it is recorded as appearing in Greek.

Kyrnos, this city is pregnant, and I fear that she may bear a man
Who will correct our wicked presumption (hubris).

For even if her citizens are still prudent, her leaders
Have descended to great wickedness.
Good men, Kyrnos, have not yet destroyed a city;
But when it pleases the base to be insolent,
And they corrupt the people and give judgement in favour of the unjust
For the sake of their own gains and advancement,
Do not hope that that city will remain long untroubled,
Not even if it now lies in great tranquility,
When these things become dear to base men,
Gains which bring with them public misfortune.
For from such come discords and kindred murders
And sole rulers (mounarchoi); may they never be pleasing to this city!

7.20 Pausanias *Description of Greece* 1.40.1: The Fountainhouse of Theagenes

Theagenes built a 'fountain house', with two reservoirs, 14 by 21 metres in size. It will have been an important part of Megara's water supply, and the fact that it was remembered as a work of Theagenes indicates that the tyrants were known for their public buildings.

1.40.1 In the city there is a fountain, which Theagenes built for them, who as I mentioned before married his daughter to Kylon the Athenian. When Theagenes became tyrant, he built the fountain which is remarkable for its size, beauty and number of pillars; and the water which flows into it is called the water of the Sithnid nymphs. The Megarians say that these nymphs belong to that region and that Zeus had intercourse with one of them.

KYLON'S ATTEMPTED TYRANNY AT ATHENS

Kylon attempted to become tyrant at Athens some time after he won an Olympic victory in the foot-race, diaulos, in 640 BC. The date of 632 BC or a little later for the attempt is usually preferred. An individual acquired status by athletic success: doc. 1.78. Kylon's failed coup seems to be the first instance of stasis, civil strife, which was to be the dominant feature in Athenian politics until Peisistratos' third attempt to become tyrant.

7.21 Herodotos 5.71.1–2: Why the Alkmeonidai were 'Accursed'

There are significant differences between the accounts of Herodotos and Thucydides: Herodotos does not mention Theagenes, the oracle, the festival, or the escape of Kylon and his brother. For the naukraroi, see doc. 8.18.

5.71.1 The 'accursed' Athenians were so named for the following reason: Kylon was an Athenian who had won a victory at the Olympic games. He aimed at becoming tyrant, so he collected a hetaireia of men of his own age and attempted to seize the acropolis. However, he was unable to hold it and sat as a suppliant at the statue there. **2** The chief administrative officials (the prytaneis of the naukraroi), who then governed Athens, persuaded them to leave by promising to spare their lives; but they were murdered and the Alkmeonidai are said to have been responsible. All this happened before the time of Peisistratos.

7.22 Thucydides 1.126.3–12: The Reasons for the Failure of Kylon's Attempt

Thucydides' account of Kylon is in the context of the Spartan demand, prior to the outbreak of the Peloponnesian War, that the Athenians 'drive out the curse', and Thucydides explains that the curse had arisen because of the way in which Kylon's attempted tyranny had been put down. Perikles was the great-great-great-grandson of Megakles, who brought the curse upon the Alkmeonidai (Thuc. 1.127.1; Table I). While Herodotos gives charge of the affair to the prytaneis of the naukraroi, Thucydides states that the nine archons took over the siege, apparently correcting Herodotos' account.

1.126.3 In former times there was an Athenian, Kylon, an Olympic victor, of noble family and powerful, who had married the daughter of Theagenes, a Megarian, who at that time was tyrant of Megara. **4** When Kylon consulted the oracle at Delphi the god ordered him to seize the Athenian acropolis during 'the greatest festival of Zeus'. **5** He obtained troops from Theagenes and persuaded his friends to help, and when it was time for the Olympic festival in the Peloponnese, seized the acropolis with the idea of setting himself up as tyrant, thinking that that was 'the greatest festival of Zeus' and that it was an appropriate time for himself as he was a past Olympic victor. **6** That the 'greatest festival' which was spoken of might be in Attica or somewhere else, he did not consider nor did the oracle make clear (in fact the Athenians celebrate the Diasia, which is called the greatest festival of Zeus the Protector (Meilichios), and this takes place outside of the city, and all the people make many sacrifices, though not of victims but offerings from the countryside). But Kylon considered that his view was right and went ahead with his attempt at power.

7 When the Athenians realised what had happened they all came in from the country to oppose them and settled down and besieged them. **8** As time went by, the Athenians grew tired of the blockade and the majority withdrew, leaving the nine archons in charge of the siege, with the power to manage everything on their authority, however they thought best; at that time the nine archons handled most political matters. **9** Kylon and his associates who were under siege were badly off through lack of food and water. **10** So Kylon and his brother succeeded in making a run for it; the others, as they were in such a bad way, some even dying of hunger, sat as suppliants at the altar on the acropolis. **11** When those Athenians who were in charge of the guard saw them dying in the temple they got them to leave, promising that they would suffer no harm, but killed them as they conducted them out; they even killed some who sat down at the altars of the august goddesses (the Erinyes) as they passed by. Because of this they and their descendants were called accursed and offenders against the goddess. **12** So the Athenians drove out these accursed men, as did Kleomenes the Spartan later on with his Athenian supporters, driving out the living and taking up and throwing out the bones of those who died there; afterwards, however, they returned from exile and their family is still in the city.

7.23 [Aristotle] *Athenaion Politeia* 1: Epimenides Purifies the City

1 ... With Myron as prosecutor a court, chosen by birth, was sworn in upon the sacrifices. The verdict was that sacrilege had been committed, and the offenders were thrown out of the tombs, while their descendants went into permanent exile. On account of these events Epimenides the Cretan purified the city.

TYRANNY AT MYTILENE

The Penthilidai, because of their habit of striking people with clubs (which implies a repressive form of government), had been overthrown at Mytilene by one Megakles and his associates some time in the seventh century; this seems to have ushered in a period of unrest in the city. A tyrant Melanchros arose (*c.* 612–608 BC), who was overthrown by Pittakos, with the assistance of the brothers of the aristocratic lyric poet Alcaeus. Pittakos allied himself with the next tyrant Myrsilos, and himself became tyrant (590–580 BC). Strabo *Geog.* 13.2.3 notes that there were several tyrants at Mytilene: Melanchros, Myrsilos, Pittakos and others, and that Alcaeus reviled them all in his poetry.

7.24 Alcaeus 70: Pittakos' Betrayal of Alcaeus and his Associates

After the overthrow of Melanchros, another tyrant had arisen, Myrsilos, and Alcaeus fled to Pyrrha on Lesbos. Pittakos had become associated with Myrsilos, and, moreover, he had married into the Penthilidai, who claimed descent from Atreus, the father of Agamemnon.

Now a kinsman by marriage of the Atreidai,
Let that man (Pittakos) devour the city just as he did with Myrsilos;
Until Ares wishes to turn us to arms,
May we completely forget this anger;
Let us have a remission from heart-gnawing sedition
And internecine fighting, which one of the Olympians
Has inspired, leading the people to ruin
But giving Pittakos the glory which he loves.

7.25 Alcaeus 129: Pittakos Breaks His Oath

Pittakos had sworn with Alcaeus and the others to fight against those in power, but had broken his vow, presumably in order to ally himself with Myrsilos, and now 'devours the city'. Alcaeus, however, in exile again, hopes that the 'Fury' of those comrades whom Pittakos betrayed will avenge them. Alcaeus is in exile in this poem but still on Lesbos. For further abuse of 'pot belly' Pittakos, see doc. 7.30.

1 … the Lesbians set up this great precinct for everyone and they placed in it altars of the immortal gods
5 And they named Zeus god of suppliants and you Aeolian glorious goddess, mother of all and this […] third they named Dionysos,
9 Who eats raw flesh. Come with kindly spirit, and hear our prayers, and save us from these labours and painful exile;
13 Let their Fury (Erinys) pursue the son of Hyrrhas (Pittakos) as we once swore, […] never any of our comrades,
17 But either to lie dead and wrapped in earth at the hands of men who then were masters(?) or to kill them and deliver the people from their distresses.
21 Pot-belly (Pittakos) did not reckon with his heart but, having readily trodden underfoot the oaths, devours our city …
25 Unlawfully … Myrsilos …

7.26 Alcaeus 130, lines 16–27: Alcaeus in Exile

This poem belongs to one of Alcaeus' periods of exile on Lesbos, after the failure of a conspiracy against Myrsilos.

... I poor wretch,
Live a rustic life
Desiring to hear the assembly
Being summoned, Agesilaidas,
And boule; what my father and father's father
Have grown old possessing, amongst
These citizens who wrong each other,
From this I have been driven out
An exile at the world's end, and, like Onymakles,
I dwelt alone among wolf-thickets
... war; for it is not good to renounce
Strife (stasis) against ...

7.27 Alcaeus 332: When Myrsilos Died, Alcaeus Celebrated

This song dates to Alcaeus' return from his first exile after the death of Myrsilos. Alcaeus' audience consisted of relatives and friends, his hetaireia, who dined together as frequently as possible and whose kinship was outwardly displayed in common military action.

Now everyone should be drunk and with all their might
Drink, since Myrsilos has died.

7.28 Alcaeus 69: The Lydians Finance Alcaeus' Attempt to Return

At some stage Alcaeus and others attempted to gain control of Mytilene with the aid of the Lydians, who provided 2,000 staters in assistance.

Father Zeus, the Lydians, indignant at our misfortunes, gave us 2,000 staters, if we could enter the holy city,
Though they had had nothing good from us nor are acquainted with us; but he (?Pittakos), like a wily fox, predicted easy things, and hoped to escape notice.

7.29 Alcaeus 348 (Aristotle *Politics* 1285a29–b3): Pittakos Elected as Tyrant

Pittakos, as the following passage indicates, was an aisymnetes, an elected tyrant, whom the Mytilenaeans chose as their leader 'against the exiles' Antimenidas and Alcaeus; for Pittakos, see also doc. 2.18. Alcaeus refers to Pittakos as a tyrant (tyrannos) and this is the first occurrence of the word used to refer to a specific Greek ruler. Alcaeus, as an aristocrat, objected to Pittakos as low-born (kakopatrides).

1285a29 So these are the two kinds of monarchy, and there is a third called 'aisymnetes' which existed among the Greeks of ancient times. This can be described in simple terms as an elective tyranny, which differs from the barbarian type of kingship not by being in opposition to the law, but only in not being ancestral. Some of these rulers kept their power throughout their lives, others until certain stated times or events. It was in this way that the Mytilenaeans chose Pittakos against the exiles who were led by Antimenidas and the poet Alcaeus. Alcaeus makes clear that they chose Pittakos as tyrant in one of his drinking songs; for he makes the complaint that 'with great praises of the low-born Pittakos the masses set him up as tyrant of their easy-going and ill-fated city'. **1285b1** This type of rule is and was like that of tyranny in being despotic, but royal in being chosen and over willing subjects.

7.30 Alcaeus 429: Alcaeus' Judgement of Pittakos

Pittakos was aisymnetes for ten years, organised the affairs of Mytilene, and then relinquished the office, living for another ten years, and dying in 570 BC. His election is therefore to be dated to 590. The only specific law that is attributed to him was that offences committed while drunk incurred a double penalty (Arist. *Pol.* 1274b18–23; Diog. Laert. 1.76). After relinquishing office he was given a grant of land, and he was numbered amongst the Seven Sages (Diog. Laert. 1.74). Clearly Alcaeus' insults must be set against the favourable tradition concerning this tyrant. [Diog. Laert. 1.81.]

Alcaeus calls him (Pittakos) 'splay-footed' and 'splay feet' (because he had flat feet and trailed his feet), 'chapped-feet' (because of the cracks in his feet, which they call chaps), 'braggart' (because he pranced around at random), 'pot belly' and 'fat belly' (because he was overweight), 'diner in the dark' (because he did not use a light) and 'swept and garnished' (since he was slovenly and filthy).

POLYKRATES OF SAMOS

The aristocrats, geomoroi (landowners), of Samos were overthrown *c.* 600 BC by the generals. In 532 BC Polykrates disposed of one brother and exiled another, Syloson, before assuming sole rule, suggesting that the brothers had a hereditary power, devolved to them from their father.

7.31 Polyaenus *Strategemata* 1.23.2: Polykrates and Lygdamis of Naxos

In this account, Polyaenus has Polykrates plan for the destruction of the Samians who have armour, who would have been the ones most likely to present a threat to his power. His brothers, here Syloson and Pantagnostos (called Pantagnotos in doc. 7.32), killed those of the Samians who had put aside their armour at a festival (cf. docs 9.13, 9.30). He received military assistance from Lygdamis, who had been made tyrant of Naxos by Peisistratos in return for help he had rendered him in his third coup (in 547/6; Hdt. 1.64.2, see doc. 9.13).

1.23.2 Polykrates, when the whole Samian people were going to make a sacrifice in the temple of Hera, an occasion upon which they used to participate in a procession with their weapons, having collected as many weapons as possible on the pretext of the festival, ordered his brothers Syloson and Pantagnostos to take part in the procession as well. When the Samians were going to sacrifice after the procession, the majority of them put aside their armour beside the altar as they paid attention to the libations and prayers. Syloson and Pantagnostos and those who were with them, who had all held onto their weapons, stood each by a man and killed them one after the other. Polykrates gathered those in the city who had been involved in the plot, occupied the most advantageous spots of the city, and was joined by his brothers and allies as they ran in haste from the temple with the weapons. After fortifying the acropolis known as Astypalaia and summoning soldiers from Lygdamis, tyrant of the Naxians, he then became tyrant of the Samians.

7.32 Herodotos 3.39.1–4: Polykrates Comes to Power

The date of Polykrates' accession to power is given by Eusebius as 532 BC, which is generally accepted as his activities coincided with the reign of Cambyses, who reigned from 530 to 522 BC.

3.39.1 While Cambyses was making war on Egypt, the Spartans made an expedition against Samos and Polykrates son of Aiakes, who had risen up and taken control of Samos. **2** Initially he divided control of the city into three parts and shared it with his brothers Pantagnotos and Syloson, but later on he killed the former and banished Syloson, the younger of the two, and controlled all Samos. He then made a treaty of friendship with Amasis, king of Egypt, sending him gifts and receiving others in exchange. **3** In a short time Polykrates' power quickly increased and he was celebrated throughout Ionia and the rest of Greece. Wherever he chose to wage war, everything turned out successfully for him. He possessed a hundred pentekonters and a thousand archers. **4** He used to rob and plunder everyone indiscriminately; for he said that he would oblige a friend more by giving back the things he had taken from him than if he had not taken them to begin with. He had captured many of the islands and also many of the cities of the mainland. He even captured the Lesbians who had come to the help of the Milesians with all their forces after conquering them in a sea-battle, and it was they who, in chains, dug the whole moat which surrounds Samos' wall.

7.33 Thucydides 1.13.6, 3.104.2: The Thalassocracy of Polykrates

Polykrates had a large and powerful navy, with which he established control over several islands. He was clearly the most important ruler in the Aegean, and also engaged in piracy (doc. 7.32). His conquest of Delos may have been provoked by Peisistratos' purification (doc. 9.17).

1.13.6 And afterwards the Ionians had a large fleet in the time of Cyrus (559–546 BC), first king of the Persians and of Cambyses his son, and when they were fighting against Cyrus they had control of the sea in their region for some time. Polykrates, the tyrant of Samos in the time of Cambyses, also had a powerful navy; he made a number of the islands subject to himself, including Rheneia which he took and dedicated to Delian Apollo ... **3.104.2** Rheneia is so little distant from Delos that Polykrates, the tyrant of Samos, during the time of his naval supremacy, not only ruled the rest of the islands, but, when he took Rheneia, dedicated it to Delian Apollo by attaching it to Delos by a chain.

7.34 Herodotos 3.44.1–46.2, 3.54.1–2, 3.56.1–2: Spartans Attempt to Interfere

The Spartans in 525/4 BC attempted to overthrow the tyranny of Polykrates, encouraged by Samian exiles, potential rebels whom Polykrates had sent to Cambyses to aid in the conquest of Egypt. At Sparta the exiles encountered the famous Spartan taciturnity. The Spartans claimed not to be able to understand long speeches — here they criticise the Samians for using three words (in the Greek) when two would have sufficed.

3.44.1 So the Spartans made an expedition against the all-successful Polykrates. They had been called in by the Samians, who afterwards built Kydonia on Crete. Polykrates had sent a herald without the knowledge of the Samians to Cambyses, son of Cyrus, who was raising an army against Egypt, requesting that Cambyses should send to Polykrates at Samos as well and ask for an army. **2** When Cambyses heard this he gladly sent to Samos to ask Polykrates to send a naval force against Egypt alongside his own. Polykrates then picked out those of the citizens whom he suspected in particular of rebellious tendencies and sent them off in forty triremes, instructing Cambyses not to send them back.

3.45.1 Some say that those Samians who were sent off never arrived in Egypt, but when they had sailed as far as Karpathos deliberated and preferred not to sail any further; others say that they arrived at Egypt, where they were guarded, but escaped from there. **2** As they were sailing home, Polykrates encountered them with his ships and engaged battle; the Samian exiles won and landed on the island, but in a battle on land they were defeated and accordingly sailed to Sparta. **3** Some say that the men from Egypt defeated Polykrates, but in saying so they seem to be wrong. For they had no need to call in the Spartans, if they were themselves able to bring Polykrates to terms. Moreover, it is unreasonable to suppose that a man who had a large force of hired mercenaries and his own archers would be defeated by the small number of returning Samians. **4** Polykrates shut up in the boat-sheds the children and wives of the citizens under his control and had them ready to burn, boat-sheds and all, should the citizens betray him to the Samian exiles. **3.46.1** When the Samians who had been driven out by Polykrates reached Sparta, they went before the magistrates and spoke at length like men in great need. But at this first presentation of their case the Spartans replied that they had forgotten what had been said to begin with, and not understood the rest. **2** Later on, when the Samians came before them for the second time carrying a sack, they said nothing else but 'The sack needs meal.' The Spartans replied that the word 'sack' was unnecessary; but they decided to help them …

3.54.1 The Spartans arrived with a large fleet and besieged Samos. They made an attack against the wall and set foot on the tower standing near the sea on the suburban side of the city, but then, when Polykrates came to the rescue with a large force, they were driven off. **2** The mercenaries and many of the Samians themselves sallied out near the upper tower which stands on the ridge of the hill and held the Spartans for a short time before retreating; but the Spartans followed and killed them … **3.56.1** When the Spartans had been besieging Samos for forty days and had made no progress, they went back to the Peloponnese. **2** A foolish report exists that Polykrates coined a large amount of native coinage in lead which he gilded and gave to them, and they took it and it was for that reason they departed.

7.35 Herodotos 3.120.1, 3.122.1–4, 3.125.1: The Murder of Polykrates

Hdt. 3.120.1 dates Polykrates' murder to the time of Cambyses' (last) illness in 522 BC. His death ushered in a period of Persian domination of Samos and gave rise to further Persian expansion against the Greeks. For the dream of Polykrates' daughter foretelling her father's fate and his refusal to listen to her warning, see Hdt. 3.124, 125.4; for Polykrates' successors, Maiandrios and Syloson, see doc. 7.36.

3.120.1 At about the time of Cambyses' illness the following events occurred. A Persian, Oroites, had been appointed viceroy (hyparchos) of Sardis by Cyrus. He became possessed of an unlawful desire; for although he had not suffered any wrong or heard any rash word from Polykrates of Samos, and had not even previously seen him, he desired to capture and kill him … **3.122.1** Oroites was then in Magnesia, which lies above the Maiander river, and sent Myrsos son of Gyges, a Lydian, to Samos with a message, having learned Polykrates' intention. **2** For Polykrates was the first of the Greeks we know of who planned to dominate the sea, except for Minos of Knossos and anyone else who may have ruled the sea before him. In what is called the historical age Polykrates was the first, and he had many hopes of ruling over Ionia and the islands. **3** Oroites learned that he was planning this and sent him the following message: 'Oroites says this to Polykrates: I hear that you are planning great things, but that you do not have enough money for your designs. If you do as I suggest, you will ensure your own success and save me; for King Cambyses plans my death and this has been plainly reported to me. **4** If you now get me and my money away, you can have some of it for yourself and leave me the rest; and through this money you will rule all Greece.'

3.125.1 Polykrates paid no regard to any advice, but sailed to Oroites, taking with him a large number of companions, among whom was Demokedes, son of Kalliphon, from Croton, who was a doctor and the most skilful practitioner of his time. When Polykrates arrived at Magnesia, he was cruelly murdered, which neither he nor his designs had deserved; for except for the tyrants of Syracuse there is no other Greek tyrant worthy of being compared to Polykrates for magnificence. After killing him (in a manner not fit to be narrated) Oroites had him crucified; all of those with him who were Samians Oroites let go, telling them to be grateful to him for their freedom; those who were not Samians or were slaves of Polykrates' companions he kept, considering them as prisoners of war.

7.36 Herodotos 3.139.1–149.1: Polykrates' Successors

After Polykrates' murder, Syloson then became tyrant with Darius' support: similarly, many tyrants were used by the Persians to control the Greek cities of Asia Minor. His son Aiakes succeeded him and was deposed as tyrant of Samos by Aristagoras of Miletos, but the Samians decided to desert the Ionian cause during the Battle of Lade as a belated response to Syloson's proposal to do so: Hdt. 6.13.1–2, 14.2; as a result, Darius spared Samos alone of the Ionians who had rebelled. Aiakes was reinstated as tyrant, and in *c.* 513 BC, at the time of Darius' ill-fated Scythian expedition, is found in the company of other pro-Persian tyrants waiting at the Danube.

3.139.1 After this King Darius conquered Samos, the first of all Greek and non-Greek cities, for this reason: when Cambyses, son of Cyrus, was making war against Egypt a number of Greeks went to Egypt, some, as was natural, for trade, some on the expedition, and some to see that country. Syloson, son of Aiakes and brother of Polykrates, an exile from Samos, was one of the latter. **2** The following piece of luck fell to Syloson when he was in the market at Memphis wearing a red cloak. Darius, who was then one of Cambyses' bodyguard (doryphoroi) and not yet of any importance, saw him, desired the cloak and came up and tried to buy it. **3** When Syloson saw that Darius greatly wanted the cloak he was inspired by providence to say, 'I won't sell this for any money, but if you really must have it, I will give it to you for nothing.' Darius commended him for this and took the garment … (**3.139.3–140.2:** *Syloson hears of Darius' accession and presents himself at* *the palace.*) **3.140.3** The gatekeeper brought in Syloson and as he stood before them the interpreters asked him who he was and what he had done that he could say he was the king's benefactor. So Syloson recounted the whole incident of the cloak and that he was the person who had given it. **3.140.4** In reply to this Darius said, 'Most high-minded of men, you are the person who made me a gift when I yet had no power, and even if it was small my gratitude is such as if you had now given me something great. As repayment I give you boundless gold and silver so you shall never repent of having done a service to Darius, son of Hystaspes.' **5** Syloson said to him, 'Do not, O King, give me gold or silver, but recover for me my fatherland Samos, which, since Oroites killed my brother Polykrates, is now held by one of our slaves, and give it to me without murder or enslavement.' (**3.141.1:** *Darius dispatches a force under the command of Otanes to carry out what Syloson has requested.*)

3.142.1 Maiandrios son of Maiandrios held power in Samos, Polykrates having delegated the government to him; even though he wished to be the most just of men he was not allowed to be so. **2** For when Polykrates' death was reported, he acted in the following way; he first set up an altar to Zeus the Liberator (Eleutherios) and marked out the precinct around it, which is still there in the suburb; after doing this, he called an assembly of all the citizens and addressed them as follows: **3** 'To me, as you all know, has been entrusted the sceptre and all the power of Polykrates and it is now in my power to be your ruler; but as far as I am able I will not do what I would blame my neighbour for doing; for I did not approve of Polykrates being the master of men like himself, nor that anyone else should do the same. Now that Polykrates has fulfilled his destiny, I give power in common to all and proclaim you all to have equal rights (isonomia).' … **5** When he proclaimed this to the Samians, one of them stood up and said, 'But you are not fit to rule us, you who are of base birth and a pest, but rather you ought to give us an account of the money you have handled.' **3.143.1** The man who said this was a notable citizen, called Telesarchos. Maiandrios realised that if he surrendered power someone else would make himself tyrant instead, and thus decided not to give it up, but withdrew into the acropolis, summoned each man as if to give an account of the monies, and seized and imprisoned them. **2** After the arrests Maiandrios fell ill. His brother, whose name was Lykaretos, hoping he would die so he might more easily take over power in Samos, killed all the prisoners; so it appears the Samians did not wish to be free.

3.144.1 So when the Persians arrived at Samos bringing back Syloson, no one resisted them, but Maiandrios' supporters and Maiandrios himself said that they were prepared to leave the island under a truce. Otanes (the Persian captain) agreed to these conditions, made the treaty, and the highest-ranking Persians then seated themselves on thrones placed opposite the acropolis. (**3.144.2–148.2:** *Maiandrios is encouraged by his brother Charilaos to resist and Charilaos attacks and kills a large number of high-ranking Persians. Maiandrios flees to Sparta and unsuccessfully asks Kleomenes for help (see doc. 6.73). The Persians, despite Darius' promise to Syloson of a bloodless takeover, take retribution on the population.*)

3.149.1 The Persians swept Samos clear of its population and handed it over, empty of men, to Syloson. But some time later Otanes peopled it as the result of a dream and an illness he had contracted in his genitals.

POLYKRATES' PATRONAGE OF THE ARTS

Several poets are heard of at the court of Polykrates. Anacreon of Teos is mentioned several times; Strabo writes: 'the poet Anacreon lived together with Polykrates and indeed all his poetry is full of references to him' (Strabo *Geog.* 14.1.16). Most of Anacreon's poems are concerned with love and wine, and were written for drinking parties, symposia; see docs 4.81–2. Polykrates' court had a luxurious lifestyle: Herodotos states of Maiandrios, 'it was he who not long afterwards (i.e., after Polykrates' death) sent as an offering all the remarkable adornment of Polykrates' men's apartments to the Heraion' (Hdt. 3.123.1).

7.37 Alexis of Samos F 2: Luxury Goods on Samos

Polykrates also attracted Demokedes, the well-known medical practitioner, from Athens by offering him a salary of two talents; Demokedes had previously held a state appointment in Aegina, where he was paid one talent per annum, and his salary in Athens under Peisistratos was 100 minas (Hdt. 3.131.2). Obviously tyrants were willing to pay to acquire the best professional services from doctors as well as poets. [*FGH* 539 F2; Athen. *Deip.* 540d–e.]

Alexis, in the third book of his *Samian Annals*, says that Samos was embellished from many cities by Polykrates, who imported Molossian and Lakonian hounds, goats from Skyros and Naxos, and sheep from Miletos and Attica. He says that he also summoned craftsmen at very high wages. Before he became tyrant he had extravagant carpets and cups and used to allow them to be used by those celebrating a marriage or the larger sort of receptions. From all of this it is worthy of remark that the tyrant is nowhere recorded as having sent for women or boys, although he was passionately excited by the society of males, so that he was even a rival in love of Anacreon the poet, when, in a rage, he cut off the hair of his beloved boy. Polykrates was the first to construct certain ships called Samainai, after his country.

7.38 Ibycus 282: Polykrates Honoured in Song

Ibycus is believed to have arrived on Samos *c.* 547/6 BC or perhaps before, and may have left, as Anacreon did for Athens, at the murder of Polykrates in 522 BC. He may have been the earliest composer of victory odes, epinicians (i.e., writing before Simonides), though his works generally feature either mythological or erotic themes. The mythical references in the poem relate to the Trojan War: Cassandra and Troilos were children of the Trojan king Priam.

10 Now it is not my desire to sing of Paris, who deceived his host, or slender-ankled Cassandra or the other children of Priam,
14 Or the inglorious day when high-gated Troy was captured; nor yet of the proud courage of the heroes whom the hollow
18 Many-nailed ships brought to be an evil for Troy, noble heroes; Lord Agamemnon commanded them, of the house of the Pleisthenidai, a king, chief of men, the son born of noble Atreus …
40 … he whom golden-haired Hyllis bore, to him, like already thrice refined gold to mountain copper,
44 The Trojans and Greeks (Danaoi) compared Troilos of similar and lovely form. They will always have beauty hereafter and you, Polykrates, will have undying renown, just as I too shall have renown through my song.

7.39 Aelian *Varia Historia* 9.4: Polykrates and Anacreon

Polykrates the Samian was given to the arts and he honoured Anacreon the Teian and treated him with esteem and took pleasure in the man and his songs. But I do not praise Polykrates' luxurious lifestyle.

THE EARLIER SICILIAN TYRANTS

7.40 Aristotle *Rhetoric* 1393b10–22 (Stesichoros 281): Phalaris of Akragas

Phalaris was tyrant of Akragas (Agrigentum) in south-west Sicily *c.* 570–554 BC and a byword for a bad ruler, roasting his enemies in a bronze bull over a fire; see docs 7.59, 7.72.

When the Himerians had chosen Phalaris general with absolute powers and were about to give him a bodyguard, Stesichoros after other arguments told them this fable ... 'thus you,' he said, 'look out lest in wishing to avenge yourselves on your enemies you suffer the same fate as the horse; you already have the bridle, in choosing a general with absolute powers; if you give him a bodyguard and allow him to mount you, you will already have become Phalaris' slaves.'

7.41 Polyaenus *Strategemata* 1.28.2: Theron of Selinous

Theron attempted to become tyrant of Selinous, in western Sicily, towards the end of the sixth century. The use of slaves is unusual, but falls into a typical pattern of tyrants having armed supporters. The slaves were presumably rewarded with their freedom and possibly citizenship, given the number of citizens killed in the coup.

1.28.2 When the people of Selinous were doing battle against the Carthaginians, many of the fallen lay unburied and they were not sufficiently bold to bury the corpses as the enemy were pressing upon them. However, they were unable to endure leaving them unburied and debated what they ought to do. Theron promised that if he could take three hundred slaves, capable of felling timber, he would go with them and both burn the bodies and erect a communal tomb; and if the enemy should get the better of them, there would be no great danger to the city, for it would only lose one citizen and the value of three hundred slaves. The people of Selinous praised this proposal and allowed him to take his choice of slaves. He picked out those who were robust and in their prime and led them out equipped with scythes and axes, as if they were going to fell timber to make a funeral pyre for so many corpses. When they had left the city, Theron persuaded them to attack their masters and returned to the city late in the evening. The guards on the walls recognised them and let them in. After Theron slew these guards and killed the majority of the citizens while they were asleep, he took the city and became tyrant of Selinous.

7.42 Herodotos 5.46.1–2: A Spartan Expatriate Aims at Tyranny in Sicily

Euryleon set up a short-lived tyranny at Selinous in 507/6 BC. The population rebelled against him, possibly disliking both tyranny and a foreigner in the position. For Dorieus (half-brother of the Spartan king Kleomenes) in Sicily, see doc. 2.22.

5.46.1 Other Spartiates sailed with Dorieus to help found the settlement, Thessalos, Paraibates, Kelees and Euryleon, who arrived at Sicily with their whole fleet but were defeated by the Phoenicians and people of Egesta and died in battle; the only one of the founders to survive this disaster was Euryleon. **2** He gathered the survivors of the army and took Minoa a colony of Selinous and joined in freeing the people of Selinous from their sole ruler (monarchos) Peithagoras. Afterwards, when he had deposed him, he made an attempt at the tyranny of Selinous and ruled alone for a short time; however, the people of Selinous rose up and killed him, although he had taken refuge at the altar of Zeus guardian of popular assemblies (Agoraios).

7.43 Herodotos 7.153.1–156.3: Gelon Comes to Power

Of the numerous Sicilian tyrannies, Gelon (*c.* 491–478 BC), Hieron (478–466) and Dionysios I (405–367) ruled Syracuse, the most important Greek city in Sicily. Gelon, a commander (hipparchos) of the cavalry made himself tyrant of Gela *c.* 491, and in 485 moved his base of operations to Syracuse. He carried out a synoikismos here, bringing in new citizens to add to the existing population. The context of Herodotos' account here is the Greek appeal in 481 BC for help against the Persians; for the foundation of Gela, see docs 2.6, 2.12.

7.153.1 Other messengers from the allies arrived at Sicily to confer with Gelon, including Syagros from the Spartans. The ancestor of Gelon, the founder of Gela, was from the island Telos, which lies near the Triopion; he was with the people of Lindos, from Rhodes, and Antiphemos, when they founded Gela. … **7.154.1** When Kleander son of Pantares died, who had been tyrant of Gela for seven years, he was killed by Sabyllos, a man of Gela, and Hippokrates, Kleander's brother, then took over the sovereignty. While Hippokrates was tyrant, Gelon, who was a descendant of Telines the priest, with many others, including Ainesidemos son of Pataikos, was a member of Hippokrates' bodyguard. **2** Not long afterwards because of his excellence he was appointed commander (hipparchos) of all the cavalry; for when Hippokrates was besieging Kallipolis and Naxos and Zankle and Leontinoi and fighting the Syracusans and many of the barbarians, Gelon appeared the most distinguished man in these battles. They said that of all the cities none except Syracuse escaped servitude under Hippokrates. **3** The Corinthians and Corcyraeans saved the Syracusans after their defeat at the river Eloros; they saved them by negotiating these terms: that the Syracusans give up Camarina to Hippokrates; for in the old days Camarina belonged to the Syracusans.

7.155.1 When Hippokrates had been tyrant for the same number of years as his brother, it was his fate to die at the city Hybla, while making war against the Sicels, and thus Gelon pretended to be protecting Hippokrates' sons Eukleides and Kleander, as the citizens were no longer willing to be subject to them, but in fact when he had conquered the people of Gela in battle he deprived the sons of Hippokrates of their rights and ruled them himself. **2** After this piece of good luck, Gelon brought back the wealthy landowners (gamoroi, as they were called), who had been expelled by the people and their own slaves, who were known as Kyllyrioi, from the city Kasmenai to Syracuse and took possession of it; for the Syracusan people handed over the city and themselves to Gelon as he approached. **7.156.1** When he had taken over Syracuse, he was less concerned with ruling Gela and handed it over to his brother Hieron, while he strengthened Syracuse, which meant everything to him. **2** It immediately began to shoot up and flourish; for he brought all the Camarinians to Syracuse and made them citizens, and razed the city of Camarina to the ground, and did the same to half the inhabitants of Gela; and he brought to Syracuse the wealthy men of Sicilian Megara, which had been besieged and come to terms, and made them citizens, although they had started the war against him and expected to be killed because of this; while the people of Megara, who were not responsible for this war and were not expecting any bad treatment, he also brought to Syracuse and sold them for export out of Sicily. **3** He did the same, using the same distinction, to the Euboeans in Sicily. He did this to them both as he thought the people a most unpleasant living companion. In this way Gelon became a great tyrant.

7.44 Herodotos 7.165–166: Gelon Refuses to Help the Greeks

Prior to Xerxes' invasion Herodotos states that Gelon agreed to come to the aid of the Greeks — with 200 ships, 20,000 infantry, 2,000 cavalry, 2,000 archers, 2,000 slingers and 2,000 light horsemen — and to feed the entire Greek army, if he were made strategos and hegemon, leader, of the Greek forces, but the condition was rejected (7.158.4–5). But the Sicilians were later able to claim that Gelon would have fought under the Spartans, if the Carthaginians had not kept him occupied in Sicily at the battle of Himera in 480 BC (doc. 7.45, *cf.* 11.55).

7.165 It is said by the inhabitants of Sicily that Gelon, even if he had to serve under the Spartans, would still have helped the Greeks, if Terillos, son of Krinippos and tyrant of Himera, had not been expelled by Theron son of Ainesidemos, ruler (mounarchos) of Akragas. At about this time Terillos brought with him 300,000 Phoenicians, Libyans, Iberians, Ligurians, Elisykans, Sardinians and Corsicans with Hamilcar son of Hanno, himself a Carthaginian king, as their general … In this situation, as it was not possible for Gelon to help the Greeks, he sent the money to Delphi. **7.166** They also say that it happened that Gelon in Sicily conquered Theron and Hamilcar the Carthaginian on the same day that the Greeks conquered the Persians at Salamis.

7.45 Simonides 34: A Dedication in Honour of Sicilian Victory

The poet Simonides was born on Keos and *c.* 556–*c.* 468 are generally accepted as his dates. Like Anacreon and Lasos, he was in Athens in the time of the Athenian tyrant Hipparchos (527–514 BC), after which he seems to have gone to Thessaly. He spent his last years in Sicily, where he was a friend of Hieron. This fragment purports to be a Delphic inscription written by him, but it is probably not genuine.

I say that Gelon, Hieron, Polyzelos and Thrasyboulos,
The sons of Deinomenes, set up these tripods,
After defeating barbarian countries, and provided a great
Hand as allies to the Greeks in regard to liberty.

7.46 Meiggs & Lewis 29: Hieron Defeats the Etruscans

This inscription is on a captured Etruscan helmet, sent to Olympia as a dedication. Hieron defeated the Etruscans off Cumae, which they were attacking, in 474/3 BC (Diod. 11.51). [*SIG*[3] 35 B, a.]

Hieron son of Deinomenes
And the Syracusans (dedicated these)
Etruscan spoils from Cumae to Zeus.

7.47 Aristotle *Politics* 1312b9–16: The End of the Deinomenids

Hieron took over the tyranny from Gelon in 478 and died in 467 BC. His brother and successor Thrasyboulos was overthrown in 466 BC. The tyranny collapsed as two factions in the Deinomenids ('sons of Deinomenes') struggled for power and the Syracusan rule (epicracy) over much of Sicily fell apart.

1312b9 Another way to destroy a tyranny is from within, when there is dissension among those who have a share in it, as with the tyranny of Gelon and in our day that of Dionysios. In Gelon's case, Thrasyboulos, Hieron's brother, won the support of Gelon's son and impelled him towards the enjoyment of pleasures, so he might rule. The family united to make sure that Thrasyboulos but not the tyranny itself was put down, but their fellow conspirators, having the opportunity, expelled them all.

THE FOURTH-CENTURY SICILIAN TYRANTS

In 466 BC tyranny at Syracuse came to an end, to re-emerge sixty years later when Dionysios I seized power in the stress of Carthaginian conquests of Greek cities on the island. He was twenty-four years old when he came to power, surely the youngest Greek ruler, and had been appointed as strategos autokrator (general with absolute powers; doc. 7.49) in 405 BC. Dying as tyrant in 367 he passed power to his son Dionysios II (367–357). Dionysios I was an extremely active military campaigner aiming to extend Syracusan power, amongst the Greek cities as well as by fighting numerous campaigns against the Carthaginians on the island.

7.48 Diodorus *Library of History* 11.72.1: The Wealth and Power of Sicily

Diodorus connects the lack of tyranny with prosperity, which could reflect his bias. In the fifth century Sicily and southern Greece were more prosperous than mainland Greece, with the exceptions of Athens and Corinth. The wealth of Sicily attracted the Athenians to invade, first in 427–424 and then in the well-known Sicilian Expedition of 415–413 BC.

11.72.1 As soon as the tyranny in Syracuse had been overthrown and all the island's cities liberated, the whole of Sicily started making great advances towards prosperity. The Siceliot Greeks were at peace and because they farmed excellent land and enjoyed plentiful harvests their estates soon flourished and they filled the country with slaves, flocks and herds, and all other forms of prosperity, and they acquired vast revenues while spending nothing on the wars to which they had been accustomed.

7.49 Diodorus *Library of History* 13.92.1–96.4: Dionysios I becomes Tyrant in 405 BC

Dionysios I used his military position to seize power; the Carthaginian conquest of the Greek cities of Himera and Selinous in 409, and Akragas and Gela in 406 BC, provided the background to his takeover (*cf.* doc. 13.32). Like Peisistratos at Athens, he made use of a bodyguard in seizing power (see doc. 9.3).

13.92.1 In all these speeches in the assembly Dionysios catered to his hearers' predilections and his own designs and raised the anger of those in the assembly to boiling point — for the people, who for a considerable period had hated the generals for what they saw as their bad leadership of the war, and who had now been inflamed by his words, removed some of them from office and chose other generals, including Dionysios, who had the reputation of great courage in the battles against the Carthaginians and who was greatly admired by the Syracusans. **2** Now that his hopes had been raised he tried everything in his power to become tyrant of his country. For instance, after taking up office, he neither took part in the generals' meetings nor associated at all with them, and while acting like this he spread word that they were corresponding with the enemy. His hopes were that in this way he could strip them of their power, while retaining the office of general for himself alone ...

94.2 When the assembly had been adjourned, more than a few Syracusans began to criticise its decisions, as if they themselves had not been responsible. For, as their thoughts turned to their own situation, they began to foresee the regime which was to eventuate. In their desire to ensure their liberty they had given their state a tyrant. **3** Dionysios of course wanted to forestall any change of heart on the part of the populace and so started to find a way by which he could request a bodyguard — if this were granted he would easily be able to establish himself as tyrant. So he straightway ordered that everyone of military age up to forty should get hold of thirty days' worth of rations and report to him under arms at Leontinoi. At that point Leontinoi was a Syracusan outpost, as it was full of exiles and foreigners. As these were all in favour of revolution Dionysios hoped that they would join his side and that the majority of the Syracusans would not even bother to go to Leontinoi. **4** So when he was camped out at night in the countryside he pretended that there was a conspiracy against him and set up an outcry and uproar using his own slaves. Once he'd done this he took refuge on the acropolis and spent the night there with fires burning, summoning his most trustworthy soldiers. **5** At dawn, when the Syracusan populace had gathered at Leontinoi, by presenting a long and plausible speech in pursuance of his plan, he persuaded the people to give him 600 soldiers of his own choosing to be a bodyguard, doing this, it is reported, in imitation of Peisistratos the Athenian... **6** At this period Dionysios fooled the people by employing a similar trick and put his tyranny into place.

96.1 He straightway picked out more than 1,000 citizens who lacked property but were bold in spirit, armed them with expensive weapons, and raised their hopes through extravagant promises, while he also summoned the mercenaries and got their support through friendly words. Additionally he made alterations in the ranks of the military, giving leading positions to those most loyal to him. As for Dexippos the Spartan he sent him back to Greece, being suspicious of this person in case he took the chance to give the Syracusans back their liberty. **2** He also called to himself the mercenaries at Gela, and gathered from all sides the exiles and ungodly, in the hope that these would prove to be the tyranny's most certain supporters. While he was still in Syracuse he made the naval station his quarters after openly proclaiming himself tyrant. Although the Syracusans were disgusted at this, they had to keep quiet as they were no longer able to do anything about it. Not only was the city full of foreign troops, but they had fears of the Carthaginians as their forces were so great. **3** Dionysios immediately married the daughter of Hermokrates, who had overcome the Athenians, and married off his sister to Polyxenos, the brother of

Hermokrates' wife. He did this because he wanted to forge a relationship with a distinguished family with a view to securing his tyranny. After this he called an assembly and had his most influential opponents, Daphnaios and Demarchos, put to death.

4 And so Dionysios, from having been a scribe and normal private citizen, became tyrant of the largest polis in the Greek world, and he kept himself in power until his death, at which point he had been tyrant for thirty-eight years.

7.50 Diodorus *Library of History* 14.7.1–5, 18.1, 18.4–8: Strategies for Retaining Power

Dionysios made peace with the Carthaginians in 392 BC, but from 383 to 375 again waged war against them. After a short peace, he attacked Carthaginian possessions again in 368 but was defeated. His role in keeping eastern Sicily for the Greeks was crucial. Here Diodorus describes Dionysios' 27 kilometre-long fortification of Epipolai, north of Syracuse, bringing it into the city walls.

14.7.1 In Sicily Dionysios, tyrant of the Sicilian Greeks, planned to spend more time on strengthening his tyranny after concluding peace with the Carthaginians, since he considered that now the Syracusans were relieved of the war they would have leisure to attempt to recover their freedom. **2** Realising that the Island was the strongest part of the city and could be easily defended, he separated it from the rest of the city by a costly wall, with high towers set into it at frequent intervals, while in front of it were business offices and colonnades which could accommodate a huge number of the populace. **3** He also built on the Island, at great expense, a fortified acropolis as a place of refuge in a crisis, and within its wall he enclosed the dockyards connected with the small harbour called Lakkion. These could hold sixty triremes and had an entrance blocked off, through which only one ship could enter at a time. **4** With regard to the territory of Syracuse he picked out the best of it and gave it away to his friends and the higher officers, and divided the rest of it in equal portions both to foreigners and citizens, including in the term 'citizens' the manumitted slaves whom he called New Citizens. **5** He also distributed the houses among the common people, except for those on the Island, which he gave to his friends and his mercenaries. When he considered that he had organised his tyranny properly he led his army out against the Sikels, as he was eager to bring all the independent peoples under his control, and the Sikels especially because of their previous alliance with the Carthaginians…

18.1 In Sicily Dionysios, tyrant of the Sicilian Greeks, decided to make war on the Carthaginians since he felt his government was progressing well, and, as he was not yet sufficiently prepared, he concealed his plans while making necessary steps towards the forthcoming dangers… **4** As he wanted to complete the construction of the walls quickly, he gathered a crowd of people from the countryside, from whom he chose 60,000 competent men, and divided out between them the space to be walled. **5** For each stade he appointed a master builder and for each plethron a mason and for each plethron to assist these 200 of the common people. Apart from these, a vast number of other workers quarried out the unworked stone, and 6,000 yoke of oxen conveyed it to the designated place. **6** The combined labour of these workmen greatly astonished those who observed it, as everyone was eager to complete their assigned task. For Dionysios, to make the crowd of workers enthusiastic, offered great rewards to those who finished first, with special ones for the master builders, others for the masons and still others for the workmen. Along with his friends he personally oversaw the work each and every day, visiting every section and always helping out those hard at work. **7** On the whole he laid aside the weight of his rank and showed himself an ordinary citizen, lending a hand with the toughest tasks and enduring the same labour as the other workers, so that great rivalry arose and some even added part of the night to the labours of the day, so much enthusiasm had been inspired in the multitude. **8** In consequence, against all expectation, the wall was completed in twenty days. In length it was thirty stades and of corresponding height, and the added strength of the wall made it impregnable to force, as there were high towers at frequent intervals and it was constructed of stones four feet in length and carefully fitted together.

7.51 *Inscriptiones Graecae* II^2 105, 523: Alliance between Athens and Dionysios I

This treaty of alliance was made between Athens and Dionysios I in 368 BC. Athens had also honoured Dionysios in 393 BC (Tod II.108). Dionysios had sent troops in 369 and 368 BC to assist the Spartans against the Thebans, and Athens in 368 BC had granted him and each of his sons the honour of a gold crown and Athenian citizenship (*IG* II^2 103). [*SIG*^{3} 163; Tod 2.136; R&O 34.]

In the archonship of Nausigenes, in the seventh prytany of Aiantis, Moschos of Kydathenaia was secretary ... The people resolved, Pandios proposed the motion: to the Good Fortune of the Athenians. The people has resolved to commend Dionysios, ruler of Sicily, because he is a good man towards the people of the Athenians and the allies. He and his descendants are to be allies of the people of the Athenians for all time on the following conditions: if anyone moves against the land of the Athenians in warfare either by land or by sea, Dionysios and his descendants shall give assistance in whatever manner the Athenians request both by land and by sea with all his forces to the best of his ability; and if anyone moves against Dionysios or his descendants or any place that Dionysios rules in warfare either by land or sea, the Athenians shall give assistance in whatever manner the Sicilians request both by land and by sea with all their forces to the best of their ability. Neither Dionysios nor his descendants are permitted to bear weapons against the land of the Athenians with hostile intent either by land or by sea; nor are the Athenians permitted to bear arms against Dionysios or his descendants or any place that he rules with hostile intent either by land or by sea. The oath concerning the alliance is to be sworn to the envoys who have come from Dionysios, and be sworn by the Council and the generals and the hipparchs and the taxiarchs; Dionysios and the magistrates and the Council of Syracuse and the generals and the trierarchs are to give their oath; each shall swear the legal oath and the oaths are to be sworn to the Athenian envoys who sail to Sicily. The secretary of the Boule is to inscribe this decree on a stone stele and set it up on the acropolis and to pay for the inscription the treasurer of the people is to give forty drachmas.

7.52 Plato *Seventh Letter* 326b–d: Plato's View of Sicily

Of all the letters of Plato this has the best claim to being authentic. Written in 343 BC during Plato's second visit to Syracuse, it is a defence of his participation in Sicilian politics and his attempt to train the young Dionysios II as a 'philosopher-king'.

326b This was my opinion when I came to Italy and Sicily, on my first visit. And when I arrived, what is there called the 'happy life', full as it is of Italian and Syracusan banquetings, was not at all to my liking, as you spend your time gorging on food twice a day, and never sleeping alone at night, **326c** and in all those occupations which accompany this sort of lifestyle. There is no man, of all those who live beneath the heavens, that could be wise if he had kept up this lifestyle since his youth — since no one could possess such a remarkable character — nor would he ever be likely to be temperate, while the same could be said of every other virtue as well. No state would remain at peace under such laws, whose people thought that they had to spend to excess in every way, **326d** while showing a total lack of exertion in everything other than banquets, drinking parties and love affairs.

7.53 Plutarch *Life of Timoleon* 1.1–2.2, 3.1–2: Sicily before Timoleon

Dionysios I was succeeded by his son Dionysios II in 367 BC, who had a chequered career as tyrant of Syracuse. While in Italy, he was deposed by Dion, his uncle, in 357 BC. He briefly returned in 346, but his family was massacred and he surrendered to Timoleon in 344 (doc. 7.54), and spent the rest of his life in Corinth. Timoleon was sent by Corinth to Sicily when Syracusan exiles appealed to their mother-city for assistance against Dionysios II.

1.1 The state of affairs in Syracuse before Timoleon's expedition to Sicily was as follows. **2** After Dion had driven out the tyrant Dionysios he was immediately killed by treachery and those who had helped him to liberate Syracuse were divided among themselves. The city was continually exchanging one tyrant for another and was virtually abandoned because of its numerous misfortunes, **3** while, as for the rest of Sicily, part of it was ruined and completely devoid of cities because of the wars, while most of the cities were occupied by barbarians of different races and unemployed soldiers, who readily went along with the changes in dynasties. **4** Finally, in the tenth year of his exile, Dionysios gathered some foreign mercenaries, drove out Nysaios, who was ruling Syracuse at the time, took over power again, and established himself once more as tyrant. The fact that he had been deprived by a small force of the greatest tyranny of all time was totally unexpected, and now even more unexpectedly he had, from the position of a humble exile, become master of those who had thrown him out. **5** Accordingly those Syracusans who remained in the city were the slaves of a tyrant who at the best of times was unreasonable and whose temper misfortunes had made altogether savage. **6** The best and most distinguished Syracusans, however, turned to Hiketas, the ruler of Leontinoi, put themselves under his protection and chose him as general for the war — not that he was better than any of the acknowledged tyrants, but because they had no other recourse, and they had some faith in one who was a Syracusan by birth and who possessed an army that could match that of the tyrant.

2.1 Meanwhile the Carthaginians had arrived in Sicily with a great fleet and were watching events with interest. The Sicilian Greeks were alarmed and wanted to send an embassy to Greece and ask the Corinthians for assistance, **2** not only because they trusted them because of their relationship and the benefits they had often received from them, but also, more generally, because they saw that the city always loved freedom and hated tyranny and had waged most of its wars, and the greatest ones, not for supremacy and gain, but for the liberty of the Greeks…

3.1 When the ambassadors arrived, the Corinthians, who always took care of the cities they had founded as colonies, and Syracuse in particular, and because it happened that there was nothing in Greece to trouble them and they were enjoying peace and leisure, voted with enthusiasm to assist them. **2** While they were searching for a commander, and the magistrates were writing down those in the city who were eager for the honour and proposing them for election, one of the ordinary citizens stood up and named Timoleon, son of Timodemos, although he no longer participated in public affairs and had no hope or expectation of this happening: some god, it would seem, put this into the man's mind, such was the kindness of Fortune that shone on his election and such the grace that accompanied his other actions and adorned his virtues.

7.54 Plutarch *Life of Timoleon* 13.3–10: The Downfall of Dionysios II, 346 BC

Hiketas, tyrant of Leontinoi, was instrumental in removing Dionysios from his second, brief, rule as tyrant of Syracuse in 346 BC.

13.3 Dionysios himself had now become despondent and was on the point of surrender. He despised Hiketas for his disgraceful defeat (by Timoleon), and as he admired Timoleon sent to him and his Corinthians, offering to give up himself and his citadel. Timoleon accepted this unexpected good fortune, **4** and sent Eukleides and Telemachos and their Corinthian associates into the acropolis, along with four hundred soldiers, not all together or in plain view, for that was impossible because of the enemy blockade, but they sneaked in secretly a few at a time. **5** So the soldiers took over the acropolis and the tyrant's palace with all its equipment and supplies for the war; **6** there were numerous horses in there, all sorts of engines of war and a great quantity of missiles, while enough armour for seventy thousand men had been stored there for a long period. **7** Dionysios also had with him two thousand soldiers whom, along with the rest, he handed over to Timoleon, while he took his treasure and a few friends and sailed off without Hiketas noticing. **8** And after he had been transported to Timoleon's camp, and appeared for the first time as an ordinary lowly person, he was dispatched to Corinth with just one ship and a small amount of treasure — **9** he who had been born and raised in what was the most magnificent and greatest of all tyrannies, which he had held for ten years and then another twelve following Dion's expedition, and who, after being harassed by conflicts and wars, surpassed in his sufferings all the acts he had committed as tyrant. **10** For he lived to see the deaths of his grown-up sons, and the rape of his daughters, and his wife, who was also his sister, while still alive being physically subjected to the most outrageous actions of his enemies and then murdered and thrown into the sea along with her children.

7.55 Plutarch *Life of Timoleon* 22.7–24.2: Sicily Regenerated

The Corinthians organised a recolonisation of Syracuse and the rest of Greek Sicily; this was especially important as the Carthaginians were preparing for further campaigns against the Greeks. Timoleon reorganised the Syracusan constitution, put down tyrannies in Sicily and died in Syracuse in the 330s BC (doc. 7.56).

22.7 Timoleon and the Syracusans decided to write to the Corinthians asking them to send settlers to Syracuse from Greece. **8** The countryside would otherwise be uncultivated and they were anticipating a great war from Libya, as they had heard that, after Mago had committed suicide, the Carthaginians had impaled his corpse in their anger over his conduct of the campaign and were gathering a huge force with the aim of crossing to Sicily in the campaigning season.

23.1 When these letters from Timoleon had arrived, accompanied by Syracusan envoys who begged them to show concern for their city and become its founders (oikistai) again, the Corinthians did not seize the opportunity for their own profit, **2** or appropriate Syracuse for themselves, but first of all visited the sacred games in Greece and the greatest festivals and proclaimed through heralds that they, the Corinthians, had overthrown the tyranny in Syracuse and expelled the tyrant, and were now inviting Syracusans and any other Sicilian Greeks who wished to settle in the city as free and independent citizens, allocating the land amongst themselves on equal and equitable terms. **3** Secondly they sent messengers to Asia and the islands, where they had heard that most of the dispersed exiles were living, and invited them all to go to Corinth, stating that the Corinthians at their own expense would provide them with a safe passage, ships and generals. **4** With these announcements the city acquired the most well-earned and highest praise and glory, as it was liberating the country from its tyrants, saving it from the barbarians and returning it to its citizens.

5 When these had gathered at Corinth, there were not enough of them and they begged that they might receive fellow-colonists both from Corinth and the rest of Greece. After their numbers had increased to not less than 10,000 they sailed to Syracuse. **6** Many people from Italy and Sicily had already joined Timoleon, and when their numbers reached 60,000, according to Athanis, Timoleon divided up the land and sold the houses for 1,000 talents, **7** at the same time allowing the original Syracusans to purchase their own houses, and cleverly providing plentiful funds for the community: this was so impoverished because of the war and other circumstances that it had sold off its public statues, passing a vote of condemnation against each of them as if they were magistrates submitting accounts. **8** It was at this point, it is said, that the Syracusans preserved the statue of Gelon, their tyrant of olden times, though they convicted the rest, because they admired and honoured him for the victory he had won over the Carthaginians at Himera.

24.1 Seeing the city revitalised and filling up, with citizens flowing into it from all sides, Timoleon wanted to liberate all the other cities as well and to eradicate tyrannies from Sicily. So he marched into their territories and forced Hiketas to defect from Carthage and agree to demolish his citadels and live in Leontinoi as a private citizen. **2** As for Leptines, who was tyrant of Apollonia and many other fortresses, when he was in danger of being captured by force he surrendered. Timoleon spared his life and sent him off to Corinth, considering it a good thing to have the tyrants of Sicily in the mother-city, where they could be seen by the Greeks living the lowly life of exiles.

7.56 Plutarch *Life of Timoleon* 35.1–3, 39.3–7: Magna Graecia

35.1 This was how Timoleon eradicated the tyrannies and put a stop to the wars. He had found the whole island in a state of savagery caused by its troubles and loathed by its inhabitants, and humanised it to such an extent and made it so universally desirable that others sailed there to settle in the actual places from which the old inhabitants previously used to run away. **2** Akragas and Gela, for example, great cities laid waste after the Attic (Peloponnesian) War, were now repopulated, one by Megellos and Pheristos and their companions from Elea, the other by Gorgos and others who sailed from Keos bringing with them the original citizens. **3** To these settlers Timoleon not only provided security and calm after so long a period of warfare, but also was so committed to supplying them with everything else they needed that he was revered as a founder (oikistes).

39.3 His funeral was attended by many thousands of men and women, whose appearance befitted a festival, as everyone wore garlands and was dressed in white, while cries and tears which mingled with blessings on the dead were evidence not just of formal respect, or of a service they had been commanded to perform, but of a just grief and gratitude based on genuine goodwill. **4** Finally, when the bier had been placed on the pyre, Demetrios, who had the loudest voice of any herald at that time, read out the following written decree:

5 'The people of Syracuse here buries Timoleon, son of Timodemos, from Corinth at a public cost of two hundred minas, and honours him for all time with musical, equestrian and athletic contests because he overthrew the tyrants, defeated the barbarians, refounded the greatest of the devastated cities, and gave the Greeks of Sicily back their laws.'

6 They buried him in the agora and afterwards, when they had surrounded it with porticoes and built palaistras in it, they made it into a gymnasium for their young men and called it the Timoleonteion. **7** And they themselves observed the constitution and laws he laid down and enjoyed a long period of uninterrupted prosperity.

SICILIAN TYRANTS AND THE PAN-HELLENIC GAMES

The Sicilian tyrants sent chariots, their drivers and representatives to compete at the Pan-Hellenic festivals, but did not attend themselves. They thus maintained links with the 'motherland', which was clearly important to them, and publicised their own wealth and importance. The following passages are examples of poems written for tyrants to celebrate such victories, and are evidence for patronage of the arts by Hieron, tyrant of Syracuse, 478–467 BC.

7.57 Bacchylides 4: Hieron's Victory in 470 BC at the Pythian Games (1)

This victory at Delphi was also commemorated by Pind. *Pyth.* 1 (see doc. 7.58). Hieron had also won the chariot-race there in 482 and 478 BC. The term navel (omphalos) refers to Delphi, which was commonly considered the centre of the world (the same term was also applied to Delos). Bacchylides of Keos, the nephew of Simonides, wrote for patrons all over Greece, including Athens, Sparta, Thessaly, Macedon and the west. His most important patron was Hieron, for whom he composed Epinicians 5, 4 and 3 in 476, 470 and 468 BC, respectively.

Golden-haired Apollo
Still loves the Syracusan city
And honours Hieron, just ruler of his city;
For the third time beside the navel of the high-cliffed land
He is sung as a Pythian victor
Through the excellence of his swift-footed horses.

7.58 Pindar *Pythian* 1: Hieron's Victory in 470 BC at the Pythian Games (2)

This victory of Hieron was also celebrated in Bacchylides 4; Deinomenes was Hieron's son. Aeschylus wrote a play (*The Women of Aetna*) on the refoundation of Aetna. He visited Sicily on more than one occasion and died there (doc. 11.11). Hieron is compared to the wealthy and hospitable Croesus, king of Lydia, and contrasted with Phalaris of Akragas, *c.* 570–*c.* 549, known for roasting his enemies alive in a bronze bull.

56 Thus may god be Hieron's preserver in the coming time,
Giving him due measure of his desires.
Muse, obey me and sing in the house of Deinomenes
The reward for his four-horse chariot;
59b His father's victory is a source of joy which belongs to no one else.
60 Come then, for the king of Aetna
60b Let us invent a loving song.
…
92 The glory of renown that lives after men
Is what reveals the way of life of the departed
Both in words and songs. The friendly virtue of Croesus does not fade.
95 But that ruthless mind, who burned victims in a brazen bull,
Phalaris, is everywhere the subject of hostile talk.
No lyres in the house welcome him
Mingling his name softly with the songs of boys.
99 To be fortunate is the first of prizes;
99b The next most fortunate destiny is to be well spoken of; the man
100 Who has met with both and keeps them
Has won the highest crown.

7.59 Bacchylides 3: Hieron's Victory in 468 BC at the Olympic Games

Hieron had also been victorious in the Olympic chariot-races in 476 (commemorated in Bacchylides 5) and in 472 BC. Lines 9–12 bear out the power and influence of Sicilian tyrants.

Sing of Demeter, the lady of fair-fruited Sicily,
And of violet-garlanded Persephone,
Clio of sweet gifts, and of the swift
Horses of Hieron which ran at the Olympic games.
For they sped with prominent Victory
And Glory beside the wide-eddying
Alpheios, and there made the son of Deinomenes
Prosperous in the successful attaining of garlands;
And the people cried aloud!
Ah, thrice-happy man,
Who obtained from Zeus
The honour of holding widest sway over Greeks
And does not know how to hide his towering wealth
In gloom-shrouded darkness.

...
Hieron, you have displayed
The most beautiful flowers of worldly happiness to mortal men;
Silence does not bring ornament to a man who has done well;
And with the true account of your success
Someone will also celebrate the grace of the honey-tongued
Nightingale of Keos (i.e. Bacchylides of Keos himself).

TYRANTS AND PUBLIC WORKS

In addition to the public works of tyrants at Samos, Athens and Megara, note also the walling of the Island of Syracuse by Dionysios I and his 27 kilometre fortifications which brought the area of Epipolai into the city (doc. 7.50).

7.60 Herodotos 3.60.1–4: Construction Work on Samos

It is commonly supposed that the three works mentioned in the following passage of Herodotos are to be dated to Polykrates' reign, though Herodotos does not actually state this. The temple is that to Hera, the Heraion.

3.60.1 I have written somewhat at length concerning the Samians, because they have the three greatest constructions of all the Greeks: first a channel with two mouths dug beneath a mountain a hundred and fifty fathoms high. **2** The length of the channel is seven stades, the height and breadth each eight feet. Through its whole length another channel is dug twenty cubits in depth, and three feet in breadth, through which the water coming from an abundant spring is carried through pipes to the city. **3** The architect of this channel was a Megarian, Eupalinos son of Naustrophos. This is one of the three, and the second is a breakwater in the sea around the harbour, twenty fathoms in depth, while the length of the breakwater is more than two stades. **4** Their third construction is the greatest of all known temples, of which the first master builder was Rhoikos son of Phileus, a Samian. It is because of these that I have written at length about the Samians.

7.61 Strabo *Geography* 8.2.1: The Diolkos at the Isthmus

The Isthmus of Corinth at its narrowest is 6 kilometres wide. The Corinthians, almost certainly during the Kypselid tyranny, constructed a stone road, the diolkos, across it. Ships could be dragged along this or, alternatively, goods from a ship unloaded, taken by cart across the diolkos and loaded onto another ship. This saved ships having to sail all around the Peloponnese: *cf.* doc. 1.62.

The Isthmus at the Diolkos where the boats are hauled across from one sea to the other is forty stades, as previously stated.

7.62 Aristotle *Politics* 1313b18–32: Public Works as Good Government

In this passage, Aristotle claims that tyrants' public works played a role in keeping their subjects busy, though the examples do not prove this. The temple of Zeus was not completed until the reign of Hadrian; and even if Polykrates is credited with all the works on Samos, it is doubtful how much employment this would have provided (and he used slaves captured in war for the moat around Samos: doc. 7.32). The pyramids are also incorrectly interpreted: they were built for religious reasons and did not employ a huge labour force.

1313b18 It is in a tyrant's interests to impoverish those he governs, so that he can afford to keep his bodyguard and so that the people are so busy with their daily lives that they have no time for plotting. An example is the pyramids of Egypt and the dedications of the Kypselids and the construction of the temple of Olympian Zeus by the Peisistratidai, and the works on Samos owed to Polykrates (for all these achieved the same, the lack of leisure and impoverishment of their subjects); another method is the payment of taxes, as at Syracuse (for in five years under Dionysios the whole value of property there was paid in). The tyrant is also an instigator of wars, as this keeps his subjects busy and continuously in need of a leader. And while kingship is preserved through friends, the policy of a tyrant is especially to distrust friends, as, what all men want, these in particular have the ability to put into practice.

ARISTOTLE ON TYRANNY

7.63 Aristotle *Politics* 1285a25–29: Tyrants as Employers of Mercenaries

While it is clear that many tyrants had bodyguards (docs 7.15, 7.19, 7.49, 7.64, 9.3), that they employed mercenaries as Aristotle claims was certainly not always the case. Aristotle is here employing anachronistic definitions of kingship and tyranny.

1285a25 Kings are guarded by armed citizens, but mercenaries guard tyrants; for kings rule willing subjects according to the law, but tyrants rule the unwilling, so that the first have a bodyguard from the citizens and the latter a bodyguard against them.

7.64 Aristotle *Rhetoric* 1357b30–36: Tyrants Come to Power by Armed Force

Most tyrants came to power with the aid of armed force, sometimes provided in the form of bodyguards by the people over whom the tyrant was to assume power. In Peisistratos' case, his bodyguard allowed him to seize power, but only temporarily (see doc. 9.3). Aristotle in this passage is illustrating logical syllogisms.

1357b30 For example (we can adduce) the statement that Dionysios is aiming at becoming tyrant because he requests a guard; for earlier Peisistratos, when he was aiming at being tyrant, requested a guard and, once he had it, became tyrant, and Theagenes in Megara also; and the others, as many as are known, all become a precedent for Dionysios, although it is not yet known if he made his request for this reason. All these are under the same general proposition, that anyone aiming at becoming tyrant requests a guard.

7.65 Aristotle *Politics* 1305a7–27: Tyrants as Champions of the People

Aristotle notes that tyrannies could arise from a constitutional position, in the past tyrants having often been generals entrusted with great powers by the populace. His reference to Miletos may be to Thrasyboulos, who was tyrant while Miletos withstood twelve years of devastation by Alyattes.

1305a7 In ancient times when the popular leader (demagogos) was himself the general as well, this caused the change from democracy to tyranny; nearly all the earlier tyrants had been popular leaders. This past cause does not exist today, because at that time the popular leaders were from those who were generals (as there were not yet any brilliant speakers), but now oratory has become so widespread those who are able to speak are the popular leaders, but through inexperience of warfare they do not make an attempt at power, except in some minor instance. Tyrannies occurred in the past rather than now because great powers were entrusted to some people, as in Miletos tyranny arose from the office of chief magistrate (prytanis) (for the prytanis had authority over many important matters). Another reason is that no great cities existed at that time, the people living in the country occupied with their work, and because of this the champions of the people, when they were warlike, used to aim at tyranny. They all did this with the full confidence of the people, and this trust stemmed from hatred of the wealthy. For instance at Athens Peisistratos formed his party against the plain-dwellers, and Theagenes in Megara took the flocks of the rich grazing beside the river and slaughtered them, and Dionysios was thought fit to be tyrant because he accused Daphnaios and the wealthy, and because of this hostility was trusted as a man with the people's interests at heart.

7.66 Aristotle *Politics* 1311a8–22: The Evils of Tyranny

For tyrants keeping the citizens out of the city as a means of controlling them, see doc. 7.15 (Periander). Here Aristotle records that Periander was the instigator of numerous methods of suppressing opposition, including giving this advice to Thrasyboulos, reversing the roles as given by Herodotos (doc. 7.13); this is part of Aristotle's conception that Periander developed many of the characteristic features of tyranny.

1311a8 It is clear that tyranny possesses both the evils of democracy and those of oligarchy; from oligarchy it derives the idea of wealth as a goal (for only thus is it possible to maintain both a bodyguard and a luxurious way of life), while the mistrust of the masses (which results in the removal of their weapons), and the mistreatment of the mob and their removal from the city and dispersal are common to both oligarchy and tyranny. From democracy it derives conflict with the distinguished and their destruction both in secret and openly, and their being exiled as rivals and hindrances to the tyrant's power. It is these who originate plots, both those who themselves wish to rule and those who do not wish to be in servitude. Hence Periander's advice to Thrasyboulos, in his cutting off of the tallest ears of corn, that one should always dispose of all outstanding citizens.

7.67 Aristotle *Politics* 1311a25–1311b6: Tyrants Bring about Their Own Destruction

Aristotle incorrectly ascribes the fall of the Peisistratidai to Harmodios and Aristogeiton; in fact, they only killed Hipparchos, after which the tyranny became harsher (doc. 9.33). For Periander of Ambracia, see also 1304a31–33, where the people joined Periander's attackers and took control of the state *c.* 581 BC, which suggests that it was not merely an affronted lover who was discontented. Evagoras was ruler of Salamis in Cyprus from 411 to 374 BC.

1311a25 As a result of injustice and fear and contempt many subjects attack their ruler, particularly if injustice is caused by arrogance, while a further cause is being deprived of one's possessions. And the aims are the same too, just as in constitutional change in general, both for tyrannies and kingships; for an immensity of wealth and honour belongs to sole rulers, which are things all men desire. Of the attacks on rulers, some may be against them physically, others against their government. Those which result from arrogant treatment are physical. There are many kinds of arrogance, and each of them provokes an angry reaction; nearly all these angered subjects attack for the sake of revenge, not pre-eminence. Examples of this are the fall of the Peisistratidai because of their insulting treatment of Harmodios' sister and insolence towards Harmodios (for Harmodios turned tyrannicide for his sister's sake, and Aristogeiton for Harmodios'); the plot against Periander, tyrant of Ambracia, resulted from his asking his young boyfriend while they were drinking together if he was yet pregnant by him; **1311b1** ... Amyntas the Small was killed by Derdas for having boasted about his youthful prime, and Evagoras of Cyprus by the eunuch, who slew him out of anger because his son had seduced his wife.

7.68 Aristotle *Politics* 1312b17–23, 1312b29–34: Why Tyrants Are Hated

Aristotle assumes that all tyrants are hated. But this was certainly not the case. The rule of Peisistratos went down in tradition as an Age of Kronos (a 'Golden Age'; doc. 9.16), and even if Hippias' tyranny became harsher after the assassination of Hipparchos, there is no evidence for popular discontent: it was the disgruntled Alkmeonidai and the Spartans who brought down this tyranny. Once again, he misleads the reader with his account of the downfall of the Peisistratidai and his assumption that tyrants are generally hated by their subjects.

1312b17 Two of the reasons why tyrants are especially attacked are hatred and scorn, one of which, hatred, is always felt for tyrants. This is illustrated by the fact that of those tyrants who gained power for themselves the majority managed to keep it, while those who inherited it all lost it immediately, so to speak ... Angry men more quickly attack because their passion does not make use of reason (which hatred does to some extent), and men are especially led by their anger when it stems from an insult. This was the reason the tyranny of the Peisistratidai was put down as well as many other tyrannies.

7.69 Aristotle *Politics* 1313a34–1313b16: How Tyrants Maintain Power

Aristotle was keen to attribute to Periander methods which tyrants commonly employed to maintain their power over their subjects (cf. doc. 7.66). Keeping the 'outstanding', i.e., the aristocrats or charismatic figures, under control deprived the populace of alternative leaders, while keeping the people occupied was a device used by Peisistratos (doc. 9.16) and Periander (doc. 7.15). The farmers were kept in the country, while the city-dwellers were to be accustomed to servile behaviour. Hieron seems to have been the first to use spies and eavesdroppers to learn what was happening amongst his subjects (Polyaen. *Strat.* 5.2.13 states that Dionysios improved on this by having singing girls and prostitutes report to him about the views of his opponents).

1313a34 Tyrannies on the other hand are maintained by two opposing methods, of which one is traditional and used by the majority of tyrants in exercising their authority. They say that Periander of Corinth instituted most of its details, though a lot of them can be found under Persian rule. Here follow the old dicta about preserving tyranny, as far as is possible: to cut off any who are outstanding and dispose of the high-spirited; allow neither messes, nor clubs, nor education, nor anything similar, **1313b1** but watch everything which is likely to inspire courage and confidence; do not permit schools or other associations for the purpose of learning, and do everything you can to make sure that people do not get to know each other (for acquaintance gives rise to confidence in each other); the city-dwellers should always be in sight and spend their time at your gate (for in this way they will have least chance of all of doing anything secretly, and by always being servile they will become accustomed to being poor-spirited); and there are other similar Persian and barbarian approaches to tyranny (all of similar efficacy); and you should attempt to make sure that nothing said or done by your subjects escapes you, and have spies like the women in Syracuse called 'tale-bearers', and the eavesdroppers whom Hieron used to dispatch wherever there was a gathering or meeting (for there is less free speech when people are frightened of such men, and if there is free speech, it is less likely to escape notice).

7.70 Aristotle *Politics* 1315b11–18, 1315b21–39: The Short-Lived Nature of Tyranny

While individual tyrants could have lengthy reigns, tyrannies in Greek cities seldom lasted more than two or three generations.

1315b11 Of all constitutions, however, oligarchy and tyranny are the shortest-lived. The tyranny at Sicyon, that of Orthagoras and his sons, was the longest; it lasted a hundred years. The reason for this was that they treated their subjects moderately and in many respects observed the laws ... **1315b21** Secondly we have the tyranny of the Kypselids in Corinth, which lasted seventy-three years and six months, with Kypselos as tyrant for thirty years, Periander for forty and a half, and Psammitichos, son of Gorgos, for three. There are the same reasons for this; Kypselos was a popular leader and continued throughout his reign without a bodyguard, while Periander was more tyrant-like, but warlike too. The third was that of the Peisistratidai at Athens, though this was not continuous, for Peisistratos twice as tyrant went into exile. As a result he was tyrant for seventeen years out of thirty-three, and his children for eighteen, which makes the total thirty-five years. Of the rest there was the tyranny of Hieron and Gelon in Syracuse, though even this did not last many years, only amounting to eighteen. Gelon was tyrant for seven years and died in the eighth, Hieron for ten, and Thrasyboulos was expelled in the eleventh month. But the majority of tyrannies are all extremely short-lived.

7.71 Aristotle *Politics* 1316a25–39: Tyranny and Constitutional Change

Aristotle is here discussing the views of Socrates on tyranny as presented by Plato in the *Republic* 562a–576b. Charillos was actually an early king of Sparta and Lykourgos was said to have been his guardian (Plut. *Lyk.* 3–4, cf. doc. 6.3); for Panaitios, see doc. 7.2; for Kleander, see doc. 7.43.

1316a25 Furthermore, Socrates does not say of tyranny whether it will undergo change nor, if it does, for what reason and into what constitution, and the reason for this is that he would not find it easy to say; for tyranny is indeterminate, since according to him it should change into the constitution which is first and best; for thus it (the sequence of change) would be continuous and a circle. But tyranny changes into tyranny, like the tyranny in Sicyon changed from that of Myron to that of Kleisthenes; and into oligarchy, like the tyranny of Antileon in Chalkis; and into democracy like that of the family of Gelon in Syracuse; and into aristocracy, like that of Charillos in Sparta and in Carthage. Change can also take place from an oligarchy into a tyranny, like nearly all the ancient oligarchies in Sicily, in Leontinoi to the tyranny of Panaitios and in Gela to the tyranny of Kleander and in Rhegium to the tyranny of Anaxilaos and in many other cities likewise.

7.72 Plutarch *On Divine Vengeance* 7: Plutarch on Tyranny

Plutarch here sees tyrants as a divine scourge, sent by providence to punish and purge the wickedness of the peoples over whom they rule. Consideration of a number of the passages in this chapter will demonstrate that his concepts (e.g. that tyrants are necessarily harsh and oppressive rulers) are inappropriate and that his views of the personalities and deeds of specific tyrants (such as the Orthagorids) are not necessarily accurate. His inclusion of Marius as a tyrant might also interest Roman historians. [*Mor.* 552f–553b.]

552f Indeed the divine Power has availed itself of some people as chastisers of the wickedness of others, like executioners, and then destroyed them, as in the case, I think, of most tyrants. Just like the bile of the hyena and the rennet of the seal, **553a** in other respects impure animals, they have a use in the case of illnesses, so on some peoples who need a sting and punishment the god has fastened on them the unappeasable bitterness of a tyrant and the painful harshness of a ruler, nor has he taken away the pain and distress before he has removed and purified what is diseased. Such a medicine was Phalaris for the people of Akragas and Marius for the Romans … **553b** But when Orthagoras became tyrant of the Sicyonians and after him Myron and Kleisthenes and their colleagues, the Sicyonians ceased their wickedness; while the Kleonaians, who did not meet with the same cure, have come to nothing.

8

THE LAWGIVERS OF ATHENS: DRAKON AND SOLON

Despite the fact that colonisation and tyranny were common phenomena in Greece in the eighth and seventh centuries, these were developments which largely passed Athens by in that period. When Kylon attempted to set up a tyranny at Athens with the support of his father-in-law Theagenes the tyrant of Megara, the attempt failed miserably (docs 7.21–23). But it did have an important long-term political repercussion, the curse which lay upon the Alkmeonidai for their role in killing Kylon's supporters (docs 10.2–3, 10.6, 13.4). It is also possible that Drakon was appointed to codify the laws in 621/0 BC as a result of the Kylonian conspiracy, to prevent blood feuds that might have taken place as a consequence. Little is known of Drakon's laws because they were superseded by those of Solon (doc. 8.15), except for the law on homicide, which remained in force and was in fact republished in the year 409/8 BC (doc. 8.3). There was a later tradition that Drakon's laws were harsh (doc. 8.4), but such a tradition can be discounted, as the law on involuntary homicide seems humane; it may simply have arisen out of a feeling that any older set of laws was bound to be harsher than the present code. Drakon was not archon when he was lawgiver, and in this sense differed from Solon, who carried out his reforms as archon. Drakon's Law Code was not unique in the Greek world in the seventh century: at Dreros a law was passed c. 650 about the holding of office (doc. 1.45), and Zaleukos of Locri in southern Italy, who was known as the first lawgiver, also belongs to this period.

By the 590s BC Attica was engulfed in a struggle between the rich and the poor, with Athenians being sold into slavery for failing to meet their obligations to wealthy landowners (doc. 8.5). The poor also had a political grievance: not being allowed political rights exacerbated their downtrodden economic status, and for the *Athenaion Politeia* both the political and economic problems were to be viewed in terms of a struggle between the rich and the poor (doc. 8.7, cf. 8.9). In 594/3 BC, the Athenians chose Solon as archon and mediator to resolve the crisis facing Attica. Prior to this he had been active in the prosecution of the war against Megara for control of the island of Salamis, though his self-appointed role as public critic, as evidenced in his poems (docs 8.5–6, 8.8–9, 8.12, 8.20), is a more probable reason for his election.

Like poets such as Archilochos, Alcaeus, Theognis and Hesiod, Solon used poetry to convey his ideas and feelings about the current political situation and his poems provide a first-hand account of his reforms, though they do not give a detailed analysis of their contents, which helps to explain why there is debate about their actual nature. Moreover, the fourth-century BC tendency at Athens to attribute all ancestral laws to Solon, regardless of their true origin, means that many laws attributed to Solon may not have been his.

Solon, as archon, lawgiver and mediator, attempted to address the various problems facing Attica, and carried out a significant series of reforms, both economic and political. It is better not to divide them into two distinct categories, as his economic reforms benefited the poor by freeing them from the fear of enslavement and so defused the worst of the political agitation. The poor had the status of pelatai and hektemoroi, and the *Athenaion Politeia* describes the status of the hektemoroi, but not of the pelatai, so that their precise standing is not known: perhaps the pelatai were clients partially or completely dependent on a wealthy landowner (doc. 8.6). The hektemoroi paid one-sixth of the produce of their land over to the wealthy landowners and slavery resulted if this was not paid. Why the oppression of the poor by the rich had reached the stage where the poor were being enslaved is not quite clear. But Solon identified the excesses of the wealthy as the chief cause of strife in Attica (doc. 8.5), and criticised those who wanted to have twice as much wealth as they already had (doc. 8.6). He saw the practice of enslavement as a 'public evil' from which no one was safe, and (like the Spartans concerning their own city) he was concerned that the city be governed with eunomia, 'good order' (doc. 8.5).

Solon's main reforms were the seisachtheia (docs 8.11–13), the classification of political privilege according to wealth (doc. 8.16), the creation of a council of 400 (doc. 8.19) and a system of appeal against decisions of the public officials (docs 8.22–23). The seisachtheia, the 'shaking off of burdens', cancelled debts and entailed drawing out from the 'black earth' the horoi (boundary-markers) which enslaved her. That is, land belonging to the poor no longer carried an agricultural obligation towards the local wealthy landowner. There were now no pelatai and hektemoroi, and the farmers could work their land free of the fear of enslavement; a class of independent farmers with small plots of land was thereby established (this may have been a re-establishment of the situation before the status of hektemoros was created). Solon did not redistribute the land, as demanded by some Athenians (doc. 8.12), but he did 'free' it: clearly the land had belonged to the hektemoroi but was encumbered by obligation to wealthy landowners.

Prior to Solon, Athenian society had been controlled by the aristocrats, the eupatridai or 'well born', a group closely knit by intermarriage and kinship ties, which dominated Athens after the downfall of the monarchy, and ruled the state through the archonship and the Areiopagos (doc. 8.1). The Kylonian conspiracy was the result of one man's ambition for tyranny (docs 7.21–23), not the work of a dissatisfied group of aristocrats. In Solon's time the wealthy seem to have closed ranks against the poor; there is no indication under Solon that the eupatridai felt that one of their number would rally the poor, and the aftermath of Solon's reforms show that the eupatridai were not looking for a protector against one of their own number championing the people. In the political struggles following Solon, Megakles and Lykourgos ignored the people as a group, and while Peisistratos attached them to his own following the people, though Peisistratos' loyal supporters were never strong enough in their own right for Peisistratos' rule as tyrant to be based simply on their support. If the eupatridai feared one of their number rallying the poor, their fears (with the benefit of hindsight) were groundless. Solon himself thought he gave the people 'as much privilege as was appropriate' (doc. 8.20).

His reforms meant that each of the four property classes — the pentakosiomedimnoi, hippeis, zeugitai and the thetes — each had specific political privileges, rights and duties (docs 8.16, 8.22). The public officials were drawn from the wealthy, but the people chose them; there was also appeal to the demos (people) against the decisions of officials. Solon's empowerment of the demos as a court of appeal, the heliaia, became the basis for the fifth- and fourth-century legal system in which juries drawn from the demos made judicial decisions. This power was seen in the fourth century as being, without Solon intending this, his most democratic reform (docs 8.22–23). His was not a democratic but a timocratic system, but the potential for extending this system into a democratic one was to be realised: in less than a century Athens was a democracy.

There could be mobility between the four property classes, because they were based on how much wealth one's land produced: if a citizen became wealthier, he went into a higher property class, as in the case of Anthemion son of Diphilos (doc. 8.16). The possibility of changing class if one's land became more productive might in itself have been an incentive to make one's farm more productive (doc. 8.29). Solon prohibited the export of grain from Attica (which by the beginning of the fifth century was already heavily reliant on grain imports: doc. 1.71), and this seems to have led to a greater interest in growing olives and grapes, which suit marginally fertile soils. His orientation was in fact agricultural, concerned with the plight of the poor farmers; while craftsmen were invited into Athens, his archonship did not usher in a period of industrialisation in the city (docs 8.27–28).

Solon left Athens after his archonship; whether the Athenians swore to obey his laws for ten years or a hundred is immaterial (doc. 8.32), as these laws remained the basis of the political system for about three hundred years. Solon is often said to have been 'a failure' as the strife within Attica continued after his archonship in 594/3. However, he had largely defused the struggle between the rich and the poor, and while post-Solonian Attica had political troubles, with open rivalries amongst the wealthy becoming evident, there was no more enslavement for agricultural debt, resulting in a more stable society. Solon had refused to become a tyrant (doc. 8.38), and clearly hated tyranny as a form of government. Within decades, however, Peisistratos set up a tyranny; in this sense, Solon had not been successful. But it is important that Solon's laws remained more or less in force, and that by the time the tyranny ended in 511/0 Attica had been under Solonian laws for more than eight decades.

DRAKON THE LAWGIVER

8.1 [Aristotle] *Athenaion Politeia* 3.6: The Council of the Areiopagos

The *Ath. Pol.* here describes the functions of the Areiopagos prior to Drakon; see also doc. 8.2. The pre-Solonian Areiopagos, chosen by birth, was purely an aristocratic body, which ruled Athens; all other offices were held for a period of one year. The Areiopagos began as a council that advised the kings of Athens and continued after the downfall of the monarchy (in 682 BC according to the archon list), and the archons automatically joined the Areiopagos.

3.6 The council of the Areiopagos had the task of keeping watch over the laws, and it controlled the majority and the most important of the city's affairs, having full authority to punish and fine all the disorderly. For the selection of the archons was by birth and wealth, and the Areiopagos was made up of these; for this reason this is the only office to have remained until this day one held for life.

8.2 [Aristotle] *Athenaion Politeia* 4.1–5: The Constitution of Drakon

The *Athenaion Politeia* 7.1 (doc. 8.15) states that Solon's constitution did away with Drakon's laws apart from that on homicide (doc. 8.3). This deals with involuntary homicide, so presumably there was at least one other axon dealing with intentional homicide; the axones were rectangular wooden beams, with four faces, fixed so the reader could revolve them, probably on a horizontal axis. Drakon's laws belong to the archonship of Aristaichmos, which can be dated to 621/0 BC (*Ath. Pol.* 4.1). The constitution of Drakon as presented here contains anachronisms: there was no coinage in Attica at the time and, three decades later, Solon still defined the classes in terms of produce not money; a council of 401 members, chosen by lot, is unlikely in a period dominated by the aristocrats.

4.1 So this is the outline of the first constitution. After this only a short time passed before Drakon enacted his ordinances in the archonship of Aristaichmos (621/0 BC); his political organisation had the following form. **2** A share in the constitution had been given to those who supplied their own arms. They chose the nine archons and the treasurers from those who had an unencumbered property of not less than ten minas, the other lesser officials from those who supplied their own arms, and the generals (strategoi) and cavalry commanders (hipparchoi) from those who could declare an unencumbered property of not less than 100 minas and had legitimate sons over ten years of age from a wedded wife; the prytaneis had to take security from these and from the generals and cavalry commanders of the previous year until they had been publicly examined, accepting as guarantors four men of the same class as the generals and cavalry commanders. **3** There was to be a council of 401 members appointed by lot from those who had citizenship. The men over thirty were to draw lots for this and the other magistracies, and the same man could not hold office twice before everyone had been in office; then they were again appointed by lot from the beginning. If any of the council members was absent from a meeting when a session of the council or assembly was being held, he was fined three drachmas if he was one of the pentakosiomedimnoi, two if one of the hippeis, and one if one of the zeugitai. **4** The council of the Areiopagos was the guardian of the laws and supervised the officials to make sure that they ruled in accordance with the laws. Anyone who had been wronged was able to lay information before the council of the Areiopagites declaring the law under which he was wronged. **5** Loans were made on the security of the person, as has already been said, and the country was in the hands of a few.

8.3 *Inscriptiones Graecae* I^{3} 104: Republication of Drakon's Law of Homicide, 409/8 BC

A revision of the laws of Solon took place after the fall of the Four Hundred in 411 BC, and Drakon's law on homicide in 621/0 was republished as part of this. The person guilty of involuntary homicide was to be exiled (not killed) but could be pardoned if the relatives of the victim permitted (father, brothers or sons are listed), but not if one of them opposed the pardon. Provisions were also made if there were no relatives. A connection between this code and the Kylonian affair is usually assumed (docs 7.21–23). The anagrapheis were recorders; the poletai let out state contracts and sold confiscated property; the hellenotamiai were the 'Hellenic Treasurers'; the nature of the ephetai remains obscure. [*IG* I^{2} 115; Meiggs & Lewis 86.]

Diogn[e]tos of Phrearrhioi was secretary; Diokles was archon. It was resolved by the boule and the people; (the tribe) Akamantis held the prytany, [D]io[g]netos was secretary, Euthydikos presided, [..]e[..ph]anes proposed the motion: let the anagrapheis record the law of Drakon concerning homicide, when they have received it from the basileus archon together with the secretary of the council, on a stone stele and set it up in front of the stoa basileios; let the poletai put this out to contract in accordance with the law; let the hellenotamiai provide the money.

First Axon. Even if without premeditation someone kills someone, he is to go into exile; the basileis are to pass judgement on him as guilty of homicide either … or he who planned it; the ephetai are to give the verdict. He may be pardoned if the father is alive or brothers or sons, all of them, otherwise the one opposing it is to prevail; if these are not alive, then (by the male relatives) as far as the cousin's son and cousin, if all are willing to pardon, the opposer is to prevail; and if not even one of these is alive and the killing was involuntary and it is judged by the Fifty-One, the ephetai, that it was involuntary homicide, let the phratry members admit him into the country, if ten are willing; these the Fifty-One are to choose according to their merit. And those who before this were **20** also killers let them be bound by this ordinance. Let proclamation be made against the killer in the agora (by the male relatives) as far as the degree of cousin's son and cousin; and let the prosecution be made jointly by cousins and sons of cousins and sons-in-law and fathers-in-law and phratry members ... guilty of homicide ... the Fifty-One ... **25** convicted of homicide ... If anyone kills the murderer or is responsible for his death, when he has kept away from the agora on the frontier and the games and the Amphictyonic rites, let him be treated the same as one who has killed an Athenian; the ephetai are to judge the case ... the aggressor ... kills the aggressor ... **35** the ephetai are to give the verdict ... is a free man. And if a man immediately defends himself against someone who is unjustly plundering him by force and kills him, that man shall die without a penalty being paid ... **56** Second Axon ...

8.4 Plutarch *Life of Solon* 17.1–3: Laws 'Written in Blood'

Drakon's laws were renowned in antiquity for their severity: hence the term 'draconian'. Scholars, however, have argued that this tradition is incorrect, and the law about unintentional homicide shows the lawgiver in a humane light. Plutarch's examples can therefore be taken as unreliable accretions. For Solon's law on idleness, see doc. 8.25.

17.1 So first of all Solon repealed all Drakon's laws, except those concerning homicide, because of their harshness and the magnitude of their penalties. **2** For one punishment, death, was laid down for nearly all offenders, with the result that even those convicted of idleness were put to death and those who stole vegetables or fruit were punished just like those who committed sacrilege or murder. **3** That is why Demades was later on well known for his remark that Drakon wrote his laws in blood, not ink.

POVERTY AND INEQUALITY IN ATTICA BEFORE SOLON

The *Athenaion Politeia* 2.1 is essentially a description of a typical class struggle between rich and poor: the crisis which Solon attempted to solve in 594/3 BC was one between exploiters and exploited (doc. 8.7). Regional tendencies in archaic Attica accordingly emerged *after* Solon, and political trouble before this was not along these or factional or family lines. Both sides chose Solon as the mediator in the class strife (*Ath. Pol.* 5; doc. 8.9); the poor to gain redress, the rich so that the people would be restrained (*Ath. Pol.* 12.4; doc. 8.12). The poor particularly would have feared enslavement.

8.5 Solon *Poem* 4: Social Disorder in Attica

In addition to his poems urging the Athenians to action over Salamis (doc. 8.8), Solon wrote many verses about the state of affairs in Attica, attempting to point out the various problems of his time. It was presumably because of his prominence as a critic that he was appointed as mediator and archon (*Ath. Pol.* 5.1; doc. 8.9).

Our city will never perish in accordance with the decree of Zeus
And the will of the blessed immortal gods;
For such a great-hearted guardian, daughter of a mighty father,
Pallas Athena holds her hands over us;
But to destroy a great city by their thoughtlessness
Is the wish of the citizens, won over by gain,
And unrighteous is the mind of the people's leaders, who are about
To suffer many pains from their great presumption (hybris);
For they know not how to restrain excess or
Arrange in peace the present good cheer of the feast.
. . .
This is an inescapable wound which comes to every city,
And swiftly brings it to wretched slavery,
Arousing civil discord and sleeping war,
Which has destroyed the lovely prime of many;
For by men of ill will a much-loved city is swiftly
Consumed in the gatherings of those who harm their friends.
These evils are at large amongst the people; and of the poor
Many arrive at a foreign land
Sold for export and bound in unseemly chains.
Thus the public evil comes to each at home,
And house doors can no longer keep it out,
It has leapt over high fences, found people in all ways,
Even one who runs and hides in his chamber's recess.
This my spirit bids me tell the Athenians,
That most evils are brought to a city by bad order (dysnomia);
But good order (eunomia) makes all things well run and perfect,
And frequently puts fetters on the unrighteous;
She smooths the rough, stops excess, obscures presumption (hybris),
Withers the growing flowers of ruin,
Straightens crooked judgements, proud deeds
She softens; she stops the works of sedition,
Ends the wrath of painful strife, and by her
All is made perfect and prudent amongst mankind.

8.6 Solon *Poem* 13: Greed and Injustice in Attica

Solon praises wealth, but only if gained legitimately. He appears to be criticising 'new' wealth, gained unjustly, perhaps referring to extortionate methods of dealing with dependants. The simile in lines 17–25 is typically Homeric and shows Solon's debt to traditional poetry.

Glorious children of Memory and Olympian Zeus,
Pierian Muses, listen to my prayer;
Give me prosperity at the hands of the blessed gods, and
At the hands of all men let me have always good repute;
Make me very dear to my friends, and bitter to my enemies,
Reverenced by those, and to these dreadful to behold.

I desire to possess money, but to have acquired it unjustly
I do not choose; for justice always comes afterwards.
Wealth which the gods give stays with a man
Lastingly from the lowest foundation to the peak;
While that which man values from presumption (hybris), comes not
By right, but, persuaded by unjust deeds,
Follows unwillingly, and soon is mixed with ruin;
Which from a small beginning grows like fire,
Trivial at first, but grievous in the end;
For the presumptuous deeds done by mortals do not last,
But Zeus watches over the end of everything, and, suddenly,
Just as a wind has quickly scattered clouds
In spring, and has stirred the unharvested many-waved ocean
To its depths, and throughout the wheat-bearing land
Laid waste the good lands, reaching the high seat of the gods,
Heaven, and again has made the aether clear to view,
And the strength of the sun shines down on land rich and
Fair, but not a single cloud is still to be seen —
Such is the vengeance of Zeus;
. . .
For men there is no limit apparently laid down as to wealth;
For those of us who now have greatest means,
Are eager for twice as much; who could satisfy everyone?
The immortals have granted men gains,
But these produce ruin, which when sent by Zeus
As retribution, is possessed now by this man and then that one.

8.7 [Aristotle] *Athenaion Politeia* 2.1–3: The Enslavement of the Masses

The account of the *Athenaion Politeia* needs some qualification. The poor were not 'slaves' of the rich in a literal sense, nor was 'all the land' in the hands of the rich. The peasants owned their own land but were required to pay one-sixth of their produce to the local wealthy landowner. In return for this one-sixth hektemoroi would originally have received various benefits and protections.

2.1 After this there was a long period of strife between the notables (gnorimoi) and the populace. **2** For not only was their state oligarchic in all other respects, but the poor were also slaves of the rich, both themselves, their children and their wives. They were called dependants (pelatai) and sixth-parters (hektemoroi), as it was for this rent (of one-sixth of their produce) that they were working the fields of the rich. All the land was in the hands of a few; and if they did not pay the rents, both they and their children were liable to seizure. Also all loans were made on the security of the person until Solon's time; he was the first champion of the people. **3** For the masses the harshest and most unbearable aspect of the constitution was their enslavement, though they were discontented on other grounds as well; for they had, so to speak, no share in anything.

SOLON AND HIS BACKGROUND

8.8 Solon *Poems* 1–3: 'A Herald from Lovely Salamis'

These fragments are from the 'Salamis', a 100-line poem justifying Athens' conflict with Megara; after a long struggle the Athenians had decreed that the matter was no longer open for discussion; Solon evaded this by pretending madness and reciting these verses exhorting the Athenians to action. The Athenians recaptured Salamis, and eventually both sides agreed to have the Spartans arbitrate the matter; they awarded the island to Athens. At about the same time the Athenians were also fighting against the Mytilenaeans for control of Sigeion; see doc. 2.18 [Plut. *Sol.* 8.3. Diog. Laert. 1.47.].

I have come as a herald from lovely Salamis,
And have composed a song, an ornament of words, instead of speech (*Poem* 1).
May I be then a man of Pholegandros or Sikinos
Instead of an Athenian, after changing my native land;
For this would shortly be men's common talk:
'This man is an Athenian, one of the letting-Salamis-go family' (*Poem* 2).
Let us go to Salamis, to fight for an island
That is lovely, and repel grievous shame (*Poem* 3).

8.9 [Aristotle] *Athenaion Politeia* 5.1–2 (Solon *Poem* 4a): 'Mediator and Archon'

As at *Athenaion Politeia* 2 (doc. 8.7), the crisis is here viewed in socio-economic terms. Solon clearly had a vision of healing the divisions in Athenian society. That both sides could agree to appoint him as the archon and mediator to deal with the situation reflects well on Athenian good political sense and explains the overall acceptance of his reforms when implemented in 594 BC.

5.1 So with the constitution organised in this way, and the many enslaved to the few, the people rose up against the notables. **2** As the dissension (stasis) was fierce and they remained opposed to each other for a long time, both sides agreed to choose Solon as mediator and archon and they entrusted the state to him, after he had composed the elegy of which this is the beginning (*Poem* 4a):

'I look on, and pains lie within my breast, as I behold Ionia's eldest land being slain.'

In this he fights with each side on behalf of the other and debates the points at issue, afterwards exhorting them to join together and put an end to their contention.

8.10 [Aristotle] *Athenaion Politeia* 5.3 (Solon *Poem* 4c): Solon's View of the Wealthy

The *Athenaion Politeia* here describes Solon as well born but not especially wealthy; Solon advised the wealthy to set limits to their quest for property.

5.3 By both birth and reputation Solon was one of the leading men, but in wealth and occupation he was middle class, as other evidence confirms and as he himself admits in his poems, when he advises the rich not to be grasping (*Poem* 4c);

'But calm your mighty hearts in your breasts,
You who have pushed on to surfeit yourselves with many good things,
Set your ambitious mind within limits; for
We will not allow you, nor will all this turn out according to your wishes.'

On the whole he always lays the responsibility for the dissension on the rich; accordingly, even at the beginning of his elegy, he says that he fears 'their avarice and their arrogance', implying that these had been the cause behind the ill feeling.

THE SEISACHTHEIA

The seisachtheia or 'shaking off of burdens' was a cancellation of debts. It must have encompassed the obligation of the hektemoroi, for the horoi (boundary-markers) on their land were uprooted. Before Solon's archonship those hektemoroi who could not meet their obligations were enslaved.

8.11 [Aristotle] *Athenaion Politeia* 6.1–4: The 'Shaking off of Burdens'

The charge of corruption levelled against Solon is clearly anachronistic; it is also found in Plut. *Sol.* 15.7–9, *Mor.* 807d–e; cf. doc. 8.13. Land might well have been inalienable at this time, and 'buying up' would have been difficult in a pre-monetary economy. In Solonian Athens there would not have been huge estates up for sale, and the wherewithal to purchase them through borrowing would not have been available at such short notice (there was also no coinage; doc. 8.24). The story is not intended so much to discredit Solon, and those who profited, but the descendants of those named at Plut. *Sol.* 15.7, especially Konon, Alkibiades and Kallias, all important in the Peloponnesian war: the slander is clearly fifth century in origin.

6.1 When Solon gained control of affairs, he liberated the people both immediately and for the future, by preventing loans on the security of the person, and enacted laws and brought about a cancellation of debts both private and public, which they call the 'shaking off of burdens' (seisachtheia), since they shook off their load. **2** Some people in this try to discredit Solon; for when he was about to bring in the seisachtheia he first spoke of it to some of the notables, and then, according to the popular party, he was outmanoeuvred by his friends, or, as those wishing to slander him say, he joined in it. For these men borrowed money and bought up large amounts of land, and not long after became rich through the cancellation of debts; in this way men who were later thought to be of ancient wealth are said to have become rich. **3** But the popular version is certainly the more probable; for it is not likely that he, who was so moderate and impartial in other respects, and who could have subordinated the rest of the people to himself and become tyrant of the city, but chose to be hated by both sides and considered right and the safety of the city of more importance than his own aggrandisement, should sully himself with such petty and easily detectable matters. **4** That he had this power is made clear by the unhealthy state of affairs, and he refers to it in many places in his poems and everyone else agrees with him. This charge must therefore be considered to be false.

8.12 [Aristotle] *Athenaion Politeia* 12.3–5 (Solon *Poems* 34, 36, 37): Solon's Achievements

At the end of his archonship Solon clearly wrote some poems to 'set the record straight' about his term of office. The call for redistribution of the land which he rejected could have come from the hektemoroi, who had their own land but might have wished to increase their holdings by a distribution of the land of the wealthy, or from a group of landless poor (perhaps the pelatai), or perhaps both groups. The horoi marked the produce obligation which a hektemoros was bound to make to a local landlord and their uprooting cancelled the obligation and created a freehold peasantry unencumbered by obligations to the wealthy.

12.3 Again he speaks elsewhere concerning those who wanted the land to be redistributed (*Poem* 34):

'Those who came for plunder had rich hope,
Each of them expecting to find great prosperity,
And that, despite smooth words, I would show an intransigent mind.
Then they contrived vainly, and angry with me
All looked at me askance as at an enemy.
It is not right. For what I said, I achieved with the gods' help,
But did nothing in vain, nor with the force of tyranny
Did I choose to act, nor that the rich earth
Of our native land should equally be shared by base and good.'

12.4 Again regarding the cancellation of debts and liberation of those previously enslaved through the seisachtheia, he says (*Poem* 36):

'Of those things for the sake of which I gathered together
The people, which did I abandon unaccomplished?
May she bear witness to these things in the tribunal of time
The greatest mother of the Olympian gods
And the best, black Earth, from whom I once
Removed markers (horoi) fixed in many places,
She who before was enslaved, and now is free.
To Athens, their god-built native land, many
I brought back who had been sold, some unjustly,
Some justly, and some who constrained by debt
Had gone into exile, who no longer spoke the Attic tongue,
So widely had they wandered;
And some who here suffered shameful slavery
Trembling before their masters' ways,
I made free. And these things by the power
Of law, by a combination of force and justice,
I accomplished, and completed them as I promised.
Ordinances for bad and good alike,
Setting up straight justice for each man,
I wrote. Another man taking up the goad like I,
A foolish and greedy man,
Would not have restrained the people; for if I had been willing to do
What then pleased their opponents,

Or again what the other side contrived for them,
This city would have been bereft of many men.
For this reason making a defence on every side,
I turned about like a wolf among many hounds.'

12.5 And again, reproaching both sides for their later fault-finding (*Poem* 37.1–5):
'If it were right to reproach the people openly,
What they have now, they would never with their eyes
Have seen even in their sleep.
While all those who are greater and more powerful
Should praise me and should make me their friend;' for if another man, he says, had achieved this position (*Poem* 37.7–10):
'He would not have restrained the people or stopped,
Before he had stirred up the milk and taken off the cream.
But I between them on neutral ground
Stood like a marker (horos).'

8.13 Plutarch *Life of Solon* 15.2–5 (Androtion F34): A Fourth-Century View

Androtion's interpretation of the seisachtheia, that it was only a partial reduction of debt, was due to a desire to downplay the radical nature of Solon's reforms, so that he would not provide inspiration for radical reform in fourth-century Athens. Interest rates would be an anachronism in Solonian times when there was no money; the devaluation referred to at 15.4 should therefore be ignored. [Androtion *FGH* 324 F34.]

15.2 For this was the first measure that Solon instituted, decreeing that existing debts should be cancelled, and that for the future no one could lend money on the security of the person. **15.3** And yet some people have written, of whom Androtion is one, that the poor were so pleased at being relieved not by a cancellation of debts, but by a reduction of interest rates, that they gave the name of 'seisachtheia' to this philanthropic act, as well as to the increase of measures and rise in value of the coinage which took place at the same time. **4** For he made the mina a hundred drachmas, it having previously been seventy-three, with the result that people paid back an equal amount numerically speaking, but less in value, and greatly benefited those paying off debts, while not disadvantaging those who recovered their money. **5** But most writers say that the seisachtheia was the removal of all debts, and Solon's poems tend to confirm this, as in them he boasts that from the mortgaged land:

'he removed the horoi which were everywhere fixed —
the earth which was in slavery, now is free'.

8.14 Aristotle *Politics* 1266b14–24: Land as the Source of Political Power

According to Aristotle, Solon realised that equality of property was an issue of political significance; Aristotle is presumably referring to the seisachtheia and the uprooting of the horoi. Solon's reforms meant that there was from that point on a freehold peasantry in Attica. For Aristotle on property in Sparta, see doc. 4.18.

1266b14 Accordingly the equality of property has some effect on the political community, and some men of former times seem to have discerned this, such as Solon in his legislation, while other places have a law which prevents people obtaining as much land as they wish, and similarly laws prevent the sale of property, like that at Lokri forbidding you to sell property unless you can show that an obvious misfortune has taken place, as well as those which preserve ancient estates (this was repealed at Leukas and made their constitution over-democratic; for it was no longer possible to appoint officials from the specified property classes).

SOLON'S CONSTITUTIONAL REFORMS

8.15 [Aristotle] *Athenaion Politeia* 7.1: Drakon's Laws Superseded

Solon's legislation superseded that of Drakon, except for the law on homicide (doc. 8.3). For the oath taken by the archons, which became a traditional procedure, cf. Plut. *Sol.* 25.3. The stone mentioned here has been identified with the large limestone block discovered outside the Stoa Basileios; for the kyrbeis, see doc. 8.33.

7.1 Solon established a constitution and made other laws, and they stopped using the ordinances of Drakon except those concerning homicide. They inscribed the laws on the tablets (kyrbeis) and set them up in the stoa of the basileus archon and everyone swore they would observe them. The nine archons used to swear their oath at the stone and declare that they would dedicate a golden statue, if they transgressed any of the laws; and even today they continue to swear in the same manner.

8.16 [Aristotle] *Athenaion Politeia* 7.3–4: The Four Property Classes

Four property classes apparently already existed in Attica according to the *Athenaion Politeia*, and what was new was that Solon made these classes the basis of political privilege, organising them on the criterion of wealth, measured in terms of annual agricultural produce. This new system was timocratic in nature. Solon allowed the top two classes, the pentakosiomedimnoi ('500 bushel-men') and the hippeis ('cavalry', 'knights'), to stand for election to the archonship (the inclusion of the zeugitai came later). The thetes, the lowest property qualification, were ineligible for any of the political offices. The reform involving the four classes presupposes more than conflict between the rich and the poor: the classification of offices by wealth and not birth suggests that there was a group of wealthy non-eupatridai in Attica, and that Solon thought that the extension of political power to this group would be of benefit to Attica.

7.3 By a property assessment he divided everyone into four classes, as they had been divided before: pentakosiomedimnoi, hippeis, zeugitai and thetes. The magistracies he assigned to the pentakosiomedimnoi, hippeis and zeugitai, that is, the nine archons, the treasurers, the poletai (sellers), the Eleven and the kolakretai (financial officials), allocating the magistracies to each class according to the size of their property assessment. But to those registered in the class of thetes he only gave a share in the assembly and law courts. **4** Whoever made five hundred measures of dry and liquid goods both together from his property was to belong to the pentakosiomedimnoi, while those who made three hundred belonged to the hippeis, though some people describe them as those who were able to keep horses. They mention the name of the class as proof, and as confirming the fact, as well as the dedications of former times; for dedicated on the acropolis there is a statue of Diphilos, on which this has been inscribed:

'Anthemion son of Diphilos dedicated this to the gods,
After exchanging the labourers' class for the hippeis.'

And a horse stands beside him as witness that this is what the hippeis class means. Nevertheless it is more reasonable that this class should have been differentiated by measures like the pentakosiomedimnoi. Those who made two hundred measures both together belonged to the zeugitai; and the others belonged to the thetes and had no share in the magistracies. Accordingly when anyone who is about to draw lots for a magistracy is asked what class he belongs to, he would never say the thetes.

8.17 [Aristotle] *Athenaion Politeia* 8.1–2: The Election of the Archons

According to the *Athenaion Politeia* the tribes elected an initial number of candidates for office, and lots were then used for the final choice.

8.1 He laid down that the magistrates were to be appointed by lot from a preliminary list of candidates, whom each of the tribes had pre-selected. Each tribe chose ten candidates for the nine archons, and they appointed by lot from these; from which the practice still continues that each of the tribes selects ten men by lot, and then they choose by lot from them. Proof that he made the offices appointed by lot from the propertied classes is the law concerning the treasurers, which is still in force even today; for it says that the treasurers should be chosen by lot from the pentakosiomedimnoi. **2** So this was how Solon legislated regarding the nine archons. In former times the Council of the Areiopagos according to its own judgement summoned people and appointed the most suitable person to each of the magistracies for the year.

8.18 [Aristotle] *Athenaion Politeia* 8.3: The Four Tribes and the Naukraroi

This passage describes some features of the Solonian constitution; little is known of the phylobasileis. There were originally four tribes, the typical Ionian ones, at Athens.

8.3 There were four tribes as before and four heads of tribes (phylobasileis). Each tribe was divided into three thirds (trittyes) and there were twelve naukrariai in each (tribe). There were officials, the naukraroi, in charge of the naukrariai, who were responsible for income and expenditure; accordingly, in Solon's laws, which are no longer in force, there is often written, 'the naukraroi shall exact' and 'expend from the naukraric fund'.

8.19 [Aristotle] *Athenaion Politeia* 8.4: The Four Hundred and the Areiopagos

The council of the Areiopagos had clear functions under Solon, in particular the general oversight of the state. The separate council of 400 was the Council, or boule, and when Kleisthenes reorganised the Athenians into ten tribes its number was increased to 500. A Council would have been needed to organise the agenda for the ekklesia. Solon may have thought that the Areiopagos, dominated by the aristocrats and likely to remain so for some time (because members were chosen for life), was unsuitable for this purpose.

8.4 He created a Council of Four Hundred, with one hundred men drawn from each tribe, and assigned the council of the Areiopagites to guard the laws, just as previously it had been guardian of the constitution. It used to watch over the majority and the greatest of the city's affairs and chastise wrongdoers, having full power to impose fines and punishments, and it deposited the fines on the acropolis, without recording the reason for the fine, and judged those who had conspired to put down the democracy, Solon having made a law of impeachment for such cases.

8.20 [Aristotle] *Athenaion Politeia* 12.1–2 (Solon *Poems* 5, 6): Solon's View of the People

Solon criticised the excesses of the wealthy, but nevertheless created a political system where wealth was the prerequisite for office, while the poor had power in the ekklesia and law courts (cf. doc. 8.23). Solon thought that the people had a specific place in society, and that they ought not to exceed their 'station in life'. He saw himself as standing between the two opposing groups, the wealthy and the 'ordinary' people, and his legislation, which enshrined the right of the wealthy to rule but protected the people by giving them specific rights, is reflected in his poetry.

12.1 Everyone agrees that this is what he did and he himself refers to it in his poetry in the following lines (*Poem* 5):

'To the people I gave as much privilege as was appropriate,
Neither taking from their honour nor reaching out to do so;
And those that had power and were admired for their possessions,
I also made sure that they should suffer nothing unseemly.
I stood firm holding my strong shield in defence of both,
And did not allow either to conquer unjustly.'

12.2 And again he makes clear how to deal with the populace (*Poem* 6):
'In this way the people will best follow their leaders,
If they are neither left too free nor restrained too much.
For surfeit breeds presumption (hybris), when too much prosperity comes
To men whose mind is not sound.'

8.21 [Aristotle] *Athenaion Politeia* 8.5: Solon's Law against Political Apathy

This law against political apathy is also given at Plut. *Sol.* 20.1 (cf. Plut. *Mor.* 550c). If genuine, it seems to have been a response to the civil disorder of his period and could have stemmed from a belief that if everyone became politically involved there would be more stability in society. The notion of participation in public affairs was also a theme in Perikles' Funeral Oration (see doc. 1.17).

8.5 Seeing that, although the city was often in dissension (stasis), some of the citizens, through reluctance to take action, were happy to accept whatever happened, he made a particular law with them in mind, that whoever did not take up arms at the service of one side or the other when the city was in dissension would be deprived of civic rights and have no share in the life of the city.

8.22 Aristotle *Politics* 1273b35–1274a21: The 'Founder of Athenian Democracy'

Aristotle views the Solonian constitution as a mixed one, with oligarchic, aristocratic and democratic features. Similarly, he sees the Spartan constitution as mixed (doc. 6.25). He notes that Solon did not intend his constitution to become a democracy, as Solon gave 'the people just the power that was absolutely necessary', and this theme is found in Solon's poems (doc. 8.20).

1273b35 Some people think that Solon was an excellent lawgiver, for he put an end to the oligarchy that was too elitist, and he stopped the people being enslaved, and he established the traditional democracy by a good constitutional mixture; for the Council of the Areiopagos is oligarchic, the elective magistracies aristocratic and the law courts democratic. But it seems probable that Solon merely did not abolish the first two, which were already in existence, **1274a1** that is, the council and the election of magistrates, but that he did establish the democracy by having the law courts drawn from everybody. Accordingly some people blame him, in that he undid his other reforms by making the law court, which is chosen by lot, supreme over everything. For when the law court became powerful, the constitution was changed into the present democracy to please the people, just as if it were a tyrant; and Ephialtes curtailed the power of Council of the Areiopagos, as did Perikles, while Perikles instituted payment for the law courts, and in this way each of the popular leaders (demagogoi) enlarged and promoted it into the democracy we have now. But it appears that this happened not according to a plan of Solon's, but rather by chance (for, as the people were responsible for naval supremacy in the Persian wars, they became presumptuous and chose inferior men as popular leaders when reasonable men pursued opposing policies), since Solon seems to have given the people just the power that was absolutely necessary, that of electing officials and of examining their conduct (for if the people were not supreme in this they would have had the status of slaves or enemies), and he ensured that all the magistracies would be filled by the notables and wealthy, that is, the pentakosiomedimnoi and zeugitai and the third class called that of the hippeis; the fourth class were the thetes, who had no share in office.

SOLON'S SOCIAL AND JUDICIAL LEGISLATION

8.23 [Aristotle] *Athenaion Politeia* 9.1–2: Judicial Reforms

The *Athenaion Politeia* defines three features of Solon's reforms as particularly 'democratic', though Solon will not have intended them to be so; the laws would certainly not have been deliberately obscure, and are only so from a fifth- and fourth-century BC perspective, probably relating to the archaic vocabulary employed by Solon. This was the first time that the ordinary people of Athens had been given any judicial competence and the fact that Athenians could now appeal against decisions of the magistrates was meant to be a curb on the power of the wealthy.

9.1 So this was what he did with regard to the magistracies. In Solon's constitution these three features seem to be the most democratic: first and greatest was not allowing loans on the security of the person, the next was that it was possible for anyone who wished to seek vengeance on behalf of those who were being wronged, and the third, the one by which they say the populace became especially powerful, was the right of appeal to the law court (dikasterion); for when the people have control of the vote they come to have control of the state. **2** Furthermore, because the laws were not written simply and clearly, but were like the one concerning legacies and heiresses, there was need for many disputes and for the court to decide on all matters both public and private. So some people think that he made his laws obscure on purpose, so that the people would be in control of the decisions. Nevertheless this is not likely, but rather it is likely that he was unable to formulate what was best in general terms; for it is not right to judge his intention from present-day occurrences, but from the rest of his constitution.

8.24 [Aristotle] *Athenaion Politeia* 10.1–2: Reform of Athenian Weights and Measures

There was no coinage in Athens in Solon's time and the *Athenion Politeia* is incorrect in attributing a reform of Athenian currency to Solon; the system used before the invention of coins would have been iron spits (originally known as 'obols'). It is clear that coinage was not introduced at Athens until at least 560 BC on the earliest dating now advocated by numismatists.

10.1 So these seem to be the democratic aspects of Solon's laws, but even before his legislation he had brought in the cancellation of debts and afterwards the increase in measures and weights and in the coinage. **2** For it was under Solon that the measures became greater than those of Pheidon, and the mina which had previously had a weight of seventy drachmas was made up to a hundred. The old standard coin was the two drachma piece. He made the weights in respect of the coinage sixty-three minas to a talent, and the three extra minas were apportioned to the stater and the other weights.

8.25 Herodotos 2.177.1–2: Law on Idleness

Drakon was said to have enacted a similar law on idleness, 'nomos argias' (doc. 8.4). The law was still in force in the fourth century BC, and there is other evidence for measures against idleness in ancient Greece.

2.177.1 It is said that Egypt under King Amasis was particularly prosperous both in what the river Nile gave the land and what the land gave the people, and the total number of its inhabited cities was 20,000. **2** Amasis was the one who established this law for the Egyptians, that every year each of the Egyptians should inform the governor (nomarch) of his source of livelihood; if he did not do this or was unable to show that his way of life was honest he was condemned to death. Solon the Athenian copied this law from Egypt and put it into force in Athens; it is still in use, being an excellent law.

8.26 Plutarch *Life of Solon* 24.3: Canine Control in Sixth-Century Athens

The perennial nuisance of the badly behaved urban dog is here dealt with in novel fashion. A cubit is roughly half a metre — hence the dog was unable to bite the person controlling him.

24.3 He also composed a law concerning injury from animals, in which he said that a dog who had bitten anyone had to be tied up with a wooden dog-collar and pole three cubits long and be delivered up (to the victim); this clever device was for safety.

SOLON ON TRADE AND AGRICULTURE

The evidence of Solon's poetry shows that he was very much concerned with the exploitation of the poor by the rich, and with the plight of the farmer. Athenian trade was relatively backward in the seventh century, which can be ascribed to her lack of colonies; compare Corinth's flourishing commercial life: docs 1.61–62. Solon encouraged manufacturing, according to Plutarch, and there was a distinct increase in the distribution of Athenian pottery in the sixth century, but that Athens was becoming a manufacturing centre is incorrect: Solon was more concerned with agriculture than with manufacturing; Peisistratos' main 'economic' concern was also with farmers (doc. 9.16). Attica was always primarily a land of farmers: Thuc. 2.14 (doc. 9.4), 2.16.

8.27 Plutarch *Life of Solon* 22.1: Solon Encourages Trade

Plutarch's colourful account of Greeks pouring into Attica can be discounted; Solon may have encouraged potters to come to Athens but there was no surge in manufacturing and Solon did not usher in an industrial age.

22.1 Seeing that the city was filling up with men who kept pouring into Attica from every side on account of its secure conditions, but that most of the country was poor and undeveloped, and that those who sail the seas are unaccustomed to send their goods to those who have nothing to give in exchange, he encouraged the citizens to turn to manufacture and made a law that there was no compulsion for a son to maintain his father if he had not had him taught a trade.

8.28 Plutarch *Life of Solon* 24.4: Restrictions on Immigrants

Access to citizenship was always restricted during Athens' history, and non-Athenians coming to Attica could not usually hope for citizenship. Solon granted citizenship to some, especially those with a trade, the tyrants guaranteed this grant, and Kleisthenes re-enfranchised those who lost their citizenship with the downfall of the tyranny (docs 9.2, 10.15).

24.4 The law concerning new citizens is a puzzling one, because it only granted citizenship to those who had been exiled for good from their country or those who emigrated to Athens with their entire families to practise a trade. They say that Solon did this not so much to exclude other people as to invite these to Athens with the certainty of becoming citizens, at the same time considering that those who had been forcibly expelled from their own countries and those who had left there for a specific purpose would be loyal.

8.29 Plutarch *Life of Solon* 24.1–2: Legislation against Exports

Plutarch gives as his authority for the following law the first axon, implying its genuineness. He does not actually state that Solon encouraged oleoculture (the cultivation of olives: see doc. 1.15); rather the law provided for the prohibition of the export of agricultural products (cf. doc. 1.65 for Teos). Already, by 594 BC, Attica's population may have been outstripping its food supply and this could explain the prohibition on exporting produce such as grain. With this prohibition, olives may have come to be cultivated more extensively and intensively and an increase in Athenian pottery exports might be so explained.

24.1 He allowed the sale of products to foreigners only in the case of olive oil, and prohibited their export, and he ordered the archon to lay curses against those who exported them, or else pay a fine of hundred drachmas to the public treasury; **24.2** the first tablet (axon) is that which contains this law. So one should not consider entirely improbable the view of those who say that even the export of figs (syka; sing.: sykon) was forbidden in former times, and that anyone informing against the exporters was called a 'sycophant' or 'fig-declarer'.

8.30 Plutarch *Life of Solon* 23.7–8: Agricultural Legislation

The precise details given here might argue against the authenticity of these measures. They may, however, preserve the tradition of Solon's very real concern with day-to-day aspects of agriculture.

23.7 He also laid down rules about distances for planting with great expertise, stating that anything planted in a field had to be five feet away from the neighbour's property, and nine feet away, if a fig or an olive tree; for these reach further with their roots and cannot be placed next to all plants without harm, because they deprive them of nutriment and give off an emanation, which is harmful to some. **8** He stated that anyone who wished to dig pits or trenches had to do so the equivalent of their depth away from someone else's property, and anyone positioning beehives had to keep them 300 feet away from any previously put in position by someone else.

SOLON'S 'APODEMIA'

8.31 Herodotos 1.29.1–30.1: Solon Leaves Athens for Ten Years

After instituting his reforms in 594/3, Solon left Athens. As archon and lawgiver in 594/3 Solon cannot have visited Croesus, king of Lydia (*c.* 560–546), and Amasis of Egypt (570–525) in a trip beginning soon after this date. These stories are not historical, therefore, but a literary device by which the sagacity of Solon can be illustrated.

1.29.1 With these peoples subdued and added by Croesus to the Lydian kingdom, all the wise men of that time from Greece, one after another, came to Sardis, which was now at the height of its wealth, including Solon the Athenian, who made laws for the Athenians at their request and then went abroad for ten years, sailing away on the pretence of seeing the world, but really in order not to be compelled to repeal any of the laws he had made. **2** For the Athenians were unable to do this, as they had constrained themselves by solemn oaths to keep the laws Solon had made for them for ten years. **1.30.1** For this reason and in order to travel Solon went abroad and visited Amasis in Egypt and, furthermore, Croesus in Sardis.

8.32 [Aristotle] *Athenaion Politeia* 7.2: Laws Observed for 100 Years

Herodotos says the Athenians swore to observe the laws for ten years, rather than one hundred as here (doc. 8.31). Ten might seem more likely, as individuals could hardly swear to observe the laws for one century, but the tyrants are said not to have changed Solon's laws (doc. 9.21), and these were still in use under the classical democracy.

7.2 He made the laws unalterable for a hundred years and organised the constitution in the following way.

8.33 Plutarch *Life of Solon* 25.1–2: Solon's Law-Tablets: The Axones

Like Drakon's homicide law (doc. 8.3), Solon's laws were also recorded on axones (law-tablets) and numbered according to axon.

25.1 He laid down that all his laws were to remain in force for a hundred years, and they inscribed them on wooden axones which revolved in the oblong frames which surrounded them, of which small remnants were still preserved in the prytaneion in my time, and which were called, as Aristotle says, kyrbeis. **25.2** And Kratinos the comic poet wrote somewhere:

> 'By Solon and by Drakon, by virtue of whose
> Kyrbeis they now roast their barley.'

But some people say that the kyrbeis are specifically those recording sacred ceremonies and sacrifices, and that the others are called axones.

8.34 Plutarch *Life of Solon* 26.1 (Solon *Poem* 28): Solon in Egypt

So first he went to Egypt and spent time there, as he himself says (*Poem* 28):

> 'At the Nile's outpourings, near the Canopic shore.'

REACTIONS TO SOLON'S LEGISLATION

Solon's seisachtheia adversely affected wealthy landowners (not necessarily only the eupatridai), who no longer received the one-sixth of the produce previously paid by the hektemoroi (cf. doc. 9.2). More serious was the discontent with Solon's constitution, politeia, which had widened the basis for political participation; presumably this made the eupatridai, with their monopoly on political power broken, 'discontented'. Some of Solon's poems seem to have been written in reaction to this discontent (cf. doc. 8.12).

8.35 [Aristotle] *Athenaion Politeia* 11.1–2: Discontent with Solon's Reforms

Plut. *Sol.* 16.1 also mentions the discontent of both 'sides', but also that soon afterwards the Athenians established a festival called the 'Seisachtheia' to celebrate the measure (Plut. *Sol.* 16.4–5).

11.1 When Solon had organised the constitution in the manner narrated, since people kept approaching him and making a nuisance of themselves over the laws, criticising some and querying others, and he wanted neither to alter them nor to stay there and be the object of attack, he went on a journey to Egypt for trade and to see the country, saying that he would not be back for ten years, as he did not think it right that he should stay there to interpret his laws but rather that everyone should follow what was written down. **2** Moreover many of the notables happened to be at variance with him because of the cancellation of debts, and both sides had changed their minds because what had been established had turned out contrary to their expectations. For the people had thought that he would have everything redistributed, while the notables had thought that he would put them back in the same position or change things only slightly. But Solon was opposed to both, and though he could have become tyrant by joining whichever side he chose, he preferred to antagonise both sides by saving his native land and passing the best laws.

8.36 [Aristotle] *Athenaion Politeia* 13.1–3: Political Troubles after Solon

In the fifth year after Solon's reforms, there were troubles over the election of officials, but it was not until the late 560s that rivalry between specific individuals emerged, and Solon's reforms seemed to have generally worked in bringing unity to Athens.

13.1 So these were the reasons why Solon went abroad. After he had left, the city continued to be in turmoil, though they continued for four years in peace; but in the fifth year after Solon's archonship they did not appoint an archon because of the dissension (stasis), and again in the fifth year after that there was no archon for the same reason. **2** Then, after the same lapse of time, Damasias was chosen as archon and remained in office for two years and two months, until he was expelled from his office by force. Then, as a result of the dissension, they decided to choose ten archons, five from the well born (eupatridai), three from the farmers (agroikoi), and two from the craftsmen (demiourgoi), and these held office for the year after Damasias. From this it is clear that the archon had the greatest power; for dissension always appears to have occurred over this office. **3** On the whole, however, their relations with each other continued in an unhealthy state, some having the cancellation of debts as the origin and reason for their unhappiness (for they had become poor because of it), while others were discontented with the constitution because of the great change that had taken place, and yet others because of their personal rivalries with one another.

SOLON AND TYRANNY

Fragments 9 and 11 were said by Diodorus (9.20.2–3) to have been written to warn the Athenians of the impending tyranny of Peisistratos. Solon may well have been alive when Peisistratos first seized power in 561/0 BC (cf. doc. 9.4) and the historical context of Fragment 10, according to Diogenes Laertios 1.49, was Solon's rushing armed into the ekklesia to warn the Athenians about Peisistratos; the Council (boule) said that he was mad.

8.37 Solon *Poems* 9–11: 'Time Will Prove My Madness'

From cloud comes the force of snow and hail,
And thunder arises from brilliant lightning;

A city of great men is perishing utterly, and through ignorance
The people have fallen into servitude to a ruler (monarchos).
For the man who has gone too far it is not easy for him to make land
Afterwards, but he should already have had all good things in mind (*Poem* 9).

A short time will prove my madness to the citizens —
It will be proved when truth comes to the fore (*Poem* 10).

If you have suffered dreadfully through your own baseness,
Do not ascribe this destiny to the gods;
You have yourselves exalted these men by giving them protection.
And because of this you now have wretched servitude.
Each one of you walks with the steps of a fox,
Every one of you has an empty mind;
For you look to the tongue and the words of a wily man,
But see nothing that takes place in actions (*Poem* 11).

8.38 Plutarch *Life of Solon* 14.4–9 (Solon *Poems* 32, 33): Solon Refuses to Become Tyrant

Solon refused to act as a tyrant, as he relates in his poetry; some people apparently ridiculed him for refusing to become a tyrant; others encouraged him to seize power. For Pittakos, see docs 7.24–30.

14.4 The leaders of both sides kept urging Solon, recommending tyranny and persuading him to seize control of the city more boldly now he had become powerful … **6** And some say that Solon received this oracle at Delphi:

'Seat yourself in the middle of the ship, steering
As the helmsman; many of the Athenians are your allies.'

7 His associates in particular reproached him, if he fought shy of sole rule (monarchia) because of its name, as if the virtues of the man who took it did not immediately turn it into a kingship, as had happened earlier in the case of Tynnondas in Euboea and in their own time in the case of Pittakos, whom the Mytilenaeans had chosen as their tyrant. **8** None of this moved Solon from his resolution, but he said to his friends, it is reported, that tyranny is a fine place to be, but there is no way down from it, writing to Phokos in his poems (*Poem* 32):

'If I have spared (he says)
My country, and of tyranny and cruel violence
Not laid hold, defiling and disgracing my good name,
I am not ashamed; for thus I think I shall be more superior
To all mankind.'

From this it is obvious that even before his legislation he had a great reputation. **9** And as to what was said by many who mocked him for shrinking from tyranny, he wrote as follows (*Poem* 33):

'Solon was not a deep thinker or a wise man;
For when the god gave him good fortune, he did not accept it.
After encompassing his prey, out of amazement he did not pull in the great
Net, failing in spirit and deprived of wits.
I would have chosen to have power, to have taken limitless wealth
And been tyrant of Athens only for a single day,
And then to have been flayed for a wineskin and had my posterity wiped out.'

8.39 Solon *Poem* 23: Solon: The Man and His Priorities

Solon's travels are attested by these lines, as well as his love of the aristocratic sport of hunting.

Fortunate he who has dear children, and whole-hoofed horses
And hunting hounds and a friend in foreign parts.

9

PEISISTRATOS AND HIS SONS

The archonship and legislation of Solon in 594/3 BC did not mean the end of strife in Attica, though the conflict between the rich and the poor was certainly defused to a great extent. In subsequent decades, there were difficulties over the archonship in some years (doc. 8.36), and as this office was the privilege of the wealthy, both the eupatridai and non-eupatridai, dissension amongst the wealthy must have been at the root of the problem. At the same time, even after Solon's reforms, there remained a group of dissatisfied poor. Three important political figures emerged by the 560s BC: Megakles, Lykourgos and Peisistratos. According to Herodotos (doc. 9.1), there were three staseis (sing.: stasis), a term which can be translated as factions or parties: those of the coast, 'hoi paraloi', under the leadership of Megakles the Alkmeonid, and those of the plain under Lykourgos, 'hoi ek tou pediou', while Peisistratos formed a third stasis, 'hoi hyperakrioi', meaning 'those from beyond the hills', also known by the *Athenaion Politeia* (doc. 9.2) as 'hoi diakrioi', 'men of the diakria'. The coastal region, paralia, stretches from Phaleron to Sounion, the west coast of Attica; it is here that the Alkmeonidai would have had their adherents, with their main centre probably at Alopeke, south of Athens. The plain referred to is the central plain, the valley of the Kephissos river, which adjoins the city, and Lykourgos probably had his main centre at Boutadai. The diakrioi were the inhabitants of the diakria, the area from Parnes to Brauron, the hilly north-east part of Attica; this area is separated from the plain of Athens by intervening hills.

Herodotos concentrates on the regional distinctions between the three groups (doc. 9.1). The *Athenaion Politeia* 13.4 (doc. 9.2) also emphasises the regional distinction, stating that the name of each group came 'from the areas in which they farmed', but also gives a distinct political affiliation to each group. Lykourgos is described as the leader of the inhabitants of the plain, presumably conservative landowners who desired oligarchy, while Megakles pursued a 'middle-of-the-road' policy. Megakles, in fact, was able to ally himself both with Lykourgos, in overthrowing Peisistratos' first and second tyrannies, and also with Peisistratos, whom he helped to establish in power a second time through a marriage alliance, and then deposed when the marriage was, supposedly, not consummated (docs 9.6, 9.8). Peisistratos' stasis, or party, consisted of the 'diakrioi' and he was 'a friend to democracy'. His party included not only regional adherents, but, as the *Athenaion Politeia* notes, the poor as well, and Peisistratos combined leadership of the 'diakrioi' with the support of those economically disadvantaged by Solon's reforms, and those afraid of losing citizen rights. Peisistratos succeeded where Megakles and Lykourgos failed because he was able to transcend regionalism. While both Lykourgos and Megakles may have had adherents outside of their main area of support, where Peisistratos had the advantage was in being able to project himself as the leader not only of a certain region, but also of the poor and the discontented, and probably therefore of Athenians in general, whose support for him can be seen in the motion to award him a bodyguard.

Peisistratos' first two attempts at tyranny involved charades: on his first attempt he wounded himself and his mules and drove his chariot into the agora (doc. 9.3), and in the second the 'goddess Athena' herself restored him to power (doc. 9.6). His third tyranny was established through battle, bloodshed and the use of outside military assistance; once in power he disarmed the people (docs 9.9–13). Hostages were taken and sent to Naxos, and the Alkmeonidai and others went into exile (docs 9.14–15). Later Athenians looked back upon Peisistratos' reign as a 'Golden Age' (doc. 9.16), in which the tyrant ruled mildly, gave financial aid to poor farmers (though not from disinterested motives) and was popular with both the ordinary people and the wealthy class (or at least with those of this class who were not in exile).

Peisistratos was succeeded by his sons, the Peisistratidai, of whom Hippias and Hipparchos were the most important. Thucydides gives a favourable opinion of their reign (doc. 9.21), and they were known for their building projects (docs 9.28–29). The Peisistratidai continued to rule by making use of the existing laws and by ensuring that 'one of their own people' was one of the archons (doc. 9.21). One of these was Peisistratos, son of Hippias, who held the archonship sometime between 522/1 and 511/0 BC, possibly in 522/1 (docs 9.24–26). A fragment of the archon-list gives the name of Miltiades as archon in 524/3; more surprising is the possible presence of Kleisthenes the Alkmeonid as archon in 525/4. The Alkmeonidai maintained that they had been in exile for the duration of the tyranny, but apparently a reconciliation had taken place by the year 525/4, and this and Miltiades' archonship seem to mark attempts at reconciliation with the aristocratic families who had previously left Athens (doc. 9.14). Hippias and Hipparchos ruled jointly until, in 514/3, Hipparchos was assassinated by Harmodios and Aristogeiton (docs 9.30–31), after which the tyranny became harsher and Hippias took revenge through killing and exiling opponents (docs 9.32–33), and planned a place of retreat for himself (doc. 9.34, cf. 9.39). An attempt by exiles, including the Alkmeonidai, to end the tyranny failed at Leipsydrion (doc. 9.35) and Hippias was finally overthrown with Spartan help (docs 9.36–38). He made his way to Persia (doc. 9.39), from where he was to return in 490 with the Persians in their attack at Marathon (doc. 11.8).

Peisistratos and his sons ruled over Athens as tyrants, and yet the Solonian constitution continued to operate with elections held and the rights and privileges of each of the four Solonian classes intact. Peisistratos' first attempt at tyranny took place in 561/0, and the deposition of his son Hippias in 511/0; the family had accordingly determined Athenian politics for half a century. When their tyranny was overthrown, the demos did not accept a pro-Spartan regime in its place but rose up, and democracy was established.

THE THREE 'PARTIES'

While Herodotos 1.59.3 (doc. 9.1) writes of Peisistratos' supporters as hoi hyperakrioi, 'those from beyond the hills', the *Athenaion Politeia* 13.4 (doc. 9.2) writes of diakrioi, 'hillsmen'; cf. Plut. *Sol.* 29.1. The diakrioi were the inhabitants of the diakria, the area from Parnes to Brauron. The *Ath. Pol.* is thus more correct in referring to the diakrioi, in that diakria is the actual name of a specific area, though the translation 'hillsmen', used here and by others, needs caution: poor hillsmen existing on a subsistence livelihood is not an appropriate picture, as the diakria was as prosperous as the rest of Attica. Support for each of the three groups could also have come from outside their area; Peisistratos certainly had support from malcontents, as well as a group who were concerned about the possibility of losing citizen rights (doc. 9.2). Aristotle (*Politics* 1305a22–24) has Peisistratos as a tyrant exploiting the hatred of the wealthy; this might overstate the case, but the sources agree that the poor were amongst his adherents.

9.1 Herodotos 1.59.3: Peisistratos and His Rivals

By the end of the 560s BC three individuals with support based on their regional areas were rivals for power in Athens; doc. 9.3 follows on from here.

1.159.3 When the Athenians were in a state of dissension between the people of the coastland under Megakles, son of Alkmeon, and those of the plain under Lykourgos, son of Aristolaides, Peisistratos fixed his sights on the tyranny and formed a third party, collecting partisans and coming forward representing himself as champion of the people beyond the hills (the hyperakrioi).

9.2 [Aristotle] *Athenaion Politeia* 13.4–5: Peisistratos as Popular Leader

The term demotikotatos ('concerned with the interests of the people') is used here of Peisistratos, and given that he had the poor and underprivileged amongst his followers this is a reasonable description from a fourth-century BC point of view. After the overthrow of the tyranny there was a review of the citizen body, and those who could not prove their citizenship were disenfranchised. Solon had encouraged immigrants to Attica (see doc. 8.28), and Peisistratos might also have done so. The disenfranchisement presumably took place because these individuals were guaranteed their citizenship by the tyrants. It was presumably to these that Kleisthenes gave back citizenship (doc. 10.15). Doc. 9.4 follows on from here.

13.4 There were three parties; the first was that of the men of the shore, led by Megakles, son of Alkmeon, and they seemed in particular to want a middle-of-the-road constitution. The second was that of the men of the plain; they wanted oligarchy, and were led by Lykourgos. The third was that of the hillsmen (diakrioi), with Peisistratos as their leader, who was apparently a great friend to democracy. **5** The latter had, moreover, been joined by those who had lost debts they were owed and were now poor, and by those who were not of pure Athenian descent, who were now afraid; proof of this is that, after the tyrants were deposed, they held a vote on claims to the registration of citizens, on the grounds that many who were not entitled to were sharing citizen rights. Each party took its name from the area in which it farmed.

PEISISTRATOS' FIRST TYRANNY

According to Herodotos (doc. 9.3), the character of Peisistratos' first tyranny was similar to that of his third: he governed moderately and well, and it is stressed that Peisistratos made use of the existing (that is, Solonian) laws and usages (doc. 9.3, cf. 9.5, 9.16), which must mean that the ekklesia met, the heliaia functioned and elections were held for magistracies (but see doc. 9.21). The first tyranny lasted from 561/0 to his expulsion, 556/5, with a brief reinstatement in the same year 556/5, and the third period of tyranny from 546 to 527, when his sons succeeded him until 510 BC.

9.3 Herodotos 1.59.3–6: Peisistratos as 'national hero'

The Athenian capture of Nisaia, the main port of Megara, was part of a long-running dispute between Athens and Megara, which centred on Salamis; for Solon's part in this, see doc. 8.8. That Peisistratos was a general in this campaign indicates that he must already have had a public profile and influence in Attica. Peisistratos' first bodyguard were club-bearers, armed to protect him from the attack of his rivals; his sons had spear-bearers, doryphoroi, like other tyrants (doc. 9.30); for such bodyguards, see docs 7.15, 7.19, 7.49, 7.64.

1.59.3 Peisistratos devised the following plan: **4** he wounded himself and his mules and drove his cart into the agora, as if he had escaped from his enemies, who had tried to murder him as he was driving into the country, and asked the people to grant him a bodyguard; he had previously won a good reputation in his command against the Megarians, by his capture of Nisaia and other great deeds. **5** The people of the Athenians, deceived, picked out and gave him some of the citizens, who became not Peisistratos' spear-bearers, but his club-bearers; for they followed him around with wooden cudgels. **6** These joined in the revolt with Peisistratos and seized the acropolis. And so Peisistratos was master of the Athenians, but he neither disturbed the existing magistracies nor changed the laws, and governed the city in accordance with the status quo, and made it fine and beautiful.

9.4 [Aristotle] *Athenaion Politeia* 14.1–3: Solon's Advice to the People

Peisistratos gained power in 561 BC with a bodyguard and popular support; he is described as 'demotikotatos' once again here (as at doc. 9.2). According to Plutarch (*Sol.* 30), Aristion had proposed a bodyguard of fifty club-bearers. The *Athenaion Politeia* gives the duration of this first period of tyranny as five years.

14.1 Peisistratos, who seemed to be a great friend to democracy and had won an excellent reputation in the war against the Megarians, wounded himself and convinced the people that this was the work of his political opponents and that they should give him a bodyguard, Aristion proposing the motion. Once he had these 'club-bearers', as they were called, he rose up with their help against the people and seized the acropolis in the thirty-second year after the enactment of Solon's laws, in the archonship of Komeas (561/0 BC). **2** It is said that when Peisistratos requested the guard, Solon spoke against it, and said that he was wiser than some and braver than others — he was wiser than all those who did not realise that Peisistratos was making an attempt on the tyranny and he was braver than all those who realised but were keeping quiet. When his words did not convince them, he brought out his weapons and placed them in front of his door, saying that he had helped his fatherland as far as was in his power (for he was already a very old man), and that he called on the others to do the same. **3** Solon's appeal at that point had no effect; Peisistratos took over the government and administered public affairs constitutionally rather than like a tyrant. But, before his power had taken root, the parties of Megakles and Lykourgos came to an agreement and sent him into exile in the sixth year after his first coming to power, in the archonship of Hegesias (556/5 BC).

9.5 Plutarch *Solon* 30.5, 31.2–5: Peisistratos Preserves Solon's Politeia

Plutarch here stresses that Peisistratos maintained Solon's laws. Clearly the oath that the Athenians had sworn to observe the laws for ten (or a hundred) years (docs 8.31–32), had its desired effect. For Solon's views on tyranny, see docs 8.37–38. [Herakleides: Wehrli F149.]

30.5 The people ratified the proposal and did not even deal grudgingly with Peisistratos over the number of club-bearers, but allowed him to keep and openly take about with him as many as he wanted, until he seized the acropolis ... **31.2** When Peisistratos came to power, he won over Solon by treating him with respect and kindness and sending for him, with the result that Solon became his adviser and praised many of his acts. **3** For he preserved most of Solon's laws, abiding by them himself and compelling his friends to do so; for example, after he became tyrant he was even summoned to trial at the Areiopagos on a charge of murder and turned up to defend himself in due form, but his accuser failed to turn up in court; he wrote other laws himself, one of which lays down that those maimed in war should be maintained at the public expense. **4** Herakleides says that Peisistratos was copying Solon, who passed this law earlier in the case of Thersippos, who had been maimed. **5** But according to Theophrastos' account it was not Solon who was responsible for the law against unemployment, but Peisistratos, by which he made the country more productive and the city more peaceful.

PEISISTRATOS' SECOND TYRANNY

Megakles and Lykourgos joined forces in 556 BC to bring about the end of Peisistratos' first tyranny. They soon fell out, however, no doubt due to their different political ambitions, and because Megakles was losing out in the power struggle he patched up his differences with Peisistratos. The incident is an interesting insight into the 'balance of power' within Athenian society. Lykourgos and Megakles had to join forces to throw out Peisistratos, as neither of them was strong enough to dominate the state, but Lykourgos seems to have been more powerful than Megakles.

9.6 Herodotos 1.60.1–5: 'Athena' Restores Peisistratos

Even Herodotos found it difficult to believe that the Athenians could be so easily tricked by the ruse which Megakles and Peisistratos employed to effect his return. As a cynical act of political manipulation of religious sensibilities, it had no equal in Greek history.

1.60.1 Not long afterwards the parties of Megakles and Lykourgos came to an agreement and drove Peisistratos out. Thus, when Peisistratos was tyrant at Athens for the first time, he was expelled because the tyranny was not yet deeply rooted, but those who drove Peisistratos out then began a fresh quarrel with one another. **2** As this discord was making life difficult for him, Megakles made proposals to Peisistratos asking if he were willing to marry his daughter and regain the tyranny on that condition. **3** When Peisistratos approved the idea and agreed to the conditions, they worked out for his return the most simple-minded ruse by far that I have encountered (since the Greek nation has been distinguished from earliest times by being both cleverer and more superior to silly foolishness than the barbarian), and yet these men devised the following trick against the Athenians, who are supposed to be the wisest of the Greeks. **4** There was a woman in the village Paiania, whose name was Phye, who only lacked three fingers of four cubits in height (she was five feet six inches tall) and was handsome in other respects as well. They dressed this woman up in full armour and mounted her on a war-chariot, and, when they had got her to pose in the attitude that would appear most distinguished, they drove into the city, having sent ahead advance messengers, who on their arrival in the city kept making the following announcement, as they had been instructed: **5** 'O Athenians, gladly welcome Peisistratos, whom Athena herself has honoured above all men and whom she restores to her own acropolis.' The messengers went around broadcasting these reports, and immediately rumour reached the villages that Athena was restoring Peisistratos. Those in the city were convinced that the woman was really the goddess, and offered this female their prayers and took Peisistratos back.

9.7 [Aristotle] *Athenaion Politeia* 14.4–15.1: Phye: A Thracian Garland-Seller

The *Athenaion Politeia* here gives Herodotos (1.60.4) as his source for one version of Phye's background, the only occasion on which he mentions Herodotos. The story that Phye was a Thracian garland-seller (that is, not an Athenian citizen), from Kollytos, a deme of the city, is probably a slander. Giving the demotic for a foreigner would be unusual (see doc. 10.7).

14.4. In the twelfth year after this Megakles, harassed by strife between the parties, again made proposals to Peisistratos and, on the condition that Peisistratos married his daughter, restored him in a primitive and extremely simple-minded way. He broadcast the tale that Athena was restoring Peisistratos, and, after discovering a tall and handsome woman called Phye, who according to Herodotos was from the deme Paiania, though some say that she was a Thracian garland-seller from the deme Kollytos, he dressed her up to resemble the goddess and brought her into the city with Peisistratos; and so he drove into the city on a war-chariot with the woman standing beside him, while those in the city fell down in worship and received him with awe. **15.1** This was how Peisistratos' first return took place.

9.8 Herodotos 1.61.1–2: Peisistratos Loses the Tyranny a Second Time

The fact that Herodotos specifically states that Peisistratos 'left the country completely' seems to imply that after he was ousted from his first tyranny he had simply retired to his estates. The details of the non-consummated marriage are very compatible with Greek notions of virginity and family honour, and so, as in the case later with the basket-bearer sister of Harmodios, they are almost certainly true.

1.61.1 After recovering the tyranny in the manner described above, Peisistratos in accordance with his agreement with Megakles married Megakles' daughter. But since he had sons who were already young men, and the Alkmeonidai were said to be accursed, he did not want to have children by his new bride and therefore did not have intercourse with her in the normal way. **2** Initially his wife kept this a secret, but afterwards, whether in answer to a question or not, she let it out to her mother and she to her husband. He was indignant at being insulted in this way by Peisistratos, and was so angry that he made up his differences with his political opponents. When Peisistratos learned of the actions taken against him, he left the country completely, and on his arrival at Eretria took counsel with his sons.

PEISISTRATOS IN EXILE

After fleeing from Attica and arriving in Eretria, Hippias persuaded his father Peisistratos to win back the tyranny. Herodotos mentions that he was assisted by money from the Thebans and by Argive mercenaries, while the *Ath. Pol.* 15.2 (doc. 9.10) adds that the hippeis of Eretria also assisted him, but does not explain why. Lygdamis was clearly acting from personal motives in assisting Peisistratos, for Peisistratos installed him as tyrant over the Naxians when he regained the tyranny at Athens (doc. 9.14).

9.9 Herodotos 1.61.3–4: Peisistratos Gains Outside Assistance

The *Athenaion Politeia* 17.4 (doc. 9.18) states that Peisistratos had an Argive wife, and it was on account of this friendship (philia) that Hegesistratos, Peisistratos' son, was able to bring 1,000 Argives to Pallene. Perhaps the marriage alliance was important, but some money may also have changed hands. Hegesistratos was later sent to govern Sigeion: doc. 2.18.

1.61.3 Convinced by Hippias' opinion that they should try to win back the tyranny, they started collecting contributions from all the cities which were at all under obligations to them. Many supplied large sums of money, the Thebans surpassing everyone else in their gift of money. **4** And then, to cut a long story short, time passed and everything was ready for their return. For Argive mercenaries had arrived from the Peloponnese and a man from Naxos called Lygdamis turned up of his own accord and exhibited great eagerness to help, bringing with him both money and men.

9.10 [Aristotle] *Athenaion Politeia* 15.2: Peisistratos' Movements While in Exile

The *Athenaion Politeia* here states that Peisistratos began his period in exile by settling a colony in Thrace; he returned to Attica via Eretria; see doc. 9.11.

15.2 First of all Peisistratos helped settle a colony at a place called Rhaikelos near the Gulf of Thermai, and from there he went on to the region about Pangaion, from where, after raising money and hiring mercenaries, he returned to Eretria. In the eleventh year he for the first time attempted to recover power by force, with the support of many others, especially the Thebans and Lygdamis of Naxos, as well as the hippeis who controlled the government in Eretria.

PEISISTRATOS RETURNS TO POWER FOR THE THIRD TIME

Peisistratos' third attempt at tyranny was not gained on the basis of popular support, but through the use of violence, backed by foreign supporters. But popular support for Peisistratos seems to have followed his third coup (though see doc. 9.14). The difficulties which Peisistratos had in retaining the tyranny on the first and second occasions indicate that Athenian politics were operating on a more sophisticated level than at Corinth or Megara, where tyrants came to power by attacking the wealthy; at Athens there was clearly not as much dissatisfaction amongst the poor as there had been in Solon's time.

9.11 Herodotos 1.62.1–63.2: The Battle at Pallene

Peisistratos landed at Marathon, both because of its proximity to Eretria, the hippeis of which were supporting his return, and because Marathon was in Peisistratid territory, where he would presumably still have been popular with the diakrioi. The opposing forces met at the temple of Athena Pallenis, in the deme Pallene. His policy of clemency and non-retribution was reflected in his method of government once tyrant (doc. 9.16). Hexameters were the standard epic poetic line, of six 'feet'.

1.62.1 They set out from Eretria and arrived back in the eleventh year after their departure. The first place they took in Attica was Marathon. While they were encamped there, their supporters from the city arrived, while others streamed in from the villages who preferred tyranny to freedom. **2** These assembled; meanwhile the Athenians from the city, while Peisistratos was collecting money and even afterwards when he occupied Marathon, took no action, but when they learned that he was marching from Marathon towards the city, they came out to meet him. **3** They marched in full battle array against the returning exiles, while Peisistratos and his men, who had set out from Marathon and were marching against the city, met them at the temple of Athena Pallenis, where both sides took up their positions against each other. **4** There, under divine guidance, Amphilytos, a seer from Akarnania, came up to Peisistratos, and pronounced the following oracle in hexameters:

'The cast is thrown, the net is spread,
The tuna-fish will come darting through the moonlit night.'

1.63.1 When he pronounced this with divine inspiration, Peisistratos understood the prophecy and saying that he accepted the oracle led his army into battle. The Athenians from the city were occupied with lunch at that point, and following their meal some of them were occupied with dice and others having a siesta. Peisistratos' men fell on the Athenians and routed them. **2** As they were fleeing Peisistratos came up with a most ingenious ploy, so the Athenians would be unable to rally in the future and would remain dispersed. He mounted his sons on horseback and sent them on ahead. Whenever they caught up with the fugitives, they told them as instructed by Peisistratos to be of good courage and each return home.

9.12 Herodotos 1.64.1: Peisistratos' Sources of Revenue

The river Strymon is in Thrace, and this is usually taken to mean that Peisistratos had access to silver mines in Thrace while in exile.

1.64.1 The Athenians did as they were told, and in this way Peisistratos for the third time became master of Athens and established the tyranny on a firm footing with a large number of mercenaries and revenues from Attica and the river Strymon.

9.13 [Aristotle] *Athenaion Politeia* 15.3–5: Peisistratos Disarms the People

The *Ath. Pol.* here has Peisistratos disarming the people (cf. doc. 9.30 for Hippias). The account of Peisistratos' ruse can perhaps be accepted given his previous success with the Athena charade (docs 9.6–7). For tyrants preferring citizens not to become involved in public affairs, cf. doc. 2.11. The *Ath. Pol.* speaks of Pallenis, rather than Pallene.

15.3 Now that he had won the battle at Pallenis, and captured the city and removed the people's weapons, he held the tyranny securely; he also seized Naxos and established Lygdamis as ruler. **4** He removed the people's weapons in the following way: he held a review in full armour at the Theseion and began to speak to the people, addressing them for a short time; when they said that they couldn't hear him distinctly, he told them to go up to the entrance gate (propylon) of the acropolis so he could make himself better heard. And while he was taking up time making his speech, the men assigned to this duty picked up the weapons and shut them up in the buildings near the Theseion and came and indicated this to Peisistratos. **5** When he had finished the rest of his speech, he told them about what had happened to their weapons, saying that they shouldn't be surprised or distressed, but should go away and see to their own affairs, as he was going to take care of all public business.

9.14 Herodotos 1.64.1–3: The Alkmeonidai Go into Exile

While the source tradition regarding Peisistratos is quite favourable (see doc. 9.16), the third period of tyranny began with an act of violence at the battle of Pallene, and amongst those who fled were the Alkmeonidai: Megakles' role in overthrowing the second tyranny made their position in Attica untenable; they were to go into exile again under Hippias.

1.64.1 He also took as hostages the sons of the Athenians who had remained and not immediately fled, and sent them off to Naxos **2** (for Peisistratos had conquered this island in warfare and put Lygdamis in power there). ... **3** So Peisistratos was tyrant of Athens, while as to the Athenians some of them had fallen in the battle and others had left the country and gone into exile with the Alkmeonidai.

9.15 *IG* I^3 1469: A Dedication of Alkmeonides Son of Alkmeon

A dedication by Alkmeonides, son of Alkmeon and the brother of Megakles, was inscribed on a marble Doric capital at the sanctuary of Apollo Ptoios in northern Boeotia, celebrating a victory in the chariot-race at the Great Panathenaia in Athens. The dedication may have been made here rather than at Athens as the Alkmeonidai had fled Athens with Peisistratos' victory in the battle at Pallene in 546. [*IG* I^2 472.]

I am the fair statue of Phoibos son of Leto;
Alkmeonides, son of Alkmeon
Who conquered with his swift horses dedicated me,
Which Knopiadas the son of ... drove,
When the festival of Pallas (Athena) was held in Athens.

PEISISTRATOS AS TYRANT

9.16 [Aristotle] *Athenaion Politeia* 16.1–10: The 'Golden Age' of Peisistratos

This section of the *Athenaion Politeia* is extremely important for Peisistratos' reign. It stresses the assistance Peisistratos gave to the farmers, but also his policy of conciliating the wealthy. The deme or village judges will have precluded the necessity of disputants coming to the city (cf. *Ath. Pol.* 16.3). More importantly, judicial authority was not in the hands of the local nobility, to whom the disputants probably would otherwise have turned.

16.1 This is how Peisistratos' tyranny was established initially and those were the changes it experienced. **2** Peisistratos, as I have said previously, administered the city's affairs with moderation and constitutionally rather than like a tyrant; for in general he was philanthropic and kind, and compassionate to wrongdoers, and moreover used to lend money to the poor to help them in their work, so they could make a living from farming. **3** He did this for two reasons, so that they would not spend time in the city but be scattered throughout the countryside, and, as they were moderately prosperous and busy with their own affairs, they would have neither the inclination nor the time to care about public business. **4** At the same time it happened that his revenue increased because the country was well cultivated; for he exacted a tenth of the produce in tax. **5** On this account also he set up judges in each village and he often used to go himself into the country, to see what was going on and to reconcile disputants so that they would not come to the city and meanwhile neglect their work.

6 It was during one such tour by Peisistratos that they say occurred the incident involving the man on Hymettos, who cultivated what was afterwards known as the 'tax-free farm'. For seeing someone labouring to dig land that was nothing but rocks, he was so amazed that he told his slave to ask what the farm produced; 'Nothing but aches and pains,' replied the man, 'and it's of these aches and pains that Peisistratos ought to take his 10 per cent!' The fellow said this without recognising him, but Peisistratos was pleased with his outspokenness and industry and made him exempt from all taxes. **7** And in general he did not impose burdens on the populace during his rule, but always maintained peace and made sure things were tranquil; for this reason it was often said in his praise that Peisistratos' tyranny was like 'life under Kronos'; for when his sons succeeded their government became much harsher. **8** And the most important of all his qualities mentioned was his natural benevolence and concern for the people. For in all matters he wanted to administer everything in accordance with the laws, not giving himself any advantage, and once, when he was summoned to trial before the Areiopagos on a charge of murder, he turned up to make his defence, which frightened his accuser, who stayed away.

9 For this reason he remained in power for a long time and whenever he was expelled from power easily recovered it. For the majority of both the notables and the populace supported him; he won the former's support by associating with them socially, and the latter's by his assistance with their private affairs, and he was fair to both. **10** In those times all the Athenians' laws concerning tyrants were lenient, especially the law regarding the establishment of a tyranny. For the law went like this: these are the ordinances and ancestral customs of the Athenians, that if any persons should aim at being tyrant or if anyone should aid in setting up a tyranny, both he and his family shall be deprived of civic rights.

9.17 Herodotos 1.64.2: Peisistratos and Delos

The Athenian purification of Delos by Peisistratos may have provoked Polykrates' conquest of the island in a tyrant tête-à-tête (doc. 7.33).

1.64.2 In addition Peisistratos purified the island of Delos, in consequence of an oracle, in the following way: he dug up the dead from the whole area within sight of the temple and transferred them to another part of Delos.

PEISISTRATOS' FAMILY

Peisistratos was married three times. The name of the first wife, an Athenian, is (typically) unknown; the sons of this marriage were Hippias, Hipparchos and Thessalos. Timonassa was the second wife, and mother of Iophon and Hegesistratos. Thirdly, Peisistratos married Megakles' daughter, by whom there were no children (see Table II). The Peisistratidai were the sons of Peisistratos, of whom the two most important were the eldest, Hippias and Hipparchos, who shared power, with Hippias as the senior 'partner'. Peisistratos was probably born 605–600 BC, and Hippias in the late 570s, for he was old enough to counsel his father after the overthrow of the second tyranny, and was still alive in 490, when he landed at Marathon with the Persians. Hippias' son, Peisistratos, held an archonship before 511/0 BC, possibly in 522/1 (see doc. 9.24).

9.18 [Aristotle] *Athenaion Politeia* 17.1–4: Peisistratos' Three Wives

Hegesistratos was sent to be tyrant of Sigeion (doc. 2.18); of Iophon nothing is known. Hegesistratos and Thessalos (Thettalos in the *Ath. Pol.*) were two separate sons, despite the *Ath. Pol.*, who considers them to be the same person, and the *Ath. Pol.*'s story (doc. 9.31) that it was Thessalos who propositioned Harmodios flatly contradicts Thucydides (doc. 9.30); cf. doc. 16.7.

17.1 Accordingly Peisistratos grew old in power and died after an illness in the archonship of Philoneus (528/7 BC), having lived thirty-three years from the time when he first set himself up as tyrant, of which he had spent nineteen years in power, for he was in exile for the rest. **2** For this reason those who say that Peisistratos was loved by Solon and was a general in the war against the Megarians over Salamis are clearly talking nonsense; for this is impossible in view of their ages, as one can see from reckoning up the life of each and the archonship in which he died. **3** After Peisistratos died, his sons held onto power, carrying on managing affairs in the same way. By his legal wife he had two sons, Hippias and Hipparchos, and by the Argive wife another two, Iophon and Hegesistratos, whose surname was Thettalos. **4** For Peisistratos had married Timonassa, daughter of an Argive man whose name was Gorgilos, who had previously been married to Archinos of Ambracia, a man of the Kypselid family; a consequence of this was his friendship with the Argives, and a thousand Argives brought by Hegesistratos fought on his side at the battle at Pallenis. Some say that he married the Argive woman when he was first in exile, others while he was in power.

9.19 Thucydides 1.20.1–2: Misconceptions about the Peisistratidai

Here, and in doc. 9.20, Thucydides corrects what he states are incorrect notions about the Peisistratidai. The Leokoreion (also at Thuc. 6.57.3; *Ath. Pol.* 18.3 (docs 9.30–31)) was a shrine to the three daughters of Leos, sacrificed at a time of famine or plague to save the city. This passage is the beginning of a section in which Thucydides criticises popular opinions about history and the work of his predecessors, and discusses his own methodology (Thuc. 1.20–22); see doc. 16.4.

1.20.1 These are the historical facts I have discovered, though it is difficult to believe every single piece of evidence about them. For men accept each other's accounts of things of old, even if they took place in their own country, equally uncritically. **2** For instance the majority of Athenians think that Hipparchos, who was killed by Harmodios and Aristogeiton, was tyrant, and do not know that Hippias was ruling as the eldest of Peisistratos' sons, and Hipparchos and Thessalos were his brothers, and Harmodios and Aristogeiton on that very day and on the spur of the moment, having suspected in some way that information had been laid before Hippias by their fellow conspirators, kept away from him as aware of the plot, but wishing to achieve something and run the risk before their arrest, killed Hipparchos when they came upon him as he was marshalling the Panathenaic procession near the place called the Leokoreion.

9.20 Thucydides 6.55.1–3: The Evidence for Hippias' Seniority

Thucydides uses the evidence of an altar and stele on the acropolis to argue against the misconception that Hipparchos was the elder brother. The altar was presumably a thanksgiving for liberation from the tyrants and the stele outlawed them.

6.55.1 That Hippias was the eldest and ruler I contend strongly as I know it by report more accurately than others do, and anyone might learn it from this point: for he appears to have been the only one of the legitimate (gnesioi) brothers who had children, as is shown by both the altar and the stele concerned with the injustice of the tyrants which stands on the Athenian acropolis, on which no child of Thessalos or Hipparchos is listed, but five of Hippias, who were born to him by Myrrhine daughter of Kallias, son of Hyperochides; for it was likely that the eldest would marry first. **2** And on the same stele he is listed first after his father, which is again not unnatural as he was the eldest son and the tyrant. **3** Nor does it seems reasonable to me that Hippias could have seized the tyranny easily and on the spur of the moment, if Hipparchos had been in power when he was killed, and Hippias attempted to establish himself that same day; but he was an object of fear to the citizens and of obedience to his mercenaries because of his previous habits and took control because his position was secure, not being at a loss as a younger brother would have been, who had not previously had any experience of government.

THE REIGN OF THE PEISISTRATIDAI

Thucydides, in the passage below, sets out to correct what he claims are mistaken views about the tyranny. It is clear that the rule of the Peisistratidai was acceptable to the majority, and Thucydides briefly dwells on the main themes of their civic programme of beautifying the city, their military success and their worship of the gods.

9.21 Thucydides 6.54.1–6: Thucydides' Judgement on the Peisistratidai

Some Athenians thought that Hipparchos was the elder brother (Thuc. 6.54.1). The 'inconspicuous manner' (Thuc. 6.54.4) in which Hipparchos insulted Harmodios was the slighting of Harmodios' sister, described at Thuc. 6.56.1–2 and *Ath. Pol.* 18.2 (docs 9.30–31). *Ath. Pol.* 16.4 mentions a 10 per cent tax (dekate) levied by Peisistratos; the Peisistratidai taxed at 5 per cent, perhaps a decrease as a result of the presumed discovery of silver at Laureion (Thuc. 6.54.5); certainly the introduction of the fine 'owl' coin series seems to indicate a greater wealth for the tyranny of the sons than that of Peisistratos (see doc. 9.12). The meaning of 'one of their own' is unclear (Thuc. 6.54.6); certainly the eponymous archonship was held by prominent members of other families (doc. 9.24), so supporters are presumably meant.

6.54.1 Aristogeiton and Harmodios' deed of daring was undertaken because of an incident concerning a love affair, and through a detailed description of it I will show that neither the other Greeks nor the Athenians themselves give an accurate account of their tyrants or their history. **2** After Peisistratos died, still tyrant despite his advanced age, it was not Hipparchos, as most people think, but Hippias, as the eldest, who was in power. Aristogeiton, one of the citizens and a man of middling rank, was the lover and possessor of the beautiful Harmodios, then in the prime of youth. **3** Harmodios was solicited by Hipparchos, son of Peisistratos. He was not won over and denounced him to Aristogeiton. Suffering the pains of love and fearful of the power of Hipparchos in case he might procure Harmodios by force, Aristogeiton immediately started plotting the downfall of the tyranny as far as was possible by someone in his position. **4** Meanwhile, after Hipparchos had again tried but got nowhere with Harmodios, he preferred to avoid violence and prepared in some inconspicuous manner, and as if unconnected with his actual motives, to insult Harmodios. **5** Hipparchos' manner of government was not burdensome to the majority, and he ruled without exciting hatred; and these tyrants practised virtue and sagacity to the greatest extent, for they exacted from the Athenians only a twentieth of their produce, beautified their city, prevailed in their wars and made sacrifices at the temples. **6** And in other respects this city continued to use the pre-existing laws, except in so far as they always made sure that one of their own people was in office.

9.22 [Aristotle] *Athenaion Politeia* 18.1: The Politician and the Aesthete

As with other tyrants, the Peisistratidai promoted culture and encouraged poets to come to Athens, fostering the development of poetry and the arts. The editing and establishing of the text of Homer's epics was ascribed to Peisistratos in antiquity; this has been both accepted and rejected by scholars; there are firmer grounds for accepting that Hipparchos organised the recitation of the Homeric epics at the Panathenaia ([Plato] *Hipparch*. 228b).

18.1 Hippias and Hipparchos were then in control of affairs owing to their positions and ages, but Hippias, being the elder and a natural politician and man of sense, was in charge of government. Hipparchos on the other hand was fond of amusement and engaged in love affairs and loved the arts; he was the one who brought the circle of Anacreon and Simonides and the other poets to Athens.

9.23 [Plato] *Hipparchos* 228c: Poets at the Court of the Peisistratidai

Hipparchos sent a pentekonter for Anacreon of Teos to bring him to Athens, and persuaded Simonides of Keos to be his continual associate by great payments and gifts.

9.24 *Inscriptiones Graecae* I³ 1031a: The Archon-List of 527/6–522/1

Miltiades is securely dated as archon in 524/3 BC and this serves to date the other archons in the list. While retaining the existing laws, the Peisistratidai, as Thucydides 6.54.6 states, ensured that 'one of their own people' held the public offices (doc. 9.21). Peisistratos, son of the tyrant Hippias, held the eponymous archonship (Thuc. 6.54.6–7; doc. 9.25) and the name Peisistratos can be restored here as the eponymous archon of 522/1. For 525/4 BC, Kleisthenes, leader of the Alkmeonidai and the reformer of 508 BC, is generally restored. The Alkmeonidai had gone into exile with Peisistratos' third attempt at the tyranny in 546 BC (doc. 9.14), and the sources state that they were in exile for the duration of the tyranny. So it is possible that the restoration here is incorrect and

Kleisthenes was not archon (or that it is *a* Kleisthenes but not Kleisthenes the reformer). The orthodox scholarly opinion since the discovery of this inscription is, however, that the Peisistratidai may have pursued a policy of reconciliation towards the Alkmeonidai and other aristocrats, with Kleisthenes holding the archonship in 525/4; the claim that they were in exile for the entire duration of the tyranny would then be false. At any rate the Alkmeonidai were certainly in exile again sometime after 514 BC. [Meiggs & Lewis 6C.]

527/6	[On]eto[r ...]
526/5	[H]ippias
525/4	[K]leisthen[es]
524/3	[M]iltiades
523/2	[Ka]lliades
522/1	[Peisi]strat[os]

9.25 Thucydides 6.54.6–7: Literary Evidence for the Archonship of Peisistratos

The altar of the 'Twelve Gods' was presumably for the Twelve Olympians; located in the agora, it was a place of refuge and supplication (see Hdt. 6.108.4). The archonship of Peisistratos, son of Hippias, can be dated to 522/1 but his name is heavily restored in this inscription. [Simonides 26b; *IG* I^2 761; Meiggs & Lewis 11; Friedländer 100; Page 240–41; Hansen 305.]

6.54.6 Those who held the Athenians' yearly archonship included Peisistratos, son of Hippias the tyrant, who had the name of his grandfather, and who as archon dedicated the altar of the twelve gods in the agora and that of Apollo in the Pythion. **7** Afterwards the Athenian people built an additional length to the altar in the agora and erased the altar's inscription; but the inscription of the altar in the Pythion even today still clearly says in faint letters:

> 'Peisistratos son of Hippias as a memorial of his archonship
> Erected this in the precinct of Pythian Apollo.'

9.26 *Inscriptions Graecae* I^3 948: Archaeological Evidence for the Archonship of Peisistratos

Thucydides 6.54.7 states that the Athenians 'erased' the inscription on the agora altar, and that the letters were 'faint' on the Pythian altar, but ever since its discovery it has been noted that the letters of this inscription belonging to the Pythian altar are clearly cut and easy to read. The letters must have been painted and Thucydides refers to the paint having faded and not having been touched up.

> Peisist[ratos s]on [of Hippias] as a memorial of his archonship
> Erected this in the precinct of Pythian Apollo.

9.27 Herodotos 6.103.1–4: The Philaidai and the Tyrants

Miltiades the Elder, of the clan (genos) of the Philaidai (Table III), had established an Athenian presence in the Chersonese, presumably with Peisistratos' agreement, as Athenians accompanied him there. He was succeeded as tyrant by his nephews Stesagoras and Miltiades the Younger.

Herodotos records a story that Kimon, the father of Miltiades the Younger, was murdered by the Peisistratidai, after being allowed to return by Peisistratos (cf. Hdt. 6.39.1). The fact that Miltiades the Younger was archon in 524/3 shortly after his father's 'murder' casts some doubt on Herodotos' story, especially since he was then sent officially to the Chersonese as tyrant. The dates of the three Olympic victories of Kimon were 536, 532 and 528, with his recall dated to 532; The context of this document is Hippias directing the Persians to land at Marathon (see doc. 11.8).

6.103.1 Miltiades' father Kimon, son of Stesagoras, had, it so happened, been banished from Athens by Peisistratos, son of Hippokrates. **2** While an exile Kimon won the prize at the Olympic games for the four-horse chariot race, and in winning this victory he carried off the same prize as Miltiades, his half-brother from the same mother. Later, at the next Olympic festival, he won with the same mares but waived the victory in Peisistratos' favour. **3** For handing over the victory Peisistratos allowed him to return home with safe conduct. He won at the next Olympic festival too, with the same mares, but was killed by Peisistratos' sons, after Peisistratos' death; they set men to ambush him and killed him at night outside the prytaneion. Kimon was buried outside Athens, on the other side of the road known as 'the one through the hollow'; right opposite him are buried those mares who won the three Olympic victories. **4** The mares of Euagoras of Sparta did the same, but they were the only ones. The elder of Kimon's sons, Stesagoras, was then living in the Chersonese with his uncle Miltiades, and the younger, Miltiades, who was named after Miltiades the founder of the Chersonese, with Kimon himself in Athens.

THE TYRANTS AND PUBLIC WORKS

The Athenian tyrants, like other Greek tyrants, were involved in public building projects (cf. docs 7.60–62); while these projects at Athens would not have created widespread employment, they would have been important for the tyrants' 'public image' (cf. Thuc. 6.54.5, doc. 9.21), and it is possible that the tyrants may have deliberately vied with each other in their public works.

9.28 Thucydides 2.15.3–5: The Enneakrounos, or 'Nine-Spouts'

Thucydides attributes the enneakrounos to 'the tyrants'; Pausanias 1.14.1 to Peisistratos. Black-figure vases of this period begin to depict Athenian women and slaves at fountains, indicating that the tyrants built several of these and that the fountain house was an important public amenity. Cf. Hdt. 6.137.3; Paus. 1.14.1. Other tyrants such as Theagenes (doc. 7.20) and Polykrates (doc. 7.60) also engaged in such works.

2.15.3 Before the time of Theseus the city comprised what is now the acropolis, together with the area below it, especially that facing south. **4** This is the proof: the temples of the other gods as well (as that of Athena) are on the acropolis and those outside it are generally situated in that part of the city, including the temples of Olympian Zeus and the Pythion and Earth (Ge) and Dionysos at Limnai (the 'marshy' quarter) ... The other ancient temples are also situated here. **5** Also the fountain, which is now called Enneakrounos ('Nine-Spouts'), since the tyrants built it like this, but which of old when the springs were visible was called Kallirrhoe ('Beautiful Stream'), used to be used for all purposes since it was so near, and from ancient times, as even today, it was customary to use the water before weddings and in other religious ceremonies.

9.29 [Plato] *Hipparchos* 229a–b; *Inscriptiones Graecae* I³ 1023: Hipparchos' 'Hermai'

Hipparchos set up hermai (sing.: hermes) throughout Attica, according to [Plato] *Hipparchos* 228c–229b, to educate the country Athenians, with each hermes having some moral maxim inscribed on one side, and a direction on the other to the effect that the hermes stood midway on the road between Athens and the relevant Attic deme. [**1–2:** [Plato] *Hipparch.* 229a–b; **3**: Friedländer 149; *LSAG* 75, 78n.35; Hansen 304; *IG* I³ 1023 (*IG* I² 837).]

1 'A reminder of Hipparchos: walk thinking just thoughts.'
2 'A reminder of Hipparchos: do not deceive a friend.'
3 'Bright Hermes in between Kephale and the city.'

THE ASSASSINATION OF HIPPARCHOS

Thucydides insists that the motive of the tyrannicides was not political but stemmed from a homoerotic love affair, when Harmodios' rejection of Hipparchos' advances led to the insulting treatment of Harmodios' sister. The assassination took place in 514/3, and four years later, in 511/10, the tyranny came to an end.

9.30 Thucydides 6.56.1–58.2: Thucydides on Hipparchos' Assassination

The context for Thucydides' digression on the tyrants is the investigation following the mutilation of the hermai in 415 BC, when the Athenians were suspicious that it was part of an attempt to overthrow the democracy. Thucydides describes the original plan for the assassination and what went wrong (cf. docs 9.19–21). According to Thucydides, Hippias was at the Kerameikos, outside the city walls, organising the procession: it was the potters' quarter and a cemetery. Harmodios' sister was to be a kanephoros, basket-bearer, in the Panathenaia: cf. doc. 3.61.

6.56.1 So Hipparchos, as he intended, insulted Harmodios for having refused his offer; first they summoned his sister, an unmarried girl, to come and carry a basket in a procession, and then they sent her away saying that they had not invited her in the first place because she was not fit to take part. **2** Harmodios took this badly, and Aristogeiton was even more incensed on his behalf. They had now arranged everything with those who were going to join with them in the deed, and were waiting for the Great Panathenaia, which was the only day on which those citizens who were to take part in the procession could gather in arms without arousing suspicion. They were to start, and the others immediately join in against the bodyguard. **3** For safety's sake the conspirators were few in number; for they hoped that, if they started the venture off, those who had no prior knowledge of the plot would use their weapons and choose to liberate themselves. **6.57.1** When the day of the festival arrived, Hippias was outside the city in what is called the Kerameikos with his bodyguard, arranging how each part of the procession should move forward, while Harmodios and Aristogeiton, already holding their daggers, proceeded to action. **2** When they saw one of their fellow conspirators talking to Hippias in a friendly manner (Hippias being approachable by everyone) they were afraid, thinking that their secret had been disclosed and that they were already on the point of being arrested. **3** They wanted first, if they could, to take revenge on the man who had wronged them and for whom they were risking everything. As they were they rushed inside the gates, came upon Hipparchos beside what is known as the Leokoreion, and immediately fell upon him rashly, one inspired by the anger of a lover and the other by insult, and struck and killed him. **4** The mob gathered, and Aristogeiton at that point got away from the bodyguard, but was afterwards captured and roughly treated; Harmodios was straightway killed on the spot. **6.58.1** When the news was brought to Hippias at the Kerameikos, he immediately proceeded not to the site of the incident but to the armed participants in the procession before they, being at a distance, perceived what had happened. He composed his countenance to give nothing away about the tragedy, pointed to a piece of ground and told them to move over there without their weapons. **2** They went over there thinking that he had something to say, and he told his mercenaries to seize the weapons, and at once picked out those whom he blamed and anyone who was found carrying a dagger; for it was usual to carry shields and spears in the procession.

9.31 [Aristotle] *Athenaion Politeia* 18.2–6: Hipparchos' Assassination

The account of the *Ath. Pol.* varies from that of Thucydides in several respects, with Thucydides' account doubtless to be preferred.

18.2 Thettalos was much younger and rash and insulting in his lifestyle, and it was from this that all their troubles started. He fell in love with Harmodios, but as he failed to obtain his friendship he could not contain his anger, but showed his bitterness in a number of ways and finally prevented Harmodios' sister from being a basket-carrier at the Panathenaia, as she was going to be, and cast some insult at Harmodios about being effeminate. Because of this provocation Harmodios and Aristogeiton perpetrated their deed, in which they had many accomplices. **3** During the Panathenaic festival, while they were lying in wait for Hippias on the acropolis (for Hippias happened to be the one welcoming the procession and Hipparchos the one starting it off), they saw one of their fellow conspirators go up to Hippias in a friendly manner and thought that he was revealing the secret. As they wanted to achieve something before being arrested, they went down and killed Hipparchos as he organised the procession near the Leokoreion, acting without waiting for the others and thus ruining the whole plot. **4** Harmodios was killed immediately by the bodyguard, while Aristogeiton was afterwards captured and tortured for a long period. Under torture he accused many who were of distinguished birth and friends of the tyrants. At first it was impossible to find any trace of the plot, but the story which is told, that Hippias made the participants in the procession stand away from their weapons and searched out those that had daggers, is not true; for at that point they did not carry arms in the procession, and it was not until later that the democracy instituted this. **5** Aristogeiton accused the friends of the tyrant, according to the democrats, on purpose, so the tyrants might act impiously and weaken themselves by killing innocent men who were their friends; others say that he did not make this up, but was actually disclosing his fellow conspirators. **6** And finally, as he was not able to die, do what he might, he stated that he would betray many others and persuaded Hippias to give him his right hand as a sign of good faith. As Aristogeiton took it, he taunted Hippias for having given his right hand to the murderer of his brother and so annoyed Hippias that he could not control his anger but drew his dagger and killed him.

THE TYRANNY BECOMES HARSHER

After Hipparchos' death the tyranny became oppressive; however, Hippias feared not popular unrest but the aristocracy. It is this period which laid the foundation for the Athenians' later conception of tyranny as harsh. The group of exiles, who wished to overthrow the tyranny in order to return to Attica, made their first attempt at Leipsydrion, failed there and then sought outside help. Herodotos focuses attention on the Alkmeonidai, while the *Ath. Pol.* notes that they were the leaders of the exiles. This leadership will have derived from their prominence in Athenian society and presumably their previous role as rivals to Peisistratos.

9.32 Thucydides 6.53.3, 59.1–2: The Harsh Tyranny of Hippias

There is no evidence as to who lost their lives: perhaps it was those who were considered to have been implicated in the assassination conspiracy.

6.53.3 For the people, as they knew by report that the tyranny of Peisistratos and his sons had become harsh at the end and, besides, that it was not put down by themselves and Harmodios but by the Spartans, were always afraid and suspicious of everything ... **6.59.1** In such a way, a lover's distress caused the beginning of Harmodios and Aristogeiton's plot and fear at the time their reckless venture. **2** Following this the tyranny became harsher for the Athenians, and Hippias was now frightened enough to kill many of the citizens, at the same time looking outside Athens for some chance of refuge should a revolution take place.

9.33 [Aristotle] *Athenaion Politeia* 19.1 : Hippias Is 'Hated by Everyone'

Compare *Ath. Pol.* 16.7 (doc. 9.16), where the tyranny is said to have become harsher after the death of Peisistratos. Nevertheless, it was not until after Marathon that the tyrants became especially hated and there was a party of Peisistratid supporters that remained in Athens after their expulsion (see doc. 10.9).

19.1 After this the tyranny became much harsher; for to avenge his brother Hippias killed and exiled many people and became mistrusted and hated by everyone.

9.34 Thucydides 6.59.3: Hippias Seeks a Connection with Persia

Hippias married his daughter to Aiantides of Lampsakos. This connection would give Hippias useful contacts with Persia (see doc. 9.39). Thucydides' comment 'though an Athenian' is out of context here and relates to the period after 451/0 BC when Perikles' citizenship law (doc. 1.36) made marriages between Athenians and non-Athenians unattractive. [Simonides 26a; Friedländer 138; Page 239–40; cf. Thuc. 6.59.2 (doc. 9.32).]

6.59.3 At any rate after this, though an Athenian, he gave his daughter Archedike to a Lampsakene, Aiantides, son of Hippokles tyrant of Lampsakos, realising that they had great influence with the Persian king Darius. Her grave is in Lampsakos and has this inscription:

'This dust covers Archedike daughter of Hippias,
A man who was greatest in Greece of those of his time.
Though her father, husband, brothers and sons were tyrants,
She was not given to unseemly arrogance.'

9.35 [Aristotle] *Athenaion Politeia* 19.2–3 : A Drinking Song about Leipsydrion

This skolion (drinking song) refers to one of several aristocratic attempts after 514 BC to oust the tyrants. Mounichia is a hill on the eastern side of the Piraeus, facing Phaleron Bay. As a result of the failure of the exiles at Leipsydrion the Alkmeonidai sought outside intervention (docs 9.36–38).

19.2 In about the fourth year after Hipparchos' death, affairs in the city were so bad that Hippias attempted to wall Mounichia, so he could move there; while he was doing this, he was expelled by Kleomenes, king of the Spartans, as oracles kept being given to the Lakonians to put an end to the tyranny for the following reason. **3** The exiles, of whom the Alkmeonidai had assumed the leadership, were by themselves unable to manage to bring about their return, but were always suffering defeats. Among their other unsuccessful attempts they walled Leipsydrion, a place in the country below Mount Parnes, where they were joined by some of the men from the city, but the tyrants besieged them and forced them to capitulate. As a result, after this disaster, they used to always sing the following in their drinking songs:

Alas! Leipsydrion, betrayer of comrades,
What men you have destroyed, brave
In war and of noble family,
Who then showed what their ancestors were like.

THE OVERTHROW OF THE TYRANNY BY THE SPARTANS

The Alkmeonidai sought outside assistance. They did this, according to the Athenians, by bribing the Pythian priestess; see doc. 10.1, where Kleisthenes was the person responsible. The Peisistratidai were able to call in outside help, and the Thessalians helped to defeat the first Spartan invasion, but were then defeated by Kleomenes. Though the Peisistratid domination of Athens ends here, the Spartans c. 505–501 proposed to restore Hippias (see docs 10.5, 6.59).

9.36 Herodotos 5.62.2–64.2: The Alkmeonidai Bribe the Pythia

Phaleron at this time was Athens' main port. Anchimolos, like other Spartans (except the kings) who died abroad, was buried where he fell (cf. doc. 6.18). The gymnasium at Kynosarges was across the Ilissos stream, south-west of the Olympieion, the temple of Olympian Zeus; the Pelargic (or Pelasgic) wall was the Mycenaean wall of the acropolis. At Hdt. 5.90.1 the Spartans, learning that the Pythia had been bribed, come to regret expelling the tyrants.

5.62.2 Then in their efforts to devise every scheme possible against the Peisistratidai, the Alkmeonidai got a contract from the Amphictyons to build the temple at Delphi, which is there now but was not then in existence. **3** As they had become wealthy and were of a family which had always been well regarded, the temple they completed was actually better than the plan, both in other respects and in the façade's being constructed of Parian marble, though it had been agreed that the temple was to be made of ordinary conglomerate. **5.63.1** The Athenians indeed maintain that, while these men were staying at Delphi, they bribed the Pythia to tell any Spartiates who came to consult the oracle either on private or public business to liberate Athens. **2** As the Spartans always received the same response, they sent Anchimolos, son of Aster, a distinguished citizen, with an army to drive the Peisistratidai out of Athens, although they shared strong ties of hospitality with them; they considered the divine injunction more important than human relationships. **3** They sent them by sea in transport ships. Anchimolos put in at Phaleron and disembarked his troops, while the Peisistratidai, who had already learned of this, summoned help from Thessaly, as there was an alliance between their two states. The Thessalians consented to their request and sent off a thousand cavalry and their king Kineas of Konde; when these allies arrived, the Peisistratidai devised the following plan: **4** they cleared the plain of Phaleron of all trees and crops and made the area fit for riding, and then sent a cavalry charge against the Spartans. It fell on them and destroyed many of the Spartans, including Anchimolos, driving the survivors back to their ships. That was the end of the first expedition from Sparta, and Anchimolos was buried at Alopeke in Attica, near the temple of Herakles at Kynosarges. **5.64.1** Later (511/10 BC), however, the Spartans dispatched a greater force against Athens, appointing King Kleomenes, the son of Anaxandridas, as the army's leader, and sending it this time not by sea but by land; **2** as they entered Attica the Thessalian cavalry were the first to engage with them, but were quickly overwhelmed, losing over forty of their men; the survivors immediately departed for Thessaly. When Kleomenes arrived at the city accompanied by those Athenians who wanted freedom, he besieged the tyrants, whom he had confined within the Pelargic wall.

9.37 Herodotos 5.65.1–5: The Peisistratidai Surrender

Herodotos discusses the ancestry of the Peisistratidai: they were descended from Neleus of Pylos (the most famous son of Neleus was Nestor the aged Homeric hero). Peisistratos obviously emphasised this heroic-age ancestry. For the Athenian colony at Sigeion, see doc. 2.18.

5.65.1 The Spartans would never have managed to dislodge the Peisistratidai at all (for they had not planned on a siege, and the Peisistratidai were well supplied with food and water) and after a few days' siege would have departed for Sparta; but at this point an incident fortuitously occurred which was unfortunate for the Peisistratidai, but of use to the Spartans, for the children of the Peisistratidai were captured as they were being conveyed out of the country. **2** As a result of this all their plans were thrown into confusion, and in return for the children they submitted on the conditions the Athenians wanted, that they should leave Attica in five days. **3** They afterwards departed to Sigeion on the river Skamander, after ruling the Athenians for thirty-six years. In origin they came from the men of Pylos and were descended from the sons of Neleus, from whom came Kodros and Melanthos, who in former times as incomers became kings of the Athenians. **4** For this reason Hippokrates gave his son Peisistratos the same name in memory of this, calling him after Peisistratos, the son of Nestor. **5** This was the way the Athenians were rid of their tyrants.

9.38 [Aristotle] *Athenaion Politeia* 19.4–6 : Delphic Money Pays the Spartans

The *Athenaion Politeia* alleges that the Alkmeonidai made money from contracting to build the temple of Apollo at Delphi, and used this money 'to pay for the Spartans' help'. Herodotos' account implies the opposite, that *because* the Alkmeonidai were wealthy they were able to complete the temple to grander specifications than necessary, and that while they were at Delphi, 'so the Athenians say', they took the opportunity to bribe the Pythian priestess. The *Athenaion Politeia* notes that the Athenian friendship with Argos was also a factor in the Spartans attacking Athens (see docs 9.9, 9.18): the Spartans and Argives were old enemies and Kleomenes mounted a successful campaign against the Argives (see doc. 6.77, cf. 7.4).

19.4 So, as they kept failing in all else, they contracted to build the temple at Delphi, and thus acquired plenty of money to pay for the Lakonians' help. The Pythia used always to command the Spartans, when they consulted the oracle, to liberate Athens, to the point where she persuaded the Spartiates, although they had ties of hospitality with the Peisistratidai; the friendship which existed between the Peisistratidai and the Argives played no less a part in the Spartans' decision. **5** So first of all they sent off Anchimolos with an army by sea. When he was defeated and killed, because the Thessalian Kineas came to the assistance with one thousand cavalry, they were so angry at what had happened that they sent Kleomenes the king with a larger army by land. When he had defeated the Thessalians' cavalry, which were preventing him from marching into Attica, he shut Hippias up within what is called the Pelargic Wall and began to besiege it with the help of the Athenians. **6** While the siege continued, the children of the Peisistratidai happened to be captured as they were trying to get to safety; when they had been caught, the Peisistratidai came to terms on condition that their children not be harmed and, after having five days to remove their possessions, they surrendered the acropolis to the Athenians in the archonship of Harpaktides (511/0). Their tyranny had lasted for about seventeen years after the death of their father, making, when added to the time their father had ruled, a total of forty-nine years altogether.

9.39 Thucydides 6.59.4: Hippias Goes to Persia

Hippias made use of his family connections, his brother Hegesistratos at Sigeion (doc. 2.18) and then Aiantides, his son-in-law (doc. 9.34), before making his way to Persia, which was to be the home of many Greek exiles (for example Demaratos and Themistokles: docs 6.75, 11.29). He accompanied Darius on his expedition to Marathon; from his flight in 511/0 BC to his return in 490 BC was roughly a twenty-year period (Thucydides has 'nineteen years').

6.59.4 When Hippias had been tyrant of the Athenians for three more years and his reign had been ended in the fourth year by the Spartans and Alkmeonid exiles, he left under safe conduct, going to Sigeion and then to Aiantides at Lampsakos, and from there to King Darius. From there he set out with the Persians on their expedition to Marathon nineteen years later as an old man.

THE CULT OF THE TYRANNICIDES

The role of Harmodios and Aristogeiton in killing Hipparchos found public expression in state cults, honours for their descendants and statues in the agora, and they came to be accepted as a symbol of freedom and democracy in the fifth century. By comparison, the role of the Alkmeonidai in organising the expulsion of the Peisistratidai with Spartan assistance found no equivalent public expression. The tyrannicides were buried in the Kerameikos, the resting place of other important Athenians.

9.40 [Aristotle] *Athenaion Politeia* 58.1: Harmodios and Aristogeiton as Heroes

The polemarch (war-archon) made offerings to those who had died for the state in war and was also responsible for the offerings to the tyrannicides as heroes; enagismata (sing.: enagisma, also enagismos) were sacrifices to chthonic deities and heroes.

58.1 The polemarch makes the sacrifices to Artemis Agrotera (the huntress) and to Enyalios and organises the funeral games for those that have died in war, and is responsible for making the offerings (enagismata) to Harmodios and Aristogeiton.

9.41 *Inscriptions of Graecae* I^3 131, lines 1–15 : Maintenance for the Tyrannicides' Descendants

This decree lists those who were entitled to dine in the Athenian prytaneion ('town hall') at the expense of the state and is dated c. 440–432. Victors at the four Pan-Hellenic festivals and other benefactors of the city of Athens, such as Kleon after his victory at Pylos (doc. 1.29), were granted perpetual dining rights; cf. doc. 1.47 for the same privilege for a benefactor at Cyzicus. [*IG* I^2 77.]

… was secretary. It was resolved by the boule and the people: (the tribe) Erechtheis held the prytany, … was secretary, […]thippos presided, […]ikles proposed the motion: there shall be public maintenance in the prytaneion, first for … in accordance with ancestral custom; then the descendants of Harm[odios and Aristogei]ton, whoever is nearest in descent, if there are no legitimate sons, shall have public maintenance, and anyone else who receives maintenance from the Athenians in accordance with what has been granted … whom Apollo has appointed while they expound (the oracles) … maintenance, and for the future whomever he appoints, these are also to have maintenance in the same way. And all those who have won a victory at the festivals at Olympia or Delphi or the Isthmus or Nemea or shall win a victory in future shall have public maintenance in the prytaneion and the other privileges in addition to public maintenance in accordance with what has been written on the stele in the prytaneion.

9.42 *Inscriptions of Graecae* I^3 502 : Inscription for the Statue Base of the Tyrannicides

A base for the statues of the tyrannicides has the inscription below. The first two lines of the following epigram were attributed in antiquity to Simonides, though Hipparchos, whom the tyrannicides killed, was in fact Simonides' patron (docs 9.22–23; Ael. *VH* 8.2). [Simonides 1; Friedländer 150; Page 186–89; Hansen 430.]

> A great light arose for the Athenians, when Aristogeiton
> And Harmodios slew Hipparchos;
> The two of them made their native land equal in laws.

DRINKING SONGS IN PRAISE OF THE TYRANNICIDES

Athenaeus *Deipnosophistae* 694c–696a collected several drinking songs (skolia), four of which (695a–b) concern the tyrannicides Harmodios and Aristogeiton, indicating that their deed was celebrated and honoured by future generations at private symposia (dinner parties).

9.43 Athenaeus *Deipnosophistae* 695a–b: Athens Attains Isonomia

At drinking parties, singers traditionally carried a branch of myrtle; it is not an indication that the tyrannicides hid their daggers in myrtle. Isonomia, the establishment of 'equality before the laws' or 'equal rights' (also doc. 9.46), was a result of Kleisthenes' political reforms, but in this drinking song the tyrannicides are credited with this by reason of their killing of Hipparchos.

In a branch of myrtle I shall bear my sword
Like Harmodios and Aristogeiton,
When the two of them slew the tyrant
And made Athens a city of equal rights.

9.44 Athenaeus *Deipnosophistae* 695b: The Tyrannicides in the Islands of the Blest

The tyrannicides are equated with the heroic warriors of the *Iliad*, some of whom after death dwelled in the Islands of the Blessed.

Dearest Harmodios, surely you are not dead;
They say that you are in the Islands of the Blessed,
Where dwells swift-footed Achilles
And, they say, brave Diomedes son of Tydeus.

9.45 Athenaeus *Deipnosophistae* 695b: The Murder of the Tyrant

In a branch of myrtle I shall bear my sword
Like Harmodios and Aristogeiton
When at Athena's festival
The two of them slew the tyrant Hipparchos.

9.46 Athenaeus *Deipnosophistae* 695b: Renown Throughout the World

You both will always have renown throughout the world,
Dearest Harmodios and Aristogeiton,
Because the two of them slew the tyrant
And made Athens a city of equal rights.

9.47 Aristophanes *Pelargoi* F444: The Song of Harmodios

Admetos was a Thessalian king (cf. doc. 4.71) and the Peisistratidai had Thessalian connections (docs 9.36, 9.38). Here one character is singing a Peisistratid song but is forced to change to one in favour of the tyrannicides. [Kassel & Austin F444; Kock F430; Schol. Ar. *Wasps* 1238a.]

One was singing the 'Tale of Admetos' to a myrtle-branch,
But the other forced him to sing the 'Song of Harmodios'.

10

KLEISTHENES THE REFORMER

While Solon may have inadvertently done much to lay the foundations of Athenian democracy (docs 8.22–23), it was the reformer Kleisthenes the Alkmeonid who established the democracy as such. After the overthrow of the tyranny of the Peisistratidai, Kleisthenes and another eupatrid, Isagoras, vied for power. Isagoras' election to the archonship in 508/7 BC must have been a great setback to Kleisthenes' political ambitions. The people had been overlooked in this rivalry between Isagoras and Kleisthenes, and so when Kleisthenes began losing out in the political struggle for influence among the aristocratic hetaireiai (political clubs), he countered with a masterstroke, gaining the support of the people by taking them into his own hetaireia (docs 10.1–2, 10.6). Not only were Kleisthenes' overtures welcomed, but the people were willing to besiege the Spartans on the acropolis rather than submit to Isagoras' planned oligarchy.

Isagoras persuaded the Spartan king Kleomenes to come to Athens to 'help in driving out the curse' (docs 10.2–3, 10.6). The events of the Kylonian coup were still hanging over the Alkmeonidai (docs 7.21–23), and Kleomenes drove out 700 families as accursed. His attempt to dissolve the boule, however, was met with resistance and the council refused to be disbanded (docs 10.3, 10.6). Kleomenes, Isagoras and his supporters seized the acropolis, where they were besieged by the people. Kleomenes had apparently come with only a limited force, obviously unprepared for a siege, and on the third day the Spartans were allowed to leave under a truce, but those with them were 'imprisoned under sentence of death' (doc. 10.3). Isagoras left with Kleomenes, but in 506 Kleomenes attempted to establish Isagoras as 'tyrant' at Athens. This attempt failed through the opposition of the Corinthians and of Demaratos, Kleomenes' fellow king (doc. 10.5; cf. 6.31). Later, c. 505–501, a Spartan proposal to restore Hippias was rejected by Sparta's allies (doc. 6.59). With the departure of Isagoras and the Spartans, and the return of Kleisthenes (still in 508/7), his reforms could proceed unhindered.

Kleisthenes' reforms resulted in the political system undergoing major changes: the four Ionian tribes were abolished and replaced by ten new ones, involving a division of Attica into trittyes and demes. Each new tribe was to contribute fifty members each year to the new boule, and the boule was increased in size, from 400 to 500 members. The main building blocks of the new organisation were the demes, the villages of Attica, and in the new system there were 140 demes. These were grouped into thirty units known as trittyes (sing.: trittys). There were ten city, ten inland and ten coastal trittyes (from the asty, mesogeios and paralia); the number of demes in each trittys varied, but three trittyes went to make up each tribe. Each deme elected a number of members to the boule and was, in fact, a miniature polis, with its own assembly and officials, which voted on deme issues.

The purpose of this reorganisation was to reorientate Athenian politics and weaken regional ties. Each citizen was a member of a tribe, which was made up of one city, one inland and one coastal trittys, and thus each tribe brought together Athenians from all over Attica into one group. Regional ties which were thought to be particularly strong received special attention (see doc. 10.16) and the tribes also obscured the origins of individual citizens: it was not possible to tell from the tribal affiliation whether someone was a new citizen or not. Kleisthenes encouraged the Athenians to call one another by their deme names, but was not quite successful in this, and while they adopted the deme appellation they still retained the patronymic (see doc. 10.7).

Kleisthenes also introduced the procedure of ostracism according to the *Athenaion Politeia*. The Athenians did not make use of this procedure for many years, and the first ostracism actually took place after the battle of Marathon (490 BC), in 488/7; the *Athenaion Politeia* (doc. 10.9) states in explanation that the Athenians only then gained the confidence to make use of the procedure, and that they had hitherto been lenient towards the 'friends of the tyrants', who were its first victims. There was a quorum of 6,000 citizen voters. The procedure involved a debate in the ekklesia in the sixth prytany of the year as to whether or not an ostracism would be held, with the ostracism, if voted for, actually held in the eighth prytany. This means that someone ostracised in a particular archonship was actually ostracised in the second half of the year, and sometimes, as with other dates known to fall in a particular half of an archon year, this is indicated by underlining the second year: for example, Hipparchos was ostracised in 487: 488/7. While it is possible that ostracism was introduced as a means of preventing those hostile to the demos from becoming too powerful, it is unlikely that it was advanced directly against the supporters of the tyranny. The people had not been opposed to the tyranny and had not effected its downfall, and an attempt to ostracise the tyrants' supporters would have created a struggle between them and Kleisthenes. Hipparchos, possibly Hippias' grandson, the first to be ostracised, had in fact been eponymous archon in 496/5, indicating that the friends of the tyrants were still influential in the 490s. It will only have been Hippias' involvement with the Persian invasion at Marathon that discredited the tyrants and their friends in the popular imagination.

The constitution established by Kleisthenes was definitely democratic in character, though the four Solonian census classes remained in use as the determinant of qualification to office. Further changes were to take place in the fifth century, notably the appointment of archons by a procedure using both direct election and lot on a tribal basis (doc. 10.9), extension of eligibility for the archonship to the zeugitai, Ephialtes' changes to the powers of the Areiopagos and the introduction of pay for jury service (see docs 1.24, 1.26, 12.26). Yet it was the reforms of Kleisthenes that made Athens a democracy and subsequent changes were only aimed at making the state even more democratic.

KLEISTHENES, ISAGORAS AND KLEOMENES

10.1 Herodotos 5.65.5–67.1: Kleisthenes Renames the Athenian Tribes

The deposition of the tyrants had been largely carried out through the machinations of the Alkmeonidai (though cf. docs 9.35, 11.10), but this was not enough to secure their political prominence: Isagoras, son of Teisander, was politically powerful after 510 BC. It was the political struggle between Isagoras and Kleisthenes which led directly to the transformation of Attica into a democratic state. Isagoras was archon in 508/7, and this election indicated his prominence; scholars generally agree that Kleisthenes had been archon in 525/4 BC. The reforms of Kleisthenes, since he was not archon, would have been introduced by him as a member of the ekklesia, backed by 'the people', who now supported him. The Ionian tribes were named after the four sons of Ion (5.66.2). Ajax would have been one of the 100 names submitted to the Delphic oracle (see doc. 10.7). He is termed 'a neighbour' because of his association with Salamis.

5.65.5 This is how the Athenians were delivered from the tyrants; whatever they did or experienced worthy of being narrated after they had been liberated, prior to Ionia's revolt from Darius and Aristagoras the Milesian's arrival in Athens to ask for their help, I shall now recount. **5.66.1** Athens, which had previously been great, now became greater still after her deliverance from the tyrants. Two men held sway in Athens, Kleisthenes, one of the Alkmeonidai, who was the one who according to report bribed the Pythia, and Isagoras, son of Teisander, a man of reputable family, but the origins of which I am unable to recount; however, his relatives sacrifice to Carian Zeus. **2** These men began a struggle for power, and Kleisthenes, who was getting worst of it, took the people into his hetaireia. And later on he changed the Athenians' four tribes into ten, getting rid of the names derived from the sons of Ion — Geleon, Aigikores, Argades and Hoples — and finding them the names of other heroes, who were Athenians, except Ajax; and he added him as a guest-friend (xenos), because he was a neighbour of the city and an ally. **5.67.1** I think that Kleisthenes in this was imitating his maternal grandfather Kleisthenes, tyrant of Sicyon.

10.2 Herodotos 5.69.1–70.2: Kleisthenes and Isagoras Struggle for Control

Despite Herodotos' account, Kleisthenes of Athens' motives in renaming the tribes were very different from those of Kleisthenes of Sicyon (doc. 7.5). Isagoras had learned the value of Spartan intervention, and the curse (docs 7.21–23) was brought up against the Alkmeonidai.

5.69.1 This is what the Sicyonian Kleisthenes did, and the Athenian Kleisthenes, being the son of Kleisthenes of Sicyon's daughter and named after him, seems to me to have imitated his namesake Kleisthenes because he despised the Ionians and did not want the Athenians and Ionians to have the same tribes. **2** So, as soon as he had added the Athenian people, which had previously been entirely left out of account, to his own party (moira), he renamed the tribes and increased their number. He created ten tribal leaders (phylarchs) instead of four, and divided the demes into ten and assigned them to the tribes. After winning the support of the people he was far more powerful than his opponents. **5.70.1** Having got the worst of it in his turn, Isagoras countered with this plan: he called for the help of Kleomenes the Spartan, who had been his guest-friend since the siege of the Peisistratidai. It was even rumoured that Kleomenes had had an affair with Isagoras' wife. **2** Kleomenes first sent a herald to Athens and expelled Kleisthenes and many other Athenians with him, calling them the 'accursed'. He did this at the suggestion of Isagoras, for the Alkmeonidai and their supporters were held to be guilty of this murder (of Kylon and his associates), while Isagoras and his friends had not been involved.

10.3 Herodotos 5.72.1–2, 5.72.4: Kleomenes Attempts to Interfere Again

As well as the Alkmeonidai, the 700 'accursed' families expelled from Athens may have included families which had marriage ties with or politically supported the Alkmeonidai. Isagoras was obviously seeking to destroy the influence of Kleisthenes in the state altogether. The boule – council – referred to here must have been the Solonian boule.

5.72.1 On the arrival of Kleomenes' order that Kleisthenes and the 'accursed' should be expelled, Kleisthenes himself withdrew from the city; but nonetheless Kleomenes then came to Athens with a small band of men, on arrival driving out, as under a curse, seven hundred Athenian families as Isagoras had suggested. After doing this he then attempted to dissolve the boule and entrust government to three hundred of Isagoras' adherents. **2** When the council resisted and refused to co-operate, Kleomenes, Isagoras and his supporters seized the acropolis. The rest of the Athenians, all of one mind, besieged them for two days; but on the third all the Spartans amongst them left the country under a truce … **4** The Athenians imprisoned the others under sentence of death, amongst them Timesitheos of Delphi, of whose prowess and courage I could recount great things.

10.4 Herodotos 5.73.1–3: A Proposed Alliance with Persia

The Athenian embassy to Persia was asked for earth and water as these were the usual symbols of submission to the Persians.

5.73.1 After their imprisonment these were executed, after which the Athenians recalled Kleisthenes and the seven hundred families expelled by Kleomenes and sent messengers to Sardis, as they wished to make an alliance with the Persians; for they knew that they had made enemies of the Spartans and Kleomenes. **2** When the messengers arrived at Sardis and spoke as they had been instructed, Artaphernes son of Hystaspes, viceroy (hyparchos) of Sardis, inquired who these men were and what part of the world they inhabited who sought the Persians as allies; when he learned this he gave the messengers this pointed reply: if the Athenians gave King Darius earth and water, he would conclude an alliance with them, but, if they did not, then he bade them depart. **3** The messengers, on their own responsibility, said they would do so, as they wanted to make the alliance. But when they returned home, they were severely blamed on this account.

10.5 Herodotos 5.74.1–76: The Return of Kleomenes

Kleomenes' second expedition to Athens is generally dated to 506/5 BC, but the campaigning season of 507/6, the year after his previous expedition, is more likely; clearly he was unhappy at his ignominious defeat in 508/7. The Spartans not only took their allies with them (the defection of the Corinthians and Demaratos' support of them led to the aborting of the attack) but arranged for the Boeotians and Chalkidians to attack on two other fronts.

5.74.1 Kleomenes felt that he had been treated insultingly by the Athenians in both word and deed and started collecting an army from the whole Peloponnese, without saying why he was collecting it, as he wanted to take vengeance on the Athenian people and establish Isagoras as tyrant; Isagoras had escaped from the acropolis with him. **2** So, while Kleomenes marched to Eleusis with a large force, the Boeotians by a preconcerted plan seized Oinoe and Hysiai, the furthermost villages in Attica, and the Chalkidians from the other side attacked and pillaged the Attic countryside. Although they were being attacked from both sides, the Athenians decided to put off dealing with the Boeotians and Chalkidians till later, and made a stand against the Spartans who were at Eleusis. **5.75.1** But when the two armies were just on the point of conflict, the Corinthians were the first to deliberate, coming to the conclusion that they were not acting rightly, and changed their minds and left, followed by Demaratos son of Ariston, who was king of the Spartiates and had jointly led out the expedition from Sparta, and who had not previously had a disagreement with Kleomenes. (**5.75.2**: *The Spartans thereupon make a law that both kings may not accompany the army.*) **5.75.3** At this point, when the rest of the allies at Eleusis saw that the Spartans' kings were not in agreement and that the Corinthians had abandoned their post, they also withdrew. **5.76** This was the fourth time that the Dorians had come to Attica, twice invading as an act of war and twice for the good of the Athenian populace: the first occasion was when they founded Megara (this expedition is correctly dated to the time when Kodros was king of the Athenians), the second and third were when they came from Sparta to expel the Peisistratidai, and the fourth was this present occasion when Kleomenes led the Peloponnesians and invaded as far as Eleusis; this then was the fourth time the Spartans entered Attica.

10.6 [Aristotle] *Athenaion Politeia* 20.1–5: Kleisthenes, Isagoras and Kleomenes

Herodotos' statement (doc. 10.1) that Kleisthenes took the people into his hetaireia is more specific than the *Athenaion Politeia* 20.1, which states that he 'brought over the people to his side'.

20.1 After the tyranny had been overthrown, Isagoras, son of Teisander, who had been a friend of the tyrants, and Kleisthenes, of the family of the Alkmeonidai, were political rivals. As Kleisthenes was getting the worst of it from the hetaireiai he brought the people over to his side by promising to hand the state over to the populace. **2** Isagoras, who was losing out in the power struggle, then called again for the help of Kleomenes, with whom he had ties of hospitality, and persuaded him to join in driving out the curse, since the Alkmeonidai were thought to belong to the 'accursed'. **3** Kleisthenes secretly left the country, and Kleomenes arrived with a few men and expelled 700 Athenian families as under a curse; after doing this he attempted to dissolve the boule, and make Isagoras with 300 of his friends masters of the city. However, when the council resisted and the populace gathered in force, the supporters of Kleomenes and Isagoras fled to the acropolis and the people settled down and besieged them for two days, but on the third allowed Kleomenes and all those with him to leave under a truce, and recalled Kleisthenes and the other exiles. **4** Once the people had gained control of affairs, Kleisthenes became their leader and champion of the people. The Alkmeonidai had been primarily responsible for the expulsion of the tyrants and had consistently opposed them for most of the time. **5** Even before the Alkmeonidai Kedon had made an attack on the tyrants, and for this reason he too was celebrated in drinking songs:

> 'Pour in honour of Kedon as well, steward, don't forget him,
> If it is right to drink a toast to courageous men.'

TRIBES, BOULE AND STRATEGIA

10.7 [Aristotle] *Athenaion Politeia* 21.1–6: Kleisthenes' Reforms

In this passage, crucial for an understanding of Kleisthenes, the *Athenaion Politeia* deals with several of his reforms. The names and official order of the ten new tribes, which replaced the old four Ionian tribes of Attica, were (modern scholars give each tribe a Roman numeral): Erechtheis (I), Aigeis (II), Pandionis (III), Leontis (IV), Akamantis (V), Oineis (VI), Kekropis (VII), Hippothontis (VIII), Aiantis (IX), Antiochis (X). To inquire into an individual's citizenship background was now no longer feasible through tribes and to be a member of a tribe did not mean that one's ancestors had always been citizens. Each tribal contingent to the boule held a particular prytany, one-tenth of the year; these fifty members were known as prytaneis during their term of office. Newly enfranchised citizens of non-Athenian background presumably had fathers with foreign names, hence Kleisthenes wanted the demesmen to address each other not by the formula, for example, 'Aristeides, son of Lysimachos', but by the formula 'Aristeides, of the deme Alopeke'.

21.1 So for these reasons the people put their trust in Kleisthenes. Then, as leader of the populace in the fourth year after the overthrow of the tyrants, in the archonship of Isagoras (508/7 BC), **2** he first of all assigned everyone to ten tribes instead of four, his aim being to mix them up, so that more might have a share in the constitution; from which comes the saying 'Don't investigate by tribes' to those wishing to inquire into family backgrounds. **3** Then he made the council (boule) instead of four hundred, fifty from each tribe; previously there were one hundred (from each tribe). He did not organise them into twelve tribes because he wished to avoid dividing them according to the pre-existing trittyes; for the four tribes consisted of twelve trittyes, with the result that he would not have succeeded in mixing up the population. **4** He also divided the country by demes into thirty parts, ten of them from the city area (asty), ten from the coast (paralia) and ten from the inland region (mesogeios), and he named these trittyes and assigned three by lot to each tribe, so that each tribe would have territory in all three regions. And he made those living in each of the demes fellow demesmen, so that they should not address each other by their fathers' names and thus show up the new citizens, but would use the names of their demes; this is the reason why the Athenians call one another by their demes. **5** He also instituted demarchs, who had the same responsibilities as the former naukraroi; for he created the demes to replace the naukrarioi. He named some of the demes after their localities and others after their founders, for not all of them were still connected with their localities. **6** But he allowed everyone to retain their clans, phratries and priesthoods according to ancestral custom. He assigned to the tribes ten eponymous heroes, whom the Pythia chose out of the one hundred founders (archegetai) who had been pre-selected.

10.8 [Aristotle] *Athenaion Politeia* 22.1–2: The Oath of the Boule and the Strategia

Kleisthenes' reforms certainly made the Athenian politeia (constitution) 'more democratic' than it had been before; Solon's constitution was timocratic, with democratic elements. The statement here that the tyrants did away with 'some of Solon's laws' contradicts the statements of other sources, including the *Ath. Pol.* 16.8 itself (docs 9.16, cf. 8.31–32). The oath of the boule was introduced in the archonship of Hermokreon (501/0 BC); and another change after Kleithenes' reforms was the introduction of a board of ten strategoi (generals) in 501/0 BC. Each tribe now elected a strategos, and fought as a military unit.

22.1 Following these reforms, the constitution was far more democratic than that of Solon; for Solon's laws had been forgotten under the tyranny through lack of use, and Kleisthenes had made other new ones with the aim of winning popular support, amongst which the law concerning ostracism was enacted. **2** First of all, in the fifth year after these had been established, in the archonship of Hermokreon (501/0), they imposed on the boule of five hundred the oath which they still swear even today. Then they began electing the generals by tribes, one from each tribe, though the polemarch was in command of the whole army.

OSTRACISM

The Athenians employed ostracism in the fifth century to send certain political figures into exile for ten years. These retained control of their property in Attica, and at the end of the ten years could return. A quorum (minimum number of participants) was required for an ostracism, and an ostracism could take place once a year. Each of the voters wrote on one ostrakon (pl.: ostraka), a piece of pottery, the name of the candidate whom they wished to ostracise, usually by scratching with an instrument; only a handful are painted, but painted ostraka are less likely to have survived (for example doc. 10.14.xii). Numbers of ostraka have been discovered in the Agora, on the north slope of the acropolis and in the Kerameikos. The actual voting was termed an ostrakophoria.

10.9 [Aristotle] *Athenaion Politeia* 22.3–8: The *Athenaion Politeia* on Ostracism

There is a discrepancy between a Kleisthenic date for the introduction of ostracism and its first use, nearly two decades later. According to the *Athenaion Politeia*, the law of ostracism was specifically introduced by Kleisthenes to drive out Hipparchos, son of Charmos, but it was not until 488/7 BC that the Athenians in fact first made use of ostracism. The recall of the ostracised, so that they could assist against Xerxes' forthcoming invasion, is also found in the 'Themistokles Decree' (doc. 11.35).

22.3 In the twelfth year after this, in the archonship of Phainippos (490/89 BC), they won the battle of Marathon, and after waiting two years after the victory, when the people were already more confident, they then (487 BC) first used the law concerning ostracism, which was enacted because of suspicion of men in positions of power, because Peisistratos, from being a popular leader and general, had set himself up as tyrant. **4** The first man to be ostracised (487 BC) was one of his relatives, Hipparchos, son of Charmos of Kollytos, on whose account in particular Kleisthenes had made the law, as he wanted to drive him out. For the Athenians, employing the tolerance characteristic of a democracy, allowed those friends of the tyrants who had not taken part in their crimes during the disorders to continue living in the city; of these Hipparchos was leader and champion. **5** In the year immediately following, in the archonship of Telesinos (487/6 BC), for the first time after the tyranny, they appointed by lot the nine archons by tribes from the 500 pre-selected by the demesmen; previous ones had all been elected; and Megakles, son of Hippokrates of Alopeke, was ostracised. **6** So for three years they continued to ostracise the friends of the tyrants, on whose account the law was enacted, but after that in the fourth year they started removing anyone else who appeared too powerful; the first of those unconnected with the tyranny to be ostracised was Xanthippos, son of Ariphron. **7** In the third year after that, when the mines at Maroneia were found (483/2 BC), ... Aristeides, son of Lysimachos, was ostracised. **8** But three years later, in the archonship of Hypsichides (481/0 BC), they recalled all those who had been ostracised, because of Xerxes' expedition; and for the future they resolved that anyone who was ostracised must not live within the limits of Geraistos and Skyllaion, or else they would entirely lose all citizen rights.

10.10 [Aristotle] *Athenaion Politeia* 43.5: The Date When Ostracism Was Decided

The *Athenaion Politeia* is describing the situation in the second half of the fourth century BC, which is generally assumed to apply also to the fifth century. In the sixth prytany of the year a vote about whether to hold an ostracism was taken, and, if there was support for this, the actual procedure took place in the eighth prytany (see doc. 10.11).

43.5 In the sixth prytany, in addition to the matters already mentioned, they take a vote concerning ostracism, whether an ostracism should be held or not, and hear complaints about informers (sykophantai), both Athenians and metics, up to three of each, and against anyone who has made a promise to the people but failed to keep it.

10.11 Philochoros *FGH* 328 F30: Philochoros on Ostracism

There is disagreement in the ancient sources about the number of votes required for an individual to be ostracised; Philochoros (and Pollux 8.19–20) has 6,000 votes required against an individual, while Plut. *Arist*. 7.6 (doc. 10.12) has a quorum of 6,000 in total, which seems more plausible; the individual who received most of the 6,000 votes would be ostracised.

The method of ostracism: Philochoros explains ostracism in his third book, writing as follows: 'Ostracism was like this; the people took a preliminary vote before the eighth prytany, to decide whether to hold an ostracism. When it was resolved to do so, the agora was fenced with planks, and ten entrances were left, through which they entered by tribes and deposited their ostraka, inscription side down; the nine archons and the boule presided. When the ostraka had been counted up, whoever had received the most and not less than six thousand had to settle his obligations regarding lawsuits in which he was a prosecutor or defendant within ten days and leave the city for ten years (but afterwards it became five), during which he could receive the income from his property, but not come any closer than Geraistos, the promontory of Euboea. Hyperbolos was the only disreputable man to be ostracised because of his depraved character, not on suspicion of aiming at tyranny; after him the custom was stopped. It had begun when Kleisthenes was passing laws, when he did away with the tyrants and wanted to expel their friends as well.'

10.12 Plutarch *Aristeides* 7.1–8: Aristeides 'the Just' Is Ostracised

While the story below is obviously an invention to illustrate Aristeides' character, it does provide support for the fact that the illiterate – who would have comprised the bulk of Athens' citizen population – participated in ostracisms.

7.1 So Aristeides at first found that he was loved because of his surname, but later envied, especially when Themistokles started spreading around the rumour to the people that Aristeides had done away with the law courts by his judging and deciding everything and that, without anyone noticing, he had made himself sole ruler, without a bodyguard; and the people, proud because of their victory and thinking nothing too great for them, already found it hard to bear any name which had a reputation above the ordinary, **2** and they came together into the city from all sides and ostracised Aristeides, giving their jealousy of his reputation the name of fear of a tyranny. For banishment by ostracism was not a punishment for wickedness, but it was called for the sake of appearances the means of lowering and curtailing pride and power which had become too difficult to bear. In fact it was a humane way of relieving jealousy, which thus directed its malignant wish to cause harm, not into doing anything fatal, but into getting the person to change his residence for ten years. **3** And when ignoble and base men started being subjected to the practice, they stopped it, Hyperbolos being the last one to be banished by ostracism. The story is that Hyperbolos was ostracised for the following reason: Alkibiades and Nikias, the most powerful men in the city, were at odds. **4** So when the people were about to carry out an ostracism and were clearly going to write one or the other, they came to terms with each other and combined their two parties into one, and caused the ostracism of Hyperbolos. The people, incensed at this, left it off completely as a practice which had been abused and degraded, and abolished it. **5** What happened, to give a general account, was as follows. Each man took an ostrakon and wrote on it the name of the citizen he wished to get rid of, and brought it to a place in the agora which had been fenced round in a circle with railings. **6** The archons first counted up the total number of the ostraka there; if there were less than six thousand voters, the ostracism was invalid; then they sorted each of the names separately, and proclaimed the man whose name was written by the most people banished for ten years, but able to receive the income from his property. **7** So when the ostraka were being inscribed, it is said that one of the illiterate, a complete rustic, handed his ostrakon to Aristeides as one of the crowd, and requested him to write 'Aristeides' on it. He was surprised and inquired what harm Aristeides had ever done him. 'None,' was the answer, 'I don't even know the fellow, but I'm tired of hearing him called "the Just" everywhere.' **8** When Aristeides heard this he said nothing, but inscribed his name on the ostrakon and gave it back.

10.13 Scholiast to Aristophanes *Knights* 855 : Ostrakinda, A Children's Game

Here Aristophanes is playing on words. That individuals had to have 6,000 votes against them is almost certainly incorrect (cf. doc. 10.11).

Ar. *Knights*: 855: And if you are indignant and look to play 'ostrakinda'.

Scholiast: Ostrakinda is the name of a children's game. He means to say should you wish him to be ostracised. The method of ostracism was like this: the people voted to hold an ostracism, and, when it was resolved, the agora was fenced with boards and ten entrances left. They entered through these by tribes and deposited the ostrakon, after placing their inscription on it. The archons and boule presided. When six thousand had been counted up (there could be more than this but not less), that man had to leave the city in ten days; if there were not six thousand, he was not banished. Not only the Athenians used to hold ostracisms, but also the Argives and Milesians and Megarians. Nearly all the most accomplished men were ostracised — Aristeides, Kimon, Themistokles, Thucydides (son of Melesias) and Alkibiades.

10.14 Ostraka: Examples of Individual Ostraka

i. Lang 134, no. 1065. An elegiac couplet. There are difficulties of interpretation: the voter perhaps regarded Xanthippos, Perikles' father, as 'accursed' due to his connection with the Alkmeonidai through his wife (see doc. 13.4); alternatively and more probably, he believed that all the leaders were accursed.

> This ostrakon says that Xanthippos, son of Ariphron,
> Does most wrong of the accursed leaders.

ii. Lang 36, no. 34: a more educated writer has helped out by adding 'son of Lysimachos' at the bottom.

Aristeides	(correctly spelled)
son of Lysi ...	(left incomplete and crossed out)
of Alopeke	(crossed out)
son of Lysimachos	(correctly spelled)

iii. Lang 138, no. 1097.

Vengeance on Hippokrates!

iv. Several of the Kerameikos ostraka have 'Kallias the Mede' (ie, Persian): this Kallias is thought to be the 'friend of the tyrants' ostracised in 486/5 (doc. 10.9).

Kallias the Mede

v. Lang 33, no. 14. Only five ostraka with the name of Alkibiades, son of Kleinias, are attested in the agora and none elsewhere.

Alkibiades
son of Kleinias

vi. Lang 98, no. 651. From the foot of a black-glazed skyphos vase, and hence presumably the ostrakon of one of the more well-to-do citizens. Perikles was never ostracised, though he must on a number of occasions have been a candidate at ostrakophoriai. This ostrakon may date to the ostrakophoria that he is said to have brought about to get rid of his rival Thucydides son of Melesias in 444/3 (Plut. *Per.* 14.3; doc. 12.27).

Perikles
son of Xanthippos

vii. Lang 116, no. 841. Ostraka to the number of 386 bearing Themistokles' name have been found in the agora and 1893 elsewhere. While he was actually ostracised in the late 470s, the large numbers of ostraka bearing his name found in the agora, and perhaps those from the Kerameikos, may possibly come from the ostrakophoriai of the 480s. This, the rim and neck of a pithos, was the largest ostrakon found in the agora, weighing 522.5 grams.

For Themistokles
son of Neokles
of Phrearrioi

viii. Lang 94, no. 630. From the wall of a coarse unglazed pot; the fact that Megakles' patronymic is inscribed as son of Hippokartes rather than son of Hippokrates may imply an uneducated writer. Megakles, according to the *Ath. Pol.* 22.5 (doc. 10.9), was the second friend of the tyrants to be ostracised and his ostrakophoria took place in 486 BC.

[Me]gak[les]
[son of Hip]pokar[tes]

ix. Lang 89, no. 592. From a roof tile with black glaze, incised on the glazed side. Kimon was probably ostracised in 461 (doc. 12.11), after the Ithome debacle.

Kimon
son of Miltiades

x. Lang 32, no. 10. From the knob of a large black-glazed lid. The elder Alkibiades had the same name, patronymic and demotic as his grandson Alkibiades the younger and was ostracised, possibly in 460 and perhaps for the same reason as Kimon.

[Alkibi]ades son of K[leinias]
[of Skamb]o<n>i<d>ai

xi. Lang 133, no. 1051. From a tile with a dull black glaze on its upper surface, incised through the glaze. Thucydides, son of Melesias was ostracised in 443 BC, after setting himself up as a champion of the aristocracy and political rival to Perikles (see doc. 12.27).

For [Thucy]dides
[son of Mele]sias

xii. Lang 64, no. 308; 418/7 BC.

Hyperbolos
son of Antiphanes

10.15 Aristotle *Politics* 1275b34–38: Citizenship Extended to Foreigners and Slaves

Kleisthenes gave Athenian citizenship to many metics 'both foreigners and slaves'. The *Ath. Pol.* 13.5 (doc. 9.2) notes that after the tyranny many who were not of pure Athenian descent, and who had supported Peisistratos and his sons, were disenfranchised. Kleisthenes gained their support by granting them citizenship. The slaves referred to by Aristotle are presumably manumitted slaves or their descendants; manumitted slaves received the status of metics. The foreigners would have been metics who came to Attica of their own free will.

1275b34 But perhaps there is even more of a difficulty here, regarding those who have obtained a share in the citizenship because change has taken place, for example Kleisthenes' actions at Athens after the expulsion of the tyrants; for he enrolled into the tribes a large number of metics, both foreigners and slaves. The doubt in respect of them is not who became citizens, but whether they are so unjustly or justly.

10.16 Aristotle *Politics* 1319b19–27: Kleisthenes Strengthens the Democracy

Aristotle considered as a characteristic of extreme democracy the policy of increasing the number of tribes and phratries (brotherhoods), and the incorporation of private religious rites into public ones.

1319b19 And there are also further practices like these which are useful with regard to this kind of democracy, which Kleisthenes employed in Athens when he wished to strengthen the democracy, like those who established democratic rule at Cyrene. For other tribes and phratries should be created, more than before, and private religious rites should be channelled into a few public ones, and everything should be contrived so that everyone mixes in with each other and former intimacies are dissolved.

DEMES AND TRITTYES

Attica's territory was divided into thirty trittyes under Kleisthenes' reforms, with ten city trittyes, ten inland trittyes and ten coastal trittyes (sing.: trittys). Each trittys was made up of one but generally more demes, with a deme generally being one village or town and its surrounding territory. There were 140 demes, and the number of demes per trittys varied. Deme membership was hereditary, and all Athenians remained registered in the deme in which their ancestor in the time of Kleisthenes had been enrolled. The most important duty of the demes was the registration of its members, the demotai, especially after Perikles' citizenship law of 451/0 BC; the list of demotai in each deme constituted a record of Athenian citizens (doc. 1.38). The main purpose of the system of demes and trittyes was to undermine regional loyalties.

10.17 *Inscriptiones Graecae* I³ 1127, 1131: Trittys Markers

The evidence for the names of trittyes (eighteen of the thirty names are known and several other possible identifications have been made) comes largely from fifteen trittys markers found in Athens and the Piraeus. They do not actually mark boundaries between trittyes; rather, they mark points where citizens would assemble when called up for military service. Seating arrangements on the Pnyx, however, were not by tribe or trittyes, but were random.

1127: *A Trittys Marker (Paianieis — Myrrhinousioi)*

Mid-fifth century; found in the Piraeus. Myrrhinousioi is the coastal trittys and Paianieis the inland trittys of the tribe Pandionis (III). [*IG* I² 898; Traill 1986, 102, no. 12.]

> Here the tri/ttys Pai/anieis en/ds, and the trit/tys My/rrhinousioi begins.

1131: *A Tribe and Trittys Marker*

Mid-fifth century; found in the Piraeus. Tetrapoleis was the coastal trittys of Aiantis (IX); Cholargeis was the city trittys of Akamantis (V). [*IG* I² 900; Traill 1986, 103, no. 13.]

> Here the tribe / Aiantis ends, / and the trittys T/etrapoleis, and the tribe Akama/ntis beg/ins, and the trittys / Cholargeis.

10.18 *Agora* XV.38, lines 1–77: Catalogue of the Prytaneis of Tribe Aigeis (II)

A deme provided members to the Council (boule) according to the population of that deme. This means that there were quotas for the deme, which are called bouleutic quotas; they are assumed to have been set by Kleisthenes. Each deme was responsible for sending a certain number of men as its share of the fifty for its tribe to the Council. The bouleutic and prytany lists provide evidence for how many members a particular deme sent to the boule. In the prytany list of Aigeis (II) below, there are four names under the heading of the deme Gargettos, indicating that this deme elected four members to the boule in 341/0 BC. City trittys (Kollyteis), demes: Kollytos, Kolonos, Bate, Upper and Lower Ankyle, Erikeia, Hestiaia, Otryne, Ikarion, Plotheia; Inland trittys (Gargettioi), demes: Gargettos, Erchia, Philaidai, Ionidai, Kydantidai; Coastal trittys (Halaieis), demes: Halai Araphenides, Teithras, Phegaia, Araphen, Myrrhinoutta, Diomeia; note that there are two pairs of brothers serving as prytaneis. For these demes, see Map IV: note that the location of Otryne, one of the city demes, is unknown. [*IG* II^2 1749.]

The prytaneis of Aigeis, who were crowned by the boule and the people in the archonship of Nikomachos (341/0) because of their virtue and justice, dedicated (this).

Column 1:

ERCHIA
Tharrias son of Tharrias
Kydias son of Lysikrates
Chaireas son of Paramythos
[Ph]ylarchos son of Paramythos
Xenokl[e]s son of Kallias
Polykleid[e]s son of Kallistratos
GA[RG]ETTOS
Diodoros son of Philokles
Meixias son of Hegesias
Smikrias son of Philokedes
Ar[e]sias son of Pausias
PHILAIDAI
Dionysios son of Hephaistion
Euthykles son of Ameinias
Euthydikos son of Ameinias
[K]YDANTIDAI
Pythion son of Aischronides
Demostratos son of [D]emost[r]atos
IONIDAI
Melieus son of Il[i]oneus

Column 2:

IKARION
Timokritos son of Timokrates
Aristophanes son of Eukleides
Archenautes son of Archenautes
Eraton son of Eration
[A]rignotos son of Babyrias
HESTIAIA
Poseidippos son of Kallikrates
BATE
Lysistratos son of Polyeuktos
FROM KOLONOS
Kalliphanes son of Kallikles
Theages
KOLLYTOS
Chairephon son of Thrason
Alexis son of Sosiades
Pherekrates son of Philokrates
PLOTHEIA
Chairias son of Chairias
OTRYNE
Philinos son of Theodoros
ERIKEIA
Epameinon son of Epainetos

Column 3:

HALAI
Lysimachos son of Lysipolis
Eubios son of Autosthenes
Apollodoros son of Archias
Eunostides son of Theophantos
Kallimedes son of Archemachos
TEITHRAS
Theomnestos
Theodoros son of Theognis
ARAPHEN
Elpinos son of Sosigenes
Kallimachos son of Mnesitheios
FROM MYRRINOUTTA
Theophilos

Demosthenes son of Demopho[n]
Demophilos son of Demokles
Ka[l]listratos
Prokleides son of Proxenides
PHEGAIA
Akeratos son of Archedemos

FROM ANKYLE
Eubios son of Eubiotos
DIOMEIA
Dorotheos son of Theodoros
FROM ANKYLE
Melesippos son of Melesias

71 [Th]arrias of Erchia proposed the motion: that the tribesmen should decree, that since Poseidippos of Hestiaia, the treasurer (tamias) of the tribe, had performed his duties for the tribesmen well and justly and conducted on behalf of the prytaneis all the sacrifices which had to be made, he should be commended for his virtue and justice regarding the prytaneis and be crowned with a crown of olive.

10.19 *Inscriptiones Graecae* I³ 258: The Finances of the Deme Plotheia, *c.* 420 BC

The deme Plotheia of the city trittys of Aigeis (II) had a bouleutic quota of one (that is, it elected one person to the boule), as doc. 10.18 indicates, and thus was one of the smallest demes. This is a decree of the deme assembly of the Plotheians. Lines 2–10 list the 'capital' of the deme; the capital itself is not to be spent, but rather the interest on each of the sums listed is to be utilised for the purpose decreed: the demarch and two treasurers have funds, and money is put aside for five festivals (the Herakleion, Aphrodisia, Anakia, Apollonia, Pandia) and an 'immunity' fund. In lines 30–31 the Plotheians make provision for participating in sacrifices with the Athenians as a whole. [*IG* I² 1172.]

Capital:
For the demarch 1,000 drachmas
For the two treasurers for the hiera throughout the year 5,000 drachmas
For the Herakleion 7,000 drachmas
For the Aphrodisia 1,200 drachmas
For the Anakia 1,200 drachmas
For the immunity 5,000 drachmas
For the Apollonia 1,100 drachmas
For the Pandia 600 drachmas
Of leases 134 drachmas and 2 ½ obols.

It was resolved by the Plotheians: Aristotimos proposed the motion; that the officials capable of handling the money are to be elected by lot for each office, and these are to look after the money for the Plotheians; concerning whatever is decreed they are to assign loan or interest in accordance with the decree loaning and exacting, and as much as is lent each year they are to lend to whomever gives most interest, and who persuades the officials who lend the money either by security or by giving sureties. And from both the interest and the leases, instead of purchases from the capital or what comes in from income, they are to sacrifice the hiera at the common festivals for the Plotheians and for the Athenians on behalf of the community of the Plotheians and for the quadrennial festivals. And for the other sacrifices, wherever it is necessary for all the Plotheians to pay money for the sacrifices, either to the Plotheians, or the Epakreans, or the Athenians, the officials, who control the money for the 'immunity', are to pay it from the common fund on behalf of the demesmen; and for all the public sacrifices, in which the Plotheians feast, they are to provide sweet wine from the common fund, and for the other sacrifices up to half a chous for each of those Plotheians present.

10.20 *IG* I^{3} 244: Law of the Deme Skambonidai, Tribe Leontis (IV), *c.* 460 BC

This is one of the earliest extant deme laws. Demes had their own officials, including the demarch (*Ath. Pol.* 21.5), and also their own assemblies, which passed decrees organising local affairs. Here, in [A] and [C], religious observations of the deme are provided for, such as the distribution of meat from the sacrifices, and the deme's participation in the Synoikia, the festival celebrating Attica's unification under Theseus. Section B indicates that an official — the euthynos — conducted the euthynai (examinations or audits) of deme officials and their handling of the deme's finances. [*IG* I^{2} 188; *LSCG* 10.]

A ... the end ... and allot the meat until the sun (sets). And if not ... se(l)l in the agora and ... let out for contract these ... except the ... the skin belongs to the demarch ... offer whatever sacrifice it is necessary to perform and allot at the Dipolieia and Panathenaia in the agora of Skambonidai as much as ... a half-chous ...

B to be proclaimed and sworn: I will also keep safe the common funds of Skambonidai and I will render the necessary to the euthynos and I swear these things by the three gods that they are not to render any of the common funds to the euthynos before ...

C ... the demarch and the hieropoioi are to offer to Leos a perfect victim; allotment ... obols to each of the men of Skambonidai and the metics are to receive a share; in the agora of Skambonidai ... offer a perfect victim and allot ... at the Synoikia in the city a perfect victim and sell the meat raw at the Epizephyria in the temple of Pythian (Apollo); ... and sell the meat raw ... in the same way.

11

THE PERSIAN WARS

For the Greeks the Persian Wars were of great significance, for in 490 and 480–479 BC the city-states of mainland Greece were faced with the prospect of becoming vassals of the Great Kings of Persia, Darius and Xerxes respectively. The failure of the Persian invasions meant that the Greeks of the mainland remained free — and that they went on to liberate their fellow Greeks of the islands, and the cities of the Asia Minor coast. Prior to his Marathon campaign in 490 BC Darius had already undertaken an expedition against the European Scythians c. 513 BC (which takes up most of Book 4 of Herodotos' *Histories*) and he remained interested in Europe generally. By about 500 BC, just prior to the Ionian Revolt, the Persians had control over the Greek cities of the Hellespont, Thrace and Macedon (docs 11.1–2). While the Ionian Revolt, led by Aristagoras of Miletos (doc. 7.3), brought the Athenians, and Eretrians, to Darius' attention, it is important to note that the Persian empire had already been expanding in that direction and it was probably inevitable that sooner or later it would have attempted to bring the Greeks of the mainland and the still unconquered islands under its sway. Persian activity north of Greece in the last two decades of the sixth century BC strongly suggests that the campaign at Marathon was intended as the start of Persian annexation of the Greek mainland. After the Ionian Revolt collapsed in 494 BC with the defeat of the Ionians at the battle of Lade and the capture of Miletos, various islands were reconquered in 493 BC by the Persians, and in 492 BC Mardonios, a son-in-law of Darius, set up democracies in many of the Greek states of Asia Minor.

In 490 BC the Persians, having sacked Eretria, landed at Marathon in Attica, the place where Peisistratos and his sons, including Hippias, had landed many decades previously in 546 (doc. 9.11). The region may still have retained Peisistratid loyalties. While the Athenians, with the Plataeans, were preparing to fight the Persians, the messenger Philippides was sent to seek aid from Sparta, but the Spartans had to wait for the full moon and could not come (doc. 11.8). Miltiades, the former tyrant of the Chersonese but now elected a strategos (general) for 490, was the hero of the day (see doc. 11.9 for details of the battle). A shield signal to the Persians was said to have been made during the course of the battle of Marathon; responsibility for this was attributed to the Alkmeonidai, but Herodotos attempted to absolve them from blame over this incident (doc. 11.10). The Persians, defeated at Marathon, managed to board their ships and made for Phaleron, the main Athenian port at the time, but the Athenians reached there before them. The Spartans arrived too late for the engagement but did tour the battlefield and congratulate the Athenians on their achievement.

The next Persian king, Xerxes, Darius' son, also demanded the submission of the Greek states (doc. 11.19). Among the cities who 'medised', or went over to the Persians, were the Boeotians, except for the Thespiaians and Plataeans (doc. 11.19) while the Greeks who were determined to oppose Persia formed the 'Hellenic League' (doc. 11.24). The western Greeks were occupied with the Carthaginians and so did not come to the aid of the mainland, except for a single ship from Croton (docs 11.24, 11.45): tradition recorded that Gelon and the Silicians defeated the Carthaginians at Himera on the same day as the battle of Salamis (docs 11.20, 11.55; 7.44–45). The Athenians sent to Delphi for an oracle in their hour of need, but the first that they received was so pessimistic that they requested a second (docs 11.21–22). Themistokles was able to persuade the Athenians to accept the interpretation that the wooden walls, mentioned by the Pythia, referred to the Athenian fleet; he had already been instrumental in building up the Athenian navy (doc. 11.23).

The Greeks decided to make a stand at Thermopylai, and the Greek fleet was stationed close by, off northern Euboea. At Thermopylai the allies, under the command of King Leonidas of Sparta, held off the Persians until they were betrayed by a local, Ephialtes, who showed the Persians a path through the mountain. Leonidas then dismissed most of the Greek forces who were with him; all those with Leonidas fell, and Simonides later composed their epitaphs (docs 11.31–33). Stories of Spartan calmness before battle and their bravery passed into Greek history (docs 11.29–30, 11.53). While Leonidas fought the Persians heroically at Thermopylai, a naval battle took place at Artemision, the northern cape of the island of Euboea. Here the result was inconclusive (doc. 11.34). During the night after the battle the Greeks fled from the Persians after hearing of the disaster at Thermopylai and made their way to Salamis. Serious divisions between the Greeks were revealed there, centring around the best strategy with which to oppose the Persians.

At this point the evacuation of Athens took place (docs 11.35–36), and shortly afterwards the Persians sacked and occupied it. With the Persian forces so near, many of the Peloponnesians wanted to retreat from Salamis to the Isthmus, along which a wall had been built, but Themistokles threatened that the Athenians would sail off in their ships, and establish a new Athens in Italy and so the decision was made to fight at Salamis. To ensure that the battle took place, Themistokles sent a message to the Persians that the Greek fleet was about to sail away, and that they should act quickly to stop this. The Persian fleet trapped the Greek fleet at Salamis, and there was now no choice: the Greeks had to fight (doc. 11.38). The campaign of Salamis was by no means the end of the war but it was a turning point, and the Persians were now on the retreat. There were two more important battles, the campaigns at Plataea (docs 11.46–48) and at Mykale (doc. 11.51), which took place on the same day. The death of Mardonios at Plataea contributed significantly to the Greek victory, but the Greeks came extremely close to defeat. At the battle of Mykale the Greeks defeated the Persians and gained control of the Hellespont and the Aegean islands. The allied fleet then sailed for the Hellespont; when the allies reached Abydos, they found Xerxes' bridges already destroyed, and the Spartan king Leotychidas and the Peloponnesian allies returned home, while the others stayed to besiege Sestos (see Hdt. 9.106, 114.1–2). Herodotos' narrative ends soon after this, and is taken up by Thucydides, in the section known as the 'pentekontaetia' (Thuc. 1.89–117).

Herodotos claimed that the Athenians played the greater role in defeating the Persians in 480–479 BC because of the part they played at Salamis (doc. 11.54): the Athenians, by fighting at Salamis, won the struggle against the Persians, because the Peloponnesian strategy of retreating to the Isthmus would have ended in an easy Persian victory. Themistokles, by dramatically increasing the size of the Athenian navy and engineering that the naval battle against the Persians be fought there, was in every sense the one individual who could take credit for Salamis. For this reason Thucydides praised him (doc. 12.1). But the Persian land forces were still in central Greece, and they were defeated at Plataea, where the Spartans could take the main responsibility for the victory which led to the retreat of the Persians to Asia Minor (doc. 11.47). Aristophanes in the Peloponnesian War could write with longing of the time when the Athenians and Spartans had fought together to drive the Persians from Greece (doc. 11.57).

While the Greeks fought well together in the land and sea battles, the dissensions about whether to fight at Thermopylai and Salamis indicate the problems involved for those who wanted to employ an offensive strategy as opposed to those Peloponnesians who saw a retreat to the Isthmus as the safest defensive option. While Greek unity is often cited as a reason for the Greeks' defeat of the Persians, this unity was limited in a numerical sense: many Greek states medised or did not participate. The Serpent Column inscription lists the Greeks who fought the Persians (doc. 11.49), but in some ways it was a limited number of Greek cities which fought off the Persians (doc. 11.56). It is factors such differences in leadership styles, command structures, weaponry, tactics and strategy that explain why the Greeks were victorious in both Persian Wars.

DARIUS AND THE PERSIANS

11.1 Aeschylus *Persians* 853–908: Persia, Darius' Mighty Empire

Aeschylus' play *The Persians* was produced in Athens in 472 BC and so was presented to participants in the battle of Salamis only eight years after the event. Aeschylus himself served at Marathon (doc. 11.11). The chorus of Persian elders, in lamenting the defeat, recalls the glories of Darius' reign, emphasising his sway over all his subject territories, especially those of the Greeks in Asia Minor and the islands.

Alas!, it was a glorious and good
Life of social order that we enjoyed, while our aged
All-powerful, guileless, unconquerable King,
God-like Darius ruled the land;
Firstly, we displayed glorious armies,
Which everywhere administered tower-like cities,
And returns from war brought home
Unwearied, unscathed men who had achieved much,
And how many cities he captured, without crossing Halys river's ford
Or rising from his hearth,
Such as the Acheloan cities of the Strymon sea which neighbour
The Thracians' dwellings;
And those outside the marshes on the mainland built round with walls
Obeyed him as lord,
As did outspread Helle around the broad strait, and the embayed Propontis
And the mouth of the Black Sea,
And the sea-washed islands opposite the sea's headland
Lying close to this land,
Such as Lesbos and olive-planted Samos, Chios and Paros,
Naxos, Mykonos and Andros, Tenos' nearby neighbour,
And he ruled the sea-girt isles lying in mid-ocean,
Lemnos and the abode of Ikaros,
Rhodes and Knidos and the Cypriot cities Paphos and Soloi
And Salamis, whose mother-city is now a cause of lamentation;
The wealthy and populous cities, too, in the Ionian lands
Of the Greeks he ruled by his own will,
And possessed the unwearied strength of armed warriors

And allies of different nations;
While now in no doubtful manner
We suffer in war
These divine changes of fortune,
Overcome woefully
By disasters on the sea.

11.2 *The Bisitun Rock Inscription* 1–9, 52–53, 58, 71–75

This inscription of King Darius I the Great (522–486 BC) was engraved on the Behistun Rock between Teheran and Baghdad. Darius was succeeded by his son Xerxes. Ahura Mazola was the Persians' supreme deity.

1 I am Darius (Dârayavaush), Great King, King of Kings, King of Persia, King of Nations; son of Hystaspes (Vishtâspa), grandson of Arsames (Arshâma), an Akhaemenian (Hakhâmanishiya). **2** King Darius says: My father was Hystaspes (Vishtâspa); Hystaspes' father was Arsames (Arshâma); Arsames' father was Ariaramnes (Ariyâramna); Ariamnes' father was Teispes (Chishpish); Teispes' father was Akhaemenes (Hakhâmanish). **3** King Darius says: For that reason we are called Akhaemenians; from of old we have been nobly born, from of old our family have been kings. **4** King Darius says: Eight in our family were kings before me; I am the ninth; nine in succession we have been kings. **5** King Darius says: By the will of Auramazdâ I am king; Auramazdâ bestowed kingship on me. **6** King Darius says: These are the countries that came to me; by the will of Auramazdâ I am king over them: Persia, Elam, Babylonia, Assyria, Arabia, Egypt, those by the Sea, Sardis, Ionia, Media, Armenia, Cappadocia, Parthia, Drangiana, Aria, Khorasmia, Bactria, Sogdiana, Gandara, Scythia, Sattagydia, Arakhosia, Maka; twenty-three countries in all. **7** King Darius says: These are the countries that came to me; by the will of Auramazdâ they became my subjects; they brought tribute to me; whatever was said to them by me, by day or by night, that was done. **8** King Darius says: Within these countries, the loyal vassal I rewarded well; the one who was evil I punished severely; by the will of Auramazdâ these countries respected my law; as it was said to them by me, so was it done. **9** King Darius says: Auramazdâ bestowed kingship on me; Auramazdâ brought me help, till I gained possession of this kingdom; by the will of Auramazdâ I hold this empire.

The victories of King Darius

52 King Darius says: This is what I did by the will of Auramazdâ in one and the same year, after I became king: nineteen battles I fought, and by the will of Auramazdâ I overthrew and captured nine kings. One was named Gaumâta, a Magian; he lied, saying he was Smerdis (Bardiya), son of Cyrus (Kurush); he made Persia rebellious. One was named Âsina, an Elamite (Ûvjiya); he lied, saying he was king in Elam (Ûvja); he made Elam rebellious. One was named Nidintu-Bêl, a Babylonian; he lied, saying he was Nebukadressar, son of Nabunaid; he made Babylonia rebellious. One was named Martiya, a Persian; he lied, saying he was Imanish, king in Elam; he made Elam rebellious. One was named Phraortes (Fravartish), a Mede; he lied saying he was Khshathrita, of the family of Cyaxares; he made Media rebellious. One was named Chisantakhma, a Sagartian; he lied, saying he was king in Sagartia, of the family of Cyaxares (Uvakhshtra); he made Sagartia rebellious.

One was named Frâda, a Margian; he lied, saying he was king in Margiana; he made Margiana rebellious. One was named Vahyazdâta, a Persian; he lied, saying he was Smerdis, son of Cyrus; he made Persia rebellious. One was named Arkha, an Armenian (Arminiya); he lied, saying he was Nebukadressar, son of Nabunaid; he made Babylonia rebellious. **53** King Darius says: These nine kings I took prisoner in these battles.

58 King Darius says: By the will of Auramazdâ there is also much else done by me which has not been engraved in this inscription; it has not been written down, lest he who shall hereafter read this inscription should think what has been done by me is too much and will not believe it, but take it to be falsehood. . . .

The conclusion of the inscription

70 King Darius says: By the will of Auramazdâ this is the inscription that I made. In addition, it was composed in Aryan on clay tablets and on parchment; furthermore, I made a sculptured image of myself; moreover, I gave my lineage. It was inscribed and read out before me. Afterwards I sent this inscription everywhere through the provinces. The people worked upon it unitedly.

The addition to the inscription

71 King Darius says: This is what I did in the second and third year after I became king. The province named Elam (Ûvja) became rebellious. A man named Atamaita, an Elamite, they made their leader. Thereupon I sent forth an army. A man named Gobryas (Gaubaruva), a Persian, my servant, I made their leader. After that, Gobryas marched forth with the army to Elam; he joined battle with the Elamites. Then Gobryas smote and crushed the Elamites, and he captured their leader. He brought him to me, and I slew him. Thereupon the land became mine. **72** King Darius says: Those Elamites were faithless and Auramazdâ was not worshipped by them. I worshipped Auramazdâ; by the will of Auramazdâ I did to them according to my desire. **73** King Darius says: Whoever worships Auramazdâ, divine blessing shall be upon him, while alive and when dead. **74** King Darius says: Thereafter with an army I went to Scythia (Saka), against the Scythians, who wear the pointed cap; these Scythians went from me. When I arrived at the sea, I crossed over it with all my army. Then I utterly defeated the Scythians; another leader I captured, who was brought in fetters to me, and I slew him, their leader named Skunkha, he it was that they seized and brought to me. Then I made another man their leader, according to my desire. Thereupon the land became mine. **75** King Darius says: Those Scythians were faithless and Auramazdâ was not worshipped by them. I worshipped Auramazdâ; and by the grace of Auramazdâ I did to them according to my desire.

THE IONIAN REVOLT

Aristagoras, tyrant of Miletos, was approached for aid by aristocrats exiled from Naxos; he sought assistance from Artaphernes the satrap of Lydia at Sardis and Darius King of Persia agreed to the plan. However, the expedition failed. Realising the implications of his failure, and encouraged by Histiaios, the previous tyrant of Miletos, Aristagoras decided to stir up a rebellion of the Greek cities under Persian rule and most of the tyrants in these cities were deposed. The adoption of isonomia, democracy, at Miletos and presumably in the other Greek cities indicates that there was a political desire for such a form of government, and that, whereas Herodotos gives a great deal of emphasis to the motives of Aristagoras, and to a lesser extent Histiaios, the cities involved had grievances. Because of the involvement of Athens and Eretria, the Ionian Revolt brought the Greeks of the mainland to the close attention of Darius (see doc. 11.5), who had already been involved in extending his empire in the expedition against Scythia *c.* 513.

11.3 Herodotos 5.97.1–3: Aristagoras at Athens

Hippias, deposed as tyrant at Athens in 510 BC, had briefly returned to Greece in *c.* 505–501 BC for the abortive Spartan plan to restore him; following this he urged Artaphernes to arrange for the subjugation of Athens: Athenian representatives sent to Sardis were told by Artaphernes to take Hippias back, but they refused (Hdt. 5.96). For Aristagoras' visit to Sparta, see doc. 6.74.

5.97.1 At this point, while the Athenians were thinking in this way and had already been brought into discredit with the Persians, Aristagoras, the Milesian who had been driven out of Sparta by Kleomenes, arrived at Athens ... (**5.97.1–2**: *he convinces the people of the wealth to be found in Asia and of the ease with which they will beat the Persians.*) It seems to be easier to impose on many people than on one, if he was unable to mislead Kleomenes, one man, and yet managed it with 30,000 Athenians. **5.97.3** The Athenians were persuaded and voted to send twenty ships to assist the Ionians, appointing as their commander Melanthios, a distinguished citizen in every respect. But these ships were the beginning of troubles for both the Greeks and the barbarians.

11.4 Herodotos 5.100–101.1, 101.3–103.1: The Burning of Sardis

Athens' position as mother-city of the Ionians may have been a factor in its support of the revolt; desire for control of the Hellespont region probably also played a part. Twenty Athenian ships (plus five from Eretria) made their way in 498 BC to Ephesos, and the troops disembarked and marched to Sardis.

5.100 The Ionians arrived with this fleet at Ephesos and left their ships at Koressos in Ephesian territory, while they marched upcountry with a large force, using Ephesian guides. They marched along the river Cayster, crossed the Tmolos range, and when they arrived captured Sardis without opposition, everything, that is, except the acropolis; Artaphernes himself saved the acropolis with a large force of men. **5.101.1** They were prevented from plundering the city after its capture by the following: most of the houses in Sardis were made of reeds, even those made of brick having roofs of reed. A soldier set light to one of these and immediately the fire went from house to house until it spread over the entire town ... **5.101.3** When the Ionians saw some of the enemy defending themselves and others approaching in large numbers, they withdrew afraid to the mountains called Tmolos, from there by night departing to their ships. **5.102.1** And Sardis was burned, and in it a temple of the local goddess Cybele, which the Persians later used as an excuse for burning the temples in Greece in return. (**5.102.1–3**: *The Ionians are severely beaten by the Persians at Ephesos.*) **5.103.1** After this the Athenians completely abandoned the Ionians, and even though Aristagoras kept sending messengers calling for their aid they refused to help him. But though the Ionians were deprived of the alliance of the Athenians, nonetheless, in view of what they had already done against Darius, they carried on preparing for war against the king.

11.5 Herodotos 5.105.1–2: 'Sire, Remember the Athenians'

Athenian involvement in the Ionian Revolt meant that Athens was brought to Darius' direct attention. By Zeus, Herodotos means Ahura Mazda, Zeus' Persian equivalent. Cf. Hdt. 6.94.1.

5.105.1 When it was reported to King Darius that Sardis had been taken and burned by the Athenians and Ionians, and that the leader of the joint attempt to bring this about was Aristagoras of Miletos, it is said that, first, when he learned this, he paid no attention to the Ionians, knowing well that they would not escape punishment for their revolt, but asked who the Athenians were, and, after learning this, called for his bow, took it, fitted an arrow and shot it up to the sky, and as he did so said, **2** 'Zeus, grant that I may punish the Athenians!' After saying this, he ordered one of his servants to say to him three times every day before dinner, 'Sire, remember the Athenians.'

11.6 Herodotos 6.18, 6.21.2: The 'Capture of Miletos'

The battle of Lade in 494 BC was decisive: many of the Greeks deserted, and the Persians were victorious, going on to sack nearby Miletos. After the revolt collapsed Mardonios established democracies in many of the Greek cities.

6.18 When the Persians had conquered the Ionians in the sea battle (at Lade), they besieged Miletos by land and sea and dug under the walls and brought up all kinds of siege engines, taking the entire city five years after the revolt of Aristagoras; and they enslaved the city, so the fate foretold by the oracle for Miletos took place … **6.21.2** The Athenians made it clear that they were very distressed by the capture of Miletos in a number of ways and especially when Phrynichos wrote and produced his play *The Capture of Miletos*, at which the theatre was moved to tears, and they fined him a thousand drachmas for reminding them of a domestic disaster and forbade anybody ever again to use this as a subject for a play.

11.7 Herodotos 6.98.1–2: A Troubled Time for Greece is on the Way

Mardonios was sent westwards by the king in 494/3 BC. Thasos submitted, as did Macedonia. But in 492 BC Mardonios' fleet was wrecked rounding Mount Athos (Hdt. 6.44–45). He returned to Persia, and Datis took command. He sailed directly to Naxos, and destroyed it for the part it had played in the Ionian Revolt, and then subdued Eretria, sacking the city, including the temples, but was lenient at Delos.

6.98.1 After Datis had set sail from Delos, it was the first and last occasion (up to my time anyway) that Delos was shaken, according to the Delians, by an earthquake. God perhaps sent this to men as a portent of the evils that were going to follow. **2** For in the time of Darius, son of Hystaspes, and Xerxes, son of Darius, and Artaxerxes, son of Xerxes, three generations in succession, Greece suffered more evils than in the twenty generations preceding Darius, some of which were caused by the Persians, others by the leading states themselves fighting for supremacy.

MARATHON, 490 BC

The Persian force proceeded from Eretria to Marathon, where the Athenians and the Plataeans alone faced them. The Spartans could not come to the assistance of the Athenians because the moon was not yet full. The still surviving earth mound in which the Athenians were buried at Marathon probably marks the location of the battle area. The Athenians relied on weakening their centre, strengthening their wings, and so defeated the Persians (doc. 11.9).

11.8 Herodotos 6.101.1–103.1, 105.1–107.1: The God Pan Helps the Athenians

Hippias landed at Marathon, as he had with Peisistratos and his other sons in 546 BC (6.102). Herodotos mentions the epiphany, manifestation, of Pan. There were three other epiphanies at Marathon: a giant hoplite, Theseus and the hero Echtelos, as well as at Artemision and Salamis. The Spartans frequently cancelled or broke off campaigns for religious reasons (6.106.3).

6.101.1 The Persians brought their ships in to land in Eretrian territory at Tamynai, Choireai and Aigilia, and having put in at these places they immediately disembarked their horses and made preparations to attack their enemy … **2** A fierce attack took place against the wall and many on both sides fell over a six-day period; on the seventh, Euphorbos, son of Alkimachos, and Philagros, son of Kyneas, both notable citizens, betrayed the city to the Persians. **3** They entered the city and stripped and burned its temples, taking revenge for the temples burned at Sardis, and enslaved the inhabitants, in accordance with Darius' orders. **6.102** After conquering Eretria and waiting a few days they sailed to Attica, pressing the Athenians hard and thinking that they would do the same to the Athenians as they had to the Eretrians. Marathon was the most suitable part of Attica for riding and the closest to Eretria, and here Hippias, son of Peisistratos, brought them in to land. **6.103.1** When the Athenians learned this, they too set off to Marathon. They were led by ten generals, of whom the tenth was Miltiades, whose father Kimon, son of Stesagoras, it so happened, had been banished from Athens by Peisistratos, son of Hippokrates … **6.105.1** First, when they were still in the city, the generals sent to Sparta a herald Philippides, an Athenian and experienced long-distance runner; as Philippides reported to the Athenians, Pan met him on Mount Parthenion above Tegea. **2** Calling Philippides by his name, he told him to ask the Athenians why they paid him no attention, even though he was well disposed to the Athenians and had already often been of service to them, and would be again in the future. **3** And the Athenians believed this to be true and when their affairs settled down again properly they set up a shrine to Pan under the acropolis, and from the time of this message have propitiated him with yearly sacrifices and a torch-race. **6.106.1** So Philippides was sent by the generals, on which occasion he said Pan appeared to him, and was in Sparta on the second day after leaving the Athenians' city. On arriving he said to the authorities: **2** 'Spartans, the Athenians request you to help them and not to look on as the oldest city of the Greeks encounters slavery at the hands of barbarians; for even now Eretria has been enslaved and Greece is the weaker by a famous city.' **3** He addressed them as he had been ordered, and they were willing to help the Athenians, but they were unable to do it immediately because they did not wish to break the law; for it was the ninth day of the month, and they said that on the ninth day they could not march out until the moon became full. **6.107.1** So they waited for the full moon, and meanwhile Hippias, son of Peisistratos, brought the barbarians in to land at Marathon.

11.9 Herodotos 6.107.2–117.1: Marathon: The Battle

The complex tactic which the Athenians executed in strengthening their wings will have been the result of forward planning and not a chance manoeuvre. The absence of the Persian cavalry in Herodotos' account of the actual battle is the subject of debate (cf. Hdt. 6.102). This absence is usually interpreted as one, if not the main, reason for the Greek success. Herodotos' figure of 192 Athenian dead is normally accepted. The figure of about 6,400 Persian dead is also credible.

(**6.107.2–109.2**: *The night before landing Hippias had a dream that he was sleeping with his mother, which he took to portend success. However, he lost a tooth on arrival and reinterpreted the dream as foreshadowing failure. The Athenians were joined by the Plataeans, with every available man. The Athenian generals were against risking a battle, until Miltiades addressed the following speech to the polemarch Kallimachos.*) **6.109.3** 'Kallimachos, it is now up to you either to enslave Athens or to liberate her and leave behind such a memory for all the life of men as not even Harmodios and Aristogeiton left behind them. Now indeed the Athenians are facing the greatest danger of any in their history, for if they submit to the Persians they will be handed over to Hippias and there is no doubt what they will suffer, but, if this city prevails, she has it in her to become the first among Greek cities' … **6.110** By these words Miltiades won over Kallimachos; and with the opinion of the polemarch added to his it was determined that they should attack. After this the generals whose opinion had been on the side of attacking, when their day for presiding came round, each offered it to Miltiades; he accepted it but would not join battle until it was his day for presiding. **6.111.1** When it came round to his turn, the Athenians were then drawn up into position for attacking; the polemarch Kallimachos was in charge of the right wing; for the Athenians at that time had a law that the polemarch commanded the right wing. Next to him came the tribes, in their correct order, following closely on each other; and last of all the Plataeans were drawn up on the left wing. **2** Ever since this battle, whenever the Athenians conduct sacrifices at their four-yearly festival, the Athenian herald prays that the Plataeans too, like the Athenians, will have good fortune. **3** The Athenians' order of battle at Marathon had the following consequence: as the army was stretched out to equal the Persian army, its centre was only a few lines deep, so the army was weakest at this point, while each wing was numerically strong. **6.112.1** When they were drawn up and the sacrificial omens were favourable, the Athenians were then given the word to move and advanced at a run against the barbarians. The space between the armies was not less than eight stades. **2** When the Persians saw them attacking at a run they prepared to meet them, imputing total destructive madness to the Athenians, when they saw that they were so few, and that they were hastening on at a run with not even a horse or any archers in support. **3** That was the barbarians' view, but the Athenians in close order engaged with the barbarians, and fought in a manner worthy of note. For they were the first Greeks, that we know of, to meet the enemy at a run, and the first to endure seeing Persian dress and the men who wore it; until then even to hear the name 'Persian' gave the Greeks cause for fear. **6.113.1** The fighting at Marathon went on for a long time. The barbarians prevailed in the centre of the army, where the Persians themselves and the Sakai were stationed; here the barbarians were victorious, breaking through and pursuing them inland, but on each wing the Athenians and Plataeans were victorious. **2** As they conquered, they allowed the routed enemy to flee, and drawing both wings together fought those that had broken through their centre, and the Athenians were victorious. They followed the fleeing Persians, cutting them down, until they arrived at the sea, where they called for fire and took hold of the ships. **6.114** It was in this struggle that the polemarch Kallimachos was killed, after fighting with bravery, and also Stesilaos, son of Thrasylaos, one of the generals; Kynegeiros, son of Euphorion, took hold of the stern of a ship and had his hand cut off and died, and many other famous Athenians also lost their lives. **6.115** In this way the Athenians took possession of seven ships, but the barbarians backed water in the rest of the ships and got away, picked up the Eretrian prisoners from the island on which they had left them and sailed round Sounion to Athens, aiming to arrive at the city before the Athenians. Amongst the Athenians the Alkmeonidai were blamed for a plot which suggested this plan to the Persians; they were said to have come to an agreement with the Persians and to have held up a shield to them as a signal once they were on board. **6.116** ... The barbarians in their ships lay off Phaleron (which was at that time the Athenians' port) riding at anchor, and then sailed back to Asia. **6.117.1** In this battle at Marathon, about 6,400 of the barbarians were killed, and 192 of the Athenians.

11.10 Herodotos 6.120–121.1, 123.1–124.2: The Shield Signal

There was a strong tradition that a shield signal was made to the Persians during the battle of Marathon. Herodotos does not believe the, to him, scandalous story that the Alkmeonidai were responsible. That there was a shield signal at all could be dismissed, but the tradition at Athens was obviously strong and there is nothing intrinsically implausible about its having taken place. An obvious candidate is the pro-tyrant group at Athens, still strong in the 490s, as attested by the election of Hipparchos, probably the grandson of Hippias, as archon in 496/5 BC. For the bribery of the Pythia, see docs 9.36, 9.38, 10.1.

6.120 Two thousand Spartans arrived at Athens after the full moon, and were in such haste to get there that they were in Attica on the third day after leaving Sparta. They had come too late for the encounter, but desired to see the Persians; they went to Marathon and looked at them. They then praised the Athenians' good work and went back home. **6.121.1** I cannot accept the story, which I find quite astonishing, of the Alkmeonidai signalling to the Persians with a shield, wanting the Athenians to be subject to the barbarians and Hippias; these men appeared to be greater tyrant-haters than even Kallias son of Phainippos and father of Hipponikos. **2** Kallias was the only one of all the Athenians who dared, when Peisistratos was expelled from Athens, to buy any of his property when it was publicly advertised for sale, and who devised all sorts of other forms of hostility towards him ... **6.123.1** And the Alkmeonidai were no less tyrant-haters than he was. So the slander surprises me and I cannot believe it, that they should give a shield signal, they who were in exile for the whole period of the tyrants and through whose plan the Peisistratidai gave up the tyranny. **2** So they were thus the liberators of Athens far more than Harmodios and Aristogeiton, in my view. For the latter aggravated the remaining members of the Peisistratidai by killing Hipparchos, and did not actually put an end to the tyrants at all, while the Alkmeonidai clearly did achieve liberation, if they did in truth bribe the Pythia to tell the Spartans to liberate Athens, as I stated earlier. **6.124.1** Perhaps, however, they betrayed their country because they had some complaint against the Athenian people. But not so, because they had a better reputation among the Athenians and were more honoured than any others. **2** So logic proves that they would not signal with a shield for any reason of that sort. A shield was held up, and it cannot be said otherwise; for it was; but as to who held it up I am unable to say more than this.

11.11 Aeschylus *Poem 2*: Aeschylus' Epitaph

Despite his being one of the greatest of Greek tragedians from 484 until his death in 456/5 BC, Aeschylus' epitaph focuses only on his service at Marathon. His brother Kynegeiros also served at Marathon and was killed there (Hdt. 6.114: doc. 11.9). Aeschylus visited the Sicilian tyrant Hieron more than once and died in Sicily. [Athen. *Deip.* 627c.]

Aeschylus, son of Euphorion, an Athenian, is covered by
This tomb; he died in wheat-bearing Gela.
The famous grove of Marathon can tell his valour
As can the long-haired Persian who knew it.

11.12 Simonides 5: Miltiades Dedicates an Offering to Pan

This is a dedication in return for Pan's help at Marathon (docs 11.8, 11.38, line 449); Miltiades was to die of gangrene after being fined fifty talents for not taking Paros: Hdt. 6.136; Plut. *Kim.* 4.4; doc. 3.59. [Page 194–95.]

I, goat-footed Pan, the Arkadian, the enemy of the Persians
And ally of the Athenians, was set up by Miltiades.

11.13 Simonides 21: The Athenians' Epitaph at Marathon

This epigram was probably inscribed with a list of the fallen on a stele at the grave-mound at Marathon. [Page 225–31.]

Fighting as Greece's champions the Athenians at Marathon
Laid low the might of the gold-apparelled Persians.

11.14 *Inscriptiones Graecae* I^{3} 784: The Memorial of Kallimachos

This inscription is on the remains of an Ionic column dedicated on the Athenian acropolis after the victory at Marathon, possibly in 489 BC. Kallimachos died at Marathon, but it seems that he vowed the offering before the battle and it was made on his behalf subsequently. The dedicated 'messenger' could be Iris or Nike (Victory). [*IG* I^{2} 609; Meiggs & Lewis 18; Hansen 256; Paus. 1.15.3.]

Kallimachos of Aphidna dedicated me to Athena,
The messenger of the immortals who have homes on Olympus,
… polemarch of the Athenians, the battle
At Marathon …
To the sons of the Athenians …

11.15 Meiggs & Lewis 19L An Athenian Thanks-Offering for Marathon

This thanks-offering was inscribed on a limestone base at the south wall of the Athenian treasury at Delphi, *c.* 490 BC. The present letters were later reinscribed over the original ones in the third century. Pausanias 9.11.5 has the treasury being built from the spoils taken from the Persians at Marathon. [*SIG*[3] 23b.]

The Athenians (dedicated this) to Apollo as first fruits from the Persians
From the battle of Marathon.

11.16 *Inscriptiones Graecae* I[3] 503: An Athenian Epigram on Marathon (?)

This is an inscription on one of two fragments of an Athenian monument base. The date is subject to much controversy, but the first part of the inscription (doc. 11.40) could refer to Salamis and the second, though inscribed later than the first, is apparently an epitaph for the dead at Marathon, possibly added after the original Marathon monument was destroyed by the Persians in 480 BC. [Meiggs & Lewis 26 (II); Hansen 2; Simonides 20b; Page 219–25; *IG* I[2] 763.]

They truly had an adamant ... when the spear
Was set in front of the gates ...
To burn the sea-girt ...
City, turning back by force the Persians.

11.17 Thucydides 2.34.1–5: Marathon 'the Victory'

This passage is part of the Funeral Oration delivered by Perikles in 431/0 BC (doc. 1.17). The war dead were given a public funeral and buried in Athens. A notable exception were the war dead who fell at Marathon who were buried there.

2.34.1 In the same winter the Athenians, following their ancestral custom, held a public funeral for those who had been the first to die in the war in the following way: **2** two days beforehand they put up a tent in which they place the bones of the dead, and each person makes what offering he wishes to his own departed; **3** then there is the funeral procession, in which wagons carry coffins of cypress wood, one for each tribe, which holds the bones of that tribe's members. One empty bier, decorated, is carried for the missing, whose bodies could not be recovered. **4** Any one who wishes, both citizens and foreigners, can join in the procession, and women related to the dead are present, lamenting at the tomb. **5** They place them in the public grave, which is in the city's most beautiful suburb, and they always bury there those who died in war, except those at Marathon: as they judged *their* valour to be outstanding, they made their tomb on the spot.

11.18 Aristophanes *Acharnians* 692–701: Old Marathon Men Discounted

Marathon and Salamis became events hallowed by tradition at Athens. The *Acharnians* was produced in 425 BC, and here the chorus of elderly men from the deme Acharnai protest about the way elderly men are treated by young upstarts in the law courts. [Cf. Ar. *Knights* 781–85, 1333–34.]

How can it be proper to destroy a grey-haired old man

By using the water-clock,
Who has played his part well,
Often wiping off the warm sweat of manly toil,
And who was a brave man
At Marathon for his city?
Then, when we were at Marathon,
We were the ones prosecuting the attack,
But now we are the ones wicked men prosecute,
— and get convicted too.

XERXES' CAMPAIGNS

Darius was apparently more determined than ever to deal with the Greeks, especially the Athenians (Hdt. 7.1). When he died in 486 BC, his son Xerxes inherited the Persian empire and his father's grudge against the Greeks (though see Hdt. 7.5–7). The Egyptian, Jewish and Babylonian rebellions did not deter Xerxes.

11.19 Herodotos 7.32, 131–133.1: Xerxes Demands Submission

Xerxes' heralds secured the submission of several Greek states, many of which were neighbours of Persian-dominated areas of northern Greece. To 'medise' was to go over to the Persian side, to give signs of submission (earth and water) and/or to collaborate with the Persians. The Greeks normally regarded heralds as inviolable; for the divine consequences for the Spartans, see Hdt. 7.133–137.

7.32 When Xerxes arrived at Sardis, he first sent heralds to Greece demanding earth and water and ordering that they prepare meals for the king; he sent the demand everywhere except Athens and Sparta. He sent a second time for earth and water because he thought that all those who had not earlier given them to Darius when he sent would now be frightened into co-operating; so he sent his heralds as he wanted to find this out …

7.131 Of the heralds who had been sent out to Greece to make the demand, some arrived back empty handed, others bearing earth and water. **7.132.1** Of those who gave them, there were the following: Thessalians, Dolopians, Ainianes, Perraibians, Lokrians, Magnetes, Malians, Achaeans of Phthiotis, Thebans and the rest of the Boeotians except for the Thespiaians and Plataeans. **2** Against these the Greeks who were undertaking to fight the barbarians swore an oath. This oath said that they would make all those Greeks who gave themselves up to the Persians without being compelled to do so give a tithe of their property to the god at Delphi, if matters went well for them. This was the Greeks' oath; **7.133.1** Xerxes did not send heralds to Athens and Sparta to make this demand because when Darius had sent earlier for the same purpose the former had thrown those making the demand into a pit, and the latter into a well, telling them to take earth and water from there to the king.

11.20 Diodorus *Library of History* 11.1.2–5: The Carthaginians Threaten Sicily

Xerxes' alliance with the Carthaginians is not mentioned by Herodotos. Certainly, the Greeks in the west did not come to the aid of the other Greeks and in 480 BC the Sicilian Greeks fought a decisive battle against the Carthaginians at Himera (see doc. 11.55, cf. 11.24, 7.44).

11.1.2 It was in this year that King Xerxes made his expedition against Greece for the following reason. **3** Mardonios the Persian, who was Xerxes' cousin and related to him by marriage, was greatly admired by the Persians for his wisdom and courage. Buoyed up by his pride and at the height of vigour he was eager to be the leader of a great army. In consequence he persuaded Xerxes to enslave the Greeks, who had always been enemies of the Persians. **4** As Xerxes was won over by him and wanted to drive all the Greeks from their homes, he sent an embassy to the Carthaginians to ask them to undertake a joint expedition and made a treaty with them that he would campaign against the Greeks who lived in Greece, while at the same time the Carthaginians should prepare great forces and conquer the Greeks who lived in Sicily and Italy. **5** The Carthaginians, in accordance with this treaty, collected vast sums of money and gathered mercenaries from Italy and Liguria, as well as from Galatia and Iberia, and to augment these they enlisted their own citizens from Libya and Carthage. After three years of preparing for war they had finally collected more than 300,000 infantry and 200 warships.

GREECE PREPARES FOR THE ATTACK

In 480 BC the Persian army crossed the Hellespont; Xerxes had two bridges of boats constructed, which were subsequently destroyed in a storm — he had the Hellespont lashed and branded as a punishment for this, and the engineers beheaded (Hdt. 7.33–36); the bridges were rebuilt. To prevent a reoccurrence of the disaster which befell Mardonios' fleet (Hdt. 6.44), Xerxes had a canal cut through the Mount Athos peninsula. Aeschylus gives the number of Persian ships as 1,207 (*Pers.* 341–43).

11.21 Herodotos 7.140.1–3: The Delphic Oracle Counsels Flight

The Athenians consulted Delphi in either 481 or 480 BC; the latter date is probably to be preferred, being closer in time to the approach of the Persians. The Athenians received no comfort from Delphi; the oracle, in counselling the Athenians to flee, did not so much medise as give an answer appropriate to the situation. Given the odds, the Pythia's first reply was understandable.

7.140.1 The Athenians sent envoys to Delphi as they wanted to consult the oracle; and once they had performed the customary rites at the temple, as they entered the sanctuary and sat down, the Pythia, whose name was Aristonike, proclaimed as follows:

2 'Wretched men, why do you sit down? Fly to the ends of the earth and leave
Your homes and the high peak of your circular city.
For neither the head nor the body remains firm,
Nor the lowest feet nor the hands nor is anything left
In the middle, but all are in an evil plight; for it is being devastated
By fire and wrathful Ares, driving his Syrian chariot.
3 Many other towers too he will destroy, not merely yours;
He will give many shrines of the immortals to raging fire,
Which now stand drenched in sweat,
Shaking with fear, and down from the topmost roofs
Pours black blood, foreshadowing evil necessity.
But leave the shrine and spread a brave spirit over your ills.'

11.22 Herodotos 7.141.1–143.2: The Delphic Oracle and the 'Wooden Wall'

In an unprecedented move the Athenians, unhappy with the oracle which they had received, approached the Pythia for a second. There were two interpretations at Athens of the second oracle: one was that the acropolis was meant, which was originally hedged round with a thorn-bush palisade (cf. Hdt. 8.51.2, where a number of Athenians remained on the acropolis), but others took the 'wooden wall' as meaning the fleet.

7.141.1 When they heard this the Athenian envoys were in a dreadful plight. They were about to give themselves up for lost under the evil which was prophesied, when Timon, son of Androboulos, one of the most respected men in Delphi, advised them to carry olive-branches and go a second time to consult the oracle as suppliants. **2** The Athenians followed his advice and said, 'Lord, respect these olive-branches which we are carrying and give us a better prophecy concerning our country; otherwise we shall not leave the shrine, but remain here until we die.' When they said this the prophetess prophesied for a second time as follows:

3 'Pallas is not able to propitiate Olympian Zeus,
Though entreating him with many words and her shrewd wisdom.
But again I will speak this word to you, having made it firm as adamant:
Though all else shall be taken which the boundary of Kekrops
Has within it and the hollow of sacred Kithairon,
Far-sounding Zeus grants to the Trito-born (Athena) that the wooden wall
Only shall be unsacked, and help you and your children.
4 Do not await the cavalry and infantry which come,
A great host from the mainland, at your ease, but withdraw
And turn your back; at some point you will meet it face to face.
O divine Salamis, you will destroy women's children
Either when corn is scattered or when it comes together.'

7.142.1 This seemed to be, and was, milder than the earlier oracle, so they had it written down and returned to Athens. (**7.142.1–3**: *There was debate in Athens as to whether the 'wooden wall' referred to the acropolis or to ships: those who believed the latter were concerned by the implication that they would be defeated.*) **7.143.1** But there was a certain Athenian who had recently come to the fore, whose name was Themistokles, called the son of Neokles. He said that the diviners' opinions were not entirely correct, pointing out that if the pronouncement was really meant for the Athenians it would not have been expressed so mildly, but as 'O *cruel* Salamis' instead of 'O *divine* Salamis', if the inhabitants were going to die for its sake. **2** But it was to their enemies that the god really referred in the oracle, not the Athenians. Accordingly he advised them to be prepared to fight at sea, as the 'wooden wall' did mean this.

11.23 [Aristotle] *Athenaion Politeia* 22.7: Themistokles Builds the Fleet in 483/2 BC

This is part of doc. 10.9. Themistokles was the architect of the build-up of the Athenian navy prior to the second Persian invasion and responsible for Athens becoming a maritime power; he had persuaded the Athenians to use the money from the mines to build 100 ships for use against Aegina (Plut. *Them.* 4.3: 100 ships; Hdt. 7.144: 200; cf. Thuc. 1.14.3).

22.7 In the third year after this (the ostracism of Xanthippos, son of Ariphron), in the archonship of Nikodemos (483/2), when the mines at Maroneia were found and the city had a surplus of a hundred talents from the workings, some people advised that the money should be divided up between the people, but Themistokles prevented this, refusing to say what he would use the money for, but telling them to lend the hundred wealthiest Athenians a talent each; if they were happy with the way the money had been spent, the cost would be the city's, and if not they could take back the money from the people to whom it had been lent. Getting it on these conditions, he had a hundred triremes built, each of the hundred men building one of them, and with these they fought the naval battle at Salamis against the barbarians.

11.24 Herodotos 7.145.1–2: The 'Hellenic League' (the Greek Alliance)

The unity which (some of) the Greeks were able to achieve in the face of the Persian invasion of 480 BC is usually cited as the main reason why they were victorious, but this unity was in fact limited (cf. doc. 11.56). The 'Hellenic League' seems to have met first in 481 BC, for the spies sent out to Persia as a result of this meeting found Xerxes still in Sardis (Hdt. 7.146). The League also sent ambassadors to various Greek states; for the oath sworn by the Greeks, note Hdt. 7.132.2 (doc. 11.19). Argos had a Delphic oracle excusing it from participation (because they were short on manpower after Kleomenes' massacre: doc. 6.77), and their demand for an equal share in the command of the forces was rejected (Hdt. 7.148–152). Gelon, tyrant of Syracuse, also refused to send aid: see docs 7.44–45. The Cretans also received a Delphic oracle not to become involved: Hdt. 7.169.

7.145.1 The Greeks who were loyal to the Greek cause now assembled and gave each other promises and guarantees, deciding in their discussion that the most important thing of all was to reconcile enmities and put a stop to existing wars between each other; of such wars which were taking place the most serious was that between the Athenians and Aeginetans. **2** Later on, when they learned that Xerxes and his force were at Sardis, they decided to send spies to Asia to learn of the King's actions, and envoys to Argos to make an alliance against the Persians, and to send others to Sicily to Gelon, son of Deinomenes, and others to Corcyra and to Crete, bidding them to come to the rescue of Greece. They hoped that Greece would be united and that they would all, in concert, take the same action, in as much as these dangers threatened all the Greeks alike. Gelon's power was said to be immense, greater by far than that of any other Greek.

11.25 Aeschylus *Persians* 73–91, 101–14: The Magnificent Persian Force Goes Forth

The Persian elders, who are speaking here, are anxious about what is happening in Greece, having received no news; parents and wives are missing the Persian soldiers, and the whole country regrets the absence of the stalwart warrior Xerxes, 'the godlike light of a gold-begotten race' (line 80).

The impetuous ruler of populous Asia
Against the whole earth
Is driving his wondrous army
In two parts, confident in those in charge on land and those strong by sea,
His stern commanders, himself a godlike light of a gold-begotten race.

Flashing from his eyes the dark glare of a deadly dragon
With many men and many sailors and urging on his Syrian chariot
He leads on a warrior host of archers against men famed for the spear.
No one's of such tried valour that he can withstand a mighty flood of men
And ward off with strong defences the unconquerable wave of the sea;
Persia's host is hard to fight and her soldiers are stout-hearted.
By the gods' will Destiny has prevailed
From times of old, and imposed upon the Persians
The conduct of wars which destroy towers
And the turmoil of horsemen and the desolation of cities;
And they have learned, when the broad-pathed sea
Grows white with a furious storm
To look upon the ocean plain
Trusting in their finely turned cables and man-conveying devices.

11.26 Aeschylus *Persians* 230–55: Persia's Target

Atossa, the Persian queen mother, has had an unfavourable dream portending Xerxes' defeat, and she therefore asks the chorus for information about Athens. This is obviously a dramatic device: as Darius' wife (also Cyrus' daughter, and previously wife of Cambyses, her brother) she should have known about Athens, and Darius' earlier invasion. At the end of the conversation a messenger arrives with the news of the battle of Salamis. This is clearly written from the point of view of the Athenian audience.

Atossa: I would like to learn this:
My friends, where on the earth do they say that Athens lies?
Chorus: Far off, at the setting point of our Lord the Sun, as he declines.
Atossa: Does my son really desire to destroy this city?
Chorus: Yes, for all Greece would then be subject to the king.
Atossa: Do they then have such a multitudinous army?
Chorus: Yes, such an army that has driven off the Persians with great disaster.
Atossa: Is the bow-stretching arrow suited to their hands?
Chorus: Not at all; lances for close fight and shield-bearing armour.
Atossa: What else in addition? Sufficient wealth at home?
Chorus: They have a spring of silver, the earth's treasure.
Atossa: And who is their chief and lord over their army?
Chorus: Of no man are they called the slaves or subjects.
Atossa: How then can they await the approaching enemy?
Chorus: Well enough to have destroyed Darius' large and splendid host.
Atossa: Your words give dire food for thought for the parents of those going there.
Chorus: But I think you will soon know the whole account in truth;
For the running of this man seems to be Persian,
And he bears clear news of something, whether good or ill.
Messenger: O cities of all the land of Asia,
O Persian land, great haven of wealth,
How at one blow your great prosperity has been destroyed,

The flower of the Persians fallen and departed.
Alas!, it is bad to be the first to report bad news,
But I must unfold the whole catastrophe,
Persians — the whole barbarian host has perished!

THERMOPYLAI AND ARTEMISION

The Thessalians sent representatives to the Hellenic League at the Isthmus, where it was decided to send a force by sea to the pass at Tempe in May 480 BC. The Athenians were commanded by Themistokles. The force of 10,000 returned soon after and Thessaly passed into Persian hands, largely due to Persian sympathisers (Hdt. 7.172–174). The Greeks met again at the Isthmus and discussed war strategy, deciding to hold the pass at Thermopylai ('Hot Gates') and to send the fleet to Artemision (Hdt. 7.175–177). Both battles, Thermopylai and Artemision, took place in September 480 BC.

11.27 Herodotos 7.204–222: Thermopylai

King Leonidas of Sparta went north, but the festival of the Karneia prevented the rest of the Spartan force from marching; 19 September, 480 BC was the final day of the battle at Thermopylai. Neither the Thespiaians nor the Plataeans medised and it is sometimes overlooked that not only the Spartan force died, but also the Thespiaians (7.222), as well as helots (8.25.1). Leonidas probably had several motives in making a stand here: this allowed for the retreat of the other Greeks from the pass, losses were inflicted on the Persians, and Leonidas presumably felt that flight was ignominious and would be bad for the morale of the Greeks.

7.204 The other states each had their own generals, but the most generally respected was the Spartan Leonidas, son of Anaxandridas, who was commander of the whole army … **7.205.2** He then went to Thermopylai with the 300 men he had chosen, who were in their prime and had living sons. He arrived also having picked up from the Thebans a force whose size I have mentioned, of whom Leontiades, son of Eurymachos, was in command. **3** Out of all the Greeks the reason why Leonidas took pains to take only these was because it was strongly alleged that they were medising; so he summoned them to the war wishing to find out whether they would send help or would openly disown the Greek alliance. They did send troops, but their sympathies were elsewhere. **7.206.1** The Spartiates had sent Leonidas and his 300 men on ahead, in order that the other allies might see them and join the expedition, and not medise, as they might do if they learned that the Spartans were delaying; and afterwards, when the Karneia, which was what was preventing them, was over, they were going to leave guards in Sparta and come to the rescue as quickly as possible with their whole force. **2** The rest of the allies also planned to do the same themselves; for the Olympic festival fell at the same time as these events; so because they did not expect the battle at Thermopylai to be decided so quickly they sent only advance parties. (**7.207–220.4**: *Xerxes' initial attacks were unsuccessful, but finally the Persians learn of a track leading over the hills. Leonidas deliberately dismisses all the allied troops.*) **7.221** Not the least evidence of this in my view is the case of the seer who accompanied this army, Megistias the Akarnanian, said to be descended from Melampous, who had foretold what was going to happen to them from the sacrificial victims, whom Leonidas clearly sent away so he should not die with them. Despite being dismissed he did not leave, but sent away his son, his only child, who was serving with him. **7.222** The allies then were dismissed and left in obedience to Leonidas, and only the Thespiaians and Thebans remained except for the Spartans. Of these the Thebans remained unwillingly and against their wishes (for Leonidas kept them as hostages), but the Thespiaians stayed of their own accord, refusing to go and desert Leonidas and his companions, and instead remained and died with them.

11.28 Simonides 6: The Epitaph of Megistias the Seer

Megistias of Akarnania, a seer, had predicted his own death (Hdt. 7.219, 221); the Spercheios is just north of Thermopylai. Of all the epigrams ascribed to Simonides, this has one of the strongest claims to authenticity (as has 22: doc. 11.32). [Page 195–96; Hdt. 7.228.3–4.]

This is the tomb of famous Megistias, whom once the Persians
Killed when they crossed the river Spercheios;
A diviner, who then clearly knew that the Fates of Death were approaching
But could not endure to forsake Sparta's leaders.

11.29 Herodotos 7.207.1–209.3: The Spartans at Thermopylai

Leonidas' decision to stay and fight at Thermopylai contrasts with the general Peloponnesian inclination to flee, which was also demonstrated just prior to the battle of Salamis. The story of the Spartans calmly grooming themselves was and is a famous one (cf. doc. 6.17). Demaratos was a Spartan king in exile: doc. 6.75.

7.207 The Greeks at Thermopylai, as the Persian army approached the pass, began to be afraid and debated whether to withdraw. The other Peloponnesians wanted to return to the Peloponnese and guard the Isthmus, but the Phokians and Lokrians were angered by this viewpoint and Leonidas decreed that they should stay where they were and send messengers to the cities demanding assistance, as there were too few of them to ward off the Medes' army.

7.208.1 While they were discussing this, Xerxes sent a spy on horseback to see how many were there and what they were doing, as he had heard while he was still in Thessaly that a small force had gathered here and that its leaders were Spartans, including Leonidas, who was a descendant of Herakles. **2** The horseman rode up to the camp and looked down to survey it, but could not see all of it, because those drawn up inside the wall, which they had rebuilt and were now guarding, were out of sight. But he observed those outside, whose weapons were lying in front of the wall. It happened that, at the time, the Spartans were stationed there. He saw some of them exercising, and others combing their hair. He was amazed at this sight and took note of their numbers. **3** After these observations he rode back quietly, as no one pursued him or paid him any attention, and so he returned and told Xerxes all he had seen.

7.209.1 When Xerxes heard this he was unable to comprehend the truth, that they were preparing to the best of their ability either to die or to kill. What they were doing seemed to him to be ridiculous, and so he summoned Demaratos son of Ariston, who was in his camp. **2** When he arrived Xerxes questioned him about all these details as he wanted to understand what it was that the Spartans were doing. 'I told you about these men before,' Demaratos replied, 'when we were setting out for Greece, and when I told you you laughed, even though I clearly saw what was going to eventuate — for I try as hard as I can, O King, to speak the truth in your presence. **3** So listen once again: these men are here to fight us for the pass, and it is for this that they are getting ready. It is their custom, when they are going to endanger their lives, to groom their hair. Believe me — if you can defeat these and the rest of those who have remained behind at Sparta, there is no other race of men, O King, that could raise their hand to withstand you: you are now facing the Greeks' finest monarchy and city and their most valiant men.'

11.30 Herodotos 7.229.1–2, 7.231–232: The Three Hundred — Minus Two

These stories of the bravery of Spartans at Thermopylai and Plataea, and the consequences of cowardice no doubt formed part of the Spartan repertoire of stories encouraging bravery in battle (cf. doc. 6.50). Ophthalmia is an eye infection.

7.229.1 There is a tale told of two of the Three Hundred, Eurytos and Aristodemos, that Leonidas had allowed them both to leave the camp and they were lying ill at Alpenoi, with a severe attack of ophthalmia. They could have come to an agreement with each other and returned together to the safety of Sparta, or if they preferred not to return they could have died with the rest, but instead of pursuing either of these alternatives they were unable to agree. When Eurytos heard of the Persians' finding the way round he demanded his armour, put it on and ordered his helot to lead him amongst the fighters. The helot took him there and then left him and fled, while Eurytos rushed into the fray and was killed. Aristodemos, in contrast, lost his courage and stayed behind. **2** Now if Aristodemos had been the only one to be sick and had returned to Sparta, or if they had both done so together, in my view the Spartiates would not have shown any anger towards them: but now that one of them had died and the other had the same excuse but would not die, they had to display severe anger against Aristodemos …

7.231 When Aristodemos returned to Sparta he suffered disgrace and dishonour. This was the way he was treated: none of the Spartiates would give him fire or would speak to him, and he had the disgrace of being called 'Aristodemos the coward'. But he removed all the guilt that he was charged with at the battle of Plataea. **7.232** It is also said that another of the Three Hundred had been saved because he had been sent as a messenger to Thessaly: his name was Pantites. He returned to Sparta, but because he was disgraced, he hanged himself.

11.31 Simonides 7: Leonidas 'King of Spacious Sparta'

This epitaph for Leonidas might not be by Simonides but is perhaps hellenistic in date. The epitaph for the Spartans as a body at Thermopylai was Simonides 22b (doc. 11.32). [Page 196–97.]

The earth hides glorious men, Leonidas, who with you
Died here, king of spacious Sparta,
After they had awaited in war
The might of the Persians' many bows and swift-footed horses.

11.32 Simonides 22 a & b: Epitaphs for the Greek army and the Spartans

The Spartan dead were buried where they had fallen (Hdt. 7.228). The epitaph 22*a* was an inscription for the whole force left with Leonidas, while 22*b* was for the Spartans. These have very strong claims to being authentic works of Simonides. [Page 231–34.]

a. Here against three million once fought
Four thousand from the Peloponnese.

b. Stranger, tell the Spartans that here
We lie, obeying their orders.

11.33 Simonides 23: Epitaph for the Lokrians

Herodotos (7.203.1) mentions that the Opountian Lokrians (that is, from Opous in Lokris) were amongst those with Leonidas at Thermopylai, but they were not at the final stand; the Lokrians commemorated here must have died in previous engagements as the Lokrians subsequently went over to the Persians (Hdt. 8.66.2). [Page 235–36; Strabo *Geog.* 9.4.2.]

These men who died for Greece against the Persians are mourned
By Opous, mother-city of the righteous-judging Lokrians.

11.34 Herodotos 8.16.1–3, 8.18: Artemision

Artemision is the cape at the northern point of the island of Euboea; a naval battle was fought there at the same time as at Thermopylai. For Themistokles' bribery of Eurybiades and the Corinthian leader Adeimantos to stay and fight at Artemision, see Hdt. 8.4–5. The battle at Artemision was inconclusive, though there had been some Greek successes in naval engagements on previous days. As at the battle of Salamis, Xerxes' large fleet hindered its own efforts by its lack of ability to manoeuvre.

8.16.1 As the forces of Xerxes sailed in their battle order to the attack, the Greeks at Artemision stayed quiet. The barbarians formed a crescent shape with their ships and encircled them to try to surround them. Thereupon the Greeks put to sea against them and engaged them. The two sides were about equal in this naval battle. **2** For Xerxes' fleet because of its size and numbers kept harming itself, with the ships in confusion continually falling foul of one another; nevertheless it kept fighting and did not yield; for they considered it dreadful to be turned to flight by fewer ships. **3** Many of the Greeks' ships were destroyed, and many men, but far more of the barbarians' ships and men … **8.18** Thus they disengaged, with both sides glad to hasten to their anchorage.

SALAMIS

Even after Themistokles had convinced Eurybiades, the Spartan commander, that the allied fleet had to fight the Persians at Salamis, there were those who disagreed, and the decision was almost reversed. Themistokles' message to the Persian king encouraged Xerxes into a trap and ensured that the battle took place. Themistokles was the architect of the defeat of the Persians: by choosing the scene of the battle, where the smaller and fewer Greek ships had the advantage, he made victory over the Persians possible.

11.35 Meiggs & Lewis 23: The Themistokles Decree, 480 BC

This decree was inscribed in the third century BC (less probably the late fourth century), and there is much debate about whether it is or at least reflects a fifth-century original. It makes arrangements for the evacuation of women, children and old people from Athens (cf. Hdt. 8.41.1; Paus. 2.31.7), and for the able-bodied males to man the ships to 'resist the barbarian on behalf of freedom' (line 15). The inscription (lines 44–47) refers to the recall of the ostracised in 481/0 BC; cf. *Ath. Pol.* 22.8 (see doc. 10.9); Plut. *Them.* 11.1, *Arist.* 8. One of the recalled was Aristeides, ostracised in 483/2 (see docs 10.9, 10.12, 5.14.ii), who played an important role in capturing Psyttaleia at the eastern end of the Salamis channel. The foreigners (lines 14, 30) must be metics.

Gods. It was resolved by the boule and the people: Themistokles son of Neokles of Phrearrhioi proposed the motion: to entrust the city to Athena who protects Athens and to all the other gods to guard and keep off the barbarian in defence of the country; and that all Athenians and the foreigners living in Athens should place their children and wives in Troizen ... in the protection of Theseus the founder of the land; and that they should place the old people and the moveable possessions on Salamis; and that the treasurers and the priestesses should remain on the acropolis guarding the belongings of the gods; and that all the other Athenians and the foreigners who have reached adulthood should embark on the prepared two hundred ships and resist the barbarian on behalf of freedom, both their own and that of the other Greeks, along with the Spartans and Corinthians and Aeginetans and the others who wish to share in the danger; and that the generals should appoint two hundred trierarchs, one for each ship, beginning tomorrow, from those who own both land and home in Athens and who have children who are legitimate and who are not more than fifty years of age, and should assign the ships to them by lot; they should also choose ten marines for each ship from those between twenty and thirty years of age and four archers; they should also appoint by lot the officers for the ships when they also appoint the trierarchs by lot; the generals should also list the others ship by ship on noticeboards, the Athenians according to the deme (lexiarchic) registers and the foreigners from those registered with the polemarch; they should list them, assigning them to two hundred divisions of up to one hundred men each and inscribe for each division the name of the trireme and the trierarch and the officers so that they may know on which trireme each division should embark; and when all the divisions have been assigned and allocated to the triremes, the boule and the generals are to man all the two hundred ships after sacrificing to propitiate Zeus the Almighty (Pankrates) and Athena and Victory (Nike) and Poseidon the Preserver (Asphaleios); and when the ships are manned, with one hundred of them they are to assist Artemision in Euboea, and with the other one hundred around Salamis and the rest of Attica they are to lie in wait and guard the country. So that all Athenians may be united in resisting the barbarian, those who have changed their residence for ten years are to go to Salamis and stay there until the people should decide about them; and those deprived of civic rights ...

11.36 Plutarch *Themistokles* 10.8–10: The Athenians Abandon Their City

The fact that the incident with the dog is supposed to have happened to Xanthippos, Perikles' father, rather detracts from than adds to its credibility; however, such a feat is not intrinsically impossible, and Plutarch here well portrays the anguish with which the Athenians abandoned their city. For the warning of the serpent on the acropolis (its failure to eat the honey-cake persuaded the Athenians that Athena was in favour of their abandoning the city), see Hdt. 8.41.2–3.

10.8 As the whole city sailed off, the sight filled some with pity, others with amazement at their courage, as they sent off their families in one direction, and themselves crossed over to the island without flinching at the lamentations, tears and embraces of their parents. **9** Those of the citizens left behind because of their old age were most pitiable, while the affectionate disposition of the tame, companionable animals was also touching, as, howling and longing to be with their owners, they ran alongside them as they embarked. **10** Among these was a dog belonging to Xanthippos, Perikles' father, who, the story goes, could not endure being parted from him, and who jumped into the sea and swam alongside the trireme and was cast ashore at Salamis, where he fainted and immediately died; they say that its tomb is the place named the Dog's Mound, which even today is pointed out.

11.37 Plutarch *Themistokles* 11.2–3, 11.5: Themistokles Carries the Day

This discussion between the allies took place at Salamis; cf. Hdt. 8.57–63, for presumably a more accurate and detailed account, where it was Adeimantos the Corinthian commander (not Eurybiades) who made the initial remark and then accused Themistokles of being a man without a polis, to which Themistokles replied that the Athenians would sail to Siris in Italy. For Adeimantos, see doc. 11.41.

11.2 Eurybiades had command of the ships because of Sparta's reputation, but he was faint-hearted in the face of danger, wanting to set sail for the Isthmus, where the Peloponnesians' infantry was gathered, but Themistokles spoke against him. **3** It was at this point that he made the remark which has often been quoted; for when Eurybiades said to him, 'Themistokles, at the games they thrash those who start before the signal,' Themistokles replied, 'Yes, but they don't crown those who are left behind'. And when Eurybiades raised his staff as if to hit him, Themistokles said, 'Strike me if you like, but listen' … **5** When someone then said that it wasn't proper for a man without a city to instruct those who had one to abandon it and desert their country, Themistokles turned to him and said, 'We have abandoned our homes and walls, you rascal, because we did not want to be enslaved by lifeless things; but we have the greatest city in Greece, our two hundred triremes, which are now ready to help you, if you want to be saved by them, but if you go away and betray us again, the Greeks will soon hear that the Athenians have acquired a city as free and land no worse than that we cast off.' When Themistokles said this, Eurybiades was afraid that the Athenians might leave and abandon them.

11.38 Aeschylus *Persians* 348–471: The Battle of Salamis

Atossa, the Persian queen, mother of Xerxes, here asks a Persian messenger about the action at Salamis. Hdt. 8.90.4 (cf. 8.86) mentions that Xerxes watched the battle from the base of a hill across from Salamis; compare lines 466–67 below. The details about how the Greek ships defeated the Persians are important ones.

Atossa: Is the city of Athens then still not sacked?
Messenger: Its defences are secure, while it has its men.
Atossa: And, tell me, what began the naval engagement?
Who started the battle, whether the Greeks,
Or my son, exulting in his multitude of ships?
Messenger: The whole evil was begun, my lady,
By some avenging spirit or evil genius that appeared from somewhere;
For a Greek man from the Athenian host
Came and said this to your son Xerxes:
That when the blackness of dark night should descend
The Greeks would not remain, but on the decks
Of their ships they would leap, one one way, one another,
And each would save his life in secret flight.
Straightway as he heard this, not knowing of the guile
Of this Greek or the jealousy of the gods,
Xerxes proclaimed this speech to all his captains:
That when the sun ceased illuminating the earth with his beams,
And darkness covered the precinct of the sky,
They should marshal the close array of ships in three lines
With other ships in a circle around the island of Ajax (Salamis)
To guard the entrances and surging straits;
If the Greeks should avoid an evil fate
And find some means of flight secretly with their ships,
It was decreed that each captain should lose his head.
Xerxes spoke this from a very cheerful heart,
For he did not know the future destined by the gods.
And they not in disorder but with obedient minds
Prepared their dinner, and meanwhile the seamen
Were fastening their oars around the well-fitting pins.
Now as the sun's light dwindled
And night came on, every man who was lord of the oar,
Every man who was master of arms, went to his ship;
Rank of each long ship encouraged rank,
And they sailed as each had been commanded;
All night long the ships' commanders
Kept all the mariners cruising at the oar.
And night was passing, and the Greek host did not at all
In any way attempt a secret exit;
But when, however, white-horsed day,
Brilliant to behold, shone over the whole land,
First of all, resoundingly, a noise from the Greeks
Echoed in praise like song, and at the same time clearly
The echo of the mountain rock returned the cry,
And fear seized all the barbarians, who

Had been deceived in their opinion; for not in flight
Were the Greeks then chanting the solemn battle-hymn,
But rushing into battle with cheerful courage.
And the trumpet with its battle-cry inflamed them all;
Immediately with the stroke of the dashing oar
They struck the deep seawater at command.
Swiftly all were clearly plain in view;
First the right wing, well disciplined,
Led on in good order, and next the whole fleet
Advanced, and one could hear in unison
A mighty shout: 'Forward, O sons of Greece, forward,
Liberate your native land, and liberate your
Children and your wives, the seats of your ancestral gods,
Your forebears' tombs; now the struggle is for your all.'
And from us a roar of Persian voices
Rose in answer, and no longer did time permit delay.
Immediately ship struck into ship its bronze-tipped
Prow; a Greek ship began the attack,
Smashing the whole of a Phoenician ship's
High stern, and each side directed one ship against another.
Initially, the stream of the Persian fleet managed to stand its
Ground; but when in the narrow strait the multitude of ships
Were gathered, and no help could be given to one another,
They struck each other with their bronze-tipped
Rams, and all their rowing gear was broke to pieces.
Meanwhile the Greek ships, with deliberation,
Circled and battered them on every side, ships' hulls
Were overturned, and no longer could one see the sea
Now filled with shipwrecks and men's slaughter;
And shores and reefs were full of corpses.
Each of our ships started rowing off in disorder,
As many as survived from the barbarian fleet.
...
Those Persians in the prime of life,
Bravest in spirit and notable in birth,
And always amongst the first to show loyalty to the king,
Have died disgracefully by a most inglorious fate.

Atossa: This dreadful calamity has made me wretched, friends.
But by what death do you say that these men perished?

Messenger: There is an island (Psyttaleia) in front of Salamis,
Small, poor anchorage for ships, which the dance-loving
Pan frequents along its sea-washed shore;
Here Xerxes sent these men, so that, when from the ships
The shipwrecked enemy might seek safety on the isle,
They could slay the easily mastered host of Greeks,
And save their own friends from the narrow straits of the sea,
Badly forecasting the future; for when god

Gave the Greeks the glory of the battle of the ships,
They straightway fenced their bodies round with well-wrought brazen
Armour, bounded from their ships, and
Encircled the whole island, so our men were at a loss
Where they might turn. Many times they were struck
By hand-thrown rocks, and from the bow's bowstring
Arrows fell upon them and destroyed them;
At last the Greeks rushed on them all at once
And struck them, cutting to pieces the wretches' limbs,
Until they utterly destroyed the life of all.
Now Xerxes, seeing the depths of his misfortunes, groaned lamentation;
For he had a seat in view of the whole host,
A high hill near the shore of the open sea;
Rending his garments, uttering a loud wail,
He gave orders immediately to his infantry,
And dismissed them in disorder and in flight. Such now,
Besides the previous one, is the disaster you must mourn.

11.39 Thucydides 1.73.2–74.3: The Athenians Review their Past Services to Greece

The context here is the debate at Sparta in 432 BC when the Spartans voted that the Athenians had broken the Thirty Years' Peace made in 446/5 BC. The Athenians' statement that 'we were the only ones to face up to the barbarian' (1.73.4) neglects the help given by the Plataeans, but is basically true (esp. Hdt. 6.108.6). Herodotos (doc. 11.54) makes a similar assessment of the Athenians' role in the second Persian invasion, probably derived from Athenian sources.

1.73.2 We must speak of the Persian Wars, events which you yourselves know well, even though you may be tired of always hearing them referred to … **4** Our view is that at Marathon we were the only ones to face up to the barbarian and when he came later, and we were not able to keep him off by land, we got into our ships with all our people and joined in the naval battle at Salamis, which prevented him from sailing against the Peloponnese and ravaging it city by city, for they would have been unable to come to each other's aid in the face of such a number of ships. **5** The best proof of this is the barbarian's own actions: once he had lost at sea, he withdrew as quickly as possible with the greater part of his host because his force was no longer adequate. **1.74.1** This then was the outcome, and it clearly demonstrated that Greece's destiny depended on her ships, and we contributed to this in the three most useful ways: in providing the greatest number of ships, the most intelligent general and our resolute courage; for of the 400 ships a little less than two-thirds were ours, Themistokles was in command, who was primarily responsible for the sea-battle taking place in the narrow straits, which was very clearly what saved the situation, and because of this you yourselves gave him more honour than any other foreigner who visited you, **2** and we displayed by far the most audacious courage, we who, since no one helped us by land and the other states right up to our borders were already enslaved, decided to abandon our city and destroy our homes, not in order to forsake the common good of the rest of the allies, nor by dispersing to become useless to them, but by getting into our ships and encountering danger and not being angry with you that you had not come to our aid earlier. **3** So our view is that we have helped you no less than you have helped us. For you came to fight from inhabited cities and ones you wanted to preserve for the future, and because you were afraid on your own behalf much more than on ours (at any rate when we were still safe you didn't appear); while we set out from a city that no longer existed and encountered danger on behalf of one for which there was little hope, and joined in saving you as well as ourselves.

11.40 Simonides 20a: An Athenian Epigram on Salamis (?)

If this inscription is accepted as pertaining to Salamis, the mention of footsoldiers refers to the fighting on Psyttaleia. The Athenians set up a trophy on Psyttaleia, and one on Salamis to commemorate the victory. [*IG* I[3] 503; Meiggs & Lewis 26 (I); Hansen 2; *IG* I[2] 763; *SEG* 40.28.]

The glory of these men's valour will always be undying
... the gods allot;
For both as foot soldiers and in quick-sailing ships they prevented
All Greece from seeing the day of slavery.

11.41 Simonides 10: Adeimantos, the Corinthian Commander at Salamis

Herodotos records that the Corinthians at Salamis fled as soon as battle was joined and only returned once the Greeks were victorious, which sounds very much like a story the Athenians invented during the Peloponnesian War (Hdt. 8.94). Adeimantos commanded the Corinthians at Artemision and Salamis and Plutarch, who records this epigram, notes that Herodotos pours abuse on Adeimantos for fleeing from Artemision (Plut. *Mor.* 870f (*On the Malignity of Herodotos* 39); Hdt. 8.5.1, 59, 61, esp. 94, esp. 94.1). [Page 200–2.]

This is the tomb of the famous Adeimantos, through whom
All Greece put on the garland of freedom.

11.42 Simonides 11: Epitaph of the Corinthians Who Died at Salamis

Plutarch *Mor.* 870e (*On the Malignity of Herodotos* 39) gives this epitaph and writes that the Athenians allowed the Corinthians to bury their dead on Salamis near the city. A marble block on Salamis has the remains of letters of the first two lines of this epitaph. [Page 202–04; Hansen 131; Meiggs & Lewis 24; *IG* I[2] 927; *IG* I[3] 1143.]

Stranger, we once lived in the well-watered city of Corinth,
But now Salamis, island of Ajax, holds us;
Here we took Phoenician ships and Persians
And Medes and saved holy Greece.

11.43 Simonides 14: A Prayer by Corinthian Women

Simonides wrote the epigram for the bronze statues which the Corinthian women dedicated to Aphrodite (Kypris) in thanks for the safety of Corinth. [Page 207–11; Schol. Pind. (on *Ol.* 13.32b); Plut. *Mor.* 871a–b (*On the Malignity of Herodotos* 39).]

These women on behalf of the Greeks and their fellow citizens who fight hand-to-hand
Stand praying with heaven-sent power to Kypris;
For the goddess Aphrodite did not choose to the bow-carrying
Persians to hand over the acropolis of the Greeks (Corinth).

11.44 Simonides 19a: The Naxians Fight with Honour

Plut. *Mor.* 869a–c (*On the Malignity of Herodotos* 36), uses another epigram of Simonides to attempt (unsuccessfully) to discredit Herodotos, who states (8.46.3) that the Naxians were initially sent to fight for the Persians, but Demokritos persuaded them to join the Greeks. Diodoros 5.52.3 writes that the Naxians were the first to withdraw from Xerxes' fleet, and participated at Salamis with distinction. [Page 219.]

Demokritos was the third to begin the battle, when off Salamis
The Greeks met the Persians at sea;
He took five of the enemy's ships, and saved a sixth,
A Dorian, from capture at barbarian hands.

11.45 *Inscriptiones Graecae* I³ 822: A Western Greek at Salamis

This heavily restored inscription is from an inscribed statue base of the athlete Phayllos, found on the acropolis at Athens. Herodotos 8.47 says that of the western Greeks only the Crotoniates came to help, and he mentions Phayllos as a past victor in the Pythian festival at Delphi. For Alexander's generosity to Croton on this account, see doc. 15.18. [*DAA* 76; Moretti 11; *IG* I² 655; Page 407–08; Hansen 265.]

Phayllos was admired by all,
For he was thrice victor in the games
At Delphi, and captured ships
Which Asia sent forth.

PLATAEA

After the defeat of the Persian navy at Salamis in 480 BC, Xerxes himself left Greece, leaving behind an army under the command of Mardonios to continue operations. Mardonios sent Alexander, king of Macedon, to Athens to suggest an alliance; the Spartans in turn sent an embassy to Athens, which was assured that the Athenians had no intention of going over to the Persians (Hdt. 8.136, 140–144; doc. 3.90). Mardonios then recaptured Athens ten months after Xerxes had first entered it. Before leaving, he burned the city, which was thus sacked a second time. When Mardonios again made overtures to the Athenians,

Lykidas, a member of the boule who proposed accepting the terms, was stoned to death by the Athenians (as was his family; see doc. 4.26). The Spartans, after some delay, sent a force, once they had been convinced that if the Athenians went over to the Persians the Isthmus wall would be of no avail. With news of the Peloponnesian forces at the Isthmus (where the Peloponnesians received favourable omens), Mardonios retired to Boeotia. Here, Greeks who had medised joined him. See Hdt. 9.1–27; for the allied numbers at Plataea, see Hdt. 9.28–30.

11.46 Tod 2.204, lines 21–51: Oath of the Athenians before Plataea

The authenticity of this oath is contested, but while Herodotos does not mention the oath before Plataea he speaks of a similar oath sworn before Thermopylai (Hdt. 7.132.2: doc. 11.19), and its formula is quoted in almost identical terms by the Athenian orator Lykourgos (*Leok.* 81) and Diodorus (9.29.2–3). To 'tithe' a city was to sell it and its inhabitants and give a tenth of the proceeds to the gods.

The oath which the Athenians swore when they were about to fight against the barbarians: 'I shall fight as long as I live, and shall not consider it more important to be alive than to be free, and I shall not desert the commanding officer (taxilochos) nor the leader of the division (enomotarch), whether he is alive or dead, nor shall I depart unless the leaders (hegemones) go first, and I will do whatever the generals command, and those of the allied fighters who die I shall bury on the spot and I shall not leave anyone unburied; and after conquering the barbarians in battle I shall tithe the city of the Thebans, and I shall not harm Athens or Sparta or Plataea or any of the other cities who joined in the battle, nor shall I suffer their being coerced by famine nor shall I keep off from them flowing waters whether they are friends or enemies. And if I abide by the things written in the oath, may my city be free from sickness, and if I do not, may it be sick; and may my city not be sacked, and if I do not, may it be sacked; and may my land bear fruit, and if I do not, may it be unfruitful; and may women bear children like their parents, and if I do not, monsters; and may cattle bear young like cattle, and if I do not, monsters.' After swearing this, they covered the sacrificed victims with their shields and at the signal of the trumpet called down a curse, that if they should transgress anything of what was sworn and should not abide by the things written in the oath, pollution should be on those that swore it.

11.47 Herodotos 9.46.1–63.2: The Battle of Plataea

The battle of Plataea was said to have taken place on the same day as the one at Mykale (Hdt. 9.100.2; doc. 11.51); Hdt. 9.48–63 deserves to be read in full. The Persian cavalry, which presented the greatest threat to the Greeks, harried them and fouled the spring from which they drew water. The Greeks therefore decided to move position to the 'Island', formed by two channels of the river Asopos. This led to their forces splitting up, and most of the Greeks fled instead to Plataea, stopping outside the walls near the temple of Hera. When Pausanias ordered the Spartans to move, one of the commanders, Amompharetos, refused to obey, causing a delay. They finally reached the temple of Demeter, and here the Persians pressed their attack.

9.46.1 The Athenian generals came to the right wing and told Pausanias what they had heard from Alexander (commander of the Macedonians). He was fearful of the Persians at their account and spoke as follows: **2** 'Since the engagement will be at dawn, you Athenians should stand opposite the Persians and we against the Boeotians and the other Greeks drawn up against us' ... **9.47.1** As this pleased both, when dawn broke they changed their positions. But the Boeotians noticed what they were doing and reported to Mardonios. And when he heard, he himself tried to change position, placing the Persians so they faced the Spartans. When Pausanias learned that this had happened, realising that his manoeuvre had not escaped notice, he led the Spartans back to the right wing; and Mardonios did likewise on the left. **9.48.1** When they were back in their original positions, Mardonios sent a herald to the Spartans (**9.48.1–61.3**: *Mardonios rebuked the Spartans for trying to give the place of danger to the Athenians. After heavy Persian harassment, the allied troops moved position to Plataea. As the sacrifices remained unfavourable Pausanias called on Hera for help.*) **9.62.1** While he was still asking her help, the Tegeates rose first and moved against the barbarians, and immediately after Pausanias' prayer the omens were favourable for the Spartans as they sacrificed. When this occurred they too moved against the enemy and the Persians left off their bows and met them face to face. **2** At first the battle took place at the Persians' shields (from behind which they were shooting). When these had fallen, a fierce battle took place near the temple of Demeter over a long period, where they came to close quarters; for the barbarians took hold of the Spartans' spears and broke them. **3** In courage and strength the Persians were not inferior, but they were without armour and untrained and not equal in skill to their opponents. Singly or in groups of ten, both more and less, they dashed out and threw themselves in a body at the Spartans and were killed. **9.63.1** Mardonios happened to be there, fighting from a white horse and with his 1,000 best hand-picked Persians around him, and here particularly the Persians pressed hard on their opponents. While Mardonios was alive they resisted and defended themselves and killed many of the Spartans; **2** but when Mardonios was killed and the troops drawn up around him, which were the strongest, fell, then the others took to flight and yielded to the Spartans. What most greatly disadvantaged them was their clothing, being without armour; for they were fighting without armour against hoplites.

11.48 Simonides *Elegy* 11: Their Glory Will Be Immortal

Several papyrus fragments of Simonides include elegies celebrating the battles of Artemision and Plataea. Simonides is also known to have written poems on Thermopylai, Salamis and perhaps Marathon (in addition to the inscribed epigrams). The elegy on Plataea here begins with a hymn to Achilles, son of Thetis. The (statues of the) Tyndaridai, Castor and Pollux, traditionally accompanied the Spartan kings on campaign; for Pausanias, the Spartan commander at Plataea, see docs 6.35–36.

But now farewell, son of the glorious goddess,
Daughter of Nereus of the sea; while I,
Summon you to my help, illustrious Muse,
If you have any care for men who pray;
Make ready too this delightful song of praise
Of mine, that men may remember ...
Those who for Sparta ... day of slavery
...
They did not forget their courage ... high as heaven,
And their glory amongst men will be immortal.

Leaving the Eurotas and the town of Sparta
They hastened accompanied by the horse-taming sons of Zeus
The Tyndarid heroes and mighty Menelaos
... Leaders of their fathers' city,
Led by the noble son of divine Kleombrotos, ... Pausanias.

11.49 Meiggs & Lewis 27: The Serpent Column

Three intertwined serpents, worked in bronze and standing about six metres high with a golden tripod atop, had the names of thirty-one of the Greek states who had fought against the Persians inscribed on the coils. This was dedicated by the allies after Plataea in 479 BC, but refers to the whole of the war and not just to this battle. There are also some absentees from the list — Croton, Pale, Seriphos, Mantineia and the Lokrians. Pausanias attempted to dedicate this on his own behalf: doc. 6.35.

These the | war | fought:
Spartans | Athenians | Corinthians
Tegeates | Sicyonians | Aeginetans
Megarians | Epidaurians | Orchomenians
Phleiasians | Troizenians | Hermionians
Tirynthians | Plataeans | Thespiaians
Mycenaeans | Keians | Melians | Tenians
Naxians | Eretrians | Chalkidians
Styrians | Eleians | Potidaeans
Leukadians | Anaktorians | Kythnians | Siphnians
Ambraciots | Lepreates.

11.50 Simonides 8 & 9: Epitaphs from Plataea (?)

Although attributed to Thermopylai in antiquity these verses probably refer to Plataea; the first is the epitaph of the Athenians, the second of the Spartans (cf. Paus. 9.2.5). [Page 197–200.]

8 If dying nobly is the greatest part of valour,
To us above all others Fortune has granted this;
For after striving to crown Greece with freedom
We lie here enjoying praise that will never age.

9 These men gave their beloved country inextinguishable fame
And encompassed themselves with the dark cloud of death.
They died but are not dead, since their valour glorifies them from above
And brings them up from the house of Hades.

11.51 Herodotos 9.101.3–102.3: The Battle of Mykale

At Mykale in 479 BC the Greeks defeated the Persians and gained control of the Hellespont and the Aegean islands. The Ionians and Aeolians fighting with the Persians deserted and fought for the Greeks; Hdt. 9.104 noted that this was the second time the Ionians had revolted against the

Persians. Here, in 479, Herodotos ends his narrative. In the following year (or 477), Leotychidas campaigned in Thessaly and was disgraced, ending his reign in exile (doc. 6.76).

9.101.3 Both Greeks and barbarians hastened to meet in battle, as the islands and the Hellespont were the prizes for victory. **9.102.1** For the Athenians and those drawn up next to them up to about half way, their line of advance was along the beach and level plain, while for the Spartans and those next to them in the line it was across a gully and mountains; so while the Spartans were still on their way round, those on the other wing were already engaged. **2** As long as the Persians' shields remained upright, they were able to repel the attack and did not have the worst of the battle; but when the host of the Athenians and their neighbours, so that the victory might be theirs and not the Spartans', encouraged each other and battled even more eagerly, from that point the affair had already changed markedly. **3** For they forced their way through the shields and made a massed attack upon the Persians, who repelled them for some time but finally fled to the wall. The Athenians, Corinthians, Sicyonians and Troizenians (for they were drawn up in this order) followed and rushed in alongside them. Once the wall was taken, the barbarians were no longer concerned with resistance, but all except the Persians turned and fled.

11.52 Simonides 16: Inscription on the Megarian Dead

The introduction, dating to the fourth or fifth century AD, to this epigram, states that it was reinscribed by the high priest Helladios because it 'had been destroyed by time', and was the work of Simonides. Lines 3–4 refer to Artemision; lines 7–8 refer to Plataea (cf. Hdt. 9.69). Paus. 1.43.3 writes of a mass grave at Megara for the Megarians who died in the Persian Wars. [Tod 1.20.]

While striving to strengthen the day of freedom
For Greece and the Megarians, we received the fate of death,
Some under Euboea and Pelion, where stands
The precinct of the holy archer Artemis,
Some at the mountain of Mykale, some before Salamis,
< >
Others on the Boeotian plain, who dared
To come to blows with enemies fighting on horseback.
The citizens granted us together this privilege around the navel
Of the Nisaians in their people-thronged agora.

11.53 Plutarch *Sayings of the Spartans* (*Moralia* 225a–d, 230e–f): Spartan Commanders

Leonidas, son of Anaxandridas **(cf.** ***Hdt. 7.226.2*****)**

4 When the ephors said, 'Haven't you decided to do anything other than block the passes against the barbarians?' he said, 'In theory no, but in actual fact to die for the Greeks.' **6** When someone said, 'It isn't possible even to see the sun because of the barbarians' arrows,' he said, 'How nice, then, that we are to fight them in the shade.' **10** When Xerxes wrote to him, 'If you do not fight against the gods, but side with me, you can be monarch of Greece,' he wrote back, 'If you knew what was good in life, you would refrain from desiring what belongs to other people; as for me it is better to die for Greece than be monarch of the people of my race.' **11** When Xerxes wrote again, 'Hand over your weapons,' he wrote back, 'Come and take them.'

Pausanias, son of Kleombrotos (cf. *Hdt. 9.82*)

6 After his victory over the Persians at Plataea, he ordered that the dinner prepared beforehand for the Persians should be served to his staff; as this was amazingly extravagant, he said, 'By the gods, these Persians are gluttonous fellows, in that they had so much and still came after our barley-bread!'

11.54 Herodotos 7.139.1–6: Herodotos' Assessment

Herodotos in ascribing the real credit for the overall victory over the Persians to the Athenians may be recording ideas he had heard at Athens. He similarly states that the outbreak of war between Athens and Aegina, which led Themistokles to argue successfully for the proceeds of the Laureion silver mines to be used to construct a fleet of 200 ships (see doc. 11.23), was what 'saved Greece' (Hdt. 7.144.2), because the outbreak of war compelled Athens to become a sea power, which meant that Athens had a fleet when the Persians invaded.

7.139.1 Here I feel compelled to express an opinion, which will be resented by most people, but nevertheless as it seems to me true I will not suppress it. **2** If the Athenians had dreaded the approaching danger so much that they had abandoned their country, or if they had not abandoned it but stayed and submitted to Xerxes, no one would have attempted to resist the king by sea. And if no one had opposed Xerxes by sea, events on the mainland would have taken place like this: **3** even if a number of walls had been built across the Isthmus by the Peloponnesians, the Spartans would have been betrayed by their allies, not willingly but by necessity, as one by one their cities were taken by the barbarian fleet, and the Spartans would have been isolated, and being isolated would have performed great deeds and died nobly. **4** Either this would have happened, or before this, seeing the other Greeks medising, they would have come to terms with Xerxes. In either case, Greece would have become subject to the Persians. I simply cannot understand the use of the walls built across the Isthmus when the king had control of the sea. **5** And so anyone who said that the Athenians were the saviours of Greece would be perfectly correct: whichever side they had turned to would have prevailed; they chose that Greece should remain free, and they roused all the rest of Greece, which had not medised, and played the main part, after the gods, in driving off the king. **6** Not even the dreadful and frightening oracles which came from Delphi persuaded them to abandon Greece, but they stayed firm and dared to await the invader of their country.

11.55 Pindar *Pythian* 1.71–75: The Greeks' Debt to Sicily

Hieron, tyrant of Syracuse (478–466 BC), won the chariot-race at Delphi in 470 BC (Gelon had died in 478): docs 7.57–58. He took part in the defeat of the Carthaginians (in the inscription referred to as Phoenicians) at Himera in 480, and defeated the Etruscans at sea in 474 near Cumae; hence he claimed that the victories at Himera and Cumae were equal to those of Plataea and Salamis.

I beseech you, son of Kronos, grant that quietly
At home the Phoenician and Etruscan war-cry will remain, now they have seen what loss of ships came from their arrogance before Cumae,
And their sufferings, when overcome by the Syracusans' leader
Who cast their youth into the sea out of their swift-sailing ships
Delivering Greece from grievous slavery.

11.56 Plato *Laws* 692d–693a: Greece's Finest Hour?

In the discussion about the governments of the Peloponnesian states Argos, Messene and Sparta, the Athenian suggests that if the three states historically had combined into a single authority, the Persians would never have attacked Greece.

692d After all, Kleinias, they defended themselves against the Persians disgracefully. By disgraceful, I don't mean to say that those who conquered the Persians at that time both by land and by sea did not win splendid battles. But what I mean when I say disgraceful is that first of all only one of those three states fought to defend Greece, and the other two were so corrupted that one (Messene) even tried to prevent Sparta's attempts to come to Greece's aid, fighting her with all her might, **692e** while the other, Argos … was called on to fight off the barbarians and yet neither answered nor helped out. Anyone who gave a lengthy account of the events of that war would have to criticize Greece for very unbecoming behaviour: in fact, to speak accurately, one might say that it didn't make any defence at all, but if it hadn't been for the joint determination of the Athenians and Spartans to ward off the approaching slavery, **693a** now nearly all the races of the Greeks would be mixed up with each other, as well as barbarians with Greeks and Greeks with barbarians, just like those nations whom the Persians rule over, who have been split up, then awkwardly mingled together, and who now live in scattered groups.

11.57 Aristophanes *Lysistrata* 1242–70: A Spartan Remembers the Old Days

In the final scene of the play *Lysistrata*, performed in 411 BC, after the celebratory banquet signalling the return of peace, a Spartan sings of the past triumphs of the alliance. The dipodia is a Spartan dance. Cf. doc. 6.19 for a further passage from the *Lysistrata*, praising the Spartans.

Spartan: My dear chap, take your pipes,
So I can dance the dipodia and sing
A fine song for the Athenians and us together.
Prytanis (to the piper):
Take your pipes then, by the gods,
As I take pleasure in seeing you dance.
Spartan: Send to this youth, O Memory,
Your Muse, who
Knows us and the Athenians,
When they at Artemision
Threw themselves like gods
Against the ships and beat the Persians;
While us Leonidas

Led like boars as we sharpened,
I think, our tusks; and much
Foam flowed around our jaws,
As well as down our legs.
For the Persian soldiers were as numerous
As the sands.
Huntress, beast-slayer,
Come hither, virgin goddess,
To our treaty,
To keep us united for a long time. And now
Again may fruitful friendship exist
Through our compacts,
And may we put an end to wily foxes.
O come hither, come,
O virgin huntress.

12

THE DELIAN LEAGUE AND THE PENTEKONTAETIA

In 478 BC the Spartan regent Pausanias was dispatched as commander of the Hellenes, but at Byzantium his arrogance made him unpopular with the Ionians, and Athens began to assume the leadership of the recently liberated Greeks (doc. 12.4). The rationale behind the Delian League was the continuation of the war against the Persians, although the Athenians obviously realised at the time the benefits to be gained from such an alliance. However, that the league was intended primarily to pursue a war of liberation is implicit in its subsequent military activities, in which the last remnants of Persian power in Greek territory were defeated.

The states that joined Athens, the islands and Greek cities of Asia Minor that had been liberated from the Persians did so of their own free will (except for Phaselis; doc. 12.29) and were autonomous, while league decisions were made in general meetings. As the allies grew tired of fighting, many commuted their contributions to money, rather than supplying men and ships (doc. 12.4). The league undertook numerous military activities against the Persians and its own members, and the number of wars in which the Athenians engaged in this period is indicated by the casualty list for the Erechtheid tribe, commemorating in 460 or 459 BC those who died in Cyprus, in Egypt, in Phoenicia, at Halieis, on Aegina and at Megara 'in the same year' (doc. 12.14). The most important campaigns against the Persians were those of the Eurymedon (docs 12.7–8), Cyprus (doc. 12.15) and Egypt (doc. 12.13). The first steps in turning the Delian League into the Athenian empire were taken when allies who revolted were forced back into the league. Naxos, for example, lost its autonomy, and had no choice as to whether to be a member: it had to pay tribute, participate in league military activities and follow Athens' lead (doc. 12.4), and the Athenian action against Thasos (doc. 12.9) strongly suggests that Athens was motivated to engage in economic imperialism and to take over Thasos' mines for its own benefit.

In either 460 or 459 BC, another important development took place, when Megara allied itself with Athens (doc. 12.18); this is considered to be the incident which heralded the start of the First Peloponnesian War. Athens welcomed the alliance as control of Megara was important for forestalling a Spartan invasion of Attica. There was direct conflict between Athens and Sparta at the battle of Tanagra in 458/7 (doc. 12.20), in which the Spartans were victorious, but this was only a temporary setback for the Athenians, who shortly afterwards established themselves as masters of Boeotia. This was followed, c. 457, by the Athenian victory over Aegina, which was forced to tear down its walls, give up its fleet and pay tribute. Aegina was amongst the states which later encouraged Sparta to declare war on Athens. But Athenian control of Boeotia was short-lived, ending in 446, and Megara returned to the Peloponnesian fold in the same year. In 446/5 a Thirty Years' Peace was agreed upon (doc. 12.22) and Athens returned to the Peloponnesians the places it had seized during the conflict.

The pentekontaetia (the term is used by the scholiast on Thucydides 1.89.1), the fifty years between the Persian invasions and the Peloponnesian War, is marked by a number of outstanding statesmen in Athens. After the repulse of the Persians, Themistokles set about rebuilding the walls of Athens (doc. 12.1), and Aristeides and Kimon took over direction of military campaigns. Themistokles was ostracised some time in the 470s, indicating that political initiative had passed to others, in particular to Kimon. Though a conservative politician and a philo-Spartan, Kimon was nevertheless an ardent supporter of the growth of Athenian power. He commanded the fleet in the 470s and 460s and was responsible for successful campaigns against the Persians. His downfall occurred when he persuaded the Athenians to assist the Spartans against the helots and perioikoi who had revolted, probably in 465. Ephialtes took advantage of his absence to carry out reforms to the Areiopagos which reduced its powers, which were then distributed to the boule, assembly, and law courts (doc. 12.12). When the Spartans 'became afraid of the Athenians' boldness and revolutionary spirit' and sent them away from Ithome (docs 12.9, 12.11), Kimon's opponents seized upon the opportunity to have him ostracised. Ephialtes' reforms meant that political decisions were made solely by the people, either in the assembly or in the law courts.

But the statesman who particularly dominated Athenian politics in the 440s and 430s BC was Perikles. He was opposed principally by Thucydides, son of Melesias (not the historian; doc. 12.27), whose attacks on Perikles had little effect in an era in which the demos was confident about its role in the state; Thucydides was ostracised (doc. 10.14.xi). Perikles was instrumental in completing Athens' transformation into an imperialist power and fully fledged democracy. He was an outstanding general, especially at Samos (doc. 12.24). Under him, cleruchies were sent out to allied states to assist in their control (doc. 12.25). His introduction of pay for jury service was crucial in extending participation in the democratic process (doc. 12.26); the ekklesia ran the empire by passing decrees. Despite Thucydides' criticisms of those who were Perikles' successors in Athenian politics, they basically followed his policies of imperialism and confrontation with Sparta (see doc. 13.9).

The period 500–431 BC was dominated by several key figures, of whom Miltiades, Themistokles, Aristeides, Kimon, Ephialtes and Perikles were the most prominent, and each played an important role in the history of the period and the growth of Athenian power. Miltiades was the architect of the victory at Marathon; Themistokles saved the day at Salamis; Aristeides was instrumental in organising the Delian League, which the Athenians transformed into an empire; Kimon extended Athenian control through the Aegean; and Ephialtes strengthened the democracy by giving more of the powers of the state to popular bodies. But each of these six individuals suffered the ebbs and flows of the political game: Miltiades was fined fifty talents and died in prison of gangrene, Aristeides, Themistokles and Kimon were ostracised, and Ephialtes was assassinated. Perikles was to die of the plague in 429, but he and his associates had also faced prosecution and fines, and on one occasion Perikles was possibly even demoted from the strategia: political life in Athens, even for a champion of the people, was certainly no sinecure.

12.1 Thucydides 1.89.3–93.7: The Athenians Rebuild Their Walls

Athens had been sacked first by Xerxes and later by Mardonios. After the Persian invasions, the rebuilding of Athens' walls was opposed by the Spartans, while Sparta's allies, according to Thucydides, were already wary of the growing power of Athens. Themistokles' stratagem of delaying tactics (cf. Plut. *Them.* 19.1–3; Diod. 11.39–40) allowed the Athenians time to rebuild their walls; the Athenian assumption that the Spartans might attack is understandable given the Spartan invasions of Attica in the sixth century.

1.89.3 The Athenian people, when the barbarians had left their country, immediately started bringing back their children and wives and their remaining property from the places to which they had removed them for safety, and prepared to rebuild their city and walls; for only small sections of their surrounding wall were still standing and most of their houses were in ruins, with only a few surviving, in which the important Persians had had their quarters. **1.90.1** But when the Spartans heard what was being planned, they sent an embassy, partly because they would not have been pleased to see either the Athenians or anyone else with a wall, but more because the allies were stirring them up, because they were afraid both of the size of the Athenians' fleet, which had previously not existed, and of the courage which they had displayed in fighting the Persians. **2** The Spartans, without showing the Athenians their wishes and their underlying suspicion, proposed that the Athenians should not fortify their city, but rather join them in pulling down any walls outside the Peloponnese which were still standing, so that the barbarians, if they should again invade, would not have a stronghold which they could use as a base, as they had recently been able to do from Thebes; and, they said, the Peloponnese would be sufficient for everyone both as a refuge and as a base of operations. **3** After the Spartans made these proposals, by Themistokles' advice the Athenians immediately sent them away with the reply that they would dispatch envoys to them to discuss these matters, and Themistokles told them to send him to Sparta as quickly as possible; the other envoys, however, who had been chosen to go with him should not be dispatched immediately, but should delay until such time as the Athenians had raised the wall to a height sufficient for them to fight from. Meanwhile the entire population of the city should build the wall, sparing neither private nor public buildings which might be of some use in the work, but demolishing everything ... **1.93.1** In this way the Athenians fortified their city in a short time. **2** Even today it is clear that the construction took place in a hurry; for the foundations are laid in all sorts of stone and these were not shaped so as to fit together, but each was laid just as it was brought forward, and many stelai from tombs and pieces of sculpture were built into the wall. For the boundaries of the city were greatly extended on all sides, and because of this they used everything they could find in their haste. **3** Themistokles also persuaded them to build the rest of the walls of the Piraeus (which had been begun earlier, during the year in which he was archon), thinking that it was a good site, having three natural harbours, and, now they had become a seafaring people, it would greatly benefit their acquisition of power **4** (for he was the first who dared to say that they should cleave to the sea), and he directly helped to establish their empire ... **7** He thought that the Piraeus was a more valuable place than the upper city, and often advised the Athenians that if they were ever hard pressed on land they should go down to the Piraeus and resist everyone in their ships.

THE ORIGINS OF THE DELIAN LEAGUE

The Delian League began as a voluntary organisation, when the allies approached Athens to replace the unpopular leadership of the Spartans under Pausanias. It was established in 478/7 BC. The allies were at first autonomous and made their decisions in general meetings, but Athens no doubt from the very beginning was the most influential member. Whether the league was unicameral (Athens and the allied representatives meeting as one) or bicameral (the allies meeting and coming to decisions separately from the Athenians, as in the Second Athenian Confederacy) is debated.

12.2 [Aristotle] *Athenaion Politeia* 23.3–24.3: Aristeides Sets up the League

Aristeides had been ostracised in 482 BC, but was recalled before the Persian invasion (docs 10.12, 10.14.ii). He encouraged the Athenians to become the leaders of the Ionians. The oaths between the Ionians and the Athenians were cemented by lumps of iron being thrown into the sea as part of a treaty, symbolising a permanent alliance, to last until the iron floated (see Plut. *Arist*. 25.1).

23.3 At that time the leaders of the people were Aristeides, son of Lysimachos, and Themistokles, son of Neokles. Themistokles' reputation was based on his military skill, Aristeides' on his statesmanship, as well as on his being the most upright man of his time; for this reason the Athenians used the one as their general and the other as their adviser. **4** So these two organised the building of the walls together, although they were political rivals, but it was Aristeides who urged the Athenians to separate the Ionians from their alliance with the Spartans, after watching for the moment when the Spartans were in discredit because of Pausanias. **5** Accordingly it was also Aristeides who assessed the first tribute contribution from the cities in the third year after the naval battle at Salamis, in the archonship of Timosthenes (478/7 BC), and he swore the oaths to the Ionians that they would have the same enemies and the same friends (as the Athenians), upon which they also threw the lumps of iron into the sea. **24.1** After this, now the city had become confident and much wealth accumulated, he started advising them to grasp the leadership and to leave their farms behind them and live in the city, telling them that everybody would have a livelihood, with some of them performing military service, others serving in garrisons, and yet others taking part in public affairs, and in this way they would hold on to the leadership. **2** They followed this advice and seized their empire, behaving in a tyrannical manner towards their allies, with the exception of Chios, Lesbos and Samos, which they made use of to help guard their empire, allowing them to keep their own constitutions and rule whatever subjects they had. **3** They also put into place a system whereby the populace could have a comfortable livelihood.

12.3 Herodotos 8.111.1–3: Persuasion and Necessity

The island of Andros, south of Euboea, had supported the Persians with its fleet and so in 480 BC the Greeks besieged the island, but unsuccessfully. It joined the Delian League a few years later.

8.111.1 Now that the Greeks had decided not to pursue the barbarians' fleet any further or sail to the Hellespont to break down the bridge, they surrounded Andros with the intention of capturing it. **2** The Andrians were the first islanders from whom Themistokles demanded money to refuse to give it. Themistokles alleged as his reason that the Athenians had come with the support of two great gods, Persuasion and Necessity, and so they had no choice but to pay up. The Andrians in their response stated that it was quite reasonable that Athens was great and prosperous as it had the blessing of effective gods; **3** as for themselves they had the supreme blessing of a total lack of land and two completely ineffectual gods who so loved their island that they never went away — Poverty and Helplessness. As they possessed these gods the Andrians would give no money: in fact, the power of Athens could never overcome the Andrians' lack of it.

12.4 Thucydides 1.96.1–99.3: The Beginnings of Athens' Empire

The details which Thucydides provides in this extract and the rest of the section on the pentekontaetia are the basis for the history of the Delian League (Thuc. 1.89–117). The revolt of Naxos was the first occasion when the independence of an ally was not observed. The meaning of 'against the terms of the existing agreement' is debated, and there may have been a clause guaranteeing the allies' freedom; a more appropriate interpretation is perhaps that such action was 'unprecedented' and that the autonomy of the allies had been taken for granted (1.98.4).

1.96.1 After the Athenians took over the leadership in this way, with the allies willing that Athens should do so because of their hatred of Pausanias, they assessed which cities had to provide money and which provide ships for the war against the barbarian; for the pretence was that they were retaliating for what they had lost by ravaging the king's country. **2** And then for the first time the Athenians instituted the class of officials known as the Treasurers of Greece (hellenotamiai), who received the tribute (phoros); for that was what contributions in money were called. The tribute fixed at first was 460 talents. Their treasury was at Delos, and the meetings used to take place in the temple. **1.97.1** The Athenians were the leaders of the allies, who were at first autonomous and made their decisions in general meetings, and achieved many great things both in war and in the handling of affairs in the period between the current war and the Persian War, against the barbarians, their own allies who revolted and the Peloponnesians whom they came up against on various occasions. **2** I have written this and made this digression because this subject has been omitted by those writing before me, who have either narrated the events of Greek history before the Persian Wars or the Persian Wars themselves; the only one who has touched on this, in his *History of Attica*, is Hellanikos, and he mentioned it briefly and without chronological accuracy. At the same time it will show the way in which the Athenians' empire was established.

1.98.1 First of all the Athenians, with Kimon son of Miltiades in command, took by siege Eion on the Strymon, which was held by the Persians, and enslaved the inhabitants (476 BC). **2** Then they enslaved the inhabitants of Skyros, the island in the Aegean, which was inhabited by the Dolopians, and settled it themselves. **3** Next there was a war between them and the Karystians, without any of the other Euboeans being involved; eventually the Karystians surrendered on terms. **4** After this they made war on the Naxians who had revolted and brought them to terms after a siege (467 BC). This was the first allied city that was enslaved against the terms of the existing agreement, and then it happened to each of the others as well. **1.99.1** There were various reasons for the revolts, the most important of which were falling into arrears with the tribute or contribution of ships and sometimes refusal to serve; for the Athenians were strict in exacting payment and, in applying compulsion, made themselves unpleasant to those who were not accustomed or willing to endure hardships. **2** In other ways, too, the Athenians were no longer as popular as rulers as they had been, and as they did not take a share in expeditions as equals it was easier for them to bring back to their side those who revolted. **3** For all this the allies themselves were responsible; for most of them, because they shrank from campaigns so they might not be away from home, agreed to pay a corresponding sum of money instead of ships. Thus the Athenians' fleet grew powerful from the money the allies contributed, and the allies had made themselves inadequately prepared and inexperienced in war when they revolted.

12.5 Thucydides 1.135.2–138.6: Thucydides Praises Themistokles

Themistokles fell victim to ostracism in the late 470s BC, after having been a candidate in the 480s as well (see doc. 10.14). After he was ostracised, Themistokles was tried *in absentia* on a charge of intriguing with the Persians; he was linked with the treason of Pausanias: Plut. *Them.* 22.1–23.6, *Arist.* 25.10 (1.135.2). For Themistokles' meeting with the King, see Plut. *Them.* 28 (1.137.3-4). This extract follows on from doc. 6.35, Pausanias' treasonable conduct. Thucydides' eulogy of Themistokles is unusual in his *History*.

1.135.2 As a result of Pausanias' medising, the Spartans sent envoys to the Athenians to accuse Themistokles also, because of what they had discovered from the evidence against Pausanias, and urged that Themistokles be punished in the same way. **3** The Athenians agreed and sent men with the Spartans, who were prepared to help in catching him, with orders to bring him from wherever they should come across him (as it happened he had already been ostracised and was living in Argos, as well as travelling to the rest of the Peloponnese). But Themistokles became aware of this beforehand and fled from the Peloponnese to Corcyra, as he was the Corcyraeans' benefactor. (**1.136.1–137.2**: *He has to take refuge with his enemy Admetos, King of the Molossians, and then takes passage in a merchant ship and is conveyed, past the siege of Naxos, to Ephesos.*) **1.137.3** Themistokles rewarded the captain by a gift of money (after it had reached him from his friends at Athens and also from what he had deposited at Argos) and travelled inland with one of the Persians from the coast, sending ahead a letter to King Artaxerxes, Xerxes' son, who had recently come to the throne. **4** The letter said: 'I, Themistokles, have come to you, I who did most harm of all the Greeks to your house, during the time that I was compelled to defend myself against your father's invasion, but still more good, when his retreat took place and I was safe but he was in danger. My benefaction should be repaid (here he wrote of the advance warning of the withdrawal from Salamis and how the bridges had not been destroyed, which he pretended, falsely, was his doing), and now I am here, pursued by the Greeks because of my friendship for you, and able to do you much good. But I want to wait a year before I show you, in person, why I have come.'

1.138.1 The king, it is said, was amazed by his resolve and told him to do this. And Themistokles, while he was waiting, learned as much as he could of the Persian language and the customs of the country; **2** at the end of the year he arrived at court and became more important there than any other Greek has ever been, both because of the reputation he already had and the hope which he held out of subjugating Greece to Artaxerxes, but mainly because he gave proof of his intelligence in his behaviour. **3** Indeed, Themistokles displayed very clearly the force of his natural powers and in this, more than anyone else, he deserves admiration; through his native intelligence, and without studying something beforehand or considering it later, he was outstanding in judgements that had to be settled immediately with the least possible discussion, and by far the best forecaster of what was going to happen in the future; he had the ability to explain things he was engaged in, and even in things he had no experience of he did not fail to make satisfactory judgements; in particular he could see beforehand the better or worse in what was as yet unseen. To sum him up, because of the strength of his natural genius and his capacity for instant action, this man was outstanding in extemporising whatever was needed. **4** He died through an illness; some people say that he intentionally took poison, when he considered it impossible to accomplish what he had promised the king.

5 There is a monument to him in Asian Magnesia in the agora; this was the country he ruled, as the king gave him Magnesia for his bread, which brought in fifty talents a year, Lampsakos for his wine (which was thought to be the best district of all for wine at that time) and Myous for his meat. **6** They say that his relatives brought his bones home, at his request, and buried them without the Athenians' knowledge in Attica; for it was not possible to bury him as he was in exile for treason. So the careers of Pausanias the Spartan and Themistokles the Athenian, the most illustrious of any of the Greeks of their time, in this way came to an end.

12.6 Timokreon 727: Themistokles: 'Liar, Criminal and Traitor'

This piece was probably composed *c.* 478 BC by Timokreon of Ialysos on Rhodes, who had medised and was known for his invective against Themistokles. It refers to Themistokles demanding money with threats from the islands after the Persians were driven out of Greece (Hdt. 8.112.2). Leto was the mother of the gods Apollo and Artemis, who were born on Delos, and hence there is perhaps a reference to the Delian League here, but more probably Timokreon is referring to Leto as the oath-giver: Timokreon was exiled for medising and Themistokles took a bribe of three talents not to restore him from exile, despite being Timokreon's xenos (friend). After the Persians were defeated, the allied commanders met at the Isthmus to cast votes for the prize of valour, voting for first and second place; each commander voted himself first, and most for Themistokles as second (Hdt. 8.123–124.1; Plut. *Them.* 17.2, *Mor.* 871 d–e). The phrase 'cold meats' presumably refers to a banquet given by Themistokles in the hope of being awarded first place. [Plut. *Them.* 21.4.]

Well, you may commend Pausanias and you Xanthippos
Or you Leotychidas, but I praise Aristeides
As the one best man
To come from sacred Athens, since Themistokles has earned the enmity of Leto,
That liar, criminal, and traitor, who did not restore Timokreon though his friend,
— Because he had been bribed with knavish silver —
Back to his homeland Ialysos,
But took three talents of silver and sailed off to the devil,
Restoring some unjustly, and expelling and killing others;
At the Isthmus, loaded up with silver, he made a ridiculous innkeeper
And served up the meat cold;
So they ate up, and prayed for Themistokles' ruin.

THE AFTERMATH OF THE PERSIAN WARS

12.7 Thucydides 1.100.1: The Battle of the Eurymedon

The years 469, 466, or *c.* 465–460 BC are all suggested as dates for the battle of the Eurymedon. Under Kimon, the Persians were defeated on both land and, spectacularly, at sea. The campaign brought new members into the Delian League; Athens next had to turn its attention to Thasos and the campaign against Persia ended for the time. See also Plut. *Kim.* 12–13.3; Diod. 11.61.

1.100.1 After this there occurred the battles on land and sea at the Eurymedon river in Pamphylia, in which the Athenians and their allies fought against the Persians, and the

Athenians were victorious in both on the same day under the command of Kimon son of Miltiades, and they captured and destroyed some two hundred triremes, the whole Phoenician fleet.

12.8 Simonides 46: Victory at the Eurymedon

This epigram was associated with Simonides and the Eurymedon in antiquity. The dead of the Eurymedon were buried in the Kerameikos at Athens: Paus. 1.29.14. [Page 268–72; *Anth. Pal.* 7.258.]

These men beside the Eurymedon lost their splendid youth
Doing battle against the vanguard of the Persian archers
As spearmen, both on foot and in their swift ships,
And, dying, left behind the finest memorial of their prowess.

12.9 Thucydides 1.100.2–101.3: The Revolt of Thasos

The revolt of Thasos, probably in 465 BC, was another instance in which Athens used league resources to force a seceding member back into the league. The Athenian attempt to establish a colony in Thrace dates to 465, with the massacre at Drabeskos occurring soon after.

1.100.2 Some time after this (the battle of the Eurymedon) it happened that the Thasians revolted from the Athenians because of a dispute concerning the trading-stations on the coast of Thrace opposite and the mine which they worked. With their ships the Athenians sailed against Thasos, won a naval battle and landed, **3** while at about the same time they sent ten thousand settlers of their own and their allies to the river Strymon to colonise what was then called Nine Ways (Ennea Hodoi), but now Amphipolis; they gained control of Nine Ways, which was held by the Edonians, but when they advanced into the interior of Thrace their force was destroyed at Drabeskos in Edonian territory by all the Thracians acting in concert, who saw the colonising of the site of Nine Ways as an act of hostility. **1.101.1** Meanwhile the Thasians, who had been defeated in battle and were now under siege, called on the Spartans and urged them to come to their aid by invading Attica. **2** This the Spartans promised to do without the Athenians knowing, and were about to do so when they were prevented by the earthquake which took place, in which both the helots, and the Thouriatans and Aithaians among the perioikoi, revolted and withdrew to Ithome. The majority of the helots were the descendants of the Messenians of old times who had then been enslaved; because of this they were all known as Messenians. **3** So the Spartans had a war on their hands with those at Ithome, while the Thasians, who were in the third year of the siege, came to terms with the Athenians, demolishing their wall and handing over their ships, and agreed to pay whatever they had to immediately as well as tribute for the future, and to give up both the mainland and the mine.

12.10 Diodorus *Library of History* 11.50.1–3: The Spartans Consider Invading Attica

According to Diodorus the Spartans in 475/4 BC regretted allowing the Athenians to take over command of the sea; the gerousia considered making war on the Athenians and the ekklesia was enthusiastic about the proposal. Some historians have doubted this story, for it finds no echo in

Thucydides. But it is plausible that a few years after 478 the Spartans, seeing the growth of Athenian power, may have regretted giving up the command of the war against the Persians to the Athenians.

11.50.1 In this year the Spartans began to be angry about the fact that they had unaccountably lost the command of the sea; accordingly they were displeased with the Greeks who had rebelled from them, and kept threatening them with fitting punishment. **2** When the gerousia was convened they debated about whether to make war against the Athenians over the command of the sea. **3** Similarly, when the common assembly (ekklesia) met, the younger men and most of the others were ambitious to regain the leadership, considering that if they could do this they would have more wealth, and Sparta in general would become greater and more powerful, and the estates (oikoi) of its private individuals be greatly increased in prosperity.

12.11 Thucydides 1.102.1–103.3: The Helot Revolt

The expedition to help Sparta cope with the revolt of the helots and perioikoi in the mid 460s at Mount Ithome was opposed by Ephialtes (Plut. *Kim*. 16.9). Kimon was successful in having it sent, but was ostracised in the following year after the Spartans dismissed the Athenian force (cf. doc. 10.14.ix).

1.102.1 As their war against those at Ithome was dragging on, the Spartans called on their allies, including the Athenians, for help; **2** and the Athenians came with a large force, under Kimon's leadership. The Spartans particularly called on the Athenians' help because they were thought to be good at siege operations, and from the length of the siege to date it was clear that the Spartans were not, or they would have taken the place by storm. **3** And it was because of this expedition that open dispute between the Spartans and Athenians first arose. For when the Spartans were still unable to take the place by storm, they became afraid of the Athenians' boldness and revolutionary spirit (as well as considering them at the same time not to be of the same race as themselves), in case, if they stayed on, they might be won over by those at Ithome and attempt some sort of revolution. So alone of all their allies they sent the Athenians away, not revealing their suspicions, but saying that they no longer had any need of them. **4** The Athenians, however, realised that they were not being sent away on any such acceptable grounds, but that some suspicion of them had arisen, and were offended, not considering it right that they should be treated like this by the Spartans. So, as soon as they returned home, they dissolved the alliance which had been formed against the Persians and became allies instead of the Argives, who were the Spartans' enemies; at the same time both the Athenians and Argives made a sworn alliance on the same terms with the Thessalians. **1.103.1** However, the rebels at Ithome were unable to hold out any longer and in the tenth year they came to terms with the Spartans, on condition that they left the Peloponnese under a truce and never set foot in it again; if any of them were caught there, he was to be the slave of the man who captured him. **2** The Spartans had also had an oracle from Delphi prior to this that they should let the 'suppliant of Zeus' leave Ithome. **3** So the rebels left with their children and wives and the Athenians took them because of the hostility which they now felt towards the Spartans and settled them at Naupaktos, which they had captured from the Ozolian Lokrians, who had recently taken it.

CONSTITUTIONAL CHANGE IN ATHENS

Before Ephialtes' reduction in the powers of the Areiopagos, this council of ex-archons had guardianship of the laws, oversaw the magistrates (conducting dokimasiai and euthynai: see docs 1.19, 1.22) and had supervision of the citizens (cf. docs 8.1–2, 8.17). Ephialtes had led a campaign against the Areiopagos and its members prior to the introduction of his reforms. In addition to the constitutional changes made by Ephialtes in 462/1 BC to the powers of the Areiopagos, other significant reforms include: *Ath. Pol.* 22.2 (501/0): the oath imposed on the Council and the election of strategoi, one from each tribe; 22.5 (487/6): use of partial sortition (selection by lot) to elect archons (500 candidates directly elected and then nine chosen by lot); 26.2 (458/7): the zeugitai made eligible for the archonship; 26.3 (453/2): thirty circuit judges reintroduced; 26.4 (451/0): Perikles' citizenship law; 27.4: pay for jury service.

12.12 [Aristotle] *Athenaion Politeia* 25.1–4: The Reforms of Ephialtes

Ephialtes was the champion of the demos, and a strategos in the 460s BC, possibly in 465/4; see Plut. *Kim.* 13.4; during the absence of Kimon and 4,000 hoplites at Mount Ithome Ephialtes put through legislation to curb the powers of the Areiopagos (Plut. *Kim.* 15.2, cf. *Per.* 7.8).

25.1 For about seventeen years after the Persian Wars the constitution remained unchanged under the supervision of the Areiopagos, although the Areiopagos was gradually declining. (And, as the populace increased in strength, Ephialtes, son of Sophonides, who had a reputation for being incorruptible and upright with regard to the constitution, became champion of the people and attacked the (Areiopagos) council. **2** He first removed many of the Areiopagites, by bringing them to trial on the grounds of administrative misconduct; then in the archonship of Konon (462/1) he took away all the council's additionally acquired powers, through which it was the guardian of the constitution, and gave some of them to the Five Hundred (the Council) and some to the people and the law courts.) **3** He did this with the assistance of Themistokles, who was a member of the Areiopagos and was about to be tried for collaboration with Persia … **4** and not long afterwards Ephialtes too died, murdered by Aristodikos of Tanagra.

ATHENIAN MILITARY CAMPAIGNS

12.13 Thucydides 1.104.1–2, 109.1–110.4: Athenian Disaster in Egypt

Egypt became a Persian satrapy in 525 BC; its revolt in 485 delayed the second Persian invasion of Greece. Thucydides places Inaros' revolt after Megara's alliance with Athens; the Athenians became involved in Egypt from *c.* 460 to 454 BC. Amongst the Athenian allies were the Samians; see Meiggs & Lewis 34 with addenda, a dedication from Samos in which Inaros awards a prize to a Samian commander: 'Around lovely Memphis a battle was brought about / by impetuous Ares between the ships of the Persians and the Greeks, and the Samians / took fifteen ships of the Phoenicians'.

1.104.1 Inaros, son of Psammetichos, a Libyan, king of the Libyans who live near Egypt, set out from Mareia, the city beyond Pharos, and organised the revolt of most of Egypt from King Artaxerxes, and became its ruler, bringing in the Athenians as his allies. **2**

They happened to be engaged in a campaign against Cyprus with two hundred ships of their own and their allies, and they left Cyprus and came to Egypt. After sailing from the sea up the Nile they gained control of the river and of two-thirds of Memphis, and started attacking the third part, which is called the White Tower, inside which were those Persians and Medes who had escaped, as well as those Egyptians who had not joined in the revolt ... **1.109.1** Meanwhile the Athenians and allies were still in Egypt, and suffered all the different experiences of war. **2** At first, as the Athenians were in control of Egypt, the king sent to Sparta Megabazos, a Persian, with money to bribe the Peloponnesians to invade Attica so that the Athenians would have to return from Egypt. **3** But as this was unsuccessful, and the money was spent without results, Megabazos and the remainder of the money were recalled to Asia, and the king sent another Persian, Megabyzos son of Zopyros, with a large army (to Egypt); **4** he arrived and defeated the Egyptians and their allies in a battle on land, drove the Greeks from Memphis and finally shut them up on the island of Prosopitis, where he besieged them for a year and six months, when he drained the water from the channel and diverted it elsewhere, thus leaving the ships on dry land and turning most of the island into mainland, and crossed and captured the island on foot. **1.110.1** In this way the Greeks' venture failed after six years of fighting; a few out of the many involved got through Libya to Cyrene and were saved, but the majority were lost. **2** Egypt was again controlled by the king except for Amyrtaios, who was king of the marshes; it was impossible to capture him because of the size of the marshes, and the men of the marshes are the most warlike of the Egyptians. **3** Inaros the Libyan king, who had been responsible for these affairs in Egypt, was captured by treachery and crucified. **4** Meanwhile fifty triremes from Athens and the rest of the alliance had sailed out to relieve the force there and put in at the Menesian mouth (of the Nile), having no idea what had happened; and they were attacked by the infantry on land and the Phoenician fleet by sea and the majority of the ships were lost, though a few managed to get away. So ended the great expedition of the Athenians and their allies to Egypt.

12.14 *Inscriptiones Graecae* I[3] 1147: A Casualty List of the Erechtheid Tribe

This inscription lists the war dead from the tribe Erechtheis (I) in 460 or 459 BC; the army was organised along tribal lines. The names of the war dead of all ten tribes were usually inscribed on one stele or adjacent stelai, but perhaps the great number of casualties explains this separate stele. The widespread nature of Athenian campaigns is seen here; Thucydides mentions all these except for Phoenicia. The Athenians may have seen themselves as fighting a single 'war' (line 2), defending themselves against the Peloponnesians while they 'championed' Greece against barbarians: cf. Thuc. 1.104. [*IG* I[2] 929; Meiggs & Lewis 33.]

1 Of (the tribe) Erechtheis
These died in the war: in Cyprus, in Egypt, in Phoenicia, at Halieis, on Aegina, at Megara
in the same year.
5 Of the Generals:
Ph[...]chos ... (*there follows a list of 176 soldiers' names in three columns*)
62 General:
Hippodamas

12.15 Simonides 45: The Campaign against Cyprus

Simonides probably died shortly after 468 BC so obviously this is not his work (cf. Diod. 11.62.3). [Page 266–68.]

From the time when the sea separated Europe from Asia
And impetuous Ares held sway over the cities of mortals,
No such deed of earthly men ever took place
On land and sea at the same time;
For on Cyprus these men destroyed many Persians
And took a hundred Phoenician ships at sea
Full of men; and Asia groaned loudly because of them,
Struck with both hands with the strength of war.

12.16 Isocrates 4 *Panegyricus* 117–18: The 'Peace of Kallias', 449/8 BC (I)

All the evidence for the 'Peace of Kallias' between Athens and Persia, brokered by the Athenian ambassador Kallias, is from the fourth century and later, which has led some scholars – even an ancient one, Kallisthenes – to doubt its historicity; it is otherwise usually dated to 449/8 (Diod. 12.4.4), and is held to have caused a crisis in the empire as the tribute lists can be interpreted to mean that in that year the allies refused to pay tribute because peace with Persia had been made. See esp. *ATL* 3.277–81.

117 Our treatment of the barbarians for having dared to cross into Europe and for their excessive arrogance **118** ensured that they not only ceased making expeditions against us but even suffered their country to be ravaged; and we so abased their pride that they who had once taken to the seas with 1,200 ships launched no ship this side of Phaselis, but stayed quiet and waited for better times, rather than trust in the forces they then possessed.

12.17 Plutarch *Kimon* 13.4–5: The 'Peace of Kallias', 449/8 BC (II)

The Kyaneai are at the entrance to the Black Sea; the Chelidoniai are islands between Lycia and Pamphylia. [Kallisthenes *FGH* 124 F16; Krateros *FGH* 342 F13.]

13.4 This achievement (the encounter at the Eurymedon followed by one at Syedra) so humbled the will of the king that he made that peace, which is much talked about, undertaking to keep a day's journey by horse away from the sea, and not to sail with a bronze-beaked warship past the Kyaneai (the Blue Rocks) or the Chelidoniai. Yet Kallisthenes denies that the barbarians made this peace, but says that he simply acted like this out of fear resulting from that defeat, and stayed so far away from Greece that Perikles with fifty ships and Ephialtes with thirty sailed beyond the Chelidoniai without a fleet from the barbarians coming to meet them. **5** But in the *Decrees*, which Krateros put together, copies of the agreements are described as having been made. It is also said that the Athenians dedicated an altar of peace as a result, and voted especial honours to Kallias the ambassador.

THE FIRST PELOPONNESIAN WAR, 460–445 BC

The dismissal of the Athenians from Ithome resulted in their allying themselves with Sparta's enemy, Argos. The Megarians approached Athens for an alliance in 460 or 459 BC, as they were being attacked by Corinth; this alienated Corinth from Athens, and led to the outbreak of the First Peloponnesian War (which is a modern term). This war consisted of a series of conflicts, the main Spartan–Athenian confrontation being at Tanagra. In 451 BC the Athenians and Spartans agreed to a Five Years' Peace; Sparta did not take the war into Attica until 446 BC; in that year the Thirty Years' Peace was signed.

12.18 Thucydides 1.103.4: The Megarians Join the Athenians, *c.* 460 BC

Thucydides 1.105 and following deals with clashes between the Athenians and Corinthians, important background in the lead-up to the Peloponnesian War. Megara was important to Athens for it could block the invasion route from the Peloponnese; Pegai was at the eastern end of the Corinthian Gulf, and had strategic value: Athenian control of it (lost under the peace treaty of 446/5 BC) meant that, as in Perikles' Corinthian Gulf expedition, the Athenians could avoid the long sail around the Peloponnese.

1.103.4 The Megarians also left the Spartans' side and allied themselves with the Athenians, because the Corinthians were attacking them in a war concerning boundary land. Thus the Athenians held both Megara and Pegai, and they built the Megarians the Long Walls from the city to Nisaia and manned them themselves. And it was primarily from this that the Corinthians' violent hatred for the Athenians first came into being.

12.19 Diodorus *Library of History* 11.78.1–79.4: Athenian Engagements in 459 and 458 BC

The Megarian alliance with the Athenians actually dated to *c.* 460–459 BC. Thucydides says the Athenians were defeated at Halieis (Thuc. 1.105). The campaigns against the Peloponnesians in these years must on the whole have been satisfactory from the Athenian point of view.

11.78.1 During this year (459 BC) a war began between the Corinthians and Epidaurians, on the one hand, and the Athenians, on the other, and the Athenians made an expedition against them and were victorious after a fierce battle. **2** With a large fleet they sailed to the place known as Halieis, landed in the Peloponnese, and killed a large number of the enemy. The Peloponnesians rallied their troops and gathered a considerable force, and a battle took place against the Athenians at a spot called Kekryphaleia, in which the Athenians were again victorious. **3** After achieving such successes, the Athenians, seeing that the Aeginetans were priding themselves on their former achievements, as well as being hostile towards Athens, decided to reduce them in war. **4** Accordingly the Athenians dispatched a considerable fleet against them, but the inhabitants of Aegina, who had great experience and a fine reputation for naval battles, were not frightened at the Athenians' superiority, as they had an adequate number of triremes and had constructed others, and so met the Athenians at sea, but were defeated with the loss of seventy triremes. Their spirits were downcast at the extent of the disaster and they were compelled to join the league, which paid tribute to the Athenians. Leokrates, the general who achieved this for the Athenians, was engaged for a total of nine months in war against the Aeginetans.

11.79.1 During this year (458 BC) a dispute arose between the Corinthians and Megarians over border territory and the cities went to war. **2** To begin with they kept making raids on each other's territory and engaging in skirmishes, but as the conflict increased, the Megarians, who were continually getting the worst of it and were afraid of the Corinthians, made an alliance with the Athenians. **3** In consequence the strength of the cities was again evenly balanced, and when the Corinthians, along with other Peloponnesians, advanced into the Megarid with a considerable force, the Athenians sent an army to help the Megarians under the command of Myronides, a man admired for his valour. A fierce engagement which lasted a long time took place, in which the two sides matched each other in courageous actions, but finally the Athenians were victorious and killed many of the enemy. **4** After a few days there was another fierce battle at the place called Kimolia and the Athenians were again victorious and killed many of the enemy.

12.20 Thucydides 1.107.1–108.5: Tanagra and Oinophyta, 458/7 BC

There were two parallel 'Long Walls' from Athens to the city, as well as the Phaleric 'Long Wall' from Athens to the eastern side of the Phaleron harbour (cf. Thuc. 2.13.7). The northern Long Wall and the Phaleric Wall were built first, being commenced before the battle of Tanagra and completed after Oinophyta. The Middle Wall (the southern Long Wall) was commenced in 446/5 BC after the Thirty Years' Peace (1.107.1). The Athenians' capture of Boeotia led to a ten-year domination there (1.108.2–3), which is referred to as the 'land empire', and the Boeotians as Athenian allies provided military contingents (Thuc. 1.111.1; cf. Arist. *Pol.* 1302b25; [Xen.] *Const. Ath.* 3.11); Boeotia was later lost in 447 BC (Thuc. 1.113). The lengthy conflict between Athens and Aegina ended (1.108.4); Aegina henceforth paid an annual tribute of thirty talents. Tolmides' expedition was in 456/5 BC. Corinthian Chalkis is on the northern side of the Corinthian Gulf. The Spartans' dockyards were at Gytheion (1.108.5).

1.107.1 At about this time the Athenians began to build their Long Walls down to the sea, one to Phaleron and the other to the Piraeus ... (**1.107.2–3**: *Phokis had captured one of the towns belonging to Doris, the mother-city of the Spartans, and Sparta came to its assistance. The Spartans then had to consider how to return home.*) **1.107.4** The Spartans decided to remain in Boeotia and see what the safest line of march would be. Apart from anything else, they were urged in secret to do this by some Athenians who had hopes of overthrowing the democracy and preventing the building of the Long Walls. **5** But the Athenians marched out against them with their whole force, together with 1,000 Argives and contingents from their other allies: altogether they came to 14,000 men. **6** They made this attack because they thought that the Spartans had difficulties in getting back and because they had some suspicions about the plot to overthrow the democracy. **7** Some Thessalian cavalry also came to aid the Athenians in accordance with the alliance, though in actual fact they deserted to the Spartans. **1.108.1** A battle took place at Tanagra in Boeotia and the Spartans and their allies were victorious, though there were heavy losses on both sides. **2** The Spartans then went into the Megarid, cutting down trees as they went, and returned home through Geraneia and the Isthmus; the Athenians on the sixty-second day after the battle marched into Boeotia with Myronides in command, **3** and defeated the Boeotians in a battle at Oinophyta, gaining control of the country of Boeotia and Phokis. They demolished the walls of Tanagra and took as hostages 100 of the richest of the Opountian Lokrians, and then completed their own Long Walls. **4** After this the Aeginetans surrendered to the Athenians, which involved destroying their walls and handing over their ships and agreeing to pay tribute for the future. **5** And the Athenians sailed around the Peloponnese, with Tolmides son of Tolmaios in command, and burned the Spartans' dockyards and took Chalkis, a Corinthian city, and, landing, defeated the Sicyonians in battle.

12.21 Thucydides 1.112.5: The Second Sacred War, 449 BC

This was the second 'Sacred War', which took place in 449 BC. Delphi was to give its blessing to Sparta's declaration of war against Athens: Thuc. 1.118.3, cf. 121.3.

1.112.5 After this the Spartans took part in what was called the Sacred War, and gained control of the temple at Delphi and handed it over to the Delphians; and once they had withdrawn, the Athenians then took the field, gained control of it and handed it back to the Phokians.

12.22 Thucydides 1.114.1–115.1: The Revolts of Euboea and Megara, 446 BC

In 446 BC, the revolts of Euboea and Megara, and the invasion of Attica by the Spartan king Pleistoanax (458–446, 428–409 BC) were important factors leading to the Thirty Years' Peace. It is not stated why Euboea revolted, unless the generic statements at Thuc. 1.98.4–99.2 (doc. 12.4) account for it; the establishment of a cleruchy on the island *c*. 450 BC may have helped to provoke the revolt (1.114.1). Perikles may have bribed Pleistoanax to withdraw from Attica (1.114.2); see Thuc. 2.21.1, 5.16; Plut. *Per*. 22.2–4. For the Hestiaians' capture of an Athenian ship and killing of the crew, see Plut. *Per*. 23.4. The Athenians settled at Hestiaia will have been cleruchs (1.114.3). In 446/5 the Athenians and Peloponnesians signed a Thirty Years' Peace (1.115.1) which lasted for fourteen years (Thuc. 2.2.1). In 425 BC Athens demanded that Nisaia, Pegai, Troizen and Achaea, which had been surrendered by the terms of the truce, be returned (Thuc. 4.21.3).

1.114.1 Not long after this Euboea revolted from the Athenians; Perikles had already crossed over with an Athenian army, when it was reported to him that Megara had revolted and the Peloponnesians were about to invade Attica, and that the Athenian garrison troops had been destroyed by the Megarians, except for those who had managed to escape to Nisaia; the Megarians had brought in as allies the Corinthians, Sicyonians and Epidaurians. So Perikles swiftly brought the army back from Euboea. **2** And after this the Peloponnesians, with Pleistoanax, son of Pausanias, in command, did invade Attica, laying it waste as far as Eleusis and Thria, but they came no further than that and departed for home. **3** The Athenians again crossed to Euboea under Perikles' leadership and subdued the whole island, drawing up treaties with all the cities except the Hestiaians, whom they drove out and whose land they occupied. **1.115.1** Not long after returning from Euboea the Athenians made a Thirty Years' Peace with the Spartans and their allies, and gave back Nisaia, Pegai, Troizen and Achaea, all of which they had taken from the Peloponnesians.

12.23 *Inscriptiones Graecae* I^3 1353: A Memorial for Pythion of Megara, 446 BC

After Megara revolted, Athens sent a force into the Megarid under the command of Andocides; this army was guided back to Athens by Pythion, through a roundabout route, presumably because of

Pleistoanax's march to Eleusis. Athens continued to control Pegai despite Megara's revolt, but it was given up to Sparta when the Thirty Years' Peace was made. The lines of verse, which do not correspond with the lines of the inscription, are followed here. [*IG* I^2 1085+; Hansen 83; Meiggs & Lewis 51; cf. Diod. 12.5.2.]

This memorial is set over the body of the bravest of men.
Pythion of Megara killed seven men,
And broke seven spears in their bodies,
Choosing valour and bringing his father honour among the people.
This man, who saved three Athenian tribes
By leading them from Pegai through Boeotia to Athens,
Brought honour to Andocides with two thousand prisoners.
Having harmed no one among earthly men
He descended to Hades most blessed in the sight of everyone.
These are the tribes: Pandionis, Kekropis, Antiochis.

PERIKLES 'THE OLYMPIAN'

Perikles took over leadership of the democratic group at Athens some time after the assassination of Ephialtes. The institution of jury pay and his citizenship law of 451/0 BC (docs 1.27, 1.36) were Perikles' two known political reforms. Another measure to advantage the people was his establishment of cleruchies in allied territory. Despite the ostracism of his political opponent Thucydides, son of Melesias (docs 10.14.xi, 12.27), Perikles still faced opposition, with indirect attacks on him being made through prosecutions of his associates Pheidias and Anaxagoras.

12.24 Thucydides 1.115.2–117.3: The Revolt of Samos, 440 BC

The Athenians supported the Samian democrats, who wanted a change in government, not simply on ideological grounds but because the 'private individuals' were presumably of sufficient prominence to be potentially powerful friends in the new political set-up. The Samian campaign provides the first example of borrowing temple funds for the prosecution of a war (cf. doc. 1.10). The cost was around 1,200 or 1,400 talents. This document follows on from doc. 12.22. See also for the revolt, Diod. 12.27–28; Plut. *Per.* 24.1–2, 25.1–28.8.

1.115.2 In the sixth year (of the peace) war broke out between the Samians and Milesians over Priene, and, after getting the worst of the war, the Milesians came to Athens to protest loudly against the Samians. Some private individuals from Samos itself, who wished to install a democratic form of government, also supported them. **3** So the Athenians sailed to Samos with forty ships and set up a democracy, and took fifty children and an equal number of men from Samos hostage, and left them for safe keeping on Lemnos. They then left a garrison behind (on Samos) and returned home. **4** Some of the Samians, however, had not stayed behind but fled to the mainland, and they made an alliance with the most influential men (leading oligarchs) in the city and with Pissouthnes, son of Hystaspes, who was then governor of Sardis, gathered about 700 mercenaries, and crossed to Samos during the night. **5** First they rose up against the leaders of the democracy and seized most of them, and then they rescued the hostages from Lemnos and declared a rebellion, and handed over to Pissouthnes the Athenian garrison and officials who were there, and made immediate preparations for an expedition against Miletos. The Byzantines also joined with them in the revolt ... (**1.116.1–117.1**: *The Athenians sent sixty ships, which were reinforced by others, under Perikles and nine other generals. Samos was blockaded, but while Perikles was preventing the arrival of the Phoenician fleet, the Samians defeated the Athenian fleet.*) **1.117.2** But, when Perikles returned, the Samians were again blockaded by the Athenians' ships. Later forty ships came to assist them from Athens under the command of Thucydides, Hagnon and Phormio, twenty more under Tlepolemos and Antikles, and thirty from Chios and Lesbos. **3** The Samians put up a brief fight at sea, but were unable to hold their own, and in the ninth month of the siege had to come to terms. They pulled down their walls, gave hostages, handed over their ships and agreed to pay back by instalments the money which the campaign had cost the Athenians. The Byzantines also agreed to return to subject status, as before.

12.25 Plutarch *Perikles* 11.4–6: Perikles Sends out Cleruchies

The Athenians established several settlements abroad, both cleruchies and colonies, in the fifth century. Cleruchies were usually sent to the territory of allies who had revolted and involved the allocation of land to Athenian citizens who retained their citizenship, and would be loyal garrisons in allied states. They were an important part of Athenian control and were obviously unpopular with Athens' fifth-century allies.

11.4 For this reason Perikles chose at this point to relax the reins on the people more than ever before and aimed his policy towards their gratification, by constantly providing public festivals, feasts and processions in the city, thus keeping the city occupied with cultural pleasures, and by sending out sixty triremes each year, in which many of the citizens sailed with pay for eight months, and at the same time learned and practised seamanship. **5** Besides this he sent 1,000 cleruchs (lot-holders) to the Chersonese, 500 to Naxos, half this number to Andros, 1,000 to Thrace to live alongside the Bisaltai, and others to Italy, when Sybaris was being resettled, which they named Thourioi. **6** In this way he lightened the city of an idle mob, who were troublemakers because they had leisure, and relieved the poverty of the people, and by sending out settlers to live alongside the allies installed both fear and a garrison to prevent their rebellion.

12.26 [Aristotle] *Athenaion Politeia* 27.3–4: Perikles Institutes Jury Pay

Ephialtes' transference of judicial functions from the Areiopagos to the jury-courts gave the courts more political power and importance. The amount of jury pay was initially two obols per day: see docs 1.24, 1.26–28.

27.3 Furthermore, Perikles was the first person to introduce pay for serving in the law courts, as a measure to win popular favour and counteract the generosity of Kimon. For Kimon, who was as wealthy as a tyrant, not only performed his public liturgies munificently but maintained many of his fellow demesmen; for any of the men from Lakiadai who wished could go to him each day and obtain enough for his needs, and all his land was unfenced, so anyone who wished could enjoy its produce. **4** Perikles lacked the resources for this kind of expenditure and he was advised by Damonides of Oe (who seems to have been the instigator of many of Perikles' measures, and it was for that reason that he was later ostracised) that since he was less well provided with private property he should give the people their own, and therefore Perikles brought in payment for the jurors; it was because of this, some people allege, that the courts deteriorated, as it was always the ordinary people rather than the better off who wanted to be chosen.

12.27 Plutarch *Perikles* 11.1–2, 14.1–3: Perikles and Thucydides, Son of Melesias

Thucydides, son of Melesias, was Perikles' main opponent, and, after his ostracism in 443 BC, Perikles was the outstanding figure in Athenian politics. His citizenship law of 451/0 indicates his importance by that date, and the 440s BC were dominated by him. Thucydides does not seem to have held any military commands; he was the champion (prostates) of the aristocrats. His main point of attack against Perikles seems to have been the misuse of allied funds for the adornment of Athens, but these accusations were doubtless greatly exaggerated as political invective.

11.1 The aristocrats had even before this recognised that Perikles had already become the most important of the citizens, but they were nevertheless anxious that there should be someone in the city to stand up to him and blunt his power, so it should not become an outright monarchy. They put forward Thucydides of Alopeke, a moderate man and relative of Kimon's, to oppose him. Thucydides was less of a soldier than Kimon, but was more effective as a speaker and politician, and by keeping his eyes open in the city and coming to grips with Perikles on the speakers' platform he soon introduced a state of balance into the political arena. **2** He did not allow the so-called 'landed gentry' to be scattered and mixed up with the people as they were before, resulting in their influence being overshadowed by the populace, but by separating them out and assembling them into a single entity he made them collectively into an important power group, a counterweight in the scale, so to speak ... **14.1** Thucydides and his supporters kept denouncing Perikles for squandering money and wasting the revenues, and so Perikles asked the people in the assembly if they thought too much had been spent; when they all replied far too much, he said, 'Then let the cost be put down to my account, not yours, and I will have the inscriptions of the buildings dedicated to the gods made in my name.' **2** When Perikles said this, either they were amazed at his munificence, or else they wanted to vie with him for the repute from the public works, and they made an uproar telling him to spend from state funds and spare nothing in his expenditure. **3** And finally he took the risk of setting up a competition against Thucydides with an ostracism, and had him banished and put down the party (hetaireia) formed against him.

THE TRIBUTE

The first tribute-quota list inscribed on stone dates to 454/3 BC; it is generally assumed that the treasury was moved in that year to Athens because of the disaster which the Greeks suffered in Egypt (doc. 12.13). The Athenian tribute-quota lists provide evidence for the annual payment of tribute, phoros, by the allies and record the dedication by the Athenians of one-sixtieth of the phoros of each allied state to the goddess Athena (this was the aparchai, 'first fruits'). For example, in the first entry of doc. 12.28, the 200 drachmas of the Pedasians represents one-sixtieth of the phoros they actually paid: their phoros was thus 12,000 drachmas (two talents). The actual records of the full phoros amounts as paid have disappeared; the fact that the one-sixtieth was a dedication to Athena explains why these were inscribed on stone.

12.28 *Inscriptiones Graecae* I[3] 259: The First Tribute-Quota List, 454/3 BC

It appears that 454/3 BC was the only year in which the aparchai were totalled (*ATL* 1, p. vii). The rather full preamble of the first list is also not repeated in subsequent years. A new fragment gives the archon as Aris[ton], which had previously been a restoration only. The preamble to the list and part of column III follow. [Meiggs & Lewis 39; *ATL* 2.1.]

These quotas, separately and all together from the hellenotamiai for whom … was secretary, were the first to be audited by the thirty commissioners for the goddess from the allied tribute, when Ariston was archon for the Athenians, a mina from (each) talent:

Pedasians 200 dr.
Astyrenians 8 dr. 2 ob.
Byzantines 1500 dr.
Kamirians 900 dr.
Thermaians
on Ikaros 50 dr.
Daunio
-teichitians 16 dr. 4 ob.
Samothracians 600 dr.
Astypalaians 200 dr.
Mendaians 800 dr.
Selymbrians 900 dr.
Aigantians 33 dr. 2 ob.
Neapolitans from
Miletos on White
Peninsula 300 dr.
Kolophonians 300 dr. …
(*6 names follow*)
Neopolitans 50 dr.
Maiandrians 66 dr. 4 ob.

ATHENIAN DECREES CONCERNING ATHENS' ALLIES

These decrees reveal how Athens regulated its affairs with the allies. The democratic constitution imposed on Erythrai indicates Athens' trust in the demos (doc. 12.30). It appears that revolts against Athens and the imposition of democratic governments are linked (as at Erythrai and Samos), suggesting that oligarchs throughout the empire were less well disposed to Athens than the demos and its leaders. The dating of many important inscriptions of the fifth century is subject to debate; some of those dated to the period of the pentekontaetia almost certainly do not belong there.

12.29 *Inscriptiones Graecae* I[3] 10: Relations with Phaselis, *c.* 469–50 BC

The orthodox dating for this decree is 469–450 BC, though after 428/7 is also possible. Phaselis was a Greek city that had not wanted to leave the Persian fold for the Greek, and was besieged by Kimon. The Chians intervened on Phaselis' behalf, and Kimon came to terms in return for ten talents and the Phaselites' help against the Persians; this provides an appropriate historical context for the decree (Plut. *Kim.* 12.3–4; cf. Thuc. 2.69.1). [*IG* I[2] 16; Meiggs & Lewis 31.]

It was resolved by the Council and the people; (the tribe) Akamantis held the prytany, [.]nasippos was secretary, Ne[…]des presided, Leon proposed the motion: this decree is to be recorded for the Phaselites; whatever cause of action arises at Athens involving one of the Phaselites, the case shall be tried at Athens before the polemarch, just as for the

Chians, and in no other place whatsoever. Other cases will be tried on treaty terms in accordance with the existing treaty with the Phaselites; the … shall be abolished. And if any other of the magistrates accepts a case against any Phaselite …, if he convicts him, the conviction shall be void. And if anyone violates what has been decreed, he shall owe ten thousand drachmas sacred to Athena. This decree is to be recorded by the secretary of the Council on a stone stele and set up on the acropolis at the expense of the Phaselites.

12.30 *Inscriptiones Graecae* I[3] 14: Regulations for Erythrai, *c.* 453/2 BC

This decree sets down the obligation of Erythrai to bring grain, or victims for sacrifice (depending on the restoration) to the Great Panathenaia: the offering of a cow and panoply (a set of armour) at the Panathenaia was to become a standard obligation for the allies (cf. doc 12.31). The city was Ionian and a member of the Delian League; Athens' interference in its internal affairs presupposes that Erythrai had revolted. [*IG* I[2] 10; Meiggs & Lewis 40.]

It was resolved by the Council and the people; … held the prytany, … presided, L …; the Erythraians are to bring wheat to the Great Panathenaia worth not less than three minas and it is to be distributed to those Erythraians present … by the hieropoioi … and if (they) bring … worth (less) than three minas in accordance with the … the priest is to buy wheat; and the people … drachmas … of meat … for anyone who wishes; of the Erythraians by lot … there is to be a Council of one hundred and twenty men; and the … in the Council and … to be able to be a member of the Council … nor anyone who is less than thirty years of age; and prosecution will take place against anyone who is found guilty. No one is to be a member of the Council within four years … and the supervisors (episkopoi) and the garrison commander (phrourarch) shall choose by lot and set up the new Council, and in future the Council and the phrourarch will do it, not less than thirty days before the Council goes out of office; and (the councillors) shall swear by Zeus and Apollo and Demeter calling down utter destruction if they forswear themselves … and utter destruction on their children … over sacrificial victims … and the Council is to burn in sacrifice not less (than) … and if not, it shall be liable to a fine of a thousand drachmas … the people are to burn in sacrifice not less. And the Council is to swear as follows: 'I shall deliberate as best and as justly as I can for the Erythraian populace and that of the Athenians and their allies, and I shall not revolt against the populace of the Athenians nor the allies of the Athenians, neither I myself nor shall I be persuaded by anyone else nor … neither I myself nor shall I be persuaded by anyone else … nor shall I receive back even one of the exiles either … shall I be persuaded by anyone of those who fled to the Persians without the approval of the Council of the Athenians and the people, nor shall I banish any of those who remain without the approval of the Council of the Athenians and the people. And if any Erythraian kills another of the Erythraians, he shall be put to death if he is judged guilty … if he is sentenced (to exile) he shall be exiled from all the Athenian alliance … and his property shall become state property of the Erythraians. And if anyone … to the tyrants … of the Erythraians and … he shall be put to death … children from him … the children from him …

12.31 *Inscriptiones Graecae* I[3] 46: The Foundation of the Colony at Brea

This decree, which appears to belong to between *c.* 445 and the late 430s BC, provides important information about fifth-century Athenian colonisation; an amendment (B) provides that Brea's colonists were to be from the thetes and zeugitai. The colonists are to bring a model phallos to the City Dionysia: the carrying of the phallos, phallophoria, was part of the festival procession. The site of Brea is not known; Brea is sometimes identified with the colony 'amongst the Bisaltai', near Amphipolis: Plut. *Per.* 11.5. [*IG* I^2 45; Meiggs & Lewis 49.]

A

... in respect of which he denounces or indicts (someone), let him prosecute. If he prosecutes ... let pledges be taken from him by the denouncer or the prosecutor. ... are to be provided for them by the apoikistai (leaders) to obtain good omens on behalf of the colony, however many they resolve. They shall elect ten men as geonomoi, one from each tribe; these are to distribute the land. And Demokleides shall have full powers to establish the colony, in the best way he can. They shall leave the precincts which have been set apart as they are, and not consecrate others. And they shall bring a cow and a panoply to the Great Panathenaia and a phallos to the Dionysia. If anyone wages war against the colonists' territory, the cities shall come to their aid as quickly as possible in accordance with the agreements which when ... was secretary were drawn up for the cities in Thrace. And they shall write these things on a stele and set it up on the acropolis; the colonists are to provide the stele at their own expense. And if anyone proposes a decree contrary to the stele or a speaker counsels or attempts to invite (someone else) to rescind or put an end to anything of what has been voted, he is to be deprived of citizen rights, as are his children, and his property is to belong to the state and a tithe be given to the goddess, unless the colonists themselves ... request. All the soldiers who are enrolled to go as settlers, when they have come to Athens, are to be at Brea as settlers within thirty days. They shall lead out the colony within thirty days. And Aeschines shall accompany them and provide the money.

B

Phantokles proposed the motion: concerning the colony at Brea, let it be as Demokleides proposed; and Phantokles shall be introduced by the tribe Erechtheis, the tribe holding the prytany, to the Council in its first session; and thetes and zeugitai are to go to Brea as the colonists.

12.32 *Inscriptiones Graecae* I^3 53: An Athenian Alliance with Rhegium, 433/2 BC

This treaty was made in the archonship of Apseudes, 433/2 BC. But the preamble is reinscribed over an earlier version of the preamble, and the text following it is older, so in 433/2 the treaty must have been renewed; this is also the case for the treaty with Leontinoi: see *IG* I^3 54. Possibly Athenian involvement in Corcyra alerted the Greek world to impending war between Athens and Sparta, and Rhegium and Leontinoi (and other Ionian cities in Sicily) may have feared 'that Syracuse would take advantage of Athens' preoccupation to try to swallow them' (Meiggs & Lewis p. 173). [*IG* I^2 51; Meiggs & Lewis 63.]

Gods. The envoys from Rhegium who made the alliance and took the oath were Kleandros son of Xen ..., ... (son of) ... tinos, Silenos son of Phokos, ... in Apseudes' archonship and in the Council of which Kritiades was secretary for the first time. It was resolved by the Council and the people, (the tribe) Akamantis held the prytany, Charias was secretary,

Timoxenos presided, Kalli (10 spaces) as proposed the motion: there shall be an alliance between the Athenians and Rhegians. And the Athenians shall swear the oath so that everything may be trustworthy and without deceit and straightforward on the part of the Athenians forever towards the Rhegians, swearing as follows: 'As allies we shall be trustworthy and just and steadfast and sincere forever to the Rhegians and we shall give assistance if they require anything ...'

12.33 *Inscriptiones Graecae* I^{3} 1178: Death of an Envoy

One of the envoys from Rhegium who arranged the alliance between Rhegium and Athens in 433 BC died in Athens and was publicly buried. 'Spacious' is an unusual term to use for Athens; as it is frequently applied to Sicily it is possible that the envoys here have adapted a pre-existing epigram to suit their colleague. [*IG* II^{2} 5220; Meiggs & Lewis 63 p. 175; Hansen 12.]

Spacious Athens buried this man
Who came here from his native land for an alliance;
He is Silenos son of Phokos, who was raised
By fortunate Rhegium as its justest citizen.

13

THE PELOPONNESIAN WAR AND ITS AFTERMATH

Thucydides viewed the Peloponnesian War, 431–404 BC, as the greatest disturbance that had ever affected the Greeks (doc. 13.1): 'both states were in their prime' and the rest of the Greeks joined either Athens or Sparta. A detailed reading of Thucydides' work is necessary for an in-depth understanding of his views of the war and of Athenian imperialism; Xenophon in his *Hellenika* continued where Thcydides' narrative ends in 411 BC. This chapter assumes that Thucydides' history is an essential background to the study of this period and concentrates primarily on a few of the main historical events, and particularly on the epigraphic evidence which complements Thucydides' narrative. One of the main themes which emerges is the enhanced Athenian imperialism which accompanied the Peloponnesian War, particularly with regard to tribute payment, which became of prime importance for Athens' prosecution of the war.

The Thirty Years' Peace of 446/5 BC did not last, and in 431 the Peloponnesian War broke out. Thucydides distinguishes between underlying and immediate causes of the war (doc. 13.2), and states that he is going to explain the grievances of each side against the other and the occasions when their interests clashed. These specific instances were disputes over Epidamnos, Corcyra and Potidaea. But Thucydides also states that these specific instances obscure the real reason for the war, and at 1.23.6 (doc. 13.2) he observes that the 'truest reason' for the war was the growth of Athenian power and the fear that this caused at Sparta. Some scholars are inclined to reject this argument, because in the ten years leading up to the outbreak of war in 431 Athens had not extended her power base. The Spartans, however, were aware that the Athenians were more powerful than they had been in 479 (cf. doc. 12.10) and Thucydides in writing of Spartan fear is not speaking of the short period immediately prior to the outbreak, for Athens had in half a century become a city with a far-flung empire which had challenged Spartan supremacy.

Sparta did not begin the war by itself. The Corinthians and other allied representatives went to Sparta in 432 BC and here encouraged the Spartans to declare war on the Athenians; representatives of the Athenians were also at Sparta and made a formal reply to the Corinthians (doc. 13.3). The Spartans decided on war but first sent an ultimatum to the Athenians in the same year. Whether war could have been avoided if Athens had acquiesced in the terms or whether the Spartans would have kept increasing their demands until war came anyway, as Perikles suspected, is a purely academic argument. Their ultimate demand was expressed by the last embassy to Athens from Sparta: that there would be peace if the Athenians 'would allow the Greeks to be autonomous' (doc. 13.4); and Epameinondas had a similar wrangling with Agesilaos over the meaning of Greek freedom in 371 BC (doc. 14.16). Sparta wanted Athens to give up its empire; Athens chose not to do so.

Athens began the war optimistically, the first phase of which is known as the Archidamian War (431–421 BC) after King Archidamos of Sparta; he had attempted to prevent the Spartans declaring war on the Athenians but led the invasions of Attica in 431, 430 and 428 BC. Perikles informed the Athenians that they had ample financial and manpower resources to prosecute the war (doc. 1.10), including the gold plates on the statue of Athena in the Parthenon (doc. 1.12; cf. 13.7). His strategy was not to fight the Spartans on land, but on sea (doc. 13.5). After the first year of war he was chosen to deliver the eulogy over the Athenian soldiers who had lost their lives (doc. 1.17). In 429 BC the plague struck Athens with great loss of life but the Athenians continued the war and soon recovered from its effects, except that Perikles died of it (doc. 13.6). To what extent his death affected the course of the war is impossible to determine, but Athens' subsequent leaders, such as Kleon, continued his policies.

Kleon pursued the same imperialistic policies that Perikles had: whereas Perikles had said the empire was *like* a tyranny, Kleon is made by Thucydides to say that it *is* a tyranny. The context was the debate about Lesbos, which had revolted from Athens in 428 BC (doc. 13.9). Revolts amongst the allies had to be taken seriously because of the tribute, manpower and naval resources that would be lost.

In 425 BC the Athenian general Demosthenes had fortified Pylos in the Peloponnese in order to harass the Peloponnese; the Spartans landed a garrison on the nearby island of Sphakteria to neutralise the threat. Kleon roundly abused the Athenian generals for making no progress; forced to take the command himself, he captured Sphakteria and, spectacularly, 120 Spartans (doc. 13.11). Shields captured from the Spartans were dedicated at Athens (doc. 13.12). It was a stunning endorsement of Kleon's leadership.

Brasidas took the war against Athens to the north in 424 BC and met with some success; even though he died in the battle at Amphipolis in 422 this Athenian possession went over to the Spartans (doc. 13.20; see 2.7). Philip II of Macedon was to capture it in 357; Athens did not formally relinquish its claim to the city until the Peace of Philokrates (doc. 14.34). Brasidas and Kleon were the main impediments to peace and their simultaneous deaths at Amphipolis in 422 BC opened the way for the Peace of Nikias (docs 3.26, 13.20).

In 418/7 Athens and Egesta made an alliance (doc. 13.22), a prelude to the disastrous Sicilian expedition of 415–413 BC (doc. 13.23), which reopened the Peloponnesian War. Athens set out to conquer Sicily: Alkibiades was the 'most enthusiastic advocate of the expedition' (doc. 13.23). But his recall from the command to face charges concerning the mutilation of the hermai and profanation of the Eleusinian Mysteries (doc. 13.24) proved to be a poor decision. Nikias, who had opposed the expedition, did not prosecute it vigorously enough, and the Syracusans with Spartan help defeated the Athenians and their allies in a naval battle in the great harbour of Syracuse in 413 BC. A lunar eclipse interpreted negatively condemned the survivors to defeat and many to their deaths in the Syracusan stone quarries (doc. 13.26; cf. doc. 3.24). On the advice of Alkibiades, in exile at Sparta, Dekeleia, some 23 kilometers (14 miles) north of Athens, was fortified by the Spartans, who harried the Athenians from this base.

The Athenians did not give up when news reached them of the Sicilian debacle (doc. 13.27), but an oligarchic revolution, of the Four Hundred, took place in 411 BC (doc. 13.28). In 409 BC Phrynikos was assassinated and the democracy restored (doc. 13.31). The Athenians won a notable victory at Arginousai in 406 BC, though six of the eight generals were executed on their return to Athens for not having been able to rescue Athenian sailors from drowning (doc. 1.20). However, the end came quickly when Lysander, with a Persian-sponsored fleet, defeated the Athenians at Aigospotamoi in 405 and starved the Athenians into submission (doc. 13.35). There were atrocities and retribution against the Athenians who survived the battle (docs 13.36, 13.38). Lysander imposed Spartan regimes on Athens' former allies (doc. 13.37) and was honoured by the Greeks (docs 13.38–39), being accorded greater honours than any Greek hitherto. The Thirty

Tyrants were installed by Lysander at Athens and they instituted a bloody regime for some eight months (doc. 13.40). Thrasyboulos, who had been a strategos, led Athenian exiles from Thebes to Phyle and then to the Piraeus; the civil war that ensued was ended by the Spartan king Pausanias, who was opposed to Lysander; Pausanias organised a reconciliation, and democracy was restored in 403 BC (doc. 13.41).

The Peloponnesian War was dominated by great statesmen and generals, and in Thucydides' narrative figures such as Perikles, Kleon, Brasidas, Nikias and Alkibiades are seen dominating the stage. But at Athens the war was conducted by the ekklesia, and it was there that debates were conducted and decisions made. Many decrees were passed in the course of the Peloponnesian War, and of particular importance are those concerning tribute payment (docs 13.15–17, 13.21). But the dating of many important Athenian inscriptions is subject to intense scholarly debate. Here the lower dating of decrees is accepted as these dates make better historical sense, and many decrees originally thought to belong to before the Peloponnesian War clearly belong to it and help elucidate its many complexities. The best example is the coinage decree (doc. 13.13), which laid down that Athenian coinage and measures were to be used throughout the empire, prohibiting other silver coinage. There may have been distinct advantages to enforcing uniformity throughout the empire, but this nevertheless reflects an infringement of the freedom of the cities, which had hitherto minted their own currency. The date of the decree is debated, but a date in the 420s is to be preferred to an earlier date *c.* 450–446, and decrees seen traditionally as signs of Athens' increasing imperialism in the 450s and 440s can now be dated to the 420s, with important implications for the conduct of the Peloponnesian War.

Two of the major preoccupations throughout the war for the Athenians were the tribute and the allies. Tribute collectors were appointed in 426 BC (doc. 13.15); the amounts paid were reassessed in 425 (doc. 13.16). Kleinias proposed a decree in the 420s which provided for seals to ensure that the tribute arrived and no quarrels could arise about the amount which had actually been sent; ships were to be sent from Athens to collect unpaid tribute (doc. 13.17). Aristophanes ridiculed Kleon, accusing him of an obsession with tribute, watching out for it as if it was a catch of tuna fish (doc. 13.18); comedy played an important part in political invective at Athens during the war. The Athenians dedicated one-sixtieth of the tribute from each state to the goddess Athena: this dedicated amount was recorded on stone. The amount listed for each ally can be multiplied by sixty to arrive at the actual amount of tribute it paid (doc. 13.21).

The allies, the tribute they paid and the manpower they provided were crucial for Athens' conduct of the war. The Kolophonians loyal to Athens when the city went over to the Persians in 427 BC were assisted (doc. 13.8); Neapolis in Thrace was loyal even late in the war and honoured as such by Athens (doc. 13.31). In particular the demos of Samos, the refuge of the fleet in the 411 oligarchic revolution, stayed loyal to the end (doc. 13.34), but under Lysander's dekarchy gave him expansive honours (doc. 13.38). Specific regulations were drawn up for allies who unsuccessfully revolted, to try to bind them more closely to Athens, as in the case of Chalkis in 424/3 BC (doc. 13.19). A decree aimed to ensure that Miletos was to stay loyal in 426/5 BC and dealt with judicial arrangements in the case of someone behaving in a way detrimental to Athens (doc. 13.10). Revolts such as that of Eretria were particularly harmful to Athens' interests (doc. 13.29). After the war, Athens lost all its allies.

To the music of flute girls, Athens' Long Walls and those of the Piraeus were demolished in 404 BC (doc. 13.35). Sparta's allies, particularly Thebes and Corinth, were disappointed that their suggestion that Athens be completely destroyed and its inhabitants enslaved was not followed; the Athenians themselves in fact had feared enslavement when the news of Aigospotamoi reached them (doc. 5.5). Sparta feared Boeotian power: the destruction of Athens would allow Boeotia, particularly Thebes, to dominate central Greece. Athens never regained the leading position and power of the 440s and 430s. Sparta was hegemon of Greece for about ten years and, despite some reassertion of its power after that, notably with the King's Peace in 386 BC, by 371 BC its power was effectively broken by Thebes at Leuktra (doc. 14.18). It played an important role in the fourth century but, despite its attempts to regain old glories, new powers emerged which played a greater role in shaping fourth-century history: Thebes, Iason of Pherai and Philip of Macedon, succeeded by his son Alexander.

THE OUTBREAK OF THE PELOPONNESIAN WAR

13.1 Thucydides 1.1.1–3: Thucydides and His History

Thucydides' exile, incurred for his failure to come to the relief of Amphipolis in time in 424/3 BC, gave him the opportunity of seeing the war from both points of view, and of speaking to participants regardless of their side (Thuc. 5.26.5, cf. 4.104.4–105.1, 106.3–107.1; doc. 16.4).

1.1.1 Thucydides the Athenian wrote the history of the war between the Peloponnesians and Athenians, how they fought each other, beginning at the very outbreak, in the expectation that it was going to be a great war and more worth writing about than those of the past, judging from the fact that both states were in their prime and at the peak of preparation and seeing that the rest of the Greek world was aligned with one of the two, even those that were not immediately committed having it in mind to commit themselves. **2** This disturbance was the greatest which ever affected the Greeks, as well as affecting a great part of the barbarian world, and thus, so to speak, most of mankind. **3** For it has been impossible because of the passage of time to discover precisely what took place before this war or still earlier, yet the evidence, from looking into it as far back as I can, leads me to conclude that these were not great periods in warfare or anything else.

13.2 Thucydides 1.23.4–6: The 'Truest Cause' of the War

The 'truest cause' ('alethestate prophasis') of the Peloponnesian War was Spartan fear of the growing power of Athens, and the specific causes of complaint (aitiai) were Corinth's colonies, Epidamnos, Corcyra and Potidaea, for which see Thuc. 1.24–65 (docs 2.8–9); cf. 1.33.3, 88, 118.2.

1.23.4 The Athenians and Peloponnesians began the war when they broke the Thirty Years' Peace, which had been made after the capture of Euboea. **5** Regarding the reasons for their having broken it, I have already recorded first their causes of complaint and disputes, so that no one ever has to ask why such a great war came upon the Greeks. **6** For its truest cause, although the one least mentioned, I consider to have been that the Athenians, by growing powerful, and making the Spartans afraid, compelled them to go to war. The causes of complaint which were openly expressed by both sides, because of which they broke the truce and went to war, were as follows.

13.3 Thucydides 1.70.1–8: Athens versus Sparta: The Corinthian View

The Corinthians, because of Athens' siege of Potidaea, encouraged the Peloponnesian allies to send representatives to Sparta in 432 BC, where the Corinthians attacked the Athenians (Thuc.

1.66–71), and Athenian delegates made a reply (1.72–78). The Spartans voted that the Athenians had broken the Thirty Years Peace of 446/5 (1.87–88) and then having sought Apollo's approval for the war called a meeting of their allies, at which the Corinthians made a second speech (1.118–24) and the Peloponnesian League voted for war (1.125, cf. 7.18.2–3). The Corinthians, in contrasting the policies and behaviour of the Spartans and the Athenians, clearly intended to frighten and goad the Spartans into war.

1.70.1 'Besides, we believe we have the right to criticise our neighbours, particularly because the stakes are so high, though in our view you seem to fail to perceive these risks, having never considered what sort of people these Athenians — whom you will have to fight — really are, and how much, how totally different they are from yourselves. **2** They are innovators, quick thinkers and swift at putting their plans into action, while you like to hold on to what you have, come up with no new ideas, and when you do take action never achieve as much as you should have done. **3** They are daring beyond their resources, face dangers they should think better of, and confident in desperate circumstances. Your way is to do less than you could, mistrust your own sound judgement, and believe that from a crisis there is no escape. **4** What's more, they are unhesitating, while you hold back, and are happy to leave Athens, while you never leave Sparta; they think that they can only gain by not staying at home in Athens, while you think that by leaving home you will lose what possessions you already have. **5** When they overcome their enemies they pursue their advantage to the utmost, and when beaten give as little ground as possible. **6** What's more, when their city is at stake, they treat their bodies with as little regard as though they belonged to somebody quite different, but their minds are quite focused with a view to achieving some success on the city's behalf.

7 'Whenever they think of a plan but do not carry it through, they think that they have been deprived of something they actually possessed, while if they try and are successful they consider that this success is minute compared with what the future has in store, and if they fail in an enterprise they compensate for this by forming other hopes instead. They are the only ones for whom to hope for a thing is to achieve it, since they undertake in haste whatever they decide to do. **8** So they keep working hard, through difficulties and dangers, all their lives, and enjoy their possessions less than any other men because they are always looking for more, since they consider that their only holiday is to do their duty, and see peace and inactivity as a greater calamity than hardship and action — and so, if someone described them by saying that they are incapable of leading a quiet life themselves or of allowing anyone else to do so, he would be speaking the absolute truth.'

13.4 Thucydides 1.139.1–3: Sparta's Ultimatum in 432 BC

The Spartans made several demands if the Thirty Years' Peace of 446/5 BC was to be preserved. The 'accursed' refers to the Alkmeonidai (see docs 7.21–23), of whom Perikles was a descendant. Megara had gone back to the Spartan alliance prior to 446 BC, and the Athenians passed a decree against it, probably in or shortly before 432 BC. The 'sacred land' was a piece of land near Eleusis which the Athenians claimed the Megarians were cultivating and hence committing sacrilege.

1.139.1 These were the demands which the Spartans made on the occasion of their first embassy and, like the demands which the Athenians made in return, they concerned the expulsion of the 'accursed'; later the Spartans came to the Athenians and demanded that they abandon the siege of Potidaea and allow Aegina to be autonomous, while above all and most explicitly they proclaimed that if the Athenians revoked the Megarian decree, in which the Megarians were forbidden to make use of the harbours of the Athenian empire and the Athenian agora, there would be no war. **2** But the Athenians did not give in on the other points and did not revoke the decree, accusing the Megarians of cultivating the sacred land and boundary land and of harbouring runaway slaves. **3** Finally, the last embassy came from Sparta, consisting of Ramphios, Melesippos and Agesander, who said none of the things that the Spartans had usually raised earlier, but simply this: 'The Spartans want the peace to continue, and it will, if you allow the Greeks to be autonomous.'

THE ARCHIDAMIAN WAR, 431–421 BC

The first phase of the Peloponnesian War is named after King Archidamos, who invaded Attica in the early years of the first phase of the war, which began with Thebes' attack on Plataea in 431. Perikles advised the Athenians not to give in to the Spartan demands, but adopted a passive rather than an aggressive strategy in the defence of Attica; the first invasion took place in summer, when the grain was ripe, and the Spartans hoped that they would defeat Athens in a few years (Thuc. 5.14.3).

13.5 Thucydides 2.14.1–2, 2.65.6–7: Perikles' Strategy

Perikles successfully argued that the Athenians should not give in to Spartan demands, and also that they should not meet the Spartans in battle outside the walls (Thuc. 1.81.6, 139–44, 2.13, 21–23, 59–65). The Athenians moved into the city, even into temples and shrines except where it was absolutely forbidden.

2.14.1 The Athenians took Perikles' advice and brought their children, women and other household possessions in from the country, even removing the woodwork from the very houses; they sent their sheep and cattle across to Euboea and the neighbouring islands. **2** But they found this removal hard, as the majority of them had always been used to living in the country ... **2.65.6** Perikles lived on for two years and six months (after the start of the war); and when he died, his foresight regarding the war became even more apparent. **7** For he had said that they would come out of it on top if they bided their time, and looked after the fleet, and did not try to extend the empire while the war was on, and did nothing to endanger the city.

13.6 Thucydides 2.47.2–3, 52.1–53.4: The Plague Strikes Athens

Perikles' plans for the conduct of the war could not take into account unforeseen events such as the plague, exacerbated by the overcrowding in Athens (Thuc. 2.52.1–2, cf. 17.1), and this was the first setback in the Periklean strategy. In Thucydides' discussion of the plague there is a 'scientific' description of the symptoms, but it is also concerned with the impact of the plague on society: Perikles himself died of it.

2.47.2 At the beginning of the following summer, the Peloponnesians and their allies, with two-thirds of their forces as before, invaded Attica (the Spartan king Archidamos, son of

Zeuxidamos, was in command), and they took up their positions and started devastating the country. **3** And after they had been in Attica for only a few days the plague made its first appearance among the Athenians. It was said that it had previously broken out in a number of other places, such as Lemnos, but nowhere else was it recorded to have been so virulent or caused such numbers of deaths …

2.52.1 The existing suffering had been made far worse by the removal of people from the country to the city, and the incomers were worst affected. **2** There were no houses for them, and, living as they did in the summer season in stifling huts, they died without hindrance, corpses of the dying lay on corpses, and the half-dead staggered around the streets and around all the fountains in their desire for water. **3** The temples in which they were living were full of the corpses of people who had died inside them; for, as the disaster weighed so heavily upon them, men, not knowing whether they would continue to live, turned to neglect of sacred and holy things alike. **4** All the funeral customs, which had been followed up to now, were thrown into disorder and they buried the dead as best each could. Many turned to disgraceful means of disposing of the dead through lack of relatives because of the number of those who had already died; for they got to other people's pyres, before those who had piled them up, and placed their own corpse on them and set them alight, or when someone else was being burned they threw on top the body they were carrying and made off.

2.53.1 In other respects as well, for the city the plague was in great measure the beginning of lawlessness. For seeing the swift change of fortune of those who were rich and died suddenly, and of those who had earlier possessed nothing and then all at once inherited what the others had had, people began to venture more readily on acts of self-indulgence, which they had previously kept secret … **4** Neither fear of the gods nor law of men was any restraint, and they considered it the same whether one worshipped the gods or not, since they saw everyone dying equally, and no one expected to live long enough for a trial to take place or to be punished for their offences, but they rather thought that the punishment had already been decreed and was hanging over them, and that it was reasonable to enjoy life a little before it arrived.

13.7 *Inscriptiones Graecae* I^{3} 52: The Financial Decrees of Kallias, 434/3? BC

The dating of these decrees is a matter of debate: they either belong to the Peloponnesian War or are a preliminary to it. The usual interpretation is that the treasures of temples in rural demes and the lower city have been moved onto the acropolis (cf. doc. 1.11) and this is seen as a security measure in the event of invasion. The Opisthodomos is the inner treasury chamber of the Parthenon. [*IG* I^{2} 91, 92; *ATL* 2.D1–2; Meiggs & Lewis 58.]

It was resolved by the Council and the people; (the tribe) Kekropis held the prytany, Mnesitheos was secretary, Eupeithes presided, Kallias proposed the motion: repayment is to be made to the gods of the money which is owed, since Athena's 3,000 talents, which have been voted, have been brought up to the acropolis in our coinage. And it is to be repaid from the money which has been voted for repayment to the gods, both that which is now in the hands of the hellenotamiai and the rest of this money, and also the money from the 10 per cent tax when it has been farmed out. The thirty auditors (logistai) who are now in office are to calculate precisely what is owed to the gods, and the Council is to have full powers over the meeting of the auditors. The prytaneis together with the Council are to pay back the money and cancel the debt when they pay it back, after searching the registers and account books and anywhere else it might be recorded. The priests and the temple overseers (hieropoioi) and anyone else who knows of the records are to produce them. And the treasurers of this money are to be chosen by lot at the same time as the other magistrates, as are those of the sacred money of Athena.

These on the acropolis in the Opisthodomos are to administer the money of the gods as efficiently and piously as possible, and are to share in the opening and closing and sealing of the doors of the Opisthodomos with the treasurers of Athena. As they receive the treasures from the current treasurers, superintendents (epistatai) and priests in the temples, who now have charge of them, they are to count them up and weigh them in front of the Council on the acropolis, and the treasurers who have been chosen by lot are to take them over from the current officials and record on one stele all the treasures, both that according to each of the gods, how much belongs to each, and the entire sum, with the silver and the gold both separate.

And in future the treasurers who are in office are to record this on a stele and draw up an account of the balance of the money and the revenue of the gods, and whatever is spent during the year, for the auditors, and submit to an examination at the end of their term. And they are to draw up accounts from Great Panathenaia to Great Panathenaia, just like the treasurers of Athena. And the stelai, on which they have recorded the sacred treasures, are to be set up by the treasurers on the acropolis. When the money has been repaid to the gods, they are to use the surplus money for the dockyard and the walls.

B

It was resolved by the Council and the people: the tribe Kekropis held the prytany, Mnesitheos was secretary, Eupeithes presided, Kallias proposed the motion: ... of stone and the golden Victories (Nikai) and the Propylaia; ... completely ... are to use ... according to what has been decreed, and the acropolis ... and they are to restore it by spending ten talents each year until it has been ... and has been restored as well as possible; and the treasurers and the superintendents are to jointly supervise the work. The architect is to make the plan just as for the Propylaia; and he is to see to it with the superintendents that the acropolis is ... as well and as economically as possible and that restoration is done to whatever is required. And the rest of the money of Athena's which is now on the acropolis and whatever may be brought up in the future they are not to use or to borrow from it for any other reason than this more than 10,000 drachmas, except for restoration if any is necessary; and they are to use the money for no other reason unless the people decree immunity, as when they decree concerning the property tax.

And if anyone proposes a motion or puts it to the vote that without immunity having been decreed they should use the money of Athena's, he shall be liable to the same penalty as someone who proposes a motion or puts it to the vote concerning the property tax. For all the gods the hellenotamiai are to deposit during the year what is owed to each with the treasurers of Athena. When from the 200 talents which the people decreed for repayment what is owed has been paid back to the other gods, the treasures of Athena shall be stored in the area on the right-hand side of the Opisthodomos, and those of the other gods on the left. However many of the sacred treasures are unweighed or uncounted, the current treasurers together with the four boards which draw up the accounts from Panathenaia to Panathenaia are to weigh how much gold there is and silver and silver gilt, and count the rest.

13.8 *Inscriptiones Graecae* I³ 37: Kolophon Swears Loyalty to the Athenians, 427 BC

Thucydides 3.34 describes the foundation in 427 BC of a colony under Athenian direction at Notion, Kolophon's port: a pro-Persian group had seized upper Kolophon, and the citizens loyal to Athens fled to Notion, and there split into two groups, one of which received assistance from the pro-Persian group, while the other group fled. The Athenian general Paches took Notion and handed it over to this latter group. The Athenians sent out settlers to join them, with oikistai (founders), and gathered together all the Kolophonians found in other cities for the purpose of the new settlement. Another possible date for the inscription is 447/6. [*IG* I² 14, 15; *ATL* 2.D15; Meiggs & Lewis 47.]

The secretary of the Council is to record this decree and the oath on a stone stele on the acropolis at the expense of the Kolophonians; and at Kolophon the oikistai sent to Kolophon are to record these things and the oath on a stone stele and set it up in a place which the law of the Kolophonians assigns. The Kolophonians are to swear: 'I shall act and speak and advise as fittingly and best I can concerning the people of the Athenians and concerning the colony; and I will not rebel against the people of the Athenians either in word or in deed, either I myself, nor shall I be persuaded by anyone else; and I will cherish the people of the Athenians and I shall not desert to the enemy; and I will not put down democracy at Kolophon, either I myself, nor shall I be persuaded by anyone else, either by revolting and going over to another city or by stirring up dissension here. And in accordance with the oath I shall confirm these things as true without deceit and without violating the terms, by Zeus and by Apollo and by Demeter, and if I should transgress these things may both I myself and my family be utterly destroyed for all time, but if I keep the oath may many good things be mine.'

13.9 Thucydides 3.36.2–4, 39.1–4: The Mytilene Debate in 427 BC

In 428 BC Lesbos (except Methymna) under the leadership of Mytilene revolted from Athens (Thuc. 3.2–19, 26–28, 35). Kleon, who argues strongly for the death penalty for the entire population, states that the empire is a tyranny (37.2: 'What you fail to perceive is that your empire is a tyranny imposed on people who plot against you and are governed unwillingly') and in this echoes Perikles (compare Thuc. 2.63.2 with 3.37.2, cf. 40.4; 2.61.2 with 3.38.1). After the surrender of Mytilene, the Athenians, on the motion of Kleon, decided to deal harshly with the Mytilenaeans. On the next day, many regretted the decision, and the debate was reopened. On the previous day Kleon had proposed (and carried) the decree for the executions, and Diodotos had opposed it. They both spoke again. Diodotos is otherwise unknown.

3.36.2 They then discussed what to do with the other prisoners and in their anger decided to put them to death, not only the ones in their hands but all the other adult male Mytilenaeans and sell the children and women into slavery. Their anger against Mytilene was caused by their revolt, even though they were not subject-allies like the others, and the Athenians' violent reaction was particularly reinforced by the fact that the Spartans' ships had dared to venture to Ionia to support them; for they thought that this showed that the revolt had been long premeditated. **3** So they sent a trireme to Paches to tell him what had been decided, ordering him to kill the Mytilenaeans immediately. **4** On the following day, however, there was a sudden change of heart and they began to reflect upon the cruelty and severity of the decision, destroying a whole city rather than just those responsible ...

3.39.1 After opposing views had been delivered on both sides with almost identical forcefulness, the Athenians were in such a conflict of opinion that they were about equally divided in the count of hands; that of Diodotos, however, prevailed. **2** They immediately dispatched another trireme with all haste, in the hope that the first trireme, which had a head start of a day and a night, might not get there first and the second arrive to find the city destroyed. **3** The Mytilenaean envoys supplied them with wine and barley and promised them great rewards should they arrive in time. Such was their haste on the voyage, that they ate their barley cakes kneaded with wine and olive oil as they rowed, and took turns at sleeping and rowing. **4** Since, by good fortune, they were not opposed by any contrary wind, and the first ship was not in any hurry to sail on this unpleasant errand, while the second ship pressed on in the way described above, though the earlier ship did arrive first so that Paches had time to read the decree and was about to put the instructions into execution, the later one put in shortly afterwards and was able to prevent the destruction — that was how close to danger Mytilene came.

13.10 *Inscriptiones Graecae* I^3 21: Agreement with Miletos in 426/5 BC

This is a poorly preserved text, but despite the many restorations much of importance about the empire can be gleaned from it, especially details concerning judicial arrangements between Miletos and Athens. This inscription has been dated to the mid-fifth century. The archon's name in line 86, cf. 61, is, however, Euthynos, who was archon in 426/5 BC. Another possible date sometimes given for the inscription is 450/49. [*IG* I^2 22; *ATL* 2.D11.]

Agreement with the Milesians. It was resolved by the Council and the people; ... is held the prytany, ... was secretary, ... or presided, Euthynos was archon; the commissioners (syngrapheis) drew up as follows: the customary sacrifices are to be paid to the gods, and the people are to elect immediately five men from everyone **5** over fifty years of age, and refusal shall not be allowed them or substitution, and these are to be officials and ... (*lines 10–24 appear to deal with the supply of troops by Miletos*). **26** ... of the allies what would not be (good) for the Athenians ... he shall be deprived of citizen rights and his property belong to the state and a tithe be given to the goddess; and the trials for Milesians are to be ... **30** drachmas from the tithe ... the court fees are to be deposited with the officials ... and the trials are to be at Athens in ... Anthesterion and Elaphebolion; and the ... having distributed and allotted ... **35** two of the archons and ... and the payment is to be given to the jurors from the court fees ... they are to provide the law court ... in the months that have been laid down or they shall be liable to examination ... to the archons of the Athenians ... **40** to Athens to the epimeletai ... just as before and ... the five are to see that ... law court sits ... shall be for those who proceed ... **45** the officials of the Athenians ... to be paid; and the (cases) over one hundred drachmas ... on a stele and for the decrees ... not to destroy or to deal fraudulently.

And if anyone transgresses them in any way, there shall be an indictment against him before the ...; **50** they shall bring him forward either to one ...; and the court is to assess what penalty or fine is proper ... (*lines 52–70 and 72–82 are not translated here*). **71** ... and the five are to administer the oath ... **83** ... the Council ... the garrison; of the decrees ... may be accomplished, the Council is to have full powers ... **85** let them send off the two guardships and the ... in the archonship of Euthynos ...

13.11 Thucydides 4.27.5–28.5, 38.5–39.3: Pylos, 425 BC

The general Demosthenes was responsible for the fortification at Pylos in the Peloponnese; the Spartans responded to this by putting troops onto the nearby island of Sphakteria. When events turned against the Athenians, Kleon accused the strategoi of incompetence, at which Nikias challenged him to take the command himself. For the whole episode, see Thuc. 4.3–41; Plut. *Nik.* 7.1–6.

4.27.5 Kleon pointed at Nikias, son of Nikeratos, who was one of the generals, and an enemy of his, and attacked him with the comment that if the generals were men it would be easy to take out a force and capture the men on the island, and that is what he would have done had he been in charge.

4.28.1 The Athenians then began clamouring against Kleon, asking him why he didn't sail right away, if he thought it was so easy, and Nikias responded to this attack of Kleon's by telling him that as far as the generals were concerned he was welcome to take whatever force he liked and try for himself. **2** At first Kleon thought that Nikias' offer to give up the command was in word only and stated that he was ready to go, but when he realised that it was actually being offered to him he started to back out, saying that it was not he but Nikias who was the general, being alarmed because he had never imagined that Nikias would have gone so far as to retire in favour of himself. **3** But Nikias again told him to go and called the Athenians to witness that he was resigning from the command against Pylos. In the usual way of crowds, the more Kleon tried to get out of the voyage and take back what he had said, the more the Athenians urged Nikias to give up the command and shouted at Kleon that he had to sail. **4** As a result, as there was no way now of going back on his proposal, Kleon undertook the expedition, and came forward to say that he was not frightened of the Spartans and would sail without taking a single citizen, but just the Lemnians and Imbrians currently in Athens, the peltasts come to help from Ainos, and 400 archers from elsewhere. With these, he said, together with the soldiers now at Pylos, in twenty days he would either bring the Spartans back alive or kill them there. **5** The Athenians greeted his boasting with a shout of laughter, but the prudent men amongst them realised that one of two good outcomes was bound to eventuate; either they would be rid of Kleon (which was their preferred option) or if they failed in this he would at least beat the Spartans for them...

4.38.5 The numbers of those who were killed and taken alive on the island were as follows: altogether 420 (Spartan) hoplites had crossed to Sphakteria; of these 292 were captured alive and the rest were killed. About 120 of those taken alive were Spartiates. Few of the Athenians had been killed, as no pitched battle had taken place. **4.39.1** The total period of the siege on the island, from the sea-battle up till the battle on the island, was seventy-two days. **2** For about twenty of these days, in which the (Spartan) envoys had been absent over the peace treaty, the Spartans were allowed provisions, but for the rest of the time they lived on what was smuggled in ... **3** The Athenians and Spartans now both withdrew their forces from Pylos and returned home, and Kleon's promise, although a mad one, had been fulfilled; for he had brought the men back, as he had undertaken to do, in twenty days.

13.12 *Agora* B, 262: Athenian Spoils from Sphakteria

The Athenians inscribed and dedicated the shields which they had taken from the Spartans at Sphakteria; Ar. *Knights* 846–49 mentions the captured shields. Pausanias saw them in the Stoa Poikile (1.15.4) and one of these has been discovered in the agora.

'The Athenians from the Spartans at Pylos (dedicated this).'

13.13 *Inscriptiones Graecae* I^3 1453: Athenian Decree on Coins, Weights and Measures

This decree forbids the minting of silver coinage in the allied cities and imposes the use of 'Athenian coins, measures and weights' (12). The Athenian officials in the cities or otherwise the local officials are to be responsible and copies are to be set up in the agora of each city (10). The dating of the decree is a matter of controversy: 425 BC is preferable to before *c.* 445 BC. [*ATL* 2.D14; Meiggs & Lewis 45.]

1 … governors in the cities or (local) officials … **2** The hellenotamiai … are to make a record; if not … of any of the cities, anyone who wishes shall immediately bring the offenders before the heliaia of the thesmothetai; and the thesmothetai within five days shall institute trial proceedings for the informers against each (offender). **3** If anyone, either one of the citizens or a foreigner, other than the governors in the cities does not act in accordance with what has been decreed, he shall be deprived of citizen rights and his property be confiscated and a tithe (given) to the goddess. **4** And if there are no Athenian governors, the officials of each city shall see that all that is in the decree is carried out; and if they do not act in accordance with what has been decreed, there shall be a prosecution at Athens against these officials, the penalty being loss of citizen rights. **5** In the mint after receiving the silver they shall mint no less than half and … the cities; the superintendents (of the mint) shall always exact a fee of three drachmas per mina; they shall convert the other half within … months or be liable … **6** Whatever is left over of the silver that has been exacted they shall mint and hand over either to the generals or to the … **7** When it has been handed over, … and to Hephaistos … **8** And if anyone proposes or puts it to the vote regarding these things that it be permissible to use or lend foreign currency, he shall be denounced immediately before the Eleven; and the Eleven shall punish him with death; and if he disputes this, let them bring him before the jury-court. **9** The people shall elect heralds … what has been decreed, one to the islands, one to Ionia, one to the Hellespont and one to the region of Thrace; the generals are to prescribe the route for each of these and send them off; and if they do not, each one shall be liable at his examination (to a fine of) ten thousand drachmas.

10 The officials in the cities are to set up this decree after recording it on a stone stele in the agora of each city and the superintendents (are to do this) in front of the mint; the Athenians shall see to this, if they themselves are not willing. **11** The herald who makes the journey shall request of them all that the Athenians command. **12** The secretary of the Council shall make an addition to the oath of the Council for the future as follows: 'If anyone mints silver coinage in the cities and does not use Athenian coins, weights and measures, but foreign coins, measures and weights, I will punish and fine him in accordance with the former decree which Klearchos proposed.' **13** Anyone is to be allowed to hand over the foreign money which he possesses and convert it in the same way whenever he wishes; and the city is to give him in exchange our own currency; each man shall bring his (money) to Athens and deposit it at the mint. **14** The superintendents (of the mint) are to record everything handed over by each person and set up a stone stele in front of the mint for whoever wishes to look at it; and they are also to record the total of the foreign currency, both the silver and the gold separately, and the total of our silver ...

13.14 Aristophanes *Birds* 1035–42: New Laws in Cloud-Cuckoo-Land

Performed at the Great Dionysia, 414 BC, these lines from the *Birds* are clearly a reference to the coinage decree, which must have been relatively recent.

Decree-seller: If an inhabitant of Cloud-Cuckoo-Land commits an offence against
an Athenian—
Peisthetairos: What is this dreadful thing now, this book?
Decree-seller: I am a decree-seller and I have come here
Bringing new laws to sell you.
Peisthetairos: What?!
Decree-seller: That you shall use the measures of Cloud-Cuckoo-Land
And its weights and decrees just like the Olophyxians.
Peisthetairos: As for you, you're going to use those of the Olotyxians ('always
weeping'), right now!

THE TRIBUTE IN THE PELOPONNESIAN WAR

The tribute was vital to the Athenian conduct of the war, and various measures were taken to ensure its efficient collection. Kleonymos moved a decree for the election in allied cities of tribute collectors along with various measures designed to ensure effective collection (doc. 13.15). This was followed by a reassessment of the tribute in 425 (doc. 13.16). Kleinias' decree (doc. 13.17) almost certainly dates to after Kleonymos' and further tightens up tribute payments.

13.15 *Inscriptiones Graecae* I³ 68: Appointment of Tribute Collectors in 426 BC

Each of the allied states were to elect tribute collectors in their cities, who were made responsible for the collection of tribute. Note the various other provisions to ensure that the tribute is paid; these provisions are further strengthened in Kleinias' decree. The importance of collecting the tribute for the war is made explicit (lines 28–29). [*ATL* 2.D8; Meiggs & Lewis 68.]

... Tribute; it was resolved by the Council and the people; (the tribe) Kekropis held the prytany, Polemarchos was secretary, Onasos presided, **5** Kleonymos proposed the motion: all the cities that bring tribute to the Athenians are to elect in each city tribute collectors, so that from all parts the whole tribute may be collected for the Athenians or the collectors will be held liable ... **11** ... for the hellenotamiai, whichever prytany is in office shall of necessity hold an assembly concerning the cities twenty days after the Dionysia; and they shall publicly make known those cities which pay the tribute, and those which do not pay, and those which (pay) in part; and they shall send five men to the defaulters in order that they may exact the tribute; and the hellenotamiai are to record on a noticeboard the cities that have failed to pay the tribute and the names of those that bring it and place it on each occasion in front of the (statues of) the heroes. There is also to be a similar decree for the Samians and Therans concerning the money which it is necessary for them to pay except for the election of the men, and the same for any other city which has agreed to bring money to Athens. The prytany of Kekropis is to set up this decree on a stele on the acropolis.

P[...]kritos proposed the amendment: that the rest be as Kleonymos proposed; and so that the Athenians may as well and as easily as possible carry on the war, an assembly is to be held tomorrow and (this) resolution brought before the people; it was resolved by the Council and the people: (the tribe) Kekropis held the prytany, Polemarchos was secretary, Hygiainon presided, Kleonymos proposed the amendment: that the rest be as in the previous decree ... ... epimeletai shall be elected for the other cases concerning the Athenian monies in accordance with the decree which has been enacted and one of the generals shall be assigned to sit alongside them whenever a case is to be judged concerning one of the cities; and if anyone schemes to prevent the tribute decree from being effective or the tribute from being brought to Athens, anyone who wishes from that city may indict him for treason before the epimeletai; and the epimeletai shall bring him before the jury-court within a month of the arrival of the summoners (kleteres). There shall be twice as many summoners as there are men against whom anyone wishes to bring an indictment; and if it convicts anyone the jury-court is to decide his proper punishment or fine; and the heralds, however many there might be, whom the prytaneis with the Council have elected, are to be sent to the cities in the prytany of Kekropis, so that the men who are to collect the tribute may be elected, and (their names) be recorded in the council chamber; the poletai are to let out the contract for the stele. Collectors of tribute from the cities.

13.16 *Inscriptiones Graecae* I[3] 71: Reassessment of Athenian Tribute, 425/4 BC

The amount of tribute being collected had become inadequate (lines 16–17), and a new assessment was made, probably under Kleon's influence; note the various measures outlined in the decree to this effect, in particular that reassessment must take place at every Great Panathenaia, and allied states are to bring a cow and panoply (a full suit of armour) to the Great Panathenaia. Eisagogeis (sing.: eisagogeus) were magistrates who brought cases into court. [*IG* I[2] 63; *ATL* 2.A9; Meiggs & Lewis 69.]

Gods. Assessment of tribute. It was resolved by the Council and the people; (the tribe) Leontis held the prytany, ... on was secretary, ... presided, Thoudippos proposed the motion: that heralds be sent out of the contractors (?) whom the Council elects, to the cities, two to Ionia and Caria, two to Thrace, two to the islands, and two to the Hellespont; and these are to announce in the government of each city that ambassadors are to arrive (in Athens) in the month Maimakterion. They are to choose by lot thirty eisagogeis; and these are to elect a secretary and assistant secretary from amongst themselves; and the Council is to immediately elect ten men as assessors (of the tribute); these within five days from when they have been elected and sworn their oaths shall record (the names of) the cities or for each day each shall pay a thousand drachmas. The commissioners for oaths (horkotai) are to administer the oath to the assessors on the same day that they are elected or each will be liable to the same penalty. The eisagogeis are to be responsible for the lawsuits concerned with the tribute, as the people should decree; and the eisagogeus who is chosen by lot and the polemarch are to prepare the cases for trial in the heliaia just like the other cases judged by the heliasts; and if the assessors do not assess the cities in accordance with the lawsuits, each of them will be fined ten thousand drachmas at their examination in accordance with the law; and the nomothetai are to establish a new jury-court of a thousand jurors.

As the tribute has become too little, the new assessments are to be drawn up all proportionately with the help of the Council, as was done in the last magistracy, during the month Posideion; and they are to conduct business every day from the new moon in the same way in order that the tribute may be assessed in the month Posideion; and a full Council is to conduct business continuously in order that the assessments may be made, unless the people decrees otherwise; and they are not to assess the new tribute for any city at less than it paid before unless some difficulty is shown, such as its region being unable to pay more. This resolution and this decree and the tribute which is assessed for each city the secretary of the Council shall record on two stone stelai and set up, one in the council chamber and one on the acropolis; and the poletai are to let out the contract and the kolakretai are to provide the money. In future a declaration is to be made to the cities concerning the tribute before the Great Panathenaia; and the prytany which happens to be in office shall introduce the assessments during the Panathenaia; and if the prytaneis do not at that time introduce them to the people and do not decree a law court concerning the tribute and do not conduct the business at that time during their period in office, each of the prytaneis shall owe a hundred drachmas sacred to Athena and a hundred to the public treasury and at their examination each of the prytaneis shall pay a fine of a thousand drachmas.

And if anyone else brings a motion that the assessments of the cities shall not be made during the Great Panathenaia in the prytany which first holds office, he is to be deprived of citizen rights and his property be confiscated with a tithe given to the goddess. The prytany of (the tribe) Oineis is of necessity to bring these proposals before the people, when the expedition has arrived, on the second day directly after the sacrifices. And if it is not completed on this day, it is to be dealt with first on the next day continuously until it has been completed during the aforesaid prytany; and if they do not bring it before the people or do not complete it during their term of office, each of the prytaneis at their examination are to be fined ten thousand drachmas for preventing the contribution of tribute for the expeditions. The heralds who are summoned are to be brought by the public summoners (kleteres) in order that the Council can judge whether they appear not to be performing their duties correctly. The routes for the heralds who are to set out are to be prescribed according to the oath by the assessors, (indicating) to where they should proceed, so that they shall not proceed in undisciplined fashion; and the heralds are to be compelled to proclaim the assessments to the cities wherever the magistrates think best; and the people is to decree whatever is to be said to the cities concerning the assessments and the decree and anything else which the prytaneis introduce concerning what is necessary.

The generals are to see that the cities pay the tribute as soon as the Council has jointly made the assessment of the tribute, in order that there may be sufficient money for the people for the war; and the generals are to be obliged to give consideration every year concerning the tribute, investigating by land and sea first of all how much it is necessary to expend either on the expeditions or on anything else; and they are always to introduce cases concerning this at the first session of the Council without consulting the heliaia and the other jury-courts, unless the people decrees that they introduce them once the jurors have first made a decision. The kolakretai are to pay to the heralds who are to set out their remuneration … proposed the amendment: that the rest be as the Council resolved; but the assessments, as many as are made on individual cities, are to be declared to the jury-court, when it is dealing with assessments, by the prytaneis who happen to be in office and the secretary of the Council, so that the jurors can approve them. It was resolved by the Council and the people: (the tribe) Aigeis held the prytany, Philippos was secretary, … oros presided, Thoudippos proposed the motion: all the cities whose tribute was assessed during the Council of which Pleistias was secretary for the first time, in the archonship of Stratokles, are to bring a cow and panoply to the Great Panathenaia; and they are to take part in the procession in the same way as colonists. The Council of which Pleistias was secretary for the first time and the heliaia assessed as follows the tribute for the cities in the archonship of Stratokles in the period of office of the eisagogeis of whom Ka[…] was secretary.

(There follows a list in four columns of the cities, according to district.)

Tribute from the Islands (col. I, lines 61–101):

New tribute	Islanders	Assessments from the 430s
30 T	Parians	18 T
15 T	Naxians	6 T, 4,000 dr.
15 T	Andrians	6 T
15 T	Melians	–
9 T	Siphians	3 T
15 T	Eretrians	3 T
5 T	Therans	–
10 T	Ceians	4 T
5 T	Karystians	5 T
10 T	Chalkidians	3 T
6 T	Kythnians	3 T
10 T	Tenians	2 T
2 T	Styrians	1 T
[2 T]	Mykonians	1 T
[2 T]	Seriphians	1 T
[1 T]	Ietians	3,000 dr.
[1 T]	Dians	2,000 dr.
1 T	Athenitians	2,000 dr.
1 T	Syrians (Syros)	1,500 dr.
2,000 dr.	Grynchians	1,000 dr.
1,000 dr.	Rhenaians	300 dr.
2,000 dr.	Diakrians from Chalkis	800 dr.
1,000 dr.	Anaphaians	–
v	Keria	10 dr. 3 ob.

2,000 dr.	Pholegandros	–
300 dr.	Belbina	–
1,000 dr.	Kimolos	–
1,000 dr.	Sikinetians	–
100 dr.	Posideion in Euboea	–
1 T 2,000 dr.	Diakrians in Euboea	–
–	Hephaistians	–
4 T	Those on Lemnos	3 T
–	Myrinaians	1 T, 3,000 dr.
[1 T]	Imbrians	1 T
OF ISLAND TRIBUTE:	TOTAL 163 talents, 410 drachmas, (3 obols)	
181	GRAND TOTAL: 1,460 talents	

13.17 *Inscriptiones Graecae* I³ 34: Kleinias' Decree on Tribute Payment, 420s BC

Kleinias' decree was aimed at ensuring that the tribute was paid and in the correct amount. The date of this decree is also disputed, but the 420s BC is preferable to 447 BC. [*IG* I² 66; *ATL* 2.D7; Meiggs & Lewis 46.]

Gods. It was resolved by the Council and the people: (the tribe) Oineis held the prytany, [Sp]oudias was secretary, [...]on presided, Kleinias proposed the motion: the Council and the officials in the cities, and the commissioners (episkopoi) are to see that the tribute is collected each year and brought to Athens; they are to arrange seals for the cities, so that it is impossible for those bringing the tribute to do wrong; and after the city has written on a tablet whatever tribute it is sending, it is to seal it with its seal and send it off to Athens; those who bring it are to give up the tablet in the Council to be read when they pay the tribute. The prytaneis, after the Dionysia, are to call an assembly for the hellenotamiai to report to the Athenians which of the cities have paid their tribute in full and which defaulted, separately, however many there may be; and the Athenians are to choose four men and send them to the cities to give a receipt for the tribute which has been paid and to demand what was not paid from the defaulters, two of them to sail to the cities of the islands and to Ionia on a swift trireme, and two to the cities of the Hellespont and to Thrace; the prytaneis are to bring this matter before the Council and the people immediately after the Dionysia and consider it continuously until it is completed. If any Athenian or ally commits an offence with regard to the tribute, which the cities must send to Athens after writing it on a tablet for those bringing it, he is to be prosecuted before the prytaneis by anyone who wishes, Athenian or ally.

The prytaneis are to bring before the Council any indictment which has been brought or each will be liable at their examination to a fine of ten thousand drachmas for bribery; the Council is not to have the power to decide sentence on anyone it convicts, but is to immediately bring him before the heliaia; and, when someone is found guilty, the prytaneis should make proposals as to what punishment or fine they think right for him. And if anyone commits an offence regarding the bringing of the cow or the panoply, there shall be a similar indictment against him and punishment in the same way. The hellenotamiai are to record and display on a whitened noticeboard **45** both the assessment of the tribute and the cities as many as pay in full and record … (c. *10 lines are missing*) **57** … the Council entering office is also to deliberate concerning the men who bring the tribute; the Council is to report to the people for each city in turn all those of the men who bring money to Athens who have been recorded on the noticeboard in the Council as owing (money). And if any of the cities disputes the payment of the tribute, saying that it has paid … the government of the city; … the cities and **65** … not be permitted to prosecute … the prosecutor shall be liable for the fine of the defendant, if he is acquitted; the prosecution is to take place before the polemarch in the month Gamelion; if anyone disputes … summons, the Council after deliberating …, **70** the eisagogeis are to bring before the heliaia in turn those who owe tribute to the Athenians in accordance with the noticeboard for information; … of the current and last year's tribute …; the Council after framing a preliminary decree is to introduce … **75** on the next day to the people; … of the election to conduct business …

13.18 Aristophanes *Knights*, 303–27, 1030–34, 1067–72: Kleon and Athenian Tribute

Kleon held a military command at Pylos in 425 BC, as a strategos, but this is best viewed as an extraordinary command; he was also strategos in 424/3, 423/2 and 422/1; Kleon's influence was primarily due to his ability in the ekklesia. The *Knights* was performed at the Lenaia in 424, winning first prize. It was an attack on Kleon, who was now at the peak of his reputation because of the victory at Sphakteria. The son of Hippodamos, line 327, is Archeptolemos, who tried to end the war. In the second passage the sausage-seller is quoting oracles which supposedly concern the state; presumably Kleon used to call himself the watchdog of the people. In lines 303–27 the chorus of knights (hippeis) is addressing Kleon.

You loathsome blackguard,
You loudmouth, of whose audacity
305 The whole world is full, and the entire assembly, and taxes
And lawsuits and law courts! You muckraker,
310 You have stirred up our entire city,
And quite deafened our Athens with your shouting,
313 As from the rocks above you keep a lookout for tribute as if it were tuna fish …
Haven't you from the very beginning shown your shamelessness,
325 Which is the orator's only protection?
Trusting in this you milk all the foreigners from whom you can get money,
Being first and foremost; and the son of Hippodamos weeps as he looks on.

The Sausage-seller:
1030 'Watch well, Erechtheides, the dog Cerberus, the kidnapper,
Who wags his tail and keeps his eye on you, while you dine,
And gobbles up your meat, when your attention wanders;
And like a dog always creeps round to the kitchen unnoticed

At night-time to lick clean the plates — and the islands' …

1067 'Aigeides, watch the dog-fox, lest he trick you,
Who bites silently, the crafty thief, the wise and wily one.'
Do you know what this means?
Demos: Philostratos the dog-fox!
Sausage-seller: It doesn't mean that — but Kleon here who on each occasion
Asks for swift ships to levy money;
Apollo Loxias tells you not to give him them!

13.19 *Inscriptiones Graecae* I³ 40: Athenian Regulations for Chalkis, 424/3 BC

This is extremely important evidence for Athens' treatment of an ally which had revolted. Athens swears to guarantee certain rights for the Chalkidians as long as they 'obey' the Athenians. The Chalkidians promise not to revolt, and to pay their tribute. Another possible date for the inscription is 446/5 [*IG* I² 39; *ATL* 2.D17, 3 p. 297; Meiggs & Lewis 52.]

It was resolved by the Council and the people: (the tribe) Antiochis held the prytany, Drak[on]tides presided, Diognetos proposed the motion: that the Council and the jurors of the Athenians are to swear the oath as follows: 'I shall not expel the Chalkidians from Chalkis, nor shall I lay waste the city, nor shall I deprive any individual of his citizen rights, nor shall I punish anyone with exile, nor shall I arrest anyone, nor shall I kill anyone, nor take anyone's property without trial without the consent of the people of the Athenians, nor shall I put anything to the vote without due notice either against the state or even against a single individual, and if an embassy arrives I shall introduce it to the Council and the people within ten days, when I hold the prytany, as far as is possible. I shall guarantee these things to the Chalkidians while they obey the people of the Athenians.' An embassy is to arrive from Chalkis and administer the oath to the Athenians along with the commissioners for oaths and record the names of those who took it. The generals are to see that everyone takes the oath. The Chalkidians are to swear as follows: 'I shall not revolt from the people of the Athenians by any means or device either in word or deed, nor shall I obey anyone who does revolt, and if anyone revolts I shall denounce him to the Athenians, and I shall pay the tribute to the Athenians, which I persuade them (to accept), and I shall be as good and upright an ally as I can, and I shall help and defend the people of the Athenians, if anyone does wrong to the people of the Athenians, and I shall obey the people of the Athenians.' All the Chalkidians who are adults are to swear; and whoever does not swear is to be deprived of citizen rights and his property belong to the state and a tithe of his property be consecrated to Zeus Olympios. An embassy of Athenians arriving at Chalkis is to administer the oath along with the commissioners for oaths at Chalkis and record the names of those Chalkidians who took it.

Antikles proposed the motion: with good fortune for the city of the Athenians. The Athenians and Chalkidians are to take the oath, just as the people of the Athenians decreed for the Eretrians; and the generals are to see that it takes place as soon as possible. The people are to immediately choose five men to administer the oath when they arrive at Chalkis. Regarding the hostages, they are to reply to the Chalkidians that the Athenians have for now resolved to leave things as decreed; but, when it seems good, after deliberation they will make the exchange as seems good and suitable for the Athenians and Chalkidians. And the foreigners in Chalkis, who living there do not pay taxes to Athens, or who have been granted exemption from tax by the people of the Athenians, are otherwise to pay tax to Chalkis, just like the other Chalkidians. The secretary of the Council is to inscribe this decree and oath at Athens on a stone stele and set it up on the acropolis at the expense of the Chalkidians, and at Chalkis the Council of the Chalkidians is to inscribe it and set it up in the temple of Zeus Olympios; this has been decreed for the Chalkidians. The sacrifices prescribed by the oracles on behalf of Euboea are to be made by Hierokles and three others, whom the Council is to choose from its own members, as soon as possible; the generals are to join in seeing that this takes place as quickly as possible and supply the money for this.

Archestratos proposed the amendment: that everything else should be as Antikles proposed, but that the Chalkidians are to have control of punishments against their own people at Chalkis just like the Athenians at Athens, except for cases where the penalty is exile, death or loss of civic rights; and concerning these there is to be a right of appeal to Athens to the heliaia of the thesmothetai in accordance with the decree of the people; and concerning the defence of Euboea the generals are to see to this as best they can, so that everything be as excellent as possible for the Athenians. The oath.

13.20 Thucydides 5.16.1: The End of the Archidamian War, 421 BC

Brasidas was successful in Thrace in detaching several cities from the Athenian alliance, notably Amphipolis in 424/3 BC. Kleon as strategos in 422/1 led his troops against Amphipolis, and thus forced Brasidas to battle, in which the two leaders lost their lives. This enabled Pleistoanax and Nikias to bring about peace. For the terms of the Peace of Nikias and the fifty-year alliance into which the Athenians and Spartans subsequently entered, see Thuc. 5.14–24.

5.16.1 Now the Athenians had been defeated again, at Amphipolis, and both Kleon and Brasidas were dead. They were the two men, one on each side, who had been most opposed to the peace, Brasidas because of the success and honour he had gained from the war, and Kleon because he thought that in peacetime his villainy would be more obvious and his attacks on others less credible. Now, then, was naturally the time when the men who aimed at the leadership in each city, Pleistoanax, son of Pausanias, king of Sparta, and Nikias, son of Nikeratos, who had had more success in his military commands than anyone else, made even greater efforts to secure peace.

13.21 *Inscriptiones Graecae* I³ 287: Athenian Tribute Quota-List of 418/7 BC

This document is important for the light it throws on Athenian tribute assessment policy. It shows that the figures of 425 BC have been scaled down, as many had proved too high to collect. The reduction seems to be from a total of 1,460+ talents to rather less than 1,000 talents. It is the quota for the goddess Athena which is listed here; the actual tribute from each people recorded was sixty times the amount listed here. [*ATL* 1 & 2, List 33; Meiggs & Lewis 75.]

1 In the year of the Council for which ... of Aphidna was first secretary, the archon at Athens was Antiphon of Skambonidai in the thirty-seventh board, the hellenotamiai were for whom Ant[...] [... of Perg]ase, Mnesitheos of Araphen, ... [... of Eupy]ridai, Aeschines of Perithoidai, ... of Thymaitadai, Ergokles of Besa. These cities paid the quota to the goddess, a mina from each talent.

column I		column II	
Of the Islands		Of the Hellespont	
...	Anaph[aians]	100 dr.	Si[gei]ans
...	Ther[ans]	2,000 dr.	Ky[zi]kenes
...	Seriph[ians]	66 dr. 4 ob.	Arta]kenians
...	Ietia[ns]	16 dr. 4 ob.]	Kia[n]ians
...	Tenia[ns]	...	Bys[b]ikenes
...	Siphnia[ns]	300 dr. ...	Pro[k]onnesians
...	Andria[ns]	... 5 dr. 4 ob.	Par[ia]nians
8 dr. 2 ob.	Sikine[tians]	600 ...	Chalk[ed]on[ian]
...	Kythni[ans]	...	Sely[mbrians]
		...	Seri[oteichitians]
		200 ...	Didy[moteichitians]
		200 ...	Daunio[teichitians]
		66 dr. 4 ob.	Sombia
		... 18 dr. 2 ob.	Perinth[ians]
400 dr.	[Kythera]	... 1 dr. 4 ob.	Bryll[eianians]
		1,200 dr.	Lampsak[enes]
		...	[Aby]denes
		...	[]e[...]
		166 dr.3 ob.	Che[rronesites] of [Agora]
		...	K[allipolitans]

THE SICILIAN EXPEDITION AND ITS AFTERMATH

13.22 *Inscriptiones Graecae* I^3 11: Alliance of Athens and Egesta, 418/7 BC

Thucydides does not mention the alliance of Athens and Egesta, though on the 418/7 BC dating it must have been recent when the Egestaeans came to Athens from Sicily to seek Athenian help in 416/5 (Thuc. 6.6.1: the Athenians aimed at conquering Sicily, and wanted to make it look as if they were sending help to their kinsmen and newly acquired allies). A date of 418/7 BC would fit the historical context of the Sicilian Expedition, which Egesta played an important role in starting. Another possible date for the inscription is 458/7 or 454/3. [Meiggs & Lewis 37.]

The alliance and oath of the Athenians and Egestaeans. It was resolved by the Council and the people; ... is held the prytany, ... was secretary ... o ... presided, ... on was archon, Archias proposed the motion: concerning the Egestaeans ... to take the oath ... as many victims ... to swear the oath. The generals are to see that all swear ... with the oath-commissioners so that ... Egestaean. ... the secretary of the Council is to inscribe this decree and the oath on a stone stele on the acropolis; and the poletai are to let out the contract; and the kolakretai are to provide the money. The Egestaean embassy is to be invited to hospitality in the prytaneion at the customary time. Euphemos proposed the amendment: that the rest be as the Council resolved; and in future when envoys of the

Egestaeans arrive, the herald is to introduce … the envoys … These are the envoys of the Egestaeans who swore the oath: **20** […]ikinos, Ap[…].

13.23 Thucydides 6.1.1, 15.2–4: The Sicilian Expedition of 415–413 BC

The most ardent supporter of the Sicilian expedition was Alkibiades. His removal from command, because of his implication in the mutilation of the hermai and the profanation of the Eleusinian Mysteries in 415 BC (Thuc. 6.28–29, 53, 60–61), was one of several factors which led to its failure. Nikias opposed the expedition, but his advice that the expedition needed to be greater than the Athenians thought led to the Athenians voting a large force (see esp. 6.24.1).

6.1.1 In the same winter (416/5) the Athenians again started wanting to sail against Sicily, with a greater force than that which Laches and Eurymedon had had, and conquer it, if they could. The majority of them were ignorant of the size of the island and the large numbers of its inhabitants, both Greek and barbarian, and of the fact that they were taking on a war not much less in scope than that against the Peloponnesians … **6.15.2** The most enthusiastic advocate of the expedition was Alkibiades, son of Kleinias, who wanted to oppose Nikias, since he was Nikias' constant opponent in political life and because Nikias had attacked him in his speech. Additionally, he desired to be in command and hoped that Sicily and Carthage would be captured through his agency, which would, if he were successful, simultaneously bring him personally wealth and fame. **3** For he was held in high esteem by his fellow citizens, and was thus more enthusiastic about his horse-breeding and other expenses that his estate warranted, which was mainly responsible for the later destruction of the Athenians' city. **4** For the majority were afraid of the extent of the lawlessness of his lifestyle and his attitude towards every single thing in which he was involved, and turned against him, thinking that he was aiming at tyranny.

13.24 Thucydides 6.27.1–28.2: The Mutilation of the Hermai in 415 BC

The property of those convicted of the mutilation and profanation of the Mysteries was confiscated and sold (docs 1.32, 5.18).

6.27.1 Meanwhile, all the stone hermai in the city of Athens (these are typically Athenian square pillars, many of which stand both at the doorways of private houses and in temples) in a single night had their faces mutilated. **2** No one knew who had done it, but large public rewards were offered to informers to find out who the offenders were and, furthermore, a decree guaranteed immunity to anyone, whether citizen, foreigner or slave, who knew of any other act of impiety which had taken place and wanted to give information about it. **3** They took the matter extremely seriously; for it seemed to be an omen for the expedition and at the same time part of a revolutionary conspiracy to overthrow the democracy. **6.28.1** Information was accordingly presented by some metics and slaves, not about the hermai at all, but about the mutilation of some other statues which had been carried out by young men as a drunken jest and also about the sacrilegious celebration of the Mysteries in private houses. **2** One of the people they accused was Alkibiades. And those who particularly disliked him, as an obstacle in the way of their acquiring firm control of the people, took this up, thinking as well that if they could drive him out they would step into first place, and so they exaggerated the affair and cried up the (profanation of the)

Mysteries and the mutilation of the hermai as part of a plan to overthrow the democracy, pointing out as proof of the fact that Alkibiades had had a hand in it the rest of the lawless and undemocratic behaviour apparent in his lifestyle.

13.25 Thucydides 7.19.1–2, 27.3–4: The Fortification of Dekeleia in 413 BC

Recalled from Sicily to face trial, Alkibiades went instead to Sparta (Thuc. 6.88.9–92) and argued that the Spartans should send aid to the Sicilians and fortify Dekeleia, about 22 kilometres north of Athens (6.91); this was undertaken in 413 (7.19–20.1; cf. Plut. *Alk.* 23.2).

7.19.1 At the very beginning of the following spring, as early as possible, the Spartans and their allies invaded Attica; the Spartan king Agis, son of Archidamos, was in command. They first ravaged that part of the country which lay around the plain, and then they fortified Dekeleia, assigning the work city by city. **2** Dekeleia is approximately 120 stades from the Athenians' city, and is about the same, or not much further, from Boeotia. The fort was built to do damage to the plain and the best parts of the country and was visible from the Athenians' city … (*1,300 Thracian peltasts arrive in Athens for the Sicilian Expedition; as they are each paid a drachma a day, they are thought too expensive to use against Dekeleia*).

7.27.3 From the time when Dekeleia had been initially fortified in this summer by the whole army, then to be occupied by garrisons from the different cities in succession attacking the country, it had done a great deal of harm to the Athenians, and amongst the worst had been the destruction to property and the loss of manpower. **4** For previously the invasions had been short and for the rest of the time had not prevented the enjoyment of the land; but now the Spartans were stationed there continuously; sometimes an even greater force invaded, and sometimes out of necessity the existing garrison overran the country and plundered it, and with Agis, king of the Spartans, actually present, who considered the war a very high priority, the Athenians were done a great deal of harm.

13.26 Thucydides 7.87.1–6: Death in the Stone Quarries

The 7,000 Athenians and their allies were detained in the stone quarries at Syracuse, where they suffered miserably as prisoners of war and many died. Nikias, who relied too much on divination, had prevented the force from retreating in time (doc. 3.24), and he and Demosthenes were put to death. The Spartans captured on Sphakteria were given four pints of barley-meal and a pint of wine by the Athenians (Thuc. 5.16.1), more than double what the Syracusans gave their prisoners.

7.87.1 At first the Syracusans treated those in the stone quarries harshly. As there were many of them in a deep, narrow hole with no roof, they suffered at first from the sun and stifling heat, while the nights which followed were in contrast autumnal and cold, with the change in temperature causing illness. **2** Lack of space meant that they had to do everything in the same area, and, besides, the corpses of those who had died of their wounds or the change in temperature or other causes were heaped up on top of each other, resulting in an unbearable stench. They also suffered at the same time from hunger and thirst (for eight months the ration for each man was half a pint of water and a pint of grain) and they escaped none of the other evils men thrown into such a place would experience. **3** For some seventy days they lived all together in this way; then the

Syracusans sold them all except for the Athenians and any Siceliots and Italiots that had joined the expedition. **4** The total number of prisoners, though it is difficult to speak with precision, was nevertheless not less than seven thousand. **5** This was the greatest action that had taken place during the war and, it appears to me, the greatest in all Greek record — the most glorious for the victors and the most catastrophic for the vanquished. **6** For those who were defeated were defeated utterly in every way and suffered on a vast scale in every respect — as the saying goes it was total ruin, with army, fleet and everything entirely destroyed and few of the many returning home. This is what took place in Sicily.

13.27 Thucydides 8.1.1–2.2: The Failure of the Sicilian Expedition in 413 BC

Thucydides, in Books 6 and 7, gives a detailed account of the Sicilian expedition and its failure. Athens refused to give in, despite the enormous losses in Sicily, and seems to have recovered quickly from the disaster. Given that Athens was not defeated for another eight years (Thuc. 2.65.12), and when in 410 the Athenians defeated the Spartans at Cyzicus Sparta wanted peace (Diod. 13.52), it is possible that Thucydides has exaggerated the extent of the losses suffered. The older men (8.1.3) were probouloi, 'preliminary advisers'.

8.1.1 When the news reached Athens, for a long time they did not believe that the expedition could have been so utterly destroyed, even when this was clearly reported to them by those soldiers who had been there and escaped; and when they did recognise the facts, they were angry with the speakers who had been united in favour of the expedition, as if they had not voted for it themselves, as well as furious with the soothsayers and seers and all the others who had originally by means of divination led them to believe that they would take Sicily. **2** They had nothing but grief on every side and after what had happened they were not only frightened but, quite naturally, extremely shocked ... **3** Nevertheless, they resolved, as far as circumstances allowed, that they would not give in, but equip a fleet, getting the timber from wherever they could, and raise money, and make sure that their allies, especially Euboea, stayed loyal, and reduce the expenses of government in the city and appoint a board of older men, who would be able to give them preliminary advice on the present situation, whenever there was occasion. **4** Because of their immediate fear, as is always the way with a democracy, they were ready to behave in an orderly manner. They carried out what they had resolved upon and so ended the summer.

8.2.1 But in the following winter, because of the great disaster that the Athenians had experienced in Sicily, all the Greeks suddenly turned against them, those that were not allies of either side thinking that they should not stay out of the war any longer, even if they were not invited to join in, but should attack the Athenians of their own accord, for they believed that, if things had gone well in Sicily, each of them would have been attacked by the Athenians, and they also thought that the rest of the war would be brief and it would be good to participate in it. The Spartans' allies, for their part, were even more eager than before to be quickly relieved from the sufferings they had long endured. **2** And in particular the subjects of the Athenians were ready, even if not able, to revolt, because they were not judging dispassionately, and would not even countenance the possibility that the Athenians would be able to survive the coming summer.

13.28 [Aristotle] *Athenaion Politeia* 29.5–30.2, 31.1, 32.3: The Four Hundred in 411 BC

The Athenians were unwilling to abolish the democracy in 411 BC, but gave way when confronted by the argument that this was the only way of obtaining financial aid from the Persians (Thuc. 8.53–54, cf. 47–48, noting that the suggestion originally came from Alkibiades). The oligarchy of the Four Hundred failed: the majority of the fleet at Samos was opposed to oligarchy; one of the oligarchs, Theramenes, later one of the Thirty, expressed dissatisfaction with it, and there was rivalry amongst the Four Hundred, and Phrynichos, one of the main movers of the oligarchy, was assassinated (see doc. 13.30; Thuc. 8.92.2). The hoplites were unhappy with the thought of surrender to Sparta. The revolt of Euboea (cf. doc. 13.29) was also important and the Five Thousand took over, a constitution of which Thucydides approved (8.97.2). Full democracy was soon restored in 410 BC. See also Thuc. 8.48–54, 63–77, esp. 65.3, 81–82, 86, 89–98; *Ath. Pol.* 29.1–34.1; Plut. *Alk.* 25–27. One of the main features of the politeia under the Four Hundred was the suspension of payment for political office, indicating its importance to the notion of participatory democracy.

29.5 Following this they organised the constitution in the following way: revenue was not to be spent on anything other than the war; no public officials were to receive salaries for the duration of the war, with the exception of the nine archons and the prytaneis in office, and these should each receive three obols a day; all the rest of the administration for the duration of the war should be entrusted to those Athenians who were most capable of serving the state both physically and financially, who should comprise not less than 5,000; these should have the power to ratify treaties with whomever they wished; and ten men over forty years of age should be elected from each tribe to enrol the 5,000 after swearing an oath over unblemished sacrificial victims.

30.1 The committee drew up these proposals, and when they had been ratified the 5,000 elected from amongst their number 100 men to draw up the constitution. The chosen men drafted and publicised the following guidelines: **2** those over thirty years of age were to constitute the council and serve for a year without pay; they were to include the generals, the nine archons, the hieromnemon, the taxiarchs, the hipparchs, the phylarchs, the garrison commanders, the ten treasurers of the funds sacred to the goddess and the other gods, the hellenotamiai, the twenty who managed all the other secular funds, and the overseers of sacrifices and superintendents, ten of each. All of these were to be elected from a preliminary list of candidates chosen from amongst the council members at the time. All other officials were to be chosen by lot and not from the council. The hellenotamiai who managed financial matters were not to be council members… **31.1** The committee drew up this constitution for the future and the following for the present crisis: there would be a council of 400 in accordance with tradition, forty from each tribe, appointed from a pre-selected number of the age of thirty or more elected by their fellow tribesmen… **32.3** Once this constitution was established the 5,000 were chosen, but only nominally, while the 400, together with the ten generals with full powers, entered the council chamber and started ruling the city.

13.29 Meiggs and Lewis 82: Eretria Revolts from Athens in 411 BC

In the summer of 411 BC thirty-six Athenian ships were defeated off Eretria by the Spartan admiral Agesandridas, and Eretria immediately revolted followed by the rest of Euboea except for Oreus

(Thuc. 8.95); this caused panic at Athens as Euboea was of more use to the Athenians than Attica itself (8.96.2). The Spartan fleet included some ships from Taras (Tarentum), of which Hegelochos may have been in command. Other allies were more loyal: see docs 13.31, 13.34. [*IG* XII.9, 187A.]

Gods. It was resolved by the Council: Hegelochos of Taras is to be proxenos and benefactor, both he and his sons, and both he and his sons shall be granted public maintenance, whenever they stay here, and immunity from public burdens (ateleia), and the privilege of front seats (proedria) at the games, since he joined in liberating the city from the Athenians.

13.30 *Inscriptiones Graecae* I^3 102: Phrynichos' Assassins Honoured, 409 BC

Phrynichos was assassinated on his return from Sparta in the autumn of 411 BC; this was followed by other events leading to the overthrow of the Four Hundred. This decree of 409 BC grants Thrasyboulos, of Kalydon (that is, not the Thrasyboulos who led the Athenian exiles in 403 BC), Athenian citizenship for his role in the restoration of democracy (see Thuc. 8.73.4, 75.2, 76.2, 81.1); it also gives honours to other conspirators involved in the assassination of Phrynichos. [Meiggs & Lewis 85; Osborne 1981–82 D2.]

In the archonship of [Glauki]ppos. [Lobon of] Kedoi was secretary. It was resolved by the Council and the people: (the tribe) Hippothontis held the prytany, Lobon was secretary, Philistides presided, Glaukippos was archon, Erasinides proposed the motion: that Thrasyboulos, who is a brave man with regard to the people of the Athenians and eager to do whatever good he can, is to be commended; and in return for the good he has done both the city and the people of the Athenians he is to be crowned with a golden crown, and the crown be made at a cost of a thousand drachmas; and the hellenotamiai are to give the money. And the herald Dionysios is to proclaim at the festival the reasons why the people have crowned him. Diokles proposed the amendment: that the rest be as the Council resolved; and that Thrasyboulos should be an Athenian, and he should be enrolled in whichever tribe and phratry he wishes; and that the rest which has been decreed by the people should be valid for Thrasyboulos; and he should be able to acquire from the Athenians anything else as well which seems right on account of his good deeds towards the people of the Athenians. And the secretary is to record what has been decreed; and five men are to be elected immediately from the Council, who are to determine what portion shall belong to Thrasyboulos.

13.31 *Inscriptiones Graecae* I^3 101: Athens Honours Neapolis (Thrace) in 409–407 BC

The first decree dates to 409 BC; the date of the second decree (lines 48–64) is uncertain, but Thasos revolted after the Sicilian expedition and was regained by Athens in 407 BC. The decrees praise Neapolis (modern Kavalla) for not revolting from Athens despite being besieged by Thasos and the Peloponnesians, noting its continued loyalty, and promise protection by Athenian generals and officials. Even late in the war, Athens could rely on the loyalty of at least some of its allies. [*IG* I^2 108; Meiggs & Lewis 89.]

Gods. The Neapolitans near Thasos. It was resolved by the Council and the people; (the tribe) Leontis held the prytany, Sibyrtiades was secretary, Chairimenes presided, [Glau] kippos was archon, [...]theos proposed the motion: the Neap[olitans] near Thasos are to be commended, firstly because they are colonists of the Thasians and though besieged by them and the Peloponnesians they did not choose to revolt from the Athenians, and also because they have been good men towards both the army and the people of the Athenians and the allies ...

and lent four talents, 2,000 drachmas ... as the generals of the Athenians requested so that they might have it for the war; instalments shall be made to them from the monies which come from the harbour of Neapolis. The generals on Thasos each year are to record what has been received from them until it has been completely repaid; and they are to do this as long as they are at war with the Thasians. That which the Neapolitans from Thrace are now giving, they gave both willingly and voluntarily to the hellenotamiai — five talents, 4,800 drachmas — and they are eager to do whatever good they can, having themselves promised this in both word and deed to the city of the Athenians. In return for this benefaction they shall now and in the future have favours from the Athenians because they are good men, and they are to have access to the Council and people first after the sacrifices, because they are benefactors of the Athenians. The envoys are to hand over to the secretary of the Council all the records of what the Neapolitans gave, what is now being given separately and the rest separately, and the secretary of the Council is to inscribe this decree on a stone stele and set it up on the acropolis at the expense of the Neapolitans; and in Neapolis they are to inscribe it and set it up on a stone stele in the temple of the Parthenos. The embassy is also to be invited to hospitality at the prytaneion tomorrow. To Oinobios of Dekeleia, general, three talents, six hundred and thirty-four drachmas, four obols.

48 Axiochos proposed the motion: the Neapolitans from Thrace are to be commended because they are good men both to the army and the city of the Athenians, and because they have made war against Thasos and besieged it with the Athenians, and because when they fought at sea with the Athenians they were victorious, and they joined in the fighting by land the whole time, and because they are benefactors of the Athenians in other respects. And in return for these good deeds they shall have favours from the Athenians just as was voted by the people. And so that they are not wronged in any way either by a private individual or by the government of a city, both the generals who hold office at any given time are all to see to whatever they might require, and also the officials of the Athenians who provide for their city at any given time shall protect the Neapolitans and be eager to do whatever they bid them. And now they shall acquire from the people of the Athenians whatever seems good ... Concerning the first fruits for the Parthenos which were before given to the goddess the matter shall be considered in the assembly for them. In the earlier decree the secretary of the Council shall make a correction and on it write instead of 'the colony of the Thasians' that 'they fought through to the end of the war with the Athenians'. And ... and P[...] and [...]ophantos are to be commended in as much as they now say and do good on behalf of the people of the Athenians and because they are eager to do whatever good they can to the army and the city for the future just as in the past. And they are to be invited to hospitality tomorrow ... proposed the amendment: the rest to be as the Council resolved; and the first fruits which the people of the Neapolitans vows is to be set apart for the Parthenos just as before

13.32 Diodorus *Library of History* 13.57.1–58.2: The Carthaginians Sack Selinous, 409 BC

Selinous in Sicily had attacked Egesta in 416 BC; Athens in fact had used this as a pretext for attacking Syracuse in the following year. Carthage agreed to help Egesta when Selinous attacked Egesta again in 410, and Hannibal attacked Selinous in 409. Falling after a nine-day siege, Selinous was brutally sacked. The horrific nature of the warfare between the Greeks, Sicels and Carthaginians in Sicily is made all too clear from this account of the city's destruction.

13.57.1 While Selinous was being captured, lamentation and tears could be observed among the Greeks, while amongst the barbarians there were war-cries and confused shouting. As the former saw with their eyes the extent of the disaster surrounding them they were terrified, while the latter, delighted at their success, urged the slaughter onwards. **2** The Selinountians fled in a body to the agora and there all died fighting; the barbarians, scattering throughout the whole city, plundered everything of value in the houses, while some of the inhabitants they found they burned along with their homes, and of the others who forced their way into the streets they took no notice of gender or age but killed them all without compassion, infants, women and the elderly. **3** They even mutilated the dead according to their country's practices, and some carried around bunches of hands on their bodies, while others had heads they had spitted on their javelins and spears. The women that had taken refuge with their children in temples they seized, urging that they not be killed, and only to these did they promise to spare their lives. **4** They did this not out of compassion for these unfortunates, but as a precaution in case the women, in despair for their lives, should burn down the temples and they would not be able to plunder the great wealth of dedications in them. **5** The barbarians differed so greatly from other men in their cruelty, that, while everyone else spares those who have taken refuge in shrines so as not to commit sacrilege against the deity, the Carthaginians, in contrast, spared the enemy so as to plunder the temples of the gods. **6** By nightfall the city had been sacked and some of the dwellings burned and others razed to the ground, while the whole place was full of blood and corpses. Sixteen thousand were found to have been killed, not including the five thousand who had been taken captive.

13.58.1 The Greeks who were serving with the Carthaginians as allies, as they looked on the reversal in their lives, felt pity for the fate of the unfortunates. The women, deprived of their usual luxurious lifestyle, spent their nights in the power of their enemies' lust, suffering frightful indignities, while some were forced to see their marriageable daughters enduring treatment inappropriate for their age. **2** For the barbarians' savagery spared neither freeborn boys nor maidens, but exposed the poor creatures to terrible experiences. In consequence, as the women reflected on the slavery they were to face in Libya, they saw themselves and their children in a condition where they would be without rights, subject to the insolent treatment of masters they would be forced to obey, and when they observed that these possessed unintelligible speech and a brutish character they mourned for their living children as if they were dead.

13.33 *Inscriptiones Graecae* I³ 118: An Athenian Treaty with Selymbria in 407 BC

Selymbria is on the north shore of the Propontis and appears in the tribute quota-lists from 451–430 BC, generally as a fairly high payer (five to nine talents), but abnormally in 435 and 433 it shows a mere 900 drachmas. which may indicate that it was at risk. By 410 it was in revolt from Athens and refused to admit Alkibiades, paying him money instead. In ?408 he recaptured the town aided by treachery: note the conciliatory nature of the treaty. It is in two parts, the settlement at its capitulation (lines 1–31) and its ratification in Athens in 407. It includes the restoration of hostages (8–10) and an undertaking not to take any in future; a guarantee of autonomy (10–12); a possible cancellation of debts to Athens (12–14); lines 14–18 seem to imply a restitution of civil rights for exiles and the disenfranchised; the abandonment of Athenian and allied claims to property except houses and land (18–22); and all other disputes are to be settled by agreement (22–26). The second part is proposed by Alkibiades ratifying the settlement and ordering its publication. A proxenos was a citizen of another state, appointed by Athens to look after visiting Athenians (doc. 1.54). [*IG* I^2 116; Meiggs & Lewis 87.]

8 ... hostages which the Athenians hold are to be given back, and for the future not to be taken, **10** and the Selymbrians shall establish their constitution autonomously in whatever manner they know ... is owed by the state of the Selymbrians or by one of the private individuals of the Selymbrians ... **14** if anyone's property has been confiscated or if anyone owed (money) to the government or if anyone was deprived of citizen rights ... exiles of the Selymbrians ... (the same) enemies and friends ... **18** and as to what was lost in the war, whether the property of the Athenians or of the allies or if there was anything owed or a deposit of anyone's which the magistrates exacted, **21** there shall be no recovery except for land and house. All other causes of dispute previously between private individual and private individual or of a private individual against the state or of the state against a private individual, **24** or if any other should arise, are to be settled between themselves; and as to whatever is in dispute, there are to be lawsuits in accordance with the agreements (symbolai). The compact is to be recorded on a stele and placed in the temple of ... **28** The generals of the Athenians swore and the trierarchs and the hoplites and any other of the Athenians who was present and all the Selymbrians.

31 Alkib[iades] proposed the motion: what the Selymbrians agreed with the Athenians is to be carried out, and the generals with the secretary of the Council are to record the compact and this decree on a stone stele, at their expense, ... and set it up on the acropolis. **36** And [Apo]llodoros son of Empedos is to be commended and to be removed from the condition of being a hostage and the secretary of the Council is to erase tomorrow the names of the Selymbrian hostages and their guarantors wherever they are recorded in the presence of the prytaneis; ... **42** and [...]omachos the Selymbrian is to be recorded on the same stele as proxenos of the Athenians; and the status of proxenos is to be given also to Apollodoros just as to his father. **45** The envoys and Apollodoros are to be invited to the prytaneion for hospitality tomorrow.

13.34 *Inscriptiones Graecae* I^3 127: Athens Honours Samos for Its Loyalty, 405/4 BC

This grant of 405/4 BC was reaffirmed in 403/2, the date of this inscription. The Samian demos overthrew the oligarchy which came to power there in or before 412, and Athens conferred autonomy on the democracy. In this decree the Athenians honour their loyalty, for after the battle of Aigospotamoi, in which Lysander defeated the Athenians, the Greek states deserted Athens except for Samos, where the people slaughtered the aristocrats and seized the city, though later many of the people left under an agreement with Lysander, who besieged the city in 404 (Xen. *Hell.* 2.2.6, 3.6) and imposed a decarchy (a government of ten men) here as elsewhere. See Thuc. 8.21. [*IG* II^2 1; Meiggs & Lewis 94; Osborne 1981–82 D4–5.]

Kephisophon of Paiania was secretary. All the Samians who were on the side of the people of the Athenians … It was resolved by the Council and the people; (the tribe) Kekropis held the prytany, Polymnis of Euonymon was secretary, Alexias was archon, Nikophon of Athmonon presided; proposal of Kleisophos and his fellow prytaneis: the Samian envoys, both those who came here formerly and those here now, and the Council and the generals and the other Samians shall be commended because they are good men and eager to do whatever good they can, and because in their actions they seem to have acted rightly for the Athenians and Samians; and in return for the benefits they have given the Athenians, because of their high esteem for them and the good things they are proposing for them, it has been resolved by the Council and the people that the Samians are to be Athenians, governing themselves however they wish; and so that these things may be as advantageous as possible for both, as these men themselves say, when peace comes, then concerning the other matters there shall be common deliberation. They shall use their own laws and be autonomous, and act in other respects in accordance with the oaths and the treaties which have been agreed by the Athenians and Samians. Concerning the disputes which might take place against each other they are to grant and submit to lawsuits according to the existing agreements. If any emergency arises on account of the war and earlier about the constitution, just as the envoys say themselves, they are to deliberate and act according to present circumstances as seems to be best. Concerning the peace, if it should come, it is to be on the same terms for those who now inhabit Samos just as for the Athenians. If it is necessary to wage war, they are to make preparations as best they can acting with the generals. If the Athenians send an embassy anywhere, the Samians present are also to send with it anyone they wish, and shall offer whatever good advice they can. They shall be given the use of all the triremes which are now at Samos when they have had them refitted as they think fit; and the names of the trierarchs whose ships these are shall be recorded by the envoys for the secretary of the Council and the generals, and if there is any … (debt) recorded in the public treasury from when they took over the triremes, the dockyard superintendents are to wipe all of it out totally, but they are to get in the equipment as quickly as possible for the public treasury and compel those who possess any of it to hand it over intact.

An amendment proposed by Kleisophos and his fellow prytaneis: the rest to be as the Council proposed, but a privilege is to be granted to those Samians who have come, as they themselves request, and they are to be assigned immediately in ten parts to the demes and the tribes. The generals are to provide travelling expenses for the envoys as quickly as possible, and Eumachos and all the other Samians who have come with Eumachos are to be commended since they are good men with regard to the Athenians; and Eumachos shall be invited to dinner at the prytaneion for tomorrow. The secretary of the Council, with the generals, is to inscribe what has been decreed on a stone stele and set it up on the acropolis, and the hellenotamiai are to provide the money; and (the Samians) are to inscribe it at Samos in the same way at their own expense.

THE FALL OF ATHENS

Alkibiades was recalled to Athens and elected strategos for 407/6 BC (cf. doc. 3.35). But the defeat of the Athenian fleet at Notion led to his deposition as strategos in 406 and his self-imposed exile in the Chersonese. The Athenians won the battle at Arginousai in 406 (cf. doc. 1.20) but in the following year Lysander was victorious at Aigospotamoi.

13.35 Xenophon *Hellenika* 2.2.10–11, 2.2.16–23: The End of the Line for Athens

Lysander in 405 BC sailed to the Hellespont to prevent grain ships sailing down the Hellespont to Athens (cf. doc. 1.71). The Athenians sailed to Aigospotamoi opposite Lampsakos; several days later Lysander launched a surprise attack and captured most of the ships and their crews (Xen. *Hell*. 2.1.21–32; Diod. 13.105.1–106.5). This, in 405, was the last battle of the Peloponnesian War and the Athenians now feared that they would suffer what they had inflicted on their own enemies (doc. 5.7). Theramenes participated for a second time in an oligarchic revolution (see doc. 13.28).

2.2.10 The Athenians, under siege by land and sea, were at a loss what to do, since they had neither ships nor allies nor food; they thought that there was no escape from suffering what they had done to others, not out of revenge but wrongly and arrogantly to men from small cities, for no other reason than that they were allies of the Spartans. **11** Because of this they held out, restoring citizen rights to those deprived of them, and although many were dying of starvation in the city they did not start discussions about peace terms. (**2.2.11–15**: *The Athenians send envoys to the Spartans declaring their willingness to become their allies while retaining their walls, but this proposal is rejected by the ephors, and they are reduced to despair.*) **2.2.16** With affairs in Athens in this state, Theramenes said in the assembly that, if they were willing to send him to Lysander, he would return with the information as to whether the Spartans were holding out over the walls because they wanted to enslave them or to obtain a guarantee of good faith. He was sent and spent three months or more with Lysander, waiting for the time when the Athenians would be ready to agree to anything that was said because of their lack of food. **17** And, when he returned in the fourth month, he reported in the assembly that Lysander had kept him for that period, and then told him to go to Sparta as he did not have the authority to answer a question of that sort, only the ephors. After this Theramenes was chosen as one of ten ambassadors to Sparta with full powers.

18 Meanwhile Lysander sent Aristoteles, an Athenian exile, with others who were Spartans, to report to the ephors that he had told Theramenes that they had full authority to decide on matters of war and peace. **19** When Theramenes and the other ambassadors were at Sellasia and were asked with what proposals they had come, they replied that they had full powers to make peace, and so the ephors ordered them to be summoned. And when the envoys arrived, they called an assembly, in which the Corinthians and the Thebans in particular, and many others of the Greeks as well, spoke against making peace with the Athenians, and in favour of destroying the Athenians. **20** But the Spartans refused to enslave a Greek city which had done great service at the time of Greece's greatest danger, and offered peace on condition that they pull down the Long Walls and those of the Piraeus, hand over all except twelve ships, take back their exiles, have the same enemies and friends as the Spartans, and follow them by land and sea wherever they should lead. **21** So Theramenes and his fellow ambassadors brought these terms back to Athens. As they entered the city a great crowd gathered around them, afraid that they had returned unsuccessful; for it was not possible to delay any longer because of the number who were dying of starvation.

22 On the following day the ambassadors announced the terms on which the Spartans would make peace; Theramenes was their spokesman, and said that it was necessary to obey the Spartans and destroy the walls. Though a few people opposed him, a far greater number agreed with him, and it was resolved that they should accept the peace terms. **23** After this Lysander sailed into the Piraeus and the exiles returned and with great enthusiasm they began to tear down the walls to the music of flute-girls, thinking that that day was for Greece the beginning of freedom.

13.36 Xenophon *Hellenika* 2.1.31–32: A Response to Athenian Brutality, 405 BC

In 405 BC after Aigospotamoi, the Spartans and their allies were in the position of victors and able to take vengeance. The 3,000 Athenian prisoners were executed (docs 13.36, 13.38).

2.1.31 Lysander gathered the allies together and instructed them to decide what to do with the prisoners. At this many accusations were made against the Athenians, both for crimes already committed and for what they had voted to do should they win the naval battle — to cut off the right hand of everyone taken alive — as well as the fact that they had captured two triremes, one Corinthian, the other Andrian, and thrown the whole of both crews overboard. Philokles, one of the Athenian generals, was responsible for their deaths. **32** Many more episodes were recounted and it was resolved that they should execute all the prisoners who were Athenian, except Adeimantos, who was the only person in the assembly who had opposed the decree to cut off hands: he was accused by some, however, of betraying the fleet. Lysander first asked Philokles, who had thrown the Andrians and Corinthians overboard, as to what his punishment should be for initiating such crimes against Greeks, and then had his throat cut.

LYSANDER 'WHO CROWNED UNSACKED SPARTA'

Lysander, though belonging to the line of the kings at Sparta, the Herakleidai, came from an obscure family; he was the lover (erastes) of Agesilaos II, later king. Appointed an admiral of the Spartan fleet in either 408 or 407 BC, he defeated the Athenians at Notion in 406 and again at Aigospotamoi in 405, which led to Athens' complete defeat. He established the dekarchies, boards of ten men, to rule Athens' possessions, now under Spartan control. He was accorded divine honours on Samos and died in battle against the Boeotians in 395 BC.

13.37 Diodorus *Library of History* 14.10.1–2: Lysander Imposes Spartan Control

The Athenian empire was defeated and its possessions came under Spartan authority; Lysander imposed oligarchies on Athens' allies and put Spartan governors (harmosts) in place.

14.10.1 In Greece, now that the Spartans had brought the Peloponnesian War to an end, they had the acknowledged supremacy both by land and sea. They appointed Lysander as admiral and instructed him to visit each of the cities where he had established the men whom the Spartans call harmosts; for the Spartans had a dislike of democracies and wanted the cities to have oligarchic governments. **2** They also levied tribute from the peoples whom they had conquered, and, despite the fact that up to this time they had not used coined money, they now collected from the tribute more than 1,000 talents.

13.38 Plutarch *Life of Lysander* 13.1–7, 18.1–10: Lysander, General of Greece

Lysander after Aigospotamoi was the most important and powerful person in Greece, and cult honours were paid to him.

13.1 After the three thousand Athenian prisoners Lysander had captured (at Aigospotamoi) had been condemned to death by the (allied) counsellors, he called Philokles the general and asked him what punishment in his view should be inflicted on him for giving advice to his fellow citizens to treat Greeks in such a way. **2** But Philokles ignored his misfortune and told him not to act as prosecutor when there was no juror, but to do as victor what he would have suffered as the vanquished. Then having bathed and put on a splendid garment he went as first person to the slaughter, as Theophrastos records. **3** Lysander then sailed to the different cities and told all the Athenians he met to return to Athens, saying that he would spare no one he caught outside the city but would kill them all. **4** He did this to drive them all into the city because he wanted there to be a great scarcity of food and famine in the city in a short time, so that they might not delay his plans by having provisions to withstand his siege.

5 He also suppressed democratic and other forms of government and left one Spartan harmost in each city with ten magistrates chosen from the political associations he had set up in each. **6** He did this in the cities which had been his enemies and his allies alike, and sailed round at his leisure as if establishing his supremacy over Greece. **7** In appointing magistrates he regarded neither birth nor wealth, but put affairs into the hands of his associates and partisans, and made them sovereign in matters of rewards and punishments. He also took part in numerous massacres and helped drive out his friends' enemies, giving the Greeks a demonstration of the injustice of Spartan rule. …

18.1 Out of the spoils of victory Lysander set up at Delphi bronze statues of himself and of each of his admirals, as well as golden stars of the Dioskouroi which disappeared before the battle of Leuktra. **2** Also, in the treasury of Brasidas and the Akanthians, there was placed a trireme made of gold and ivory, two cubits long, which Cyrus sent Lysander to mark his victory. **3** And Anaxandrides the Delphian writes that money of Lysander's was deposited there, comprising a talent of silver, fifty-two minas and eleven staters besides — a statement that contradicts the accepted view of his being poor. **4** At any rate Lysander was now more powerful than any Greek before his time had been and was thought to possess a pride and self-importance that were even greater than his power. **5** For, as Duris writes, he was the first of the Greeks to whom cities erected altars and made sacrifices as if to a god, and the first to whom songs of triumph were sung. The beginning of one of these has been handed down and runs as follows:

> The general of noble Greece
> From spacious Sparta
> We shall hymn, crying
> 'O Paian'.

6 In addition, the Samians voted that their festival the Heraia should be called the Lysandreia. **7** Poets too were involved: Lysander kept Chorilos constantly with him to celebrate his achievements in poetry, while as for Antilochos, who composed some verses in his honour, he was so delighted that he filled his cap with silver and gave it to him. **8** And when Antimachos of Colophon and a certain Nikeratos of Herakleia competed against each other in composing poems in his honour, and he gave the crown of victory to Nikeratos, Antimachos was so angry that he destroyed his poem. **9** But Plato, who was then a young man, and admired Antimachos for his poetic skill, tried to cheer and console him in his disappointment at this defeat, telling him that it is the ignorant who suffer from their ignorance just as the blind do from their blindness. **10** However, when Aristonous, the harpist, who had won six times at the Pythian festival, kindly informed Lysander that if he won yet again he would have the victory announced under Lysander's name, Lysander replied, 'As my slave, I presume?'

13.39 *Fouilles de Delphes* 3.1 50: A Dedication by Lysander

This dedication inscribed on a statue base of Lysander, made by himself at Delphi, refers to the defeat of Athens (the sons of Kekrops, mythical king of Athens). Cf. Paus. 10.9.7–10; Plut. *Lys*. 18.

On this monument he dedicated his statue, after — victorious
With his swift ships — he had destroyed the power of the sons of Kekrops,
Lysander, who crowned unsacked Sparta,
His fatherland with its beautiful dancing grounds, the acropolis of Greece.
One from sea-girt Samos composed the poem — Ion.

THE RULE OF THE THIRTY TYRANTS

Intimidated by Lysander, the ekklesia voted that thirty men, the 'Thirty Tyrants', be elected to codify the ancestral laws under which they would govern (Xen. *Hell.* 2.3.2; *Ath. Pol.* 34.3: doc. 13.40); the Thirty obtained a garrison from Sparta and with its backing they arrested all their opponents (Xen. *Hell.* 2.3.13–4; cf. *Ath. Pol.* 37.2). Theramenes opposed the ruthless nature of the rule of the Thirty, but was forced to drink hemlock by Kritias (Xen. *Hell.* 2.3.15–56).

13.40 [Aristotle] *Athenaion Politeia* 34.2–35.4, 39.6: The Thirty Tyrants

Thrasyboulos, in exile in Thebes, first seized the fort of Phyle on the Athenian–Theban frontier, then Mounichia in the Piraeus. The Thirty were deposed, and replaced by a board of Ten for the purpose of ending the civil war; these, however, sent to Sparta for help, and in turn were replaced by another board of Ten, who worked for peace. King Pausanias came with a force from Sparta; after initial fighting with the democrats at Piraeus, he arranged peace and an amnesty in conjunction with the Ten. Democracy was then restored (Xen. *Hell*. 2.4.24–43; *Ath. Pol*. 38.3–4).

34.2 In the following year, the archonship of Alexias (405/4), the Athenians had the misfortune to lose the sea-battle at Aigospotamoi, as a result of which Lysander became master of the city and set up the Thirty in the following way. **34.3** Peace had been made on condition that the Athenians should live under their traditional constitution. The democrats tried to preserve the democracy, and those of the notables those who belonged to the hetaireiai and the exiles who had returned after the peace treaty were eager for oligarchy, while those who did not belong to any hetaireia and who otherwise appeared to be among the best of the citizens aimed at the traditional constitution; these included Archinos, Anytos, Kleitophon, Phormisios and many others, but their particular champion was Theramenes. But Lysander sided with the oligarchs, and the people were intimidated and compelled to vote for the oligarchy. The decree was drafted by Drakontides of Aphidna. **35.1** In this way the Thirty were established in the archonship of Pythodoros (404/3). Once they had become masters of the city, they ignored all the resolutions concerning the constitution except for appointing 500 Councillors and the other officials from a preselected 1,000, and chose as supporters for themselves ten governors of the Piraeus and eleven guardians of the prison and 300 whip-bearers as their attendants, thus keeping the city under their control. **35.2** At first they were moderate towards the citizens and pretended that they were administering the traditional constitution, and took down from the Areiopagos the laws of Ephialtes and Archestratos concerning the Areiopagites, and annulled the laws of Solon, which were ambiguous, and removed the power of the jurors, on the grounds that they were emending ambiguities in the constitution …

35.3 So this is what they did at first, and they eliminated the informers (sykophantai) and those mischievous and wicked men who gain favour with the people contrary to their best interests, and the city was pleased with this, considering that they were doing this for the best. **35.4** But when they had firmer control of the city, they spared none of the citizens, but put to death those who were noted for their property, family and reputation, because this removed their own fear and they wanted to appropriate their property; and in a short space of time they had done away with no less than 1,500 … (*Thrasyboulos and the exiles occupy Phyle and Mounichia and the Thirty are deposed.*) **39.6** There was to be a total amnesty concerning the past actions of everyone except the Thirty, the Ten, the Eleven and the governors of the Piraeus, and of these as well, if they would submit to an examination (euthyna). The governors of the Piraeus were to be examined among the men of the Piraeus, and those who held office in the city amongst those who had taxable property there. Then those who wished could leave. Each side was to pay back separately the money it had borrowed for the war.

13.41 [Aristotle] *Athenaion Politeia* 38.4–40.4: Restoration of Democracy in 403/2 BC

The factions in Athens were reconciled by the Spartan king Pausanias in 403/2 BC, undoing Lysander's arrangements in establishing the rule of the Thirty.

38.4 It was the Spartan king Pausanias, along with the ten mediators who later came from Sparta at his instigation, who brought the peace and reconciliation to a conclusion. Rhinon and his colleagues were commended for their goodwill towards the people, and though they had taken up their duties under an oligarchy they submitted their accounts for examination under a democracy, and no one – either of those who had stayed in the city or of those who had returned from the Piraeus – made any complaint against them. In fact Rhinon was actually immediately elected general because of his conduct.

39.1 The reconciliation took place in the archonship of Eukleides (403/2) on the following conditions:

those Athenians who remained in the city who wish to emigrate shall have Eleusis to live in, retain their citizen rights, be entirely sovereign and self-governing, and remain in possession of the income from their properties;

2 the temple (of Demeter and Persephone) shall be common to both parties and under the superintendence of the Kerykes and the Eumolpidai according to the traditional practice;

the men from Eleusis shall not be permitted to go into the city, nor those in the city to Eleusis, except in either case to celebrate the Mysteries;

they (the men from Eleusis) shall contribute from their revenues to the allied force just like the other Athenians;

3 if any of those who leave take a house at Eleusis they shall get the permission of the owner; if they cannot come to an agreement each is to chose three assessors and accept whatever price they settle upon. But if they choose to live with any Eleusinians they may do so;

4 there shall be a registration of those who wish to migrate within ten days of the swearing of the oaths for those currently in the country, their migration taking place within twenty days, and for those abroad the same time limits shall apply, from the time when they return to Athens;

5 it shall not be legal for anyone settling at Eleusis to hold any office in the city until he has re-registered as a resident in the city;

trials for murder shall be conducted in accordance with traditional practice, in cases where someone has killed or wounded a person with his own hands;

6 for past events there shall be a total amnesty for everyone except the Thirty, the Ten, and the Eleven, and those who governed the Piraeus (unless they submit their accounts for examination). Those who governed the Piraeus shall submit accounts to the people of the Piraeus, and those who held office in the city to those who have taxable property there, after which those who wish may migrate on these conditions;

each party shall make its own repayment of the sums borrowed for the war.

40.1 When the reconciliation had taken place on these conditions, all those who had fought on the side of the Thirty were afraid, and many of them intended to migrate, but delayed their registration until the last few days as everyone generally does. Archinos realised the numbers involved and as he wanted to stop them he cancelled the remaining days for registration, and as a result many were forced to remain against their will until they had regained their confidence. **2** This appears to have been very statesmanlike on the part of Archinos, as was his subsequent indictment of Thrasyboulos' decree as unconstitutional, in which citizenship was granted to all those who returned from the Piraeus, some of whom were obviously slaves. On a third occasion, when someone started stirring up bad feeling against the returnees, he brought him in front of the Council and persuaded it to have him executed without trial, on the grounds that it was now the time for them to show if they wanted to save the democracy and keep their oaths; for by letting this man off they would encourage others as well, while if they put him to death they were setting an example for everyone.

And this is exactly what happened, as after he was executed no one subsequently broke the amnesty, and everyone appeared in both private and public to behave in respect of past calamities with the greatest honour and statesmanship. **3** For not only did they ignore all charges relating to past events, but they also publicly returned to the Spartans the monies the Thirty had received for the war (although the agreement laid down that each party, whether in the city or Piraeus, was to make separate repayments), feeling that this was a necessary first step towards establishing concord. In the other cities, however, those who have set up democracies never think of making such payments out of their own property – all that they want to do is redistribute the land! **4** They also entered into a reconciliation with the settlers at Eleusis two years after the migration, in the archonship of Xenainetos (401 BC).

13.42 Plutarch *Life of Lysander* 24.1–25.3, 30.1–5: Lysander Discredited

Lysander's influence began to wane as soon as the Peloponnesian War was concluded. His arrangements for the Thirty to rule Athens were terminated by King Pausanias, who arranged for the restoration of democracy in 403 BC. Although Lysander had been Agesilaos' lover, as king the latter was lukewarm in his support due to Lysander's great personal influence and following at Sparta, and the dekarchies were removed soon after. The command against Persia which he was granted in 396 BC was undermined by Agesilaos, who sent him to the Hellespont. The account of Lysander's scheme to make the kingship elective might be fictional, invented after his death to ruin his reputation, but his career exemplifies the tension which arose in Sparta when an individual other than a king was a successful commander.

24.1 Lysander was sent as ambassador to the Hellespont; though he was angry with Agesilaos he did not fail to do his duty, and persuaded the Persian Spithridates, who was at odds with Pharnabazos to defect from him, and brought him to Agesilaos. **2** Agesilaos made no further use of him in the war and when his time was up he sailed back to Sparta ingloriously, not only angry with Agesilaos, but loathing the entire political structure more than ever, and so resolved to waste no time in now putting into effect the plans for change and revolution which he is thought to have come up with and devised some time before. **3** These were as follows: of the Herakleidai who had joined with the Dorians and come down into the Peloponnese there was a large and notable stock flourishing in Sparta, but not every family belonging to it shared in the royal succession. The rulers came from only two families, and were called the Eurypontidai and Agiadai, and the rest had no special role in the government because of their noble birth, while the honours arising from superior excellence were open to everyone of ability.

4 Now Lysander belonged to one of these families, and, when he had risen to great renown through his achievements and acquired many friends and a position of power, it irritated him to see the city growing through his agency but ruled by others no better born than himself. **5** So he resolved to take away the rule from the two houses and give it back to all the Herakleidai in common or, as some say, not to the Herakleidai but to the Spartiates, so that sovereignty might belong not to those descended from Herakles, but to those chosen like Herakles for superior excellence, the quality which had raised Herakles to the honours of the gods. **6** Of course he hoped that when the kingdom was decided on this criterion no Spartiate would be chosen before himself.

25.1 First of all he had to do his best to prepare to win over the citizens through his own efforts, and to this end learned by heart a speech written by Kleon the Halikarnassian. **2** Then, as he saw that the extraordinary nature and magnitude of his innovatory plan needed bolder support, he brought to bear upon the citizens the machinery of tragic drama, as it were, by gathering and preparing responses and oracles from Delphi, because he believed that Kleon's cleverness would not help him unless he first terrified and subdued the citizens by some religious fear and superstition and then led them to yield to his argument. **3** At any rate Ephoros tells us that after using Pherekles to try to bribe the Pythia and then the priestesses of Dodona and failing, he went to the temple of Ammon and talked to the god's interpreters there, but when he offered them a large amount of gold they were annoyed and sent men to Sparta to denounce him…

30.1 After Lysander had died in this way (attacking Thebes), the Spartiates initially took this very badly and summoned Pausanias, the king, to stand trial for his life; however, he avoided this and fled to Tegea, where he lived out his life in the sanctuary of Athena. **2** It was the poverty of Lysander discovered at his death that made his excellence more obvious, as from the vast wealth and power, and the homage paid him by cities and the king of Persia he had not tried in the slightest to amass money to enrich his house, as Theopompos relates, who is more to be believed when he is praising than when he is criticising, for he prefers to criticise rather than praise. **3** Some time later, according to Ephoros, some sort of dispute about the allies arose at Sparta and it became necessary to consult the documents that Lysander had possession of, so Agesilaos went to his house. **4** When he found the book in which the speech on the constitution was written, proposing that the kingship should be taken away from the Eurypontidai and Agiadai and be put up for open selection from among the best men, he was eager to show the citizens the speech and reveal Lysander's real character as a citizen. **5** But Lakratidas, a sensible man and the chief ephor at the time, restrained Agesilaos, saying that they ought not to dig Lysander up again but to bury his speech with him as it was composed with such corrupting plausibility.

13.43 Plato *Seventh Letter* 324b–325c: Plato Decides Not to Go into Politics

Of the letters of Plato, this seventh one has most claim to authenticity, and was written in 343 BC. The reference to the democracy as a 'Golden Age' compared to the rule of the Thirty Tyrants is interesting. Plato's own expectation was that he would naturally enter politics, as Kritias was Plato's mother's cousin.

324b When I was a boy I naturally felt the same as many others did, thinking that as soon as I reached independence I would immediately enter the city's public life. **324c** But then certain changes took place in the city's political situation, which affected me as follows:

A change was made to the government of the time, which was the target of abuse from a large number of people, with fifty-one men established as rulers during this change process, eleven in the City, and ten in the Piraeus (both of these groups dealing with the market and other things involved in city administration), and thirty established as absolute rulers over everything. **324d** Now some of these were relatives and friends of mine, and they immediately invited me to join them, as being entirely appropriate. What I felt at this was in no way amazing, considering my youth, for I thought they would administer the city in such a way that it would be led away from a life of injustice to a just way of living, and so I paid great attention to them to see what they would do. But in fact I saw how those men in just a short time made the previous government seem like a Golden Age, and especially in their treatment of my elderly friend Socrates, **324e** whom I would have no shame in calling the most just man of that time, yet they tried to send him along with others to fetch one of the citizens and bring him in forcibly to be executed — **325a** the object of this being of course to make him participate in their actions, whether he wanted to or not. He refused to do it, and risked every penalty rather than be party to their monstrous actions. So when I saw all this and other things of a similar gravity, I was horrified and removed myself from all the evil practices which were in train. And, not long after, the regime of the Thirty, along with the whole of the government at that time, was overthrown. Then once again, though less urgently, I was inspired by a desire to take part in public and political matters.

325b But in those times, troubled as they were, many unacceptable things were still happening, and it was not to be wondered at if on some occasions during these times of change some people took too great a revenge on their enemies; and yet even so the exiles (the democrats) who then returned showed great moderation. But by some mischance some people in power summoned our friend Socrates to court, arraigning him on a most monstrous accusation which fitted Socrates least of all men: **325c** for they summoned him on a charge of impiety, and the others condemned him and killed him — that same man who on that former occasion had refused to take part in the monstrous arrest of one of the friends of the exiles, when these very men had had the misfortune to be in exile themselves. When I thought about all this and the type of men who were administering the city, and their laws and customs, and the more I thought about them, and the older I got, the more difficult I considered it to manage government with justice.

14

THE RISE OF MACEDON

Sparta had accepted Persian gold in the war against Athens and the relationship between Lysander and Cyrus was such that in 401 BC Cyrus successfully requested Spartan assistance against his brother Artaxerxes who had taken the Persian throne in 404. In addition, a force of Greek mercenaries, the Ten Thousand, of which Xenophon was a member, was also employed by Cyrus. At Cunaxa in that year the Greek mercenaries won a major battle but Cyrus was killed. Tissaphernes as satrap of Sardis demanded control of the Ionian cities, but they had been under Cyrus' control when he was satrap, and so they appealed to the Spartans for assistance against Tissaphernes (doc. 14.1). Thibron was sent by the Spartans as harmost to Asia Minor and protected the Greek cities, and when joined by the Ten Thousand in 399 BC (doc. 14.2) achieved some further successes. The Spartan campaign against Elis took place at this time (doc. 14.3), as too did a conspiracy against the Spartan state in 397 BC (doc. 14.5).

Immediately after the Peloponnesian War, Sparta had begun to fall out with its allies; Thebes, for example, was the home to many Athenians fleeing from the Thirty Tyrants, and it was from here that Thrasyboulos had set out in 403 BC; democracy was then restored at Athens. Boeotia and Athens made an alliance in 396/5 BC (doc. 14.10), less than a decade after they had been bitter enemies, and Athens began to rebuild its demolished walls in 395/4 BC (doc. 14.11). In 395 BC war broke out between the Spartans on one hand and their former allies, Persia, Thebes and Corinth, with the addition of Athens (doc. 14.6); this is called the Corinthian War. The revival of Athenian power came in the form of Konon, a strategos who took refuge with the king of Cyprus after the Athenian defeat at Aigospotamoi in 405 BC. From 397 BC he established a good working relationship with the Persian Pharnabazos, satrap of Phrygia, and together they defeated the Spartans at Knidos in 394 BC (doc. 14.9). Pharnabazos took the Persian fleet to the Isthmous of Corinth, the closest Persian ships had been to the mainland since 480 BC at Salamis.

But in 386 BC the Spartans, who were having the worst of the Corinthian War, achieved a political and diplomatic masterstroke when they detached the Persians from Sparta's enemies; Artaxerxes II imposed the King's Peace with Spartan co-operation. The Persians gained uncontested control of the Greek cities of Asia Minor and some of the islands (doc. 14.12), for whose independence the Spartans had fought from 401 until Agesilaos' recall in 394 to fight in the Corinthian War. The other Greeks were in no position to oppose this settlement as the Persians threatened force against those who opposed the peace; the combination of Persia and Sparta was unassailable. The King's Peace guaranteed the autonomy of all the Greek cities of the mainland: the capital is always used to denote the Persian (Great) King as opposed to the kings of Sparta.

The Spartans were themselves the first to break the peace by occupying Thebes in 382 BC. Athens then took the initiative in 377 BC by forming a new league, known by scholars as the Second Athenian Confederacy (docs 14.14–15). Its aim was to oppose Spartan power and numerous states joined. Sparta's ascendancy began to unravel with Theban independence; Pelopidas liberated the city in 379 BC (doc. 14.13), and the Theban defeated a Spartan force in 375. Sparta called a peace conference in 371 BC and, while the Athenians and other Greeks accepted peace with Sparta, Epameinondas and Agesilaos quarrelled over definitions of Boeotian and Lakonian freedom (doc. 14.16). Under Agesilaos the Spartans invaded Boeotia and the Thebans met them on the plain of Leuktra, where Sparta suffered a crushing defeat from which it never recovered (doc. 14.18). The Thebans successfully invaded Sparta again in 370 and 369 BC; in 370 Messenia was freed and the helots gained their independence, as well as a new capital, Messene. The Arkadians were similarly empowered with the establishment of a federation and capital at Megalopolis (docs 14.20–24). Thebes briefly established a hegemony (supremacy) over Greece, which, however, lasted only until Epameinondas was killed in battle at Mantineia in 362 BC. Defeat of the Athenians and Boeotians at the Battle of Chaironeia against Philip II of Macedon in 338 BC was a significant blow (doc. 14.48), and Thebes' destruction by Alexander in 335 BC terminated its fourth-century history (doc. 15.4). Its role in the foundation of Megalopolis (docs 14.21–22) and Messene (docs 14.23–24), with the liberation of the helots, was Thebes' lasting contribution to Greek history.

Iason (or Jason) of Pherai, as tyrant, became tagos of Thessaly, unified it, arbitrated between Thebes and Sparta after Leuktra and seems to have aspired to a leadership role in Greek affairs. His assassination in 370 BC may have been motivated by fear of his growing power in central Greece (doc. 14.24). Tyranny continued at Pherai but Philip II later put it down and installed a Macedonian garrison. Whatever good intentions the Athenians had in establishing the Second Athenian Confederacy, these turned sour in 357–355 BC when many of their allies successfully revolted (doc. 14.28); Athens was still the most powerful naval state in Greece but was now without major maritime allies to assist it. Philip used the opportunity to seize Amphipolis.

Philip II had inherited the Macedonian throne in 359 BC in the aftermath of a major military defeat at the hands of the Illyrians, whom he was soon to conquer and incorporate into the Macedonian state. He trained the Macedonians in the use of the long spear known as the sarissa (docs 14.41–42), and in 358 inflicted a major defeat on the Illyrians (doc. 14.25); as Demosthenes notes, he used a wide variety of troops and was prepared to campaign no matter what the time of year (doc. 14.41). Territorial ambition seems to have been one of Philip's aims from the beginning, for just two years later he began a process of territorial acquisition and conquest. Illyria and Thessaly also came under his control (doc. 14.26), and access to Thrace's gold gave him resources to equip soldiers and bribe the Greeks (doc. 14.29). He made fairly quick progress in conquering his immediate Greek neighbours, such as Amphipolis, Pydna, Poteideia, Methone (docs 14.26, 14.29), and Olynthos, which had previously been in alliance with him (doc. 14.30).

The Third Sacred War broke out in 357 BC when the Delphic Amphicytony declared war on Phokis, which seized Delphi and proceeded to use the treasures there to fund its war against the Amphictyony, led mainly by Thebes (doc. 14.32). Philip was invited to deal with the matter in 346. Athens had begun negotiations with Philip for peace while the Sacred War was still in progress. Two embassies were sent to him for this purpose, on both of which Aeschines and Demosthenes served. The Peace of Philokrates was ratified, named after the Athenian politician who proposed the decree early in 346 for sending an embassy to Philip. Both sides kept what was then in their possession. But Philip immediately seized Thermopylai, and compelled the Phokians to surrender (doc. 14.33). As a result he was awarded the Phokians' place on the Amphictyonic Council (doc. 14.34) but more importantly had been shown to be the arbiter in Greek affairs. The balance of power had shifted to Philip within days of the Peace being ratified. Demosthenes indicted Aeschines for his role in the affair, but the matter only came to court in 343 BC, with Aeschines being narrowly acquitted (doc. 14.44).

Demosthenes became increasingly antagonistic towards Philip (doc. 14.40), whose intervention in Euboea in 342 BC and attacks on Perinthos and Byzantium in 340 were unsuccessful but infuriated Athens (see doc. 14.48). Matters came to a head in 339 when the Fourth Sacred War gave Philip an excuse to occupy Elateia in Phokis (doc. 14.48). This news shocked the Athenian ekklesia and only Demosthenes rose to address it, successfully urging alliance with Thebes, which did in fact join Athens (doc. 14.48). The two cities and other Boeotians fought Philip at Chaironeia and lost spectacularly, with the Theban Sacred Band annihilated to a man (doc. 14.17). Philip made peace with Athens and Boeotia; in 337 BC he formed the League of Corinth in which the Greek states accepted him as hegemon or leader (docs 14.50–51). After Chaironeia the Athenian orator Lykourgos played a major role in rehabilitating Athens' finances, and in construction projects such as an arsenal, docks and harbour works (he was one of the ten Athenian politicians whose surrender Alexander demanded in 335 BC).

Philip was assassinated in the theatre at Pella in 336 BC (docs 14.53–54). There is a very real possibility that Alexander, and even more possibly Olympias, were involved in Philip's murder, but the primary responsibility seems to lie with Pausanias. His obvious motive was Philip's refusal to punish Attalos: Pausanias had been sexually assaulted and humiliated by Attalos' muleteers after himself having verbally abused another Pausanias (whom Philip was falling in love with) as a hermaphrodite and slut; Pausanias himself was handsome and already loved by Philip. The other Pausanias, distraught, killed himself by throwing his life away in battle. In the theatre at Pella, in which Philip had a statue of himself carried around with that of the twelve Olympian gods, Pausanias struck down the king and was immediately killed himself. Philip's achievements were many and acknowledged by Alexander (doc. 14.55), who continued his preparations and plans for the attack on Persia.

SPARTA VERSUS PERSIA, 401–387 BC

Sparta had entered into alliance with Persia in the Peloponnesian War, and it was largely with Persian gold that the Spartans had financed their fleet and won the war. Sparta after the war, however, became embroiled against Persia in Asia Minor. The Athenian Konon was able to work with the Persians to crush Spartan naval power in 394 BC at Knidos. Sparta also fell out with its allies Thebes and Corinth, with war between them – the Corinthian War – from 395 BC until the King's Peace of 386, which guaranteed the freedom of the Greek cities, except those of the islands and Asia Minor. Sparta broke the terms of the peace by seizing Thebes in 382, from which the Spartans were ejected in 379 by Theban exiles under Pelopidas. Partly encouraged by this, the Athenians formed a league – the Second Athenian Confederacy – to counteract Sparta's power.

14.1 Xenophon *Hellenika* 3.1.1–8: Sparta Campaigns in Asia Minor in 401 BC

The Spartans had been victorious in the Peloponnesian War, arguably mainly because of Persian financial support received from Cyrus; he and Lysander had become friends. In 401 BC Cyrus rebelled against his elder brother Artaxerxes II with Spartan support. Xenophon and the Ten Thousand mercenaries assisted Cyrus, who won a major battle against Artaxerxes' forces at Cunaxa in 401 but was killed in the fighting. Xenophon states here that the account of the battle and the return of the Ten Thousand to Greece was written by Themistogenes the Syracusan: this is obviously a pseudonym for Xenophon himself, whose *Anabasis* covered the history of the Ten Thousand.

3.1.1 After the civil strife in Athens had ended in this way, Cyrus sent messengers to Sparta requesting that the Spartans should do the same for him as he had done for them in the war against the Athenians. The ephors considered that what he said was fair and sent orders to Samios, their admiral at that time, to take any orders from Cyrus that he might give. And Samios willingly carried out whatever Cyrus requested: with his own fleet accompanying that of Cyrus, he sailed round to Cilicia and made it impossible for Syennesis, the ruler of Cilicia, to oppose Cyrus by land while he was marching against the King. **2** The account of how Cyrus collected an army and with it marched upcountry against his brother, how the battle took place and how he died, and how the Greeks then made their way safely back to the sea, has been recorded by Themistogenes the Syracusan.

3 Now when Tissaphernes, who was considered to have been very valuable to the King (Artaxerxes) in the war against his brother, was sent down to the coast as satrap, both of the area which he had previously ruled and that of Cyrus, he immediately demanded that all the Ionian cities should be his subjects. Now they, both because they wanted to be free and because they were afraid of Tissaphernes as they had elected to support Cyrus while he was alive and not him, refused to allow him into their cities and sent envoys to Sparta requesting that, since the Spartans were the champions of all of Greece, they should also take them, the Greeks in Asia, under their protection to prevent the devastation of their land and to ensure their liberty. **4** As a result the Spartans sent Thibron as their harmost, giving him 1,000 neodameis (new citizens) as soldiers and 4,000 men from the rest of the Peloponnese. Thibron also asked from the Athenians 300 cavalry, saying that he would pay them himself, and they sent him some of those who had served in the cavalry under the Thirty, as they considered that it would be to the advantage of the Athenian people if they went abroad and died there.

5 When they arrived in Asia, Thibron also collected soldiers from the Greek cities of the mainland, for all the cities obeyed any order given them by a Spartan. With this army Thibron did not descend to the plains because he saw the strength of the enemy's cavalry, but was satisfied to keep them from devastating the territory wherever he happened to be. **6** But when the men who had returned safely after going upcountry with Cyrus joined forces with him, from then on he drew up his troops against Tissaphernes even on the plains, and took over cities, Pergamum of its own free will, as well as Teuthrania and Halisarna, which were ruled by Eurysthenes and Prokles, the descendants of Demaratos the Spartan (this territory had been given to Demaratos by the King for taking part in the expedition against Greece). The brothers Gorgon and Gongylos also gave him their support, who ruled Gambrion and Palaigambrion and Myrina and Gryneion respectively. These cities had also been a gift from the King to that Gongylos who was the only one of the Eretrians to support the cause of the Persians and had been exiled in consequence. **7** There were also some weak cities which Thibron captured by force; indeed, with 'Egyptian' Larisa, as it is called, when it refused to give in, he surrounded it with his army and besieged it … As he seemed to be achieving nothing, the ephors sent him instructions to leave Larisa and march against Caria. **8** While he was at Ephesos and about to move against Caria, Derkylidas arrived to take command of the army — a man reputed to be extremely resourceful, and hence nicknamed 'Sisyphos'. Accordingly Thibron returned home, where he was fined and exiled, for the allies accused him of having permitted his army to plunder their friends.

14.2 Xenophon *Anabasis* 4.7.21–26: The Sea!

Xenophon and the Ten Thousand Greek mercenaries who had served Cyrus now fought their way north across the interior of Asia Minor, harried by Persian forces, to Byzantium, from where they could sail home. Many of these mercenaries, including Xenophon, then joined the Spartan general Thibron in 399 BC, who operated in Asia Minor against the Persians with some success then, and again in 391 BC, when he was killed.

4.7.21 They arrived at the mountain on the fifth day; its name was Theches. When those in the vanguard reached the top, a great shout went up. **22** When Xenophon and the rearguard heard it they imagined that other enemies were attacking them from the front, for they were being followed from behind from the countryside that was in flames, and the rearguard had killed some of them and taken others alive by setting an ambush, and had captured about twenty wicker shields covered with raw, hairy ox-hides. **23** But when the shouting kept getting louder and nearer, as each rank in turn came up and began running fast toward those in front who continued to shout, and as the shouting grew louder and louder as the number of men increased, it became very clear to Xenophon that this was a matter of greater importance, **24** and he mounted a horse and went to the rescue with Lykios and the cavalry. In a moment they heard the soldiers shouting, 'The sea! The sea!' and passing the word along. Then all the rearguard started running as well, and even the baggage animals and horses began to race forward. **25** When they had all reached the top, they all started embracing each other and even the generals and captains, with tears of joy. All of a sudden someone passed the word and the soldiers began to bring rocks and build a huge heap of stones. **26** On this they placed as offerings a number of raw ox-hides, staffs and the captured wicker shields.

14.3 Xenophon *Hellenika* 3.2.21–22: Sparta's War with Elis

Derkylidas was Spartan general in Asia Minor after Thibron was exiled in 399 BC for not restraining his troops from looting Sparta's allies, but also probably because of his limited military successes in the field. Sparta settled a dispute with Elis, which had debarred it from competing in the Olympic games since 420 BC and allied itself with Sparta's enemies. This passage also makes clear the prestige attached to participating in and winning at the Olympic festival and Spartan punctiliousness in religious rites. Agis II, of the Eurypontid branch, was Spartan king from *c.* 427 to 400.

3.2.21 While Derkylidas was campaigning in Asia, the Spartans were at the same time engaged in war against the Eleians. They had been enraged with Elis for a long time, both because the Eleians had made an alliance with the Athenians, Argives and Mantineians, and because, on the excuse that a judgement had been made against the Spartans, they had barred them from taking part in the horse races and athletic contests (at the Olympic festival). Even worse than this, after Lichas (a Spartan) had made over his chariot to the Thebans and they had been proclaimed the winners, when Lichas came forward to crown the charioteer, they flogged him, despite the fact that he was an old man, and drove him out. **22** And later on, when Agis had been sent to sacrifice to Zeus in accordance with an oracle, the Eleians refused to allow him to pray for victory in war, saying that from ancient times it had been accepted as a principle that Greeks should not consult the oracle in connection with a war against other Greeks. In consequence he left without sacrificing.

14.4 Isocrates 12 *Evagoras* 51–56: The Enemies of Sparta Fight Back

Konon was the only Athenian strategos to escape from the Athenian naval disaster at Aigospotamoi in 405 BC, and took refuge with Evagoras, king of Cyprus (411–374), until 397 (Xen. *Hell.* 2.1.29). He then helped revive Persian naval power as the Persians were concerned about the Spartan attacks on Asia Minor. The combined Greek and Persian fleet defeated the Spartan fleet at Knidos on the Asia Minor coast in 394, and Konon expelled the Spartan governors from the Greek cities of the islands and Asia Minor. With the satrap Pharnbazos, he expelled the Spartan governors from the islands and cities of Asia Minor, and returned to Athens in 393. This encomium of Evagoras, who was granted Athenian citizenship in 394 BC for his role against the Spartans, was written for his son. Arrested by Tiribazos (doc. 14.12) Konon escaped to Cyprus, where he died. Xen. *Hell.* 4.3.10–12, 8.1–6; Diod. 14.79.7–85.4.

51 The greatest proof of the character and integrity of Evagoras is this: that many of the most reputable Greeks left their homelands and came to live in Cyprus, because they thought that Evagoras' rule was less harsh and more constitutional than that of their own governments at home. To go through all the others by name would be a vast undertaking — **52** but who does not know of Konon, who was pre-eminent among the Greeks because of his numerous virtues? And how when he met with misfortune he chose to go to Evagoras rather than anyone else, believing that refuge with him would be safest for his person and that Evagoras would provide the quickest help to his city? And although he had been successful many times in the past, in none of these did he appear to have made a better decision than on this occasion; **53** for this visit to Cyprus resulted in the exchange of mutual benefits. Firstly, no sooner had they met each other than they regarded each other more highly than those who had previously been their close friends. Next, not only had they passed their lives in complete agreement on all other issues, but held the same view regarding our city. **54** For when they looked at Athens as subject to the Spartans and suffering under a dreadful reverse, they were grieved and angered, as was only proper for both of them — as one of them was a native of Athens, and the other, as a consequence of his many great services, had had citizenship legally conferred upon him [actually in 394]. And while they were considering how they might release Athens from her misfortunes, the Spartans soon gave them the opportunity; for while they were ruling the Greeks by land and sea they became so greedy that they even attempted to ravage Asia. **55** So Konon and Evagoras seized this opportunity and, as the King's generals did not know how to manage matters, they told them not to make war on the Spartans by land, but by sea, as they considered that, if the Persians put together a land army and were successful with it, only the mainland would benefit, but, if they were victorious by sea, the whole of Greece would share the victory. **56** And this is exactly what happened: the generals took their advice and a fleet was gathered, the Spartans were defeated at sea, and they lost their empire, while the Greeks were liberated and our city recovered part of its old glory and became leader of the allies. And although all this took place with Konon in command, Evagoras both made it possible and provided most of the forces.

14.5 Xenophon *Hellenika* 3.3.4–11: Conspiracy in Sparta in 397 BC

Agesilaos II of the Eurypontid house succeeded his brother Agis II in 400 until 359 BC. He achieved some limited successes in Asia Minor against Persia in 396–395 but was recalled to deal with the

Corinthian War. In Sparta there was a conspiracy led by one Kinadon, who was not one of the homoioi, Spartan equals (citizens). Helots, neodameis (new citizens) and inferiors were involved. The planned revolt is an indication of the various discontented groups within Sparta. The term 'inferiors' (hypomeiones) occurs only here and its meaning is unclear; it could refer to a group of homoioi who had lost their citizen rights, perhaps because they no longer possessed an estate or had been demoted for cowardice.

3.3.4 Agesilaos, who had not yet been king for a year, was offering up one of the prescribed sacrifices on behalf of the state, when the diviner told him that the gods were revealing a conspiracy of the worst possible kind. When he sacrificed a second time the seer said that the signs were even worse. And when he sacrificed a third time the seer said: 'Agesilaos, what is foretold to me is just as if we were in the midst of our enemies.' They therefore made sacrifices both to the gods who avert evil and to the saviour deities, until they with difficulty obtained favourable omens and could stop. Within five days of the sacrifice someone informed the ephors of a conspiracy and that Kinadon was its leader. **5** He was a fine and courageous young man, but not one of the 'homoioi'. When the ephors asked how the plan was to be carried out, the informer said that Kinadon had taken him to the boundary of the agora and told him to count how many Spartiates were present there. 'And I,' he said, 'after counting the king and ephors and gerontes and some forty others, asked Kinadon why he had asked me to count them. His answer was that I should look upon these men as my enemies, and all the others in the agora, who amounted to more than 4,000, as my allies.' He also said that Kinadon pointed out of those they met in the streets one here and two there as enemies, and all the rest as allies, while of all those whom they met on the country estates of the Spartiates there was one, the owner, who was an enemy, but many others on each estate who were allies. **6** When the ephors asked how many Kinadon had said to be implicated in the conspiracy, the informer stated that he had said that in this regard there were only a trustworthy few who were in the secret with himself and the other leaders, but that in the leaders' view it was they who were in the secret of all the others – helots, neodameis, inferiors and perioikoi, for when any mention was made of the Spartiates in their presence, none of them was able to hide the fact that they would happily eat them raw. **7** The ephors then asked how they planned to arm themselves, and the informer replied that according to Kinadon it was clear that those in the army already had weapons, and as for the mob – and he then took him into the ironmonger's and showed him great quantities of knives, swords, spits, axes, hatchets and sickles – all the equipment which men use to work the land or wood and stone were also weapons, while most of the other trades also employed implements which were satisfactory weapons, especially when used against unarmed men. And when finally he was asked when all this was to eventuate, he replied that he had been instructed not to leave the city.

8 When the ephors had heard all this they concluded that he was describing a well-thought-out plan and were panic-stricken. Without even convening the so-called 'Little Assembly' they just individually gathered together some of the elders and decided to send Kinadon to Aulon with some other young men with instructions to bring back those of the Aulonians and helots whose names were written on the message-stick. They also told him to bring back the woman who was said to be the most beautiful there, who was thought to be corrupting all the Spartans who visited, whether old or young. **9** Kinadon had performed other duties of a similar sort for the ephors prior to this, so on this occasion they just gave him the message-stick on which were written the names of those to be arrested. When he asked which of the young men he should take with him, they replied, 'Go and tell the most senior of the guard-commanders to send with you six or seven of those who happen to be there.' They had of course ensured that the guard-commander knew whom he had to send and that the men who were sent knew that it was Kinadon whom they had to arrest. The ephors also said to Kinadon that they would be sending three wagons, so they would not have to bring those arrested back on foot, concealing as far as they could that they were sending for one man – himself.

10 They did not want to arrest him in the city because they were not aware of how far the plot had spread and they wanted to hear from Kinadon who his accomplices were before these could learn that they had been implicated and manage to escape. So they planned that those arresting Kinadon should detain him, and discover from him the names of the other plotters, and write them down and send them to the ephors as quickly as possible. The ephors viewed the affair with such seriousness that they sent a squadron of cavalry with the men going to Aulon. **11** Once he had been seized and a horseman had returned with the names he had listed, the seer Tisamenos and the most important of the others were immediately arrested. Kinadon was then brought back and questioned, at which he confessed everything and named his accomplices. When he was finally asked why he had chosen to act as he did, he replied, 'I wanted to be inferior to no one in Sparta.' For this he was at once bound neck and hands in a collar and driven through Sparta with his accomplices, flogged and goaded as they went. And this is how they met their punishment.

14.6 Xenophon *Hellenika* 3.5.1–2: Tithraustes Bribes the Greeks to Oppose Sparta

Agesilaos operated in Asia Minor from 396–395 BC and was then called back to Sparta in 395 to deal with the Corinthian War (395–386). Tithraustes was Tissaphernes' successor as Persian satrap of Sardis (in western Asia Minor). Cf. Diod. 14.80.6–7 (Tithraustes).

1 Tithraustes now believed that he had discovered that Agesilaos looked with contempt on the activities of the King and had no intention of leaving Asia but, on the contrary, had great hopes of overcoming the King. He was unsure of how to deal with this, so he sent Timokrates the Rhodian to Greece, giving him gold to the value of fifty talents of silver and instructions to give it to the most prominent men in the different poleis, after receipt of the most reliable pledges, on condition that they made war against the Spartans. So he went and handed over the money to Androkleidas, Ismenias and Galaxidoros at Thebes, to Timolaos and Polyanthes at Argos, and to Kylon and his supporters at Argos. **2** Though the Athenians did not receive a share of this gold, they were still eager for war, considering that the empire was theirs by rights. Those who had accepted the money started drumming up bad feeling against the Spartans in their own poleis, and once they had created this hatred of the Spartans they then brought the most important poleis into cooperation with each other.

14.7 Meiggs & Lewis 67: Contributions to the Spartan War Effort, 426 or 396–395 BC

This is a heavily restored inscription from Sparta, possibly from the temple of Athena Chalkioikos. Few public documents were inscribed at Sparta; this one records various contributions of money, grain and even raisins to the Spartans. The date cannot be ascertained with certainty, and 426 BC is often preferred, but the donations, often very small ones, come from the islands and Ephesos; Meiggs & Lewis therefore suggest the date 396–395 when Agesilaos was in Asia Minor based at Ephesos. If it dates to the Peloponnesian War it still highlights Sparta's perennial financial problems (Thuc. 1.80.4, 121.3, 141.3; doc. 6.42). [*IG* V.1 1; *SIG*[3] 84]

... to the Spartans ... darics ... to the Spartans for the war nine minas and ten staters. Given to the Spartans by ... son of Lykeidas ... from Olenos has given to the Spartans for the war for the rowers 32 minas of silver ... The friends ... at Chios ... Aeginetan staters. ... have given to the Spartans for the war 4,000 medimnoi and another 4,000 medimnoi and ... raisins ... so many talents. ... son of ... has given to the Spartans many ... and 800 darics and three talents of silver. ... for the war a talent and 30 minas of silver and 3,000 medimnoi and also ... -ty medimnoi and 60 minas of silver. The Ephesians have given to the Spartans for the war 1,000 darics.

Given by the Melians to the Spartans silver twenty minas. Given by Molon of Lokri to the Spartans ... talents of silver. Given by the Melians to the Spartans ...

14.8 Xenophon *Hellenika* 4.2.1–4: Sparta Abandons the War in Asia Minor in 394 BC

Agesilaos had been operating in Asia Minor 396–395 but was recalled to Sparta in 394 BC to assist in the Corinthian War, and the Spartans abandoned the Greek cities to the Persians, Agesilaos promising to return. But by the terms of the King's Peace of 386 BC (doc. 14.12), Sparta formally abandoned the Greeks of Asia Minor, who had to await Alexander's invasion of Asia Minor to be freed from Persian control.

1 Once the Spartans knew for certain that the money (from Timokrates) had reached Greece and that the greatest cities had combined for war against them, they realised that their city was in danger and considered it essential to mobilise their troops. **2** And, while they were making preparations for this, they immediately sent Epikydidas to fetch Agesilaos. When Epikydidas arrived he explained the state of affairs and that the polis was summoning Agesilaos to come to the assistance of his country as soon as possible. **3** When Agesilaos heard this, although he was perturbed and mindful of the honours and expectations he would be deprived of, he nevertheless assembled the allies, told them what the polis had instructed, and stated that they had to go to the assistance of his country. 'But if events turn out successfully,' he proclaimed, 'be assured, my allies, that I shall not forget you, but will come back again to perform whatever you request.' **4** When they heard this many burst into tears, but they all voted to go with Agesilaos to the assistance of Sparta, and afterwards, if all there went well, to ensure his return back to Asia.

14.9 *SIG*[3] 122: Athens' Alliance with Boeotia in 396/5 BC

In 395 BC Athens allied herself with the Boeotian league and Corinth against Sparta in the Corinthian War (395–386 BC). While the Corinthians and Thebans had been vocal in demanding the total destruction of Athens in 404 BC (doc. 13.35), Corinth, Thebes and the Persians were now in conflict with their former ally Sparta and in league with their enemy of the Peloponnesian War, Athens. Ostensibly war broke out when Lokris appealed for assistance from Thebes against Phokis, which appealed to Sparta. But the background was wide concern about the spread of Spartan power. The King's Peace concluded the Corinthian War (Xen. *Hell.* 3.5.1–5.1.24; Diod. 14.81–109). [*IG* II^2 14; Tod 2.101; Harding 14; R&O 6]

Gods. Alliance of the Boeotians and Athenians in perpetuity. If anyone comes in war against the Athenians either by land or sea, the Boeotians shall come to their help with all their strength as the Athenians request as far as possible. And if anyone comes in war against the Boeotians either by land or sea, the Athenians …

14.10 Tod 2.107: The Re-fortification of the Piraeus in 395/4 BC

Athens' walls had been demolished at the end of the Peloponnesian War (doc. 13.35). Rebuilding its fortifications was crucial to Athens' independence; Persian funds from Pharnabazos assisted the project in 393 BC. A large contingent of Boeotians was involved in this project; as is usually noted, the Thebans had been keen just a decade earlier, in 404 BC, to destroy Athens completely. Cf. Xen. *Hell.* 4.8.9–10; Diod. 14.85.2–3. [*SIG*^{3} 124–25; *IG* II^2 1656–57; R&O 9]

A In Diophantes' archonship (395/4 BC) in the month of Skirophorion the following sums were paid for the daily work: for the teams bringing the stone blocks, cost 160 drachmas; for iron tools, cost 53 drachmas.

B In Euboulides' archonship (394/3 BC) for the section beginning with the marker as far as the pillar between the gates by the shrine of Aphrodite on the right hand side as one exits, 790 drachmas. Contractor: Demosthenes the Boeotian including the transport of the stone blocks.

14.11 Xenophon *Hellenika* 4.8.8–9: Persia Interferes in Greece in 393 BC

The satrap Pharnabazos and Konon, after the naval victory at Knidos, replaced Spartan governors (harmosts) in the Greek cities along the coast of Asia Minor. Pharnabazos took the fleet to Greece in 393 to attack Spartan territory and supported Athens financially. The wall around the Piraeus had been destroyed at the end of the Peloponnesian War, but the rebuilding of the walls actually began in 395/4 BC: doc. 14.10.

8 When those who were in charge of the city of the Kytherans, afraid that they would be taken by force, abandoned their walls, Pharnabazos allowed them to leave for Lakonia under a truce, and he repaired the Kytherans' walls and left in Kythera a garrison and Nikephoros, an Athenian, as harmost. After doing this and sailing to the Isthmus of Corinth and encouraging the allies to carry on the war with enthusiasm and show themselves loyal to the King, he left them all the money he had and sailed off home. **9** But Konon said that if he would let him have the fleet, he would support its upkeep with contributions from the islands, and sail to Athens and rebuild the Long Walls and the wall around the Piraeus for the Athenians – saying that he knew there could be no heavier blow than this for the Spartans. 'So,' he said, 'by doing this you will both gratify the Athenians and take revenge on the Spartans, for you will undo the act into which they put their hardest work.' When Pharnabazos heard this he was happy to send him to Athens and also gave him money for the rebuilding.

14.12 Xenophon *Hellenika* 5.1.30–31: The 'King's Peace' of 386 BC

The Spartans were hard pressed by their enemies and sent their admiral Antalkidas to make peace between the Spartans and the Persian King Artaxerxes II in 386 BC. The Greek cities of Asia Minor, the islands and Cyprus were to be under Persian control: the Athenians and Thebans were concerned at this but the Persian threat to make war against any city that did not accept these terms pre-empted any action; the other Greeks were to be independent. Sparta's position as the leading state of Greece was re-established. Cf. Diod. 14.109.2.

30 When Tiribazos instructed all those to assemble who desired to adhere to the peace terms which the King had dispatched, everyone immediately presented themselves. When they were all together, Tiribazos showed them the King's seals and read out what was written. This was as follows:

31 King Artaxerxes thinks it right that the cities in Asia should belong to him, as well as the islands Klazomenai and Cyprus, and that the other Greek cities, both great and small, should be autonomous, except for Lemnos, Imbros and Skyros, which should belong to the Athenians as of old. I will make war on whoever does not accept these peace terms, by land and by sea, providing both ships and money for this purpose, assisted by all those who are willing to accept them.

14.13 Cornelius Nepos *Pelopidas* 16.2.5, 16.3.1–3: Pelopidas Liberates Thebes in 379 BC

The Boeotian League (cf. docs 1.57–58) was disbanded under the prescription that all Greek cities were to be free. But in 382 BC the Spartan Phoibidas captured the citadel of Thebes, the Kadmeia, in defiance of the King's Peace. Pelopidas was exiled from Thebes in that year but with a few followers seized the Kadmeia in 379. As Boeotarch he defeated the Spartans at Tegyra (375) and spectacularly at Leuktra (371). Epameinondas and he were the main leaders of Thebes during the hegemony it established in Greece from 371 to 362. The Greeks hunted hares on foot with hounds and nets. Capture of Kadmeia: Xen. *Hell.* 5.4.1–12; Diod. 15.25–27.

2.5 So these twelve men, with Pelopidas as their leader, left Athens by day in order to reach Thebes by nightfall, taking hunting hounds with them, carrying hunting nets, and wearing rustic clothing to ensure that their journey attracted less suspicion. They arrived at exactly the time planned, and stayed at the home of Charon who had given the time and the day.

3.1 At this point I would like to digress, although this is off the actual topic, to note what danger there can be in overconfidence. For the report came at once to the Theban magistrates that exiles had arrived in the city, but being seriously engaged in drinking and banqueting they considered the news so unimportant that they did not even bother to enquire into so serious a matter … **3** All these magistrates, during the course of the night, were slaughtered as they slept off their intoxication by the exiles, led by Pelopidas. With this achieved, the people were called to arms and liberty, and hastened to the spot, not just those in the city, but also those from throughout the countryside. They expelled the Spartan garrison from the citadel and freed their fatherland from occupation, with those who had brought about the takeover of the Kadmeia being slaughtered or driven into exile.

14.14 Diodorus *Library of History* 15.28.1–5, 29.5–8, 30.2: The Athenians Stir up Greece, 377/6 BC

Pelopidas' success in ousting the Spartans from Thebes led to the reforming of the Boeotian League. In addition, the Athenians founded the Second Athenian Confederacy, 'so that the Spartans may allow the Greeks, free and autonomous, to live in peace' (doc. 14.15); the Athenians were also clearly aware of the unpopularity of their cleruchies and so restored the territory to their former owners to gain their support. In reaction, Sphodrias raided Attica without the ephors' permission, but was acquitted, largely because his son and Agesilaos' son were lovers (Xen. *Hell.* 5.4.20–33).

15.28.1 After the failure of the Spartans at Thebes, the Boeotians plucked up their courage and united, forming an alliance, and gathered a considerable force, expecting that the Spartans would arrive in Boeotia with a vast army. **2** The Athenians sent their most respected men as ambassadors to the cities that were subject to the Spartans, urging them to give their support to the common freedom. For the Spartans, because of the magnitude of their forces, were governing their subjects arrogantly and harshly, and as a result many of those under Spartan rule were beginning to incline towards the Athenians. **3** The first to respond to the call for revolt were the people of Chios and Byzantium, and they were followed by the peoples of Rhodes and Mytilene and some of the other islanders; and, as the movement gathered momentum throughout Greece, many cities joined the Athenians. The Athenian people, overjoyed by the goodwill of the cities, set up a common council (synedrion) of all the allies and appointed delegates to it from all cities. **4** It was agreed by common consent that the council should meet in Athens, but that in the interests of equity each city, whether great or small, should cast only one vote and that all should be autonomous, under the leadership of Athens.

The Spartans saw that they could not prevent the cities' desire for autonomy, but through envoys, friendly words and even promises of future benefits tried their hardest to win back the peoples they had alienated. **5** They gave equal time to their preparations for war, for they anticipated that the Boeotian war would involve them in a major, lengthy conflict, as the Athenians and all the other Greeks who took part in the council were allies of the Thebans …

29.5 The truce which the Spartans and Athenians had made earlier on (387 BC) had remained in force up until now. But at this point the Spartan king Kleombrotos prevailed on Sphodrias the Spartan, who had been placed in command and who was naturally haughty and rash, to seize the Piraeus without consulting the ephors. **6** With more than 10,000 soldiers Sphodrias attempted to take the Piraeus by night, but being detected by the Athenians and failing in his attempt, had to return unsuccessful. He was prosecuted before the Spartans' council, but was unfairly acquitted because of the support of the kings. **7** As a consequence, the Athenians, who were extremely angry at what had happened, voted that the Spartans had broken the truce. They decided to make war on them and selected three of their most distinguished citizens as generals, Timotheos, Chabrias and Kallistratos, and agreed to raise 20,000 hoplites and 500 cavalry and to man 200 ships. They also allowed the Thebans to join the common council on equal terms in every respect. **8** They also voted to restore the territory settled as cleruchies to the former owners, and made a law that no Athenian should farm land outside of Attica. By this act of generosity they regained the Greeks' goodwill, and made their own leadership more secure … **30.2** Seventy cities in the end entered into an alliance with the Athenians and participated on equal terms in the common council. So, with the continual increase of Athenian power and the decrease of that of the Spartans, the two states were now well matched.

14.15 Tod 2.123: The Second Athenian 'Confederacy', 377 BC

This decree, proposed by Aristoteles (after whom it is sometimes named), concerning the foundation of the Second Athenian Confederacy, has a list of member states at the end, and new cities were added as they joined the alliance, with sixty names listed here (cf. Aeschines 2.70: 75 cities; Diod. 15.30.2: 70 cities). The gap at line 15 was erased in antiquity and is usually restored as 'in its entirety and so that there may continue in validity for all time the Common Peace that was sworn by the Greeks and the King in accordance with the agreements'. When the Athenians established this confederacy in 377 BC, they aimed at avoiding features of the Delian League which had been unpopular. They kept their promise about cleruchies: two only are known from the fourth century, and they were sent to non-allies, Samos and Potidaea (at Potidaea's request, *IG* II^2 11; Tod 2.146); but there were garrisons in some allied states. [*IG* II^2 43; Harding 35; R&O 22.]

In the archonship of Nausinikos, Kallibios son of Kephisophon of Paiania was secretary.

When Hippothontis held the seventh prytany (spring 377), the Council and the people resolved, Charinos of (the deme) Athmonon presided, Aristoteles proposed the motion: to the good fortune of the Athenians and the allies of the Athenians, so that the Spartans may allow the Greeks, free and autonomous, to live in peace, holding with security the territory which is their own ... Proposed to the people: If anyone wishes of the Greeks or barbarians who live on the mainland, or anyone of the islanders who are not subject to the King, to be an ally of the Athenians and their allies, he shall be allowed to do so, remaining free and autonomous, living under whatever constitution he wants, neither receiving a garrison nor having a governor put over him nor paying tribute, but shall become an ally on the same terms as those by which the Chians and Thebans and the other allies did. To those who have allied themselves with the Athenians and their allies, the people shall hand over the properties, however many there may be, held either privately or publicly by Athenians in the country of those who are making the alliance and shall give a pledge concerning these properties ...

If it is the case that regarding the cities who are making this alliance with the Athenians there are inscriptions (stelai) at Athens unfavourable to them, the Council at the time in office shall have the power to destroy them. After the archonship of Nausinikos it shall not be permitted for any Athenian, either privately or publicly, to possess in the lands of the allies either a house or a plot of land, whether by purchase, or as the result of a mortgage, or through any other means at all. If anyone does purchase or acquire or take such a property on mortgage through any other means at all, any of the allies who wishes shall be permitted to lay an indictment before the delegates of the allies. The delegates, after selling the property, are to give half (the amount) to the person who laid the indictment, while the rest is to belong in common to the allies.

If anyone comes with the aim of making war, either by land or by sea, against those who have made the alliance, the Athenians and their allies will assist them both by land and by sea, with all their strength and to the best of their ability. If anyone proposes or puts to the vote, whether a magistrate or a private citizen, anything contrary to this decree, that it is necessary to rescind any of the enactments laid down in this decree, the penalty for him shall be to be deprived of his civic rights and his possessions to become public property, with the goddess to take a tithe, and he shall be tried among the Athenians and the allies on the grounds of breaking the alliance and shall be punished by death or exile from all lands under the control of the Athenians and allies. If he is condemned to death, he shall not be buried in Attica, nor in the country of the allies.

With regard to this decree, the secretary of the Council shall have it inscribed on a stele of marble and have it placed next to the sanctuary of Zeus Eleutherios. The money for the inscription of the stele, sixty drachmas, shall be given out of the Ten Talents, by the treasurers of the goddess. On this stele shall be inscribed the names both of the cities that are allied and of any city that becomes an ally. This information shall be inscribed, and there shall be chosen by the people three ambassadors to go immediately to Thebes, to persuade the Thebans to do whatever good they can. Chosen: Aristoteles of Marathon, Pyrrhandros of Anaphlystos, Thrasyboulos of Kollytos.

These states are allies of the Athenians: Chians, Tenedians, Thebans, Mytilenaeans, Chalcidians, Methymnaians, Eretrians, Rhodians, Poiessians, Arethousians, Byzantines, Karystians, Perinthians, Ikians, Peparethians, Pal ..., Sciathians, ... Maroneans, ..., Dians, ..., Parians, Ol ..., ..., Athenitai, Pl ..., ... Aristoteles proposed the motion: since first ... of their own free will they join ... what has been voted by the people and the ... of islands into the alliance ... things that have been voted ...

Left side: Of the ... raians the people, Abderites, Thasians, Chalcidians from Thrace, Ainians, Samothracians, Dikaiopolitans, Akarnanians, of the Kephallenians Pronnoi; Alketas, Neoptolemos, ..., Andrians, Tenians, Hestiaians, Mykonians, Antissaians, Eresians, Astraiousans, of the Keans the Iulietai, Karthaians, Koressians, Elaiousians, Amorgians, Selymbrians, Siphnians, Sikinetans, Dians from Thrace, Neapolitans. Of the Zakynthians the people in the Nellos.

SPARTA, THEBES AND THE BATTLE OF LEUKTRA IN 371 BC

Sparta had taken possession of the Theban citadel, the Kadmeia, in 382 BC and exiled its opponents. In 379 Pelopidas and a handful of young men recovered Thebes and instituted a democracy (doc. 14.13). In 375 Pelopidas defeated the Spartans at Tegyra in Boeotia: Diod. 15.37, Plut. *Pelop.* 16–17.

14.16 Plutarch *Life of Agesilaos* 27.4–28.4: Agesilaos and Epameinondas

Epameinondas and Pelopidas dominated Theban, and in fact Greek, affairs generally, in the two decades of the 370s–360s. The peace conference in 371 BC led to war between Sparta and Thebes on the issue of Boeotian independence as interpreted by Agesilaos (see also Xen. *Hell.* 6.3.1–4.1). For the Boeotian constitution, see docs 1.57–58. Athens, concerned at the Theban treatment of their allies the Plataeans and the Phokians, accepted the peace.

27.4 In this period the Spartans suffered many defeats both by land and by sea; the worst of these was at Tegyra where for the first time they were defeated by the Thebans (under Pelopidas) in a pitched battle (375 BC). **5** Everyone thought it was a good idea to make a general peace, and ambassadors from all over Greece met at Sparta to settle the terms. **6** One of these was Epameinondas, a person renowned for his culture and philosophy, but who had not yet given proof of his skill as a general. **7** He saw all the others deferring to Agesilaos and was the only one who had the courage to speak out openly, making a speech not on behalf of the Thebans, but on behalf of the whole of Greece, declaring that war made Sparta great at the expense of the sufferings of all the rest, and asserting that peace should be made on terms of equity and justice, as it would only last if everyone became equal.

28.1 When Agesilaos saw that the Greeks listened to him with the highest approval and attention he asked him whether he thought it 'just and equal' for the cities of Boeotia to be self-governing (not ruled by Thebes). **2** Epameinondas immediately and boldly asked him in reply whether he thought it just for Lakonia to be self-governing, and Agesilaos jumped up and angrily told him to say plainly whether he was going to make Boeotia independent. **3** Epameinondas replied again in the same way by asking if he was going to make Lakonia independent, at which Agesilaos became violently angry and was glad of the excuse to immediately erase the Thebans' name from the peace treaty and declare war on them. **4** He told the other Greeks to go home, now they were at peace with each other, and deal with their curable differences in peace and their incurable ones in war, for it would be hard work to clear up and settle all their disputes.

14.17 Plutarch *Life of Pelopidas* 18.1–4, 18.7, 19.3–4: The Theban 'Sacred Band'

An elite force of 300 men, established perhaps in 379 BC by Gorgidas when the Spartan garrison was expelled from Thebes, the Sacred Band comprised 150 pairs of male lovers utilising the strengths of homosexual pair-bonding. Initially distributed through the infantry, they were used as a unit after the battle of Tegyra, and played a critical role at the battle of Leuktra. They were annihilated at Chaironeia in 338 BC. Pammenes was a Theban general in the 360/350s.

18.1 The Sacred Band, it is said, was first formed by Gorgidas from 300 chosen men, for whom the city provided training and maintenance and who encamped in the Kadmeia, which is why they were also called the city band, for in those days citadels were properly called cities. **2** And some say that this corps was made up of lovers and beloveds. A witty remark of Pammenes is recorded, where he said that Homer's Nestor was no tactician when he told the Greeks to form companies by tribes and clans, 'that clan should give support to clan and tribe to tribe' (*Iliad* 2.363), since he ought to have stationed lover by beloved. **3** For tribesmen care little for tribesmen or clansmen for clansmen in times of danger, whereas a body of men held together by the affection between lovers is indissoluble and unbreakable, since the lovers and beloveds through shame stand firm to protect each other when in danger. **4** This is nothing to wonder at since men respect their lovers even when absent more than others who are present, as in the case of the man who begged his enemy who was about to slay him where he lay to run his sword through his breast, 'so that,' he said, my beloved may not feel shame at seeing my body with a wound in the back.' … **7** It is said, too, that the band remained unbeaten until the battle of Chaironeia (338 BC); and when, after the battle, Philip was inspecting the dead and stopped at the place where the 300 were all lying in their armour mingled with each other where they had faced and met his sarissas, he was amazed, and on learning that that this was the band of lovers and beloveds he wept and said, 'May those who suspect these men of doing or suffering anything shameful perish miserably!' … **19.3** Gorgidas, then, by breaking up this sacred band among the front ranks of the whole hoplite phalanx, made the valour of these men inconspicuous, nor did he make use of their strength against a common object as it was clearly dissipated when intermixed with a large, inferior body, **4** but Pelopidas, after their valour had shone out at Tegyra, where they fought round him as an entity, never again divided or dispersed them, but treated them as a single body of men and put them at the front to bear the brunt of the danger in the most critical conflicts.

14.18 Xenophon *Hellenika* 6.4.13–16, 19–20: The Battle of Leuktra in 371 BC

The Spartan king Kleombrotos led the Spartans into southern Boeotia, and camped at Leuktra; the Thebans encamped opposite, with no allies except other Boeotians; a plain separated them. Not all the Thebans had wanted to fight the Spartans at Leuktra but Epameinondas persuaded them to do so. The Spartans put their cavalry in front of their phalanx and so too did the Thebans in response. Xenophon notes that the Theban cavalry was greatly superior to the Spartans'. The Spartan cavalry when it engaged was pushed back into the ranks of the Spartan hoplites, where the line was only twelve men deep (as opposed to the Thebans' fifty); the Spartans lost the battle; Sphodrias was killed; 400 Spartans died; and Kleombrotos later died of his wounds. The era of Spartan military supremacy was over; when a Theban messenger announced the news to the Athenian boule (Council) at Athens he was met with a stony silence and none of the usual diplomatic niceties, and left without having been given a reply: Athens was now apprehensive of Theban power. Cf. Xen. *Hell.* 6.4.1–15; Diod. 15.55–56; Plut. *Pel.* 23.

6.4.13 When Kleombrotos began to lead his men against the enemy, first of all, before his army had even noticed that he was leading them out, the cavalry had already engaged, with the Spartan horse speedily defeated. As they fled, they had fallen upon their own hoplites, and to make things worse the companies of the Thebans were already on the attack. Nevertheless, the fact that Kleombrotos and his men were victorious in the battle at first may be known by this clear piece of evidence, for his men would not have been able to pick him up and carry him off still alive, unless those fighting in front of him were getting the best of it at that point. **14** When, however, Deinon the polemarch, Sphodrias, one of the king's council, and his son Kleonymos had been killed, then the hippeis, the polemarch's so-called aides, and the rest fell back under the pressure of the Theban force, while those on the Spartans' left wing gave way when they saw that the right wing was being pushed back. But though many had been killed and they had been defeated, when they crossed the trench which happened to be in front of their camp, they grounded their arms at the spot from which they had set out. The camp was not, in fact, on level ground, but rather on a slope. Following this, some of the Spartans, thinking this disaster unendurable, said that they ought to stop the enemy from setting up their trophy, and try to recover their dead, not under a truce but by fighting.

15 The polemarchs, however, saw that out of all the Spartan army nearly 1,000 were dead, while of the 700 Spartiates on the campaign some 400 had been killed, and they realised that none of their allies had the heart for further fighting, while some of them were actually not displeased at what had happened. So they gathered together the most important men and discussed what they ought to do. As everyone considered that they should recover their dead under a truce, they accordingly sent a herald to request one. The Thebans then erected a trophy and gave back the dead under a truce.

16 Following this, the messenger sent to carry the news of the catastrophe to Sparta arrived there on the final day of the festival of the Gymnopaidia, when the men's choruses were performing. When the ephors learned of the catastrophe, they were deeply distressed, as in my view was inevitable, though they did not take the chorus off, but allowed the contest to finish. And while they gave the names of the dead to the relatives of each, they instructed the women not to lament publicly, but to bear the disaster in silence. Indeed, on the next day, the relatives of the men who had died were seen going round in public with bright and cheerful faces, while of those whose relatives had been announced as still living you saw only a few out and about, and they looked downcast and ashamed …

19 Straight after the battle the Thebans sent a messenger crowned with garlands to Athens, both to stress the importance of their victory and to urge them to come to their assistance, declaring that it was now possible for them to get revenge on Sparta for everything that had been done to them. **20** The Athenian Council chanced to be sitting at the time on the acropolis, and when they heard what had happened it was clear to everyone that they were extremely annoyed, as they did not offer the herald any hospitality, and made no reply to his request for help. So the herald left Athens without a response.

14.19 Tod 2.130: The Thebans Triumph

This epigram celebrates the part played by three Theban leaders at the battle of Leuktra. Theopompos had been one of Pelopidas' companions in the expedition leading to the expulsion of the Spartans from Thebes in 379 BC; Xenokrates was one of the Boeotarchs, who supported Epameinondas in attacking the Spartans at Leuktra: Plut. *Pelop.* 8.2; Paus. 9.13.6–7. [*IG* VII 2462; Hansen 632; R&O 30.]

Xenokrates
Theopompos
Mnasilaos.
When the Spartan spear was pre-eminent,
Xenokrates won by lot the duty of bringing trophies in honour of Zeus,
Being unafraid of both the army from Eurotas and the Lakonian
Shield. 'The Thebans are greater in war'
Announces the victory trophies won by the spear at Leuktra,
Nor in the contest did we come second to Epameinondas.

14.20 Xenophon *Hellenika* 6.5.22–32: The Thebans Invade the Peloponnese in 370 BC

After Leuktra, Thebes became the 'liberator' of Greece. Plut. *Ages*. 31 states that the Thebans had a force of 40,000 men (cf. Diod. 15.62). Due to his service with Sparta and loyalty to it, Xenophon fails to mention that Messenia became independent. Note the Spartans' fear of helots in arms even when they are on their own side (29).

6.5.22 Once Agesilaos had left and the Arkadians learned that his army had been disbanded, they made, while they were still mustered, an expedition against Heraia, not only because the Heraians were unwilling to be part of the Arkadian league but because they had accompanied the Spartans in their invasion of Arkadia. After attacking they began to burn down the houses and fell the trees. But they then heard that the Thebans who were coming to their rescue had arrived in Mantineia and so they left Heraia and joined forces with the Thebans. **23** Once the forces had united, the Thebans were pleased with their situation, since they had come to bring assistance and yet could see no one any longer around to fight in the region and were accordingly making preparations for going home. But the Arkadians, Argives and Eleians urged them to lead the way into Lakonia as quickly as possible, pointing out the size of their own forces and eulogising the Thebans' army. For the Boeotians were all now in training as soldiers in their pride at their victory at Leuktra, and they were followed by the Phokians, who had become their subjects, the Euboeans from all Euboea's cities, both sets of Lokrians, the Akarnanians, the Herakleotes and the Malians, and by cavalry and peltasts from Thessaly. Seeing this and declaring that Sparta was deserted they entreated the Thebans not to turn back before they had invaded Spartan territory ...

25 At this point men arrived from Karyai reporting the absence of the Spartans and promising to guide them themselves, telling the Thebans to put them to death if they were found to be deceiving them in any way. Some of the perioikoi as well turned up inviting their aid and declaring that they would revolt even if the Thebans only made an appearance in the region, and stating that the perioikoi were at that very moment being summoned by the Spartans and were refusing to go and help them. So as a result of hearing all this from all sides, the Thebans were convinced and with their own forces invaded by way of Karyai, while the Arkadians went via Oion in Skiritis ...

27 They did not attempt to cross the bridge and attack the city, because they could see hoplites ready to meet them in the sanctuary of Athena Alea. Instead, keeping the Eurotas on their right hand side, they went along burning and plundering houses full of many valuable items. **28** As for the people in the city, the women could not even endure looking at the smoke, for they had never seen an enemy before, while the Spartiates, whose city was unwalled, were posted at intervals here and there on guard, though there were, as was obvious, very few of them. The authorities also decided to proclaim to the helots that if any of them chose to take up arms and join the ranks they would be given a guarantee that all who participated in the fighting would be given their freedom. **29** It was reported that at first more than 6,000 enlisted, so that when they were marshalled together the Spartans were again afraid, as there seemed to be far too many of them. But when the mercenaries from Orchomenos remained loyal, and the Phleiasians, Corinthians, Epidaurians and Pelleneians and some other cities supported the Spartans, they were less concerned about those who had enlisted. **30** In the meantime the invading army had got as far as Amyklai, where they crossed the Eurotas ... On the third or fourth day the cavalry advanced in their ranks into the racecourse in the sanctuary of (Poseidon) the Earthshaker, including the full force of the Thebans, the Eleians and all the cavalry present of the Phokians, Thessalians and Lokrians. **31** The Spartans' cavalry, and very few they seemed to be, were drawn up to face them. The Spartans had laid an ambush of about 300 of their younger hoplites in the house of the Tyndaridai, and at the same moment these rushed out and the cavalry charged. The enemy did not stand to face the attack but fell back. When they saw this many of the infantry also turned to flight. But when the pursuers halted and the Theban army stayed firm they again encamped. **32** It now seemed less likely that they would make another attempt on the city, and in fact the army departed taking the direction of Helos and Gytheion. They burned any cities that were unwalled, and made a three-day attack on Gytheion, which was the site of the Spartans' shipyards. Some of the perioikoi took part in the attack and also joined the troops serving with the Thebans.

14.21 Pausanias *Description of Greece* 8.27.1–2: The Foundation of Megalopolis

Megalopolis in Arkadia was founded in the period following the Theban victory at Leuktra (between 370 and 367 BC), though Xenophon fails to mention this: *Hell.* 6.5.1–14; cf. Diod. 15.72.4. Several Arkadian cities provided oikistai, but the main role was played by Epameinondas according to Pausanias. Mantineia (also in Arkadia), whose population had been 'de-synoikoised' (split up into its original villages) and the city destroyed by the Spartans in 385 BC (Xen. *Hell.* 5.2.5–7; Diod. 15.5.3–4, 12.2), was also refounded and its walls rebuilt; Agesilaos went there and unsuccessfully attempted to stop this. Megalopolis remained the most important Arkadian city for two centuries and was the birthplace of Polybios, the historian of Rome.

8.27.1 Megalopolis is the youngest city, not only of Arkadia but of Greece as well, with the exception of those whose inhabitants have been removed by the circumstance of Roman rule ... **2** It was with this purpose (of self-defence) in mind that the Arkadians synoikised, and Epameinondas of Thebes could fairly be called their oikistes; for it was he who encouraged the Arkadians to undertake synoikismos and sent one thousand picked Thebans and Pammenes to defend them, in case the Spartans tried to prevent its foundation.

14.22 Pausanias *Description of Greece* 4.26.5–27.11: The Messenians Return Home

Epameinondas freed the Messenian helots and Messenia, and invaded Sparta's territory in 370, 369 and 367 BC. A new city, Messene, was founded as the capital on the western slopes of Mt Ithome, where the helots had revolted in the 480s BC. Most of the Messenians had of course stayed in the Peloponnese as helots. The freeing of the helots and the re-establishment of Messenia as a separate state meant the end of the helot system and undermined the basis of Sparta's agricultural system. Sparta henceforth went into decline.

26.5 After their victory at Leuktra the Thebans sent messengers to Italy, Sicily and Euesperides (Cyrene) and summoned the Messenians to the Peloponnese from everywhere else they might be. And they gathered more quickly than might have been expected because of their longing for their country and eternal hatred of the Spartans ... **27.5** As Epameinondas considered the most suitable place for the foundation to be where the city of the Messenians now stands, he instructed the diviners to make enquiry as to whether the gods' favour would follow him here. When they reported that the omens were auspicious, he started preparations for the foundation, ordering stone to be brought and summoning men skilled in laying out streets and constructing houses and temples and walls to encompass them.

6 When everything was ready, with the Arkadians providing the sacrificial victims, Epameinondas himself and the Thebans then sacrificed to Dionysos and Apollo Ismenios in their customary fashion, the Argives to Argive Hera and Nemean Zeus, the Messenians to Zeus of Ithome and the Dioskouroi, and their priests to the Great Goddesses and Kaukon.

Together they all summoned their heroes to return and dwell with them — first Messene daughter of Triopas, and after her Eurytos, Aphareus and his children, and Kresphontes and Aipytos of the sons of Herakles. The loudest summons from everyone was for Aristomenes. **7** They remained engaged in sacrifice and prayer for that day, but on the succeeding days they raised the circuit of the walls and within them built houses and the temples. They worked to the accompaniment of music, but only from Boeotian and Argive flutes — the tunes of Sakadas and Pronomos were brought into fierce competition. They gave the city itself the name Messene, but they also founded other towns. The people of Nauplia were not disturbed at Mothone; **8** and they allowed the people of Asine to remain in their country, as they remembered their kindness in refusing to make war against them with the Spartans. And when the Messenians returned to the Peloponnese the people of Nauplia brought them whatever gifts they had and, while constantly praying to the gods for their return, also begged them to give them their protection.

9 The Messenians returned to the Peloponnese and recovered their own country two hundred and eighty seven years after the capture of Eira, in the archonship of Dyskinetos at Athens and in the third year of the 102nd Olympiad (370 BC), when Damon of Thurioi was victorious for the second time ... **11** The Messenians were wanderers outside the Peloponnese for nearly 300 years, during which time it is clear that they abandoned not a single one of their customs, nor did they lose their Doric dialect, and in fact to our day they have preserved its purity more than the other Peloponnesians.

14.23 Diodorus *Library of History* 15.66.1: Epameinondas and Messene, 369 BC

15.66.1 Epameinondas, who was by nature ambitious and desirous of eternal fame, advised the Arkadians and other allies to found Messene, which had been destroyed many years before by the Spartans, for it was ideally situated as a base from which to attack Sparta. When they all agreed, he sought out those Messenians who remained, registered as citizens any of the others who so wished, and refounded Messene with a large number of inhabitants. By dividing up the land among them and constructing buildings, he restored a fine Greek city and won a great reputation among all people.

EVENTS IN NORTHERN GREECE

14.24 Xenophon *Hellenika* 6.4.27–32: Iason of Pherai, 371–370 BC

Lykophron had established a tyranny at Pherai in Thessaly *c.* 406 BC. Iason was apparently his son and became tagos (commander) of Thessaly and unified it, turning it into a significant power; conflict with Phokis ensued. Iason was allied with the Thebans, and after Leuktra they sent for him. They wished to annihilate the remaining Spartan forces at Leuktra but Iason persuaded them not to (on the grounds that the Spartans would now be desperate and might inflict a defeat on them). Peace was arranged and the Spartans withdrew. Xenophon argues that he did this so that the two sides would continue in conflict and might need his assistance. On his way back from Leuktra Iason destroyed Herakleia, ensuring his access to southern Greece, where he presumably had territorial ambitions. These were ended by his assassination in 370 – which Xenophon attributed to fears that he would become tyrant of Greece. Control of the Pythian festival showed Iason's power in Greek affairs. Cf. Xen. *Hell.* 6.4.20–32; Diod. 15.57.2, 60.1–5.

6.4.27 On his way back through Phokis, Iason seized the outer city of the Hyampolitans, ravaged their territory and killed many of them, but he crossed through the rest of Phokis without hostility. At Herakleia he destroyed the wall of the Herakleots, clearly not afraid that with this passage (Thermopylai) open anyone would march against his kingdom, but rather having in mind the probability that anyone who seized Herakleia, situated as it was in a narrow pass, could block his way if he desired to march anywhere in Greece. **28** And when he returned to Thessaly he was extremely powerful, not only because he had legally been made tagos of the Thessalians, but because he kept with him a number of mercenaries, both infantry and cavalry, all of whom had been trained to the highest proficiency. He was even more powerful due to his numerous allies, those whom he already had and those who wished to become so. And he was the most powerful of all the men of his time as there was no one who could look down on him.

29 At the approach of the Pythian festival he instructed his cities to prepare oxen, sheep, goats and pigs for the sacrifice. And it was said that, although his demands on any city were only moderate, there were no less than one thousand oxen and more than ten thousand of the other animals. He also proclaimed that there would be the prize of a golden crown for whichever city reared the finest ox to lead the sacrifice in honour of the god. **30** And he ordered the Thessalians to make preparations for an expedition at the time of the Pythian festival, for he intended, it was said, to preside over both the festival in honour of the god and the games. His intentions with regard to the sacred treasure are unclear even today, but it is reported that when the Delphians asked the god what action they should take, should he try to seize any of the god's treasure, the god replied that he would take care of it. **31** So this great man, then, who had so many and such great plans, after reviewing and inspecting the Pheraian cavalry, was sitting in judgement and responding when anyone came forward with a request, when he was struck down and killed by seven young men who came up to him as if they were quarrelling with each other. **32** When the guardsmen beside him rushed forcefully to his assistance, one of them was run through with a spear and killed while still in the act of striking Iason; another was seized while he was mounting his horse and died of the numerous wounds he received; and the rest jumped onto the horses which were in readiness and escaped. In most of the Greek cities to which they went they were honoured, from which it is clear that the Greeks were extremely afraid in case Iason became a tyrant.

14.25 Diodorus *Library of History* 16.2.1–3.3: The Accession of Philip of Macedon

Philip of Macedon (382–336 BC) was responsible for transforming Macedon, which had hitherto played a secondary role in Greek affairs, into a major power which dominated Greece and eventually comprehensively defeated the Greeks at Chaironeia in 338 BC. His brother Perdikkas was killed in a major clash with the Illyrians in 360/59 BC: this brought Philip to the throne. Philip had been a hostage at Thebes, probably in 369–367 BC, which turned out to be an important part of his upbringing. Diodorus also describes Philip's adoption of the phalanx: the Macedonian soldiers, armed with a long spear called the sarissa (doc. 14.41), were trained to fight in small units within the overall structure of the army.

16.2.1 When Kallimedes was archon of Athens (360/59 BC), the 150th celebration of the Olympic festival was held at which Poros of Cyrene won the stadion and the Romans elected as consuls Cn. Genucius and L. Aemilius. During their year of office Philip, son of Amyntas and father of Alexander who defeated the Persians in war, became ruler of the Macedonian kingdom for the following reasons. **2** Amyntas had been defeated by the Illyrians, and forced to pay tribute to his conquerors; the Illyrians took Philip, the youngest of his sons, as hostage and put him in the care of the Thebans. They in turn put the young boy in the care of the father of Epameinondas and told him to keep good watch over his charge and to oversee his upbringing and education. **3** As Epameinondas had as his tutor a philosopher who was a Pythagorean, Philip who was brought up with him shared to a great extent this Pythagorean teaching. As both pupils possessed natural ability and diligence, both distinguished themselves in deeds of valour. Of the two of them, Epameinondas endured great contests and dangers and presented his homeland almost miraculously with the leadership of Greece, while Philip by making use of the same initial advantages did not fall short of Epameinondas' fame. **4** For after the death of Amyntas, Alexander (II) the eldest of his sons took over the throne. But Ptolemy of Aloros murdered him and took over the kingdom and then in similar fashion Perdikkas got rid of him and ruled as king. But when he was defeated in a great engagement with the Illyrians and fell in the heat of battle, his brother Philip, who had escaped from his position as hostage, succeeded to the kingdom, which was now in a bad way. **5** In the engagement the Macedonians had lost more than four thousand men, while the rest of them, struck with panic, were terrified of the Illyrian forces and had lost all enthusiasm for continuing the war. **6** At about this same time the Paionians, who live close to the Macedonians, showed their contempt of them by starting to ravage their territory, while the Illyrians began assembling large forces and making preparations to invade Macedonia. Moreover a certain Pausanias, who was related to the royal house, was conspiring along with the Thracian king to put in a claim to the Macedonian throne. Similarly the Athenians (who were hostile to Philip) were also trying to get Argaios back on the throne and had already sent off Mantias as general with three thousand hoplites and a large naval force.

16.3.1 As a consequence of the disastrous outcome of the battle and the magnitude of the dangers pressing upon them the Macedonians were at a total loss. Nevertheless, despite the fears and dangers threatening them, Philip did not panic at the extent of the disasters in store, but instead gathered the Macedonians in a series of assemblies, exhorted them with persuasively crafted speeches to be men, and instilled them with courage; and when he had improved the organisation of his forces and equipped his men with appropriate weapons he held continual musters of the men under arms and competitive training exercises. **2** He also devised the close-packed structure and equipment of the phalanx, imitating the method of fighting with shields overlapping used by the heroes at Troy, and was the originator of the Macedonian phalanx. **3** He was also courteous in his dealings with men and attempted through gifts and promises to win supreme popularity with the people, while attempting to counter the host of impending dangers by skilful manoeuvring.

14.26 Justin *Epitome Historiarum* 7.5.1–6.16: Philip II's Early Years

Alexander II (370–368 BC), Perdikkas and Philip were the three sons of Amyntas III of Macedon (*c.* 393–370) and Eurydike. Alexander was succeeded by Perdikkas, who died in battle against the Illyrians, leaving behind a young son Amyntas IV. In the early years of his reign (359–352 BC), Philip overcame the Athenians, who were supporting a rival (Argaios) to the throne, defeated the Illyrians, bought off the Thracians, and acquired Amphipolis and Pydna (357), Potidaea (356) and Methone (354), where he famously lost an eye. Philip's interventions in Thessaly began in 358 BC and met with setback in 353, but in 352 he defeated Pherai, was elected archon of Thessaly for life, and henceforth Thessaly's resources of cavalry and foot soldiers were at his disposal: for the effectiveness of the Thessalian cavalry, see docs 15.7, 15.11. Justin's epitome (summary) of the lost *Philippic Histories* of Pompeius Trogus (dating to the reign of Augustus) tends towards the sensationalist and moralising.

7.5.1 Alexander (II of Macedon) at the start of his reign purchased peace from the Illyrians with a sum of money and by giving his brother Philip as hostage. **2** Some time after this he also made peace with the Thebans by giving the same hostage, **3** which gave Philip a good opportunity to improve his extraordinary abilities, as he was kept at Thebes as a hostage for three years and received the first steps in his education in a city noted for its strict discipline, and in the house of Epameinondas, who was as pre-eminent a philosopher as he was a general. **4** Not long afterwards Alexander was killed in a plot by his mother Eurydike, **5** whom Amyntas, when she was convicted of conspiring against him, had spared for the sake of their mutual children, not knowing that one day she would be their destroyer. **6** Alexander's brother too, Perdikkas, was similarly removed by cunning treachery. **7** It was dreadful that children should have been deprived of life to satisfy their mother's lust, when a regard for those actual children had saved her from the punishment of her crimes. **8** The murder of Perdikkas seemed all the more monstrous since not even the prayers of his little son could win him his mother's compassion. **9** Philip, for a long time, acted not as king but as guardian to this child. **10** But when serious wars threatened and any assistance from this child would be too long to wait for, he was forced by the people to take over the kingdom.

7.6.1 When he became king everyone had great hopes of him, both because of his abilities, which promised that he would be a great man, and because of some ancient oracles about Macedonia, **2** which foretold that, when one of Amyntas' sons was ruling, Macedonia would prosper exceedingly, to fulfil which hopes his mother's wickedness had left only him surviving. **3** Initially, when the murder of his brother, so monstrously put to death, the multitude of his enemies, and the poverty of his kingdom, so exhausted by continual wars, weighed heavily on the youth's immaturity, **4** he thought it necessary to deal with the wars, which as if by a mutual conspiracy to destroy Macedonia rose around him from different nations and various places at one and the same time, and, since he could not resist them all together, **5** he put off some by offers of peace, others he bought off, while attacking those enemies that seemed most easy to defeat, so that by a victory over them he would strengthen the unequal spirits of his soldiers and combat any disdain with which his enemies might regard him. **6** His first conflict was with the Athenians, whom he overcame by treachery and allowed to depart unharmed and without ransom, from fear of a more serious war, though he could actually have slaughtered them all. **7** After them he led his army against the Illyrians and slew several thousand of his enemies. **8** Then he suddenly attacked Thessaly which was fearing anything rather than war, not from a desire for plunder, but because he wanted to add the strength of the Thessalian cavalry to his own army, **9** and in this way brought together a force of cavalry and infantry into a single invincible army; **10** he also captured the renowned city of Larissa. **11** His undertakings having so far been successful, he married Olympias, daughter of Neoptolemos king of the Molossians (in Epiros). **12** Her cousin Arrybas, then king of the Molossians, who had brought up the girl and had married her sister Troas, supported the alliance, though this was to be the cause of his downfall and all his misfortunes. **13** For while he hoped to strengthen his kingdom by this connection with Philip, he lost his throne because of that very king and spent his old age in exile.

14 After these achievements, Philip was no longer satisfied with staying on the defensive and proactively attacked even those who had not injured him. **15** When he was besieging Methone an arrow, shot from the walls as he passed, took out his right eye. **16** But this did not make him less active in prosecuting the siege, or more incensed against the enemy, and when a few days later they asked for peace, he granted it and was not only not severe, but even merciful towards the defeated.

14.27 Diodorus *Library of History* 16.1.3–6: The Achievements of Philip II

Diodorus sums up Philip's career: 'he excelled in shrewd generalship, courage and brilliance of personality', all of which were in fact key aspects in his success. For Delphi and the Phokians, see doc. 14.32.

16.1.3 Now that I have come to the actions of Philip, son of Amyntas, I will attempt to cover all the deeds of this king in the present book. For he was ruler of the Macedonians for twenty-four years, and starting from the most insignificant beginnings made his kingdom into the greatest of the powers in Europe, and, after inheriting Macedonia when she was enslaved to the Illyrians, made her mistress of numerous powerful peoples and cities. **4** And it was through his own prowess that he took over the supremacy of the whole of Greece, with the cities willingly accepting his authority. He successfully fought against the men who had been plundering the shrine at Delphi and for this assistance to the oracle was made a member of the Amphictyonic Council, and, because of his piety towards the gods, won as his prize the votes of the Phokians whom he had defeated. **5** Then, after conquering in war Illyrians, Paionians, Thracians, Scythians and all the surrounding peoples, he planned to overcome the Persian kingdom, and after transporting his armies into Asia was in the process of liberating the Greek cities, but, cut short by fate, left behind him armies so large and powerful that his son Alexander did not need to ask for allies in his attack on Persian supremacy. **6** And King Philip accomplished all this not through Fortune, but through his own prowess, for he excelled in shrewd generalship, courage and a charismatic personality.

14.28 Diodorus *Library of History* 16.7.2–4: The Revolt of Athens' Allies in 357 BC

In 357 BC Athens' allies in the Second Athenian Confederacy rebelled, particularly Rhodes, Kos, Byzantium (its secession may in fact date earlier) and Chios. An Athenian fleet sent to deal with the revolt in 356 was defeated at Chios; another fleet sent subsequently lost to the allies at the Hellespont, who were in revolt. Peace was organised in 355 when the Persian king threatened to intervene on the allies' side and the size of the confederacy was very much reduced. The causes as to the revolt are unclear but indications are that the Athenians were encroaching on the freedoms of the allies. Philip was not inactive and seized Amphipolis, Pydna and Potidaea.

16.7.2 While these events were taking place the inhabitants of Euboea fell into a state of conflict amongst themselves, and, when one party summoned the Boeotians to their assistance and the other the Athenians, war broke out through all of Euboea. A number of battles and skirmishes took place in which the Thebans sometimes had the advantage, while in others the Athenians won the victory. No great pitched battle was fought to a conclusion, but, after the island had been devastated by the internecine warfare and numerous men had been killed on both sides, even then, despite the lessons the disasters had taught them, they found it hard to come to an agreement and make peace with each other.

The Boeotians now returned home and stayed quiet; **3** the Athenians, however, who had undergone the revolts of Chios, Rhodes and Kos, and also that of Byzantium, became involved in the so-called 'Allied' (Social) War which lasted three years. They chose as their generals Chares and Chabrias and dispatched them with an army. When these sailed to Chios, they found that allies had arrived to assist the Chians from Byzantium, Rhodes and Kos, and also from Mausolos, ruler of Caria. When they had drawn up their forces, they besieged the city simultaneously by land and by sea. Chares who led the infantry advanced against the walls by land and began to engage with the enemy who poured out against him from the city, while Chabrias, who sailed up to the harbour, fought a heavy naval battle and was worsted when his ship was shattered by rams. **4** The men on the other ships saved their lives by withdrawing in time but he chose a glorious death rather than defeat and after fighting on for his ship died of his wounds.

14.29 Diodorus *Library of History* 16.8.1–7: Philip's Resources in 356 BC

Philip captured Amphipolis, much to Athens' chagrin, in 357; the city had been its colony and Athens had never given up claiming it (cf. docs 2.7, 13.20). He took Potidaea, first enslaving the inhabitants, at the request of Olynthos, which had made an alliance with him, and expelled the Athenian garrison and cleruchy. (Olynthos was on the Chalkidike peninsula south-east of Macedonia; it later fell out with Philip and was destroyed by him in 348 BC.) In 356 BC Philip renamed Krenides in Thrace as Philippoi and began working the mines there and elsewhere in Thrace extensively, bringing himself a huge revenue; Diodorus must mean a revenue of 1,000 talents annually. As Diodorus notes, this money enabled him to employ a large army of mercenaries and in particular to bribe Greek statesmen as required.

16.8.1 At about the same time Philip, king of the Macedonians, who had overcome the Illyrians in a great engagement and had made all the people living there up to the lake known as Lychnitis his subjects, returned to Macedonia, after making a glorious peace with the Illyrians and having won great renown among the Macedonians for the achievements due to his valour. **2** Then, because the people dwelling at Amphipolis were hostile towards him and offering many reasons for going to war, he made an expedition against them with a noteworthy force. By bringing siege-engines up against the walls and making continuous heavy assaults, he demolished part of the wall with the battering rams, entered the city through this gap and eliminated many of his opponents, thus gaining control of the city and exiling those who were ill-disposed to him, but showing consideration in his dealings with the rest. **3** Because this city was well positioned with regard to Thrace and the surrounding regions, it made a great contribution to increasing Philip's power. He immediately conquered Pydna and made an alliance with the Olynthians, agreeing to take Potidaea for them, as the Olynthians had a great desire to possess that city. **4** As the Olynthians dwelt in an important city and due to its large population it was of great significance in war, the city was much contended over by those who wished to enlarge their supremacy. In consequence the Athenians and Philip were rivals against each other for the alliance with the Olynthians. **5** Nevertheless, when Philip took Potidaea by siege he escorted the Athenian garrison out of the city and behaved towards it with consideration, sending it back to Athens (for he paid particular attention towards the Athenian people because of the importance and reputation of the city). Potidaea, once he had sold the inhabitants into slavery, he handed over to the Olynthians, at the same time giving them all the properties in the region.

6 After this Philip went to the city of Krenides (in Thrace) and, when he had increased its size with a large number of settlers, changed its name to Philippoi, calling it after himself. He then so greatly increased by his improvements the output of the gold mines in the region, up to then totally unproductive and unimportant, that they were able to provide him with a revenue of more than one thousand talents. **7** So he very quickly amassed a fortune from these mines and by using this abundance of money raised the Macedonian kingdom to even greater pre-eminence; for with the gold coinage he struck, which came to be called Philippeioi after him, he organised a considerable force of mercenaries and also used it to bribe many Greeks to betray their homelands.

14.30 Demosthenes 1 *First Olynthiac* 11–13: Philip Increases His Power

Olynthos joined Philip in 357–356 BC, but changed sides to Athens as Philip's power grew, supporting rivals to the Macedonian throne; the city requested Athens' assistance, probably in 349 BC. Demosthenes delivered three speeches in 349 (*Olynthiacs* 1–3) urging the Athenians to come to the aid of the city, but was unsuccessful; Philip destroyed the city in 348 BC. In 351 BC Demosthenes had delivered his speech the *First Philippic* against Philip, urging the Athenians not to give up the struggle for Amphipolis, but this was already a lost cause.

11 And so we must, men of Athens, keep a close watch on future events, so that by restoring our past fortunes we can blot out the discredit of our past actions. **12** But if, men of Athens, we fail these men as well and Olynthos is destroyed by Philip in consequence, I would like one of you to tell me what there is that would hinder his marching anywhere he pleases. Does any of you, men of Athens, actually think about and keep an eye on the way in which Philip, who was initially so weak, has become so powerful? First of all he took Amphipolis, then Pydna, and then Potidaea, after that Methone, and finally invaded Thessaly. **13** After this he won over Pherai, Pagasai and Magnesia to his own interests and then headed off to Thrace; there he expelled some of the rulers and put others in place before falling ill. On recovering, he did not decide to take it easy, but immediately attacked Olynthos. And I will just pass over his campaigns against Illyrians and Paionians and Arybbas and any others that might be mentioned.

14.31 Diodorus *Library of History* 16.52.1–3: Philip's 'Modus Operandi', 348 BC

Philip is here portrayed by Diodorus as combining devious treachery with skill in warfare in his conquests; cf. Diod. 16.54.4 for his use of gold. Olynthos was delivered up through bribery of its chief officials, the population enslaved and the city destroyed.

16.52.1 When this year came to an end at Athens, Theophilos was archon, while at Rome Gaius Sulpicius and Gaius Quinctius were made consuls, and the 180th celebration of the Olympic festival was held at which Polykles of Cyrene won in the stadion. **2** In their year of office Philip, who wished to take over the cities on the Hellespont, gained Mekyberna and Torone without risk through treachery, and after making a campaign against Olynthos, the largest city in this region, with a huge army, first defeated them in two battles, and then shut them in for a siege, losing in the continuous assaults many of his soldiers in battles at the walls; finally he bribed the Olynthians' chief officials, Euthykrates and Lasthenes, and took Olynthos when they betrayed it. **3** He plundered it and sold the inhabitants into slavery and the property as booty. By doing this he acquired large sums of money for the war and terrified the other cities who opposed him. He rewarded with suitable gifts those soldiers who had fought bravely in the battle and handed out much money to men of importance in their cities, thus gaining numerous people prepared to betray their countries. In fact he used to say that it was far more through the use of gold than of arms that he had enlarged his kingdom.

14.32 Diodorus *Library of History* 16.23.1–5: The Third Sacred War, 357–346 BC

In 357 BC Delphi accused the Phokians of cultivating the Krisaian (or Kirrhaian) plain near Delphi. The Delphic Amphictyony ('council', made up of representatives from several Greek states) imposed a substantial fine for this, which the Phokians declined to pay. Athens and Sparta supported the Phokians who then seized the Delphic sanctuary in 356, at which the Amphictyony declared war; the Thebans were the main prosecutors and suffered numerous Phokian incursions into Boeotia.

16.23.1 When Kallistratos was archon at Athens, the Romans elected as consuls Marcus Fabius and Gaius Plautius (355/4 BC). In their consulship the so-called Sacred War started and lasted for nine years. For Philomelos, the Phokian, a man of unusual audacity and violence, seized the shrine at Delphi and kindled the Sacred War for reasons such as those that follow. **2** When the Spartans had fought the Leuktrian war against the Boeotians and been defeated (371 BC), the Thebans brought a serious charge against the Spartans in the Amphictyonic Council over their seizure of the Kadmeia (382 BC), and had them condemned to pay a heavy fine, **3** while the Phokians, who had cultivated a large part of the sacred land known as the Kirrhaian, had a case brought against them before the Amphictyons and were fined a large number of talents (357 BC). When they did not pay what was owed, the hieromnemones in the Amphictyonic Council brought charges against the Phokians and demanded that the council, if the Phokians did not pay the money to the god, should consecrate the territory of those who were robbing the god. Similarly, they said that the others, who had been condemned, should pay what they owed, among these being the Spartans, and if they did not obey they should be hated by all the Greeks together for their wickedness. **4** When the Greeks all ratified the decisions of the Amphictyons and the territory of the Phokians was on the point of being consecrated, Philomelos, who had the highest reputation among the Phokians, made a speech to his fellow countrymen, telling them that they could not pay the money because of the size of the fine, and that to allow the territory to be consecrated was not only cowardly, but dangerous as it meant the destruction of the livelihood of them all. **5** He also tried to show that the judgements of the Amphictyons were extremely unjust, since they had imposed huge fines for the cultivation of a very small piece of land. He therefore advised them to treat the fines as invalid and showed that the Phokians had strong grounds for their case against the Amphictyons — for in ancient times they had the control and guardianship of the oracle. As witness, he offered the most ancient and greatest of all poets, Homer, who said:

> 'Now Schedios and Epistrophos ruled over the Phokians,
> who held Kyparissos and rocky Pytho [Delphi]' (*Iliad* 2.517, 519).

So, he said, they should claim the guardianship of the oracle as part of the ancestral rights of the Phokians, and promised that he would succeed in this attempt if they would appoint him general with full and total powers for the whole enterprise.

14.33 Justin *Epitome Historiarum* 8.4.1–5.6: Events Prior to the Peace of Philokrates

A peace, named after the Athenian statesman Philokrates, was made between Philip and Athens in 346. Aeschines and Demosthenes had been sent as members of a ten-person embassy to Philip to seek this; Demosthenes ensured that the decree ratifying the Peace of Philokrates was passed in the ekklesia. Athens was to abandon all claim to Amphipolis (Dem. 5.25). Demosthenes and others later disowned this peace and Philokrates was attacked for his part in making it and forced into exile. The Peace had excluded the Phokians at Philip's insistence (Dem. 19.65), but the Athenians were nevertheless shocked later when Philip, soon after the peace was made, destroyed Phokis. The peace came under increasing attack at Athens. Demosthenes' and Aeschines' speeches, both called *On the Embassy*, deal with the peace.

8.4.1 During these transactions, envoys from the Athenians came to Philip seeking peace. **2** After listening to them he sent envoys to Athens with peace terms and a peace was made there to the advantage of both sides. **3** Embassies also came from other Greek cities, not from love of peace but from fear of war: **4** for with increasing anger the Thessalians and Boeotians asked him to show himself the leader of Greece, as he had professed to be, against the Phokians, **5** such being the hatred with which they were inflamed against Phokis that, forgetful of their own disasters, they preferred to perish themselves rather than not destroy the Phokians, and chose to endure Philip's cruelty rather than spare their enemies. **6** On the other side, envoys from the Phokians, joined by Spartans and Athenians, were trying to beg off the war, a postponement of which they had already bought from him on three occasions.

7 It was a shameful and wretched sight to see Greece, which even then was still the leader of the world in strength and dignity, that had always been the conqueror of kings and nations and was still mistress of many cities, in attendance at a foreign court requesting or begging off war; **8** that the champions of the whole world should place all their hopes on the assistance of someone else; that they had been reduced through their own discord and civil wars to such a condition as to flatter of their own free will what had previously been an insignificant part of their own dependencies; **9** and it was still worse that the Thebans and Spartans should be doing this, as they had formerly been rivals for power but were now rivals for a sovereign's favour. **10** To show his importance Philip put on an air of disdain for these great cities and considered which of the two he should favour. **11** So he heard both embassies in private, promising one security from war, putting them on oath to reveal his answer to no one, and the other that he would give them assistance. He told both neither to prepare for war nor to fear it. **12** After these different responses, while all was secure, he seized the pass of Thermopylai.

8.5.1 As a result, the Phokians, finding themselves trapped by Philip's cunning, were the first, in trepidation, to take up arms. **2** But they had no time to make preparations for war or to attract military aid, and Philip threatened their destruction unless they surrendered. **3** So, overcome by necessity, they surrendered, asking only for their lives. **4** But Philip kept this promise just as faithfully as he had his promises about the war they had tried to beg off. **5** They were everywhere killed or captured: children were not left to their parents, or wives to their husbands, or the statues of gods to their temples. **6** The one comfort for these poor people was that, as Philip defrauded his allies of any part of the plunder, they saw none of their property in the hands of their enemies.

14.34 Diodorus *Library of History* 16.59.4–60.5: Philip and the Third Sacred War, 346 BC

Philip, on behalf of the Amphictyonic League, moved against the Phokians, allies of Athens, who had plundered the shrine at Delphi; the Phokians surrendered, so losing the Third Sacred War. Philip took the place of Phokis on the Amphictyonic Council. He had become the arbiter of affairs in central Greece.

16.59.4 The king, after unexpectedly putting an end to the Sacred War without a battle, sat in council with the Boeotians and Thessalians. He therefore decided to call a meeting of the Amphictyonic Council and leave to it the final decision on all issues.

16.60.1 The members of the council then passed a decree admitting Philip and his descendants to the Amphictyonic Council and granted him the two votes which had previously been held by the Phokians, who had now been defeated. They also decreed that the three cities in the possession of the Phokians should have their walls removed and that the Phokians should have no participation in the shrine or the Amphictyonic Council; they should not be permitted to acquire horses or arms until they had repaid to the god the money they had stolen; those of the Phokians who had fled and any others who had had a part in plundering the shrine were to be under a curse and subject to arrest, wherever they might be; **2** all the cities of the Phokians were to be destroyed and the people moved to villages, none of which was to have more than fifty houses, with the villages to be at least a stade apart; and the Phokians were to keep their territory and pay the god every year a tribute of sixty talents until they had repaid the sum recorded in the accounts at the time the shrine was robbed. Furthermore, Philip was to hold the Pythian festival together with the Boeotians and Thessalians, since the Corinthians had shared with the Phokians in the sacrilege against the god.

3 The Amphictyons and Philip were to hurl the arms of the Phokians and their mercenaries over the cliffs and burn what was left of them and sell the horses. Following on from this, the Amphictyons laid down regulations for the guardianship of the oracle and all other matters relating to piety towards the gods and the common peace and concord of the Greeks. **4** After this, when Philip had assisted the Amphictyons to put their decrees into effect and had treated everyone with magnanimity, he returned to Macedonia not only having gained a reputation for piety and superb generalship, but also having made great preparations towards the aggrandisement which was going to be his. **5** For he desired to be appointed supreme general of Greece and prosecute the war against the Persians. And this was what actually happened.

14.35 Justin *Epitome Historiarum* 8.2.5–9: Athens' Concern at Philip's Success

Following the Phokians' defeat, the Athenians were afraid that Philip would march into Greece, and they seized the pass into central Greece at Thermopylai. Philip would, however, end up with control of the pass.

8.2.5 It was incredible how much glory this affair brought to Philip in the opinion of all people; **6** they called him the avenger of sacrilege and the defender of religion, and said that he had emerged as the only person to exact vengeance for something which should have been punished with the strength of the whole world. **7** As a result he was worthy of being ranked next to the gods, since the majesty of the gods had been vindicated by him.

8 But when the Athenians heard the outcome of the war, fearing that Philip would cross into Greece, they seized the pass of Thermopylai as they had done earlier on the approach of the Persians, but in a totally different spirit and for a different reason: **9** for on the earlier occasion they had acted in defence of the liberty of Greece, but now on behalf of public sacrilege, then to defend temples against the ravages of an enemy, now to defend the ravagers of temples against their avengers.

14.36 Tod 2.172A: The Phokians Pay Their Fine

The Phokians were ordered to pay back the sum which they had seized from Delphi during the Third Sacred War in instalments of sixty talents each year (Diod. 16.60.2), with these payments being recorded on stone at Delphi. This was later reduced to ten talents a year. Payments continued until 322 BC, the total paid apparently being 360 talents. Kleon was archon at Delphi in either 344/3 or 343/2. [*SIG*^{3} 230; R&O 67.]

While these men were in office the Phokians at the spring meeting paid thirty talents. This was the second payment of the sacred money paid in the archonship of Kleon at Delphi, when the prytaneis were Echetimos, Herakleidas, Antagoras, Ariston, Philinos, Choirikos, Ameritos, Sodamos. The following were the hieromnemones: of the Thessalians, Kottypos, Kolosimmos; of those from Philip, Eurylochos, Kleandros; of the Delphians, Damon, Mnasidamos; of the Dorians, from Matropolis Nikon, of the Argives Deinomenes; of the Ionians Timondas, Mnesilochos the Athenian; of the Perrhaibians and Dolopians, Phaikos, Asandros; of the Boeotians, Daitadas, Olympion; of the Lokrians, Pleisteas, Theomnastos; of the Achaeans, Agaskrates, Pythodoros; of the Magnesians, Philonautes, Epikratidas; of the Aenianians, Agelaos, Kleomenes; of the Malians, Antimachos of Herakleia, Demokrates of Lamia.

14.37 Athenaeus *Deipnosophistae* 557b–e: 'A Wife with Each War'

Philip practised polygamy, using marriages to strengthen his claim to Macedonia and the states he conquered. By the end of his reign he had several wives, but Olympias was his only queen; she bore him Alexander (III) and Kleopatra. The other wives were subsidiary to her, with the notable exception, towards the end of his life, of his marriage in 337 BC to (another) Kleopatra Euryolike, ward of Attalos. Olympias retired to Epiros at the time of this marriage but had her revenge on Philip's death when she had Kleopatra and her infant daughter executed (Paus. 8.7.5). Philip actually reigned for twenty-three and a half years. Alexander's elder half-brother Arrhidaios, who was born in 358 or 357, was mentally deficient. [Dikaiarchos *FHG* 2.240; Satyros *FHG* 3.161.]

557b Philip of Macedon did not take his wives on campaign as did Darius, who was deposed by Alexander, who though fighting for his whole empire took 360 concubines with him, according to the account written by Dikaiarchos in the third book of his *History of Greece*. However, Philip always married a wife with each war. 'In the twenty-two years of his reign,' Satyros says in his *Life of Philip*, **557c** 'he married Audata of Illyria and had by her a daughter Kynna; he also married Phila, a sister of Derdas and Machatas. And in his desire to make claim to the Thessalian nation he had children by two Thessalian women, one of whom was Nikesipolis of Pherai, who bore him a daughter Thessalonike, the other Philinna of Larisa, by whom he fathered Arrhidaios. He also acquired the kingdom of the Molossians by marrying Olympias, by whom he had Alexander and Kleopatra. **557d** Also, when he subdued Thrace, Kothelas the Thracian king came over to him bringing his daughter Meda and many gifts. He married her also, adding her to Olympias. After all these he married Kleopatra, with whom he had fallen in love, the sister of Hippostratos and niece of Attalos; by bringing her into his household in addition to Olympias he threw his whole life into chaos. For right away, during the actual wedding, Attalos remarked, "Now, then, there will be legitimate rulers born and not bastards." Alexander, on hearing this, threw the cup he had in his hands at Attalos, and he retaliated with his own vessel. **557e** After this Olympias fled to the country of the Molossians and Alexander to Illyria. And Kleopatra bore Philip a daughter, who was named Europe.'

14.38 Arrian *Expedition of Alexander* 4.13.1: Philip Recruits Noble Youths

The 'Royal Pages' (or squires) were the adolescent sons of the King's Companions (doc. 14.39), the noble cavalrymen. The Pages were the King's bodyguard while he was asleep. For their conspiracy against Alexander, see doc. 15.25.

4.13.1 It was a practice established in the time of Philip that when the sons of Macedonian nobles reached adolescence they should be enlisted in the King's service; besides general attendance on his person their duties included guarding him while he slept. And whenever the King rode out these boys received the horses from the grooms and led them up, mounted the King in the Persian manner and were the King's companions in the rivalry of the hunt.

14.39 Theopompos *The History of Philip*: FF224–225: The 'Companions'

The Companions (hetairoi) were aristocratic cavalrymen who served alongside the King; they were essentially his friends and associates. As Philip's power grew in the 340s, Theopompos relates that there were 800 companions, from Greece and Thessaly as well as Macedonia, who were given estates in newly conquered territory. Theopompos is clearly critical here, but did spend time at Philip's court. [Theopompos *FGH* 115 F224–225: Athen. *Deip*. 166f–167c, 260d–261a]

224 In the forty-ninth book of his *Histories*, Theopompos gives us the following details of the extravagant lifestyle of Philip and his Companions. When he became master of a great fortune, did he spend it quickly? That's not the word — he squandered it and just threw it away, for he was the worst manager in the world! His Companions were just like him — in simple terms, not one of them knew how to live decently or manage a property sensibly. Philip himself was to blame for this: he was insatiable and extravagant, doing everything rashly, whether getting or giving, for as a soldier he had no time to reckon up revenue and expenditure. Moreover, his Companions had joined him from all sorts of places, some from Macedonia, some from Thessaly, and others from the rest of Greece, and they were chosen not on merit — quite the opposite: nearly all those among the Greeks or barbarians with a lewd, disgusting or ruffianly lifestyle gathered in Macedonia and were called Philip's Companions. And even if one of them was not like this when he arrived, he soon became just like the rest under the impact of the Macedonian lifestyle and habits. It was partly the wars and campaigns, and partly the extravagant way of life that turned them into ruffians and forced them to live not in a decent manner, but like profligates and highwaymen.

225 Theopompos writes as follows about both Dionysios and Philip in his forty-ninth book: Philip rejected those of decent character who looked after their property, but he praised and honoured those who were extravagant and spent their time in dicing and drinking. Not only did he make sure that these sorts of entertainment were available for them, he even made them compete against each other in every kind of wickedness and loathsome behaviour … They loved drunkenness instead of sobriety, and would rather rob and kill than live decent lives. Being truthful and keeping agreements they saw as nothing to do with them, while they were ready to perjure themselves and cheat in the holiest places. Neglectful of what they possessed, they wanted what they had not, though they owned quite an extensive part of Europe. In my view, though there were no more than 800 Companions at that time, they enjoyed the revenue of as much territory as the 10,000 Greeks who had the best and largest properties.

14.40 Demosthenes 9 *Third Philippic* 47–50: Philip and Warfare

By 341 BC, Demosthenes was a particularly ardent critic of Philip. He notes the differences between fifth- and fourth-century warfare, especially emphasising Philip's range of troops, his disregard of the campaigning season, and his ability to bring about betrayal within cities through bribery (cf. doc. 14.31).

47 There is a ridiculous argument, put forward by those who want to reassure the city of Athens, that Philip is not yet as powerful as the Spartans were when they controlled every sea and land, had the King as their ally, and nothing could withstand them, and nevertheless our city defended itself against them and was not captured. But I believe that, while almost everything has made great advances, and nothing is like it used to be, there is nothing that has changed and advanced as much as the art of war. **48** In the first place I am told that in those days the Spartans and all the other Greeks would invade and ravage the enemy's territory with hoplites and citizen armies for just four or five months and then would go home again. They were so old-fashioned, or rather so conscious of their duties as citizens, that they did not use money to buy anything from anyone, and their type of warfare was waged according to the rules and in plain view. **49** But now you can surely see that in most cases disasters are caused by traitors and are not the result of a pitched battle, and you hear of Philip marching where he chooses, not with a phalanx of hoplites, but followed by light-armed troops, cavalry, archers, mercenaries and this type of force. **50** When he attacks a people suffering internal strife and no one goes out to defend their territory because they are suspicious of each other, he brings up his engines of war and besieges them. And I say nothing of the fact that he makes no distinction between summer and winter and has no special season for inactivity.

14.41 Polybios *Histories* 18.29.1–30.4, 31.5–7: The Macedonian Phalanx

Philip from the first year of his reign focused on the development of the phalanx; it was crucial to his defeat of the Illyrians in 358 BC. The basic Macedonian weapon became the sarissa, a six-metre pike (Diod. 16.3.1: doc. 14.25), but ranks in the phalanx had differing spear-lengths depending on their distance from the front rank (doc. 14.42). The whole effect was to produce a bristling array of close spears in front of the phalanx. Philip, in organising the Macedonian army into phalanxes, was no doubt influenced by the victories of Epameinondas of Thebes. The infantry phalanx of about 15,000 men was intended to be used alongside cavalry; Alexander certainly used the two in tandem to devastating effect against Persia. The heavy infantry were the pezetairoi (foot-companions), along with the hypaspistai (the guard corps, or shield-bearers). A cubit was approximately 1 ft 5 in., or 45 cm.

18.29.1 It can be easily understood for many reasons that when the phalanx has its unique characteristics and strength nothing can stand up to its frontal attack or withstand its charge. **2** In its dense battle formations, each man with his arms occupies a space three feet in width, and the length of the sarissas is sixteen cubits, according to the original plan, but fourteen when adapted to needs in reality, **3** and of these fourteen cubits four are taken up by the space between the hands and the weighted part of the shaft to the rear: **4** so it is clear that the sarissa has to extend ten cubits beyond the body of each hoplite when he charges the enemy holding it with both hands. **5** Consequently the sarissas of the second, third and fourth ranks extend further than those of the fifth rank, while these extend two cubits in front of the men in the front rank when the phalanx has its characteristic close order in both depth and breadth, **6** as Homer (*Iliad* 13.131–3) describes in these lines:

> 'Spear crowded against spear, helmet against helmet, man against man,
> The horsehair crests of their shining headgear touching
> As they nodded, so closely to each other did they stand.'

7 This description is true and accurate and it is clear that each man in the front rank must have five sarissas projecting in front of him, each two cubits in length different from the next.

18.30.1 From this it is easy to understand the characteristics and strength of a charge by a whole phalanx when it is sixteen deep. **2** Those further back than the fifth rank are not able to engage in the fighting with their sarissas; they do not individually level them for the attack, **3** but hold them slanting up over the shoulders of those in front of them to protect the whole formation from above, with this density of sarissas warding off all those missiles which, passing over the heads of those in the front, might fall on those standing behind them. **4** These men by their bodily weight pressing against those in front increase the force of the assault, and it is impossible for the front ranks to turn about.

18.31.5 It is agreed that the phalanx requires level, open ground which, in addition, has no obstacles such as ditches, ravines, stream-junctions, ridges and river beds, **6** for all of these are sufficient to impede and break up such a formation. **7** And everyone would agree that it is nearly impossible to find, except very rarely, spaces of some twenty stades or even more in length without such obstacles.

14.42 Asklepiodotos *Tactics* 5.1–2: The Macedonian Shield and Spear

The pike or spear was now extended to a maximum of six metres (17 to 18 feet); the small shield was 61 cm (24 in.) in diameter; a palm is 7.5cm (3in).

5.1 The best shield for use in the phalanx is the Macedonian, made of bronze, eight palms in diameter, and not too concave; the spear is not less than ten cubits, so that the part which projects in front is not less than eight cubits, and in no case is longer than twelve cubits so as to project ten cubits. When the Macedonian phalanx employed such a spear in a compact formation it appeared unbeatable to the enemy. For it is evident that the spears of the first five ranks project beyond the front, for the soldiers in the second rank, being two cubits back, project their spears eight cubits beyond the front, those in the third rank six cubits, those in the fourth rank four cubits, and those in the fifth rank two cubits, so that five sarissas extend beyond the first rank. **2** And the Macedonians, they say, with this row of spears, not only terrify the enemy at the sight of them, but also give courage to each of the men leading in the front row, protected as he is by five spears.

DEMOSTHENES

14.43 Plutarch *Life of Demosthenes* 6.1–5, 11.1: An Early Career Politician

Demosthenes, an orphan who had to take his guardians to court for appropriating his inheritance (doc. 5.19), trained under the Athenian orator Isaeus. His first major speech in the assembly was the *First Philippic*, delivered in 351 BC, which began a career of opposition to Philip: at *First Philippic* 1 he states that it was the first time that he had been the speaker in the ekklesia who opened a debate.

6.1 When Demosthenes came of age he started bringing suits and writing speeches against his guardians, who then came up with many evasions and retrials. However, after training himself, in the words of Thucydides (1.18.3), 'through exercises not without danger or toil', he was successful, though unable to recover even a small part of his inheritance. He had, however, acquired confidence in speaking and sufficient practice, as well as a taste for ambition and influence, and so made the attempt at entering public life and engaging in politics ... **2** As a result Demosthenes, who had initially applied himself to public speaking in order to recover his private property, by this means finally achieved forcefulness and authority in politics and, just like in the games where the award consists of a crown, won first place among the citizens who battled with each other from the speaker's platform. **3** At his first address to the people, however, he was interrupted by catcalls and laughed at for his inexperience. The long sentences in his speech made it complicated and seem far too pedantically convoluted in its arguments. **4** He also suffered from, it seems, a weakness in his voice and a shortness of breath which made his statements confusing because his sentences were disconnected. **5** After he had decided to leave the assembly and was just hanging around in the Piraeus, Eunomos the Thriasian (already an old man) spotted him and told him off — he had a Periklean style of speaking, said Eunomos, but was throwing himself away because of his cowardice and weakness: he should have been confidently facing up to the assembly and getting his physical constitution ready for these battles, rather than allowing it to waste away in the enjoyment of idleness.

11.1 To combat his physical disability he took to the exercises which Demetrios of Phaleron describes, who says he heard about them from Demosthenes himself in old age: the lack of clarity and lisping quality in his speech he used to correct and compensate for by putting pebbles in his mouth and then declaiming speeches. And he used to practise his delivery while running or going uphill and reciting speeches or lines of poetry without drawing breath. He also had a large mirror at home and used to stand in front of it reciting his exercises.

14.44 Aeschines 2 *On the Embassy* 34–39: Demosthenes' Speech before Philip, 346 BC

Demosthenes and Aeschines were two of the ten ambassadors sent to Philip by Athens in 346 BC to discuss peace (the 'Peace of Philokrates'), making two trips to Macedon. After the Peace was ratified, Philip occupied Thermopylai, entered Phokis, and received its surrender. It became clear that Athens had gained nothing from the peace. Demosthenes, who had supported it, now brought a charge of treason against Aeschines for his conduct during the second embassy to Philip; this came to court in 343 BC. Aeschines in return paints a very negative picture of Demosthenes' behaviour as an orator and politician. Demosthenes' corresponding speech is also called *On the Embassy*. Aeschines was narrowly acquitted by thirty votes out of the 1,501 jurors hearing the case.

34 When I had spoken to this effect and more besides, it was Demosthenes' turn to speak as part of the embassy, and everyone listened eagerly, expecting to hear an oratorical tour de force — we learned later that promises of his superior performance had been reported both to Philip and to his court. So the whole audience was in a state of anticipation — and then this creature uttered a sort of introduction, totally incomprehensible and made lifeless by his fright. He got a short way into his topic and then suddenly fell silent and stood there at a loss, finally breaking off his speech altogether. **35** Philip saw how he was situated and encouraged him, telling him not to think that he was on the stage and that he had ruined the performance, but to calm down and gradually recollect his speech and deliver it as he had planned. But once he had been thrown into confusion and lost his place in the script, he wasn't able to recover his poise: in fact when he tried a second time, the same thing happened. There was silence, and then the herald told us to withdraw.

36 When we were on our own, our respected Demosthenes, with a very grumpy expression, declared that I had ruined the city and the allies. And when not only I, but all our fellow envoys as well, were astonished at this and asked why he had said that, he enquired of me whether I had forgotten the state of affairs at Athens and whether I did not recall that the people was exhausted and desperate for peace. **37** 'Or does your confidence rest,' he asked, 'in those fifty ships that have been voted, but will never be manned? You have so infuriated Philip by what you have said that the result will be not peace instead of war, but war instead of peace — and with no holds barred!' I was just starting to answer him, when the attendants called us back.

38 When we had entered and sat down, Philip started methodically answering from the beginning every point we had made, and of course spent most of his time dealing with my arguments (for I think I can reasonably say that I left out nothing that could have been said), and repeatedly mentioned my name in his response. But as for Demosthenes, who had acquitted himself so ridiculously, he did not address, I believe, a single point of his — which pained Demosthenes extremely. **39** And when Philip began speaking on the subject of friendly relationships, and the slander which Demosthenes had earlier uttered against me in front of our fellow envoys was shown to be baseless — that I was going to be the cause of war and conflict — then everyone could see that Demosthenes was beside himself, to such an extent that even when we were invited in to dinner his behaviour was totally unacceptable.

14.45 Polybios *Histories* 18.14.1–14: Philip as Protector of Smaller States

Polybios, who came from Arkadia, had a different point of view from Demosthenes, and argued that Philip's intervention in Greek affairs was to the benefit of the smaller states. His view that Philip humbled the Spartans and guaranteed Peloponnesian freedom seems to overlook the fact that this had been established by the Thebans a generation earlier.

18.14.1 So while we have to praise Demosthenes for many things, we have to blame him on one account, which is for having unjustifiably and uncritically cast bitter reproaches at the most distinguished men in Greece, **2** by saying that Kerkidas, Hieronymos and Eukampidas in Arkadia were betrayers of Greece, **3** because they joined Philip, and the same of Neon and Thrasylochos the sons of Philiadas in Messene, Myrtis, Teledamos and Mnaseas in Argos, **4** Daochos and Kineas in Thessaly, those who supported Theogeiton and Timolas in Boeotia, **5** and several others whom he named in different cities. Yet all the above men had a perfectly clear justification for defending their own rights, especially those from Arkadia and Messene. **6** For they, by inducing Philip to enter the Peloponnese and humble the Spartans, allowed, in the first place, all the inhabitants of the Peloponnese to breath freely and grasp the concept of liberty, **7** and also, by recovering the territory and cities which the Spartans in their times of prosperity had seized from the Messenians, Megalopolitans, Tegeans and Argives, they indubitably increased the power of their cities. **8** With this object in mind it was not their duty to fight against Philip, but to do everything they could for their own honour and glory. **9** If in doing this they had allowed their native cities to be garrisoned by Philip, or abolished their laws and deprived the citizens of freedom of action and speech for the sake of their own advantage and power, they would have deserved being called traitors as he calls them. **10** But if, in protecting the rights of their native countries, they just differed in their judgement of facts, considering that the interests of Athens were not the same as those of their cities, they should not, I believe, have been called traitors by Demosthenes for this reason. **11** In measuring everything by the interests of his own city and thinking that all of Greece should have its eyes on Athens, and, if not, calling them traitors, Demosthenes seems to me to have been mistaken and to have misrepresented the truth, **12** especially since what actually happened to the Greeks did not bear out Demosthenes' foretelling of the future, but that of Eukampidas, Hieronymos, Kerkidas and the sons of Philiadas. **13** For the consequence of the Athenians' resistance to Philip was that they experienced the worst possible disasters, defeated as they were at the battle of Chaironeia. **14** And had it not been for the king's magnanimity and concern for his reputation their misfortune would have been even greater as a consequence of Demosthenes' policy.

14.46 Demosthenes 18 *On the Crown* 60–69: Demosthenes Defends His Position

In 336 BC Ktesiphon proposed a decree that Demosthenes be awarded a crown at the festival of the Dionysia in recognition of his services to the city. Aeschines brought an indictment against Ktesiphon for proposing this. The case initially lapsed, but was revived in 330, when Aeschines delivered his *Against Ktesiphon*, and Demosthenes his *On the Crown*. Demosthenes, by emphasising the great history of Athens and its glorious achievements, won the case; Aeschines received less than one-fifth of the votes and had to leave the city to go into exile.

60 I shall remind you and give you an account of the ways in which Philip was thwarted from the first day that I entered public life, starting with the initial point that Philip had a tremendous advantage. **61** In the Greek states, not just some of them but all at once, there happened to have emerged a crop of corrupt, irreligious traitors never before known in the memory of mankind. With these as his collaborators and accomplices, he made the relationships between Greek states, who were already on bad terms with each other, still worse, some by deception, some by bribes, and others by every kind of corruption, splitting them into many factions, although they had a single interest in common — to prevent his power increasing. **62** With all the Greeks in this situation and unaware of this looming and increasing threat, you had to consider, men of Athens, what was the right policy and right course of conduct for Athens to adopt: that is the question on which you should call me to account, for I was the one who took his political stand on this point. **63** Should our city, Aeschines, have abandoned her spirit and dignity and ranked herself with the Thessalians and Dolopians in helping Philip to acquire an empire over Greece, and destroy all the glory and honour of our ancestors? Or if she rejected that shameful policy, should she have looked on at what she could have foreseen well in advance would happen, if no one resisted it, and let it continue?

64 I would now like to ask the greatest critic of our past deeds which party he would have wished Athens to join — the one which shares the guilt of the ruin and disgrace of Greece, that of the Thessalians, you might say, and their associates, or the one which overlooked all these events in the hope of material advantage, that in which you could include the Arkadians, Messenians and Argives? **65** But many of these, or rather all of them, are much worse off than we are now. If after his victory Philip had immediately left Greece and then stayed at peace, with no damage either to his allies or to the rest of the Greeks, there might have been reason to blame and criticise those who opposed his actions; but if, wherever possible, he was bent on destroying the prestige, leadership, liberty and even the constitution of every state, how can it not have been the most honourable course that you chose under my guidance?

66 I will continue with my argument. What should have been Athens' duty, Aeschines, when she saw that Philip's aim was to establish despotic rule over all of Greece? What should a statesman at Athens — this is the real point at issue — have advised or proposed, who was aware, as I was, that, from its earliest times right up till the day when I first stood on the speaker's platform, our country has always striven for primacy, and honour, and renown, and that she has expended for her own glory and the welfare of all the Greeks more resources and manpower than all the other Greeks individually have expended on their own behalf, **67** and knowing that Philip, our antagonist, in his struggle for empire and supremacy had endured the loss of an eye, a broken collarbone, the mutilation of a hand and a leg, and was ready to sacrifice to fortune any part of his body if only, with what of it was left, he should live a life of honour and renown? **68** Surely no one would dare say it was fitting that a man from Pella — then a mean and insignificant village — should possess such greatness of spirit as to want to rule the whole of Greece and have this as his heart's desire, while you Athenians, who every day in every speech and spectacle see the memorials of your ancestors' prowess, should submit to such cowardice as spontaneously and willingly to surrender your freedom to Philip. **69** No one could agree to this! The only remaining, and indeed essential, course of action was that you should put up righteous resistance to every one of his unjust designs.

14.47 Plutarch *Life of Demosthenes* 20.2–5: Demosthenes' Relationship with Persia

Demosthenes was not incorruptible, and was later exiled for accepting a twenty talent bribe from Harpalos, Alexander's runaway treasurer (doc. 15.37). He was fined fifty talents, going into exile on Aegina and at Troizen, but was recalled after the death of Alexander. In 322 BC, condemned to death by a decree proposed by the Athenian orator Demades, he committed suicide. Demosthenes was not apparently running away from the battle at Chaironeia but was returning to Athens to organise its defences.

20.2 In the battle (at Chaironeia) Demosthenes showed no conduct that was honourable or which matched his speeches, but ran away, leaving his post, fleeing most disgracefully and throwing away his weapons, feeling no shame regarding the inscription on his shield which, as Pytheas says, was inscribed 'with good fortune' in golden letters.

3 Immediately after his victory Philip was arrogant with joy and held a revel (comos), in his intoxication, in the presence of the bodies of the slain, chanting the beginning of Demosthenes' decree and dividing it into feet and beating time:

> 'Demósthenes, son of Demósthenes of Paianía, here móves the mótion';

but when he sobered up and realised the extent of the crisis which had faced him he shuddered at the ability and power of the orator, by whom he had been compelled to risk his empire and person in the short compass of a single day. **4** His fame had even reached as far as the King of the Persians, who had sent letters to his satraps on the coast telling them to offer Demosthenes money and pay more attention to him than to any other Greek, since he was able to distract and occupy the Macedonian with the disruptions taking place in Greece. **5** Alexander discovered these later on, when he found at Sardis letters of Demosthenes and documents of the King's generals which showed the amount of the money which had been given him.

PHILIP AND ATHENS

14.48 Diodorus *Library of History* 16.84.1–87.3: The Battle of Chaironeia, 338 BC

Philip had unsuccessfully intervened in Euboea – literally Athens' next-door neighbour — in 342 BC (Dem. 18.87). Demosthenes in 330 BC claimed that Philip then turned to a second way of attacking

Athens: her grain supply. In 340 BC Philip unsuccessfully attacked Perinthos, located in the Propontis, the entrance to the Black Sea, but was foiled by Persian interference (Diod. 16.74). Philip then attacked Byzantium, and despite its earlier secession from the Second Athenian Confederacy, Athens sent help, being more than aware of what this implied for her grain supply (Dem. 18.87, cf. 139; Diod. 16.77.1–2; Plut. *Phok.* 14). Philip in fact in the same year seized 230 ships carrying grain (Philochoros 328 *FGH* FF54, 162). But he ended his siege of Byzantium through lack of progress; this was, however, no comfort to Athens. In 339 the Delphic Amphictyony asked Philip to lead it in a Sacred War (the Fourth) against Amphissa, and towards the end of the year Philip, with a considerable force, was in Elateia in Phokis, in a position to threaten Athens easily, as it was just two days' march away (Dem. 18.169). The Athenian ekklesia was dumbfounded when the news was announced: only Demosthenes rose to speak, enjoining alliance with Thebes (Dem. 18.170–74). He went there, and was able to persuade the city to join Athens against Philip, whose ambassadors were also at Thebes urging the Thebans to maintain their alliance with Philip; Thebes chose to ally itself with Athens. War resulted and in 338 at Chaironeia in Boeotia Philip met the Athenians and Boeotians in battle. He was victorious and gained full mastery over Greece; garrisons were placed in Corinth and Thebes, and the League of Corinth was founded the following year, which recognised him as hegemon of its member states. For the vulgar 'buffoon' Thersites, see Homer *Iliad* 2.211–77.

16.84.1 When Charondes was archon at Athens, Lucius Aemilius and Gaius Plautius became consuls (338/7 BC). In this year, King Philip, who had won the friendship of the majority of the Greeks, was desirous of possessing the undisputed leadership of Greece by terrorising the Athenians into submitting. **2** He therefore suddenly seized the city of Elateia, gathered all his forces there, and determined to go to war against Athens. He expected to have an easy victory over them, as they were not prepared for war because of the peace treaty that was in place — and this was how things turned out. For, after Elateia had been taken, some people went by night to announce that the city had been taken and that Philip would soon be arriving in Attica with his army. **3** The Athenians' generals, stunned at the unexpected turn of events, summoned the trumpeters and ordered them to sound the alarm throughout the night.

With the report having reached into every household, the city was tense with fear, and at dawn the entire population ran into the theatre, even before the archons had summoned them in the usual way. **4** And when the generals arrived and brought in the messenger and he made his announcement, silence and fear gripped the theatre and none of the accustomed speakers dared suggest a plan of action, and though the herald called time and again for people to speak with regard to the safety of them all, no one came forward with advice. **5** In great anxiety and consternation the crowd kept looking at Demosthenes. He eventually came down from his seat, told the people to have courage, and said that it was his view that they should immediately send envoys to Thebes and invite the Boeotians to join them in making a struggle for liberty. There was not enough time to send embassies to their other allies invoking the treaties, as the King could be expected to arrive in Attica in two days and the alliance with the Boeotians was their only hope left, particularly as it was clear that Philip, a friend and ally of the Boeotians, would try to get them them to join him as he passed them in his march to war against Athens.

16.85.1 When the people had approved the proposal, and the decree authorising the embassy had been drawn up by Demosthenes, the people looked for their most powerful speaker, and Demosthenes willingly undertook the duty. He represented his case strongly and returned to Athens, having won the Thebans over …

5 As Philip had failed to obtain the alliance with the Boeotians, he nonetheless decided to fight them both together; so he waited for the rest of his allies and marched into Boeotia, with more than 30,000 infantry, and no less than 2,000 cavalry. **6** Both sides were eager for the fray and were comparable in spirit, zeal and courage, but the King had the advantage in numbers and superiority in generalship. **7** He had taken part in numerous battles of all different kinds and had been victorious in most of these engagements, and as a result had wide experience of military operations. On the Athenian side their best generals were dead — Iphikrates, Chabrias and Timotheos as well — and of those who were left Chares was the best, but he was no better than any ordinary soldier in respect of the energy and judgement needed by a general.

16.86.1 The armies took the field at dawn and the King stationed his son Alexander, who was young in years but outstanding in courage and swiftness of action, on one wing, placing with him his most notable commanders, while he himself at the head of his picked men had the command of the other; he deployed individual units as required. **2** On the other side the Athenians divided their line according to nationality, assigning one wing to the Boeotians and the other to themselves. Once joined, the battle was for a long time hotly contested and many fell on both sides, so that for a while the conflict allowed both sides the hope of victory.

3 At this point, Alexander, eager to show his father his prowess and yielding to no one in his desire to win, with the advantage too of having many brave men fighting alongside him, was the first to break through the solid front of the enemy's line, and, striking down many of them, bore heavily on those opposing him. **4** As his companions had the same success, gaps in the massed front line kept being opened. Corpses piled up until Alexander and his men managed to force their way through and put their opponents to flight. Then the King himself also advanced, not conceding credit for the victory even to Alexander: he first forced back the troops drawn up against him, and then by making them take flight became the man responsible for the victory. **5** More than 1,000 Athenians fell in the battle, and no less than 2,000 were captured. **6** Many of the Boeotians were also killed and not a few taken prisoner. After the battle Philip erected a trophy, gave up the dead for burial, made sacrifices to the gods, and rewarded according to their deserts those of his men who had fought bravely.

16.87.1 It is said that in the drinking Philip downed a large amount of unmixed wine and indulged in revelry (a comus) with his friends to mark the victory, leading to their parading through the middle of the prisoners and accompanying this with insulting speeches about the misfortunes of these ill-fated men. Demades, the orator, who was then one of the prisoners spoke boldly out and uttered a remark which successfully managed to halt the King's outrageous behaviour. **2** He is reported to have said, 'King, when Fortune has cast you in the role of Agamemnon, are you not ashamed to be acting like Thersites?' Stung by this well-aimed rebuke, Philip totally altered his entire behaviour, threw off his garlands, shook off the symbols of hybris that accompanied the comus, praised the man who had dared to speak out, and released him from captivity, and then made him join his present entourage with due respect. **3** In the end, after Demades had spoken to him with Attic suavity, he released all the prisoners without ransom and completely dropped the arrogance he was displaying as a result of his victory. He sent envoys to the Athenian people and made a treaty of alliance and friendship with them; he also concluded a peace with the Boeotians, but stationed a garrison at Thebes.

14.49 *Inscriptions Graecae* II^2 5226: The Athenian Dead at Chaironeia

This inscribed epigram honouring the 1,000 Athenian dead at Chaironeia is from Athens. The last two lines are restorations based on the text at *Greek Anthology* [*Anth. Pal.*] 7.245. [Tod 2.176; Harding 98.]

O Time, Deity who sees all the things which happen to mortals,
Be a messenger to all people regarding our sufferings —
How, in our attempt to save the sacred land of Greece,
We died on the famous plain of the Boeotians.

14.50 Justin *Epitome Historiarum* 9.5.1–6: The League of Corinth

After Chaironeia, Philip made separate peace treaties with various Greek states, including Athens (Diod. 16.87.3: doc. 14.48), which had to dissolve the Second Athenian Confederacy but retained its fleet and Samos. In 337 BC Philip summoned envoys from all over Greece to Corinth and imposed peace. Demosthenes 17 *On the Treaty with Alexander* refers to some of the provisions of the league treaty: there was to be no change in constitutions in the cities (10), and no cancellation of debts, no confiscation of land, no redistribution of land, and no freeing of slaves to change constitutions (15). In short, no radical democracies were to be allowed; cf. Arr. 3.24.5. At Corinth, with Greece conquered and under control, its resources at his disposal, Philip announced his war against Persia.

9.5.1 With matters put in order in Greece, Philip ordered that envoys from all the cities be summoned to Corinth to settle the state of affairs as they stood at present. **2** Here he fixed a law of peace for the whole of Greece, according to the merits of the individual cities, and chose a council of all as a senate, as it were, from them all. **3** Only the Spartans showed contempt both for the king and the laws, considering it slavery, not peace, since it was not to the benefit of the cities themselves but was imposed by a conqueror. **4** The levies of the individual states were then determined, whether the king, if attacked by someone, was to be assisted by that force or whether war was to be declared under his leadership. **5** Nor was there any doubt that in all these preparations the empire of the Persians was the object. **6** The total of the levies was 200,000 infantry and 15,000 cavalry.

14.51 *Inscriptiones Graecae* II^2 236: The Oath of the League, 337 BC

Representatives of the members of the Corinthian League swore an oath 'to abide by the peace' imposed by Philip, who was its hegemon. Members could not attack other league states, and Philip and his descendants were not to be overthrown. Alexander became hegemon after Philip's assassination (Diod. 17.4.9; Arr. 1.1.1: doc. 15.3), and it was ostensibly in this capacity that he took war into Asia Minor. [Tod 2.177; Harding 99; Heisserer 9; R&O 76.]

Oath. I swear by Zeus, Earth, Sun, Poseidon, Athena, Ares and all gods and goddesses: I will abide by the peace and I will not break the treaty made with Philip the Macedonian, nor will I bear arms with hostile intent against any of those who abide by their oaths, either by land or sea, nor will I seize in war either a polis or fort or harbour belonging to any of those who share in the peace by any device or stratagem, nor will I overthrow the kingdom of Philip and his descendants nor the governments in place in each state, when they swore the oaths regarding the peace, nor will I myself do anything against this treaty nor will I permit anyone else, as far as is in my power; and if anyone does anything to break the treaty, I will assist those who are injured as they request and I will make war against anyone who transgresses the common peace as is agreed by the common council and as the hegemon requests, and I will not abandon … (here follows a fragmentary list of league members).

14.52 *SEG* 12.87: Athenian Legislation against Tyranny, 337/6 BC

This decree was passed in 336 BC; at the top of the stele above the inscription there is a female figure crowning another: almost certainly the personified deity Demokratia (democracy) crowning the demos. The decree was passed after the defeat at Chaironeia and is concerned with preventing the establishment of a tyranny, but in particular it targets the Areiopagos and legislates that this must not meet if the demos or democracy is overthrown. To make doubly sure the Areiopagos remained aware of this decree, one copy was set up at the entrance to this council and one in the assembly. The League of Corinth, in fact, did not allow for changes in member states' constitutions, and Philip had only changed the regime at Thebes, so the exact purpose of the decree is somewhat elusive: but there were clearly fears of tyranny at Athens and the Areiopagos was to be considered defunct if the democracy was abolished. [*Hesperia* 21, 1952: 355–6: Harding 101; R&O 79.]

In the archonship of Phrynichos, Leontis held the ninth prytany, Chairestratos son of Ameinias from Acharnai was secretary. Vote put by Menestratos of Aixone, presiding officer; Eukrates, son of Aristotemos, of the Piraeus proposed the motion.

Good fortune to the assembly of Athens. The legislators have resolved: if anyone undermines the authority of the assembly with a view to establishing a tyranny or helps to establish a tyranny or overthrows the Athenian assembly or the democracy at Athens, the killer of the person doing this shall be sacrosanct. None of the members of the Council of the Areiopagos shall be permitted, should the assembly or democracy at Athens be overthrown, to go up to the Areiopagos, sit in conclave in the Council, or transact any business. If the demos or democracy of Athens is overthrown and any member of the Council of the Areiopagos goes up to the Areiopagos, sits in conclave in the Council or transacts any business, both he and his descendants are to be disenfranchised and his property confiscated, with a tithe to the goddess [Athena]. This law is to be inscribed on two marble pillars by the secretary of the Council and one copy set up at the entrance to the Areiopagos as you go into the Council chamber and the other in the assembly. To cover the cost of the inscription on the pillars the treasurer of the assembly is to give twenty drachmas from the money granted for public expenditure.

14.53 Diodorus *Library of History* 16.92.5, 16.93.7–95.1: Philip's Murder

The occasion is the magnificent celebration of the marriage, at Aigeai in Macedonia, of Philip and Olympias' daughter Kleopatra to Olympias' brother Alexander, king of Epiros. As Demosthenes noted in his *First Philippic* of 351 BC, Philip's power was not unchangeable like that of a god, and his supporters were prone to the same passions as other men (Dem. 4.8). The motive for the assassination was purely personal, with Pausanias feeling aggrieved that the sexual assault on him by Attalos' muleteers had not been avenged by Philip, who was his lover, though of course rumours arose of wider involvement in the plot, including that of Olympias and Alexander (doc. 14.54). Here Diodorus states that Attalos was Kleopatra's nephew, not her uncle.

16.92.5 Finally, with the drinking at an end and the games on the following day about to start, the multitude raced into the theatre while it was still dark, and the procession began at dawn. Along with his other magnificent preparations, Philip included in the procession statues of the twelve gods, fashioned with superb craftsmanship and adorned with an incredible display of wealth — and with these was carried a thirteenth statue, appropriate for a god, that of Philip himself, with the King thus showing himself enthroned beside the twelve gods.

16.93.7 Attalos, who was one of those at court who were particularly influential with the King, invited Pausanias to dinner and after giving him plenty of unmixed wine handed his body over to his muleteers to abuse in their cups. **8** On recovering from his inebriation he was shocked and pained at this outrageous treatment and accused Attalos before the King. Philip was furious at this shameless crime, but preferred not to take action because of his relationship to Attalos and the current need he had of his services, **9** for Attalos was the nephew of Kleopatra, whom Philip had just married, and had been chosen as general of the advance force to be sent into Asia, for he was valiant in conflict. The King, therefore, tried calming Pausanias' reasonable anger at this treatment of him by making him splendid presents and promoting him amongst the bodyguards. **16.94.1** Pausanias, however, kept his anger burning hot and focused on getting revenge not just on the person who had committed the outrage, but on the person who had not avenged him … **3** He posted horses at the gates, and came to the theatre entrance with a Celtic dagger concealed about his person. When Philip directed the friends who were accompanying him to precede him into the theatre, and the bodyguards kept their distance, Pausanias saw the King on his own, hurried forward, gave him a blow right through his ribs, and laid him out dead, and then ran towards the gates and the horses prepared for his escape. **4** One group of the bodyguards hastened to the King's corpse, while the others streamed out in pursuit of the murderer, among them Leonnatos, Perdikkas and Attalos. Pausanias had a head start and would have jumped on his horse before they could reach him, if his boot had not got caught in a creeper and made him fall. As a result, Perdikkas and the others caught up with him as he was getting up from the ground and killed him with their javelins. **16.95.1** It was through such a disaster that Philip, who had become the greatest of the kings of Europe in his time, and who, because of the extent of his kingdom, had made himself a throned companion of the twelve gods, met his end, after a reign of twenty-four years.

14.54 Plutarch *Life of Alexander* 10.6–8: Was Olympias Implicated?

On Philip's marriage to Kleopatra, Olympias withdrew to Epiros, and Alexander (the heir) to Illyria; Alexander later returned to Pella and was formally reconciled with his father, but the court situation must have been strained. At Euripides *Med*. 289, Medea kills Creusa's father, Jason, and Jason's new bride Creusa, and by quoting the line Alexander was supposedly encouraging Pausanias similarly to kill the giver of the bride (Attalos, as Kleopatra's guardian), the bridegroom (Philip) and the bride (Kleopatra): cf. doc. 4.70. Alexander is hardly likely to have openly encouraged the assassination in this way.

10.6 When Pausanias, who had been treated outrageously at the instigation of Attalos and Kleopatra and was unable to obtain reparation for this, murdered Philip, most of the guilt revolved around Olympias as she had encouraged the young man's wrath and spurred him on, but some slander also attached itself to Alexander. **7** It is said that when Pausanias encountered him after the outrage and passionately expressed his grief at the occurrence, Alexander quoted the iambic verse from the *Medea*:

> 'the giver of the bride, the bridegroom and the bride.'

8 But he did seek out the conspirators in the plot and punish them, though he was annoyed with Olympias for the brutal way she had treated Kleopatra while he was away.

14.55 Arrian *Expedition of Alexander* 7.9.1–5: Alexander's View of Philip's Achievements

Alexander's troops mutinied at Opis (Babylonia) in 324 BC (doc. 15.32); Alexander at this point reminded them how much they owed to Philip, who had been responsible for the creation of the Macedonian empire. In sections (4) and (5) he gives a brief history of Philip's path to the mastery of Greece.

7.9.1 'It is not to change your minds about wanting to go home, Macedonians, that I shall make this speech, for you may go wherever you wish as far as I am concerned; I just want to make you aware of your character and ours and the way you have behaved — as you leave for home. **2** First I shall begin my speech with Philip my father, as is proper. Philip took you on when you were penniless vagabonds, mostly clothed in skins, grazing a few sheep up on the mountains and on their behalf fighting — with poor results — Illyrians and Triballians and the neighbouring Thracians. He gave you cloaks to wear in place of skins; he brought you down from the mountains to the plains; he trained you so you could engage with the barbarians on your borders, and no longer relied for your safety on your strongholds rather than on your innate courage; he made you inhabitants of cities and gave you good laws and customs. **3** It was he who made you masters, and not the slaves and subjects of those barbarians who previously used to harry and plunder yourselves and your property; he also added most of Thrace to Macedonia, and by capturing the most advantageous places by the sea opened the country up to trade; he ensured that you could work the mines in safety; **4** he made you rulers of the Thessalians, who in the old days used to frighten you to death; by humbling the Phokian people he made you a pathway into Greece which was broad and easy instead of narrow and rough; the Athenians and Thebans who were always lying in wait to attack Macedonia he so greatly humbled, — and we were part of these campaigns — that instead of paying the Athenians tribute and taking orders from the Thebans it was our turn to give *them* security. **5** He also invaded the Peloponnese and settled matters there as well, and his recognition as absolute leader over the whole of Greece conferred renown not so much upon himself as upon the Macedonian state.

15

ALEXANDER 'THE GREAT' OF MACEDON, 336–323 BC

Alexander succeeded Philip as king of Macedon and hegemon (leader) of the League of Corinth on his father's assassination in 336 BC. He was the son of Olympias, who claimed that his was a divine conception (doc. 15.1). Estrangement between Philip and Olympias complicated Alexander's relationship with his father; this was particularly so when Philip married the Macedonian Kleopatra Eurydike, who bore him a daughter. It seems reasonably clear, however, that Philip always considered Alexander his true heir. Philip prepared him for the throne by arranging that Aristotle should be his tutor (doc. 15.1) and by allowing him to govern Macedonia in his absence in 340 BC. Most particularly, Alexander proved his military mettle at Chaironeia in 338 BC (doc. 14.48), and showed he was a worthy military successor to his father.

The circumstances surrounding Philip's assassination are unclear, but it is doubtful that Alexander was involved. Olympias, however, certainly took the opportunity to dispose of her rival Kleopatra Eurydike. Attalos (with Parmenion) had been appointed by Philip to take charge of the invasion of Asia Minor, but he was now killed, paying with his life for his connection with Kleopatra and his comments that with the marriage a true Macedonian heir to the throne would be born (doc. 14.37): Olympias was from Epiros. Alexander was also faced with a number of possible revolts, with which he dealt firmly on his accession (docs 15.2–3).

Though Alexander succeeded his father as hegemon of the League of Corinth, Thebes rebelled in 335 BC while he was campaigning on the Danube. The other Greeks did not join the revolt, and he moved quickly to sack Thebes mercilessly, except for its temples and the descendants of Pindar; 6,000 Thebans were killed and 30,000 enslaved (doc. 15.4). With Greece quiet, Alexander left Macedonia and Greece in the hands of Antipater, a wise choice as in the event Antipater dealt swiftly with the Thracian and then the Spartan revolt under Agis III, both in 330 BC (doc. 15.19). By 324, however, Alexander and Antipater had fallen out and he was replaced by Krateros. Because of differences with Antipater in 331 BC Olympias returned in Epiros, though she remained in correspondence with Alexander.

In 334 BC Alexander launched his invasion of the Persian empire, crossing the Hellespont with a reasonably modest military force in comparison to the Persian forces he would encounter (doc. 15.6). The Macedonians formed the greater part of the army but the Greek allies of the League of Corinth supplied troops as well. The first encounter with Darius was at the Battle of Granikos in 334 BC, not far from where Alexander had crossed into Asia Minor (doc. 15.7). Granikos was the first of three set-piece battles which dealt the death blows to Darius and the Persian empire (the other two were Issos and Gaugamela). Darius had moved quickly to stem the Macedonian invasion, clearly aiming for a decisive victory here. Having crushed the Persian cavalry and thus Darius' army, Alexander was able to move on the great cities of Asia Minor: Sardis, Ephesos and Miletos. At Priene he dedicated the temple to Athena Polias (doc. 15.8), and the city honoured his second-in-command

Antigonos (doc. 15.9). Control of the Aegean islands was, however, hotly contested, yet Alexander disbanded his fleet. Memnon of Rhodes' defence of Halikarnassos with the Persian fleet in 334 BC stalled Alexander's progress for several months; the city was captured in that year but when Memnon redeployed he captured Chios and Lesbos, and urged a Persian attack on Macedonia itself. Affairs in the Aegean islands and coastal cities were complicated, as is indicated by events at the city of Eresos on Lesbos, where Alexander was concerned to replace tyranny with democracy (doc. 15.36). Further Persian attention to this area could have reaped solid benefits but Darius crippled the Persian fleet by withdrawing its manpower. Darius' decision to use the mercenaries in the fleet to fight in the next land battle handed the cities of the islands and Asia Minor coast to Alexander, who had pushed on eastwards, taking Lycia, Pamphylia and Phrygia. Here he cut the so-called Gordion knot and so claimed for himself the prophecy that the person who achieved this would rule Asia (doc. 15.10).

In Cilicia Alexander took the initiative and choice of battleground, tempting Darius into terrain completely unsuitable for the Persian forces at Issos in November 333 BC (doc. 15.12). Yet Darius caught the Macedonian forces in the rear by not taking the pass into the area which Alexander had expected him to use. If Darius had avoided confrontation for the moment he might well have had Alexander cornered here. But the Great King decided on battle; the Persian army was routed but the Macedonians turned to plundering the Persian camp and a sizeable section of the Persian army successfully retreated. Darius' mother, wife and children were captured but were treated well. Alexander and Hephaistion later each married one of his daughters in the Macedonian–Persian weddings at Susa (doc. 15.32). Darius made overtures of peace to Alexander which the latter, from a position of overwhelming military superiority and confidence, emphatically rejected (docs 15.13, 15.15).

Persia to the Euphrates river was now Alexander's. The siege of Tyre on the Phoenician coast was vigorously prosecuted in 332 BC in a famous struggle in which a population sought to defend its freedom against a determined conqueror (doc. 15.14). Alexander then marched south to Egypt, where he was greeted in October 332 BC as pharaoh and crowned at Memphis. He was now, like all Egypt's kings before him, officially 'Son of Re' and the living incarnation of the god Horus. He founded Alexandria in 331 on the Mediterranean coast, which was to become one of the most famous and cultured Greek cities of antiquity (doc. 15.16). Then he travelled to the oracle of the god Ammon – known to the Greeks – at Siwah, and here either received or claimed to have received confirmation that he was Zeus' son (doc. 15.17, cf. 15.1); at Gaugamela he was to pray for Zeus' assistance on the grounds that his 'father' should help him. Leaving Egypt, returning through Phoenicia and arriving in Mesopotamia, his last and crucial battle was fought successfully against Darius at Gaugamela (doc. 15.18). Here as victor Alexander was proclaimed 'King of Asia', and appointed Macedonians to the Persian satrapies. Memnon of Rhodes, however, organised an uprising in Thrace, and the Spartans revolted (doc. 15.10). Antipater dealt with these uprisings, and the crushing of the Spartans assured Alexander of peace in Greece for the rest of his reign, which allowed him to pursue his conquests further eastwards.

Alexander then travelled to Babylon, Susa and finally to Persepolis, the magnificent Persian capital, which was burned apparently in a drunken Macedonian riot, though this was later claimed to have been fitting revenge for Xerxes' burning of Greek temples (doc. 15.20). In August 330 BC, Bessos, satrap of Bactria, murdered Darius and proclaimed himself Artaxerxes V, but was swiftly dealt with by Alexander. Alexander was now adopting Persian dress, customs and mannerisms, and leading a more 'barbaric' lifestyle, while his appointing Persians to office also aroused Macedonian antipathy. Dissension in the Macedonian ranks had opened up. Philotas in 330 BC was apparently part of or at least aware of a plot to kill Alexander and was executed, and Kleitos the Black and Hephaistion replaced him with his command of the Companions (the cavalry) split in two.

Philotas' father Parmenion, who had commanded the Macedonian left wing at Granikos, Issos and Gaugamela, was executed and not replaced (doc. 15.21). He had perhaps disagreed with Alexander as to how far their conquest of the Persian empire should extend and whether Alexander should replace the Great King. The murder of Kleitos at Alexander's own hands followed in 328 BC; he had criticised flatterers who compared Alexander's achievements to those of his father and ancient heroes to the latter's detriment (doc. 15.22).

A major revolt in Bactria, the huge north-eastern sector of the empire, broke out in 329 BC and ended when the Rock of Sogdiana was brilliantly captured in 327 BC (doc. 15.23); here Alexander met Roxane, who became his first wife. In the same year the court historian Kallisthenes, who had detractors who criticised his historical accuracy even in antiquity (doc. 15.12), made clear his opposition to the adoption of the Persian practice of proskynesis (prostration before the king) to Alexander; Kallisthenes left 'having missed out on a kiss' (doc. 15.24). Soon he was implicated in the Royal Pages' conspiracy and lost his life. Opposition and criticism to Alexander were not to be tolerated.

Alexander moved into India, defeating King Poros (doc. 15.26), but his troops mutinied at the Hyphasis river in 326 BC and refused to conquer any further (doc. 15.29). Alexander began the march back westwards; his troops' loyalty was confirmed by their reaction to his wounding in the Mallian campaign (doc. 15.30). But their mutiny in India prompted Alexander to rely more on the Persians, and at Opis in Mesopotamia he announced his dismissal of the unfit Macedonians (doc. 15.32). Matters escalated into a second mutiny; and Arrian reports that complaints were made about his adoption of Persian dress, and the infiltration of Persians into the army – and their training and dressing as Macedonians – while Alexander was taunted about his claim to be the son of Ammon. He reacted by announcing the discharge of all the Macedonians and the complete Persianisation of the army. Preparations began for further conquests.

Harpalos, Alexander's treasurer, absconded to Athens with a huge treasure in 324 BC (doc. 15.37). In the same year Alexander promulgated the 'Exiles' Decree', which provided for the return of all but sacrilegious exiles to their home cities (docs 15.38–39). This was perhaps designed to cause civil unrest in a number of cities, which would have allowed Alexander the chance to interfere in their affairs: it certainly paved the way later for the Lamian War in Greece after Alexander's death. Alexander apparently requested too that the Greeks honour him as a god. Hephaistion died at Ecbatana (doc. 15.42), and Alexander himself soon after at Babylon in 323 BC (doc. 15.43). He ended his reign as a partly Persianised ruler, willing to rely on the Persians to maintain and extend his empire, and convinced of his own divinity. Revolt in Greece, dissension amongst his generals and the carving up of his empire into what became the great hellenistic monarchies followed swiftly upon his death.

Alexander's conquests caused the deaths and enslavement of tens of thousands of bystanders, the razing or enslaving of numerous cities, including the holocaust of arguably the ancient world's greatest city, Persepolis, the lives of tens of thousands of combatants and the destruction of an ancient culture. In return, there was the foundation of numerous Greek cities throughout what had been the Persian empire and the spread of Greek culture, and the establishment of the hellenistic kingdoms. The overall verdict of antiquity was one of admiration for Alexander (docs 15.3, 15.41), though a number of his actions did not escape criticism.

15.1 Plutarch *Life of Alexander* 2.1– 9, 7.1–8.3: Alexander's Parentage and Education

The stories concerning the omens which accompanied Alexander's birth were part of Alexander's later claim that he was the son of Zeus, and so was divine. Plutarch relates that Philip sent to Delphi to enquire as to the meaning of the snake, and was told to sacrifice to Ammon and that he would lose the eye with which he had seen the god in this form (Plut. *Alex.* 3). Alexander's earlier tutors were Leonidas, a relative of Olympias, and Lysimachos, but when Alexander was fourteen years old, Philip sent for Aristotle, who was his tutor at Pella from 342 to 335 BC. For Alexander's devotion to the *Iliad*, see doc. 15.16.

2.1 Alexander's lineage on his father's side was from Herakles through Karanos, and on his mother's side from Aiakos through Neoptolemos, and this is accepted without dispute. **2** Philip, it is said, was being initiated in the mysteries at Samothrace when he was still a young man, and she a child bereft of parents, and fell in love with her and betrothed himself to her straight away, having gained the consent of her brother Arymbas. **3** Then the bride, on the night before they went into the marriage chamber, saw a bolt of lightning, after a peal of thunder, falling on her womb, and a great fire kindled by this thunder strike which broke into flames that spread everywhere before being extinguished. **4** Philip, some time after the marriage, also had a dream that he was putting a seal on his wife's womb: the figure on the seal, he thought, was the image of a lion. **5** The other diviners suspected from the vision that Philip needed to keep a closer guard on his relations with his wife, but Aristander of Telmessos said that she was pregnant, since a seal would not be put on anything that was empty, and pregnant with a son whose nature would be ferocious and lion-like. **6** A serpent was once seen lying by Olympias' side as she lay sleeping: this, it is said, more than anything else dampened Philip's love towards her so he no longer came often to sleep by her side, either because he feared his wife might practise some spells and enchantments upon him or because he kept away from her as being united to a higher being.

2.7 There is, however, another story about this, to the effect that all the women of that region were involved in Orphic rites and the worship of Dionysos from the most ancient times, under the name of 'Klodones' and 'Mimallones', and celebrated the same rituals as the Edonian women and the Thracian women in the region of Mount Haimos, **8** from whom it would seem the name 'threskeuein' came to be applied to these immoderate and curious rites. **9** Olympias was more involved in this type of possession than other women and in a state of divine frenzy would, like a wild woman, bring great tame serpents into the Bacchic companies, which would often crawl out from amongst the ivy and the sacred winnowing-baskets or entwine themselves around the women's thyrsoi (staffs entwined with ivy) and garlands, terrifying the men.

7.1 As Philip saw that Alexander's nature was unyielding and that he could not be compelled by force, but was easily led to what was right by reasoning, he tried to use persuasion rather than command, **2** and would not completely entrust his direction and training to the teachers of poetry and music and general education, as being a question of much greater importance, and as Sophocles says, 'a job for many bridles and rudders too'. Philip therefore summoned the most famous and erudite of philosophers, Aristotle, and paid him an immense and highly prestigious salary for his tuition. **3** Aristotle's home city, Stageira, which had been destroyed by Philip, he resettled and restored those of the citizens who had been exiled or enslaved. **4** As a place where they could study and work he gave them the precinct of the nymphs at Mieza, where to this day they point out Aristotle's stone seats and shady walks.

8.1 In my view, Alexander's love of the art of medicine was primarily imparted to him by Aristotle, for he was not only fond of the theory, but actually looked after his friends when they were sick and prescribed some treatments and diets for them, as can be learned from his letters. **2** He was also naturally fond of literature and learning. He considered and called the *Iliad* the essential guide to the art of warfare, and used to take with him Aristotle's revised version of it, which is called the '*Iliad* of the casket', and always kept it lying beside his dagger underneath his pillow, as Onesikritos tells us, **3** and when he was unable to find any other books in central Asia he told Harpalos to send him some, and Harpalos sent him the books of Philistos, a number of tragedies of Euripides, Sophocles and Aeschylus, and the dithyrambs of Telestos and Philoxenos.

15.2 Diodorus *Library of History* 17.2.1–3, 3.1–6: Alexander's First Tasks as Ruler

Alexander was born in October 356 BC, and succeeded his father on the Macedonian throne in October 336 BC. At sixteen (340 BC), he was left as regent when Philip was attacking Byzantium, and earned his military credentials at Chaironeia at eighteen (338 BC). Alexander took the opportunity of Pausanias' murder of his father Philip to purge some possible rivals of his own, including his cousin Amyntas and the family of Alexander of Lyncestis. Olympias killed Philip's latest wife, Kleopatra, and her baby daughter. It was the Spartans, not the Arkadians, who had refused to accept Philip's hegemony (doc. 14.50).

17.2.1 On succeeding to the throne Alexander started by inflicting fitting punishment on his father's murderers and then turned his attention to his father's funeral, establishing his authority much more successfully than anyone had expected. **2** He was after all fairly young, and due to his age some people thought little of his abilities, but he began by winning the Macedonians' support through diplomatic statements, for, he said, the king had changed in name only, and affairs would be handled no less effectively than under his father's government. He then gave audiences to the embassies and courteously asked the Greeks to maintain toward him the goodwill they had previously shown to his father. **3** He kept his soldiers occupied with regular training in arms and military exercises, and established discipline …

17.3.1 Alexander was aware that many of the Greeks were on the point of revolt and was seriously concerned. **2** The Athenians, with Demosthenes continually stirring up opposition towards the Macedonians, were delighted when they heard of Philip's death, and, as they were not prepared to hand over their leading position among the Greeks to the Macedonians, they communicated secretly with Attalos and agreed to work together, while they urged many of the cities to hang onto their freedom. **3** The Aitolians voted to restore those people from Akarnania who had experienced exile because of Philip, while the Ambrakiots were persuaded by Aristarchos to expel the garrison Philip had established in their city and turn their city into a democracy. **4** Similarly the Thebans voted to expel the garrison in the Kadmeia, and not allow Alexander to take over the leadership of the Greeks. The Arkadians were the only Greeks who had never recognized Philip's leadership, and now did not accept that of Alexander, **5** while as far as the other Peloponnesians were concerned the Argives, Eleians and Spartans, as well as others, were set to recover their independence. Across the frontiers of Macedonia many tribes were ready to revolt and there was a sense of upheaval throughout the barbarians in that area. **6** Despite, however, all the difficulties and fears facing his kingdom on all sides, Alexander, though just a young man, dealt with all the crises to his authority with amazing speed: he gained the support of some through persuasion and diplomacy, and used terror tactics to bring others into line, while some he had to force into subjection.

15.3 Arrian *Expedition of Alexander* 1.1.1–3: Alexander and the League of Corinth

Alexander had fought at Chaironeia in 338 BC with great success (doc. 14.48). Philip's death in 336 caused unrest in Athens and the Peloponnese, so he marched to the latter; there he requested of the Peloponnesians that he should lead the expedition against Persia, which they had given to Philip. Sparta alone disagreed. Athens was restless but, when Alexander approached it, granted honours 'even greater than those they had bestowed upon Philip' (1.1.3).

1.1.1 It is reported that Philip's death took place in the archonship of Pythodelos at Athens (336 BC). Alexander, Philip's son, succeeded to the kingship and marched into Greece: he was then about twenty. **2** There he assembled all the Greeks in the Peloponnese and requested of them the leadership of the expedition against the Persians, which they had already granted to Philip. They all agreed to his request except the Spartans, who answered that it was their custom not to follow others, but to lead them. **3** There was also a revolutionary movement in Athens, but they were panic-stricken at Alexander's initial approach to the city and granted Alexander honours even greater than those they had bestowed upon Philip. Alexander returned to Macedonia and started preparing for his expedition against Asia.

15.4 Plutarch *Life of Alexander* 11.9–12.6: Timokleia and the Sack of Thebes

After Athens, Alexander marched into Thrace against the restless tribes of the Triballi and Illyrians. While he was there Thebes revolted in 335 BC, and he made an example of the city: it was destroyed and its inhabitants enslaved and this successfully cowed the other Greeks. The Kadmeia is the citadel of Thebes. Cf. Arr. 1.7–10; Diod. 17.8.3–14.1: 'Over six thousand Thebans were killed, thirty thousand were enslaved, and the amount of plunder was incredible' (14.1).

11.9 The Thebans struggled with a valour and earnestness beyond their powers against the enemy they were facing, which was far more numerous than they were; **10** but when the Macedonian garrison left the Kadmeia and fell upon them from the rear, most of them were surrounded and fell in this engagement, and the city was captured, plundered and demolished, **11** the main reason being that Alexander expected that the Greeks would be thunderstruck at such a catastrophe and keep their heads down out of fear, as well as priding himself on humouring the accusations of his allies, for the Phokians and Plataeans had made complaints against the Thebans. **12** He therefore put to one side the priests, all the guest-friends of the Macedonians, the descendants of Pindar, and those who had voted against the rebellion, and sold all the others — there were about thirty thousand. The dead amounted to more than six thousand.

12.1 Among the many dreadful disasters which held the city in their grip, some Thracians broke into the house of Timokleia, a very respectable and prudent woman, and, while the rest were seizing her property, the leader after disgracefully raping her asked if she had gold or silver hidden anywhere. **2** She admitted that she did and led him on his own into the garden and showed him a well, telling him that when the city was captured she had thrown into it her most valuable possessions. **3** As the Thracian was bent over peering in, she came up behind and pushed him in, threw a number of stones on top of him and killed him. **4** She was tied up and brought to Alexander by the Thracians, showing by her appearance and manner of walking that she was a person of great dignity and high-mindedness, so unperturbedly and calmly did she follow her escort. **5** When the King enquired of her who she was, she replied that she was the sister of Theagenes who drew up the forces that met Philip to fight for the liberty of Greece and who fell at Chaironeia. **6** Alexander was amazed at her reply and what she had done, and told her to depart with her children in freedom.

15.5 Plutarch *Life of Alexander* 14.1–5: Alexander and Diogenes the 'Cynic'

Alexander was in Corinth as head of the League of Corinth in 335 BC. Diogenes, exiled from Sinope, spent much of his time at Corinth and Athens. He believed in following the dictates of nature rather than law or convention, with minimal material possessions. The term cynic means 'dog-like'. Cf. Arr. 7.2.1.

14.1 The Greeks now assembled at the Isthmus and voted to make an expedition against the Persians with Alexander, who was proclaimed their leader. **2** Many statesmen and philosophers came to him to congratulate him and he expected that Diogenes of Sinope would do the same, as he was staying in Corinth. **3** As, however, he paid not the slightest attention to Alexander and continued to laze around at Kraneion, Alexander went to see him. He found Diogenes lying in the sunshine. **4** Diogenes just raised himself slightly at the sight of so many people approaching, and stared at Alexander, who greeted him and asked if he required anything. Diogenes just replied, 'Stand a little out of my sun.' **5** It is said that Alexander was so impressed by this and so admired the man's haughty disdain and lofty manner that he said to his companions who were laughing and making jokes as they departed, 'In truth, were I not Alexander, I would like to be Diogenes.'

THE MACEDONIAN ASSAULT ON ASIA

When news came of the destruction of Thebes, the Athenians were celebrating the Great Mysteries, and, in an unprecedented move, they abandoned the rites. On the motion of Demades they chose an embassy of ten men to send to Alexander; he replied that they should surrender to him ten Athenian politicians, including Demosthenes and Lykourgos. The Athenians did not do so but sent a second embassy and Alexander relented, perhaps in a hurry to undertake the expedition against Persia or unwilling to create further ill will in Greece (Arr. 1.10.3–6). He returned to Macedonia, and in spring 334 BC marched to the Hellespont.

15.6 Plutarch *Life of Alexander* 15.1–7: Alexander's Forces

Alexander set out for Asia with a fairly small force, first distributing land to his associates as a reward for their service. He crossed the Hellespont early in 334 BC. Antipater was left in charge of Greece, and remained the head of Macedonian forces there until 324 BC. Perdikkas was a Macedonian noble and one of the Companions of Alexander. Cf. Arr. 1.10.3–12; Diod. 17.17.3–5. [*FGH* 139 F4; *FGH* F40; *FGH* 134 F2.]

15.1 As to the number of his troops, those who put it at the lowest figure state that he had thirty thousand infantry and four thousand cavalry, and those who put it at the highest forty-three thousand infantry and five thousand cavalry. **2** To provision these, Aristoboulos writes that he had no more than seventy talents, Duris that he only had maintenance for thirty days, and Oneirokritos that he was in debt for two hundred talents as well. **3** But although he was setting out with such small and meagre resources he would not embark on the ship before he had enquired into the circumstances of his Companions (hetairoi) and allocated a farm to one, a village to another and to another the revenue from some community or harbour. **4** When nearly all the crown property had been expended or assigned, Perdikkas asked him, 'What, O King, are you leaving for yourself?' 'My hopes,' he replied. 'Then,' said Perdikkas, 'those of us who are going on campaign with you will share them with you.' **5** Perdikkas then refused to take the property which had been assigned to him and some of Alexander's other friends did the same. **6** On those who wanted and accepted his gifts Alexander bestowed them willingly and expended in these distributions most of what he owned in Macedonia. **7** This was the spirit and this the equipment with which he crossed the Hellespont.

15.7 Diodorus *Library of History* 17.19.1– 21.6: Battle at the River Granikos, May 334 BC

Alexander in 334 BC crossed the Hellespont, and fought his first engagement against the Persians at the nearby river Granikos in May, where he scored a comprehensive victory. The Persians lost the initial advantage of the high ground, and, although their infantry greatly outnumbered the Macedonians, preferred to use their cavalry. Alexander fought on the right wing, and Darius engaged him in single combat. Here at Granikos Kleitos the Black saved Alexander's life, which he reminded him of scathingly just before Alexander speared him in 328 BC (doc. 15.22). When the Persian cavalry was overwhelmed and defeated, it was the Greek mercenaries in Persian employ who fought on and were massacred. After Granikos, Miletos was captured, Alexander demobilised his fleet, and besieged Halikarnassos; he then advanced through Lycia, Pamphilia and Phrygia. Cf. Arr. 1.13.1–16.7 for a different account of Granikos; Plut. *Alex*. 16.

17.19.1 When Alexander learned that the barbarians' forces had massed there, he marched forward by the quickest route and made camp opposite the enemy, so that the Granikos flowed between the two camps. **2** The barbarians, who occupied the high ground, remained where they were, as they had decided to fall on the enemy as they crossed the river, assuming that, with the Macedonians' phalanx broken up, they would win the battle more easily. **3** Alexander, however, forestalled the enemy by boldly bringing his army over at dawn and deploying them in battle order. The barbarians on their part stationed the mass of their cavalry along the entire Macedonian front, having decided to begin the battle with these. **4** Memnon of Rhodes and Arsamenes the satrap held the left wing, each with their own cavalry, and next to them was positioned Arsites with the cavalry from Paphlagonia, then Spithrobates, satrap of Ionia, leading the Hyrkanian cavalry, while the right wing was held by one thousand Medes, and two thousand cavalry with Rheomithres as well as the same number of Bactrians. The cavalry of other races held the centre, and were numerous and chosen for their valour. All together the cavalry came to more than ten thousand. **5** The Persian infantry were not less than one hundred thousand, but they were positioned behind and stayed where they were as the cavalry were considered to be sufficient to defeat the Macedonians.

6 As each side's cavalry plunged eagerly into danger against the opposition, the Thessalian horse on the left wing under Parmenion's command met the attack of the troops ranged against them, and Alexander, who had the best of the cavalry with him on the right wing, was the first to charge upon the Persians and engage with the enemy, and inflicted great slaughter on them.

17.20.1 The barbarians put up a stout resistance and opposed the Macedonians' valour with their own spirited courage: indeed Fortune had caused the most pre-eminent men to engage at the same location to contest the victory. **2** The satrap of Ionia, Spithrobates, Persian-born and son-in-law of Darius the King, who excelled in courage, hurled himself at the Macedonians alongside his forty comrades in battle, all 'Relatives' and distinguished for their valour, pressing hard upon those opposing him, and fighting bravely, killing some of his opponents and wounding others. **3** Because the strength of the attack endangered his troops, Alexander turned his horse towards the satrap and charged at the barbarian.

The Persian thought that the gods must have given him this chance for single combat, and hoped that through his own brave deeds Asia would be liberated from this dreadful menace, Alexander's renowned daring be brought to an end by his own hands, and Persia's glory avoid disgrace. He was the first to throw his javelin at Alexander and cast it with such force and hurled the spear so violently that he pierced Alexander's shield and right shoulder and drove it through his breastplate. **4** The King threw off the weapon drooping from his arm, urged on his horse with his spurs and, making use of the momentum gained by his aggressive attack, thrust his spear through the middle of the satrap's breastplate. **5** When this happened all the nearby ranks on both sides cried out at this outstanding act of valour, but the point of the spear broke off against the breastplate with the snapped-off shaft rebounding, and the Persian drew his sword and rushed against him. The King grabbed his spear in time to thrust it at his face and drive the blow home. **6** As he was falling his brother Rhosakes charged and brought his sword down on Alexander's head with such an aggressive blow that it split his helmet open and slightly grazed his scalp. **7** As Rhosakes aimed another blow at the same weak spot, Kleitos, known as 'the Black', charged up on his horse and cut off the barbarian's arm.

17.21.1 The 'Relatives' now rallied all together around the two fallen men (Spithridates and Rhosakes), initially hurling their javelins at Alexander and then fighting in close combat, enduring every danger with the aim of killing the King. **2** But although experiencing numerous fierce attacks, he nevertheless was not overcome by the numerical force of the enemy, but taking two blows on his breastplate and one on his head and three on the shield which he had taken from the temple of Athena he still did not give in but, supported by desperate courage, surmounted every danger. **3** After this many of the other noble Persians ranged against him also fell, of whom the most renowned were Atizyes and Pharnakes, brother of Darius' wife, and also Mithrobouzanes, commander of the Cappadocians. **4** As a result of many of their commanders having been killed and all the Persian companies beaten by the Macedonians, those drawn up against Alexander were the first to be compelled to flee and then the rest. The King by common consent carried off the prize for courage and was seen as chiefly responsible for the victory in its entirety; next to him the Thessalian cavalry won a great reputation for valour due to the way they handled their squadrons to best advantage and their distinctive fighting quality. **5** After the rout of the cavalry, the infantry engaged with each other in a short contest, for the barbarians, terrified at the flight of the cavalry and broken in spirit, turned to flee. **6** The total of the Persians' infantry killed was more than 10,000 and of the cavalry not less than 2,000, with more than 20,000 taken prisoner. After the battle the King held magnificent funerary rites for the dead, in the hope of inspiring his soldiers by this type of honour to become more eager to face the dangers of battle.

15.8 Tod 2.184: Alexander Dedicates the Temple of Athena Polias at Priene

Following his victory at the Granikos, Alexander took Sardis, which the Ionians had burned in 498 BC, and which had led to Xerxes' invasion of Greece. He also took Ephesos and Miletos; then at Priene he rededicated the recently completed temple of Athena Polias, to which he had donated funds. For the cult statue, see Paus. 7.5.5.

King Alexander dedicated this temple to Athena Polias.

15.9 Tod 2.186: Priene Honours Antigonos 'the One-Eyed', 334 BC

Alexander restored democracy at Priene – as in the Greek cities of Asia Minor which he liberated – and the city honoured his general Antigonos Monophthalmos ('one-eyed') with privileges including proxenia and citizenship. He had commanded Alexander's Greek allies in the invasion of Asia, and Alexander made him satrap of Phrygia. These honours were probably meant to convey their flattery of Alexander. [*SIG*^{3} 278.]

Resolved by the Council and People, in the month Metageitnion, on the second day, at a principal meeting of the assembly, when the Prienians were autonomous, in the presidency of Hippokrates: Antigonos, son of Philip, of Macedon, since he has been a benefactor and zealous to aid the city of the Prienians, shall be given proxenia and citizenship and the right to possess land and house, and freedom from all taxation in everything to do with his household with the exception of the land, and freedom to import and export both in time of war and in time of peace with inviolability and without treaty, and right of access to the magistrates and the people of Priene first after the sacrifices. And these privileges shall belong to both him and his descendants.

15.10 Arrian *Expedition of Alexander* 2.3.6–8: A Knotty Problem

There was a prophecy that whoever undid the Gordion knot would rule Asia. Gordion is the capital of Phrygia; Alexander in 333 BC used lateral thinking to solve the problem. Cf. Plut. *Alex*. 18.2; Curt. 3.1.14–18. [*FGH* 139 F7.]

2.3.6 There was a legend about the wagon — that whoever untied the knot of the wagon's yoke would rule Asia. **7** The knot was made of cornel bark and neither its end nor its beginning were visible. Alexander was unable to find a way to untie the knot, but didn't want to leave it tied in case this caused the populace concern. Some say he struck it with his sword and cut the knot and declared that it was now untied; but Aristoboulos writes that he took out the pole pin, the bolt which goes right through the pole which held the knot together, and so pulled the yoke from the pole. **8** I cannot say with certainty how he actually dealt with the knot, but he and his entourage left the wagon as if the prophecy about the knot had been fulfilled. And during the night there was thunder and lightning as signs from heaven, so on the next day Alexander offered a sacrifice to those gods who had shown the signs and how to undo the knot.

ISSOS AND 'MISSED OUT ON A KISS'

15.11 Diodorus *Library of History* 17.32.1–34.9, 36.6: The Battle at Issos, 333 BC

After Phrygia, Alexander moved to Cilicia. Darius marched from Babylon in 333 BC and Alexander enticed the huge Persian army into the narrow coastal plain south of Issos, in south-east Cilicia, probably in November, but had not counted on Darius' forces arriving in his rear. Here the narrowness of the plain rendered Darius' overwhelming forces ineffective. Alexander broke the Persian left flank and then smashed the Persian centre, where Darius as usual was stationed: he fled. Alexander now controlled all the territory of the Persian empire up to the Euphrates river. But notably Tyre remained to be subdued (doc. 15.15). Cf. Arr. 2.6–11; Plut. *Alex*. 19–20; Curt. 3.8–11.

17.32.1 Alexander's mother wrote to him, warning him amongst other useful pieces of advice, to beware of the Lyncestian Alexander, a spirited man distinguished by his bravery, who was trusted by the king and accompanied him as part of his group of friends. **2** As there were many other reasonable circumstances leading to this accusation, he was seized, bound and put under guard, until he could be tried in court. Alexander then learned that Darius was only a few days' march away and sent Parmenion with a force to take control of the pass of the so-called ... [Cilician] Gates. When Parmenion reached the spot he forced out the barbarians who were holding the pass and took control of it. **3** Because Darius wanted his army to be unencumbered he sent off his baggage-train and camp followers to Damascus in Syria; then learning that Alexander controlled the pass he marched quickly to meet him as he thought that Alexander would not dare to fight him on the plain. **4** The local peoples were unimpressed by the small numbers of Macedonians, but were staggered by the huge size of the Persians' army and abandoned Alexander to come over to Darius. They presented the Persians with food and other supplies in their eagerness to support them and in their own view were sure that the Persians would win. Alexander, however, controlled Issos, a noteworthy city, which he had frightened into submitting.

17.33.1 When his scouts announced that Darius was thirty stades away and marching forward in a terrifying way with his army drawn up for battle, Alexander realised that the gods had given him the chance to destroy the Persian power with a single victory, and inspired his soldiers with the right words to face a contest for ultimate supremacy, positioning the battalions of infantry and the squadrons of cavalry as suited the location, putting the cavalry in the front of the entire army and instructing the infantry phalanx to remain in reserve behind it. **2** He advanced at the head of the right wing to engage the enemy, leading the best of his cavalry; the Thessalian cavalry, which surpassed all the rest in bravery and experience, were positioned on the left wing. **3** When the armies were within missile range, the barbarians let fly at Alexander and his men such a quantity of missiles that they collided with each other due to their density in flight, and weakened their effectiveness. **4** When the trumpeters on both sides sounded the signal for attack, the Macedonians let out a portentous battle cry, which the barbarians then answered so that all the mountainous region around them echoed the noise, with the loudness of the

Persians' cry surpassing the previous war cry as the 500,000 men shouted together with one voice ...

17.34.1 The officers on each side fought at the head of their men and through their own valour inspired the rest to valiant deeds. And so there were seen many sorts of wounds inflicted, and many types of struggles motivated by the desire for victory. **2** When the Persian Oxathres, the brother of Darius who was renowned for his fighting abilities, saw Alexander hastening against Darius with nothing to stop him, he was ambitious to share the same fate as his brother. **3** Taking with him the best of the cavalry in his company, he threw himself with them against Alexander and his men with the thought that this example of love for his brother would bring him high renown among the Persians, and fought in front of Darius' chariot, engaging the enemy with skill and daring and killing many of them. **4** But Alexander's men surpassed them in fighting abilities and soon a mass of bodies was heaped around Darius' chariot; all the Macedonians wanted to strike the King and in their eager rivalry with each other took no thought for sparing their lives.

5 In this contest many of the noblest Persian officers fell, among them Antixyes and Rheomithres and Tasiakas, satrap of Egypt. Many of the Macedonians fell likewise, and Alexander himself happened to be wounded in his thigh, as the enemy were crowded around him. **6** The horses yoked to Darius' chariot had numerous wounds and were terrified by the mass of corpses piled around them, shaking their bridles violently and all but carrying Darius off into the midst of his enemies. So the King himself in this ultimate danger grabbed the reins, compelled to put aside the dignity of his royal position and break the normal custom of Persian kings. **7** Another chariot was brought up for Darius by his attendants and as he transferred to this in the confusion, with the enemy pressing upon him, he fell into panic-stricken terror.

The Persians perceived the King's loss of control and turned to flee. With each unit of cavalry in turn doing the same, the entire cavalry was soon in retreat. **8** As their flight took them through narrow passes and rough terrain they clashed with and trampled each other and many died without receiving a blow from the enemy. They lay there heaped up together, some without armour, others preserving their full panoply; others who still held their naked swords killed those who spitted themselves upon them. The majority, however, escaped through these onto the plain and by driving their horses violently managed to reach the allied cities. **9** The Macedonian phalanx and the Persian infantry now met briefly in battle: the defeat of the cavalry preceding, as it were, the entire victory. All the barbarians were soon in flight and, with so many tens of thousands making their escape through narrow passes, the entire region was soon filled with corpses ...

17.36.6 During the battle more than 100,000 barbarian infantry were killed, and not less than 10,000 cavalry, while the Macedonians lost some 300 infantry and 150 cavalry. This was the outcome of the battle at Issos in Cilicia.

15.12 Polybios *Histories* 12.20.1–6, 22.1–7: Kallisthenes' Ignorance of Military Matters

In a lengthy passage Polybius criticises Kallisthenes' incorrect details of terrain, formation and length of line in his discussion of the battle at the Cilician Gates (12.17–22). Kallisthenes of Olynthos,

Aristotle's nephew, wrote a history dealing with the period 386 to 356 BC, as well as his *Deeds of Alexander*. In 327 he offended Alexander by opposing the practice of proskynesis (prostration), and was put to death for supposed involvement in the Royal Pages' Conspiracy (docs 15.24–25). [*FGH* 124 F7.]

12.20.1 After this Kallisthenes says that Alexander led his army in an extended line, being then about forty stades away from the enemy. One could hardly think up anything more ridiculous than this statement. **2** Where could one possibly find, especially in Cilicia, such an extent of terrain where a phalanx armed with sarissas could advance for forty stades in a formation twenty stades in length? **3** There are so many obstacles to such types of formation and manoeuvre that one could not easily enumerate them all. But just one, actually mentioned by Kallisthenes, is sufficient to bring conviction: **4** he actually states that the torrents coming down from the mountains had made so many crevasses in the plain that most of the Persians in their flight perished in these ravines. **5** Zeus! Alexander wanted to be ready at the appearance of the enemy. **6** What can be less ready than a phalanx arranged in formation which is broken up and disunited?

12.22.1 It would take too long to mention all the other illogicalities in his account, except for just a few final ones. **2** He states that Alexander in putting his army into formation was eager to fight opposite Darius in person; equally, Darius at first wished the same with regard to Alexander, but afterwards changed his mind. **3** But as to how they found out where the other was positioned in his army or where Darius finally went when he changed position, he says absolutely nothing. **4** And how did a formation of heavy-armed soldiers in a phalanx climb the bank of the river which was steep and full of brambles? **5** This is also totally illogical. Such an absurdity cannot be attributed to Alexander whose experience and training in the arts of war is universally acknowledged to have been acquired from his childhood, **6** but rather to the historian, whose ignorance is such that he cannot distinguish between the possible and the impossible. **7** So, let these remarks suffice for Ephoros and Kallisthenes.

15.13 Arrian *Expedition of Alexander* 2.14.1–9: Darius' Response to Defeat

After Issos, Darius fled in his chariot; his mother, wife and children had fallen into Alexander's hands, but Alexander treated them with marked respect. Alexander in his reply to Darius' letter blamed Philip's assassination on Darius. Alexander's position was uncompromising: he would not treat with Darius as an equal for Alexander was now 'King of Asia'. Cf. Diod. 17.39.1–2. The League of Corinth sent an embassy with a golden crown to congratulate him on his victory at Issos.

2.14.1 While Alexander was still at Marathos, envoys reached him from Darius, bringing a letter from Darius, while on their part the envoys were to make speeches pleading for the release to Darius of his mother, wife and children. **2** The letter went as follows: Philip had been in peace and alliance with Artaxerxes and, when Arses son of Artaxerxes became King, Philip had been the first to wrong King Arses although he had not been injured by the Persians. From the time he had been king of the Persians, Alexander had sent no one to confirm their old friendship and alliance, but had crossed with his army into Asia and occasioned the Persians many evils. **3** This was why Darius had come down to defend his country and save his ancestral empire. The battle had been decided according to the will of some god, but he as king begged him as a king to return his wife and mother and children who were now Alexander's captives, and he wished to enter into friendship with Alexander and become Alexander's ally; for these reasons he thought it appropriate for Alexander to send him, together with Meniskos and Arsimes (the envoys who had come from Persia), people who would take and give pledges on Alexander's behalf.

4 Alexander replied to this and sent Thersippos along with the envoys from Darius, telling him to give the letter to Darius but not to discuss anything with him. Alexander's letter went as follows: 'Your ancestors invaded Macedonia and the rest of Greece and did us damage though we had done nothing to you which justified this aggression; I have been appointed hegemon of the Greeks and have invaded Asia because I wished to take vengeance on the Persians for the actions you initiated. **5** You gave assistance to the Perinthians, who injured my father, and Ochos sent a force into Thrace, which was under our control. After my father was killed by conspirators, whom you organised, as you boasted in your letters to everyone, you murdered Arses with the help of Bagoas, and took the throne unjustly and against the dictates of Persian law, thus wronging the Persians, and sent mendacious letters to the Greeks about me **6** to get them to make war on me, and dispatched money to the Spartans and certain other Greeks, which the Spartans accepted though none of the other Greeks did, while persons sent by you tried to rupture the peace I had established in Greece — so while I may have invaded your country, our hostility was of your making. **7** Since I have conquered in battle first your generals and satraps, and now yourself and your army, I am master of your country, which has been given to me by the gods, and consider myself responsible for all those of your troops who did not die in battle but fled to me for refuge, who are with me of their own free will and serve voluntarily in my army. **8** Come to me, therefore, as you would to the lord of the whole of Asia. If you are afraid that in coming you may suffer some injury at my hands, send some of your friends and they will receive pledges from me. Come then, and ask me for your mother and wife and children and whatever else you want, and you will receive them, for whatever you can persuade me to give you will be yours. **9** And in future when you send to me, send your message to the King of Asia, and do not write as if to an equal, but state what you need to one who is master of everything you possess; if you do not, I shall make plans to deal with you as one who is misbehaving towards me. And if you want to contest the kingship with me, stand and fight for it without running away, because wherever you are I will come after you.'

ALEXANDER INCREASES HIS GRIP ON THE PERSIAN EMPIRE

15.14 Arrian *Expedition of Alexander* 2.18.1–19.6: The Siege of Tyre in 332 BC

The city of Tyre was situated on an island half a mile from shore and its fleet contributed greatly to the strength of the Persian navy. Alexander constructed a mole in order to capture it. Both sides used an array of ingenious tactics and engineering devices. The siege lasted seven months and the women and children were sold into slavery, and the remaining men of military age, some 2,000, were crucified. Alexander had a dream the night before that Herakles was conducting him into the city (he wanted to sacrifice to Herakles there). Cf. Diod. 17.40–46; Plut. *Alex.* 24–25; Curt. 4.2.6–4.21.

2.18.1 It was obvious that besieging Tyre would be a massive operation. **2** The city was an island, completely fortified by high walls. In addition Tyre at that point appeared to have a naval advantage, as the Persians were still in control of the sea and the people of Tyre also had many ships at their disposal.

3 However, Alexander's arguments prevailed and he decided to construct a mole from the mainland to the city. The place is a strait covered with shallow water and near the mainland there are shallows and stretches of mud, while near the city itself, where the crossing is deepest, it is about three fathoms deep. But there were plenty of stones and wood, which they piled on top of the stones, and then it was not difficult to fix stakes in the mud, with the mud helping to bind the stones together securely. **4** The Macedonians were as enthusiastic in the work as Alexander who was there in person, directing each step himself, rousing them with his words and rewarding with gifts those who were exceptional in the quality of their work. While they were building the mole near the mainland the work proceeded without difficulty, as the depth in which they were working was not great and no one was putting up any resistance. **5** But, once they got into deeper water and were at the same time near the city, they suffered badly from the missiles fired from the high walls, especially as they were appropriately dressed for working rather than for battle. The Tyrians, who were still in control of the sea, sailed in their triremes here and there along the mole and in many places made it impossible for the Macedonians to make any progress. **6** The Macedonians constructed two towers on the end of the mole, which now extended far into the sea, and placed war-engines on the towers. There were coverings of hides and skins on them to protect them from incendiary missiles fired from the wall and to shelter those working on the mole from the arrows. At the same time those Tyrians who sailed up and tried to harm those building the mole could be fired upon from the towers and driven off without difficulty.

2.19.1 The Tyrians, however, took a measure to counter this: they filled a cavalry transport ship with dry branches and other inflammable material, fixed two masts in the prow, and built it up all round as high as they could so it could contain as many wood shavings and torches as possible — in addition they loaded it with pitch, sulphur and anything else which would create a great blaze. **2** They attached a double yardarm to each mast and from it hung in cauldrons anything which could be poured or thrown on to fuel the blaze, and placed ballast in the stern to raise the height of the prow by weighing down the ship's stern. **3** They then watched for a wind blowing towards the mole and attached the ship to triremes, which towed it behind them. When they were near the mole and towers they set the material alight, pulled the ship forward with the triremes as strongly as possible, and drove it onto the end of the mole; those on the burning ship swam away without difficulty. **4** By now a massive amount of flame was falling on the towers and as the yardarms shattered they rained down onto the fire all the items intended to feed the flames. The men in the triremes stayed near the mole and shot at the towers so that it was unsafe for anyone to approach with material to extinguish the fire. **5** At this point, with the towers fully ablaze, a number of people rushed out of the city, leaping into small boats and landing here and there along the mole, and tore down without difficulty the fence that had been erected to protect it and set fire to all the war-engines which had not been set alight from the ship. **6** But Alexander told his men to make the mole broader, starting from the mainland, so it could hold more towers, and the engineers to build more engines. While these were under construction he set out for Sidon with his hypaspists and the Agrianians to collect all the triremes he had there already, since the success of the siege appeared to be hopeless as long as the Tyrians were in control of the sea.

15.15 Arrian *Expedition of Alexander* 2.25.1–3: Darius Attempts to Make Terms

Darius sought to make peace with Alexander after Issos but the latter was in a position of strength and rejected Darius' overtures. Arrian has Darius make a second peace offer after Tyre but the other sources have it before Gaugamela. Alexander wanted to conquer the entire Persian empire, and would do so. For Darius' various (rejected) peace offers, see Plut. *Alex*. 29.7–8; Diod. 17.39.1–2, 54.1–6; Curt. 4.11.1–22.

2.25.1 While Alexander was still involved in the siege of Tyre, envoys arrived from Darius who announced that Darius was prepared to give Alexander ten thousand talents in return for his mother, wife and children; that Alexander could be master of the entire country between the river Euphrates and the Greek Sea (the Mediterranean); and that Darius would marry his daughter to Alexander and Alexander could be his friend and ally. **2** When these terms were announced in the council of the Companions, Parmenion is said to have told Alexander that were he Alexander he would be pleased to put an end to the war on these terms and be freed from further dangers, at which Alexander replied to Parmenion that he would have done this had he been Parmenion, but as he was Alexander he would give Darius the answer he had actually made. **3** This was that he had no need of money from Darius, nor of a part of the country instead of all of it; the money and the country were already his; if he wanted to marry Darius' daughter he would marry her even if Darius did not give her; and he told Darius to come to him if he wanted to be treated with consideration. When Darius heard this reply, he lost hope of making terms with Alexander and again began to prepare for war.

15.16 Plutarch *Life of Alexander* 26.1–10: The Foundation of Alexandria, 331 BC

After Tyre, Alexander also besieged and took Gaza in Syria; he then travelled south to and wintered in Egypt, in 332/1 BC, where he became pharaoh and was welcomed by the inhabitants, because of the harsh and impious attitude of the Persians who had recently retaken Egypt, some twelve years previously. On the coast, he founded Alexandria, which was to become one of the largest and most important Greek cities in the Mediterranean. Cf. Arr. 3.1–2.2; Diod. 17.52 (out of chronological order); Plut. *Alex*. 26.3–10; Curt. 4.8.1–6. For Alexander and the *Iliad*, see doc. 15.1.

26.1 When a small chest was brought to him (at Issos) which seemed to those in charge of the wealth of Darius and the baggage the most valuable object there, he asked his friends what precious item would be most suitably deposited in it. **2** Many gave numerous opinions, but Alexander said that he was going to put the *Iliad* inside for safe keeping. A great many trustworthy authors have borne witness to this. **3** And if what the Alexandrians have told us on the authority of Herakleides is correct, Homer was no idle or unproductive companion for him on his expedition. **4** The story goes that after he had conquered Egypt he wanted to found a large and populous Greek city which would bear his name, and on the advice of his architects was just about to measure and mark out a particular site. **5** Then that night as he lay asleep he saw a wonderful dream: a grey-haired man of venerable appearance appeared to stand beside him and recite the following lines of verse (*Odyssey* 4.354–5):

> 'Now there is an island in the stormy sea
> in front of Egypt; men have called it Pharos.'

6 As a result he immediately got out of bed and went to Pharos, which was then still an island, a short way above the Canopic mouth of the Nile, but which now has been linked to the mainland by a causeway. **7** When he saw the unique natural advantages of the site (for it was a strip of land like a broad isthmus stretching between a large lagoon and the sea which ends in a great harbour), he said that Homer, quite apart from his other wonderful qualities, was also a very skilful architect, and ordered the plan of the city to be drawn up so it equated to this site. **8** There was no chalk at hand, so they took barley-meal and marked out a semicircle on the dark ground, with straight lines extending from the circumference making the area into equal segments, as if to produce the shape of a chlamys with the lines extending from the hem. **9** The king was delighted with the plan, but all of a sudden birds from the river and lake, in countless numbers and of every type and size, settled in that spot like clouds, leaving not the slightest grain of barley behind. Alexander was greatly troubled by this omen. **10** However the diviners urged him to take heart: the city would have abundant resources of its own, and would nurture men from countless nations. He therefore ordered those in charge of the work to carry on and himself set out for the oracle of Ammon.

15.17 Arrian *Expedition of Alexander* 3.3.1–4.5: Consultation of Ammon in 331 BC

While in Egypt, Alexander in 331 BC visited the shrine of Ammon (who was identified with Zeus by the Greeks) at Siwah. As in the case of the foundation of Alexandria, omens attended Alexander on his journey, and are a consistent feature of the narratives about him, and indicative of the divine support Alexander was considered to have. He himself believed that he was descended from both Herakles and Perseus, and was the son of Zeus. Arrian states that Alexander 'heard the response that he desired' from the oracle, while Plutarch *Alex.* 27.3 writes: 'the prophet of Ammon greeted him as a father would'. From then on Alexander styled himself the son of Zeus Ammon. This visit marks the real beginning of Alexander's belief in his own divinity. Cf. Diod. 17.49.2–51.4; Plut. *Alex.* 26.6–27.6; Curt. 4.7.5–32. [*FGH* 139 FF13–15; *FGH* 138 FF8–9.]

3.3.1 Alexander was then overwhelmed by a desire to visit the oracle of Ammon in Libya, because he wanted to consult the god (as the oracle of Ammon was said to be infallible and to have been consulted by Perseus and Herakles — the former when he was sent by Polydektes against the Gorgon, and the latter when he travelled through Libya to find Antaios and Egypt to find Bousiris). **2** Alexander wished to emulate the deeds of Perseus and Herakles, since he was a descendant of them both, and traced his own ancestry in some measure back to Ammon, as legend traced that of Herakles and Perseus back to Zeus. At any rate, he set out to visit the oracle of Ammon with this in mind, so he might acquire clearer information about his future, or at least be able to say that he had acquired it. **3** Up until Paraitonion he followed the coastline through the desert (actually, it is not entirely waterless) for 1,600 stades, according to Aristoboulos. At that point he turned into the interior towards the site of the oracle of Ammon. The route is desolate and most of it is sandy and waterless. **4** But Alexander had plenty of rain, and this was seen as a gift from the god.

The following incident was also attributed to the god: whenever a south wind blows in that region it piles sand deeply up on the track and makes its signposts invisible. The travellers are unable to find their way in this ocean of sand, where there are no markings to point out the track, or any hill or tree or prominent mounds of earth to enable travellers to recognise their route as sailors do from the stars: in fact Alexander's army got lost and the guides were unsure as to the right direction. **5** Well Ptolemy son of Lagos says that two snakes went before the army hissing on their way and Alexander told his leaders to follow them and trust the god, and the snakes led the way to the oracle and back again; **6** Aristoboulos, however, and this is the more common form of the story, records that two crows flew in front of the army and that Alexander used these as guides. I am positive that some form of divine assistance was given to Alexander because it seems the most likely scenario, but the actual details of the story cannot be ascertained, as different authors give different versions of his actions. **3.4.1** The site where the temple of Ammon is situated is surrounded by desert, sandy and waterless, but the area in the centre though small (for at its broadest it only stretches to some forty stades) is full of domesticated trees, olives and palm-trees and alone of all the surrounding countryside catches the dew. **2** Furthermore a spring wells up, though quite unlike other springs which rise from the ground. Even at midday the water is cold to the taste and even colder, as cold as can be, to the touch. When, however, the sun sinks to the west it is warmer, and from evening it gets warmer still up until midnight when it is at its warmest. From midnight in turn it grows colder, and is already cold at dawn, but coldest at midday. This cycle of change happens regularly every day. **3** There are also natural salts in this region which can be dug up; some of these are taken by priests of Ammon to Egypt. When taken to Egypt, they place the salt in woven baskets of palm leaves to be carried to the king or someone else as a gift. **4** The grains of salt are large, some more than three fingers in breadth, and as clear as crystal: Egyptians and others who are particular about their religious practices use these in their sacrifices because they are purer than sea salt. **5** Alexander was amazed at this place and consulted the oracle: he had heard the response he desired, he reported, and turned back to Egypt, by the same route according to Aristoboulos, but on a direct route to Memphis, according to Ptolemy son of Lagos.

THE FINAL CONQUEST OF PERSIA

15.18 Plutarch *Life of Alexander* 33.4–8, 34.1–4: The Battle at Gaugamela, 331 BC

Leaving Egypt, Alexander invaded Mesopotamia, where he met Darius in battle on 1 October 331 BC at Gaugamela, 35 kilometres east of the Tigris river. The two kings fought on ground that had been chosen and cleared by Darius so that the Persian cavalry and scythe-chariots could operate freely. The charge of these scythe-chariots into Alexander's centre was repulsed. He then attacked the centre of Darius' line, which was thinning as it moved to attack Alexander's deliberately weakened left and right flanks. The Persians had reacted in precisely the way Alexander had planned. Despite overwhelming Persian numerical superiority, again outmanoeuvring Darius' troops, Alexander won his third victory. He was now free to take Babylon, Persepolis and Susa. Darius had now more or less lost his empire. The reference to the Plataeans refers to 479 BC; for Phayllos, see doc. 11.45. For Gaugamela, see Diod. 17.53.1; Curt. 4.13.26–32.

33.4 Even before the foremost ranks were engaged, the barbarians turned to flee and were hotly pursued, with Alexander driving the conquered enemy into the centre where Darius was. **5** For Alexander could see him from afar through the deep ranks of the royal cavalry squadron, a handsome, tall man carried on a high chariot, surrounded by numerous magnificent horsemen, who were heavily concentrated around the chariot and drawn up to receive the enemy. **6** But when they saw the terrifying Alexander nearby, driving those who fled before him onto those who stood firm, most of them were struck with fear and scattered. **7** However, the best and most noble of them were killed in front of their king and, as they lay fallen upon each other, hindered his pursuit, twisted and tangled as they were around themselves and their horses.

8 With all these disasters before his eyes and his forces, no longer in battle-order, pushed back upon him, and as it was not easy to turn his chariot and drive off, with the wheels entangled with the innumerable corpses, and the horses, surrounded and hidden by the mass of dead bodies, rearing up and frightening the charioteer, Darius abandoned his chariot and weapons, mounted a mare which, it is said, had just given birth, and fled.

34.1 With the battle ending in this way, the Persians' empire was considered to be entirely destroyed and Alexander, proclaimed king of Asia, made magnificent sacrifices to the gods and gifts of wealth, estates, and governorships to his friends. **2** As he wanted the Greeks to honour him, he wrote to them that all their tyrannies were dissolved and they could live under their own constitutions. He wrote especially to the Plataeans that he would rebuild their city, because their ancestors had given their country to the Greeks for the struggle on behalf of Greek liberty. **3** He also sent part of the booty to the people of Croton in Italy, in honour of the commitment and valour of their athlete Phayllos, who in the Persian Wars, when the other Greeks in Italy refused to help the Greeks, had a ship equipped at his own expense and sailed to Salamis, so he could in some way participate in the danger. **4** This was how well disposed Alexander was to all kinds of valour and what a guardian and friend he was towards noble actions.

15.19 Diodorus *Library of History* 17.62.1–63.3: The Consequences of Gaugamela

Antipater had been left by Alexander as regent in Thrace. He moved to deal with Memnon's revolt in Thrace, and the Spartans and other Peloponnesians seized the opportunity to revolt. As a result of this revolt Antipater took fifty Spartiates hostage (Diod. 17.73). Alexander's suzerainty over Greece was confirmed just at the same time as he had made himself master of the Persian empire.

17.62.1 When Aristophon was archon at Athens, Gaius Domitius and Aulus Cornelius entered into the consulship at Rome [330/29 BC]. At this time the outcome of the battle near Arbela [Gaugamela] was reported to Greece, and many of the cities in their suspicion at the increase in Macedonian power decided to make a stand for their freedom while the Persians continued to hold out, **2** believing that Darius would help them and send them huge amounts of money so they could collect large mercenary armies, while Alexander would not be able to divide his forces. **3** If, however, they just looked on while the Persians were annihilated, the Greeks would be isolated and would never again be able to act to preserve their liberty.

4 At this very time there was a rebellion in Thrace which offered the Greeks a chance to revolt; **5** Memnon, who had been appointed general of Thrace, possessed an army and an independent spirit. He caused trouble among the barbarians, revolted against Alexander, and was soon in control of a large force and openly determined on war. **6** As a result Antipater mobilised his army and advanced through Macedonia into Thrace to deal with Memnon.

While this was happening, the Spartans thought it was time for them to prepare for war and called upon the Greeks to make a common stand for their liberty. **7** The Athenians, who had been granted more honours than the other Greeks by Alexander, took no action; most of the Peloponnesians, in contrast, and some of the others came to an agreement and committed themselves in writing to go to war. In line with their city's resources they enlisted the best of their young men and enrolled as soldiers no less than 20,000 infantry and some 2,000 cavalry. **8** The Spartans were in command and led out their entire citizen body for the decisive engagement, with their king Agis being commander-in-chief.

17.63.1 When Antipater learned that the Greeks had joined forces he finished the war in Thrace as best he could and marched into the Peloponnese with his whole army. He added soldiers from those Greeks who were still his allies and gathered a total force of not less than 40,000. **2** When battle was joined Agis fell fighting, but the Spartans fought with spirit and held their ranks for a long time. When their allies were pressed back, they retreated to Sparta. **3** More than three thousand, five hundred Spartans and allies were killed in the battle and three thousand, five hundred of Antipater's men.

15.20 Diodorus *Library of History* 17.72.1–6: The Burning of Persepolis, 331 BC

After Gaugamela, Alexander captured Babylon, Susa and then Persepolis, the Persian capital. Here he took possession of the Persian treasury, some 120,000 talents. The burning of Persepolis appears to have been the result of an overenthusiastic drinking party rather than a planned strategy of revenge, as it was later represented to have been: Arrian has Parmenion urging Alexander to protect what was now his own property, but Alexander setting it on fire in retaliation for the burning of the temples on the Athenian acropolis in 480 BC. Curtius is presumably nearer the truth in noting that the excuse was made up for shame at what they had done. Cf. Arr. 3.18.10–12; Plut. *Alex*. 38; Curt. 5.7.1–11.

17.72.1 Alexander put on games to honour his victories, performed magnificent sacrifices to the gods and gave his friends splendid banquets. While his companions were feasting, and they had been drinking for some time with everyone becoming intoxicated, a mad spirit starting taking over the minds of the drinkers. **2** At this point one of the women present, whose name was Thais and who was Athenian in origin, said that it would be the greatest of all his achievements in Asia, if he joined them in a comus (triumphal procession), set fire to the palaces, and let women's hands wipe out in a moment these renowned achievements of the Persians. **3** This remark was made to men who were young and whose spirits were elevated by alcohol, and so, as one would expect, someone yelled out to form the komos and light torches, urging everyone to take vengeance for the monstrous crime against the Greeks' temples. **4** Others too took up the cry, saying that this was a deed worthy only of Alexander, and, when the king caught fire at their words, they all leapt up from their drinking and told everyone to form a victory komos in honour of Dionysos.

5 A great number of torches were quickly collected, and as there were female musicians present at the party the king led the komos to the sound of singing, flutes and pipes, with the hetaira Thais leading the whole performance. **6** She was the first, after the king, to hurl her flaming torch into the palace; with the others doing the same, the whole palace area was soon consumed by fire, through the intensity of the flames. Most paradoxical of all was that the sacrilege of Xerxes, king of the Persians, against the acropolis of the Athenians was repaid by a single woman, a citizen of the land which had been wronged, in sport, so many years afterwards, and in kind.

15.21 Arrian *Expedition of Alexander* 3.26.1–4: Philotas and Conspiracy in 330 BC

In 330 BC one of Alexander's bodyguards, Dimnos, for reasons not adequately explained by the sources, decided to assassinate Alexander, and confided in his lover, the young Nicomachos, who informed his brother Kebalinos, who in turn informed Philotas of the plot on two consecutive days. Philotas did not act and so Kebalinos informed one of the 'Royal Pages' (see doc. 15.25), who informed Alexander. Dimnos committed suicide; Philotas – who had failed to report the plot and was therefore believed to be part of it – was tortured, tried by the army and speared. Philotas' father Parmenion was assassinated on the grounds of complicity, despite having commanded Alexander's left wing at all three major battles against Darius. At the same time Alexander the Lyncestian, who had been imprisoned for three years on a charge of plotting against Alexander, was also executed. Cf. Diod. 17.79–80; Plut. *Alex.* 48–49; Curt. 6.7.1–7.2.38. [*FGH* 138 F13.]

3.26.1 It was also in India that Alexander learned of the conspiracy of Philotas, son of Parmenion … **2** Ptolemy, son of Lagos, gives this account: Philotas was brought before the Macedonians, Alexander made a strong case against him, and Philotas made his defence. Then those who had laid information about the plot came forward and convicted Philotas and his associates on clear evidence, especially in view of the fact that, while Philotas himself admitted that he had heard about some sort of conspiracy in preparation against Alexander, he was condemned for having kept silent on the matter to Alexander, even though he visited Alexander's tent twice every day. **3** Philotas was speared to death by the Macedonians' javelins, together with all those who were involved in the conspiracy. As for Parmenion, Polydamas, one of the Companions, was sent with a letter from Alexander to the generals in Media, Kleander, Sitalkes and Menidas: these had been appointed to the army commanded by Parmenion. **4** They executed Parmenion, perhaps because Alexander was unable to believe that Parmenion had no part in his son's conspiracy, or perhaps because, even if he had not been involved, it was no longer safe for Parmenion to survive his son's execution, as he was held in such honour by Alexander himself and in the army's eyes too — not only the Macedonian army, but the foreign troops as well, whom he had frequently commanded in turns on Alexander's orders.

15.22 Arrian *Expedition of Alexander* 4.8.1–9.4: Alexander Murders Kleitos in 328 BC

Bessos, satrap of Bactria, murdered Darius and proclaimed himself 'King of Kings' as Artaxerxes V. In the spring of 329 BC Alexander marched through modern Iran and Afghanistan and invaded Bactria; Bessos was quickly handed over by his associates to Alexander, who gave him to Darius' relatives, who killed him and butchered his body. This was followed by a revolt in Sogdiana (modern Uzbekistan), put down in spring 327. From 330 BC Alexander had adopted some forms of Persian dress and Persian ceremonial and had promoted Persians to high rank; this aroused strong opposition amongst the Macedonians. Kleitos disapproved and at the festival of Dionysos celebrated at Samarkand in 328 he quarrelled with Alexander, especially over comparisons of Alexander's achievements with those of Herakles, the Dioskouroi and his father Philip. Plut. *Alex.* 50–51; Curt. 8.1.22–2.11.

4.8.1 Now is the time for me to relate the tragedy of Kleitos, son of Dropides, and the subsequent misfortune it caused Alexander, even though it actually occurred rather later. The Macedonians celebrated a day sacred to Dionysos and every year Alexander sacrificed to him on that day; **2** on this occasion however, the story goes, he neglected Dionysos and sacrificed to the Dioskouroi, some reason having made him decide to sacrifice to Castor and Pollux. There had been some heavy drinking (and in fact drinking was another area in which Alexander had taken to new and barbaric habits), and in the course of the drinking the question of the Dioskouroi came up in conversation and how their birth was attributed to Zeus and not to Tyndareus. **3** Some of the company, the sort of people who always have and always will injure the interests of kings, flattered Alexander by stating that even Pollux and Castor could not be compared to Alexander and his achievements. The drink made others extend the comparison to Herakles: it was jealousy, they said, which prevented living men from receiving their due honours from their associates.

4 It had, however, been clear for some time that Kleitos disapproved of Alexander's change to a more barbaric lifestyle and of the flattery of his sycophants, and under the influence of wine he would not let them insult divine beings, nor belittle the deeds of heroes of old to pay Alexander a compliment that was actually not one at all; **5** he did not, he said, think Alexander's deeds were so great and remarkable as the flatterers cried them up to be — in any case he hadn't achieved them single-handed, but rather most of them were due to the Macedonians. His words deeply hurt Alexander, and for my part I cannot approve of them and think that in this type of drunkenness it is enough for a man to keep his views to himself without engaging in the same errors of flattery as the others. **6** But when some of them turned to Philip and suggested most unjustly that *his* achievements were not great or remarkable, in the hope of ingratiating themselves with Alexander, Kleitos could no longer keep it to himself but spoke out on behalf of Philip's achievements and denigrated Alexander and his. He was by now very drunk and among much else taunted Alexander with the fact that he, Kleitos, had saved his life in the cavalry battle against the Persians at the Granikos river; **7** he even held out his right hand dramatically, telling Alexander that this was the hand that had saved him then. Alexander could not put up any longer with Kleitos' drunken abuse and jumped up in anger to hit him, but was held back by his fellow drinkers. Kleitos continued hurling insults at him. **8** Alexander shouted for the hypaspists, and when no one obeyed cried that he was in the same situation as Darius, when he was captured by Bessos and his associates, and now had nothing left of kingship but the name. The Companions could no longer restrain him — he leapt up, the story goes, snatched a spear from one of the bodyguards and struck Kleitos dead, though according to others he used a sarissa from one of the guards …

4.9.1 For myself I strongly blame Kleitos for his insolent behaviour towards his king, and pity Alexander for his misfortune, as he demonstrated that he was mastered by two vices, neither of which should be allowed to overcome a man of moderation, that is anger and drunkenness. **2** But in what follows I commend Alexander because he immediately recognised that his conduct had been inexcusable. Some relate that he leaned the sarissa against the wall intending to fall on it himself, as it was dishonourable for him to continue living after having killed his friend under the influence of wine. **3** Most historians, however, give a different account; they say that Alexander took to his bed and lay there lamenting, calling on the name of Kleitos himself and Kleitos' sister Lanike, daughter of Dropides, who had been his nurse; what a fine return for her nursing had he made her now he was a man! **4** She had seen her own sons die fighting for him, and now he had killed her brother with his own hand. He would not stop calling himself the murderer of his friends, refused all food and drink for three days, and ignored all other bodily needs.

ALEXANDER MOVES EAST

15.23 Arrian *Expedition of Alexander* 4.18.4–19.6: 'Soldiers with Wings', 327 BC

The revolt in Bactria which broke out in 329 BC ended with Alexander's conquest of the Rock of Sogdiana in 327 BC. Here Alexander met Roxane; he married her in 327 BC and she was to be the mother of his posthumous son, Alexander IV; Roxane and Alexander IV were murdered in Amphipolis in 311 BC. This campaign in Bactria ended his conquest of the north-east of the empire; pacification of the area involved the capturing of seven major fortresses in which the entire male population was massacred and the women and children sold into slavery (Arr. 4.2.1–4.3.5, esp. 4.2.4). Greek and Macedonian settlers colonised the area. Cf. Curt. 7.11.1–29.

4.18.4 As soon as spring arrived Alexander marched towards the Rock of Sogdiana, where, he had heard, many of the Sogdianians had fled for safety. The wife of Oxyartes the Bactrian and his daughters were also said to have taken refuge on this rock, as Oxyartes had removed them to that place, because at the time of his own revolt against Alexander he considered it impregnable. Once this rock was captured Alexander believed that those Sogdianians who wanted to revolt would have no resources left with which to do so. **5** But when they reached the rock Alexander realised that it provided a sheer face on all sides to attackers and that the barbarians had gathered enough provisions for a lengthy siege. In addition a heavy snowfall rendered the means of approach even more impracticable for the Macedonians, while it provided the barbarians with a plentiful supply of water. Despite all this Alexander decided to attack the place. **6** A boastful comment made by the barbarians had increased Alexander's intense desire for renown: when invited to peace talks, which Alexander offered to the effect that they would have safe conduct to their homes if they handed over the rock, they laughed at Alexander in their barbarian speech and told him to find soldiers with wings to capture the mountain for him, since they had no worries that anyone else would. **7** So Alexander announced that the first to climb the rock would receive a reward of twelve talents, the second man one less, the third one less again, until finally the last man to reach the top was to receive the reward of three hundred darics. The Macedonians were already full of enthusiasm, but this announcement made them even more determined to succeed.

4.19.1 All those who had experience in rock-climbing from earlier sieges now got together, about 300 of them, equipped with small iron pegs used to secure their tents, tied to strong linen ropes, to fix into the snow where it appeared to be frozen and in any spot which was free from snow. At night they made for the most precipitous side of the rock, as for this reason it was the least guarded. **2** They secured their pegs in the ground where they could see it, or in the snow where it seemed least likely to break away, and pulled themselves up the rock by different routes. Some thirty of them lost their lives in the ascent, falling in various places in the snow so that their bodies could not be recovered for burial. **3** The rest of them climbed up and seized the top of the mountain at about dawn, and waved bits of linen in the direction of the Macedonian camp as Alexander had told them to do. He then sent a herald with instructions to shout to the barbarians' lookouts not to waste any more time but to give themselves up: he had actually discovered the men with wings and the mountain summit was in their hands, and as he said this he pointed out the soldiers on the peak.

4 The barbarians were thunder-struck at this unexpected sight and as they suspected that the soldiers in occupation of the summit were more numerous and fully armed than they were they gave themselves up — so frightened were they at the sight of those few Macedonians. Many wives and children were captured here, including the wife and daughters of Oxyartes. **5** Oxyartes had an unmarried daughter of marriageable age named Roxane and those on campaign with Alexander said that she was the most beautiful woman they had seen in Asia after the wife of Darius, and that Alexander fell in love with her at first sight. Despite his desire he did not want to treat her with violence, although she was his prisoner, but thought it was not beneath him to marry her. **6** And I applaud rather than censure Alexander for this conduct.

15.24 Arrian *Expedition of Alexander* 4.9.9, 4.12.1–5: 'Missed out on a Kiss'

After Sogdiana, Alexander attempted to introduce proskynesis (prostrating oneself before the king), in the way that the Persians had made obeisance to the Great King. It was arranged that the topic be brought up at a symposium as a means of sounding out the opinion of the court. Arguments in favour were put forward; the Macedonians were opposed but kept silent; only Kallisthenes spoke against it. Alexander dropped the idea for the Macedonians, but the Persians made proskynesis to him from this date. Cf. Plut. *Alex*. 54.

4.9.9 The story goes that Alexander wanted people to prostrate themselves before him from his belief that his father was Ammon rather than Philip. He was already showing his admiration for the customs of the Persians and Medes, both in his change of dress and in new rules for those who paid court to him. Regarding prostration there was no lack of those willing to pay it to him out of flattery, including, among others, Anaxarchos and Agis the Argive poet, who were two of the sophists in his entourage. (*Kallisthenes, however, argued that a distinction needed to be kept between men and the gods, and that the Macedonians as free men should not be subjected to the dishonour of making proskynesis*) **4.12.1** What Kallisthenes said seriously annoyed Alexander, but pleased the Macedonians, and, realising this, Alexander sent to the Macedonians to say that prostration was no longer necessary. **2** But in the silence after this proclamation the most important Persians rose and prostrated themselves one after the other. Leonnatos, one of the Companions, thought that one of the Persians did obeisance awkwardly, and made fun of his posture as being demeaning, at which Alexander was at first angry with him though he came round afterwards. The following story has also been recorded: **3** Alexander sent a golden drinking-cup round the company, to begin with to those whom he had come to an agreement with about obeisance, and the first who drank from the cup rose, prostrated himself, and received a kiss from Alexander, and this went round all of them, one after the other. **4** When it was Kallisthenes' turn to drink his health, Kallisthenes rose, drank from the cup, and went up as if to kiss Alexander, without having prostrated himself. At that moment Alexander was talking to Hephaistion, and so was not paying attention as to whether Kallisthenes had done obeisance or not. **5**

But as Kallisthenes approached to kiss him, one of the Companions, Demetrios son of Pythonax, remarked that he was coming forward without having done obeisance. Alexander did not allow Kallisthenes to kiss him, at which Kallisthenes commented, 'So — I go away, having missed out on a kiss.'

15.25 Arrian *Expedition of Alexander* 4.13.7–14.3: The Royal Pages' Conspiracy, 327 BC

Hermolaos, one of the Royal Pages — Macedonian youths of noble birth attendant upon the king and guarding him when asleep (doc. 14.38) — when on a hunt with Alexander had killed a wild boar before Alexander had a chance to do so and was publicly whipped as a punishment. Hermolaos and his lover of the same age, Sostratos son of Amyntos, decided to conspire against Alexander and persuaded some of the other Pages to participate. They decided to kill him on the night when they were on guard duty. But a Syrian woman possessed by a divine spirit warned Alexander to stay out drinking all night; her predictions had always come true, so he obeyed her. The next day one of the conspirators Epimenes told his lover of the plot, and he turned informer. The Pages were stoned to death. Kallisthenes was implicated as having encouraged them in the view that they could gain glory by killing Alexander and having reminded them that Alexander was a mortal man like all others (and so encouraging them to oppose proskynesis and Alexander's pretensions to divinity). [*FGH* 139 FF31, 33; *FGH* 138 F17.]

4.13.7 On the following day Epimenes son of Arsaios, one of the conspirators, told his lover Charikles, son of Menander, of the plot, Charikles told Epimenes' brother Eurylochos, and Eurylochos went to Alexander's tent and revealed the whole affair to his bodyguard Ptolemy, son of Lagos, who told Alexander. He ordered that all those whose names Eurylochos had produced be arrested, and they were stretched on the rack, after which they revealed their conspiracy and gave the names of others who were involved.

4.14.1 Aristoboulos states that they said that Kallisthenes had encouraged them in this bold venture, and Ptolemy says likewise, though most writers have a different story, that it was because he had already come to hate Kallisthenes, and because Hermolaos was particularly close to Kallisthenes, that Alexander did not find it difficult to believe the worst of him. **2** Some writers have also recorded that Hermolaos, when brought before the Macedonians, confessed his conspiracy, declaring that no free man could possibly endure Alexander's arrogance any longer, and recounting all the details: Alexander's undeserved execution of Philotas, his still more criminal execution of Philotas' father Parmenion and of the others who died at the same time, his drunken murder of Kleitos, his Median costume, his wish to introduce prostration, which was still on the cards, and his drinking parties and sleeping habits — he could not endure these any longer and had been attempting to liberate himself and the other Macedonians. **3** He was then stoned to death by those present, along with those imprisoned with him. As for Kallisthenes, Aristoboulos states that he was bound in chains and carried around with the army, until he died of illness, while Ptolemy son of Lagos says he was stretched on the rack and then put to death by hanging. So not even those who are most trustworthy in their narrative and who were accompanying Alexander at the time agree in their accounts about events that were public knowledge and in which they were involved.

15.26 Quintus Curtius *History of Alexander* 8.14.31–4, 8.14.38–40, 8.14.44–46: Poros and his Faithful Elephant

After Bactria and Sogdiana Alexander moved south to India. In spring 326 BC he was at Taxila to face Poros, who held the Hydaspes River. Poros faced the Macedonians with eighty-five elephants, 300 chariots and 30,000 foot soldiers. The combat of Alexander with Poros and his elephant was recorded on Alexander's silver decadrachmas (ten-drachma pieces). Plut. *Alex.* 60; Arr. 5.8–21; Diod. 17.87–89.

8.14.31 The elephants, like cattle, more frightened than dangerous, were being driven from the battlefield, when Poros, deserted by many of his men, began from his own elephant to hurl many javelins prepared in advance at those surrounding him. While he wounded many at a distance he was himself exposed to shots from all sides. **32** He had already incurred nine wounds, some in his breast, some in his back, and had lost so much blood that his arms were weak and the javelins he was throwing were rather dropped from his hands than hurled with force. **33** His beast too was not slowed down and, roused to madness and not yet wounded, charged against the enemy's ranks until the driver of the beast saw that his king was near collapse, had dropped his weapons and was barely conscious. **34** He then urged the beast to flee, with Alexander pursuing … **38** Alexander had already come up to him and, seeing Poros' refusal to give in, ordered that no quarter be given to anyone who resisted. And so weapons were thrown from all sides both at the infantry and at Poros himself, who was at last overwhelmed and started sliding off his beast. **39** The Indian in charge of the animal thought that he was dismounting in the usual way and ordered the elephant to its knees; when it did so, all the others too let their bodies down to the ground, for they had been trained to do this. This action delivered Poros and the rest of his men to the victors. **40** The king ordered Poros' body to be stripped, as he believed him killed, and men were running up to take off his breastplate and robe when the beast began to protect his master and to attack those despoiling him, lifting the body to put it again on his back. It was therefore overwhelmed with weapons from all sides and once it was killed Poros was placed in a chariot …

44 Poros' greatness of spirit, unconcerned and unbroken even by misfortune, Alexander thought worthy to be treated not only with compassion but even with honour. **45** He had the wounded man cared for as if he had fought on his side; when against all expectation he recovered, he numbered him amongst his friends; and he later gave him a kingdom greater than the one he had possessed before. **46** And indeed there was no stronger or more constant facet of his character than admiration for true worth and glory, though he estimated reputation more sincerely in an enemy than in a fellow citizen. For he believed that his greatness could be diminished by his countrymen, but that the greater those whom he had conquered were, the more splendid his own deeds would appear to have been.

15.27 Arrian *Expedition of Alexander* 5.19.4–6: 'Ox-Head'

Plutarch *Alex.* 32 records that Alexander in the later campaigns only used Boukephalas ('Ox-Head') in battle, not in marshalling or reviewing his men, to spare him as he was getting old. Plutarch (*Alex.* 61) cites Potamon the Lesbian for the detail that he also founded a city named after a beloved dog, Peritas, whom he had reared.

5.19.4 Where the battle was fought, and in the place from which he had set out to cross the Hydaspes river, Alexander founded cities. One of these was called Nicaea to commemorate his victory ('nike') over the Indians, the other Boukephala in memory of his horse Boukephalas who died there, **5** not because he was wounded by anyone but was just exhausted by heat and age (he was about thirty years old). Up till then he had shared Alexander's toils and dangers, and had never been mounted by anyone but Alexander, since he thought no other rider worthy of him: he was a large horse with a noble spirit. His mark was an ox-head ('boos kephale') branded on him, hence, it is said, his name, though others say he was black with a white mark on his head exactly like an ox-head. **6** Alexander once lost him in the Uxians' territory and had it proclaimed throughout the country that he would kill every Uxian unless they brought him back his horse: he was returned immediately after the announcement. This was how devoted Alexander was to him, and how frightened the barbarians were of Alexander. I had to say all this in Boukephalas' honour for Alexander's sake.

15.28 Diodorus *Library of History* 17.91.7–92.3: Mighty Dogs

Directly after the defeat of Poros, Alexander intended to undertake a campaign against Sopeithes, who ruled the neighbouring kingdom in India. Sopeithes, however, surrendered his kingdom willingly to Alexander, who immediately gave it back to him. For Indian dogs, see Hdt. 1.192, 7.187.

17.91.7 Their king, Sopeithes, who was more outstandingly handsome and taller than any of his subjects, being over four cubits in height, came out of the city where he had his capital and handed himself and his kingdom over to Alexander, but received it back through the goodwill of his conqueror. **8** Sopeithes then with great enthusiasm gave an abundant banquet to the whole army which lasted several days.

17.92.1 He presented Alexander with many fine gifts, including 150 hounds remarkable for their size, strength and other fine qualities, who were said to have been interbred from tigers. **2** He wanted to give Alexander a demonstration of what these dogs could do and brought into the enclosure a lion in perfect condition and set two of the weaker dogs he had given Alexander against the lion; when these were getting the worst of the contest with the wild beast, he released two others. **3** When the four of them started getting the better of the lion, he sent in someone with a knife who started severing the right leg of one of the dogs. Alexander shouted for him to stop and his bodyguards rushed forward and grabbed the Indian's arm, but Sopeithes said that he would give him three other dogs for that one, and the huntsman seized the leg and quietly and slowly cut it through. The hound let out no yelp or whine, but held on with his teeth firmly clasped, until he became faint from loss of blood and died on top of the lion.

15.29 Plutarch *Life of Alexander* 62.1–8: The Turning Point: The Hyphasis in 326 BC

After the battle with Poros, and the death of Alexander's horse Boukephalas, Alexander continued marching eastwards. He crossed the rivers of the Punjab, but his troops mutinied at the Hyphasis river and refused to march into the Ganges river area. Alexander was bitterly disappointed but had no choice but to accede to their requests to begin the journey home. A fleet was built on the Hydaspes river, which in November took the army downstream. It then marched by land back to

Babylon, with the significant campaign against the Mallians en route (doc. 15.30). Cf. Arr. 6.1.1–5.4. The fleet was commanded by Nearchos; after Alexander left the river, Nearchos sailed along the coast of India to the mouth of the Tigris. Alexander marched his army across the Gedrosian desert with large losses and proceeded to Persepolis in 324 BC (soon after, at Susa, the Persian–Macedonian marriages took place: doc. 15.31).

62.1 The struggle against Poros had dulled the Macedonians' courage and prevented their marching further into India. **2** They had only just managed to repulse an enemy who could put twenty thousand infantry and two thousand cavalry into the field, and they vehemently opposed Alexander when he tried to make them cross the river Ganges as well, the width of which they learned was thirty-two stades, and the depth one hundred fathoms, while the opposite banks were obscured by multitudes of infantry, cavalry and elephants. **3** The kings of the Ganderites and Praisii were said to be awaiting them with eighty thousand cavalry, two hundred thousand infantry, eight thousand chariots and six thousand battle elephants — **4** and there was no boasting in this; for Androkottos, who ruled there not long after, gave Seleukos five hundred elephants as a gift, and invaded and conquered all India with an army of six hundred thousand men.

5 Consequently Alexander in despondency and ill temper initially shut himself up in his tent and lay there, knowing no thankfulness for what he had already achieved, unless he could cross the Ganges, and actually considering a retreat as tantamount to defeat. **6** But his friends gave him appropriate consolation, and his soldiers crowded at his doors and beseeched him with lamentation and cries of sorrow, until his resolution was shaken and he started breaking camp, contriving many deceitful and ingenious ways of enhancing his reputation. **7** He had arms and armour, for example, made which were larger than normal, and mangers for horses, and bits which were heavier, and left them scattered around the landscape, **8** as well as founding altars for the gods. Right up to the present time the kings of the Praisii cross the river and worship at these, sacrificing in the Greek manner.

15.30 Arrian *Expedition of Alexander* 6.12.1–13.4: The Army's Devotion to Alexander

On their journey south, Alexander in 326 BC attacked the Mallians in India, killing and enslaving the inhabitants. He then moved against their greatest city; Alexander was the first to jump the wall of the city but became isolated because the troops, rushing after him, broke the ladders with their combined weight. He was seriously wounded; every man, woman and child in the citadel was massacred by the Macedonians (Arr. 6.11.1). [*FGH* 133 F2.]

6.12.1 While Alexander stayed here getting his wound treated, the first report that arrived at the camp from which he had set out to attack the Mallians was that he had died of his wound. First of all the entire army broke into lamentation as the rumour was passed from one to another; when they stopped lamenting his demise they were disheartened and helpless, with no idea of who could lead the army, **2** for both Alexander and the Macedonians considered that there were many whose reputation was equally balanced, and with no idea of how they might get safely back to their homes, surrounded as they were by so many warlike nations, some of whom had not yet joined them and who were likely to fight with determination for their liberty, while others would revolt once they were no longer afraid of Alexander. They also believed that they were in the middle of impassable rivers and they thought that everything would be unachievable and insurmountable if they were to lose Alexander. **3** When the news finally arrived that Alexander was still alive they could hardly believe it, and could not feel confident that he would really recover. On the arrival of a letter from him stating that he would soon visit the camp, most of them could not believe it because of how frightened they were, and they considered that the letter had been fabricated by his bodyguards and generals.

6.13.1 When Alexander realised this, as soon as was possible, he had himself carried to the banks of the river Hydraotes, and sailed downstream, as the camp was at the junction of the Hydraotes and Akesines where Hephaistion was in command of the army and Nearchos had his fleet; as soon as the ship carrying the King approached the camp, he instructed them to take the awning off the stern so he could be clearly seen by everybody. **2** Even then they did not believe it and thought that what was being transported was Alexander's dead body, until the ship put in to the bank and he held up his hand to greet his men; they shouted with joy, holding their hands up to heaven or towards Alexander himself. Many in spite of themselves even burst into tears at this unexpected turn of events. As he was being carried from the ship some of the hypaspists brought him a stretcher, but he called for his horse to be led up. **3** When he was seen to have mounted his horse once more, the whole army applauded again and again, and the riverbanks and nearby glens re-echoed the sound. Once near his tent he dismounted so he could also be seen walking. They crowded around him, some touching his hands, some his knees or his clothing, while others at the sight of him standing near murmured a blessing and moved away. Some showered him with garlands and others with whatever flowers the country of India produced at that time of year.

4 Nearchos states that some of his friends annoyed him by blaming him for endangering himself ahead of his army: this, they said, was not a general's role but that of a soldier. And in my view Alexander was irritated by these comments, because he knew they were true and he had left himself open to this criticism. But, nevertheless, in his passion in battle and his love of glory, he was like men who are conquered by any other sort of pleasure and he was not strong enough to keep out of danger.

15.31 Plutarch *Life of Alexander* 70.3, 71.1–3: Marriage with Princess Stateira, 324 BC

At Susa in 324 BC Alexander and eighty of the Companions took Persian wives. Whether by this Alexander intended to 'unite' the Persians and Macedonians is unclear, but certainly the training and incorporation of Persians into his army pointed towards there being a composite army with a leadership of mixed Persian–Macedonian heritage in the future.

70.3 At Susa he brought about the marriage of his Companions, and for himself took Stateira, the daughter of Darius, as his wife, assigning the noblest women to the noblest men and holding a general wedding banquet for those of his Macedonians who had already married, at which, it is recounted, nine thousand people reclined at table, each of whom was given a gold cup for the libations. Everything else was exceptionally magnificent as well, and Alexander paid off the debts any of them owed, at a total cost of 9,870 talents …

71.1 The thirty thousand boys whom he had left behind to be trained and educated were now strong in physique and handsome in appearance, and displayed such amazing skill and agility in their exercises that Alexander was delighted, while his Macedonians were despondent and afraid, believing that the King would now view them with less regard. **2** As a result, when he sent the sick and maimed among them there down to the sea, they said it was insulting and abusive, that after making use of their services in every way he should now put them aside in disgrace and throw them back upon their native lands and parents, now they were no longer the men they were when he took them over. **3** So they told him to send them all home and consider his Macedonians as worthless, since he now had these young war-dancers with whom he could forge ahead and conquer the world.

15.32 Arrian *Expedition of Alexander* 7.8.1–3, 7.10.5–11.3: The 'Persianisation' of the Army

Alexander left Susa, sailed south down the Elaeus river (Hephaistion and most of the army marched by land) and into the Persian Gulf, thence east along the coast to the mouth of the Tigris. Sailing northwards up it, he stopped at Opis in Babylonia, and here announced the discharge of his veterans. This was not well received and became the occasion for complaints about the increasing Persianisation of his court and the army. In a move most unpalatable to the Macedonians he discharged all of them with bitter recriminations. His intention may well, in fact, have been to rely mainly on the Persians for the further conquests which he planned. Cf. Plut. *Alex.* 71.2–9; Diod. 17.109.2–3.

7.8.1 When he reached Opis he summoned the Macedonians and proclaimed that he was discharging from the army and sending to their homes all those who were unfit for war because of old age or physical disability. He would give those who stayed with him what would make them envied by those at home and inspire the rest of the Macedonians to want to share the same dangers and hardships. **2** Alexander doubtless said this as a compliment to the Macedonians, but, because they thought that Alexander no longer appreciated them and considered them totally useless in warfare, they naturally resented this speech of his, just as throughout this whole campaign they had resented many other things that he had done which annoyed them, such as his Persian dress which suggested the same thing, by his equipping the barbarian Epigonoi in Macedonian style, and the inclusion of foreign cavalry in the units of the Companions. **3** In consequence they did not endure this in silence, but told him to discharge them all from the army and campaign along with his father — taunting him by this reference to Ammon. Alexander had by this time become more short-tempered and the barbarian obsequiousness with which he was treated had made him less tolerant towards the Macedonians than of old. When he heard this he leapt down from the platform with the officers around him and ordered them to arrest the most obvious troublemakers, personally gesturing at the hypaspists whom they had to seize: these numbered about thirteen. These he ordered to be lead away to execution. The rest were shocked into dead silence, and he remounted the platform and addressed them …

7.10.5 'I had intended to discharge only those of you who were unfit for service, to be the envy of those at home. But, as you all want to go, then go — all of you! Return home and announce that your king, Alexander, defeated Persians, Medes, Bactrians, and Sakai, **6** overcame Uxians, Arachotians, and Drangians, conquered Parthyaians, Chorasmians, and

Hyrakanians right up to the Caspian Sea, passed through the Caucasus beyond the Caspian gates, crossed the rivers Oxus and Tanais, and even the river Indus which no one but (the god) Dionysos had crossed before, and the Hydaspes and Akesines and Hydraotes, **7** and would have crossed the Hyphasis as well, had it not been for your fears, and adventured into the Great Sea through both mouths of the Indus, and made it through the Gadrosian desert, where no one had ever been before with an army, and acquired Karmania and the land of the Oreitans as he passed through, while his fleet had already sailed right around the coast from India to Persia — and that when you returned to Susa you deserted him and took off, handing him over to the barbarians he had conquered as his protectors. This report will perhaps win you reputation among men and doubtless be thought pious by the gods. Go!'

7.11.1 After this speech he jumped quickly down from the platform and entered the palace, paying no attention to bodily needs or seeing any of the Companions: nor was he seen on the following day. On the third day, however, he summoned those of the Persians he had selected and allocated the commands of the battalions to them, and granted the right to kiss him only to those he declared his kinsmen. **2** The immediate effect of his speech on the Macedonians was one of shock and they stayed in silence in front of the platform, with none of them following the King as he departed, except the Companions who attended him and his bodyguard, with the rest staying there not knowing what to do or say, but not wishing to leave. **3** But when they were told about the Persians and Medes, that commands were being given to the Persians and barbarian troops enrolled in the units, and the use of Macedonian names, with an agema (squadron) called Persian, and Persians as foot-companions (pezetairoi) and others as asheteroi, and a Persian battalion of 'Silver-shields' and the Companions' cavalry having a new royal agema, they could no longer control themselves, and every one of them ran to the palace and threw down their arms in front of the doors in supplication to the King, and shouted in front of the doors begging to be let in. They said they were willing to hand over those responsible for the recent mutiny and those who began the outcry; they would not leave the doors by day or night until Alexander took pity on them.

ALEXANDER AND THE GREEK POLEIS

Alexander as hegemon of the League of Corinth and liberator of the Greek cities of Asia Minor naturally intervened in Greek affairs. When he crossed into Asia Minor, democracies were established in the freed cities of the coast and the Aegean, but, as at Chios, there was to be a Macedonian garrison which the Chians would pay for themselves; all tyrannies were dissolved (cf. docs. 15.18–19). Otherwise, Alexander paid little attention to Greek affairs until his instruction in 324 BC that all exiles be allowed to return to their home cities. This indicates that he viewed Greek affairs as his to interfere in as he wished. According to Aelian, Alexander after his defeat of Darius commanded that the Greek cities pass decrees that he was a god, to which the Spartans' response was: 'since Alexander wishes to be a god, let him be one' (*VH* 2.19).

15.33 *SIG*[3] 283: Alexander's Letter to the People of Chios, 334 BC

Alexander established a democracy on Chios in 334 BC and all exiles from the island were to return; the island was to supply ships for Alexander's fleet. The pro-Persian 'traitors' on Chios were exiled from all the cities under Alexander's control, and any that were found were to be judged by the council of the Greeks, a reference to the League of Corinth. The city was betrayed to Memnon of Rhodes in 333 BC, but in 332 BC the demos went over to Alexander. [Heisserer 80–81; Harding 107; R&O 84.]

In the prytany of Deisitheos, from King Alexander to the people of Chios.

All exiles from Chios are to return, and the government on Chios is to be a democracy. Law-writers are to be chosen, who shall draft and correct the laws, so that nothing shall be contrary to the democracy or to the return of the exiles; and the laws that are corrected or drafted are to be referred to Alexander. The Chians are to provide twenty fully manned triremes at their own expense and these are to sail as long as the other fleet of the Greeks sails alongside us. Of those who betrayed the city to the barbarians all those who have escaped are to be exiled from all the cities that share in the peace, and may be seized according to the decree of the Greeks; all those who have been captured are to be brought back and judged in the council of the Greeks. And if there is any dispute between those who have returned and those in the city they are to be judged concerning this before us. Until the Chians are reconciled with each other, they are to have a garrison from Alexander the king, of suitable size; and the Chians are to pay for this.

15.34 Tod 2.187: Aristotle and Kallisthenes Honoured at Delphi, *c.* 334 BC

Aristotle and Kallisthenes are praised in this decree for compiling a list of victors at the Pythian games and of the organisers. After Alexander's death, Delphi cancelled its honours for Aristotle. Gylidas was archon in 591/0 BC. [*SIG*^{3} 275; *FGH* 124 T23; R&O 80.]

Since Aristotle son of Nikomachos of Stageira and Kallisthenes son of Damotimos of Olynthos compiled a table of those who from the archonship of Gylidas had been victors at the Pythian Games and of those who from the beginning organised the contest, commendation shall be given to Aristotle and Kallisthenes and they shall be crowned. The treasurers shall dedicate the table in the temple after it has been copied onto stelai.

15.35 Tod 2.188: Alexander's Courier and Surveyor

This dedication was made at some date after 334, at Olympia and is described by Pausanias (6.16.5). 'Hemerodromas' means a long-distance runner (as of Philippides at Hdt. 6.105 after Marathon). Bematistes (here translated as surveyor) is literally 'route-measurer'. Alexander's courier was obviously an important enough person to make his own dedication at Olympia. Chersonesos is a town on the north coast of Crete. [*SIG*^{3} 303.]

King Alexander's courier and surveyor of Asia, Philoneides, son of Zoites, a Cretan from Chersonesos, dedicated this to Olympian Zeus.

15.36 *IG* XII 526, lines 4–28: Alexander and the Tyrants of Eresos, 332 BC

Parmenion and Attalos in 336 BC rid Eresos on Lesbos, and other cities on Lesbos, of tyranny and the cities became members of the League of Corinth. In 335 the tyrants were reinstalled in Eresos by Memnon of Rhodes fighting for the Persians; in 334 Alexander's general Alkimachos recaptured

Lesbos and installed democracies; Eresos again became a member of the League and the tyrants were expelled. Memon of Rhodes in his Aegean offensive of 333 restored a different family of tyrants who overturned the altars to Zeus Philippios (Zeus as a manifestation as Alexander's father Philip); an appeal was now made to Alexander by the author Theophrastos on behalf of his home town. The tyrants were captured in 332 by Alexander's admiral Hegelochos, who took Lesbos and sent them to Alexander in Egypt; they were then returned to their city for trial on Alexander's orders; they were there condemned to death and executed. [Tod 2.191; Heisserer 44–45; R&O 83.]

The people decreed: concerning those things on which the boule passed a resolution, or passed a decree, or made a change to its decree; the men who have been elected are to provide all the documents against the tyrants, both those who lived in the city and their descendants, and they shall introduce the documents into the assembly. And since earlier King Alexander sent back his diagrapha ('instruction') and ordered the Eresians to make a judgement on behalf of Agonippos and Eurysilaos, what punishment they should undergo, the people in accordance with the diagrapha set up a court in accordance with their laws that passed judgement that Agonippos and Eurysilaos should be put to death, and their descendants were to be liable to the law which is on the stele, and their possessions were to be sold in accordance with the law; and when Alexander sent to enquire about the family of Apollodoros and his brothers Hermon and Heraios who were previously tyrants of the city and their descendants, that the people was to decide whether they should return or not, the people in accordance with the diagrapha set up a court for them, following the law and the diagrapha of King Alexander, and this court decided, after speeches had been made by both sides, that the law against the tyrants was to be valid and they were to be exiled from the city.

15.37 Diodorus *Library of History* 17.108.6–8: The Harpalos Affair at Athens in 324 BC

Alexander's treasurer Harpalos had fled Babylon, where he had lived an extravagant lifestyle and embezzled funds, with mercenaries and a huge supply of money, on hearing that Alexander was heading back from his Indian campaigns; at Karmania Alexander had executed several satraps and Macedonian commanders. Harpalos came first to Athens with a huge force, and was not admitted; later, with only three ships, he was allowed entry. Arrested and his money placed on the acropolis, he escaped amidst accusations of massive bribes to Athenian politicians, including Demosthenes (doc. 14.47).

17.108.6 Alexander, on his return from India, put to death many of the satraps who had been accused of misconduct. Being alarmed that he might incur this punishment, Harpalos gathered together five thousand talents of silver, enlisted six thousand mercenaries, and left Asia to sail across to Attica. **7** When no one there would receive him, he sent his mercenaries off to Tainaron in Lakonia, and, with some of the money still in his possession, asked for the protection of the Athenian people. Antipater and Olympias demanded that he be handed over and, although he had given large amounts of money to the orators who made speeches to the assembly on his behalf, he had to flee and head to Tainaron and his mercenaries. **8** From there he sailed to Crete, where he was murdered by Thibron, one of his friends. The Athenians undertook an investigation into Harpalos' funds, and Demosthenes, and several other politicians, were convicted of having received money from these.

15.38 Diodorus *Library of History* 18.8.1–7: The Exiles' Decree

At the Olympic festival of 324 BC Alexander had Nikanor of Stageira read out a letter proclaiming that all Greek exiles were to be allowed to return to their home cities (except for those guilty of sacrilege). The terms of the League of Corinth denied the return of exiles if they set out with arms. Antipater, as leader of the Macedonian forces in Macedonia and Greece generally, had ably crushed the Spartan rebellion (doc. 15.19), and Alexander openly threatened that Antipater would employ violence against non-complying cities. It has been suggested that Alexander deliberately provoked this situation so as to have an opportunity to intervene further in the internal affairs of the Greek cities; more basically, it was simply an assertion of his control over Greece. When Alexander died in 323 BC, the Exiles' Decree was one of the reasons why the Greeks, particularly the Athenians and Aetolians, rebelled (unsuccessfully) in the so-called Lamian War (323–322 BC). For the Athenians' cleruchy on Samos, see docs 14.14–15, 15.39.

18.8.1 In Europe the Rhodians expelled their Macedonian garrison and liberated their city, and the Athenians commenced the war against Antipater, which is called the Lamian War. I must set out the causes of the war so that the events that took place as part of it may become clearer. **2** Shortly before his death Alexander resolved to restore all the exiles in the Greek cities, partly for the sake of his own renown, and partly because he wanted to have many personal supporters in each city whose goodwill towards himself would counter the Greeks' rebellions and revolts. **3** As the Olympic festival was imminent, he dispatched Nikanor of Stageira, with a letter about the restoration; this, he ordered, was to be proclaimed to the crowds at the festival by the victorious herald. **4** Nikanor carried out this instruction and the herald received and read out the following letter: 'King Alexander to the exiles from the Greek cities. We were not the cause of your exile, but we shall be the cause of your returning to your native cities, except for those who are under a curse. We have written to Antipater about this, so that he may use force against those cities which refuse to reinstate you.'

5 When this announcement was made the crowd showed its approval with great applause. Those at the festival welcomed the favour granted by the King with shouts of joy, and repaid his benefaction with praises. All the exiles had gathered at the festival, and numbered more than twenty thousand.

6 Most people welcomed the return of the exiles as a good thing, but the Aitolians and Athenians were angry at the action and took it badly. The Aitolians had expelled the Oiniadai from their native city and expected that their crimes would be visited with punishment, for the King had himself threatened that not the children of the Oiniadai but he himself would punish them; **7** similarly, the Athenians had divided up Samos into allotments and were most unwilling to abandon the island.

15.39 *SIG*[3] 312: Gorgos of Iasos Honoured at Samos

Gorgos and the details of his career are made evident in five inscriptions. Gorgos aided the Samian exiles to return home, under the terms of Alexander's Exiles' Decree, and gives an insight into how this process – the return of exiles – occurred with direct assistance from Alexander's court. In 366/5 BC the Athenians had taken Samos from the Persians, and five years later sent Athenian cleruchs who displaced the Samians, who became exiles, many at Iasos on the Asia Minor coast. [*IG* XII 6.17; Heisserer 184; Harding 127; R&O 90B.]

The Council and the demos decreed, Epikouros son of Drakon proposed the motion. Gorgos and Minion of Iasos, sons of Theodotos, have been good and helpful men with regard to the Samians in exile and Gorgos, who has spent time at Alexander's court, has demonstrated great goodwill and zeal regarding the demos of Samos, involving himself so that the Samians might quickly regain their native land; when Alexander announced in his camp that he would give Samos back to the Samians, because of this the Greeks crowned him, and Gorgos also crowned him, and sent to Iasos to the magistrates, so that when those of the Samians living in Iasos return to their native land they would be able to take away their possessions untaxed, and the costs of the journey would be provided for them, with the city of the Iasians covering the expense; and now Gorgos and Minion proclaim that they will do whatever good they can for the demos of the Samians. The demos has therefore decreed to give them citizenship on equal and fair terms, both to them and their descendants, and to assign them by lot to a tribe both the thousand and the hundred and the clan, and to inscribe them in the clan, which they have obtained by lot, in the same way as the other Samians, and the inscription is to be seen to by the five men chosen by lot, and this decree is to be inscribed on a stone stele and erected in the temple of Hera, and the treasurer is to see to the cost.

15.40 *IG* IV^2 616: Gorgos of Iasos Again

This inscription honouring Gorgos comes from Epidauros and refers to activities of his on the island of Kos, perhaps relating to the return of exiles to the island. Specific reference is made to his loyalty to Alexander, the 'god-like king'. [Heisserer 196.]

For the sake of good and god-wrought ordinances, Gorgos,
For your son and yourself immortal thanks is given
By vine-clad Epidauros. You, sprung from Iasos,
Were nourished and taught the deeds of war
By much-praised Kos, seat of the Meropes, and were shown to be
A servant always loyal to the godlike king.

15.41 Ephippos FF4–5: Gorgos the 'Guardian of Arms'

Gorgos as a guardian of the arms could clearly gain access to the Macedonian armoury: Ephippos describes him as one of the king's 'guardians of arms' (a hoplophylax) willing in 324 BC to provide Alexander with armour, catapults and other weapons to besiege Athens. The context for the offer may well have been the Harpalos affair, or the expectation that Athens would react violently to the Exiles' Decree. This fragment of Ephippos' work, and the inscriptions, indicates that as an individual Gorgos was useful to Alexander in dealing with Greek states and was extremely loyal to him. [Ephippos *FGH* 126 FF4–5; Athen. *Deip.* 537d–538b.]

4 (537d) Regarding Alexander the Great's luxurious lifestyle Ephippos of Olynthos in his work *On the Death of Hephaistion and Alexander* says that in the garden there was for his use a golden throne and couches with silver feet on which he used to sit when transacting business with his companions. **5 (537f)** Alexander even sprinkled the floor with expensive perfume and sweet-scented wine. **(538a)** Myrrh and other types of incense were burned in his honour; a religious silence and quiet possessed all those in his presence through fear — for he was quick-tempered and murderous, and even thought to be a manic depressive. At Ecbatana he organised a festival for Dionysos, with everything at the feast supplied lavishly, and Satrabates the satrap gave a banquet for all the soldiers. Many gathered for the spectacle, Ephippos tells us, and there were arrogant proclamations even more audacious than the usual Persian boastfulness. **(538b)** For with various people crowning Alexander and proclaiming him conqueror in different ways, one man in particular, one of the guardians of arms, surpassed all the rest of the flatterers and, after consulting with Alexander, ordered the herald to proclaim that 'Gorgos, the Guardian of arms, crowns Alexander, son of Ammon, with a crown worth three thousand gold pieces, and whenever he besieges Athens will give him ten thousand full suits of armour, the same number of catapults, and all other missiles as well sufficient for the war.'

ALEXANDER'S DEATH: 'HE DRANK AND PARTIED'

15.42 Arrian *Expedition of Alexander* 7.14.1–10: The Death of Hephaistion, 324 BC

Hephaistion was arguably Alexander's closest friend, held several important commands, and had been made chiliarch, amounting to a position of second-in-charge, of Alexander's empire. Like Alexander he married a daughter of Darius III at Susa in 324 BC (doc. 15.31). Alexander was extremely fond of him, and his excessive grief at his death may have been a deliberate imitation of Achilles' mourning for his beloved Patroklos. Cf. Diod. 17.114–115.

7.14.1 At Ekbatana Alexander performed a sacrifice, as he was accustomed to do after a successful enterprise, and held an athletic and musical competition while simultaneously engaging in drinking bouts with his companions. It was at this point that Hephaistion fell ill. His illness was in its seventh day and, according to report, the stadium was crowded, as there was an athletic contest for boys on that day, but when Alexander was told that Hephaistion was seriously ill he hurried to his side; however, he found him no longer living.

2 At this point different writers have recorded various accounts of Alexander's grief. That his grief was immense, all have reported, while there are differing accounts of his actions depending on the degree of goodwill or envy each writer felt towards Hephaistion or even towards Alexander himself. **3** Of those who narrated the excessive nature of his behaviour, some appear to me to have thought that whatever Alexander did or said under the influence of his grief for his dearest friend redounded to his credit, while others place it instead to his discredit as inappropriate either for a king or for Alexander. Some say that for most of that day he lay prostrate and in tears on his friend's body and would not leave him, until he was forcibly removed by the Companions; **4** others that he lay prostrate on the body for the whole of that day and night; still others that he hanged the doctor Glaukias for giving the wrong medicine, or because he had seen Hephaistion drinking to excess but did nothing about it. I don't consider it implausible that Alexander cut off his hair in honour of the dead and did other things in emulation of Achilles towards whom he had felt a sense of rivalry from boyhood. **5** Yet others write that he himself drove the chariot in which the body was carried — but I cannot accept this as reliable. Others tell us that he ordered the shrine of Asklepios at Ekbatana to be torn down, the act of a barbarian and in no way worthy of Alexander, but rather of Xerxes' arrogance towards the divine and the chains which they say Xerxes sank in the Hellespont in the hope that he could punish it.

6 But there is also an account which appears to me to be not entirely implausible, that when Alexander was going to Babylon many embassies from Greece met him on the road, amongst them envoys from the Epidaurians; they received what they requested from Alexander and Alexander gave them a dedication to take back to Asklepios, with the words, 'this is although Asklepios has not used me well, for he failed to save for me my friend who was as dear to me as life'. **7** Most writers have also recorded that he ordered sacrifices always be made to Hephaistion as a hero, and some say that he sent to the oracle of Ammon to ask if he permitted sacrifice to Hephaistion as to a god, but that the god refused.

8 The following facts are, however, agreed by everyone, that until the third day after Hephaistion's death Alexander tasted no food nor took care of any bodily needs, but lay there either weeping or in a mournful silence; that he ordered a pyre to be prepared for Hephaistion at Babylon at a cost of 10,000 talents, though some writers say even more, **9** and commanded mourning to take place throughout the whole barbarian country; and that many of Alexander's Companions out of respect for him dedicated themselves and their weapons to the dead Hephaistion. Eumenes was the first to begin this expedient, whose quarrel with Hephaistion I described a little earlier, and it was said that he did this so that Alexander should not think that he was pleased at Hephaistion's death. **10** At any rate Alexander never appointed anyone in Hephaistion's place as chiliarch over the Companions' cavalry, so that Hephaistion's name should never disappear from the company: the chiliarchy was still called Hephaistion's and the standard carried before it was the one made on his orders. He also planned to hold athletic and musical contests more magnificent than any before in terms of both the huge number of competitors and the expense of putting them on, making preparations for 3,000 competitors in total. These were also the men, it is said, that competed a little later at Alexander's own funeral.

15.43 Arrian *Expedition of Alexander* 7.24.4–27.3: Alexander's Death

At Babylon in June 323 BC, Alexander suddenly fell ill, and died on the tenth of that month after a ten-day illness. Poison was suspected and several parties implicated (Plut. *Alex.* 77). Alexander's empire soon fell apart in territorial squabbles amongst his generals, which led to the formation of the great hellenistic kingdoms which dominated the history of the next few centuries until the coming of Rome to the east. Arrian refers to the Royal Diaries as a source of information and there is no particular reason to deny their existence. Cf. Plut. *Alex.* 73–75; Diod. 17.117; Curt. 10.5.

7.24.4 Not many days after this Alexander made the traditional sacrifices to the gods for good fortune as well as some that were prescribed by prophecy, and began banqueting with his friends and drinking long into the night. It is said that he also gave his army sacrificial victims and wine, by companies and centuries. Some writers have recorded that he was about to leave the drinking party for his bedroom, but Medios, one of his favourite Companions at the time, met him and asked him to come and join his party, for they were going to have a great time.

7.25.1 This is the account in the Royal Diaries: he drank and partied with Medios; then after getting up and bathing, he slept, after which he dined again with Medios and drank with him far into the night; he then left the drinking party and bathed; after bathing he ate a little and slept where he was, as he was already suffering from a fever. **2** He was carried out on a couch to make the sacrifices prescribed for every day by custom, and when the offerings had been made he lay down in the men's apartments till dusk. Meanwhile he gave the officers their orders for the march and voyage: the infantry were to prepare for departure on the fourth day and those who would be sailing with him on the fifth. **3** From there he was carried on the couch down to the river, embarked on a boat and sailed across the river to the garden, where he again bathed and relaxed. On the following day he once more bathed and made the customary sacrifices, got into his canopied bed and talked with Medios, and again instructed his officers to meet him at dawn. **4** Having done this he had a light dinner, was again carried, in a fever, to his canopied bed and remained in a continual fever for the entire night; on the following day he bathed and sacrificed after bathing. He gave Nearchos and the other officers instructions for the voyage and that it was to take place on the third day.

On the next day he bathed again and made the prescribed sacrifices; once he had made the sacrifices he no longer had any break in the fever. However, he summoned his officers and instructed them to make sure that everything was ready for the voyage; he bathed in the evening and after bathing was now seriously ill. **5** On the following day he was carried to the house near the diving-spot and made the prescribed sacrifices, and though gravely ill summoned the highest-ranking officers and again gave them instructions for the voyage. Next day it was only with difficulty that he was carried to the sacrifices and conducted them, but nonetheless gave instructions to the officers about the voyage. **6** On the following day, now very seriously ill, he still made the prescribed sacrifices. He instructed the generals to wait in the courtyard and the chiliarchs and pentakosiarchs outside the doors. Then he was carried, in a critical state of illness, from the garden to the palace. When the officers entered he knew them, but said nothing more — speech was beyond him. He was in a high fever all that night and day, and the next night and day.

7.26.1 This is what is recorded in the Royal Diaries, which also say that his soldiers desired to see him, some to see him still alive, and others because it was being reported that he was already dead and they had, in my view at least, an idea that the bodyguards were hushing up his death; but most of them did all they could to see Alexander because of their grief and longing for their king. They say that he was already speechless when the army filed past him, but that he greeted them individually, raising his head with difficulty, and making signs of recognition with his eyes. **2** The Royal Diaries record that Peithon, Attalos, Demophon and Peukestas, along with Kleomenes, Menidas and Seleukos, slept in the temple of Sarapis to enquire of the god whether it would be preferable and more appropriate for Alexander to be brought into the god's temple and after supplicating to be treated by the god; the god's reply was that he should not be brought into the temple, but that it would be better for him to stay where he was. **3** Then, shortly after the Companions reported this, Alexander died — so this was what was now 'better'. Neither Aristoboulos nor Ptolemy have recorded further than this in their *Histories*, but some have written that his Companions asked him to whom he was leaving his kingdom and that he replied, 'to the strongest'; others that he added to this remark that he foresaw that there would be a great funeral contest over him.

7.27.1 I know, of course, that many other details are recorded about Alexander's death: for instance that a drug was sent to Alexander by Antipater and that it was as a result of this drug that he died, and that Aristotle, who was already afraid of Alexander because of Kallisthenes, made up the drug for Antipater, while Kassander, Antipater's son, delivered it. Others have even recorded that it was brought in a mule's hoof **2** and given by Iollas, Kassander's younger brother: Iollas was the royal cup-bearer and had been annoyed in some way with Alexander not long before his death. Still others state that Medios was part of the plot, as he was the lover of Iollas, and that he was the one who got Alexander involved in the riotous party, that Alexander felt a stab of pain after drinking down the cupful, and that he left the drinking on feeling the pain. **3** One writer has not even been ashamed to record that Alexander, realising that he was not going to live, went to the river Euphrates to throw himself in, to ensure his disappearance from amongst mankind and thus make the idea that a god sired him and that it was to the gods that he returned more credible to later generations. Roxane his wife, however, noticed that he was going out and stopped him, at which he lamented saying that she was actually grudging him the glory for all time of having been born a god. I have recorded these stories to show that I am not ignorant of their existence rather than because I believe they are credible enough to narrate.

15.44 Arrian *Expedition of Alexander* 7.28.1–3: Praise for Alexander's Reign

Arrian's encomium here reflects his overall admiration of Alexander and his achievements (cf. Arr. 7.30.3). [*FGH* 139 F61.]

7.28.1 Alexander died in the 114th Olympiad, in the archonship of Hegesias at Athens. He lived thirty-two years and eight months, according to Aristoboulos, and ruled for twelve years and another eight months. He excelled in corporeal beauty, physical exertion, shrewdness of intellect, courage, love of honour and danger, and attention to matters of religion, **2** as well as in self-restraint over pleasures of the body, insatiability (as far as pleasures of the mind are concerned) only for praise, skill in discerning what was necessary when it was still unclear, the ability to deduce from observation what was likely to occur, and the knowledge of how best to marshal, arm and equip an army, while in raising the morale of his soldiers, inspiring them with confidence, and removing their fear in dangers through his own fearlessness – in all these he showed the greatest high-mindedness. **3** Whenever it was clear what was to be done, he did it with absolute bravery, and whenever he had to steal a success from the enemy by being proactive, he had the finest ability to anticipate events before anyone could even apprehend what was going to happen. No one was more reliable in keeping terms or agreements, or safer from being taken in by deceit, while as for money no one was more sparing of money where his own pleasures were concerned, or more generous in using it to benefit those around him.

15.45 Arrian *Expedition of Alexander* 7.29.3–4, 7.30.2–3: Alexander's Divinity

Throughout his reign, Alexander seems to have increasingly regarded himself as divine. Philip, his father, had accorded himself divine honours (doc. 14.53). The oracle at Siwah in 331 BC apparently addressed him as the son of Zeus (doc. 15.18). Alexander was clearly annoyed at Kleitos for arguing that Alexander's achievements did not compare to those of the gods Herakles (from whom

Alexander claimed descent) and the Dioskouroi (doc. 15.22). In 324 BC he requested divine honours from the Greek states; both the Spartans and Athenians ironically stated that he could be a god if he wished (Aelian VH 2.19; Hypereides 5.31). The practice of proskynesis, with courtiers prostrating themselves before Alexander, as had taken place before the Great King, had been adopted by Alexander (note Kallisthenes' opposition to this, doc. 14.24) and was an aspect of his claim to divinity.

7.29.3 I do not think that his attributing his birth to a god was a serious fault of his, and in any case it might well have been a way of making his subjects reverence him. In my view he was no less distinguished a king than Minos or Aiakos or Rhadamanthys, whose birth men of olden times actually attributed to Zeus without this being considered hybris in any way, or less worthy than Theseus, son of Poseidon, or Ion, son of Apollo. **4** I also believe that his Persian dress was adopted with a view to the barbarians, so that the king might not appear to them to be totally alien, and for the Macedonians too, to give him some protection from Macedonian criticism and insolence; it was for this same reason in my view that he mingled the Persian 'apple-bearers' into the Macedonian ranks and the Persian nobles (homotimoi) into the agemas. His drinking bouts too, according to Aristoboulos, were not prolonged for the sake of wine, because Alexander drank little wine, but to enjoy the companionship of the Companions.

7.30.2 In my own view there was no nation and no city — not even a single person — whom the name of Alexander at that time had not reached. And so I believe that a man who was so unique among mankind could not have been born without divine agency. Proof of this is said to have been the oracles at Alexander's death, along with various visions which appeared to different people, and dreams to yet others, as well as the honour paid to him by mankind till this day and the remembrance of him, which is more than human: even today, after so long a stretch of time, different oracles in his honour have been given to the Macedonian people. **3** So, despite the fact that I have criticised some of Alexander's actions in my *History* of them, I am not ashamed to express my admiration of Alexander himself. Where I have faulted his deeds I have done so out of respect for truth and for the good of mankind — this is why I embarked on this *History*, and, like Alexander, have done so not without god's help.

16

THE ANCIENT SOURCES

The ancient sources for the period *c.* 800–323 BC are both varied and numerous. Literary sources are the most accessible for students, by both historical writers such as Herodotos, Thucydides, Xenophon, the *Athenaion Politeia*, Arrian, Diodorus and Plutarch, and the poets, such as Simonides, Pindar, the tragedians (such as Aeschylus and Euripides) and the comic playwrights Aristophanes and Menander; in addition, there are the speeches in the law courts, such as those of Lysias and Demosthenes. But the aim of this collection has also been to give access to other sources, such as information recorded on stone (see Epigraphy, p. 537) and papyrus (see Papyrology, pp. 537–8), as well as historians, such as Ephoros and Theopompos, whose work only survives in 'fragments', small sections quoted or cited by other ancient historians. What follows can at best be only a minimal introduction to Greek historiography (historical writing), and is aimed at helping the reader to understand the aims and methodology of ancient authors.

The beginnings of Greek historiography and how it developed are obscure. The first 'literary' compositions — those of 'Homer' — were essentially mythic, but nevertheless the *Iliad* was in a sense a 'history' of a war, and intended to convey that story to future generations; Herodotos, Thucydides and Arrian also chose war as their themes. Xenophon's *Hellenika*, an account of Greek history from 411 to 362 BC, is basically a history of war: the various conflicts between the Greek city-states. Ionian logographers began with accounts of mythology: Hekataios of Miletos (doc. 16.1) wrote both a geography, including ethnographic material, and a mythographic work, the *Genealogies*, and can probably be referred to as the first historian. While Herodotos may sometimes be termed 'The Father of History', in a very real sense he was preceded in this by others.

HISTORIANS

Brief discussions of Herodotos, Thucydides, Xenophon, the *Athenaion Politeia* (attributed to Aristotle) and Plutarch can be found in this chapter, with extracts illustrating their historical methods. But there were other ancient historians. The works of many no longer survive as a complete text such as that of Herodotos; they are known only from phrases, sentences or paragraphs quoted or paraphrased by other ancient historians or commentators. For example, the *Athenaion Politeia* quotes Androtion. Such excerpts are called fragments of the historian's work, and Jacoby (*FGH*) collected the Greek text of several hundred such authors. Contemporary histories can also be supplemented by later works. Ephoros (405–330 BC; doc. 2.11), for example, wrote a 'universal history' down to 340, which is now lost, and it was used by many ancient writers, such as Strabo, Nicholas of Damascus and Plutarch. A special subcategory of the fragmentary historians are the Atthidographers (p. 537), who wrote local histories of Athens, including myths, religious practices and historical events.

ATTHIDOGRAPHERS

The Atthis (hence Atthidographer, writer of an Atthis, pl.: Atthides) was a chronicle of Athenian history; the first Atthis may have been written by Hellanikos of Lesbos (480–395; see Thuc. 1.97.2, doc. 12.4). Other writers of Atthides were Androtion (410–340; doc. 8.13), used by the *Athenaion Politeia*, and Philochoros (340–260), who also used Androtion; Philochoros was the last of the Atthidographers. These Atthidographers survive only in fragments as quoted by later ancient historians; Plutarch made use of them in his Athenian *Lives*, and this fact increases the reliability of his *Lives*, written so long after the events described.

EPIGRAPHY

Many epigraphic sources are 'impersonal' texts, such as state decrees or laws inscribed on stone; the Athenians in the fifth and fourth centuries inscribed numerous decrees of the people, an invaluable source for political history. These involve a series of problems of interpretation, such as dating, noting in particular the crux about the date of various Athenian state decrees (eg, doc. 13.13), upon which turn a whole series of questions, such as the character of the Athenian empire at a particular time, and the date of the development of an imperial Athens. Inscriptions also present problems of interpretation, such as the meaning of a particular word, and, even more exasperating for the modern student of ancient history, missing gaps in the text, where the stone has broken or had been worn away. Sometimes inscriptions are personal, such as when they record a funerary epigram, and the deceased or their relatives speak, revealing important information about the family, though here too one needs caution, weighing up conventional ideals against reality. Inscriptions could also be in the form of graffiti, such as docs 2.32 and 4.77.

LEXICOGRAPHERS AND SCHOLIASTS

There are various works from the Byzantine period (330–1453 CE) by lexicographers, compilers of lists of Greek words, such as the *Suda* (tenth century) and *Etymologicum Magnum* (twelfth century), whose entries are often based on works by ancient authors now lost. These lexicographers also had access to previous lexicographical works of the post-Hellenistic period, such as the still extant second-century AD compilation of Harpokration and the *Onomastikon* of Pollux, which drew on Hellenistic writers. Ancient and Byzantine scholars sometimes also made explanatory notes (scholia, written by 'scholiasts') on the manuscripts of the texts of ancient authors, preserving information and interpretations which do not otherwise survive; sometimes, however, the explanations given only have the value of guesswork. The scholia on Aristophanes are, however, particularly useful (see, for example, doc. 10.13).

PAPYROLOGY

Nearly all of the papyri (sing.: papyrus) preserving Greek texts are from Egypt; these include a wide range of subjects, such as correspondence (official and private), petitions and official edicts from all periods when the Greek language was used in Egypt. Of interest here is the fact that the Greeks in Egypt had papyrus copies of numerous Greek literary texts, and in many instances these papyri are the only surviving copies; the dry climate and sand have acted to preserve them (though not always in good condition). The only text of the Aristotelian *Athenaion Politeia* is a papyrus from Egypt (there are also a few separate papyrus fragments), published in 1891. Many texts have come from

Oxyrhynchus, such as the work of the Oxyrhynchus Historian (doc. 1.58), who wrote between 387 and 346; two papyri have been found of this author, in 1906 and 1942. As recently as 1992, new fragments from Oxyrhynchus of Simonides, his elegies on the Battles of Plataea and Artemision, were published (doc. 11.48). Many ancient authors, such as Sappho and Bacchylides, are preserved mainly through papyrus copies.

ORATORS

Most of the speeches delivered in the Athenian courts date to the fourth century; Antiphon (c. 480–411 BC) is the first orator whose speeches survive. In fact, he was probably the first to write speeches for litigants. He was executed for his role in the 411 oligarchic revolution. The metic Lysias (459/8–c.380) and Andocides (c.440–390), who was accused of being involved in the profanation of the Mysteries and mutilation of the hermai, are also relevant to our period. While the orators of the late fifth and fourth centuries are an unrivalled source on Athenian social history, their speeches have to be used with caution. Usually only one side of a case survives; major exceptions to this are Aeschines' and Demosthenes' speeches *On the Embassy* delivered in the same case in 343 BC, and similarly their opposing speeches *Against Ktesiphon* (Aeschines) and *On the Crown* (Demosthenes) of 330 BC. Speeches are without the witness statements, the citations of relevant laws are generally interpolated by later editors, and it is unknown whether the speaker in fact won his case. In other words, each speech gives the orator's interpretation of the laws in favour of his client, his aim being to persuade the (all-male) jury drawn primarily from the poorer class of citizens to decide in his client's favour. In the *Wasps*, esp. 548–602, Aristophanes presents in comic fashion some of the abuses of the jury system (see docs 1.26–27).

TRAGEDIANS AND OTHER POETS

Of the three 'classic' fifth-century tragedians, Aeschylus (525/4?–456/5 BC) fought at the battle of Marathon and possibly also at Salamis (see doc. 11.11). His *Persians*, about the battle of Salamis (doc. 11.38), is an important source for the battle. In general his plays, such as the *Eumenides*, reflect a belief in democracy but also the need to reconcile groups within the polis in order to guarantee stability. Dramatically, his characters, such as Clytemnestra (doc. 4.68), are some of the most dark and compelling in Attic tragedy. His younger contemporary Sophocles (?496/5–406 BC) was a Treasurer of Athena (443–442 BC), and a general (possibly in 441/0) with Perikles during Samos' revolt (doc. 12.24, cf. 4.86). He had a remarkably long and successful career, writing more than 120 plays and never taking third (i.e., last) place. Of his seven extant works, the best known are perhaps his *Oedipus Tyrannus* and the *Antigone*, in which the heroine defends family loyalties against the dictates of the state by burying her brother Polyneikes against her uncle's explicit command (cf. docs 3.54, 4.69). Euripides (490/80–406), who wrote some ninety plays, is sometimes seen as the most 'realistic' of the tragedians and the one most interested in human psychology. Euripides is portrayed by Aristophanes as a woman-hater and poetic innovator; however, Aristophanes' frequent attacks on him in his comedies, particularly the *Frogs* and *Thesmophoriazousai* (see docs 3.64, 4.60), are in fact testimony to Euripides' popularity with the audience. The plots of all surviving Attic tragedies are set in the heroic past, and while these plays were a vehicle of public discourse and can be used to help elucidate social developments in Athens, care has to be taken in using citations out of their dramatic contexts. Stories from the mythical past could be presented in such a way as to encourage the audience to look at current tensions in their society — Euripides' *Medea* (doc. 4.70), for example, highlights those between male and female, and metic and citizen

— but quotations from the plays should never be taken as being the dramatist speaking *in propria persona* (in his own identity); in every case attention must be paid to the dynamics of the dramatic setting and the stand point of the protagonist who is voicing their views. Nevertheless the tragedies are valuable evidence for the tastes and preoccupations of fifth-century Athenians and can be taken as reflecting contemporary social conditions and religious beliefs.

Valuable evidence for historical events and contemporary responses to them can be drawn from the works of other poets, such as the epigrams and elegies of Simonides of Keos (c. 556?–*c.* 466?), who celebrated the victories and individual protagonists of the Persian Wars (see, especially, docs 11.12–13, 11.41–44, 11.50), while Solon of Athens (archon 594/3), Alcaeus of Mytilene (born c. 625) and Theognis of Megara (writing around 640–600 or 550–490) used poetry as a vehicle for comments on the current political situation in their poleis. Simonides was followed by other professional poets who celebrated the athletic victories of patrons throughout the Greek world: most notable are Pindar (*c.* 518?–c. 445) and Bacchylides of Keos (c. 520–450), nephew of Simonides, as well as the sixth-century Ibycus of Rhegium. Further evidence for aristocratic and symposiastic pursuits can be found in the works of the lyric poets Sappho, Alcaeus and Anacreon of Teos (born *c.* 575), while the seventh-century poet Archilochos of Paros, like Alcaeus and Anacreon, was noted for his satirical and abusive attacks on contemporaries.

Possibly the best known of the eleven extant plays of Aristophanes (460/50–*c.* 386 BC) is the *Lysistrata* (411), in which the women of Athens, by refusing to have sex with their husbands, force them to make peace with the Spartans (see docs 6.19, 11.57, 4.66). The advisability of peace with Sparta is a frequent theme in his comedies, such as *Acharnians* (425), in which Dikaiopolis makes a private peace treaty, *Peace* (421) and *Lysistrata*; while the *Wasps* (422) is a vicious satire on the Athenian jury-courts and the *Clouds* (revised 418–16) poked fun at Socrates and sophists generally (docs 3.80, 3.82). Aristophanes satirized numerous politicians and prominent individuals, such as Perikles, Kleon and Euripides, no doubt to the delight of his audience. In the (lost) *Babylonians* (426) he attacked public officials, and was apparently prosecuted, unsuccessfully, by Kleon as a result. The *Knights* (424) mercilessly attacks Kleon (cf. doc. 16.13); it won first prize, but Kleon was elected as general soon afterwards. Aristophanes' primary aim as a dramatist was to entertain rather than to make moral judgements; the fact that he poked fun at all classes of his audience did not detract from his success as a comic poet, though his plays do not seem to have had a marked effect on contemporary politics. Menander wrote comedies at Athens in the last quarter of the fourth century; these have domestic plots and are apolitical (docs 3.10–11, 3.63).

USE OF SOURCES

There are numerous problems associated with the sources; some, for example, were very much removed in time from the period about which they were writing. When these writers are drawing on the accounts of earlier historians — often now lost — they can, to an extent, be considered to reflect contemporary accounts. But this relies upon these later historians having accurately read, and then written up, these earlier works. The ancient historians clearly made use of their predecessors' accounts: Herodotos drew on Hekataios, and Thucydides has clearly read Herodotos and perhaps used Hekataios and Antiochos. While criticizing Herodotos (doc. 6.28), Thucydides is clearly indebted to him as providing a model for writing history. The nature of the genre within which each author is writing also has to be taken into account: Herodotos in his description of other countries is recording legends and current beliefs about the customs and history of his informants, Thucydides is undeniably writing history, while Plutarch is concerned with biography, and admits that it is not his purpose to provide a strict chronological account of his subjects' actions. Each historian has biases:

Thucydides is clearly biased towards Perikles and against Kleon, while Plutarch certainly approves of some of the individuals he is writing about more than others, and is also concerned with 'virtue and vice'.

Herodotos wrote a history that was derived from oral traditions; even if such oral traditions can be accurate, one of the factors that attracted Thucydides to recording the events of the Peloponnesian War was that he was writing contemporary history. Herodotos may to an extent have not only reflected his sources (those at Sparta, for example, being primarily but not universally hostile to Kleomenes), but also his audience and their expectations, and in view of the fact that works were primarily intended for recitation rather than for private readers the audience for whom each work was composed is an important factor. Thucydides, in contrast, implicitly reacts against the way in which his predecessors' accounts have contained the 'pleasing' and 'fabulous'; his work was not for an immediate audience, he tells us, but composed as 'a possession for all time rather than as a declamation for the moment' (1.22.4, doc. 16.3.ii).

The comments on individual authors and bibliographies that follow are of necessity brief, and the excerpts from the writers are chosen to illustrate what they say about their own techniques and methodology: the intention is that the passages should largely 'speak for themselves'.

LOGOGRAPHERS AND HISTORIANS

16.1 Hekataios of Miletos F1

Herodotos and other early Greek historians were preceded by another prose writer (one of the first writing in prose rather than poetry), Hekataios (son of Hegesander) of Miletos, who wrote a geographical work about Asia (including Africa) and Europe, as well as the *Genealogies* (or *Histories*) dealing with mythology; only fragments of Hekataios' works survive. Writers in prose were known as logographers; Thucydides (1.21.1) uses this term in criticising those prose writers who preceded him. These logographers wrote both about the mythological past and what we might call 'history'; most of them were from Ionia. Hekataios was the most important of the early logographers. Herodotos clearly made use of his works, giving Hekataios' version of a story at one point (Hdt. 6.137 (doc. 16.3.iv); see also Hdt. 2.143); in addition, Hekataios was a political figure, involved in the Ionian Revolt (499–494 BC), and opposing it (Hdt. 5.36, 125). There were several logographers, some contemporaneous with Herodotos; the more important of these were Xanthos of Sardis (*FGH* 765) and Charon of Lampsakos (*FGH* 262, 687b), both of whose works Herodotos may have used. Thucydides may well have used Hekataios in his accounts of Epiros and northern Greece. The fragment below indicates that Hekataios was concerned with ascertaining the 'truth', and in this sense he made an important contribution to the development of historical writing. Hekataios of Miletos *FGH* 264 F1 is from Diog. Laert. 1.10.

Hekataios of Miletos speaks thus: I write what seems to me to be true; for the Greeks have many tales which appear to me to be absurd.

16.2 Antiochos of Syracuse F2

Antiochos of Syracuse may have been the first historian in the western Greek world, after Hippys of Rhegium (*FGH* 554), perhaps a legendary figure. He wrote after Herodotos, who dealt with the west only in passing, and perhaps Antiochos was motivated to write to supplement Herodotos' account. His methodology was to select what seemed to him to be the most credible traditions.

Antiochos may have written both a history of Sicily (the *Sikelika*) in nine books, which Thucydides may have used for the colonisation of Sicily (doc. 2.12), and an account (the *Peri Italias*) of the foundations of some of the Greek cities of southern Italy, though these may not have been separate works. Antiochos of Syracuse *FGH* 555 F2 is from Dion. Hal. 1.12.3; see doc. 2.23.

Antiochos of Syracuse, a very early historian, in his account of the settlement of Italy recounts how each of the oldest inhabitants came to possess some part of it, and says that the Oinotrians were the first of those reported to have inhabited it in these words: 'Antiochos, son of Xenophanes, has written this down as comprising the most trustworthy and certain of the ancient tales concerning Italy; this land, which is now called Italy, the Oinotrians possessed in olden days.'

16.3 Herodotos, the 'Father of History'

Life

Herodotos was born in Halikarnassos (modern Bodrum, on the Aegean coast of Turkey); this was a Dorian city but contact occurred with the local non-Greek Carian population. The city was under Persian control; along with Panyassis, his uncle or cousin, Herodotos was involved in an attempt to depose the city's tyrant, Lygdamis; Panyassis was killed and Herodotos went into exile. He is generally considered to have been born in the 480s, and clearly lived through at least the initial stages of the Peloponnesian War; it is thought that he died in the 420s, for his references to this war do not postdate that decade.

Content and structure

Herodotos wrote his *historia* ('inquiries', 'investigation') to explain how the Greeks and the Persians came into conflict (see doc. 16.3.i). In doing this, he went back to the middle of the sixth century, and the fall of Lydia to the Persians. While readers often complain of the number of digressions from what they see to be the main narrative, the work does have a structure. In nine books Herodotos explores the theme of Persian expansion and how the Greeks and the Persians came into conflict, and he sees the Athenian and Eretrian decision to aid the Ionian revolt as the main reason for the Persian determination to annexe mainland Greece. The treatments of the customs and histories of many peoples in the *Histories* are not merely digressions, but occur in the text at the point when such peoples came into contact with the expanding Persians.

Herodotos devotes Book 1 to the development of the Persian Empire: how Croesus, king of the Lydians, had conquered the Ionian city-states of Asia Minor, but was in turn conquered by the Persians under Cyrus. This explains how the Greeks of Asia Minor came to be under Persian domination. There is also important material on Athens and Sparta, introduced because Croesus enquired which of the Greek states were the most powerful, so that he could seek their support: Herodotos therefore discusses the tyranny of Peisistratos at Athens (docs 9.1, 9.3, 9.6, 9.8, 9.9, 9.11, 9.12, 9.14, 9.17), and how the Spartans became powerful (doc. 6.2). Book 2 is a major 'digression' on Egypt, its people, gods, geography and customs, and shows Herodotos' marked ethnographic interests. The first chapter explains how Cyrus' son, Cambyses, who succeeded him, decided to send an expedition to annexe Egypt. Book 3 opens with Cambyses' defeat of the Egyptians, and Darius' succession; there are important digressions on the tyrant Polykrates of Samos (docs 7.32, 7.34–35) and Periander, the Corinthian tyrant (doc. 7.13). Book 4 deals with Darius' failed campaigns against the Scythians, and Book 5 with Persian expansion into northern Greece and the Ionian revolt (docs 11.3–5). Aristagoras' attempt to obtain help from the mainland Greeks means that Kleomenes of Sparta (docs 6.74, 6.75, 6.77), the Corinthian tyranny (docs 7.9), the liberation of Athens from the tyranny of Peisistratos' sons, and Kleisthenes' reforms (docs 9.36–37, 10.1–5) are dealt with; this book is a very important one for archaic Greek history. This brings the work towards its climax, and Book 6 deals with Marathon, including the Spartan response to the impending invasion, with more on Kleomenes and the nature of Spartan kingship (docs 6.26, 6.76, 6.77). The rest of the work, Books 7–9, covers the campaign of 480–79.

Oral tradition and Herodotos' sources

Herodotos occasionally relied on documents and inscriptions (he notes monuments and paintings commemorating historic events), and made use of the work of previous logographers, but the bulk of his history comes from oral tradition. He was also presumably aware of earlier poetic sources such as Aeschylus' *Persians*, and used the elegies of Simonides, and in a newly discovered inscription from Halikarnassos he is himself described as 'the Homer of history in prose': cf. doc. 16.6. Herodotos was not writing contemporary history, and is sometimes describing events a century or so earlier than when he is writing; even the Persian Wars took place several decades before he wrote his *Histories*. He had visited many of the places whose people and history he describes; in a famous passage, he tells his audience that everything he has related so far about Egypt in his narrative he has seen with his own eyes (2.99, doc. 16.3.iii; cf. 2.29). He travelled as far as Elephantine along the Nile, and had been to the Black Sea area, Phoenicia, Palestine, Cyrene and Metapontum in southern Italy. In Greece itself he visited many cities, including Dodona in the north-west, and his knowledge of Athens and Sparta is drawn from information he heard from local inhabitants. He often notes that he has spoken to local informants and mentions when he has not been personally to a place but is relying on 'hearsay' about it (doc 16.3.iii,). Sometimes he knows of more than one version of an event, and in such cases often gives the variants (as in doc. 16.3.iv and vi; cf. 2.29). Although historians often deal with Herodotos as a written text, his work was intended for recitation in sections in public performances and at symposia.

Religious factors

Herodotos is much less interested in the divine role in human affairs than is commonly thought. He does believe in oracles and has gods intervening in human affairs; in doing this he is clearly reflecting popular belief, such as when he records the Athenian belief that Boreas helped wreck Persian ships in storms (7.189). But on the whole, mortals and their motives dominate the *Histories*. More conspicuous than the gods, in fact, are Herodotos' pronouncements on the vagaries of human prosperity and on fate, retribution, vengeance, and figures such as Solon and Amasis, noted for their wisdom.

Bias

Herodotos, like other historians (both ancient and modern), is biased towards and against various individuals and states in his *Histories*. In general, he does not show prejudice against non-Greek cultures. Plutarch, in his *On the Malignity of Herodotos*, accuses Herodotos of prejudice on a number of occasions, and he is clearly biased against Corinth (see doc. 11.41; cf. 6.58) and Thebes, but in favour of Athens, and attributes to the Athenians the real victory over the Persians (doc. 11.54). His account has also been seen as favouring the Alkmeonidai (see doc. 11.10).

Sometimes called the 'Father of History' he has also been dubbed the 'Father of Lies', due to the incredible nature of some of the stories that are included in his narrative. Some scholars are extremely sceptical about the accuracy of Herodotos' history; others are probably too uncritical. Herodotos himself disclaims responsibility for the truth of many of the stories he included in his work (docs 16.3.iii and v), and is recording what people believed about their own cultures and history. Even when he might have disbelieved the tales himself, many were simply too entertaining to be omitted. However, oral testimony in the middle of the fifth century for the period about which

Herodotos is writing is likely to have been fairly accurate. He made use of the sources which were available to him, and to the extent that these were accurate, so too is he. It cannot be denied that he is the most valuable source for many of the topics which he covers.

i. Herodotos 1 (preface)

Herodotos of Halikarnassos here gives the results of his investigation (historia), so that men's achievements may not in time become forgotten, nor great and wonderful deeds, some displayed by Greeks and some by barbarians, lose their fame, and especially to show the cause of the war they fought against each other.

ii. Herodotos 1.5.3–4

1.5.3 This is what the Persians and Phoenicians say. And concerning this I am not going to say that they were so or not, but I myself know who was the first to act unjustly against the Greeks, and after pointing this out I will proceed onwards with my account, relating the details of small and large cities of men alike. **1.5.4** For the majority of those which were formerly large have become small, and those which used to be small were great in my own time. So, knowing that human prosperity never remains in the same place, I will make mention of both alike.

iii. Herodotos 2.99.1, 2.123.1

2.99.1 Up to this point, what I have written is based on my own observation and judgement and investigation, but from now on I am going to record the accounts I heard from the Egyptians; but I will also add to these from my own observation ... **2.123.1** Anyone to whom such things are plausible may believe the tales of the Egyptians; but my appointed task through the whole work is to record what I have been told by everyone as I heard it.

iv. Herodotos 6.137.1, 6.137.3

6.137.1 Miltiades, son of Kimon, captured Lemnos in the following way: some Pelasgians had just been driven out of Attica by the Athenians, whether justly or unjustly; for I am unable to say this, only what is said, that Hekataios, son of Hegesander, related in his account that it was unjustly ... **6.137.3** But the Athenians say that they expelled them justly.

v. Herodotos 7.152.1, 7.152.3

7.152.1 Whether Xerxes sent a herald to Argos to say this, and whether Argive messengers went to Susa to ask Artaxerxes about their friendship, I am unable to say with certainty, nor express any opinion about these events other than what the Argives say ... **3** I am obliged to record what is said, but by no means to believe it, and this statement applies to my work as a whole.

vi. Herodotos 8.83.2–84.2

8.83.2 The Greeks then put their ships to sea (at Salamis), and as they were setting sail the barbarians immediately attacked them. **8.84.1** The other Greeks put their ships astern and were on the point of running them aground, when Ameinias of Pallene, an Athenian, set sail and rammed a ship. As the ship became entangled with her opponent and the two could not be separated, the others came to his assistance and joined battle. **2** The Athenians say the sea-battle began like this, but the Aeginetans say that the ship which had gone to Aegina to fetch the sons of Aiakos was the one which made the first move. It is also said that the phantom of a woman appeared to them, and exhorted them so as to be heard by the whole Greek army, first reproaching them: 'My good men, how long are you going to keep going astern?'

16.4 Thucydides, Historian of the Peloponnesian War

Biographical data

Cf. doc. 13.1. Thucydides was born in Athens, probably in the 450s BC or a little earlier. As a general (strategos; he would need to have been thirty years old for this office) in 424 he failed to save Amphipolis from Brasidas (4.104–6); he was exiled from Athens for twenty years on account of this (5.26.5). He makes no allusion to any events after 400 and so was presumably dead by then. He was the son of Oloros (a Thracian name); he had the right of working goldmines in Thrace (4.105). Kimon's grandfather was also called Oloros, indicating a blood relationship. He was also related to Thucydides son of Melesias; it has been suggested that he was a son of one of the daughters of Thucydides son of Melesias, Perikles' main political opponent in the 440s (see docs 10.14.xi, 12.27). Aristocratic, with politicians 'in the family', wealthy from Thracian gold and prominent enough to be elected a strategos, he was a member of the Athenian elite. Thucydides made his exile into a virtue, and while it is easy to accept that it did give him access to information that he might not otherwise have had, his absence from Athens for twenty years has considerably weakened his narrative for the period after 424.

Criticism of predecessors

He justifies his digression on the pentekontaetia because no other writer had dealt with it, except for Hellanikos in his *History of Attica* (1.97.2: doc. 12.4): 'and he mentioned it briefly and without chronological accuracy'. He never mentions Herodotos by name, but is clearly indebted to him; 1.20.3 must be a correction of Hdt. 9.53.2 (doc. 6.28), and 1.20.3 and 2.8.3 probably criticise Hdt. 6.57.5 and 6.98.1, respectively (cf. doc. 9.19–20).

Content and structure

Thucydides' *History* is primarily a detailed and usually dispassionate account of the war between Athens and its allies and the Spartans and their allies, and he himself states that he is keeping to the events as they happened. The work is essential for more than just the period 432–411 (where it breaks off incomplete). Thucydides obviously lived until at least 404 BC and intended to take his account down to the end of the war. Book 1 serves more or less as an introduction to the Peloponnesian War, with Book 2 opening with the start of the war in 431. Book 1 commences with his rationale for writing the history: he began writing at the beginning of the war in the belief that it was 'going to be a great war and more worth writing about than those of the past' (doc. 13.1).

The section now called the 'Archaeology' (1.1–19) provides material on the early history of the Greeks, such as tyranny and the early history of Athens and Sparta (docs 1.56, 7.3, 7.22, 7.33). A digression on who actually succeeded Peisistratos as tyrant (doc. 9.19; cf. 9.21) is introduced to show that one cannot believe all the oral history that one hears; in addition, people have misconceptions even about contemporary history, and he gives two examples of views (presumably Athenian) about Sparta (Thuc. 1.20.3). There are then three chapters on methodology, partly given here as (ii). At Thuc. 1.23.4–6 (doc. 13.2) he outlines the immediate causes of the war, the disputes about Epidamnos, Corcyra and Potidaea (see docs 2.8–9), which take up chapters 1.24–65, and lead in chronological fashion to 432: the debate at Sparta about declaring war (1.66–88).

At this point, Thucydides decides to give an account, the so-called pentekontaetia (docs 12.1, 12.4, 12.5, 12.7, 12.9, 12.11, 12.13, 12.18–22, 12.24), of how the Athenians came to be powerful (1.89–117). He then returns to the Spartan deliberations about going to war, which were followed by demands made to the Athenians, including that they drive out the 'accursed', which Thucydides then explains by narrating Kylon's attempt (*c.* 632 BC) to set up a tyranny (doc. 7.22). Following Athenian accusations regarding Pausanias' career (docs 6.35, 12.4), and Spartan charges against Themistokles as a mediser (doc. 12.5), Thucydides returns to his main narrative and the Athenian response to the Spartan demand (1.139). The work then becomes strictly lineal, with a few major digressions: the Athenian tyranny and its overthrow (in the context of the profanation of the Eleusinian Mysteries and the mutilation of the Hermai, which the Athenians connected with an attempt to overthrow the democracy; doc. 13.24), and the colonisation of Sicily (in the context of the Athenian decision to undertake an invasion to conquer the Greek cities there; docs 2.12, 13.23).

The later division into eight books is even more artificial than Herodotos' nine. While Book 1 serves as an introduction, 2.1–5.24 deals with the Archidamian War (or, as he called it, the 'Ten Years War' (5.25.1, 5.26.3, or the 'First War' 5.24.2)), and the period of 'peace' (5.25–5.116, 421–15 BC), Books 6–7 with the Sicilian Expedition and Book 8 with the aftermath of the failed Sicilian Expedition down to 411.

Political views

An admirer of Perikles, he claimed that Athens was not really a democracy but the rule of one man (2.65.9, cf. 1.127.3); in his view the leaders who followed Perikles (and Kleon is clearly meant to be numbered amongst these) brought Athens to ruin (2.65.10), and the limited franchise under the 5,000 was the best constitution that Athens had ever had (8.97.2); it would, however, be a mistake to describe him as anti-democratic, let alone anti-Athenian, though it is almost impossible to argue that his portrait of Kleon was balanced; esp. 3.36.6; 5.10.9, 5.16.1 (doc. 13.18).

Speeches

The speeches have attracted much more attention than those which Herodotos puts into the mouths of his characters. This is not simply because Thucydides' theme is considered more important by many historians, but because Thucydides tells the reader some important things about his methodology in recording them: see (ii). The speeches are attractive to historians as sources because there is the very real possibility that they represent actual speeches, almost 'transcripts' of what was said. But Thucydides himself comments that the speeches are not 'exactly the precise words', even when he heard them himself or had good informants, and states that he chose 'the most suitable remarks for the various speakers to have made in each situation'. It is possible that he did have information about the range of topics covered in particular speeches, and worked these up in his narrative, though the way in which speakers reply to points made by other speakers despite being separated by time or distance has often been noted (1.69, 1.144; 1.121, 1.143). It is notable that Kleon, for example, sounds like Perikles, but is more direct (2.63, 3.37).

Religious beliefs

Certainly the nature of the divine which Thucydides deals with is different from the views of his predecessor Herodotos and 'successor' Xenophon; at no point in his narrative are the gods made responsible for events. But Thucydides clearly gives credence to some oracles, there are numerous references to religious matters in his work and he reports the religious convictions of his protagonists; admittedly, he is sometimes critical of these (doc. 3.24 on Nikias' devotion to divination; cf. docs 7.22, 12.21).

i. Thucydides 5.26.1, 5.26.5

5.26.1 The same Thucydides, an Athenian, has also written the history of these events in chronological order, as each happened, by summers and winters, down to the time when the Spartans and their allies put an end to the Athenians' empire, and captured the Long Walls and the Piraeus. At this point the war had gone on for twenty-seven years in total ... **5.26.5** I lived through the whole (of the war), being old enough to understand and paying attention to what was happening, so as to gain an accurate knowledge of events; it happened too that I was exiled from my country for twenty years after my command at Amphipolis, and I saw what happened on both sides, and particularly on that of the Peloponnesians, because of my being in exile and having the leisure to take notice of events.

ii. Thucydides 1.22.1–4

1.22.1 As for the speeches made by people, either just before the war started or while it was going on, it was difficult for me to remember exactly the precise words of what was said when I heard them myself, as well as for those who reported them to me from various other sources; so the speeches contain what in my view are the most suitable remarks for the various speakers to have made in each situation, while I have kept as closely as possible to the overall sense of what was actually said. **2** But as to the facts of what was done in the war I have thought it proper to write them, not after ascertaining them from just anyone, or from my own opinion, but after fully examining everything in the greatest possible detail, both in the case of those events where I was myself present and those where I had my information from others. **3** And the finding out of facts was laborious, because those who were present at each event did not say the same about them, either from partiality for one side or the other, or from faulty memory. **4** And perhaps the fact that it contains nothing fictitious may make this history less pleasing than that of others to listen to; but it will be sufficient for me that those who wish to have a clear view of what has happened in the past, and of the same or similar events which will in accordance with human nature occur at some time or other in the future, should judge this work useful. For it is as a possession for all time, rather than as a declamation for the moment, that it has been composed.

16.5 Xenophon *Constitution of the Spartans* 1.1–2, 14.1, 14.6–7: On Sparta

Xenophon was born *c.* 430 BC into a wealthy Athenian family. An associate of Socrates, he was known for his oligarchic and pro-Spartan tendencies. He fought against the democrats in 404–403, and in 402 he went to Persia and with other Greek mercenaries was in the employ of Cyrus in his rebellion against his brother Artaxerxes II. At the battle at Cunaxa, Cyrus was killed, and Xenophon led the mercenaries back to the Aegean (narrated in the *Anabasis*: doc. 14.2). He served with the Spartans in Persia from 399 and at Koroneia in 394, at which Sparta defeated several states, including Athens. It may have been this that led to his exile from Athens (or this is sometimes dated earlier): see doc. 3.52. Plutarch (*Agesilaos* 20.2) records that his two sons underwent the agoge at Sparta; however, one son was killed at Mantineia, serving in the Athenian cavalry.

Thucydides' account of the Peloponnesian War is incomplete, breaking off in 411, and was continued by Xenophon, whose *Hellenika* covers the period from 411 to 362 (the battle of Mantineia), but mentioning events after this date. The commencement of his text does not exactly match up with the end of Thucydides' (8.109); perhaps this was deliberate. The *Hellenika* is invaluable, but clearly not modelled on Thucydides' actual style. Of the seven books, Books 1 and 2 deal with 411–403 (the last phase of the war, the Thirty Tyrants, and the restoration of democracy). Thucydides was also continued by the Oxyrhynchus Historian (who was perhaps Kratippos (*FGH* 64), known to have been a continuator of Thucydides), and by Theopompos (*FGH* 115; the *Hellenika* from 411–394); both the Oxyrhynchus Historian and Theopompos survive only in a fragmentary form. The Oxyrhynchus Historian, Xenophon's *Hellenika*, and the Aristotelian *Athenaion Politeia* all help round out the details of the Peloponnesian War (note too Diodorus' reliance on Ephoros, who made use of the Oxyrhynchus Historian in preference to Xenophon).

Xenophon has been considered uncritically impressed by Sparta, but in the *Constitution of the Spartans* 14 he makes it clear that Lykourgos' laws are no longer obeyed, and that Sparta has lost her popularity in Greece due to the corruption and ambition of her leading citizens: he should therefore not be seen as uncritically praising the Spartan constitution. His various other works include the *Oeconomicus* (on agriculture and household management), the *Symposium* (with good descriptions of what a symposium — even if this one appears somewhat idealised — was like), *Revenues*, *Apology* (a courtroom defence of Socrates) and *Memorabilia* (a defence of Socrates and 'Socratic' dialogues), all useful as sources of social history. He also wrote *The Cavalry Commander*, *On Horsemanship*, *On Hunting*, *Hiero*, *Agesilaos*, *Anabasis* and the *Cyropaedia*. The political pamphlet ascribed in antiquity to Xenophon, and now known as 'The Old Oligarch' or as 'Pseudo-Xenophon's *Constitution of the Athenians*', was not by Xenophon; it is anti-democratic in sentiment, but contains useful material about the nature of Athenian democracy (see docs 1.8, 1.69, 5.35; it perhaps dates to *c.* 440–415 BC).

1.1 When I reflected on one occasion that though Sparta was one of the most thinly populated cities she was clearly the most powerful and famous in Greece, I wondered in what way this could have come about; but when I considered the practices of the Spartiates I wondered no longer. **1.2** But I do wonder at Lykourgos who gave them their laws, obeying which they prospered, and consider him wise in the extreme. For he did not imitate the other cities, but on the contrary, doing the opposite to most of them, made his country pre-eminent in prosperity … **14.1** If anyone were to ask me, if still even now the laws of Lykourgos seem to me to remain unchanged, I could not, by Zeus, say this any longer with confidence … **14.6** Accordingly Greeks in earlier times used to go to Sparta and beg her to lead them against those who were thought to be doing injustice; but now many call on one another to prevent her from a revival of supremacy. **14.7** However, there is no need to wonder that these blameworthy things have occurred, since the Spartans are clearly obedient neither to the god nor to the laws of Lykourgos.

16.6 Aristotle *Poetics* 1451a36–b11: On the Writing of History

Aristotle was born in Stageira in Chalcidice in 384 and was resident in Athens 367–347 and 335–323 BC (dying in 322), as well as tutor of the young Alexander of Macedon (doc. 15.1). Aristotle here believes poetry, in which he includes the works of the great tragedians, to be more concerned with universal truths than history.

It is also clear from what we have said that the work of a poet is not to tell what has happened, but what might or could happen either probably or inevitably. For the historian and the poet differ not in the writing of verse or prose; for the work of Herodotos could be put into verse and would be no less a kind of history whether written in metre or not; but the difference is this, that one tells what has happened, the other what might happen. For this reason poetry is more scientific and serious than history, for poetry speaks general truths, and history particular facts. By general truths I mean the sorts of things that a certain type of person will say or do either probably or inevitably, and poetry aims at this in creating characters. A particular fact is what Alkibiades did or had done to him.

16.7 [Aristotle] *Athenaion Politeia* 28.5: Constitutional History

Since its discovery this work has been ascribed to Aristotle, on the grounds that Aristotle wrote (or had attributed to him) 158 such constitutions, including one on Athens. Many modern historians are sceptical of this attribution, and the work is generally referred to as the Aristotelian *Constitution of Athens*, or [Aristotle], the square brackets indicating the disputed authorship; many consider it to be the work of one of Aristotle's pupils. The first forty-one of the sixty-nine chapters of this work are a survey of the various changes (the author at 41.2 identifies eleven 'stages' in the constitution: doc. 1.4) which the political system of Athens underwent from the attempt at tyranny by Kylon down to 403 and the restoration of democracy. The other chapters (42–69) describe the workings of the Athenian democracy at the time of the writing of the work, probably *c.* 320 BC. The surviving text, published in 1891, is a papyrus missing some material from its beginning; the text now commences with the purification of the city after the failed coup of Kylon (see doc. 7.23).

Political views
The author preferred moderate oligarchy to 'radical' democracy. At 28.1 he reflects Thucydides' judgement (2.65) that the leaders of Athens after Perikles harmed Athens, and at 28.5 (see below) his sympathies are clear. At 9.2 (doc. 8.23) Solon is acquitted of blame for the way in which the law courts became so important.

Sources
The *Athenaion Politeia* (*Ath. Pol.*) quotes the poetry of Solon, and mentions Herodotos once (16.4; doc. 9.7). The similarity in the quotations of poetry between the *Ath. Pol.* and Plutarch's *Solon* indicates that they were using a common, earlier, source. The *Ath. Pol.* would have had many other sources at his disposal: the Atthidographer Androtion is cited and chapter 22 (doc. 10.9), on ostracism, is probably indebted to him, as the lexicographer Harpokration's citation of Androtion (*FGH* 324 F6) on ostracism reads very much like *Ath. Pol.* 22.3–4. Sometimes these different sources are combined awkwardly. The most important example is in the assassination of Hipparchos: chapter 18 deals with the assassination of Hipparchos, and 18.1 is a description of Hipparchos, who 'engaged in love affairs'; the reader would therefore expect that the *Ath. Pol.* would, like Thucydides, have Hipparchos desiring Aristogeiton's eromenos Harmodios. But the *Ath. Pol.* makes Thessalos, a younger brother, the one who 'fell in love with Harmodios' (doc. 9.31). The *Ath. Pol.* has started by following one source — almost certainly Thucydides — but then has taken up another (inferior) source, and used it. In 18.5 he refers to 'democratic writers' whose account is contradicted by that of 'others' (see also 6.2–3, doc. 8.11 (where he prefers the 'democratic' version), and 28.5 below). He clearly made use of several sources but had difficulty evaluating their different worths; when they disagree, he sometimes accepts what to him is the more reasonable version. For the *Ath. Pol.*'s attempts to criticise his own sources, see doc. 9.18. The *Ath. Pol.* is an invaluable text, and chapter 21 (doc. 10.7) is the most detailed ancient source on Kleisthenes' reforms and (whatever the difficulties of his description) the basis of all modern scholarship.

The best of the politicians at Athens, after the earlier ones, appear to have been Nikias, Thucydides (son of Melesias) and Theramenes. As regards Nikias and Thucydides, nearly everyone agrees that they were not only gentlemen, but also statesmen, and behaved in a paternal manner towards the city, but concerning Theramenes there is some doubt as to the judgement because of the upheavals to the constitution that took place in his time. It seems, however, to those who do not give a cursory opinion that he did not, as those who slander him state, destroy all the regimes, but supported all as long as they did nothing unlawful, since he was able to take part in politics under them all, as is the duty of a good citizen, but when they acted unlawfully did not assent, but incurred their hatred.

16.8 Diodorus *Library of History* 17.1.1–2: Universal History

Diodorus of Sicily wrote a 'universal' history, from the mythical period to 60 BC; Books 11–20 cover the period 480–302 and can be a useful supplement for this period when recording information not found in other sources (see, for example, doc. 12.10). He has relied heavily on Ephoros, which to an extent means that his history is reliable, except that it is clear that Diodorus makes numerous mistakes of chronology, is not accurate in compiling narratives of events from his sources and sometimes describes the same event under different years (historical 'doublets').

17.1.1 The previous book, the sixteenth of these *Histories*, began with the accession of Philip son of Amyntas and covered Philip's entire career down to his death, along with events involving other kings, nations, and cities which occurred during the twenty-four years of his reign. **2** In this book we shall continue the chronological narration of events beginning with the accession of Alexander and cover both the history of this king down to his death and contemporary events in the known parts of the world — as I believe this to be the best way of ensuring that events are remembered, with the material arranged topic by topic, with each covered without interruption from beginning to end.

16.9 Arrian *Expedition of Alexander, Preface* 1.1–3: Source Criticism

Arrian (AD 86-160) was born in Nikomedia in Bithynia; his history of Alexander was and is known as his *Anabasis of Alexander*; he himself referred to it as his 'Concerning Alexander' (7.3.1; cf. 1.12.4-5). He is the major source for Alexander. At the beginning of his work in the *Preface* he establishes the source methodology which he has employed in his writing. He has selected two main sources for Alexander, Ptolemy son of Lagos and Aristoboulos son of Aristoboulos, whose works are now lost, and is satisfied when they agree. These two men accompanied Alexander, and were therefore present for the events described, and this justifies their use: Ptolemy (who became Ptolemy I of Egypt) was a boyhood friend of Alexander and a general in his army, and Aristoboulos an officer. Moreover, Arrian notes, they did not write while Alexander was alive and so did not seek his favour. In describing the fleet in India in 326 BC, Arrian states that the number of ships he gives is from Ptolemy, 'whom for my own part I am chiefly following' and this could apply simply to this part of the narrative or more probably to the work as a whole given the citations of Ptolemy elsewhere in the work (*Anab.* 6.2.4). Aristoboulos is clearly the less used of the two sources (cf. doc. 15.17). Other writers on Alexander were utilised, but only for 'stories told about Alexander', indicating that Arrian gave them less credit. The usefulness of Arrian's work, therefore, depends primarily on how accurate Ptolemy was and how well Arrian used this source.

1.1 Whenever Ptolemy son of Lagos and Aristoboulos son of Aristoboulos have reported the same accounts of Alexander son of Philip I have recorded these accounts as accurate in every way, but where they differ I have chosen the account which seems to me to be the most reliable and also the best worth recounting. **2** Other writers have given very different accounts of Alexander, nor is there any person of whom there are more historians who are so prone to contradict each other. In my opinion, Ptolemy and Aristoboulos are the most credible in their narrative, since one of them, Aristoboulos, took part in King Alexander's expedition, and the other, Ptolemy, not only took part, but as he was a king it was more disgraceful for him to lie about it than anyone else. What's more, both of them wrote once Alexander was dead, and there was no compulsion or hope of reward to make them write down anything except what had actually happened. **3** I have, however, recorded some statements made in other accounts when I have thought these worth recording and not entirely unreliable, but only as stories told about Alexander. If anyone is surprised that I should have wanted to add my own work to that of so many previous historians, he should first peruse all their works and only express his surprise once he has read mine.

BIOGRAPHY

16.10 Plutarch *Alexander* 1.1–3: Biographer of 'Great Men'

Plutarch of Chaeroneia in Boeotia was born before 50 CE and died after 120 CE. From the historical point of view, his *Lives* are the most important of his works. There are twenty-three pairs — one Greek, one Roman — of famous individuals making up the collection of *Lives*. While writing, in the case of sixth- and fifth-century Greek individuals, some 500 years or so after the events, his work is nevertheless important as he drew on much earlier sources, most of them now lost, and surviving only in fragmentary form as cited or quoted by Plutarch and other authors. Plutarch makes it clear that he was writing biography, and he has a strong emphasis on personal character (with the aim of moral edification). For Greek history down to 399, the relevant *Lives* are: *Agesilaos*, *Alkibiades*, *Aristeides*, *Kimon*, *Lykourgos*, *Lysander*, *Perikles*, *Nikias*, *Solon* and *Themistokles*. Amongst the numerous works grouped under the title *Moralia* (not all of which are his), *Sayings of Spartan Women*, *Sayings of the Spartans* and *On the Malignity of Herodotos* are also useful.

1.1 In this book my subject is the life of Alexander the king and of Caesar, by whom Pompey was defeated. Owing to the multitude of events in question, I shall say only this by way of preface, asking it as a favour from my readers that, if I do not record every one of their famous achievements or discuss each of them exhaustively, but summarise for the most part, they should not criticise me. **2** For I am not writing histories, but biographies, and the best demonstration of virtue or wickedness is by no means in the most brilliant actions, but often a trifling thing like a word or jest may give a better insight into character than battles in which thousands die or the marshalling of the greatest armies or the besieging of cities. **3** So just as painters take likenesses from the face and the appearance of the eyes, in which character is revealed, and care less for the other parts of the body, so my job is to enter into the signs of the soul, and through these portray the life of each man, leaving to others their achievements and struggles.

16.11 Xenophon *Symposium* 1.1: Xenophon on Socrates

Xenophon's *Symposium* is biographical rather than philosophical in nature and aims to present Socrates 'the man' rather than the philosopher. With his *Memorabilia* Xenophon created a new biographical genre.

In my view not only the serious deeds of great and good men are worth relating, but also what they do for amusement.

GEOGRAPHY

16.12 Strabo 1.1.1, 1.1.23: The Study of Geography

Strabo of Amaseia in Pontos was born *c.* 64 BC and wrote his *Geography* in seventeen books under the Roman emperors Augustus and Tiberius. He travelled extensively and is the most important source for ancient geography. The whole of Strabo's first book (1.1.1–4.9) is worth reading for an account of his methodology and the work of his predecessors such as the third-century geographer Eratosthenes. Strabo's *History*, in forty-seven books, is now lost. At 1.1.16–17 Strabo explains why his work is of especial use to statesmen and generals. Pausanias, who flourished *c.* 150 CE, also gave an account of extensive travels through mainland Greece in his *Description of Greece*, with particular reference to its surviving monuments from antiquity (cf. docs 3.3, 5.22, 7.20) and his accuracy has been confirmed by archaeological excavation.

1.1.1 Of concern to the philosopher, I think, if anything is, is the study of geography, which I am now going to investigate … The usefulness (of geography) is of various kinds, both in respect of the actions of politicians and commanders, and of the knowledge of the heavens and the things on land and sea, animals and plants and fruits and everything else that can be seen in each, and indicates that the geographer is a philosopher, one who is concerned with the art of life and happiness.

1.1.23 Accordingly, when I had written my *Historical Sketches*, which have made a useful contribution, I believe, to moral and political philosophy, I decided to follow it with this treatise; for it has the same form, and is addressed to the same people, and especially those in high positions. And in the same way as in my *History*, where matters concerning distinguished men and their lives are mentioned, and the petty and undistinguished are left out, so here I must omit what is petty and obscure, and employ myself amongst the glorious and great and whatever is practical and memorable and entertaining. And just as in the case of colossal statues we do not examine each part in detail, but rather pay attention to the overall effect, and whether it is good as a whole, so should this work be judged. For it too is a colossal construction, explaining the facts relating to large things, and wholes, unless some petty detail too is able to stir the interest of the man who is fond of learning or the man of affairs. I have said this to show that the present work is serious and worthy of a philosopher.

DRAMA

16.13 Aristophanes *Wasps* 1015–59: Aristophanes Reviews His Career

The *Knights* in 424 BC was the first play that Aristophanes produced by himself, though he had previously written three plays, including *Acharnians*. This passage exemplifies the sort of abuse that Aristophanes could put forth against a political figure, in this case Kleon, prominent in the 420s, who had apparently prosecuted Aristophanes for his portrayal of officials in the *Babylonians* (*Ach.* 659–64). Aristophanes depicts himself in this passage as a monster-fighter on behalf of the Athenian people, having tackled on their behalf both Kleon (in the *Knights* in 424) and informers (sykophantai), in an unknown play at the Lenaia of 423. What most concerns him, however, is his failure with the *Clouds* at the Great Dionysia of 423, which only took third prize: see *Clouds* 518–62; in *Knights* 520–40 Aristophanes also laments the Athenians' fickle treatment of their comic poets. *Peace* 753–8 essentially quotes *Wasps* 1031–35, and Aristophanes may have expected his audience to remember his description here as an abusive *tour de force*.

But now, O people, give me your attention, if you love plain speaking.
For the poet would now like to criticize his audience.
For he says that without provocation they have treated him unfairly, though he has done them much good;
Partly not openly, but helping other poets in secret,
Imitating the oracular device of Eurykles
By entering the stomachs of others to pour out many comedies,
And after that openly, venturing on his own,
Guiding with his reins the mouths not of other people's but his own Muses.
He achieved great eminence, and was honoured by you like none other,
But says he did not become overconfident, nor have a swollen head,
Nor carouse around the palaistrai making propositions; and, if some erastes
Urged him that his lover, with whom he was annoyed, should be satirized,
He denies that he's ever been won over by anyone, but has a balanced judgement,
And would not show up his associates, the Muses, as procuresses.
He states that when he first began to put on his own plays he did not attack mere men,
But, with the courage of Herakles, had a go at the greatest monsters,
Forthwith, from the beginning, having boldly joined battle with the shark-toothed monster (Kleon) himself,
From whose eyes the most dreadful Kynnine ('doggy') rays shone forth,
And a hundred heads of damned flatterers licked
All around his head, and he had the voice of a death-dealing torrent,
The stench of a seal, the unwashed testicles of Lamia, and a camel's arse.
On seeing such a monster, though frightened, he denies that he took bribes to betray you,
And even now still fights on your behalf. And he declares that after him
He last year attacked the shivers and fevers,
Which at night used to choke your fathers and strangle your grandfathers,
And which lying down on the beds of those of you who keep out of politics
Glued together court oaths and summonses and statements of evidence,
So that many of you jumped up in terror and hurried to the polemarch.
Though you'd found such an averter of evil and purifier of this country
You betrayed him last year when he sowed brand-new ideas,
Which you made fruitless, from not clearly understanding them.
And yet he makes libations upon libations, swearing by Dionysos
That no one has ever heard better comic verses than those.
This, then, is your disgrace that you did not understand them immediately,
Though the poet is thought of none the worse among the wise,
If, while overtaking his rivals, he crashed his idea.
But for the future those poets,

Good sirs, who seek
To say and discover something new
Love them rather and cherish them,
And preserve their thoughts
And put them into your boxes with citrons.
If you do this, all year round
From your cloaks,
There'll come a smell of cleverness.

LYRIC AND ELEGIAC

16.14 Pindar *Nemean* 1, lines 19–26: Poet of Athletic Victory

Pindar, who lived perhaps from 518 to after 446 BC, wrote victory odes for athletes throughout the Greek world, especially for the tyrants who sent their chariot teams to the major festivals of Greece, travelling on many occasions to the home of the victor (docs 2.30, 7.58). Herodotos knew his work (3.38). His odes contain self-praise of his own poetic ability and brief autobiographical comment: *Nemean* I was written for Chromios, general of Hieron of Syracuse, perhaps after 476, and Chromios is here praised for the hospitality which gains him many friends.

And I have taken my stand at the courtyard gates
Of a man who loves to entertain strangers, singing of noble deeds,
Where for me a fitting
Feast has been set, for frequently
This house has experience of men from overseas;
And he has been fated to bring good men against his detractors like water
Against smoke. Various men have various skills;
We must walk on straight roads and strive with all our natural powers.

16.15 Theognis 31–38: Aristocrat of Megara

Theognis was prominent in Megara as one of the aristocratic inner circle, but was forced into exile after political upheaval: he may have been a younger contemporary of Solon rather than writing c. 640–600, the traditional dating. His poetry (some of which may be later additions to his corpus) exemplifies the aristocratic and symposiastic ethos, which is found in writers such as Sappho, Alcaeus and Anacreon. Much of Theognis' poetry gives political advice to his eromenos Kyrnos, and Theognis here expounds his trust in 'good men', the aristocrats of his city; see doc. 7.19, where he disapproves of revolutionary movements in Megara, and for social history, docs 4.11, 4.74.

And don't mix with knaves,
But always hold to the men who are 'good' (agathoi);
And drink and eat with these, and with them
Sit, and do them favours, for their power is great.
For you will learn noble lessons from noble men; but if you mix
With knaves, you will lose the sense you have.
Take note of this, consort with the good, and some day you will say
That I give excellent counsel to my friends.

16.16 Aristophanes *Thesmophoriazousai* 146–167: You Are What You Write

Biographical stereotyping in antiquity was created by the tendency to make each poet's character correspond to the genre of his writing. This form of biographical fiction is parodied in Aristophanes' portrait of the tragic poet Agathon, who won his first victory in 416: see doc. 4.88. Aristophanes here presents Agathon as writing according to the needs of his drama: he is found composing poetry dressed as a woman and asked by the uncouth protagonist Mnesilochos where his breasts are. This portrait of Agathon may well be modelled on the stereotypical picture of Anacreon, poet of wine and love, who was seen as a licentious drunkard (for example by Athenaeus 600d, citing Kritias of Athens): docs 4.81–82. Phrynichos was an early fifth-century tragedian (see doc. 11.6).

Agathon: Old man, old man, the envy in your criticism
I heard, but did not let it hurt me;
I am wearing this clothing to match my inspiration.
For, with regard to the plays he has to compose, a poet
Must adapt his temperament to suit them.
So if he's composing plays about women,
His body has to model itself accordingly.

Mnesilochos: So do you ride a sexual horseback, when you're creating Phaidra?

Agathon: And if he's writing plays about men, his body's
Already got the equipment. And what we haven't got,
Can be achieved by imitation.

Mnesilochos: Call on me, when you're writing satyr plays,
So I can help you compose with some penetration from behind.

Agathon: Besides it is uncultured to see a poet
Who's boorish and hairy; look at
The famous Ibycus and Anacreon of Teos
And Alcaeus, who when they made sweet music
Wore headbands and moved in an effeminate Ionian way,
While Phrynichos, whom you must have heard,
Was both handsome and dressed so beautifully;
That's the reason his plays were so beautiful too —
You have to write in accordance with what's in you.

POLITICAL PHILOSOPHY

16.17 Aristotle *Politics* 1252a1–7, 18–23: Aristotle and the Ideal Constitution

See also under docs 16.6–7. In his *Politics*, Aristotle aims at using an analytical approach to examine past and present political constitutions and to draw conclusions about their developments and about the ideal state;. For his comments on the Spartan constitution, for example, see docs 6.37–44. Aristotle sees the polis as the supreme form of association, believing that 'man is by nature a creature of the polis' (1253a): doc. 1.1.

1252a1 Since we can see that every city is an association and every association is formed for some good purpose (for in all their actions all men act for the sake of what appears to be good), it is clear that all associations aim at some good, and especially that association which is supreme over all others and comprises all the others. This is the one we call the state and the association we call political ... **1252a18** Just as in other things we are accustomed to analyse the composite until it can no longer be subdivided, so in the same way examining the city and its components we shall see concerning these how they differ from each other and whether it is possible to deduce a working principle concerning each of the parts mentioned.

ORATORS

16.18 Lysias 1 *On the Murder of Eratosthenes* 35–36, 47–50: Lysias' Speech for the Defence

In this passage, note how Lysias, in the speech written for Euphiletos to present in court (doc. 4.54), flatters the jurors and plays on their own domestic fears of being cuckolded in order to win their support. For a speech on his own behalf, see doc. 5.41.

35 For I think that all cities make their laws in order that on any matter on which we may be in doubt we can go to them and inquire what we ought to do. So then it is they who exhort those who have been wronged in matters of adultery to exact this death penalty. **36** I think it right that you should share their opinion; if not, you will give adulterers such licence that you will encourage thieves as well to call themselves adulterers, as they will realise that, if they give this as their defence and say that they have entered other people's houses for this purpose, no one will touch them. For everyone will know that the laws on adultery have to be dismissed, and that it is your vote that they have to fear; for this has supreme authority in all the city's affairs ... **47** So, gentlemen of the jury, I do not see this punishment as being a private one enacted on my own account, but on behalf of the whole city; for those who do such things, when they see what rewards are laid down for such crimes, will be less likely to transgress against others, if they see that you share the same opinion. **48** And if not, it would be much better to wipe out the existing laws, and make others, which will inflict punishments on men who guard their wives, and give full licence to those who wish to seduce them. **49** For this would be far more just than for citizens to be ensnared by the laws, which order a man, if he catches an adulterer, to do whatever he likes with him, though the actions at law have been found to be more dangerous to those who have been wronged than to those who dishonour other people's wives in defiance of the laws. **50** For I am now risking my life, my property and everything else, because I have obeyed the laws of the city.

16.19 Demosthenes 5 *On the Peace* 4–9: You Should Have Listened to Me!

Demosthenes was even in antiquity regarded as the most important and greatest of the Athenian orators. He pursued an anti-Philip of Macedon policy from 351 BC, with his most important speeches on this being his three works entitled the *Philippics* (doc. 14.30). He struggled early in his career with speech difficulties, which he overcame (doc. 14.43). His main rival in the 340s and to a lesser degree the 330s was Aeschines. There are difficulties with the contents of the political speeches, of course, by their very nature. They aim to convince the ekklesia of Demosthenes' point of view, and, for example, in *On the Embassy* he gives his view of events, which seems very much at variance with Aeschines' account in his speech of the same name. In addition to political speeches (docs 14.30, 14.40, 14.46), there were his private legal cases, which are a prime source for social history (docs 5.19, 5.63). Demosthenes is here attacking the Peace of Philokrates, made with Philip; Demosthenes and Aeschines had been two of the envoys sent to Philip first to negotiate the Peace and then exchange oaths for it. Once it was made, Demosthenes denounced the Peace and Philip's intentions; Philip was now on the Amphictyonic Council and held the pass of Thermopylai, and Athens' ally Phokis had been humiliatingly defeated. However, while the Athenians have come to share his views, Demosthenes warns them that the Peace is in place and that there will be serious consequences if they choose to repudiate it, despite his protestations, referring back to his previous speeches on the topic and the way that his warnings have in fact been proved to be right.

4 While I am very well aware, men of Athens, that addressing you on the subject of one's previous speeches and on the topic of oneself can be extremely profitable for those who have the necessary audacity, I consider it to be so vulgar and annoying that — though I see that it is now essential — I recoil from doing it. However, I believe that you will be better able to judge what I am going to propose if I remind you about a few remarks that I have made on previous occasions.

5 In the first place, men of Athens, when Euboea was torn by rival parties and you were persuaded to go to the assistance of Ploutarchos and join in a war which would be both inglorious and expensive, I was the first and only speaker who came forward to oppose it, and nearly got torn to pieces by those who led you to commit many grievous errors for the sake of miniscule gains; and it was not long after that that you incurred disgrace and suffered indignities worse than anyone else has ever received from those whom they had assisted — and it was *then* you all realised the worthlessness of those who had got you involved and that I was the one who had given you the best possible advice. **6** And again, men of Athens, when I saw that the actor, Neoptolemos, who had immunity in the guise of his profession, was doing his very best to damage this city and was Philip's spy and agent in Athens, I came forward to address you, not because of any private agenda or love of playing the informer, as my subsequent actions have proved. **7** But in this case I shall not blame those who spoke up for Neoptolemos (for no one did), but you yourselves — for if you had been watching a tragedy in the theatre of Dionysos, and not been part of a debate on the very existence of the state itself, you could not have shown more goodwill towards him or more hostility towards me. **8** Yet I believe that by now you have all seen how he visited the enemy, as he alleged to collect monies owed to him which he was then going to expend in liturgies here, and argued persistently that it would be too bad to bring a charge against someone transferring property from Macedonia to Athens, and on being granted safe conduct because of the Peace, he then cashed up all the actual property he owned here, and headed back to Philip with it.

9 These then are two pieces of advice which are clear proof that the speeches I have delivered in the past were both sincere and based on solid facts. And thirdly, men of Athens (and when I have given just this one other example, I will go on to some of the topics I have skipped over), when we envoys returned from administering the oaths about the Peace, there were some who were promising that Thespiai and Plataea would be resettled, and that the city of the Thebans would be broken up into villages, and that Oropos would be yours, and that you would get Euboea in exchange for Amphipolis — and you were carried away by such hopes and deceptions, that you deserted the Phokians against all expediency, justice and integrity. But you will observe that I was neither part of this deception nor kept silent about it, but told you outright, as I know you can remember, that I had no knowledge or expectation of any such outcomes and that anyone who stated this would eventuate was talking rubbish.

CHRONOLOGICAL TABLE

c. 1250	The 'Trojan War'
c. 1200–1125	Destruction of Mycenean centres in Greece
c. 1200–1000	Greek colonisation of the Asia Minor coast
c. 825	Establishment of an emporion at Al Mina
776	Traditional date for the first Olympic games
c. 750–25	Foundation of Pithekoussai
c. 740–c. 720	Spartan conquest of Messenia: 'First Messenian War'
734	Foundation of Sicilian Naxos
669/8	Argive defeat of the Spartans at Hysiai
c. 680–640	Reign of Gyges of Lydia
c. 650	Second Messenian War
664–610	Reign of Psammetichos I; establishment of Naukratis
c. 658–c. 585	Kypselid tyranny at Corinth
656/5?–556/5?	Orthagorid tyranny at Sicyon
c. 640	Theagenes becomes tyrant of Megara
632?	Attempted tyranny of Kylon at Athens
631	Foundation of Cyrene
621/0	Drakon lawgiver at Athens
607/6	Athenian and Mytilenaean dispute over Sigeion
594/3	Solon's archonship and nomothesia (lawgiving)
590–580	Pittakos aisymnetes, elected tyrant, of Mytilene
c. 575	Marriage of Kleisthenes' daughter to Megakles of Athens
570–526	Amasis king of Egypt
561/0–556/5	Peisistratos' first tyranny at Athens and expulsion
560–546	Croesus king of Lydia
559–556	Miltiades the elder becomes tyrant of the Chersonese
556/5	Peisistratos' second tyranny at Athens and expulsion
546/5	Peisistratos' third tyranny at Athens; Cyrus defeats Croesus
c. 537	Battle of Alalia
532–522	Polykrates tyrant of Samos
530	Accession of Cambyses to Persian throne
528/7	Death of Peisistratos; rule of the Peisistratidai at Athens
525/4	Kleisthenes' archonship at Athens
522	Darius seizes power in Persia
521 or 520	Kleomenes becomes king of Sparta

514/3	Harmodios and Aristogeiton assassinate Hipparchos at Athens
c. 513	Darius' Scythian expedition
511/0	Expulsion of the Peisistratidai from Athens
508/7	Isagoras' archonship at Athens; reforms of Kleisthenes
505	Beginning of tyranny at Gela
499	Ionian Revolt
494	Battle of Lade and sack of Miletos
493/2	Themistokles' archonship at Athens
c. 491	Gelon becomes tyrant of Gela
491 or 490	Death of Kleomenes of Sparta
490	First Persian expedition against Greece; battle of Marathon
488/7	First ostracism at Athens (Hipparchos, ?grandson of Hippias)
486	Death of Darius; accession of Xerxes as king of Persia
485	Gelon becomes tyrant of Syracuse
483	Discovery of new vein of silver at Laureion
480	Second Persian invasion; the Carthaginians invade Sicily
	Battles of Thermopylai, Artemision, Salamis and Himera
479	Battles of Plataea and Mykale
478/7	Delian League founded under Athens' leadership
	Hieron becomes tyrant of Syracuse
c. 469–466	Persians defeated at the Eurymedon river
466	End of the Deinomenid tyranny at Syracuse
?465/4	Revolt of Thasos; helot revolt in Messenia
462/1	Reforms of Ephialtes at Athens
c. 460	Start of First Peloponnesian War
c. 460	Athenian expedition to Egypt
458/7	Battles of Tanagra and Oinophyta
454/3	First tribute quota-lists; League treasury moved to Athens
451	Five Years' Peace
447	Building of the Parthenon begun in Athens
446	Revolts of Euboea and Megara; Thirty Years' Peace
440–439	Revolt of Samos
437/6	Foundation of Amphipolis with Hagnon as oikistes
435–433	War between Corinth and Corcyra
431	Second Peloponnesian War begins with the 'Archidamian War'
429	The plague; death of Perikles
428–427	Revolt of Lesbos; the 'Mytilene debate'
426	Spartan foundation of Herakleia in Trachis
425	Athenian success at Pylos
422	Death of Kleon and Brasidas at Amphipolis
421	Peace of Nikias between Athens and Sparta and their allies
415–413	Sicilian Expedition
413	Spartan fortification of Dekeleia in Attica
411	The Four Hundred take power at Athens
406	Athenian naval victory at Arginousai
405	Athenian fleet defeated at Aigospotamoi; Athens besieged
	Dionysios I becomes tyrant of Syracuse

404	Capitulation of Athens; Rule of Thirty instigated at Athens
	Artaxerxes II becomes king of Persia
403	Thrasyboulos and the democrats take the Piraeus
	King Pausanias effects reconciliation at Athens; end of the Thirty
401	Failed rebellion of Cyrus against Artaxerxes II
	Sparta attacks Persian possessions in Asia Minor
399	Sparta defeats Elis and regains access to Olympic festival
	Execution of Socrates
397	Conspiracy of Kinadon revealed and crushed at Sparta
	Konon works with Pharnabazos against the Spartans in Asia Minor
395	Athens commences rebuilding Long Walls and Piraeus walls
	Tithraustes bribes the Greeks to oppose Sparta (or soon after)
	Athens' alliance with Boeotia
	Persia, Athens, Thebes and Corinth oppose Sparta in the Corinthian War
394	Persian fleet and Konon defeat the Spartans at Knidos in Asia Minor
	Sparta abandons the war against Persia in Asia Minor; Agesilaos II returns to Greece
	Agesilaos defeats Thebans and allies at Koroneia in Boeotia
386	The King's Peace ends the Corinthian War to Sparta's advantage
381	Sparta seizes the Kadmeia and occupies Thebes
379	Pelopidas frees Thebes and institutes a democracy
377	Athens forms the Second Athenian Confederacy
375	Thebans under Pelopidas defeat Spartan force at Tegyra
371	Spartan peace conference
	Sparta invades Boeotia and is defeated by the Thebans under Pelopidas at Leuktra
370	Messenian helots freed; Messenian exiles return
	Iason of Pherai assassinated
370–367	Megalopolis founded as capital of Arkadia
369	Messene founded as capital of Messenia
368	Alliance between Dionysios I and Athens
367	Dionysios II becomes tyrant of Syracuse
362	Battle of Mantineia; Epameinondas killed; Theban hegemony ends
359	Philip becomes king of Macedon
358	Philip defeats Illyrians and begins transformation of Macedon
357	'Social War' commences
	Philip marries Olympias of Epiros; seizes Amphipolis, Pydna and Potideia
	Third Sacred War commences
357–356	Olynthos allies with Philip
356	Alexander future king of Macedon born to Olympias and Philip
355	End of Social War
354	Philip captures Methone and loses right eye
353	Philip's alliance with Boeotian league
352	Philip elected archon of Thessaly for life
	Philip intervenes in Euboea
351	Demosthenes delivers his *First Philippic* speech
350	Philip threatens Olynthos

349	Olynthos appeals to Athens; Demosthenes delivers *First, Second & Third Olynthiacs*
348	Olynthos destroyed by Philip
346	Two Athenian embassies to Philip; Peace of Philokrates
	Third Sacred War ends with destruction of Phokis by Philip
344	Demosthenes delivers his *Second Philippic* speech
343	Trial of Aeschines (*On the Embassy*); acquitted
	Persians reconquer Egypt and rule it harshly
343–342	Philip intervenes in Euboea
341	Demosthenes delivers his *Third Philippic*
340	Philip unsuccessfully attacks Perinthos and Byzantium; captures Athenian grain fleet
339	Philip in Phokis for the Fourth Sacred War
338	Thebans persuaded by Demosthenes to join Athens
	Philip defeats the Athenians and Boeotians at Chaironeia in Boeotia
	Demosthenes delivers funeral oration for the Athenian dead
337	Formation of the League of Corinth with Philip as hegemon
	Philip marries Kleopatra, ward of Attalos; Olympias retires to Epiros
336	Parmenion invades Asia Minor as a prelude to Philip's planned campaign
	Assassination of Philip II of Macedon; Alexander III 'The Great' becomes king
	Aeschines indicts Ktesiphon for proposal to award Demosthenes a crown
	Kleopatra, wife of Philip, murdered
	Darius III becomes king of Persia
335	Alexander campaigns in the north
	Destruction of Thebes by Alexander
334	Alexander crosses the Hellespont into Asia Minor
	Alexander defeats Darius at Granikos
	Capture of Sardis
333	Alexander defeats Darius at Issos
332	Darius' first offer of peace
	Siege of Tyre
331	Alexander frees Egypt from Persian control; founds Alexandria
	Alexander visits Siwah and apparently hailed as Zeus-Ammon's son
	Darius' second offer of peace
	Alexander defeats Darius at Gaugamela
330	Persepolis burned
	Darius assassinated; Bessos becomes Persian king as Artaxerxes V
	Sparta defeated by Antipater
	Philotas executed; Parmenion assassinated
	Trial of Ktesiphon (Demosthenes *On the Crown*); Aeschines goes into exile
329	Bactrian Revolt (ends in 327)
	Bessos captured and given to Darius' relatives
328	Alexander murders Kleitos the Black
327	Rock of Sogdiana captured
	Royal Pages' Conspiracy
	Execution of Kallisthenes
326	Invasion of India; battle with Poros
	Boukephalas dies

	Macedonian mutiny at the Hypasis
324	Marriages to Persian women at Susa
	Alexander inspects 30,000 trained Persian youths; Macedonian mutiny at Opis
	Harpalos affair at Athens
	Exiles' Decree
	Alexander becomes a Greek god
323	Death of Hephaistion
	Death of Alexander
323–322	Lamian War; Greeks defeated by Antipater at Krannon
322	Demosthenes commits suicide while pursued by Antipater's henchmen
317	Philip IV (Arrhidaios, Philip's son) murdered by Oympias
316	Olympias murdered

BIBLIOGRAPHY

Abbreviations of books and journals

ATL	Meritt, B.D., Wade-Gery, H.T. and McGregor, M.F. 1939–53, *The Athenian Tribute Lists i–iv*, Cambridge, Mass.
Bogaert	Bogaert, R. 1976, *Epigraphica iii: Texts on Bankers, Banking and Credit in the Greek World*, Leiden.
Buck	Buck, C.D. 1955, *The Greek Dialects*, Chicago, second edition.
Chadwick	Chadwick, J. 1973, 'The Berezan Lead Letter', *PCPhS* 19: 35–37.
CIG	Boeckh, A. 1825–87, *Corpus Inscriptionum Graecarum* i–iv, Berlin.
Clairmont	Clairmont, C.W. 1983, *Patrios Nomos: Public Burial in Athens during the Fifth and Fourth Centuries* B.C. *Parts* i–ii, Oxford.
DAA	Raubitschek, A.E. 1949, *Dedications from the Athenian Akropolis*, Cambridge.
FD	Homille, T. 1902, *Fouilles de Delphes* iii.1. Épigraphie, Paris.
FGH	Jacoby, F. 1923–64, *Die Fragmente der griechischen Historiker*, Leiden.
FHG	Müller, C. 1841–70, *Fragmenta Historicorum Graecorum* i–iv, Paris.
Friedländer	Friedländer, P. 1948, with the collaboration of Hoffleit, H.B. *Epigrammata: Greek Inscriptions in Verse. From the Beginnings to the Persian Wars*, London.
Graham 1983	Graham, A.J. 1983, *Colony and Mother City in Ancient Greece*, Chicago, second edition.
G&R	*Greece and Rome*
Hansen	Hansen, P.A. 1983, *Carmina Epigraphica Graeca Saeculorum viii–v A. Chr. N.*, Berlin.
Harding	Harding, P. 1985, *From the End of the Peloponnesian War to the Battle of Ipsus*, Cambridge.
Heisserer	Heisserer, A.J. 1980, *Alexander the Great and the Greeks. The Epigraphic Evidence*, Norman.
IG I²	de Gaertringen, F.H. 1924, *Inscriptiones Graecae. Inscriptiones Atticae Euclidis anno anteriores*, Berlin, second edition.
IG I³	Lewis, D.M. 1981, *Inscriptiones Graecae. Inscriptiones Atticae Euclidis anno anteriores, fasc. 1* (nos. 1–500), Berlin, third edition; Lewis, D.M. & Jeffery, L. 1994, *Inscriptiones Graecae. Inscriptiones Atticae Euclidis anno anteriores, fasc. 2* (nos. 501–1517), Berlin, third edition.
IG II²	Kirchner, J. 1913–40, *Inscriptiones Graecae. Inscriptiones Atticae Euclidis anno posteriores*, fasc. 1, Berlin, second edition.
IG IV²	von Gaertringen, F.H. 1929, *Inscriptiones Graecae. Inscriptiones Argolidis*, Berlin, second edition.
IG V	Kolbe, G. 1913, *Inscriptiones Graecae. Inscriptiones Laconiae, Messeniae, Arcadiae*, Berlin.

IG IX	Klaffenbach, G. 1932, *Inscriptiones Graecae: Inscriptiones Aetoliae, Acarnaniae, Locridis Occidentalis*, Berlin.
IG XII	de Gaertringen, F.H. *et al.* 1895–39, *Inscriptiones Graecae. Inscriptiones insularum maris Aegaei praeter Delum*, Berlin.
Kassel & Austin	Kassel, R. and Austin, C. 1983, 1984, *Poetae Comici Graeci*, iv: *Aristophon–Crobylus*, iii.2: *Aristophanes*, Berlin.
Kock	Kock, T. 1880–88, *Comicorum Atticorum Fragmenta* i–iii, Leipzig.
Lang	Lang, M.L. 1990, *The Athenian Agora xxv. Ostraka*, Princeton.
LSAG	Jeffery, L.H. 1961, *The Local Scripts of Archaic Greece*, Oxford; and Johnstone, A.W. 1990, rev. edn *Supplement*, Oxford.
LSAM	Sokolowski, F. 1955, *Lois sacrées de l'Asie mineure*, Paris.
LSCG	Sokolowski, F. 1969, *Lois sacrées des cités grecques*, Paris.
LSCG Suppl.	Sokolowski, F. 1962, *Lois sacrées des cités grecques: Supplément*, Paris.
Meiggs & Lewis	Meiggs, R. and Lewis, D.M. 1988, *A Selection of Greek Historical Inscriptions: To the End of the Fifth Century BC*, Oxford, second edition.
Moretti	Moretti, L. 1953, *Iscrizioni agonistische greche*, Rome.
Osborne 1981–82	Osborne, M.J. 1981–82, *Naturalization in Athens* i–ii, Brussels.
Page	Page, D.L. 1981, *Further Greek Epigrams*, Cambridge.
PCPhS	*Proceedings of the Cambridge Philological Society.*
Pleket	Pleket, H.W. 1964, *Epigraphica i. Texts on the Economic History of the Greek World*, Leiden.
R&O	Rhodes, P.J. and Osborne, R. 2003, *Greek Historical Inscriptions* 404–323 BC, Oxford.
SEG	*Supplementum Epigraphicum Graecum.*
SIG^3	Dittenberger, W. 1915–24, *Sylloge Inscriptionum Graecarum* i–iv, Leipzig.
Tod	Tod, M.N. 1946, *A Selection of Greek Historical Inscriptions* 1, second edition; 1948, *A Selection of Greek Historical Inscriptions* 2, Oxford.
Traill 1986	Traill, J.S. 1986, *Demos and Trittys: Epigraphical and Topographical Studies in the Organization of Attica*, Toronto.

General bibliography

Buckley, T. 1996, *Aspects of Greek History 750–323 BC. A Source-Based Approach*, London.

Cartledge, P. 1993, *The Greeks: A Portrait of Self and Others*, Oxford.

Davies, J.K. 1993, *Democracy and Classical Greece*, London, second edition.

Ehrenberg, V. 1973, *From Solon to Socrates*, London, second edition.

Fine, J.V.A. 1983, *The Ancient Greeks: A Critical History*, Cambridge, MA.

Fisher, N. and Wees, H. van 1998, *Archaic Greece*, London.

Hall, J.M. 2007, *A History of the Archaic Greek World, ca. 1200–479 BCE*, Oxford.

Hornblower, S. 2002, *The Greek World 479–323 BC*, London, third edition.

Hornblower, S. and Spawforth, A. (eds) 1996, *The Oxford Classical Dictionary*, Oxford, third edition.

Levi, P. 1984, *Atlas of the Greek World*, Oxford.

Murray, O. 1993, *Early Greece*, London, second edition.

Osborne, R. 1996, *Greece in the Making, 1200–479 BC*, London.

Pomeroy, S. et al. (eds) 1998, *Ancient Greece*, Oxford.

Powell, A. 1988, *Athens and Sparta: Constructing Greek Political and Social History from 478 B.C.*, London.

Sealey, R. 1976, *A History of the Greek City States ca. 700–338 B.C.*, Berkeley.

Chapter 1 The polis: The Greek city-state

Carter, L.B. 1986, *The Quiet Athenian*, Oxford.

Freeman, K. 1950, *Greek City-States*, London.

Murray, O. and Price, S. (eds) *The Greek City from Homer to Alexander*, Oxford.

Adkins, A.W.H. and White, P. (eds) 1986, *The Greek Polis*, Chicago.

Hansen, M.H. 2006, *Polis: An Introduction to the Ancient Greek City-State*, Oxford.

Dynneson, T.L. 2008, *City-State Civism in Ancient Athens: Its Real and Ideal Expressions*, New York.

Rich, J. and Wallace-Hadrill, A. (eds) 1991, *City and Country in the Ancient World*, London: 97–118.

Stockton, D. 1990, *The Classical Athenian Democracy*, Oxford.

Chapter 2 Colonisation

Austin, M.M. 1970, *Greece and Egypt in the Archaic Age*, Cambridge.

Carratelli, G.P. (ed.) 1996, *The Western Greeks. Classical Civilization in the Western Mediterranean*, London.

Cawkwell, G.L. 1992, 'Early Colonisation', *CQ* 42: 289–303.

Demand, N.H. 1990, *Urban Relocation in Archaic and Classical Greece: Flight and Consolidation*, Norman.

Dunbabin, T.J. 1948, *The Western Greeks: The History of Sicily and South Italy from the Foundation of the Greek Colonies to 480 B.C.*, Oxford.

Graham, A.J. 1964, *Colony and Mother City in Ancient Greece*, Manchester.

—— 2001, *Collected Papers on Greek Colonization*, Leiden.

Sjöqvist, E. 1973, *Sicily and the Greeks*, Ann Arbor.

Chapter 3 Religion in the Greek world

Burkert, W. 1985, *Greek Religion*, Oxford.

Dillon, M.P.J. 1997, *Pilgrims and Pilgrimage in Ancient Greece*, London.

Guthrie, W.K.C. 1950, *The Greeks and Their Gods*, Boston.

Mikalson, J. 2004, *Ancient Greek Religion*, Oxford.

Parker, R. 2005, *Polytheism and Society at Athens*, Oxford.

Pedley, J.G. 2005, *Sanctuaries and the Sacred in the Ancient Greek World*, Cambridge.

Price, S. 1999, *Religions of the Ancient Greeks*, Cambridge.

Simon, E. 1983, *Festivals of Attica: An Archaeological Commentary*, Wisconsin.

Zaidman, L.B. and Pantel, P.S. 1992, *Religion in the Ancient Greek City*, Cambridge.

Chapter 4 Women, sexuality and the family

Blundell, S. 1995, *Women in Ancient Greece*, Cambridge, MA.

Cantarella, E. 1987, *Pandora's Daughters: The Role and Status of Women in Greek and Roman Antiquity*, Baltimore.

Clark, G. 1989, *Women in the Ancient World*, Oxford.

Cohen, D. 1991, *Law, Sexuality, and Society: The Enforcement of Morals in Classical Athens*, Cambridge.

Demand, N. 1994, *Birth, Death and Motherhood in Classical Greece*, Baltimore.

Dillon, M.P.J. 2002, *Girls and Women in Classical Greek Religion*, London.

Golden, M. 1990, *Children and Childhood in Classical Athens*, Baltimore.

Pomeroy, S. 2002, *Spartan Women*, Oxford.

Chapter 5 Labour: slaves, serfs and citizens

Austin, M.M. and Vidal-Nacquet, P. 1977, *Economic and Social History of Ancient Greece: An Introduction*, Berkeley.

de Ste Croix, G.E.M. 1981, *The Class Struggle in the Ancient World*, London.

Finley, M.I. 1980, *Ancient Slavery and Modern Ideology*, Harmondsworth.

—— 1981, *Economy and Society in Ancient Greece*, London.

Garlan, Y. 1988, *Slavery in Ancient Greece*, Ithaca.

Hunt, P. 1998, *Slaves, Warfare, and Ideology in the Greek Historians*, Cambridge.

Thompson, F.H. 2003, *The Archaeology of Greek and Roman Slavery*, London.

Whitehead, D. 1977, *The Ideology of the Athenian Metic*, Cambridge.

Wiedemann, T.E.J. 1987, *Slavery*, Oxford.

Wood, E.M. 1988, *Peasant-Citizen and Slave: the Foundations of Athenian Democracy*, London.

Chapter 6 Sparta

Fitzhardinge, L.F. 1980, *The Spartans*, London.

Jones, A.H.M. 1967, *Sparta*, Oxford.

Hooker, J.T. 1980, *The Ancient Spartans*, London.

Huxley, G. 1962, *Early Sparta*, London.

Lazenby, J.F. 1985, *The Spartan Army*, Warminster.

Lewis, D.M. 1977, *Sparta and Persia*, Leiden.

Michell, H. 1952, *Sparta*, Cambridge.

Powell, A. (ed.) 1989, *Classical Sparta: Techniques behind Her Success*, London.

Powell, A. and Hodkinson, S. (eds) 1994, *The Shadow of Sparta*, London.

Whitby, M. 2001, *Sparta*, Edinburgh.

Chapter 7 Tyrants and tyranny

Austin, M.M. 1990, 'Greek Tyrants and the Persians, 546–479 B.C.', *CQ* 40: 289–306.

Cawkwell, G.L. 1995, 'Early Greek Tyranny and the People', *CQ* 45: 73–86.

Drews, R. 1972, 'The First Tyrants in Greece', *Historia* 21: 127–44.

Caven, B. 1990, *Dionysius I: Warlord of Sicily*, New Haven.

McGlew, J. 1993, *Tyranny and Political Culture in Ancient Greece*, New York.

Snodgrass, A.M. 1965, 'The Hoplite Reform and History', *JHS* 85: 110–22.

Starr, C.G. 1977, *The Economic and Social Growth of Early Greece*, New York.

Ure, P.N. 1922, *The Origin of Tyranny*, New York.

Chapter 8 The lawgivers of Athens: Drakon and Solon

Anhalt, E.K. 1993, *Solon the Singer: Politics and Poetics*, Lanham.

Freeman, K. 1926, *The Work and Life of Solon*, Cardiff.

Gagarin, M. 1981, *Drakon and Early Athenian Homicide Law*, New Haven.

Linforth, I.M. 1919, *Solon the Athenian*, Berkeley.

Rosivach, V.J. 1992, 'Redistribution of Land in Solon, fragment 34 West', *JHS* 112: 153–57.

Almeida, J.A. 2003, *Justice as an Aspect of the Polis Idea in Solon's Political Poems*, Leiden.

Blok, J.H. and Lardinois, A.P.M.H. (eds) 2006, *Solon of Athens: New Historical and Philological Approaches*, Leiden.

Chapter 9 Peisistratos and his sons

Lavelle, B. 1993, *The Sorrow and the Pity: A Prolegomenon to a History of Athens under the Peisisitratids,* c. 560–510 BC, Stuttgart.

—— 2005, *Fame, Money, and Power: The Rise of Peisistratos and 'Democratic' Tyranny at Athens,* Ann Arbor.

Shapiro, H.A. 1989, *Art and Cult under the Tyrants in Athens,* Mainz.

Smith, J.A. 1989, *Athens under the Tyrants,* Bristol.

Taylor, M.W. 1991, *The Tyrant Slayers: The Heroic Image in Fifth Century B.C. Athenian Art and Politics,* Salem, second edition.

Sancisi-Weerdenburg, H. (ed.) 2000, *Peisistratos and the Tyranny: A Reappraisal of the Evidence,* Amsterdam.

Chapter 10 Kleisthenes the reformer

Andrewes, A. 1977, 'Kleisthenes' Reform Bill', *CQ* 27: 241–48.

Bicknell, P.J. 1972, *Studies in Athenian Politics and Genealogy,* Wiesbaden.

Develin, R. and Kilmer, M. 1997, 'What Kleisthenes Did', *Historia* 46: 3–18.

Eliot, C.W.J. 1962, *Coastal Demes of Attika: A Study of the Policy of Kleisthenes,* Toronto.

Traill, J.S. 1975, *The Political Organization of Attica: A Study of the Demes, Trittyes, and Phylai, and Their Representation in the Athenian Council,* Princeton.

—— 1986, *Demos and Trittys: Epigraphical and Topographical Studies in the Organization of Attica,* Toronto.

Whitehead, D. 1986, *The Demes of Attica 508/7–ca. 250 B.C.: A Political and Social Study,* Princeton.

Chapter 11 The Persian Wars

Balcer, J.M. 1995, *The Persian Conquest of the Greeks, 545–450 B.C.,* Konstanz.

Burn, A.R. 1962, *Persia and the Greeks,* with postscript by Lewis, D.M. 1984, London.

Balcer, J.M. 1995, *The Persian Conquest of the Greeks, 545–450 B.C.,* Konstanz.

Green, P. 1996, *The Greco–Persian Wars,* Berkeley; also published as 1970, *The Year of Salamis, 480–479 BC,* London, and as 1970, *Xerxes at Salamis,* New York.

Lazenby, J.F. 1993, *The Defence of Greece 490–79 B.C.,* Warminster.

Lenardon, R.J. 1978, *The Saga of Themistocles,* London.

Szemler, G.J. et al. 1996, *Thermopylai. Myth and Reality in 480 B.C.,* Chicago.

Strausss, B. 2002, *The Battle of Salamis,* New York.

Chapters 12 and 13 The Delian League and the Pentekontaetia; The Peloponnesian War and its aftermath

Connor, W.R. 1971, *The New Politicians of Fifth-Century Athens,* Princeton.

de Ste Croix, G.E.M. 1954–55, 'The Character of the Athenian Empire', *Historia* 3: 1–41.

—— 1972, *The Origins of the Peloponnesian War,* London.

Due, B. 1987, 'Lysander in Xenophon's *Hellenica*', *C&M* 38: 53–62.

Ellis, W.M. 1989, *Alcibiades,* London.

Kagan, D. 1969, *The Outbreak of the Peloponnesian War,* Ithaca.

—— 1974, *The Archidamian War,* Cornell.

—— 1981, *The Peace of Nicias and the Sicilian Expedition,* Cornell.

—— 1987, *The Fall of the Athenian Empire*, Cornell.
—— 1991, *Pericles of Athens and the Birth of Democracy*, New York.
Meiggs, R. 1972, *The Athenian Empire*, Oxford.
Podlecki, A.J. 1998, *Perikles and His Circle*, London.
Rhodes, P.J. 1985, *The Athenian Empire*, Oxford.
—— 1987, 'Thucydides on the Causes of the Peloponnesian War', *Hermes* 115: 154–65.
Westlake, H.D. 1968, *Individuals in Thucydides*, Cambridge.

Chapters 14 and 15 The Rise of Macedon; Alexander 'the Great' of Macedon, 336–323 BC

Ashley, J.R. 2004, *The Macedonian Empire. The Era of Warfare under Philip II and Alexander the Great, 359–323 BC*, Jefferson.
Bosworth, A.B. 1988, *Conquest and Empire. The Reign of Alexander the Great*, Cambridge.
Cargill, J. 1981, *The Second Athenian League*, Berkeley.
Cartledge, P. 1987, *Agesilaos and the Crisis of Sparta*, Baltimore.
Ellis, J.R. 1976, *Philip II and Macedonian Imperialism*, London.
Engles, D.W. 1978, *Alexander the Great and the Logistics of the Macedonian Army*, London.
Errington, R.M. 1990, *A History of Macedonia*, New York.
Green, P. 1991, *Alexander of Macedon: 356–323 BC. A Historical Biography*, rev. edn, Berkeley.
Hammond, N.G.L. and Griffith, G.T. 1979, *A History of Macedonia* ii, Oxford.
Hammond, N.G.L. and Walbank, F.W. 1988, *A History of Macedonia* iii, Oxford.
Hammond, N.G.L. 1994, *Philip of Macedon*, London.
Lane Fox, R. 1973, *Alexander the Great*, London.
Roismann, J. (ed.) 2003, *Brill's Companion to Alexander the Great*, Leiden.
Savill, A. 1993, *Alexander the Great and His Time*, New York.
Sealey, R. 19993, *Demosthenes and His Time: A Study in Defeat*, New York.
Strauss, B. 1986, *Athens after the Peloponnesian War*, Ithaca.
Tarn, W.W. 1948, *Alexander the Great*, Cambridge.

Chapter 16 The ancient sources

Crawford, M. (ed.) 1983, *Sources for Ancient History*, Cambridge.
Duff, T.E. 2003, *The Greek and the Roman Historians*, Bristol.
Grant, M. 1995, *Greek and Roman Historians. Information and Misinformation*, London.
Hornblower, S. (ed.) 1994, *Greek Historiography*, Oxford.
Luce, T.J. 1997, *The Greek Historians*, London.
Marincola, J.M. 2001, *Greek Historians*, Oxford.
Pearson, L. 1939, *Early Ionian Historians*, Oxford.
Rhodes, P.J. and Osborne, R. 2003, *Greek Historical Inscriptions 404–323 BC*, Oxford: xiii–xxvii.
Rhodes, P.J. 1994, 'In Defence of the Greek Historians', *G&R* 41: 156–71.
Turner, E.G. 1980, *Greek Papyri*, Oxford, second edition.
Usher, S. 1969, *The Historians of Greece and Rome*, New York.
Woodhead, A.G. 1981, *The Study of Greek Inscriptions*, Cambridge, second edition.

INDEX OF ANCIENT SOURCES

Numbers here refer to documents. The texts used in translations are given in brackets after each author (editor(s), publisher, date), together with the date of writing. Abbreviations used for authors and titles are given in square brackets [Aeschyl.], [*Agam.*].

Aelian, AD 165/70–230/5 (Dilts (ed.), Teubner, 1974) *Varia Historia* [*VH*] **9.4**: 7.39; **12.50**: 6.79.

Aeschines [Aesch.], fourth-century BC (Blass, Schindel (eds), Teubner, 1978)
1 *Against Timarchos* 9–11, 13–14, 19–20: 4.85; **26–32**: 1.42; **138–39**: 5.34;
2 *On the Embassy* 34–39: 14.44;
3 *Against Ktesiphon* 17–21: 1.22.

Aeschylus [Aeschyl.], ?525/4–456/5 BC (Page (ed.), OCT, 1972)
***Agamemnon* [*Agam.*] 1377–98**: 4.68;
***Libation Bearers (Choephori)* 87–93**: 3.55; **747–65**: 5.65;
***Persians* [*Pers.*] 73–91, 101–14**: 11.25; **230–55**: 11.26; **348–471**: 11.38; **852–907**: 11.1;
***Prometheus Bound* 484–95**: 3.16;
***Suppliant Women* 600–14**: 5.39;
***Myrmidons*, FF135, 136** (Radt *TrGF* 3, 1985): 4.72;
***Poem* 2** (Page *EG*): 11.11.

Agora B, 262: 13.12.

Agora XV.38: 10.18.

Alcaeus, b. *c.* 625/20 BC (Page *LGS*) **69**: 7.28; **70**: 7.24; **129**: 7.25; **130**: 7.26; **332**: 7.27; **348**: 7.29; **428**: 2.19; **429**: 7.30.

Alcman, seventh century BC (Page *LGS*) **1**: 4.14.

Alexis of Samos, ?third century BC *FGH* 539 **F1**: 4.94; **F2**: 7.37; **F103** (Kassel & Austin *PCG*): 4.100.

Anacreon, b. *c.* 575/70 BC (Page *LGS*) **357**: 4.81; **358**: 4.5; **359, 360**: 4.81; **396**: 4.82; **399**: 4.15; **407**: 4.81; **4.46**: 4.90; ***Epigrammata* 7**: 4.43.

Anaxagoras of Klazomenai, ?500–428 BC (Diels II) **12**: 3.76.

Anaximenes of Lampsakos, *c.* 380–20 BC *FGH* 72 **F26**: 2.16.

Andocides [Andoc.], *c.* 440–*c.* 390 BC (Dalmeyda (ed.), Budé, 1930)
1 *On the Mysteries* 11–12: 3.34; **133–34**: 1.68;
[Andocides] **4 *Against Alkibiades* 13–15**: 4.55.

Androtion, *c.* 410–340 BC, *FGH* 324 **F34**: 8.13.

Anthologia Palatina [*Anth. Pal.*] (Beckby (ed.), Teubner, 1966–7) **6.163**: 4.43; **7.245**: 14.49; **7.258**: 12.8.

GENERAL INDEX

Numbers refer to documents and their introductions. For ancient authors, see also the index of ancient sources.

TABLE I

The Alkmeonidai

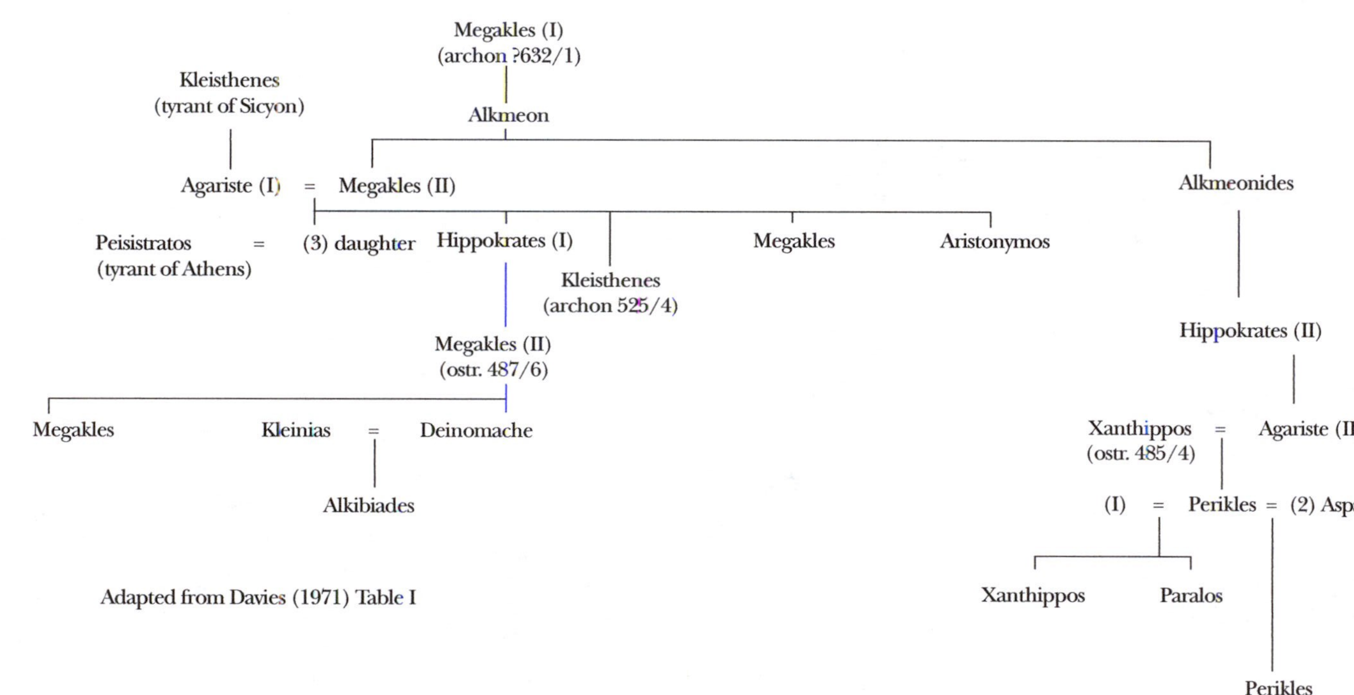

Adapted from Davies (1971) Table I

TABLE II

The family of Peisistratos

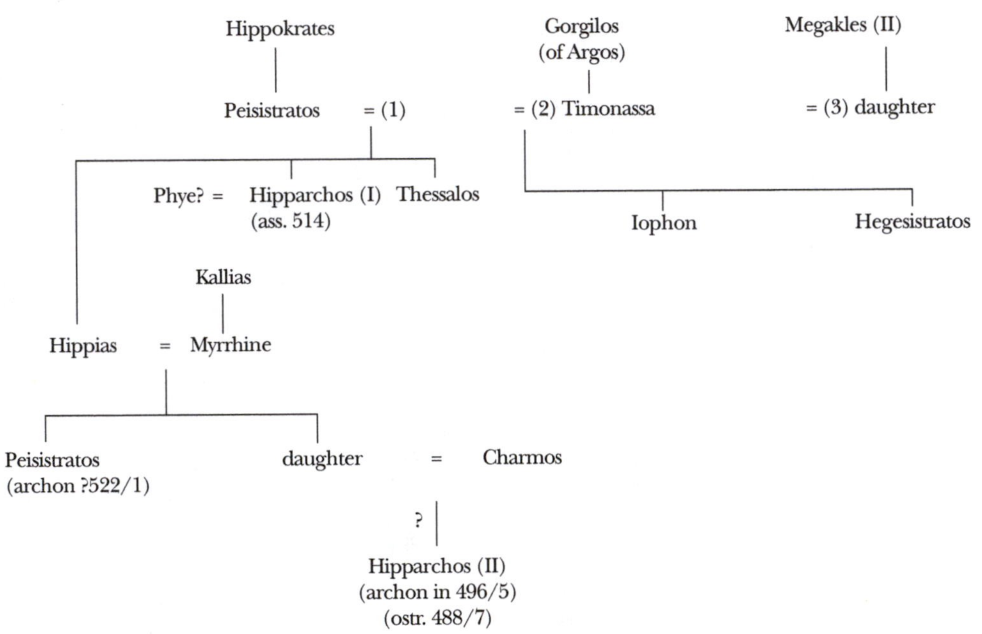

Adapted from Davies (1971) Table I

TABLE III

The Philaidai

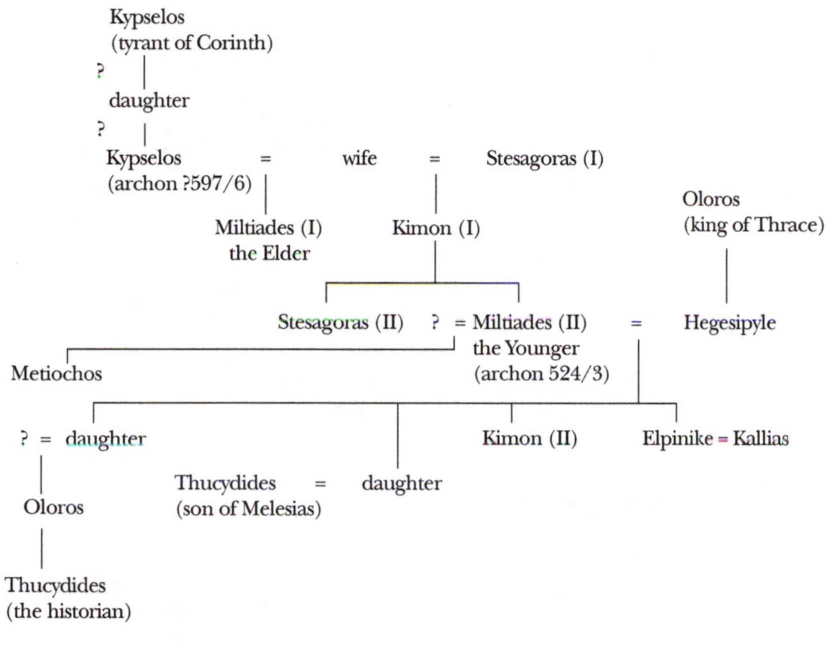

Adapted from Davies (1971) Table I

TABLE IV

The family of Kleomenes

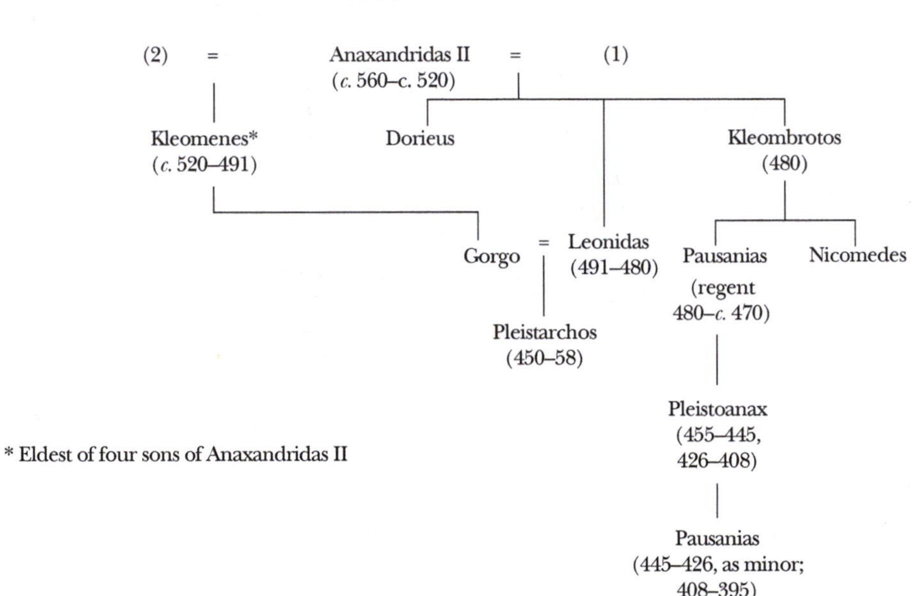

* Eldest of four sons of Anaxandridas II

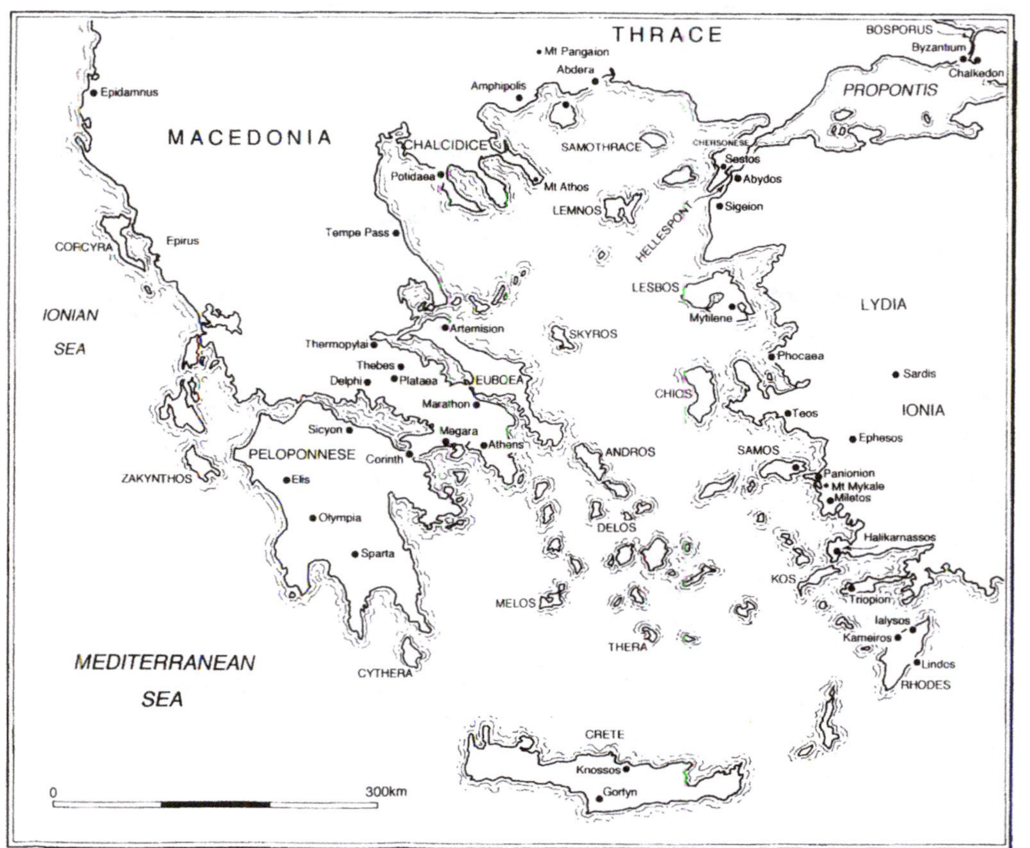

Map I The Greek world

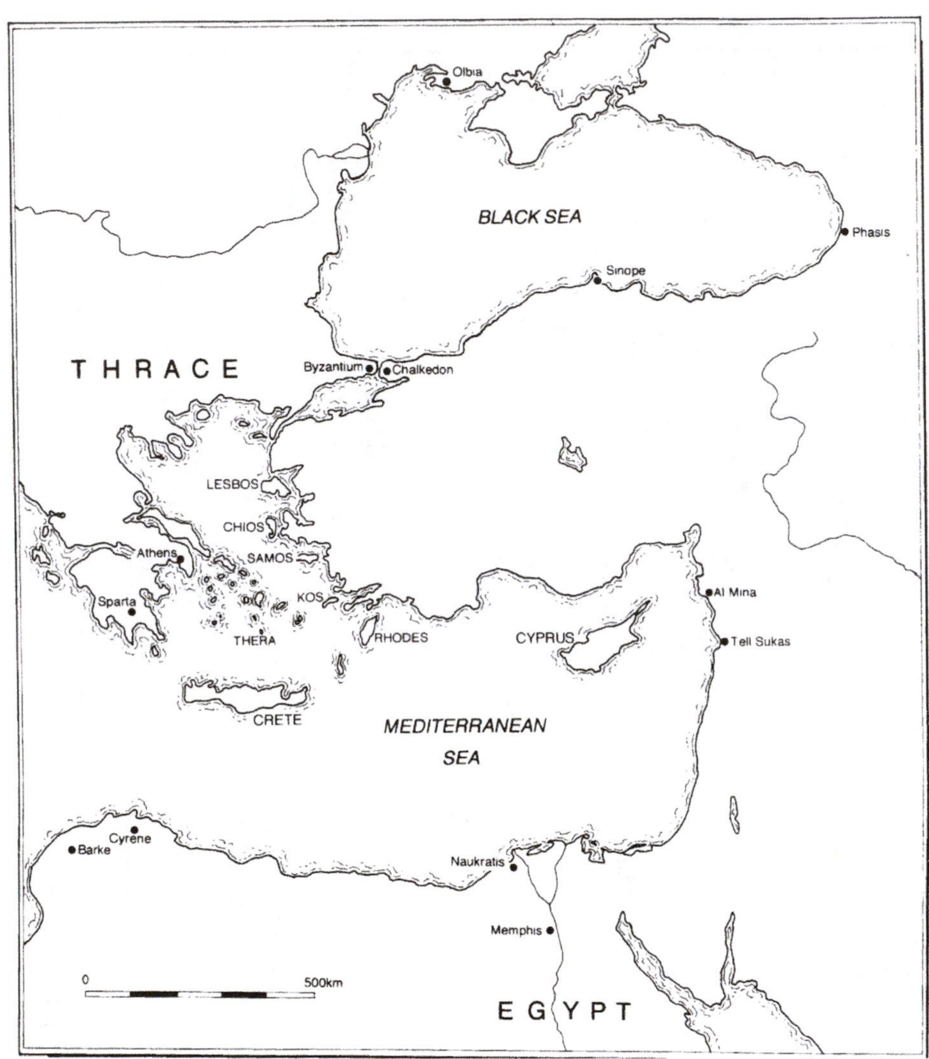

Map II The Greeks in the east

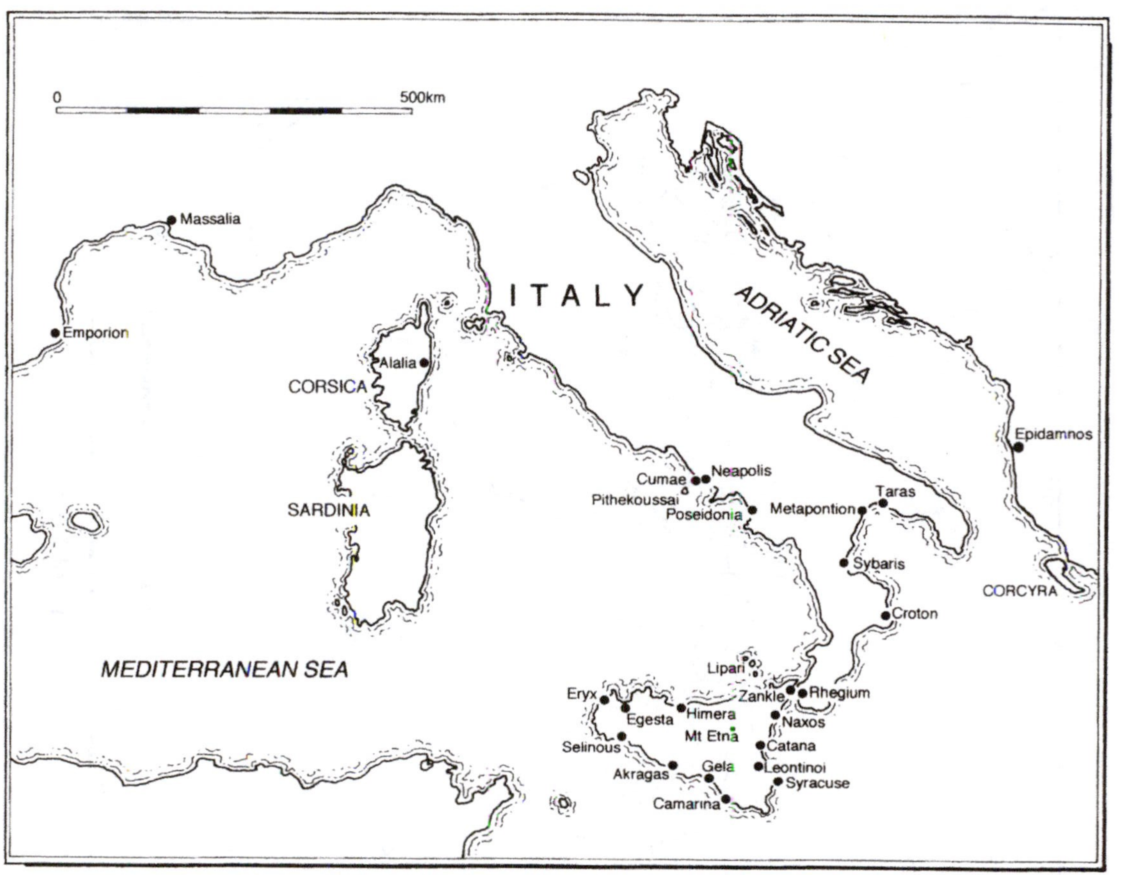

Map III The Greeks in the west

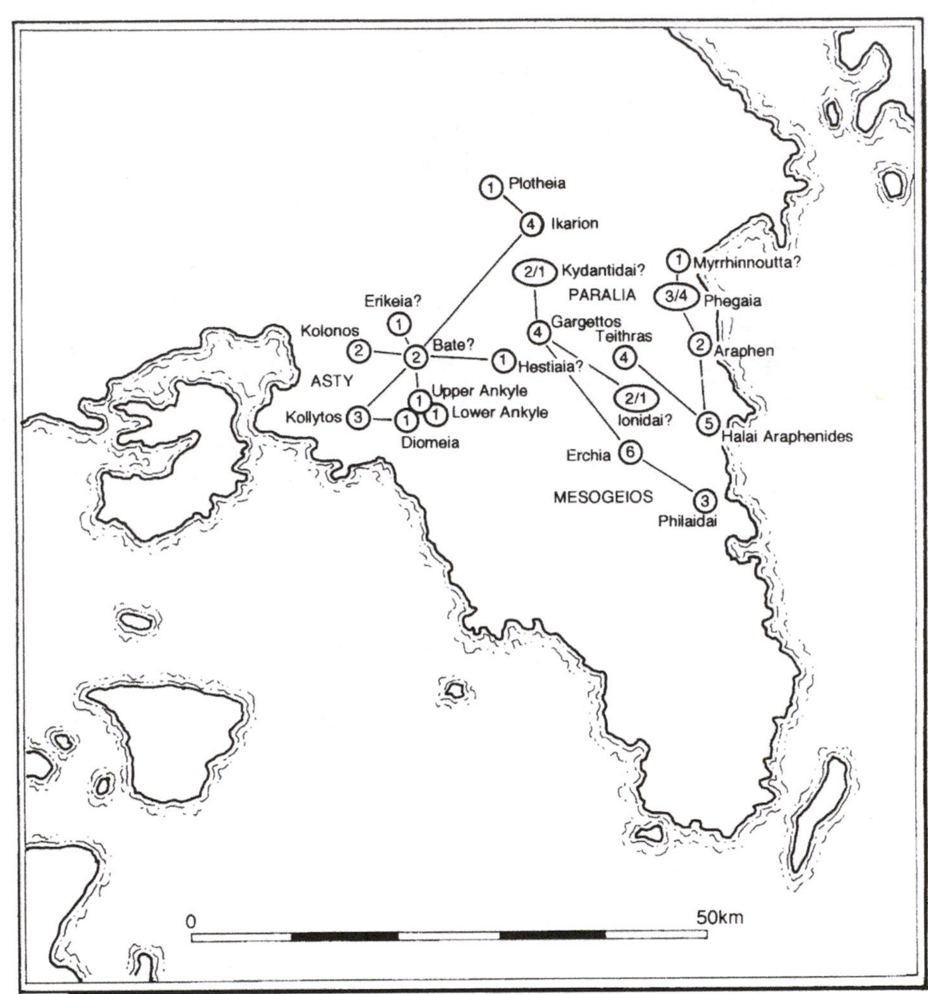

Map IV Attica and the demes of Aigeis (II)

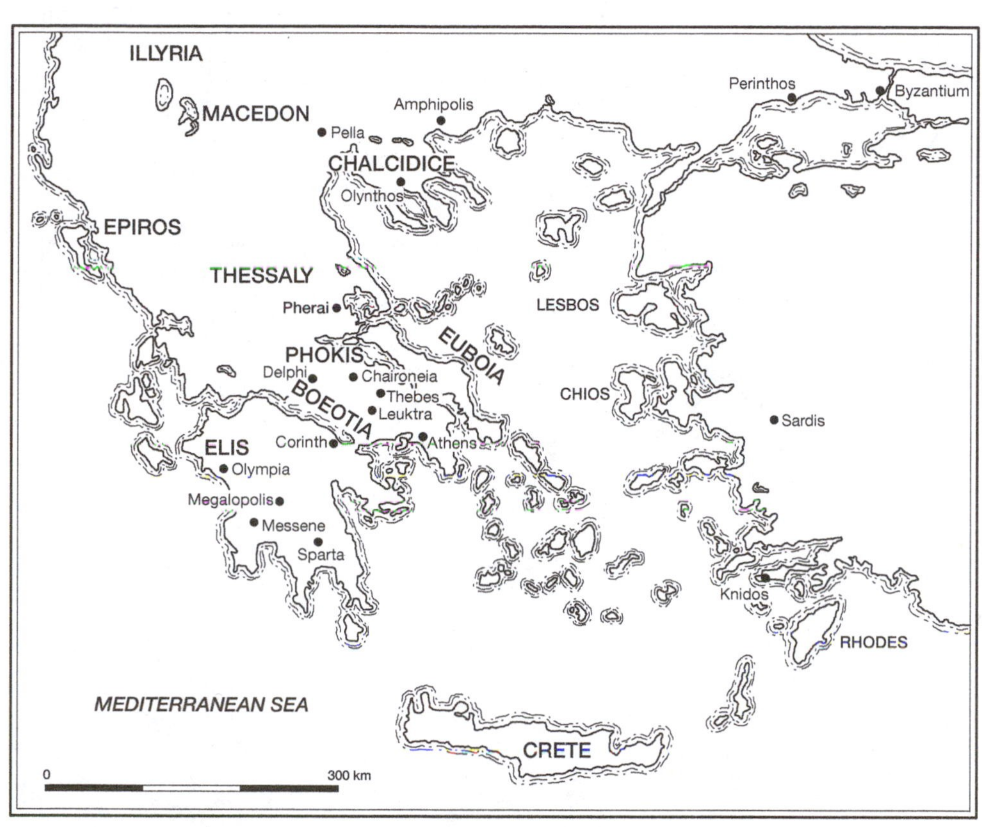

Map V Philip and the Greeks

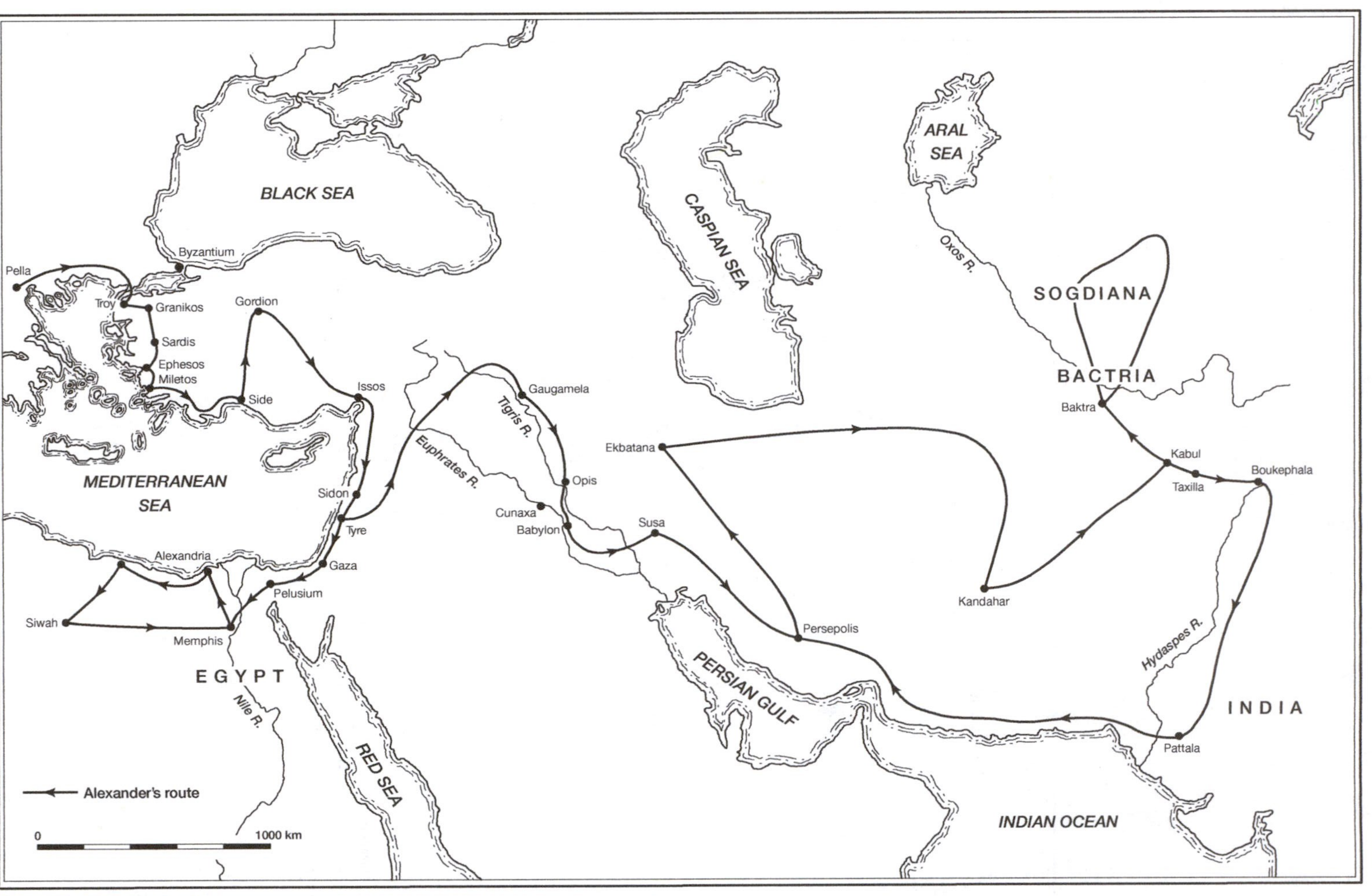

Map VI Alexander's conquests

CPSIA information can be obtained
at www.ICGtesting.com
Printed in the USA
FSHW010805180619
59155FS

9 780415 473309